CONCEPTS AND CONTROVERSY IN ORGANIZATIONAL BEHAVIOR

CONCEPTS AND CONTROVERSY IN ORGANIZATIONAL BEHAVIOR

SECOND EDITION

edited by WALTER R. NORD
Washington University

GOODYEAR PUBLISHING COMPANY, INC.
Santa Monica, California

Library of Congress Cataloging in Publication Data

Nord, Walter R comp.
Concepts and controversy in organizational behavior.

Includes bibliographies and index.
1. Organization–Addresses, essays, lectures.
2. Management–Addresses, essays, lectures. I. Title.
[DNLM: 1. Organization and administration. 2. Social behavior. HM131 C744]
HM131.N66 1976 301.18'32 75-10424
ISBN 0-87620-164-8

by GOODYEAR PUBLISHING COMPANY, INC.
Santa Monica, California 90401

Current printing (last digit):
10 9 8 7 6 5

Y-1648-8

Printed in the United States of America

DEDICATED TO

Ann Nord
Arthur Nord
Elizabeth Nord

Contents

Acknowledgments

Many people have contributed substantially to this book. Some have influenced my thinking, others have contributed specifically to the text as it appears, and many have helped with clerical and administrative problems.

I am most grateful to several people who have shaped my thinking about organizational behavior. Ned Rosen and Lawrence Williams first stimulated my interest in psychology and exposed me to the knowledge and methods of organizational behavior. In addition, Jack Glidewell, Richard Willis, and Robert Hamblin are a few of my many teachers who contributed greatly to my ideas. More recently my wife, Ann, has been a valued source of learning. Her questioning and creative approaches to human behavior have widened my horizons.

A second group of people made contributions directly to the book itself. Of special importance are Victor Gamboa, Karl Jackson, Frank Petrock, Marshall Rosenberg, Dennis Shea, and Arthur Shulman, who prepared papers specifically to help me cover topics which otherwise could not have been included. Sterling Schoen and Raymond Hilgert introduced me to several readings which appear in the compendium. Joseph Towle, Dick Beatty, Mike Rubin, Fred Russell, Jim Rhea, Pete Skoglund, Alice Yawitz, and Ken Runyon all helped in a variety of ways. I especially wish to express my gratitude to Ken Runyon, who was a valued and constructive critic of my work. In addition, I am extremely grateful to Jane Warren, whose efforts and editing skills have enabled me to express what I want to say.

Several people were extremely helpful in the compiling, clerical details, and related problems of producing a book of this kind. Those who contributed here inlcude Virginia Reed, Joan Aach, Sylvia Stephans, and Ruth Scheetz. The efforts of Ruth Scheetz, whose typing translated several revisions of barely legible drafts into a readable manuscript, are most gratefully appreciated. Also, I wish to acknowledge the help of Roger MacQuarrie, who was my first contact with the publisher.

The help of the reference department of Olin Library and the supporting services of the Graduate School of Business at Washington University are gratefully acknowledged.

As always, the errors in the book are the responsibility of the author. My hope is that those who find errors will give their best efforts to seeing that these mistakes are corrected in the literature and in the management of social organizations.

Preface

Although the structure of this revision is similar to that of the first edition, there are some important changes in content.

The major changes have been made in part 2 of this book—Formal Organizations in Theory and Practice. The readings in this volume present a much fuller picture of the history of organizational theory, the current view of organizations as socio-technical systems, and the importance of environmental factors affecting organizational performance.

There have also been substantial changes in part 3—Social Psychology in Organizational Behavior. I have expanded and updated the treatment of social power, significantly reduced the emphasis on sensitivity training, and given increased attention to recent developments in leadership theory and practice.

The remaining two sections of the book have been updated and slightly augmented. The changes in part 1—Individual Behavior—reflect my growing awareness of how environmental pressures affect the requirements for effective managerial behavior. Part 4—Toward Some Answers?—now includes a revised critique of participative management and a more systematic treatment of organizational development.

In preparing this revision I have been helped by the constructive comments of several people. Merle Ace of the University of British Columbia in particular exposed the weaknesses of the first edition. In addition, Dr. Sterling Schoen and Dr. David Luecke of Washington University have provided constructive criticisms and suggestions.

Introduction

The growth of knowledge in the behavioral sciences, accelerating since World War II, has been paralleled by an increasing recognition of the potential contributions of behavioral science to organizational effectiveness. One result has been an expanding role for psychologists and sociologists as teachers in schools of administration and as consultants to managers of organizations. The field of organizational behavior is a product of these trends.

Although we cannot separate it completely from its foundation disciplines, we can identify certain ideas shared by those who have established organizational behavior as a field of study. First, they believe that knowledge from a wide variety of disciplines is necessary for the effective study and management of organizations. Second, knowledge from these disciplines can be and should be applied to problems of the management of people. Third, the application of knowledge can result in simultaneous improvements in organizational effectiveness and in the psychological health and growth of organizational participants. Although there is disagreement as to the extent to which these two goals can be pursued concurrently, most of the work in organizational behavior is oriented to such an accommodation. Finally, the potential of organizational behavior for solving organizational problems is only beginning to be realized.

The field of organizational behavior is rife with problems. One set of problems is substantive. First, the findings in the foundation disciplines are often unreliable. Second, the reliable findings that do exist usually account for only a small part of the phenomena they are attempting to explain. Third, the problems studied are complex, and relevant findings are scattered throughout several academic disciplines.

An additional set of problems is more social-psychological in nature. Even when the subject matter is not humanity, all science is confounded by the influence of values about what can be studied, what can be changed or manipulated, and what will be accepted. Ethical issues are central in the study and practice of organizational behavior. Second, "conventional wisdom" (Galbraith, 1958) often inhibits progress. Practitioners and students often have inaccurate and incomplete understanding of how organizations really work and therefore hold tenaciously to erroneous prescriptions for effective management of people. As a result, frequently the organizational behaviorist must change and/or remove existing beliefs and feelings before progress can be made. A third social-psychological problem stems from the disparity between the needs of the client population and the existing state of knowledge. Action-oriented practitioners demand answers or solutions to complex problems with a degree of precision and authority beyond what existing knowledge can provide. Organizational behavior is only beginning to face these substantive and social-psychological problems.

IS ORGANIZATIONAL BEHAVIOR A USEFUL CONCEPT?

One controversial issue in organizational behavior is the name of the field itself, particularly the utility of the modifier "organizational." While arguing about names is often fruitless and unexciting, some attention to this question may help the reader develop a "feel" for the area.

Weick (1969) argued that the word "organizational" adds no meaning to "behavior" and therefore serves no useful guiding function. Behavior is behavior whether it occurs in organizations or not, and "organizational" often influences people to look for non-existent differences or discontinuities between behavior in general and behavior which occurs in organizations. Weick concluded that "organizational" has a negative net utility.

Weick is correct in stressing the continuity of behavior but errs in suggesting that "organizational" necessarily implies a lack of continuity. In fact, most people who use the term stress the continuity and do not find that the modifier "organizational" is a barrier to such a view. More importantly, "organizational" may prove to be an asset.

A term must be evaluated according to its worth in the relevant verbal community. "Organizational behavior" is useful in three ways. First, it suggests that problems in modern organizations must be approached at both the sociological and psychological levels.[1] Very often one finds psychologists attempting to apply their knowledge without an understanding of the requirements and forces existing in a formal organization. Similarly, sociologists have written about human organizations with only a limited understanding of individual behavior. "Organizational behavior," composed of a central word from each of the two major foundation disciplines, fosters the required interdisciplinary approach. "Organizational" reminds one of the important fact that organizations are social systems which have powerful effects on the behavior of participants.

Second, even though behavior is behavior whether it occurs inside or outside organizations some determinants are more important in organizational settings

1. This is, of course, a minimum requirement. Many other disciplines and fields—including political science, economics, anthropology, management, personnel, industrial engineering, and information systems—have much to contribute.

than in other situations. For example, formal authority has more important consequences on behavior inside organizations than it does outside. The modifier "organizational" may well direct our attention to such variables and thus provide a useful guiding function.

A third advantage of the term, although potentially a disadvantage too, is the utilitarian connotation that it tends to have in current usage. Organizational behavior courses are more likely to be offered by business and professional schools than by departments of psychology or sociology. The term directs attention to knowledge about behavior which can be used in the short run. In comparison with the foundation disciplines the emphasis of the area is more clinical and practical than theoretical. However, this practical tendency does not mean that theory is not important in organizational behavior. It is. Rather it means that a course or instructor in organizational behavior often asks questions of a theory in addition to those asked by an organizational sociologist or a research psychologist. In addition to examining its uniqueness, its scientific merit, and its explanatory value, the organizational behaviorist is apt to ask how and under what conditions the theory can be used to produce practical consequences. The applied scientist, who is interested in improving action and decisions, may find a model or a theory useful, even if it has not been "proven" or thoroughly tested. While "applied" science and "pure" science are not really separable, they emphasize different criteria of knowledge because they use that knowledge in different ways.

In summary, "organizational behavior" appears to be a useful term. First, it suggests an interdisciplinary approach. Second, while not inconsistent with the view that human behavior is continuous between different contexts, it directs attention to certain classes of variables which may be relatively more important in organizational settings than elsewhere. Finally, it may describe an orientation toward action guided by existing (albeit limited) knowledge. Thus the term has a utilitarian connotation for the people in the field.

ORGANIZATIONAL BEHAVIOR AND THE TRAINING OF MANAGERS

Managers of organizations are called on every day to make decisions concerning human behavior and to take action for which current knowledge provides no convenient guide. Courses in organizational behavior need to teach students *about* behavior, but they also need to teach students how to behave, how to learn about their own and others' behavior, and how to react to behavior and influence it by managerial action.

The emphasis on facilitating action does not indicate a non-theoretical approach. Most of the readings in this book could quite well be included in academic courses in psychology, sociology, and social psychology. In fact, many of them have been. Nevertheless, the aim of this book is to provide readings and theories which not only are academically sound but also have a high probability of aiding the management of human resources. The existing concepts of psychology and sociology are essential tools for management action, but extreme care must be exercised in any move to general principles. It is for this reason that controversy has been selected as the orienting principle of this book.

While the concepts are useful, existing knowledge does not permit certainty as to exactly what is useful exactly when and where. The literature reveals conflict among competent scholars on almost every topic. The controversy does not indicate that there is no creditable knowledge in the field. Rather, it is indicative of the complexity of human behavior in organizations, a complexity characterized by the interaction of factors varying from organization to organization and indeed from division to division and from time to time within the same organization. The best way to orient someone who must act in such systems is to increase his sensitivity to the variables, their interaction, and the variety of alternative actions which have a high probability of success under a given set of conditions. It is hoped that the emphasis on controversy will help the student to develop a "feel" for the complexity of the social systems we call organizations.

In this book the reader will not find a "best" answer; rather he will find ideas to improve his exploration in poorly mapped areas. Gouldner (1965) distinguished between "clinical" and "engineering" applications; organizational behavior, at present, is largely clinical. In other words, it is oriented to the needs of a particular client in a particular situation. Campbell, Dunnette, Lawler, and Weick (1970) pointed out that the management of people must be individualized in terms of the job, the person, and the organization.

Controversy as a guiding theme has important advantages for an exploration of organizational behavior as it now exists. Controversy should, first of all, end the prospective manager's hope that he is going to find a canned program for "instant human relations" and insulate him from those who will attempt to sell him such a program. Once students shed this expectation, they are more apt to be receptive to the ambiguity which characterizes knowledge in this field. Second, the existing controversy, rooted as it is in contradictory findings, seems to suggest that some things do "work," but only under some conditions. Thus, while extreme optimism is discouraged, all is not chaos. Controversy encourages a search for valid concepts as well as the parameters which limit their validity. Consequently, it may help us to see any particular system of thought in more realistic terms, as the great philosopher Nietzsche (Kaufman, 1968) would have had us do.

> No one system reveals the entire truth, but by surveying a number of them, we can educate our minds. . . . they [systems of thought] are good for the man who uses them intelligently but bad for the philosopher who artificially imprisons his thought in one of them (p. 81)

Controversy is also important for the development of theoretical knowledge. Boring (1929) observed that scientific truths come about through controversy; conflict stimulates thought and research. He noted that the history of science is a dialectical process, in which advances result from a long series of theses and antitheses. Often new movements are negative, overthrowing the ". . . progress of the past." The new movements must gain attention in order to overcome the "perseverative" tendency in scientific thought which, according to Boring, exists because the drive which motivates a man to do research and to publicize it also drives him to preserve his findings against criticism. New findings must fight the "establishment." Thus, science progresses by controversy of ideas but also progresses through "promoters." Ideas must be, in a sense, sold to the academic community. An important part of scientific progress is social-psychological.

The same social-psychological process characterizes organizational behavior. Interesting and valuable ideas and findings have been vigorously promoted. Evidence of promotion can be discovered in the common practice of publishing one or even a few ideas repeatedly in a variety of books and journals. In organizational behavior the established ideas are profitable economically as well as scientifically. For example, there may be strong forces which reduce the incentive to make radical changes in training programs once they have been developed and marketed. Furthermore, to the degree that a scientist becomes a practitioner, he has less time to keep up with new findings.[2] As a result, the perseverative tendency in an applied science, such as organizational behavior, may be stronger than in other types of scientific endeavor. An emphasis on controversy may help to increase the rate at which antitheses will be promoted and fruitful syntheses developed.

A further advantage to the perspective of controversy has to do with the nature of organizations themselves. Organizations are complex social systems; their actions are determined by a multitude of interacting forces. The importance and configuration of these forces are neither constant for any one organization nor identical for various organizations. Consequently, both old and new ideas and practices must be viewed in the context of the unique state of interdependent social forces operating at a given time for a given organization. Our focus on controversy can help stimulate dynamic thinking consistent with the nature of organizations. This style of thought should convey the continuing need for evaluation and adjustment of practices in light of changes at every point in the system. Moreover, by promoting the comparison of apparently conflicting theories and data, this approach may have at least two important benefits. First, it may reveal areas of at least partial agreement between principles and/or theories previously assumed to be incompatible. Second, this mode of thought may help us become aware of the degree to which differing sets of assumptions made by various theorists and different domains which they have observed have been responsible for the lack of consensus in organizational behavior.

One remaining advantage of controversy may be the most important one. Controversy may develop in the reader a feeling—or what some might wish to call an intuitive ability—about systems. Awareness that organizations are complex systems is only part of what is required. The effective application of organizational behavior requires us to do more than "think systems." Rather, we may have to employ emotional characteristics, thought patterns, and information-processing abilities which have yet to be developed.[3] Organizational participants need an ability to search out the systems variables, to "feel" the complexity and diversity of human systems. It is hoped that the focus on controversy will not only convey the current concepts but also help students to develop a better feel for organizations as systems.

2. This problem is perhaps most clearly recognized in medicine.

3. The need to train people to respond in systems terms will be more fully treated in the note to the student at the end of the work.

While the focus on controversy helps to convey the state of knowledge in organizational behavior in a realistic, comprehensive, and exciting way, it has possible disadvantages. One point of caution is especially important. The apparent lack of agreement among the "experts" can lead a beginning student to feel that organizational behavior is a chaotic field and therefore of little practical importance. Such discouragement can be a real barrier to learning unless the student is helped to search for areas of accord. The introductory sections throughout the book stress commonality and agreement as well as controversy. The concluding chapter is also designed to aid the integration process.

To be sure, teaching beginning students about the controversy in the field runs the risk of losing them through discouragement. However, failing to give them the controversy may lead them to a false sense of security and acceptance of current "knowledge." Both of these are serious errors. Given the current state of knowledge in the area, the second error would seem to be more dangerous than the first. In such a rapidly-changing, relatively immature field, questioning and analysis would seem more likely to have utility for future managers and academicians than would premature acceptance. At the present time we must develop diagnosticians. Controversy acts to stimulate creative thought and search. If nothing else, even if the student becomes discouraged by looking at the controversy, he is apt to learn something about how to learn in this field, which may well be the most important skill that can be taught.

ORGANIZATION OF THE BOOK

The readings demonstrate the major concepts in organizational behavior as well as the controversies at both the applied and conceptual levels. In some cases the controversy is contained within one selection, while in others it is between consecutive selections. The readings are organized in four parts. The first three view organizations in terms of variables commonly considered by psychologists, sociologists, and social psychologists. The final part focuses on several behaviorally-based management strategies and future possibilities. Generally, the introductory sections and the early readings attempt to develop the conceptual basis of the field. Many of the other readings are concerned with application. In several sections, short integrating selections appear after the readings, since certain points seem more appropriate as postscripts than as introductions.

Focus On The Individual

Part 1 introduces basic concepts about human behavior. The section begins with the nature-nurture controversy, moves into consideration of perception and motivation, and finally explores personal development in terms of learning and culture. The coverage of these topics, while of limited depth, does include many basic psychological issues.

The first topic, the nature and nurture question, provides a basis for evaluating assumptions which managers and students often make about human nature. The literature in organizational behavior is replete with explicit and implicit assumptions about man's nature but offers very little supporting evidence. In fact, much of the controversy among writers in this field can be traced to the authors' differing views of the nature of man. Consequently, it is important that their assumptions be understood and evaluated in a reasonable way. The study of organizational behavior must include some understanding of the properities of man and the limits of his modifiability. The next two sections in part 1 include some of the more standard readings on perception and motivation. Especially in the section on motivation, a focus on controversy encourages evaluation of the "conventional wisdom" in the field. Many books in this area limit their treatment of motivation to the work of Maslow, McGregor, and Herzberg. However, recent work dealing with motivation, in both theoretical and applied contexts, suggests just how tentative the widely accepted beliefs are. The final selections in part 1 deal with personality, learning, culture, and some ethical questions about the control of behavior. The focus on environment in this section helps to set the stage for part 2.

Organizations As Systems

Part 2 introduces the student to the properties of formal organizations—those complex social systems which are distinguished from other social groups primarily by their being deliberately structured for the achievement of stated goals. An understanding of formal organizations requires knowledge about the interaction between their deliberately created structure and their human resources. From the point of view of organizational planners, often the human beings appear to be "villains" rather than resources. Part 2 attempts to clarify the reasons for human problems in organizations. It begins with a brief overview of the study and theory of formal organizations. Then it shows how unanticipated outcomes develop in organizations and how both anticipated and unanticipated outcomes affect organizational and personal goals.

Social Processes

Successful management requires the integration of organizational and personal goals. Part 3 introduces some of the basic social-psychological variables related to this integration. The concept of influence is central to this section, which discusses power, communication, attitudes, leadership, and group behavior. In general, part 3 attempts to provide the student with some basic social-psychological concepts which are central in behavioral approaches to management.

Some Answers To Management Problems

The final part of this book deals with some common approaches that behavioral scientists have been instrumental in introducing into organizational management. The three topics dealt with extensively are participative management, management by objectives, and organizational development. Although these topics are dealt with earlier in the book, in the final part they are treated as strategies in themselves. Another paper in this section describes a newer contingency approach. A concluding note, prepared by the editor, attempts to suggest some possible directions in which the field of organizational behavior could develop.

OVERVIEW

Materials which are basic to successful management are presented in a manner which may aid the understanding and application of what we know and the exploration of what we need to know. In addition to the basic concepts, a variety of points of view are highlighted throughout this entire book. The student of organizational behavior will find selections from many "old friends," such as Maslow, McGregor, Herzberg and Argyris. However, he will find some powerful challenges to their ideas. While the "human-relations tradition" is seriously considered, so are a number of counter-arguments. Many of these new ideas have qualified and limited, rather than rejected, the human-relations view. While human relations is still an important force in the nucleus of organizational behavior, the field itself has grown well beyond its core.

The book is intended primarily for future practitioners and beginning academicians. Many competing anthologies already exist. Some are heavily oriented toward sociology or psychology, and some are well balanced. All attempt to overcome common problems. First, how can an immature and imprecise body of knowledge about complex, interacting variables be translated into action in such complex social systems as organizations? Second, in an interdisciplinary field how can one be all things to all men? This book faces the same problems and limitations but deals with them a little differently. The attempt to highlight both the concepts and controversy should promote learning, inquiry, and a realistic approach to application.

A NOTE TO THE STUDENT

Many students have shared with me their feelings about the first edition of this book; a number of them had reactions similar to what one student expressed: "As I was reading the different parts, I was often frustrated because I didn't see how all the parts fit together and how it all related to management. However, after I read the last part of the book, things really began to fit together." In preparing this edition I have tried to clarify the relationship among the various approaches discussed in the book. Since the basic concepts must be understood before they can be interrelated and applied, most in-depth analysis of the application of the material to organizations remains in part 4 of the book. Consequently, I expect that many readers still may become frustrated trying to deal with concepts which do not seem to be clearly related to the management of organizations.

You may wish to peruse part 4 before reading some other parts of the book. Unfortunately, I do not know at what point you will find this most useful. The best advice I can give you is to rely on your own feelings. If and when you feel a strong need to see how some of the various ideas in the book are directly related to current organizational practice, try reading ahead into part 4.

REFERENCES

Boring, E. G. "The Psychology of Controversy." *Psychological Review* 36 (1929): 97-121

Campbell, J. P.; Dunnette, M. D.; Lawler, E. E. and Weick, K. E. *Managerial Behavior, Performance, and Effectiveness.* New York: McGraw-Hill, 1970.

Galbraith, J. K. *The Affluent Society.* Boston: Houghton Mifflin, 1968.

Kaufman, W. *Nietzsche.* 3rd ed. New York: Vintage, 1968.

Weick, K. D. *The Social Psychology of Organizing.* Reading, Mass.: Addison-Wesley, 1969.

part 1

INDIVIDUAL BEHAVIOR

Most managers look upon individual human beings as a vital organizational resource but understand very little about human behavior. This first section explores what is known about the psychological properties of human beings and develops some implications of this knowledge for the behavior of people in organizations.

Before continuing, you might engage in a personal exercise to enhance your reading of this section. Record your answers to the following questions: What is man's basic nature, and how malleable is he? How does man view his social and physical environment and learn about it? What motivates man? In view of your answers to the first three questions, how would you design a society or a social system that could change man in any direction you consider desirable? What problems would you face in developing such a system? How would you apply the principles underlying your social system to the design and management of work organizations? These are some of the questions that organizational behaviorists seek to answer.

After reading part 1, repeat this exercise and measure your learning by comparing the two sets of answers. If your assumptions become both clearer to yourself and more complex, you will have gained a greater awareness of the variables that need to be considered in the management of human resources.

chapter **1**

Assumptions About Human Nature and the Nature-Nurture Issue

A person's decisions and actions are influenced by his or her assumptions about the nature of reality. In social interaction and the management of organizations, our assumptions about one aspect of reality—people—are especially important. What I take for granted about others influences my behavior toward them and hence their behavior toward me. For example, if I treat someone as if he were hostile, he will often become hostile. Faulty assumptions about human nature are often self-fulfilling and may therefore lead to problems which are not easily diagnosed or corrected.

Assumptions about human nature come in various sizes; some are limited to things people take for granted about themselves and those in their immediate surroundings. The behavior of individuals in similar situations differs greatly, in accordance with the nature of the assumptions that they characteristically make. For example, Rotter (1966) suggested that some people tend to see themselves as having a great deal of influence over their own fates; Rotter termed these people internals. By contrast, externals were described by Rotter as people who tend to attribute what happens to them to factors beyond their control. Other types of assumptions people make about themselves were discussed by Ellis and Harper (1970); for example, some people assume that it is important to be liked by nearly everyone; other people assume that it would be terrible to make a mistake and that they must be right all the time. Quite obviously, such assumptions will influence how these people behave. In addition to these personal beliefs, we all assume things about specific individuals with whom we deal. For example, most managers have expectations about the reliability of their various employees. They tend to assume that Person A will do a given job promptly and creatively without too much prodding while Person B will probably not complete the same assignment without a great deal of directive supervision. These are assumptions about specific individuals; the expectations we have about other people in general also affect our behavior. For example, some managers tend to perceive most of their subordinates as being like Person B.

The second set of assumptions about human beings is much broader in scope.

These tend to be more philosophically based and pertain more generally to human nature. For example, Wrightsman (1974) listed six dimensions of philosophies about human nature.

1. Trustworthiness vs. untrustworthiness
2. Strength of will and rationality vs. external control and irrationality
3. Altruism vs. selfishness
4. Independence vs. conformity to group pressures
5. Complexity vs. simplicity—by this Wrightsman means ". . . the extent to which one believes that people are complicated and hard to understand rather than simple and easy to understand." (p. 45)
6. Similarity vs. variability—by this Wrightsman means ". . . the extent to which one believes that people differ in their basic natures." (p. 45)

These more pervasive characteristics attributed to human beings influence the design of social systems. As Atyas and Wrightsman (1974) noted, our view of human nature has a strong influence on the type of social structure we attempt to create. Knowles and Saxberg (1967), focusing on both political states and business organizations, wrote:

> The quality of human relations in any organization . . . reflects first of all its members', and particularly its leaders', views of the essential character of humanity itself. . . . If we assume that man is good, we can believe that misbehavior is a reactive response rather than a manifestation of character. This will lead to a search for causes in his experience rather than in his nature. . . .
>
> If, on the other hand, we assume that man himself is bad, *a priori,* then we are prone to assume that misbehavior is caused by something within him which we cannot alter directly. Accordingly, our attention will focus on limiting his freedom to choose and to act through external curbs or controls. . . .
>
> Thus the underlying human value which predominates is readily perceived in (a) the way social relationships are structured, (b) the kinds of rewards and penalties that are used, (c) the character of the communication process which links people together, and (d) the other elements of social control that characterize a relationship or an organization. (p. 178)

However, the causal relationship between assumptions and organizational structures is not one-way. As Atyas and Wrightsman (1974) pointed out, the prevailing views of human nature are influenced by the social structures themselves; assumptions about human nature are self-fulfilling in that certain structures we create in the light of our assumptions then reinforce those beliefs.[1]

In short, a person's assumptions about human nature are apt to have important consequences for his or her managerial style, particularly the manner in

1. McGregor's discussion (in chapter 3) of the influence of Theory X and Theory Y assumptions on the motivation of employees provides a good example of the self-fulfilling nature of assumptions.

which he or she designs organizations and manages other people. Consequently, we should begin our study of individual behavior by trying to develop a useful way of discussing the nature of the human resource.

THE NATURE VS. NURTURE CONTROVERSY

There is considerable disagreement about the essence of human nature. Much of this debate has been presented as "the nature-nurture question." Those who attempt to answer this question try to determine the relative influences of heredity and environment on human behavior. Such research presents two major sets of problems. First, it is almost impossible to collect sufficiently controlled data; the only pairs of people with the same genetic compositions are identical twins, and there is rarely enough information about their environments to allow conclusive research. Moreover, our attitudes toward the use of humans for research do not permit the appropriate experiments to be conducted. Second, interpretation of the data which are available is complicated by value questions and emotionality. The controversy stimulated by the widely publicized work of Jensen (1969) demonstrated both of these difficulties. Having conducted a comprehensive review of the literature, Jensen concluded that whites tend to have significantly higher IQs than blacks and that a large portion of this difference could be attributed to genetic differences. Jensen's paper sent shock waves through the liberal community of academic psychologists and stimulated debate throughout the world.

Some of this controversy revolves around technical questions of inference and research methodology, which are well outlined in the collection of papers by Kagan, Hunt, Crow, Bereiter, Elkind, Cronbach, and Brazziel (1969), and a book edited by Cancro (1971). Several points from these papers are particularly relevant for our discussion. First, most of the data have been collected only from white populations. Estimates of the inheritability of a characteristic based on data from one population may not provide a valid estimate for another population. Second, several authors noted that, even if IQ were largely genetically determined, significant improvements could be obtained for many people if appropriate environments were provided.

In addition to raising these research issues, Jensen's work has generated strong reactions reflecting evaluative and emotional concerns. For example, consider the experiences of Harvard psychologist Richard Herrnstein. After publishing an article in which he took the position that genetic ingredients played a major role in determining mental capacity and social status, Herrnstein (1971) reported being harassed on his own campus and prevented from delivering academic lectures on other subjects at other universities.

Herrnstein (1971) charged that honest inquiry into the nature-nurture question had been choked off by value judgments. He wrote:

> The hostility of the radicals, the obscurantism of some academics, the public silence of other academics, the one-sided coverage in the news, the increasing reluctance of scientific periodicals to publish hereditarian find-

> ings or scientific agencies to support hereditarian research—these are all signs of a political orthodoxy on human equipotentiality to which scholarship has become hostage. (p. 59)

He added:

> The false belief in human equality leads to rigid, inflexible expectations, often doomed to frustration, thence to anger. . . . We call on our educational and social institutions to make everyone the same, when we should instead be trying to mold our institutions around the inescapable limitations and varieties of human ability. (p. 59)

Herrnstein's position presents a direct challenge to our belief in equal treatment for all individuals.

Clearly, the nature-nurture question is difficult to deal with, being subject to the research problems noted above and being related to so many central moral and social issues. However, research and analysis by a number of biologists, geneticists, and psychologists have resulted in the interactionist position, which provides us with a useful perspective from which to view some of these difficult issues.

One of the major contributors to the interactionist view has been the geneticist Dobzhansky (1964). He has argued that, to be dealt with adequately, the nature-nurture question must be asked in an appropriate manner. Dobzhansky maintained that almost all traits are a product of the interaction of both genetic and environmental forces. Therefore, the question is not whether a given trait is a result of nature or nurture but rather to what extent it is influenced by each. Of course, establishing the relative contribution of each is a difficult task. The reading by Dobzhansky in this section gives his argument in more detail.

The nature-nurture issue is further complicated by the conditions which are experienced between conception and birth. McCurdy (1961) argued convincingly that variations in the prenatal environment play a vital role in an individual's development. Thus, even a complete understanding of genetics and comprehensive knowledge of post-birth environments would not be enough to account for all the variation in human behavior.

Nevertheless, recent research has provided some interesting insights. In addition to the work cited in following selections, three sets of studies deserve brief mention.

First is the exploratory work of Rosenzweig (1966). He found that he could induce physical and chemical changes in the brains of rodents by varying the complexity of the environment. Animals reared in enriched environments (environments offering many stimuli) were better at solving problems than animals reared in deprived (relatively unstimulating) environments. Remarkably, certain portions of the brains of the "enriched" animals were larger than those of the deprived. Of course, it is difficult to generalize about human behavior from such experiments, but the results do suggest the possibility that environmental experience may be encoded via physiological changes, which in turn may influence the ability to learn. Again, the question with respect to intelligence is not nature or nurture but degree of nature and nurture.

A second line of inquiry, by Bell (1968), questioned the model of socialization which takes into account only the effects of parental behavior on children. Bell cited considerable evidence that certain congenital factors contribute to types of child behavior, which in turn influence parental behavior. Infants differ in assertiveness, activity, and desire for such stimuli as social reinforcement. As a result, the same parents respond differently to different children. Compare, for example, the probable adult interactions with a sickly, delicate child to those with a healthy, robust one. Thus, while environmental experience may be encoded via physiological changes, the action of a child himself may be an independent variable which partially determines the environment.

The third set of studies has been provided by ethologists, zoologists who study animal behavior. According to Tinbergen (1968), ethologists apply the methods of biology to behavior to study the relationship of behavior to the survival of the animal, the causes of the behavior at a given moment, the development of the behavioral machinery through individual growth, and the evolution of behavioral systems within a particular species. Tinbergen argued that this approach should be applied to the study of man himself. Such an application suggests some interesting ideas about the nature-nurture question and the very survival of social organization as we know it.

Tinbergen argued that certain patterns which have been regarded as innate in fact depend on interaction with the environment for their development.[2] For example, certain parts of the eye of a tadpole do not function properly unless they have been exposed to light. Also, evidence exists that birds acquire their songs in part through exposure to the full song of an adult male of the same species. Furthermore, while behavior is influenced by rewards which follow it, the particular rewards which have effects vary from one species, stage of development, or occasion to another. Thus, behavior develops as "programmed instructions" given by one's genetic membership in a species and modified in interaction with the environment. Language learning is a prime example. A human infant can make many sounds. However, the particular sounds he comes to make will be only the ones his environment supports. Again, the interplay of nature and nurture in development is clear.

Consideration of innate predispositions and mechanisms provides an important new dimension to the nature-nurture question which may have profound implications for organizational behavior. The interactionist view—that behavior is determined jointly by species characteristics, inherited individual differences, and behavioral modifications of individuals—may provide a useful model for understanding organizational behavior. Many theories of psychology and management have failed to consider the species-specific nature of behavior. Many approaches to organizational behavior tend to focus on certain variables which highlight the similarity of all men. Other theories focus on variables which highlight individual differences among men. The approach in this book is that men

2. While it is not directly relevant here, it should be noted that Tinbergen also maintained that learning at various developmental states is limited by "internally imposed restrictions."

are more homogeneous in some respects than in others and that it is important to distinguish between the two sets of characteristics in designing organizations or other social systems.

Where greater homogeneity exists, it is expected that the characteristic may be common to the species rather than peculiar to some individuals. In designing social systems, it is often best to take these characteristics as given. Some of these attributes will be useful, and a social system may be created to take advantage of them. The characteristics which are undesirable may be surpressed or at least controlled by the design of the system.

With respect to other characteristics in which there are important individual differences among people, there are two practical choices: selection of people with the desired characteristics and training of those without them.[3] In part the choice is determined by the relative contributions of heredity and environment. Obviously, training is apt to be more useful when environment contributes substantial variance. However, the species questions must still be considered. For example, even though some responses may be largely environmentally determined, often they are easier to learn at certain stages of development.

In sum, the nature-nurture question is difficult to answer even when it is appropriately phrased. The evidence suggests that species factors, individual genetics, and environment are all important. The readings which follow support this contention. Dobzhansky suggests just how complex is the interaction. Hebb, in the second article, deals indirectly with the nature-nurture question by suggesting that all behavior must be viewed in the context of the environment in which it occurs. In other words, a person is highly dependent on the state of his environment and, at least to some degree, is a different individual in every context. Changes in the protective cocoon in which the individual functions produce changes in the individual's behavior.

This argument is extremely important for managers of organizations. Changes in the organizational and social climate produce changes in the organizational participant. Each individual is a unique human being. In addition to being different from other people in many ways, an individual constantly exhibits changes in himself as he experiences new or different environments. Inappropriate assumptions about the nature-nurture issue often lead to systematic overestimation of the stability of individual characteristics and consequent underestimation of the influence of environmental factors in organizational performance. Some assumptions about the nature-nurture question, either explicit or implicit, underlie all approaches to management and organizational behavior. The following readings attempt to improve the quality of these assumptions.

REFERENCES

Atyas, J., and Wrightsman, L.S. "A Time for Taking Stock." In *Assumptions about Human Nature: a Social-Psychological Approach,* edited by L. S. Wrightsman, pp. 210-23. Monterey, Calif.: Brooks/Cole, 1974.

3. Theoretically there is at least one other alternative. Several social systems could be designed to exist side by side. Individuals could then choose that system which was best suited to their particular characteristics.

Bell, R. Q. "A Reinterpretation of the Direction of Effects of Studies of Socialization." *Psychological Review* 75 (1968): 81-95.

Cancro, R. *Intelligence: Genetic and Environmental Influences.* New York: Grune & Stratton, 1971.

Dobzhansky, T. *Heredity and the Nature of Man.* New York: New American Library, 1964.

Ellis, A., and Harper, R. A. *A Guide to Rational Living.* N. Hollywood, Calif.: Wilshire, 1970.

Herrnstein, R. J. *I.Q. in the Meritocracy.* Boston: Little, Brown & Co., 1971.

Jensen. A. J. "How Much Can We Boost IQ and Scholastic Achievement?" *Harvard Educational Review* 39, no. 1 (1969): 1-123.

Kagan, J. S.; Hunt, J. Mc.; Crow, J. F.; Bereiter, C.; Elkind, D.; Cronback, L. J.; and Brazziel, W. F. "How Much Can We Boost IQ and Scholastic Achievement? A Discussion." *Harvard Educational Review* 39, no. 1 (1969): 273-356.

Knowles, H. P., and Saxberg, B. O. "Human Relations and the Nature of Man." *Harvard Business Review* 45 (1967): 22-24, ff.

McCurdy, H. G. *The Personal World.* New York: Harcourt Brace Jovanovich, Inc., 1961.

Rosenzweig, M. R. "Environmental Complexity, Cerebral Change, and Behavior." *American Psychologist* 21 (1966): 321-32.

Rotter, J. B. "Generalized Expectancies for Internal versus External Control of Reinforcement." *Psychological Monographs* 80 (1966): Whole No. 609.

Tinbergen, N. "On War and Peace in Animals and Man." *Science* 160 (1968): 1411-18.

Wrightsman, L. S., ed. *Assumptions about Human Nature: a Social-Psychological Approach.* Monterey, Calif.: Brooks/Cole, 1974.

Theodosius Dobzhansky

HEREDITY

GENOTYPE AND PHENOTYPE

The biological inheritance of every person consists of genes received from his parents. The totality of the genes is the "genotype." The concept of the genotype framed by Johannsen (1909, 1911) is now extended beyond its initial usage: the genotype subsumes all self-reproducing bodily constituents regardless of their localization – the genes in the chromosomes as well as the plasmogenes in the cell cytoplasm.

The function of the genotype, or at least one of its functions, is to make more of itself: genes induce synthesis of their own copies. Some of the shorthand language used by biologists is grossly misleading if its metaphorical character is not understood. For example, what is the meaning of the often made statement that the genotype of a person does not change in his lifetime? Since the amount of deoxyribonucleic acids in the cell nucleus is doubled between the end of one cell division and the beginning of the next, I obviously no longer have the genes which I had as an infant or as a fertilized egg cell; what I do have, instead, are true copies of these genes. It is even less accurate to say that I carry the genes of my remote ancestors, because I possess copies of only some of their genes. My genes do not change, but solely in the sense that they make new genes just like themselves.

It is an interesting speculation, but nothing more, that the development of the body is a by-product of the self-copying of the genes. The genes reproduce themselves by converting the materials taken up from their surroundings in the cell into their replicas. But cells and organisms, any organisms whatever, grow and reproduce by assimilation of food, in other words by intake of suitable materials from the environment. However, not all cell components give rise to their replicas, as genes do; for example, muscle and nerve fibers and various secretions are not present in the sex cells but are formed by, or from, other cell constituents, ultimately by or from genes.

A long, complex, and little known sequence of processes intervene between the genotype which was present in the egg cell at fertilization and the organism as we observe it. These processes are subsumed under the name "development." Development is neither completed in the womb nor concluded at birth. Although the embryonic, or fetal, development is the period when changes are rapid and spectacular, development goes on throughout life–infancy, childhood, adolescence, maturity, senility, and inevitable dissolution. Life is unceasing development, although some organisms, such as seeds and spores of plants, may remain quiescent for more or less long periods. However that may be, the organism can be observed and studied at any stage of the eternally recurrent metamorphosis of life. To designate the sum total of the observable characteristics of the organism, Johannsen has proposed the term "phenotype."

The phenotype changes throughout time. The changes in the phenotype of a person may be shown by, for example, a series of photographs taken at different ages, but it should be stressed that the phenotype includes more than the external appearance of a person: his physiology, metabolism, gross and microscopic anatomy, bodily chemical processes, even the appearance of the chromosomes in his cells—all are aspects of the phenotype, as are his behavior, thinking processes, and adjustment or maladjustment to society. In short, the phenotype is the total of everything that can be observed or inferred about an individual, excepting only his genes. The phenotype obviously cannot be inherited; it can only develop as life goes on. As stated above, only the genes are inherited or, more precisely still, only the genes in the sex cells, of which the genes that an individual possesses are true copies.

The genes interact with the environment, and the outcome is the process of development, or aging. Development results in an orderly succession of phenotypes. The genotype determines the reactions and responses of the developing, or aging, organism to the environment: it determines the norm of reaction. My phenotype at this moment has been determined by the norm of reaction of my genotype to the succession of environments that I have met in my lifetime; my phenotype tomorrow, or a year hence, will be determined by its present state, as modified by my responses to the environments that I shall have encountered in the meantime.

All the traits, characters, or features of the phenotype are, of necessity, determined by the genotype and by the sequence of environments with which the genotype interacts. There is no organism without a genotype and no genotype can exist outside a spatio-temporal continuum, an environment.

WHICH CHARACTERISTICS ARE HEREDITARY AND WHICH ENVIRONMENTAL?

The man in the street believes that some traits are herditary and others environmental. Belief in a sharp dichotomy between hereditary and environmental traits almost invariably goes hand in hand with a misunderstanding of the roles of social conditions and medicine and education: an hereditary disease is supposedly incurable, a disease contracted by exposure to some noxious environment may perhaps be cured; if the IQ of a child depends on his schooling, then it cannot be hereditary.

The dichotomy of hereditary and environmental traits is, however, untenable: in principle any trait is modifiable by changes in the genes and by manipulation of the environment. Contrary to the . . . opinion of Adler [1927] recognition of the genotypic component in human personality need not hinder the educator nor deprive him of confidence. Education is a form of management of the human environment, and except for a pathological minority, all human genotypes respond to some extent to this management. But the educator had better recognize that not all genotypes respond uniformly and different genotypes may profit most by different forms of management.

At this point, illustrations of what is meant by the statement that all characters or traits are both genotypic and environmental are in order. It is generally agreed that at least some forms of the disease known as diabetes mellitus are genetically conditioned, although it is still uncertain whether the disease behaves as a Mendelian recessive or dominant or whether there are several varieties of the disease with different genetic causations . . . . Physiologically, the disease is due to a failure of certain cells in the pancreas to secrete enough of the hormone insulin, needed for normal utilization of blood sugars. This leads to the excretion of sugar in the urine, accumulation of fatty acids in the blood stream and blood vessels, and susceptibility to infections and other complications which may result in death. When diabetes is discovered, a reduction of sugars and starches in the diet is prescribed and in mild cases this treatment may suffice to remove the symptoms. In more severe cases regular injections of insulin are necessary to maintain health. Thus, diabetes can be "cured" by manipulation of the environment.

Most certainly neither the dietary rules nor the insulin injections change the "diabetic genes" and make the pancreas manufacture its own insulin, although they do relieve the morbid symptoms of the disease: health or disease is surely a condition of the phenotype, i.e., the well-being of persons with a certain genotype requires a sugar-free but insulin-rich environment. One may even speculate that a mankind consisting entirely of persons with diabetic genotypes could be reasonably well off in in an environment where factories maintained a regular supply of synthetic insulin. Diabetes would then be an environmental disease caused by insulin deficiency, like the once-dreaded but now fortunately preventable scurvy, which is caused by a deficiency of vitamin C.

Conversely, malaria, syphilis, and influenza are environmental diseases: they arise because of infection with specific microorganisms, and persons who live in environments free of the infecting agents are free of the diseases. And yet the microorganisms infect only possessors of certain genotypes – particularly human genotypes. (Very few other animals that can be infected with the human forms of these diseases are known, and it is surely not accidental that susceptibility to syphilis, for example, is restricted to man's closest relatives among the primates.) Furthermore, not all human beings are easily infected with malaria or influenza, and there are good reasons to think that a part of the variation in susceptibility is genetic. It has long been believed people of European origin are more likely to contract malaria and to have a severe form of the disease than natives of many tropical lands. Swellengrebel (1940) found such a situation in parts of Guiana: the human population and the malarial parasite had reached a sort of mutual accommodation, with most of the potential hosts infected but the disease rarely lethal. The discovery of Allison (1945a,b, 1955) that persons heterozygous for the sickle-cell gene are relatively immune to infection with quartan malaria is an even better example. Although this situation will be discussed in more detail later, we should here consider a population in which some persons carry the gene for sickle cells and others do not. If such a population lived in a tropical lowland where quartan malaria was pandemic, the infection or noninfection with malaria might conceivably be a matter of heredity rather than environment.

HEREDITARY AND ENVIRONMENTAL DIFFERENCES

I certainly do not maintain that the nature-nurture problem is meaningless and that all human variation is always due as much to heredity as to environment. But to make the distinction between genetic and environmental effects on the phenotype meaningful, the problem must be stated with greater care than it often is.

It is easy to observe that some people have dark and others light skins; some enjoy robust health and others are handicapped in various ways; some are bright and others dull; some have kindly and others irascible dispositions. Skin pigmentation, health, intelligence, and temperament are all, like life itself, necessarily determined by the interaction of the genotypes with their environments. A question may, however, be validly posed: To what extent are the differences observed between persons due to genotypic or to environmental causes (Fig.1)? Or to put it another way: What part of the observed variance in a given trait in a given population is due to the diversity of the genotypes and what part to the diversity of the environments?

With the problem so stated, two things become apparent. First, the contribution of the genetic and environmental variables may be quite different for different characteristics: to which blood group a person belongs is decided, as far as is known, entirely by the genotype and not at all by the environment; which language a person speaks is decided entirely by environment and not at all by genotype, except that some low-grade mental defectives may be unable to learn any language and the defect may be genetic. Second, the relative weights of the genetic and the environmental variables are not constant: they change in space and time.

Take human stature as an example. It has been known for a long time that children of tall parents are on the average taller than those of short parents, but by itself this proves nothing, since a parent-offspring correlation may be due to common genes or common environments. Studies of twins have shown, however, that monozygotic twins, when reared together or apart, resemble each other in stature more than do dizygotic twins. There is, then, a strong genetic component in the determination of stature. (The statures of the twins described in the classical work of Newman, Freeman, and Holzinger, 1937, were correlated rather more closely than in the newer study of Osborn and DeGeorge, 1959. . . .) On the other hand, children of Japanese immigrants born in the United States are taller than their parents born in Japan. The environment is clearly responsible for a part of the variance in stature. If environment becomes homogeneous, owing to more uniform diet and child care, people will differ in stature mostly

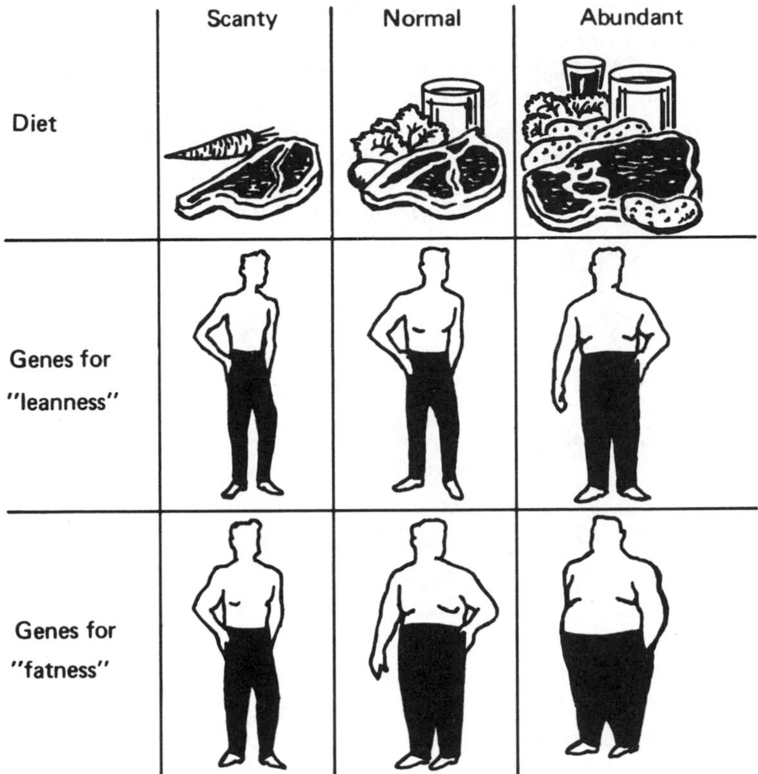

FIGURE 1. **Gene-environment interaction. A person who has a gene for "fatness" may actually weigh less than a person with a gene for "leanness," if the former lives on a scanty and the latter on an overabundant diet.**

because of the differences in their genes and, conversely, in genetically homogeneous populations the environmental differences will account for a relatively greater part of the variance in stature than in genetically heterogeneous ones. There is clearly no single solution to the nature-nurture problem, and the matter must be studied separately for each character. Even then the results may have validity only for a population studied at a certain time and place

* * *

REFERENCES

Adler A. *Understanding Human Nature.* New York: Premier Books (Fawcett), 1957.

Allison, A. C. "Protection Afforded by Sickle Cell Trait Against Subtertian Malarial Infection." *Brit. Med. J.* 1: 290-92.

—— "Notes on Sickle-Cell Polymorphism." *Ann. Human Genetics* 19: 39-57.

—— "Aspects of Polymorphism in Man." *Cold Spring Harbor Symp. Quant. Biol.* 20: 239-55.

Johannsen, W. *Elemente der exakten Erbichkeitslehre.* Jean: Fischer, 1909.

—— "The Genotype Conception of Heredity." *Am. Nat.* 45 (1911): 129-59.

Osborn, R.H., and F.V. DeGeorge. *Genetic Basis of Morphological Variation.* Cambridge: Harvard University Press, 1959.

Swellengrebel, N.H. "The Efficient Parasite." *Proceedings of the 3rd International Congress on Microbiology* 1940, 119-27.

D. O. Hebb

THE MAMMAL AND HIS ENVIRONMENT

The original intention in this paper was to discuss the significance of neurophysiological theory for psychiatry and psychology, and to show, by citing the work done by some of my colleagues, that the attempt to get at the neural mechanisms of behavior can stimulate and clarify purely behavioral—that is, psychiatric and psychological—thinking. The research to be described has, I think, a clear relevance to clinical problems; but its origin lay in efforts to learn how the functioning of individual neurons and synapses relates to the functions of the whole brain, and to understand the physiological nature of learning, emotion, thinking, or intelligence.

In the end, however, my paper has simply become a review of the research referred to, dealing with the relation of the mammal to his environment. The question concerns the normal variability of the sensory environment and this has been studied from two points of view. First, one may ask what the significance of perceptual activity is during growth; for this purpose one can rear an animal with a considerable degree of restriction, and see what effects there are upon mental development. Secondly, in normal animals whose development is complete, one can remove a good deal of the supporting action of the normal environment, to discover how far the animal continues to be dependent on it even after maturity.

THE ROLE OF THE ENVIRONMENT DURING GROWTH

The immediate background of our present research on the intelligence and personality of the dog is the work of Hymovitch (6) on the intelligence of rats. He reared laboratory rats in 2 ways: (1) in a psychologically restricted environment, a small cage, with food and water always at hand and plenty of opportunity for exercise (in an activity wheel), but with no problems to solve, no need of getting on with others, no pain; and (2) in a "free" environment, a large box with obstacles to pass, blind alleys to avoid, other rats to get on with, and thus ample opportunity for problem-solving and great need for learning during growth. Result: the rats brought up in a psychologically restricted (but biologically adequate) environment have a lasting inferiority in problem-solving. This does not mean, of course, the environment is everything, heredity nothing: here heredity was held constant, which prevents it from affecting the results. When the reverse experiment is done we find problem-solving varying with heredity instead. The same capacity for problem-solving is fully dependent on both variables for its development.

To take this further, Thompson and others have been applying similar methods to dogs (9). The same intellectual effect of an impoverished environment is found again, perhaps more marked in the higher species. But another kind of effect can be seen in dogs, which have clearly marked personalities. Personality–by which I mean complex individual differences of emotion and motivation–is again strongly affected by the infant environment. These effects, however, are hard to analyze, and I cannot at present give any rounded picture of them.

First, observations during the rearing itself are significant. A Scottish terrier is reared in a small cage, in isolation from other Scotties and from the human staff. Our animal man, William Ponman, is a dog lover and undertook the experiment with misgivings, which quickly disappeared. In a cage 30 by 30 inches, the dogs are "happy as larks," eat more than normally reared dogs, grow well, are physically vigorous: as Ponman says, "I never saw such healthy dogs–they're like bulls." If you put a normally reared dog into such a cage, shut off from everything, his misery is unmistakable, and we have not been able to bring ourselves to continue such experiments. Not so the dog that has known nothing else. Ponman showed some of these at a dog show of national standing, winning first-prize ribbons with them.

Observations by Dr. Ronald Melzack on pain are extremely interesting. He reared two dogs, after early weaning, in complete isolation, taking care that there was little opportunity for experience of pain (unless the dog bit himself). At maturity, when the dogs were first taken out for study, they were extraordinarily excited, with random, rapid movement. As a result they got their tails or paws stepped on repeatedly–but paid no attention to an event that would elicit howls from a normally reared dog. After a few days, when their movements were calmer, they were tested with an object that gave electric shock, and paid little attention to it. Through five testing periods, the dog repeatedly thrust his nose into a lighted match; and months later, did the same thing several times with a lighted cigar.

A year and a half after coming out of restriction they are still hyperactive. Clipping and trimming one of them is a two man job; if the normal dog does not stand still, a cuff on the ear will remind him of his duty; but cuffing the experimental dog "has as much effect as if you patted him–except he pays no attention to it." It seems certain, especially in view of the related results reported by Nissen, Chow, and Semmes (7) for a chimpanzee, that the adult's perception of pain is essentially a function of pain experience during growth–and that what we call pain is not a single sensory quale but a complex mixture of a particular kind of synthesis with past learning and emotional disturbance.

Nothing bores the dogs reared in restriction. At an "open house," we put two restricted dogs in one enclosure, two normal ones in another, and asked the public to tell us which were the normal. Without exception, they picked out the two alert, lively, interested animals–not the lackadaisical pair lying in the corner, paying no attention to the visitors. The alert pair, actually, were the restricted; the normal dogs had seen all they wanted to see of the crowd in the first two minutes, and then went to sleep, thoroughly bored. The restricted dogs, so to speak, haven't the brains to be bored.

Emotionally, the dogs are "immature," but not in the human or clinical sense. They are little bothered by imaginative fears. Dogs suffer from irrational fears, like horses, porpoises, elephants, chimpanzees, and man; but it appears that this is a product of intellectual development, characteristic of the brighter, not the duller animal. Our dogs in restriction are not smart enough to fear strange objects. Things that cause fear in normal dogs produce only a generalized, undirected excitement in the restricted. If both normal and restricted dogs are exposed to the same noninjurious but exciting stimulus repeatedly, fear gradually develops in the restricted; but the normals, at first afraid, have by this time gone on to show a playful aggression instead. On the street, the restricted dogs "lead well," not bothered by what goes on around them, while those reared normally vary greatly in this respect. Analysis has a long way to go in these cases, but we can say now that dogs reared in isolation are not like ordinary dogs. They are both stupid and peculiar.

Such results clearly support the clinical evidence, and the animal experiments of others (1), showing that early environment has a lasting effect on the form of adjustment at maturity. We do not have a great body of evidence yet, and before we generalize too much it will be particularly important to repeat these observations with animals of different heredity. But I have been very surprised, personally, by the lack of evidence of emotional instability, neurotic tendency, or the like, when the dogs are suddenly plunged into a normal world. There is, in fact, just the opposite effect. This suggests caution in interpreting data with human children, such as those of Spitz (8) or Bowlby (3). Perceptual restriction in infancy certainly produces a low level of intelligence, but it may not, by itself, produce emotional disorder. The observed results seem to mean, not that the stimulus of another attentive organism (the mother) is necessary from the first but that it may become necessary only as psychological *dependence* on the mother develops. However, our limited data certainly cannot prove anything for man, though they may suggest other interpretations besides those that have been made.

THE ENVIRONMENT AT MATURITY

Another approach to the relation between the mammal and his environment is possible: that is, one can take the normally reared mammal and cut him off at maturity from his usual contact with the world. It seems clear that thought and personality characteristics develop as a function of the environment. Once developed, are they independent of it? This experiment is too cruel to do with animals, but not with college students. The first stage of the work was done by Bexton, Heron, and Scott(2). It follows up some work by Mackworth on the effects of monotony, in which he found extraordinary lapses of attention. Heron and his co-workers set out to make the monotony more prolonged and more complete.

The subject is paid to do nothing 24 hours a day. He lies on a comfortable bed in a small closed cubicle, is fed on request, goes to the toilet on request. Otherwise he does nothing. He wears frosted glass goggles that admit light but do not allow pattern vision. His ears are covered by a sponge rubber pillow in which are embedded small speakers by which he can be communicated with, and a microphone hangs near to enable him to answer. His hands are covered with gloves, and cardboard cuffs extend from the upper forearm beyond his fingertips, permitting free joint movement but with little tactual perception.

The results are dramatic. During the stay in the cubicle, the experimental subject shows extensive loss, statistically significant, in solving simple problems. He complains subjectively that he cannot concentrate; his boredom is such that he looks forward eagerly to the next problem, but when it is presented he finds himself unwilling to make the effort to solve it.

On emergence from the cubicle the subject is given the same kind of intelligence tests as before entering, and shows significant loss. There is disturbance of motor control. Visual perception is changed in a way difficult to describe; it is as if the object looked at was exceptionally vivid, but impaired in its relation to other objects and the background – a disturbance perhaps of the larger organization of perception. This condition may last up to 12 or 24 hours.

Subjects reported some remarkable hallucinatory activity, some which resembled the effects of mescal, or the results produced by Grey Walter with flickering light. These hallucinations were primarily visual, perhaps only because the experimenters were able to control visual perception most effectively; however, some auditory and some esthetic hallucinations have been observed as well.

The nature of these phenomena is best conveyed by quoting one subject who reported over the microphone that he had just been asleep and had a very vivid dream and although he was awake, the dream was continuing. The study of dreams has a long history, and is clearly important theoretically, but is hampered by the impossibility of knowing how much the subject's report is distorted by memory. In many ways the hallucinatory activity of the present experiments is indistinguishable from what we know about dreams; if it is in essence the same process, but going on while the subject can describe it (not merely hot but still on the griddle), we have a new source of information, a means of direct attack, on the nature of the dream.

In its early stages the activity as it occurs in the experiment is probably not dreamlike. The course of development is fairly consistent. First, when the eyes are closed the visual field is light rather than dark. Next there are reports of dots of light, lines, or simple geometrical patterns, so vivid that they are described as being a new experience. Nearly all experimental subjects reported such activity. (Many of course could not tolerate the experimental conditions very long, and left before the full course of development was seen.) The next stage is the occurrence of repetitive patterns, like a wallpaper design, reported by three-quarters of the subjects; next, the appearance of isolated objects, without background, seen by half the subjects; and finally, integrated scenes, involving action, usually containing dreamlike distortions, and apparently with all the vividness of an animated cartoon, seen by about a quarter of the subjects. In general, these amused the subject, relieving his boredom, as he watched to see what the movie program would produce next. The subjects reported that the scenes seemed to be out in front of them. A few could, apparently, "look at" different parts of the scene in central vision, as one could with a movie; and up to a point could change its content by "trying." It was not, however, well under control. Usually, it would disappear if the subject were given an interesting task, but not when the subject described it, nor if he did physical exercises. Its persistence and vividness interfered with sleep for some subjects, and at this stage was irritating.

In their later stages the hallucinations were elaborated into everything from a peaceful rural scene to naked women diving and swimming in a woodland pool to prehistoric animals plunging through tropical forests. One man saw a pair of spectacles, which were then joined by a dozen more, without wearers, fixed intently on him; faces sometimes appeared behind the glasses, but with no eyes visible. The glasses sometimes moved in unison, as if marching in procession. Another man saw a field onto which a bathtub rolled: it moved slowly on rubber-tired wheels, with chrome hub caps. In it was seated an old man wearing a battle helmet. Another subject was highly entertained at seeing a row of squirrels marching single file across a snowy field, wearing snowshoes and carying little bags over their shoulders.

Some of the scenes were in three dimensions, most in two (that is, as if projected on a screen). A most interesting feature was that some of the images were persistently tilted from the vertical, and a few reports were given of inverted scenes, completely upside down.

There were a few reports of auditory phenomena–one subject heard the people in his hallucination talking. There are also some esthetic imagery, as when one saw a doorknob before him, and as he touched it felt an electric shock; or when another saw a miniature rocket ship maneuvering around him, and discharging pellets that he felt hitting his arm. But the most interesting of these phenomena the subject, apparently, lacked words to describe adequately. There were references to a feeling of "otherness," to bodily "strangeness." One said that his mind was like a ball of cottonwool floating in the air above him.

Two independently reported that they perceived a second body, or second person, in the cubicle. One subject reported that he could not tell which of the two bodies was his own, and described the two bodies as overlapping in space—not like Siamese twins, but two complete bodies with an arm, shoulder, and side of each occupying the same space.

THEORETICAL SIGNIFICANCE

The theoretical interest of these results for us extends in two directions. On the one hand, they interlock with work using more physiological methods, of brain stimulation and recording, and especially much of the recent work on the relation of the brain stem to cortical "arousal." Points of correspondence between behavioral theory and knowledge of neural function are increasing, and each new point of correspondence provides both a corrective for theory and a stimulation for further research. A theory of thought and of consciousness in physiologically intelligible terms need no longer be completely fantastic.

On the other hand, the psychological data cast new light on the relation of man to his environment, including his social environment, and it is this that I should like to discuss a little further. To do so I must go back for a moment to some earlier experiments on chimpanzee emotion. They indicate that the higher mammal may be psychologically at the mercy of his environment to a much greater degree than we have been accustomed to think.

Studies in our laboratory of the role of the environment during infancy and a large body of work reviewed recently by Beach and Jaynes(1) make it clear that psychological development is fully dependent on stimulation from the environment. Without it, intelligence does not develop normally, and the personality is grossly atypical. The experiment with college students shows that a short period—even a day or so—of deprivation of a normal sensory input produces personality changes and a clear loss of capacity to solve problems. Even at maturity, then, the organism is still essentially dependent on a normal sensory environment for the maintenance of its psychological integrity.

The following data show yet another way in which the organism appears psychologically vulnerable. It has long been known that the chimpanzee may be frightened by representation of animals, such as a small toy donkey. An accidental observation of my own extended this to include representations of the chimpanzee himself, of man, and of parts of the chimpanzee or human body. A model of a chimpanzee head, in clay, produced terror in the colony of the Yerkes Laboratories, as did a lifelike representation of a human head, and a number of related objects such as an actual chimpanzee head, preserved in formalin, or a colored representation of a human eye and eyebrow. A deeply anesthetized chimpanzee, "dead" as far as the others were concerned, aroused fear in some animals and vicious attacks by others(4).

I shall not deal with this theoretically. What matters for our present purposes is the conclusion, rather well supported by the animal evidence, that the greater the development of intelligence the greater the vulnerability to emotional breakdown. The price of high intelligence is susceptibility to imaginative fears and unreasoning suspicion and other emotional weaknesses. The conclusion is not only supported by the animal data, but also agrees with the course of development in children, growing intelligence being accompanied by increased frequency and strength of emotional problems—up to the age of five years.

Then, apparently, the trend is reversed. Adult man, more intelligent than chimpanzee or five-year-old child, seems not more subject to emotional disturbances but less. Does this then disprove the conclusion? It seemed a pity to abandon a principle that made sense of so many data that had not made sense before, and the kind of theory I was working with—neurophysiologically oriented—also pointed in the same direction. The question then was, is it possible that something is concealing the adult human being's emotional weaknesses?

From this point of view it became evident that the concealing agency is man's culture, which acts as a protective cocoon. There are many indications that our emotional stability depends more on our successful avoidance of emotional provocation than on our essential characteristics: that urbanity depends on an urbane social and physical environment. Dr. Thompson and I(5) reviewed the evidence, and came to the conclusion that the development of what is called "civilization" is the progressive elimination of sources of acute fear, disgust, and anger; and that civilized man may not be less, but more, susceptible to such disturbance because of his success in protecting himself from disturbing situations so much of the time.

We may fool ourselves thoroughly in this matter. We are surprised that children are afraid of the dark, or afraid of being left alone, and congratulate ourselves on having got over such weakness. Ask anyone you know whether he is afraid of the dark, and he will either laugh at you or be insulted. This attitude is easy to maintain in a well-lighted, well-behaved suburb. But try being alone in complete darkness in the streets of a strange city, or alone at night in the deep woods, and see if you still feel the same way.

We read incredulously of the taboo rules of primitive societies; we laugh at the superstitious fear of the dead in primitive people. What is there about a dead body to produce disturbance? Sensible, educated people are not so affected. One can easily show that they are, however, and that we have developed an extraordinarily complete taboo system—not just moral prohibition, but full-fledged ambivalent taboo—to deal with the dead body. I took a poll of an undergraduate class of 198 persons, including some nurses and veterans, to see how many had encountered a dead body. Thirty-seven had never seen a dead body in any circumstances, and 91 had seen one only after an undertaker had prepared it for burial; making a total of 65 percent who had never seen a dead body in, so to speak, its natural state. It is quite clear that for some reason we protect society against sight of, contact with, the dead body. Why?

Again, the effect of moral education, and training in the rules of courtesy, and the compulsion to dress, talk and act as others do, adds up to ensuring that the individual member of society will not act in a way that is a provocation to others—will not, that is, be a source of strong emotional disturbance, except in highly ritualized circumstances approved by society. The social behavior of a group of civilized persons, then, makes up that protective cocoon which allows us to think of ourselves as being less emotional than the explosive four-year-old or the equally explosive chimpanzee.

The well-adjusted adult therefore is not intrinsically less subject to emotional disturbance: he is well-adjusted, relatively unemotional, as long as he is in his cocoon. The problem of moral education, from this point of view, is not simply to produce a stable individual, but to produce an individual that will (1) be stable in the existing social environment, and (2) contribute to its protective uniformity. We think of some persons as being emotionally dependent, others not; but it looks as though we are all completely dependent on the environment in a way and to a degree that we have not suspected.

BIBLIOGRAPHY

1. Beach, F. A., and Jaynes, J. *Psychol. Bull.* 51 (1954): 239.
2. Bexton, W. H., Heron, W., and Scott, T. H. *Canad. J. Psychol.* 8 (1954): 70.
3. Bowlby, J. *Maternal Care and Mental Health.* Geneva: WHO Monogr. No. 2, 1951.
4. Hebb, D. O. *Psychol. Rev.* 53 (1946): 259.
5. Hebb, D. O., and Thompson, W. R. In Lindzey, G. (Ed.), *Handbook of Social Psychology.* Cambridge: Addison-Wesley, 1954.
6. Hymovitch, B. J. *Comp. Physiol. Psychol.* 45 (1952): 313.
7. Nissen, H. W., Chow, R. L., and Semmes, Josephine. *Am. J. Psychol.* 64 (1951): 485.
8. Spitz, R. A. *Psychoanalytic Study of the Child,* 2 (1946): 113.
9. Thompson, W. R., and Heron, W. *Canad. J. Psychol.* 8 (1954): 17.

chapter **2**

Perception

Perception is the process by which an individual gives meaning to his environment. While there are many definitions of the term, most include, at least implicitly, all of the following elements: some external stimulus, some process by which the external stimulus is transmitted into psychological experience, and some interpretation or meaning of that psychological experience given by the individual. Because they take an active part in giving meaning to stimuli, different individuals will see the same thing in different ways. How a person "sees" determines his behavior. Therefore, the way a person "sees" the situation has much greater practical significance for organizational behavior than does the situation itself. Recognition of the active role of the perceiver is important for the student and practitioner of organizational behavior.

Because it is central to our understanding of human behavior, the perceptual process has been the subject of a tremendous volume of research. In a book of this sort, only the issues which have the most clear implications for human social behavior can be dealt with. These introductory pages cover some basic ideas in the field of perception, particularly social perception.[1] The readings which follow relate these concepts to interpersonal behavior and organizational functioning.

The "mind-body" problem which underlies perception has never been fully resolved. It concerns the relationship between the "physical world" and the "experienced world" of the individual. Laymen have generally assumed that an individual's senses receive and transmit valid information about the external world to the individual. As the history of psychology and philosophy demonstrates, however, many scholars have raised serious questions about the relationship of the internal and external worlds. Some have doubted the existence of mind; others have doubted the existence of body.

Recognizing that this issue has not been settled, for present purposes we will make several assumptions consistent with the laymen's view mentioned above. First, we will assume that some material world exists and through the senses

1. For further reading, Allport (1955), Gibson (1969), Secord and Backman (1964), and Tagiuri (1969) are suggested.

people absorb forms of energy that are experienced as a representation of the material world. In addition, there is transmission of internally generated energy which may also be reported as experience. The exact relationship between the source of the energy and the reported experiences is not known, but some relationship is presumed to exist. Attempts to understand the relationship between the source and the experience are the basis of a variety of theories of perception.

Most theories agree that the psychological meaning given to an energy source is determined by the interaction of previous experiences, current states of the organism, the context in which the perceived object exists, and the unique sensing system of an individual. The variability of all these factors causes considerable intraindividual and interindividual differences in the way a given object is experienced. For example, oftentimes perception is determined by particular needs and values as well as by the stimulus itself. Furthermore, perception is selective in that people attend to only part of the stimulus situation. The expectations of an individual, his particular current interests, and the way needs have been satisfied in the past also influence what he sees.

Bruner (1958) coined the phrase "perceptual readiness" to express the requirement that what is seen will be influenced not only by needs and goals but also by the efficiency of means of goal attainment. In other words, perception is influenced by the way a person has learned to deal with his needs as well as by the factors noted above. As a consequence of variations in all these factors, there is room for considerable disagreement among people as to what is "seen." Fortunately, there is enough shared experience concerning a sufficiently large number of objects to permit social organization to exist. An adequate perceptual theory must be able to explain not only variability and uniqueness but also stability and commonality in the relationship between object or source and experience.

The complexity of the perceptual process has caused considerable controversy over competing theories of object perception. The controversy becomes more difficult to resolve when the perceived objects are people. In interpersonal perception the relationship between the source and the perceiver is more complex, because the source varies as the process evolves. Furthermore, the behavior of the perceiver influences the source, and the perceiver is also a source himself. In nonpersonal object perception the state of the source is at least more stable. However, many of the problems in organizations involve interpersonal perception, so the process must be understood.

A MODEL OF INTERPERSONAL PERCEPTION

Figure 1 summarizes the interaction of variables in interpersonal perception by describing an interaction between two individuals, named "Person" and "Other." The two lower circles in the diagram represent the inner worlds of each party, and the upper portion of the figure represents the context and interaction as they "really are."[2] Consider the lower portion first, particularly Person's inner world.

2. When I refer to things "as they really are," I am making a simplifying assumption that

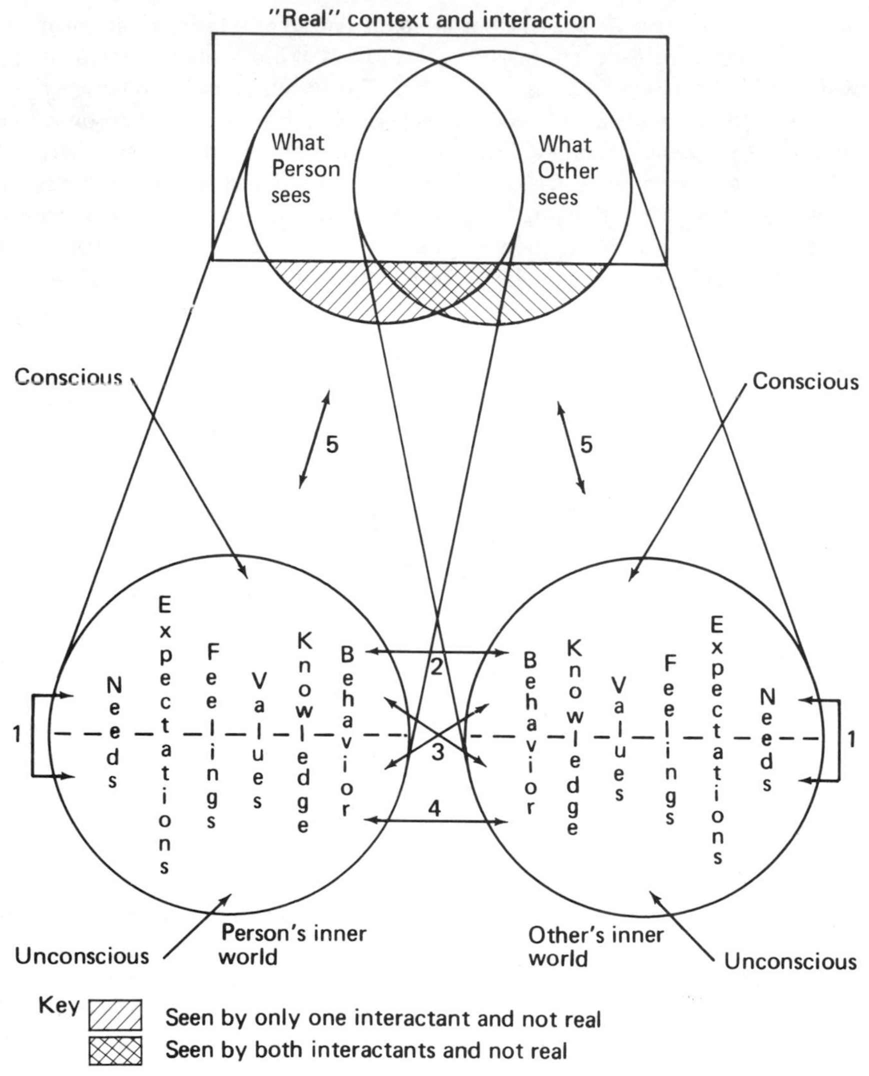

FIGURE 1. **Model of interpersonal perception.**

The Inner World

Four features of Person's inner world play a major role in the process of interpersonal perception. First, the inner world contains a number of characteristics—such as needs, predispositions to behave, expectations, feelings, values, and knowledge—which influence how he will perceive his environment. Second, Person is not equally aware of all characteristics of his own inner world. Third,

---

there is an objective reality. If the reader prefers, he may call this a consensual reality—i.e., the situation as seen by several people.

information flows between the conscious and unconscious levels (in channel 1). Fourth, the contents of Person's inner world are constantly changing. As a result, the accuracy of his perceptions of Other may vary.

As Person interacts with Other, information flows along channels 2 through 5. All such information is susceptible to two types of error. Information may be sent but not received, and information which is received may be distorted by the receiver. In addition, there are various other sources of error unique to each channel. Let us look at channels 2, 3, and 4, which link Person's and Other's inner worlds.

Channel 2 carries information which is sent consciously by one person and received consciously by the other. Such exchanges are relatively clear to both parties, although they can be a source of difficulty. For example, Person may manipulate Other's perception by consciously sending false data or withholding true information. Also, the information passing between people at the conscious level is often limited by social norms and a desire to avoid hurting the other person. Consequently, information flowing in this channel may be inappropriately positive. As Hastorf, Schneider, and Polefka (1970) observed,

> People find it more comfortable to say pleasant than unpleasant things to one another. Is is embarrassing to tell another he is wrong. If another perceives me (let us say incorrectly) as particularly intelligent, I may find it ego-enhancing and socially comfortable not to disabuse him of his incorrect perception. I would probably be more likely to try to correct his perception that I am unkind. (p. 93)

Information in this channel may understate positive feelings as well. For example, it may be difficult to tell another person that you like him a lot; consequently, overt expressions of affection are often toned down. Because these sources of distortion exist, accurate perception of others often requires the processing of information which one or both participants send and/or receive unconsciously.

The channels numbered 3 carry information between the conscious level of one party and the unconscious level of the other. Two types of discrepancy between Person's and Other's perceptions of an interaction may arise when information flows in these channels. First, Person may be consciously sending information to Other that Other is not aware of receiving. Second, Person may receive information from Other that Other is not aware of sending. For example, Other may consciously state into channel 2, "I am not angry." However, the tone of Other's voice, which Other is not aware of having introduced into channel 3, may lead Person to believe that Other is very angry. These "mixed" messages are a frequent source of difficulty in relations between people. This channel can be of great value to a manager who is aware of the nonverbal messages that another person is sending unconsciously, because these messages are less susceptible to conscious manipulation by the sender than is information sent in channel 2. Many managers favor face-to-face meetings rather than telephone conversations in order to gain access to channel 3.

Channel 4 carries exchanges between nonconscious levels. The data it carries influence how Person perceives Other, even though neither is ever fully aware of sending or receiving such information. For example, the body movements of Other may influence Person's inner world in ways which both fail to recognize. This channel carries mainly nonverbal communications.[3] Often they are very accurate, because neither party can manipulate them consciously. They may be responsible for vague feelings or intuitions we have about other people.

The "Real" Interaction and Its Context

In addition to the information transmitted in channels 1 through 4, interpersonal perception is affected by the "real" situation. The upper portion of Figure 1 represents both the context in which Person and Other are interacting and the interaction itself.[4] Information between Person and the context flows through channel 5.

Person's view of the context is influenced by things of which he is aware and unaware. This channel is two-way because, while the context influences Person and his perception, his inner world also helps shape his view of the context. The errors here are similar to those of object perception.

There are several additional, important considerations about the context itself. First, the large rectangle represents the "objective" or "real" context. Person's view of the situation coincides only partially with the "real situation." Similarly, Other's view coincides only partially with reality. Furthermore, the limited overlapping of Other's and Person's views allows only partial agreement between the two individuals. Thus Person and Other agree on only a part of reality, and both miss part of reality. It is also important to note that both Person and Other may "see" some things that are not part of reality. This possibility is represented by the cross-hatched areas extending beyond the real context. Finally, the dark area where the cross-hatched areas overlap represents the possibility that Person and Other could agree on things that do not really exist. For example, two employees may agree that their jobs are in danger when in fact they are not.

This model is really only a framework for summarizing some of the elements that influence interpersonal perception while two people interact. A number of other processes that occur before, during, and after this interaction will affect the relationship between Person and Other. Two of these—the selective process in human interaction and the attribution of causality—are especially important.

A great deal of research evidence and everyday experience supports the proposition that human interaction is selective. In the words of Hastorf *et al.* (1970):

> If I know that you perceive me as unintelligent, I would probably be offended and might avoid you, thus denying you the opportunity to correct your impression. If I perceive you as dishonest, I am likely to cease interaction with you, again denying the opportunity for correction. (p. 94)

3. See Shulman's paper in part 3.

4. It is important to emphasize that in Fig. 1 the behavior of the participants is assumed to be part of the "real" situation.

Once formed erroneous perceptions may remain unchanged if they cause interaction between the participants to cease.

Second, participants are not passive receivers of information; they attempt to organize or make sense of incoming data so they can use the information. For instance, people try to determine why someone is behaving in a particular way. These attempts to make causal inferences exemplify attribution.

In interpersonal interaction we tend to perceive other people as causal agents, and we make inferences about their intentions. As Hastorf *et al.* have noted, an important aspect is the degree to which we see the person's behavior as due to external or internal forces. Often the same type of behavior will elicit very different responses from us, depending on what we perceive to have caused the behavior. For example, consider the influence of attributions on the response of a manager to two subordinates. Subordinates A and B tend to do their assigned tasks promptly and competently. However, the manager believes that Subordinate A performs well because he is afraid that poor performance will be punished. Subordinate B is seen as working because he wants to help the department look good and he feels satisfied when he has done a good job. We can expect the supervisor to evaluate and treat these two workers very differently.

Although the example is a simple one, it indicates the importance of attribution. As Kelley (1973) wrote in concluding his excellent paper on attribution theory:

> Man's concern with the reasons for events does not leave him "lost in thought" about those reasons. Rather, his causal explanations play an important role in providing his impetus to action and in his decisions among alternative courses of action. When the attributions are appropriate, the person undoubtedly fares better in his decisions and actions than he would in the absence of the causal analysis. (p. 127)

Studies of the attribution process have revealed a great deal about the causal inferences people typically make. Two of these findings are especially relevant for the management of people. First, there is a tendency for people to prefer simple attributions over complex ones; single-cause explanations are more likely to be given than multi-cause ones. Consequently, we tend to develop rather simplistic cause-and-effect explanations. This preference is apt to lead us to attribute the behavior of other people to their personal characteristics rather than to situational forces. Second, our tendency to hold people responsible for their own behavior is apt to be stronger when we attempt to account for the behavior of others than when we explain our own behavior. We attribute our own actions to situational requirements but explain the behavior of others by their personal dispositions (Kelley, 1973).

The problems these tendencies can introduce into organizations are clear. If I as a manager fail to perceive the role of situational forces acting on others, I am prone to making inaccurate evaluations of my employees and likely to fail to manage the situation in a way that facilitates maximum performance. Moreover, to the degree that I inappropriately attribute my own actions to situational forces, I am unlikely to diagnose my own shortcomings.

PERCEPTION AND MANAGEMENT: THE READINGS

Our discussion of perception has and will continue to focus on interpersonal perception. While object and interpersonal perception are similar, the latter is more complex because of the possibility of deliberate distortion, unrepresentative behavior, changes which occur within both parties, and interplay between conscious and unconscious elements. The probability that interpersonal and organizational problems will be rooted in perception is so great that in many ways perception is a central concern for managers.

The readings in this section focus on the basic process of perception and its implications for interpersonal and organizational behavior. The process of perception is important to managers above and beyond the problems of interpersonal perception. It is not only important that people agree enough about what they "see" to be able to coordinate their efforts; it is also important that people see the "real" world accurately enough to be able to deal with it in a functional manner. Often, under certain conditions, people find it useful to defend themselves perceptually by distorting or overlooking information which threatens their view of the world or themselves. For example, a person questioning a grade given him by a professor may misinterpret the professor's statements. The teacher may be attempting to say, "You missed the point." The student may tell himself, "I just misunderstood the meaning of a word or two." The problem is compounded by the professor's own defensiveness. The student may be saying, "I don't understand your question." The teacher may be "seeing" a hostile, disrespectful, immature individual. Such a view allows the professor to defend his own self-view from the threat he perceives to his favorite exam question.

Similar perceptual defenses operate in all organizations. It is generally agreed that types of distortion are systematically related to particular needs and that distortion is often increased under conditions of psychological threat. Further, training and experience predispose people to "see" certain things and not others. Effective management of people requires an awareness of the possibility of distortion, a recognition of its probable sources, and a means to prevent and alleviate it.

The first reading is a selection by Cantril describing the nature of perception and its implications for interpersonal behavior. The Dearborn and Simon reading which follows points to the interaction between organizational and perceptual factors. Their study suggests the consequences that performance of organizational roles can have for one's ability to see the world. Their findings are supported by many other studies. For example, Toch and Schulte (1961) found that the training that policemen receive increases the probability that they will see themes of violence in ambiguous pictures. A final reading by Marshall McLuhan introduces the view that the way in which stimuli are communicated has important consequences for perception. McLuhan maintains that the technology used in communication affects the receiver's perception of the message. In his words, "The medium is the message." The implications of McLuhan's stress on the process of communication have not been fully recognized by organizational behaviorists. An example of the implications of process for organizations was provided by Postman and Weingartner (1969), who pointed out that what is learned in schools may be more a consequence of *how* things are taught than of *what* is taught. Process is thus a central variable in perception.

These selections represent only a small sampling of relevant material on perception. However, many of the issues which are partially treated here reappear in the sections on motivation, learning, personality, communication and group behavior. Many of the unanticipated consequences discussed in part 2 also have their roots in perception.

REFERENCES

Allport, F. H. *Theories of Perception and the Concept of Structure.* New York: John Wiley, 1955.

Bruner, J. "Social Psychology and Perception." In *Readings in Social Psychology.* 3rd ed., edited by E. Maccoby, T. Newcomb, and E. Hartley, pp. 85-94. New York: Holt, Rinehart and Winston, 1958.

Gibson, E. J. *Principles of Perceptual Learning and Development.* New York: Appleton-Century-Crofts, 1969.

Hastorf, A. H.; Schneider, D. J.; and Polefka, J. *Person Perception.* Reading, Mass.: Addison-Wesley, 1970.

Kelley, H. H. "The Processes of Causal Attribution." *American Psychologist* 28 (1973): 107-128.

Postman, N., and Weingartner, C. *Teaching as a Subversive Activity.* New York: Delacorte, 1969.

Secord, P. F., and Backman, C. W. *Social Psychology.* New York: McGraw-Hill Book Company, 1964.

Tagiuri, R. "Person Perception." In *The Handbook of Social Psychology.* 2nd ed., vol. 3, edited by G. Lindzey and E. Aronson, pp. 395-449. Reading, Mass.: Addison-Wesley, 1969.

Toch, H., and Schulte, R. "Readiness to Perceive Violence as a Result of Police Training." *British Journal of Psychology* 52 (1961): 389-93.

Hadley Cantril

PERCEPTION AND INTERPERSONAL RELATIONS

It is with a very profound feeling of humility that I, as a psychologist, offer any comments for the consideration of psychiatrists on the subject of perception and interpersonal relations. For the more one studies perception, the more one sees that what we label "perception" is essentially a process which man utilizes to make his purposive behavior more effective and satisfying, and that this behavior always stems from and is rooted in a personal behavioral center. Thus perception involves numerous aspects of behavior which we rather artificially and necessarily differentiate in order to get a toe-hold for understanding, but which, in the on-going process of living, orchestrate together in a most interdependent way.

This means, then, that the nature of perception can only be understood if somehow we manage to start off with what some of us call a "first-person point of view" as contrasted to the "third person point of view" represented by the traditional psychological investigator. And so my very genuine feeling of humility in accepting an invitation of psychiatrists derives from the fact that the psychiatrist, perhaps more than any other specialist concerned with the study of human beings, is primarily concerned with the first-person point of view, is skilled in the art of uncovering what this may be for his patient, and knows from his own experience the wide gap that exists between this first-person experience and the abstractions we have created as scientists in order to analyze, conceptualize, and communicate. A very nice expression of this last state of affairs was, incidentally, recently made by Aldous Huxley in his book *The Genius and the Goddess:*

> What a gulf between *im*pression and *ex*pression! That's our ironic fate—to have Shakespearian feelings and (unless by billion-to-one chance we happen to *be* Shakespeare) to talk about them like automobile salesmen or teen-agers or college professors.
>
> We practice alchemy in reverse – touch gold and it turns to lead; touch the pure lyrics of experience, and they turn into the verbal equivalents of tripe and hogwash.

Abridged from Hadley Cantril, "Perception and Interpersonal Relations," *American Journal of Psychiatry* 114 (1957):119-26.

BACKGROUND

Most of you are probably familiar to some extent with a point of view that has developed rather recently in psychology and has been dubbed "transactional psychology." While I do not want to spend time here repeating what has been published in a variety of sources, I might at least very briefly note some of the major emphases of transactional psychology before discussing certain aspects and some experimental results which may be of particular interest to psychiatrists (1, 2, 3, 4).

Here, then, are some of the emphases of transactional psychology which may give us a take-off for discussion:

Our perception depends in large part on the assumptions we bring to any particular occasion. It is, as Dewey and Bentley long ago pointed out, not a "reaction to" stimuli in the environment but may be more accurately described as a "transaction with" an environment.

This implies that the meanings and significances we assign to things, to symbols, to people, and to events are the meanings and significances we have built up through our past experience, and are not inherent or intrinsic in the "stimulus" itself.

Since our experience is concerned with purposive behavior, our perceptions are learned in terms of our purposes and in terms of what is important and useful to us.

Since the situations we are in seldom repeat themselves exactly and since change seems to be the rule of nature and of life, our perception is largely a matter of weighing probabilities, of guessing, of making hunches concerning the probable significance or meaning of "what is out there" and of what our reaction should be toward it, in order to protect or preserve ourselves and our satisfactions, or to enchance our satisfactions. This process of weighing the innumerable cues involved in nearly any perception is, of course, a process that we are generally not aware of.

CREATING CONSTANCIES

Since things in the world outside us—the physical world and more especially the social world—are by no means static, are not entirely determined and predictable, experience for most of us often carries at least some mild overtone of "concern" which we can label "curiosity," "doubt" or "anxiety" depending on the circumstances involved.

* * *

Thus we seldom can count on complete 100 percent surety in terms of a perfect correspondence between our assumptions concerning the exact experience we may have if we do a certain thing and the experience we actually do have as the consequence of the action we undertake.

In an attempt to try to minimize our potential lack of surety concerning any single occasion and thereby maximize our sense of surety concerning the effectiveness of our action in achieving our intent, we build up "constancies" and begin to count on them. While a great deal of experimental work has been done on "constancies" in the psychological laboratory, we still have much more to learn. And above all, we have a great deal to learn about constancy as we extend this concept into the field of our interpersonal relations.

Parenthetically, one of the most important things we have to learn is that the "constancy" we create and that we describe usually by means of some word, symbol, or abstract concept *is* man's creation, the validity of which can only be tested and the meaning of which can only be experienced in terms of some behavior which has consequences to us and signals to us what the concept refers to.

We create these constancies by attributing certain *consistent* and *repeatable* characteristics to what they refer to, so that we can guess with a fair degree of accuracy what the significances and meanings are of the various sensory cues that impinge upon us. We do this so that we will not have to make fresh guesses at every turn.

These significances we build up about objects, people, symbols, and events, or about ideas all orchestrate together to give us what we might call our own unique *"reality world."* This "reality world" as we experience it includes, of course, our own fears and hopes, frustrations and aspirations, our own anxiety and our own faith. For these psychological characteristics of life—as the psychiatrist knows better than anyone else—are just as real for us in determining our behavior as are chairs, stones or mountains or automobiles. It seems to me that anything that takes on significance for us in terms of our own personal behavioral center *is* "real" in the psychological sense.

ASSIGNING SIGNIFICANCES

Let me illustrate with reference to a few recent experiments the way in which the significance we attach to others "out there" seems to be affected by what we bring to the situation. Incidentally but important: I do want to underscore that the experiments mentioned here are only exploratory; are only, I believe, opening up interesting vistas ahead. I am in no sense attempting to indicate what their full theoretical implications may be. But I mention them to show how experiments designed to get at the first person point of view may suggest to the experienced psychiatrist ways of using experimental procedures in his diagnosis and possibly even in therapy. And I also mention them because of my deep conviction that psychology can be both humanistic and methodologically rigorous.

A whole series of most promising experiments now seems possible with the use of a modern adaptation of an old-fashioned piece of psychological equipment, the stereoscope. Dr. Edward Engel who devised the apparatus has already published a description of it and reported some of his first findings(5). As you know, the stereoscope in a psychological laboratory has been used to study binocular rivalry and fusion but the material viewed almost always consisted of dots and lines or geometrical patterns. Engel was curious to see what would happen if meaningful figures were used instead of the traditional material.

The results are really most exciting. In Engel's experiments he prepares what he calls "stereograms" consisting of photographs 2 x 2 inches, one of which is seen with the left eye, the other with the right. The photographs he used first were those of members of the Princeton football team just as they appeared in the football program. Although there were slight differences in the size and position of the heads and in the characteristics of light and shadow, still there was sufficient superimposition to get binocular fusion. And what happens? A person looks into the stereoscope and sees one face. He describes this face. And it almost invariably turns out that he is describing neither the face of the man seen with the left eye nor the face of the man seen with the right eye. He is describing a new and different face, a face that he has created out of the features of the two he is looking at. Generally the face seen in this particular case is made up of the dominant features of the two individuals. And generally the face created by the observer in this situation is more attractive and appealing than either of those seen separately. When the observer is shown the trick of the experiment by asking him to close first one eye and then the other and to compare the face he originally saw with the other two, he himself characterizes the face he created as more handsome, more pleasant, a fellow he'd like better, etc.

I hasten to add, however, that we should by no means jump to the conclusion that an individual picks out the "best" or "most attractive" features of figures presented to him in a situation of binocular fusion. For example, Professor Gordon Allport recently took one of Engel's stereoscopes with him to South Africa and initiated some experimental work there, using photographs of members of the different racial groups which make up that complex community.

While the experiments in South Africa have only just begun and no conclusion should be drawn, it is significant to note that in recent letters communicating the early results, Allport reported that when the stereograms consist of a European paired with an Indian, a colored person compared with an Indian, etc. the Zulus see an overwhelming preponderance of Indians. For the Zulu is most strongly prejudiced against the Indian who represents a real threat to him. Allport also reports that when Europeans in South Africa view the stereogram they tend to see more colored faces than white. It would seem, then, that a person sees what is "significant," with significance defined in terms of his relationship to what he is looking at.

One pair of slides we use in demonstrating this piece of equipment consists of two stereograms, each a photograph of a statue in the Louvre. One of the statues is that of a Madonna with Child, the other a lovely young female nude. While I am unable so far to predict what any given individual will "see," no doubt such a prediction might be made after some good psychiatric interviewing. But let me describe what happened in a typical viewing of these stereograms. The viewers happened to be two distinguished psychologists who were visiting me one morning, one from Harvard, the other from Yale. The first looked into the stereoscope and reported that he saw a Madonna with Child. A few seconds later he exclaimed, "But my God, she is undressing." What had happened so far was that somehow she had lost the baby she was holding and her robe had slipped down from her shoulders and stopped just above the breast line. Then in a few more seconds she lost her robe completely and became the young nude. For this particular professor, the nude never did get dressed again. Then my second friend took his turn. For a few seconds he could see nothing but the nude and then he exclaimed, "But now a robe is wrapping itself around her." And very soon he ended up with the Madonna with Child and as far as I know still remains with that vision. Some people will never see the nude; others will never see the Madonna if they keep the intensity of light the same on both stereograms.

In the situation described above, we do not have conditions for genuine fusion, but rather a condition which introduces conflict and choice in the possible meaning of the content represented. In order to learn whether or not there might be differences in choice that would be culturally determined, a cross cultural comparison was made by Dr. James Bagby (6). He constructed pairs of stereograms that would create binocular rivalry: in one stereogram of each pair he had a picture of some individual, object or symbol that would be of particular interest to Mexicans; in the other stereogram he had a picture that would be of particular significance to Americans. For example, one pair of slides consisted of a picture of a bull fighter matched with a stereogram picturing a baseball player. When these pairs were shown to a sample of Mexican school teachers, an overwhelming proportion of them "saw" the Mexican symbol; when the same slides were presented to a group of American school teachers, the overwhelming proportion "saw" the American symbol.

Incidentally, the Engel stereoscope is so constructed that one can get some idea of the relative "strength" of each of the stereograms by adjusting the intensity of the lighting on each. Hence, if the lighting is equivalent on two stereograms in a rivalry situation, one can reduce the amount of lighting on the one that originally predominates, increase the amount of light on the one that was not "seen" and find the point where the first one disappears and the second one "comes in."

A modification of the stereoscope has just been completed by Mr. Adlerstein in the Princeton laboratory. Our thought was that it might be extremely useful both in the clinical and social areas, if instead of having to use photographs of objects or people, a person could view the real thing—that is, the faces of real, live individuals or pairs of actual objects. So by means of prisms and mirrors this device was constructed and I have only very recently had the opportunity of experiencing the resulting phenomena. I must say it is strange and wonderful. For example, when I viewed Mr. Adlerstein and Mrs. Pauline Smith, Curator of our Demonstration Center, I seemed to be looking at a very effeminate Mr. Adlerstein who was wearing Mrs. Smith's glasses. Though weird, he was extremely "real." At one point while I was observing them Mrs. Smith began to talk yet it was Adlerstein's lips that were moving! Tingling with excitement and with a certain amount of anxiety, I drove home and asked my wife and daughter to come down to the laboratory so that I could take a look at them. I was, of course, fearful that I might see only one or the other. But fortunately, again I got an amazing fusion–a quite real and lovely head composed of a blending of my daughter's hair and chin and my wife's eyes and mouth–an harmonious composition that would do justice to any artist and which I created almost instantaneously and without any awareness of what was going on. These pieces of apparatus seem to me to have enormous potential usefulness for studying the way in which we create the world around us. I am hoping, for example, that before long someone in a position to do so may use this sort of equipment in a study of disturbed children. The child–having two eyes and two parents–might in some situations and in a very few seconds reveal a good bit about his inner life and his interpersonal family relations.

An interesting series of experiments on perception and interpersonal relations began systematically a few years ago after an observation I made one Sunday morning in our laboratory. An old friend of mine, who was a distinguished lawyer in New York and has since died, called me at home to say that he and his wife had been in town for the weekend and would I be willing to show them some of the Ames' demonstrations about which he had heard. It is important for this story to emphasize the fact that the gentleman in question was really a most unusual man in terms of his ability, charm, accomplishments, and his devotion to his family and friends.

Many of you are familiar, I am sure, with the "distorted room" designed by Adelbert Ames, Jr. which produces the same image on the retina as a regular square room if it is viewed monocularly from a certain point. Since the room is seen as square, persons or objects within the room or people looking through the windows become distorted. I had shown this room to hundreds of individuals and among other phenomena had demonstrated that when two people look through the back windows, the head of one individual appeared to be very large, the head of the other to be very small. When the individuals reversed the windows they were looking through, the size of their heads appeared to the observer to change. But on this Sunday morning when my friend's wife was observing him and me, she said, "Well, Louis, your head is the same size as ever, but Hadley, your head is very small." Then we changed the windows we were looking through and she said, "Louis, you're still the same, but Hadley you've become awfully large." Needless to say this remark made a shiver go up my spine and I asked her how she saw the room. It turned out that for her – unlike any other observer until then–the room had become somewhat distorted. In other words, she was using her husband–to whom she was particularly devoted–as her standard. She would not let him go. His nickname for her was "Honi" and we have dubbed this the "Honi phenomenon."

This observation was followed systematically in a series of experiments on married couples by Dr. Warren Wittreich. He found that if couples had been married less than a year there was a very definite tendency not to let the new marital partner distort as quickly or as much as was allowed by people who had been married for a considerable time (7). But, again, I hasten to add that it is not a simple matter of how long one has been married that determines how willing one is to distort the size or shape of one's marital partner! The original observation was made on a couple who were already grandparents. Preliminary investigation also seems to show that parents of young children will not allow their children to distort as readily as will parents of older children.

We could continue at some length reporting experiments which seem to show that what we "perceive" is, as already emphasized, in large part our own creation and depends on the assumptions we bring to the particular occasion. We seem to give meaning and order to sensory impingements in terms of our own needs and purposes and this process of selection is actively creative.

SOCIAL CONSTANCIES AND SELF-CONSTANCY

It is clear that when we look for constancies in other people either as individuals or as members of a group a variety of complications is introduced. For when people are involved, as contrasted to inorganic objects or most other forms of life, we are dealing with purposes, with motives, with intentions which we have to take into account in our perceptual process—the purposes, motives and intentions of other people often difficult to understand. The purposes and intentions of these other people will, of course, change as conditions change; and they will change as behavior progresses from one goal to another. Other people's purposes will be affected by our purposes, just as our purposes will be affected by theirs.

It is by no means a quick and easy process, then, to endow the people with whom we participate in our interpersonal relations with constancies and repeatabilities that we can always rely on. And yet we must, of course, continue the attempt to do so, so that our own purposeful action will have a greater chance of bringing about the satisfying consequences we intended. So we try to pigeonhole people according to some role, status, or position. We create constancies concerning people and social situations. These provide us with certain consistent characteristics that will ease our interpretation and make our actions more effective so long as there is some correspondence between the attribution we make and the consequence we experience from it in our own action.

The "social constancies" we learn obviously involve the relationships between ourselves and others. So if any social constancy is to be operational, there must also be a sense of "self-constancy." The two are interdependent. Since the human being necessarily derives so much of his value satisfaction from association with other human beings, his conception of his "self," his own "self-constancy" and "self-significance" is determined to a large extent by the significance he has to other people and the way they behave toward him. This point is, of course, a familiar one to the psychiatrist and has been eloquently illustrated in literature as, for example, in Shaw's *Pygmalion*.

But it seems to me of paramount importance in any discussion of perception and interpersonal relations that we should not slip into the error of positing an abstract "self" or "ego" that can somehow be isolated, pointed to, analyzed, or experienced apart from any social context. It is only through the life setting and the process of participation with others that meaning and continuity are given to the "self." If the constancy of "self" is upset, it becomes difficult for us to assess changes in our interpersonal relations and accommodate to them. We lose the compass that keeps us going in a direction. "We" are lost.

This does not mean in any sense that for self-constancy to be maintained there can be no development or growth. On the contrary, self-development and growth are themselves aspects of social constancy. But this development must, as the psychiatrist knows better than anyone, flow from form if it is to be recognized, if there is to be continuity, and if there is to be a standard for comparison. Obviously, each of us surrounds himself with anchoring points of one kind or another which help to maintain this self-constancy in the process of ceaseless change around us. In this connection I think, for example, of Konrad Lorenz' interpretation of why people like dogs. In his book *King Solomon's Ring,* he writes that we should "not lie to ourselves that we need the dog as a protection for our house. We *do* need him, but not as a watch-dog. I, at least in dreary foreign towns, have certainly stood in need of my dog's company and I have derived, from the mere fact of his existence, a great sense of inward security, such as one finds in a childhood memory or in the prospect of the scenery of one's own home country, for me the Blue Danube, for you the White Cliffs of Dover. In the almost film-like flitting-by of modern life, a man needs something to tell him, from time to time, that he is still himself, and nothing can give him this assurance in so comforting a manner as the 'four feet trotting behind.'"

This interdependent problem of social constancy and self-constancy has been submitted to some preliminary investigation. For example, when a person is wearing a pair of aniseikonic spectacles, which greatly distort the shape of the environment when familiar monocular cues are ruled out, he will generally see another person as distorted if that person is standing in an environment which has itself already become distorted. With a certain pair of these spectacles, for example, an individual will be seen as leaning forward with the upper and lower half of his body distorted in length. Dr. Wittreich set up such a situation at the Naval Training Center at Bainbridge, Maryland to see what might happen when the relationship of the person who was doing the viewing and the person being viewed was altered. His subjects were 24 white male Navy recruits. They first observed an authority figure dressed up as a first class petty officer and, second, a nonauthority figure dressed up in a white enlisted uniform with the marks of a recruit. Wittreich found that the authority figure did not distort nearly as much as the nonauthority figure. In other words, the disciplinary training imposed in an organization that depends for effective functioning on the rigid acceptance of roles had produced a "constancy" which overpowered physiological changes in the optical system.

Another finding using the aniseikonic spectacles may be of interest to psychiatrists: namely, that a person tends to report much less distortion of his own image when he looks at himself in a full-length mirror while wearing aniseikonic spectacles than he reports when he is looking at a stranger. When one looks at one's self, the changes that appear seem to be minor and detailed—for example, slight distortions in the hands or feet; when one looks at a stranger, there is the more general bodily distortion plus the leaning one way or another, depending on the kind of spectacles used.

A subsequent study by Wittreich and one which I emphasize is only suggestive, was made comparing 21 subjects obtained from the patient roster of the neuropsychiatric unit at the Bethesda Naval Hospital. When these disturbed individuals were wearing aniseikonic spectacles and saw their own image in the mirror, they tended to see the gross distortions that the "normal" population attributed to others; and, conversely, when the disturbed clinic population looked at others, they tended to see the more detailed and minor distortions which the "normal" population had seen in themselves. All I should like to conclude about this particular experiment so far is that there seems to be some difference between the normal individual and the clinical patient in the functional importance assigned to his bodily image; the patient may conceivably be operating in terms of a relatively fixed and homogeneous image of himself which does not alter readily with the demands of the environment.

PERCEPTUAL CHANGE

Laboratory experimentation as well as research in the field of opinion and attitude change seems to demonstrate beyond a shadow of a doubt that the major condition for a change in our perception, our attitudes or opinions is a frustration experienced in carrying out our purposes effectively because we are acting on the basis of assumptions that prove "wrong." For example, Dr. Kilpatrick has demonstrated that apparently the only way in which we can "learn" to see our distorted room distorted is to become frustrated with the assumption that the room is "square" in the process of trying to carry out some action in the room(8). It is clear that an "intellectual," "rational," or "logical" understanding of a situation is by no means sufficient to alter perception. The psychotherapist has taught us how successful reconditioning requires a therapy which simplifies goals so that their accomplishment can be assured through an individual's action as he experiences the successful consequences of his own behavior and thereby rebuilds his confidence in himself.

In this connection I recall a conversation I had in 1948 in Paris with an extremely intelligent woman who was at that time a staff member of the Soviet Embassy in Paris. We were at some social gathering and she began to ask me about American elections and the two-party system. She just couldn't understand it. She wasn't trying to be "smart" or supercilious. She was simply baffled. She couldn't "see" why we had to have two parties. For, obviously, one man was better than another and why wasn't he made President and kept as President as long as he proved to be the best man? It was a difficult argument for me to understand, just as my argument was impossible for her to understand. It was much more than a matter of opinion, stereotype or prejudice on either side. We were simply living in different reality worlds, actually experiencing entirely different significances in happenings which might appear to "an objective" "outside" observer to be the same for both of us.

Parenthetically, while one of the outstanding characteristics of man is often said to be his amazing capacity to learn, it seems to me that an equally outstanding characteristic is man's amazing capacity to "unlearn" which is, I think, not the exact opposite. Because man is not entirely a creature of habit, he has the fortunate ability to slough off what is no longer of use to him.

THE REALITY OF ABSTRACTIONS AND THE COMMONNESS OF PURPOSES

In order to ease our interpersonal relations and to increase the commonness of the significances we may attribute to the happenings around us, man has created abstractions in his attempt to bring order into disorder and to find more universal guides for living no matter what the unique and individual purposes and circumstances of an individual may be. Such abstractions are represented by our scientific formulations, our ethical, political, legal and religious systems. The abstractions can be recalled and repeated at will. They can be communicated. They are repeatable because they are static and have fixed characteristics.

The value of these abstractions for us in our interpersonal relations seems to be that when the tangibles of our personal reality world break down, we can turn to the intangible—to the abstractions we have learned that have been created by others and have presumably proved useful to them. We can begin to check our own particular situation, possibly a frustrating one, against the abstraction and thereby, perhaps experience for ourselves what the abstraction is referring to. Only then will the abstraction become real for us. For when it does become functional for us in our own individual lives, it *is* real as a determinant of our experience and behavior.

I will close this discussion of perception and interpersonal relations with a story which seems to sum a good deal of what I have been talking about. The story concerns three baseball umpires who were discussing the problems of their profession. The first umpire said, "Some's balls and some's strikes and I calls 'em as they is." The second umpire said, "Some's balls and some's strikes and I calls 'em as I sees 'em." While the third umpire said, "Some's balls and some's strikes but they ain't nothin' till I calls 'em."

BIBLIOGRAPHY

1. Cantril, Hadley. *The "Why" of Man's Experience.* New York: The Macmillan Company, 1950.
2. Kilpatrick, F.P. (ed.). Human Behavior from the Transactional Point of View. Hanover, N. H.: Institute for Associated Research, 1952.
3. Kilpatrick, F.P. Recent Transactional Perceptual Research, a summary. Final Report, Navy Contract N6onr 27014, Princeton University, May, 1955.
4. Cantril, Hadley. ETC: A Review of General Semantics, 12: No. 4, 278, 1955.
5. Engel, Edward. *Amer. J. Psychol.,* 69: No. 1, 87, 1956.
6. Bagby, James. A Cross Cultural Study of Perceptual Predominance in Binocular Rivalry. 1956 (to be published).

7. Wittreich, Warren. *J. Abnorm. Soc. Psychol.*, 47:705, 1952.
8. Kilpatrick, F. P. *J. Exp. Psychol.*, 47: No. 5, 362, 1954.

DeWitt C. Dearborn
Herbert A. Simon

SELECTIVE PERCEPTION: A NOTE ON THE DEPARTMENTAL IDENTIFICATIONS OF EXECUTIVES

An important proposition in organization theory asserts that each executive will perceive those aspects of the situation that relate specifically to the activities and goals of his department (2, Ch. 5, 10). The proposition is frequently supported by anecdotes of executives and observers in organizations, but little evidence of a systematic kind is available to test it. It is the purpose of this note to supply some such evidence.

The proposition we are considering is not peculiarly organizational. It is simply an application to organizational phenomena of a generalization that is central to any explanation of selective perception: Presented with a complex stimulus, the subject perceives in it what he is "ready" to perceive; the more complex or ambiguous the stimulus, the more the perception is determined by what is already "in" the subject and the less by what is in the stimulus (1, pp. 132-133).

Cognitive and motivational mechanisms mingle in the selective process, and it may be of some use to assess their relative contributions. We might suppose either: (1) selective attention to a part of a stimulus reflects a deliberate ignoring of the remainder as irrelevant to the subject's goals and motives, or (2) selective attention is a learned response stemming from some past history of reinforcement. In the latter case we might still be at some pains to determine the nature of the reinforcement, but by creating a situation from which any immediate motivation for selectivity is removed, we should be able to separate the second mechanism from the first. The situation in which we obtained our data meets this condition, and hence our data provide evidence for internalization of the selective processes.

Abridged from DeWitt C. Dearborn and Herbert A. Simon, "Selective Perception: A Note on the Departmental Identifications of Executives," *Sociometry* 21 (1958):140-44. Reprinted by permission.

METHOD OF THE STUDY

A group of 23 executives, all employed by a single large manufacturing concern and enrolled in a company sponsored executive training program, was asked to read a standard case that is widely used in instruction in business policy in business schools. The case, Castengo Steel Company, described the organization and activities of a company of moderate size specializing in the manufacture of seamless steel tubes, as of the end of World War II. The case, which is about 10,000 words in length, contains a wealth of descriptive material about the company and its industry and the recent history of both (up to 1945), but little evaluation. It is deliberately written to hold closely to concrete facts and to leave as much as possible of the burden of interpretation to the reader.

When the executives appeared at a class session to discuss the case, but before they had discussed it, they were asked by the instructor to write a brief statement of what they considered to be the most important problem facing the Castengo Steel Company—the problem a new company president should deal with first. Prior to this session, the group had discussed other cases, being reminded from time to time by the instructor that they were to assume the role of the top executive of the company in considering its problems.

The executives were a relatively homogeneous group in terms of status, being drawn from perhaps three levels of the company organization. They were in the range usually called "middle management," representing such positions as superintendent of a department in a large factory, product manager responsible for profitability of one of the ten product groups manufactured by the company, and works physician for a large factory. In terms of departmental affiliation, they fell in four groups:

Sales (6): Sales product managers or assistant product managers, and one field sales supervisor.

Production (5): Three department superintendents, one assistant factory manager, and one construction engineer.

Accounting (4): An assistant chief accountant, and three accounting supervisors—for a budget division and two factory departments.

Miscellaneous (8): Two members of the legal department, two in research and development, and one each from public relations, industrial relations, medical and purchasing.

THE DATA

We tested our hypothesis by determining whether there was a significant relation between the "most important problem" mentioned and the departmental affiliation of the mentioner. In the cases of executives who mentioned more than one problem, we counted all those they mentioned. We compared (1) the executives who mentioned "sales," "marketing," or "distribution" with those who did not; (2) the executives who mentioned "clarifying the organization" or some equivalent with those who did not; (3) the executives who mentioned "human relations," "employee relations" or "teamwork" with those who did not. The findings are summarized in the Table.

The difference between the percentages of sales executives (83 percent) and other executives (29 percent) who mentioned sales as the most important problem is significant at the 5 percent level. Three of the five nonsales executives, moreover, who mentioned sales were in the accounting department, and all of these were in positions that involved analysis of product profitability. This accounting activity was, in fact, receiving considerable emphasis in the company at the time of the case discussion and the accounting executives had frequent and close contacts with the product managers in the sales department. If we combine sales and accounting executives, we find that 8 out of 10 of these mentioned sales as the most important problem; while only 2 of the remaining 13 executives did.

Department	*Total number of executives*	*Number who mentioned* *Sales*	*"Clarify organization"*	*Human relations*
Sales	6	5	1	0
Production	5	1	4	0
Accounting	4	3	0	0
Miscellaneous	8	1	3	3
Totals	23	10	8	3

Organization problems (other than marketing organization) were mentioned by four out of five production executives, the two executives in research and development, and the factory physician, but by only one sales executive and no accounting executives. The difference between the percentage for production executives (80 percent) and other executives (22 percent) is also significant at the 5 percent level. Examination of the Castengo case shows that the main issue discussed in the case that relates to manufacturing is the problem of poorly defined relations among the factory manager, the metallurgist, and the company president. The presence of the metallurgist in the situation may help to explain the sensitivity of the two research and development executives (both of whom were concerned with metallurgy) to this particular problem area.

It is easy to conjecture why the public relations, industrial relations, and medical executives should all have mentioned some aspect of human relations, and why one of the two legal department executives should have mentioned the board of directors.

CONCLUSION

We have presented data on the selective perceptions of industrial executives exposed to case material that support the hypothesis that each executive will perceive those aspects of a situation that relate specifically to the activities and goals of his department. Since the situation is one in which the executives were motivated to look at the problem from a company-wide rather than a departmental viewpoint, the data indicate further that the criteria of selection have become internalized. Finally, the method for obtaining data that we have used holds considerable promise as a projective device for eliciting the attitudes and perceptions of executives.

REFERENCES

1. Bruner, J. S. "On Perceptual Readiness." *Psychological Review* 64 (1957): 123-52.
2. Simon, H. A. *Administrative Behavior.* New York: Macmillan, 1947.

* * *

Marshall McLuhan

UNDERSTANDING MEDIA: THE EXTENSIONS OF MAN

PREFACE TO THE THIRD PRINTING

Jack Paar mentioned that he once had said to a young friend, "Why do you kids use 'cool' to mean 'hot'?" The friend replied, "Because you folks used up the word 'hot' before we came along." It is true that "cool" is often used nowadays to mean what used to be conveyed by "hot." Formerly a "hot argument" meant one in which people were deeply involved. On the other hand, a "cool attitude" used to mean one of detached objectivity and disinterestedness. In those days the word "disinterested" meant a noble quality of fairmindedness. Suddenly it got to mean "couldn't care less." The word "hot" has fallen into similar disuse as these deep changes of outlook have developed. But the slang term "cool" conveys a good deal besides the old idea of "hot." It indicates a kind of commitment and participation in situations that involves all of one's faculties. In that sense, one can say that automation is cool, whereas the older mechanical kinds of specialist or fragmented "jobs" are "square." The "square" person and situation are not "cool" because they manifest little of the habit of depth involvement of our faculties. The young now say, "Humor is not cool." Their favorite jokes bear this out. They ask,

"What is purple and hums?" Answer, "An electric grape." "Why does it hum?" Answer, "Because it doesn't know the words." Humor is presumably not "cool" because it inclines us to laugh *at* something, instead of getting us emphatically involved in something. The story line is dropped from "cool" jokes and "cool" movies alike. The Bergman and Fellini movies demand far more involvement than do narrative shows. A story line encompasses a set of events much like a melodic line in music. Melody, the *melos modos,* "the road round," is a continuous, connected, and repetitive structure that is not used in the "cool" art of the Orient. The art and poetry of Zen create involvement by means of the *interval,* not by the *connection* used in the visually organized Western world. Spectator becomes artist in oriental art because he must supply all the connections.

The section on "media hot and cool" confused many reviewers of *Understanding Media* who were unable to recognize the very large structural changes in human outlook that are occurring today. [Slang offers an immediate index to changing perception.] Slang is based not on theories but on immediate experience. The student of media will not only value slang as a guide to changing perception, but he will also study media as bringing about new perceptual habits.

The section on "the medium is the message" can, perhaps, be clarified by pointing out that any technology gradually creates a totally new human environment. Environments are not passive wrappings but active processes. In his splendid work *Preface to Plato* (Harvard University Press, 1963), Eric Havelock contrasts the oral and written cultures of the Greeks. By Plato's time the written word had created a new environment that had grown up by benefit of the process of the *tribal encyclopedia.* They had memorized the poets. The poets provided specific operational wisdom for all the contingencies of life—Ann Landers in verse. With the advent of individual detribalized man, a new education was needed. Plato devised such a new program for literate men. It was based on the Ideas. With the phonetic alphabet, classified wisdom took over from the operational wisdom of Homer and Hesiod and the tribal encyclopedia. Education by classified data has been the Western program ever since.

Now, however, in the electronic age, data classification yields to pattern recognition, the key phrase at IBM. When data move instantly, classification is too fragmentary. In order to cope with data at electric speed in typical situations of "information overload," men resort to the study of configurations, like the sailor in Edgar Allan Poe's *Maelstrom.* The drop-out situation in our schools at present has only begun to develop. The young student today grows up in an electrically configured world. It is a world not of wheels but of circuits, not of fragments but of integral patterns. The student today *lives* mythically and in depth. At school, however, he encounters a situation organized by means of classified information. The subjects are unrelated. They are visually conceived in terms of a blueprint. The student can find no possible means of involvement for himself, nor can he discover how the educational scene relates to the "mythic" world of electronically processed data and experience that he takes for granted. As one IBM executive puts it, "My children had lived several lifetimes compared to their grandparents when they began grade one."

"The medium is the message" means, in terms of the electronic age, that a totally new environment has been created. The "content" of this new environment is the old mechanized environment of the industrial age. The new environment reprocesses the old one as radically as TV is reprocessing the film. For the "content" of TV is the movie. TV is environmental and imperceptible, like all environments. We are aware only of the "content" or the old environment. When machine production was new, it gradually created an environment whose content was the old environment of agrarian life and the arts and crafts. This older environment was elevated to an art form by the new mechanical environment. The machine turned Nature into an art form. For the first time men began to regard Nature as a source of aesthetic and spiritual values. They began to marvel that earlier ages had been so unaware of the world of Nature as Art. Each new technology creates an environment that is itself regarded as corrupt and degrading. Yet the new one turns its predecessor into an art form. When writing was new, Plato transformed the old oral dialogue into an art form. When printing was new the Middle Ages became an art form. "The Elizabethan world view" was a view of the Middle Ages. And the industrial age turned the Renaissance into an art form as seen in the work of Jacob Burckhardt. Siegfried Giedion, in turn, has in the electric age taught us how to see the entire process of mechanization as an art process. *(Mechanization Takes Command)*

As our proliferating technologies have created a whole series of new environments, men have become aware of the arts as "anti-environments" or "counter-environments" that provide us with the means of perceiving the environment itself. For, as Edward T. Hall has explained in *The Silent Language*, men are never aware of the ground rules of their environmental systems of cultures. Today technologies and their consequent environments succeed each other so rapidly that one environment makes us aware of the next. Technologies begin to perform the function of art in making us aware of the psychic and social consequences of technology.

Art as anti-environment becomes more than ever a means of training perception and judgment. Art offered as a consumer commodity rather than as a means of training perception is as ludicrous and snobbish as always. Media study at once opens the doors of perception. And here it is that the young can do top-level research work. The teacher has only to invite the student to do as complete an inventory as possible. Any child can list the effects of the telephone or the radio or the motor car in shaping the life and work of his friends and his society. An inclusive list of media effects opens many unexpected avenues of awareness and investigation.

Edmund Bacon, of the Philadelphia town-planning commission, discovered that school children could be invaluable researchers and colleagues in the task of remaking the image of the city. We are entering the new age of education that is programmed for discovery rather than instruction. As the means of input increase, so does the need for insight or pattern recognition. The famous Hawthorne experiment, at the General Electric [sic.] plant near Chicago, revealed a mysterious effect years ago. No matter how the conditions of the workers were altered, the workers did more and better work. Whether the heat and light and leisure were arranged adversely or pleasantly, the quantity and quality of output improved. The testers gloomily concluded that testing distorted the evidence. They missed the all-important fact that when the workers are permitted to join their energies to a process of learning and discovery, the increased efficiency is phenomenal.

Earlier it was mentioned how the school drop-out situation will get very much worse because of the frustration of the student need for participation in the learning process. This situation concerns also the problem of "the culturally disadvantaged child." This child exists not only in the slums but increasingly in the suburbs of the upper-income homes. The culturally disadvantaged child is the TV child. For TV has provided a new environment of low visual orientation and high involvement that makes accommodation to our older educational establishment quite difficult. One strategy of cultural response would be to raise the visual level of the TV image to enable the young student to gain access to the old visual world of the classroom and the curriculum. This would be worth trying as a temporary expedient. But TV is only one component of the electric environment of instant circuitry that has succeeded the old world of the wheel and nuts and bolts. We would be foolish not to ease our transition from the fragmented visual world of the existing educational establishment by every possible means.

The existential philosophy, as well as the Theater of the Absurd, represents anti-environments that point to the critical pressures of the new electric environment. Jean-Paul Sartre, as much as Samuel Beckett and Arthur Miller, has declared the futility of blueprints and classified data and "jobs" as a way out. Even the words "escape" and "vicarious living" have dwindled from the new scene of electronic involvement. TV engineers have begun to explore the braille-like character of the TV image as a means of enabling the blind to see by having this image projected directly onto their skins. We need to use all media in this wise, to enable us to see our situation.

On page 27 there are some lines from *Romeo and Juliet* whimsically modified to make an allusion to TV. Some reviewers have imagined that this was an involuntary misquotation.

The power of the arts to anticipate future social and technological developments, by a generation and more, has long been recognized. In this century Ezra Pound called the artist "the antennae of the race." Art as radar acts as "an early alarm system," as it were, enabling us to discover social and psychic targets in lots of time to prepare to cope with them. This concept of the arts as prophetic, contrasts with the popular idea of them as mere self-expression. If art is an "early warning system," to use the phrase from World War II, when radar was new, art has the utmost relevance not only to media study but to the development of media controls.

When radar was new it was found necessary to eliminate the balloon system for city protection that had preceded radar. The balloons got in the way of the electric feedback of the new radar information. Such may well prove to be the case with much of our existing school curriculum, to say nothing of the generality of the arts. We can afford to use only those portions of them that enhance the perception of our technologies, and their psychic and social consequences. Art as a radar environment takes on the function of indispensable perceptual training rather than the role of a privileged diet for the elite. While the arts as radar feedback provide a dynamic and changing corporate image, their purpose may be not to enable us to change but rather to maintain an even course toward permanent goals, even amidst the most disrupting innovations. We have already discovered the futility of changing our goals as often as we change our technologies.

chapter **3**

Motivation

For ages, people charged with managing others have sought an elixir for motivating people. Still today, if one is writing a book for managers, he is well-advised to put "motivation" in the title, even if that is not the subject of the book. The reasons are obvious. The concept of motivation encompasses the variables responsible for the initiation, direction, and intensity of behavior. If these variables are known, they can be more easily manipulated to bring about the maximum contribution of people toward organizational goals. With a better understanding of human motivation, we can reduce the energy expended on undesired behavior and increase the energy spent on desired behavior by effecting changes in individual characteristics and situational variables. Unfortunately, or perhaps fortunately, the problem of motivating people has proven to be too complex to permit a simple answer.

A full understanding of motivation requires answers to many of the unresolved issues of the nature-nurture question and of perception. First, any attempt to deal with causes of behavior almost inevitably gravitates to either implicit or explicit concern with the degree to which characteristics of the individual are inherited or acquired. Second, perception and motivation are treated separately here only for purposes of exposition. In reality, they are highly interdependent. Furthermore, as with perception, discussions of motivation often involve inferences about the inner world of another person.

My ability to make accurate inferences about your inner world is influenced by both my own inner world and your behavior. For example, what could I say about your motivation at the present time? Descriptively, your eyes are running across the words on this page, and your body is in some position in relation to the book. I infer that you are reading. But why? Are you reading for knowledge? to gain power over people? for fun? to improve your grades? or for some other reason? If you are pursuing any one or some combination[1] of these objectives, are you doing so out of a fear of failure, or for some more positive reason? Often I both raise and answer such questions about you to myself, without either of us being aware of it, while only infrequently do I think of testing

1. The term "combination" is important. Most behavior probably is multidetermined or overdetermined—that is to say, it occurs for many reasons.

the accuracy of my inferences with you. Rather, I infer that you are reading this book for the same reasons for which I might read it under similar conditions. Even when attempting to test my inferences, I still impute my own inner world to you on the basis of my prior experience with you and other people. Thus, when I say something about what motivates you, I am often saying more about what motivates me. Interpreting another's inner world is a risky business.

TYPES OF MOTIVES

The complexity of motivation has not prevented man's mind from attempting to impose order on the cause of behavior. These attempts are reflected in a wide variety of theories, experiments, and other communications, ranging from poems and sermons to manuals for raising children and managing people. Bindra (1959) suggested that many efforts to explain what motivates behavior do not really explain the causes but rather only verbally relate the activity to conditions or events which are considered to be goals in the culture. In other words, what are often called motives are merely classifications of acts rather than causes of acts. While Bindra's point is well taken, these "descriptions" are helpful ways of discussing behavior. The types of motivation can be grouped into four classes, according to the major inferred source. Since the major inferred source is often the only source of motivation treated in each class, any one approach taken alone is only partially adequate at best.

Instincts

While instincts are infrequently used today to explain human behavior, the concept dominated much early psychological thinking about human behavior. Instincts are generally viewed as complex patterns of unlearned behavior which have and/or had survival value for a species. Beach (1955) suggested that instinct gained an important position in scientific thought from the Darwinian approach, which assumed that behavior must be governed by either instinct or reason. Beach concluded that, as our knowledge of instinct and behavior advances, the idea of instinctive behavior will be replaced by more useful scientific explanations. The operation of instincts should not be seen as an entirely internal process. Recently the ethologists (Hess, 1962) have shown that some complex, instinctive behavior patterns may require certain environmental cues for their initiation. For example, a bundle of red feathers will produce fighting behavior in a male robin, whereas a dummy male robin without a red breast will not. Further, physical concentration of animals can produce radical changes in individual and social action, as demonstrated by the changes in parental behavior. For example severe increases in population density may reduce fertility and/or increase the eating of young by mothers. This recent ethological research has revived interest in research on instincts.

Much of the work on territorial behavior and animal communication has direct parallels in the current attention being given to the role of personal space and nonverbal communication in humans. While animals, including humans, act to define and defend territories, the characteristics of the territories and their defense may be modified by environmental factors.

Drives

A second general approach to motivation relies on such concepts as drive reduction, equilibrium creation, or homeostatic processes to account for behavior. Generally, these approaches parallel biological explanations of body functioning, which postulate that environmental changes induce physiological adjustments by the body to reduce tension or produce quiescence. For example, sensed environmental changes produce variations in the concentration of certain substances in the blood. These trigger other physiological changes, such as glandular reactions, which then produce changes in body processes to bring the body back to its prior state.

The analogy of the thermostat provides a useful illustration of such homeostatic processes. As the temperature in the room decreases, the shape of a small bar in the thermostat changes, because the two metals of which it is composed contract at different rates as the temperature falls. At a certain point, the bar has changed enough so that it closes a circuit, activating a heat-producing mechanism. The heat mechanism operates until the temperature of the room rises sufficiently to return the bar to its initial position. The desired state is maintained by repetitions of the cycle.

In the same way that the bar helps to maintain the desired internal state, physiological responses enable the body to maintain equilibrium with its environment. For example, changes in the concentration of blood sugar initiate a release of glycogen from the liver, which influences the receptors of the body to be more sensitive to signs of food. Similar mechanisms seem to operate for thirst (Hunt, 1965). While the reduction of many drives is accomplished through motor activity by the animal rather than by an automatic adjustment, the general model of producing and maintaining an equilibrium holds.

These equilibriating mechanisms are primary, in the sense that they occur without any prior learning. The body reacts automatically to reduce the state of disequilibrium. However, the means of drive reduction, such as effective techniques for obtaining food, are learned. Drive theorists have been concerned not only with learned behavior to satisfy the primary drives but also with secondary drives derived from the primary ones. For example, money, which can be used to satisfy many primary drives, may itself become the object of a drive. The drive theorists assume that deficit states of both primary and secondary drives are responsible for the motivation of behavior.

Hunt (1965) has described the drive-reduction approach well by summarizing how a typical drive theorist treats the eight basic motivational issues: instigation of activity, intensity of behavior, direction of activity, feelings about objects, choices among responses and among goals, source of behavioral change and learning, and the persistence of behavior. Generally, drive theorists maintain that strong and painful external stimuli, homeostatic mechanisms, sex, and acquired drives cause the instigation of activity, the intensity of the behavior being a function of the degree of need, the intensity of the stimuli, and the intensity of the evoked emotional responses. Behavior is directed toward the reduction of drive levels or away from drive increments. Those objects, responses, and goals which have been associated with successful drive reduction in the past tend to be favored, and the more often a response succeeds the more persistently it will be chosen in the future. Conversely, unsuccessful responses, which lead to frustration, are chosen with decreasing frequency. Learning is then said to take place.

Drive-reduction models have been and still are at the center of assumptions about motivation in American psychology. They are likely to stay there, since a primary or higher-order drive can usually be inferred to "explain" almost any behavior.[2] Thus, besides its power in generating research, and the dedication and ingenuity of its proponents, the drive-reduction view has been preferred because it is able to deal with a wide variety of behavior and is very difficult to disprove. In spite of all this, drive-reduction theory in its pure form is increasingly being challenged.

Growth, Competence, and Self-Actualization

The strongest challenge has come from theories and evidence supporting the existence of drive-seeking, self-actualization, or competence and growth motivation. This body of thought springs from diverse sources and has been, at least in part, a polemic against the drive-reduction assumptions. Support for this position has been marshalled from the work of experimental psychologists and the writings of humanistic psychologists such as Maslow and Rogers.

Many of the current theories of management, such as McGregor's and Likert's, share important commonalities with the humanistic or growth-oriented view. In fact, the humanistic assumptions about human motivation have become very important ones in organizational behavior. Although recent evidence suggests that growth models are not the sole answer to the problems of management of human behavior, it is nevertheless important to view them in some detail.

Growth models challenge the assumption that human beings (and other animals) are merely drive-reducing mechanisms and propose an alternative view that people seek novel stimuli, mastery over their environment, and growth in order to come closer to their "true essence." Growth theorists argue that, rather than attempting to reduce tension, man often acts to seek stimulation. A growing body of evidence supports this contention. Olds and Olds (1965) reported that animals will work to receive stimulation of certain areas of the brain. For example, rats will press a bar vigorously, until physically fatigued, for reinforce-

2. The drive-reduction model has played an important role in modern thinking about cognitive functioning as well as about simple behavioral events. Festinger's (1957) theory of cognitive dissonance has been one of the most important foundations for empirical reasearch in recent social psychology. This theory is based on the assumption that organisms respond to a conflict of ideas and attitudes by attempting to bring the conflicting elements into balance. In other words, cognitive conflict, like any other drive, induces organisms to reduce tension.

Festinger's work is treated in more detail in the selection by Secord and Backman in part 3 of this book.

ment by electrical stimulation to the septal area of the brain. Other work by Bexton, Heron, and Scott (1954) and Lilly (1956) demonstrated that human beings find it very difficult to tolerate a homogeneous environment.[3] White (1959) wrote of a competence motive, which stimulates men to seek and conquer challenges posed by their environment. White maintained that a persistence of behavior directed toward learning to interact effectively with the environment exists at times when the organism is not dominated by other drives. White called this need for effectiveness, not included in most instinct or drive theories, competence motivation.[4] Hunt (1965) postulated a standard of optimal incongruity, arguing that organisms perfer some tension to no tension. Berlyne's (1960) work has given strong support for an exploratory drive in animals and humans, in line with Hunt's view. Other work by Butler (1953) found that opportunities for visual exploration were rewarding to monkeys. This evidence cannot be explained by drive-reduction theory, at least in its pure form.

Considerable support for the growth model exists among personality theorists. Abraham Maslow has pioneered in proposing a need for self-actualization and growth. He and other theorists supporting this view contend that people seek "higher" goals in addition to the physiological and psychological reduction of drives, that they seek to reach their full potential as people. Maslow (1969) argued that biologists and psychologists, in accepting a normative model, have paid insufficient attention to the conditions which produce the "best" human specimens.

It should be noted that one can accept the evidence which has been collected without necessarily accepting some of the conclusions for which it has been used or the assumptions on which the theory is based. For example, it is possible to translate the concept of exploration needs into drive-reduction terms. All we need do is postualte a drive for an optimal level of stimulation. The data can be reconciled with any of several models of motivation. It may be premature for organizational behaviorists to get "locked into" any one set of assumptions about human nature and human motivation. By contrast, it is very profitable to be familiar with and draw evidence and information from a variety of approaches.

Environment As Source of Motivation

The fourth general approach to motivation is perhaps the least developed of all, since it seeks to skirt what most people mean by motivation. This approach focuses on the environment as a source of behavioral change; it does not attempt to investigate the internal processes of the organism but rather treats them as givens. This approach is perhaps best exemplified by the work of B. F. Skinner.[5] Basically this approach stresses the role of factors external to the organism in influencing behavior. For example, rather than talk about hunger,

3. Hebb's article earlier in this part dealt with this research in further detail.

4. Morse and Lorsch in part 4 rely heavily on White's concept.

5. Although his recent work (Skinner, 1969) draws heavily on ethological thinking and stresses the role of phylogeny, he still also relies greatly on external factors.

these investigators refer to the number of hours an animal has been deprived of food. No inferences are made about changes in internal states. Only changes in behavior are dealt with. This approach to motivation is viewed by many as not dealing with motivation. Nevertheless, it does direct attention to the important role of external stimuli in the initiation, direction, and intensity of behavior.

A complete view of motivation must certainly deal with external as well as internal variables. For example, some of the work of the ethologists has shown that the sex drive does not operate in a vacuum. In fact, external stimuli, such as a distinguishing characteristic of a member of the opposite sex of the same species, are necessary for triggering the sexual behavior of many animals. Similarly, Ervin (1964) measured the aggressiveness of responses to the Thematic Apperception Test (TAT) and found that bilingual subjects expressed more aggression when responding in French than when responding in English. Since the language in which one speaks is apt to be influenced by the language of the person with whom one is talking, Ervin's finding suggests that aggression, thought by many to be a personality trait, may be at least in part a function of external factors, such as the language in which one is addressed.

Berkowitz (1969) has summarized some ways in which situational factors influence motivation and behavior. He noted that traits, attitudes, and personality needs can be viewed as habitual responses to a particular set of stimuli. The stimulus factors may act as both inhibiting and disinhibiting factors. Furthermore, environmental factors may elicit behavior which would not occur in their absence. Taken together, the foregoing arguments demonstrate the importance of situational factors to motivation.

Summary

We have viewed four classes of approaches to motivation. Each approach has much to offer, and each is better in dealing with some topics than with others. At present the issue is not so much choosing the "correct" model as developing an integrated understanding of the knowledge embodied in the varied approaches. Motivation is both innate and acquired, both internal and external, and perhaps both drive-reducing and tension-producing. Vinacke's (1962) model, discussed below, is a useful tool for integrating existing knowledge. While it is unlikely to provide definitive answers, it does demonstrate the multi-factor approach that seems essential for an adequate treatment of motivation.

AN INTEGRATIVE APPROACH TO MOTIVATION

Vinacke's drive-modification theory focuses on both intrinsic and extrinsic factors as determinants of motivation. Motivation, according to Vinacke," . . . concerns the conditions responsible for variation in the intensity, quality, and direction of ongoing behavior" (p. 3). The conditions constitute an organized system of factors which determine responses at any given time. The different components of these conditions are all significantly interrelated.

Vinacke grouped the components into three intrinsic and two extrinsic classes. The first intrinsic class, instigation, corresponds to the activity of the bodily tissues. Instigation includes the components which determine ". . . the forms and degrees of fundamental energy-expenditure of the organism" (p. 4). Vinacke's description of the components of instigation parallels more traditional theories in explaining the intensity and direction of energy expenditure. However, drive-modification theory maintains that the tissues and hence the basic drives themselves are modified by learning and experience with the environment. The second intrinsic class, regulation, includes mechanisms and processes which perform the "steering" function. These include what other writers have called values, sentiments, tastes, defense mechanisms, habits and other regulative processes; they determine the direction and pattern of acts which follow instigation. Vinacke uses "attitude" as a summary term for these processes. The third intrinsic class is adjustment, which includes temporary and specific determinants of responses following instigation and regulation. Adjustment summarizes cognitive processes which ". . . focus behavior by selecting the particular act or series of acts that occurs in a given situation" (p. 9). In the same way that the attitudes or regulative processes determine the expression of energy, the adjustment process determines the expression of the attitudes. In sum, intrinsic motivation involves energy potential which is first generated, then steered in a general manner, and finally structured to deal with a given situation.

The intrinsic classes interact with two extrinsic classes, induction and situation. Induction includes conditions which influence performance by evoking changes in intrinsic variables. For example, food deprivation acts as an induction factor to produce tissue changes. Finally, motivation is influenced by situational variables involved in task performance itself. Included in situation are such factors as a person's perceptions of the goal, his relationship to the goal, his performance, and the properties of the task itself.

All of these variables operate simultaneously to determine motivation. This approach to motivation can be a useful guide to thought in organizational behavior, because it integrates the essential factors which produce motivation. The drive-modification model suggests that motivation is better described as sets of conditions which affect behavior rather than as a personality trait, because external factors should be taken into account. In sum, motivated behavior is the product of environmental conditions, physiological states, and cognitive processes. The direction, quality, and intensity of behavior are determined by a variety of factors operating simultaneously. The effects of extrinsic factors will vary with individual differences in intrinsic factors, and vice versa.

THE READINGS

The readings that follow were selected to provide an introduction to and evaluation of contemporary thought about motivation; they are divided into two sections. The first three readings, by McGregor, Herzberg, and Jackson and Shea, summarize many of the concepts from the study of motivation that have been applied to the management of people. The ideas of McGregor and Herzberg, in particular, have been widely accepted by practicing managers. The paper by Jackson and Shea expands the research on achievement motivation into an organizational framework. While the work on achievement motivation has not had nearly as great an impact on business organizations as the writings of McGregor and Herzberg, Jackson and Shea demonstrate that the ideas stemming from the study of the achievement motive may be extremely useful to organizational managers. Moreover, they point out the relationship of this approach to the more widely known models developed by McGregor and Herzberg.

The readings in the second section of this chapter summarize some of the applications of the ideas discussed in the first section. More importantly, they reveal some of the limitations of these approaches. In the first reading Maslow expresses his reservations about the application of his work to industrial organizations. This critique is especially noteworthy since McGregor, as we shall see, based his ideas on the work of Maslow. Hulin and Blood, in their paper, also question the generality of current models of motivation.

REFERENCES

Beach, F. A. "The Descent of Instinct." *Psychological Review* 62 (1955): 401-10.

Berkowitz, L. "Social Motivation." In *The Handbook of Social Psychology,* 2nd ed., vol. 3, edited by G. Lindzey and E. Aronson, pp. 50-135. Reading, Mass.: Addison-Wesley, 1969.

Berlyne, D. E. *Conflict, Arousal, and Curiosity.* New York: McGraw-Hill, 1960.

Bexton, W. H.; Heron, W.; and Scott, T. H. "Effects of Decrased Variation in the Environment." *Canadian Journal of Psychology* 8 (1954): 70-76.

Bindra, D. *Motivation: A Systematic Reinterpretation.* New York: Ronald Press, 1959.

Butler, R. A. "The Effect of Deprivation of Visual Incentives on Visual Exploration Motivation in Monkeys." *Journal of Comparative and Physiological Psychology* 46 (1953): 95-98.

Ervin, S. M. "Language and TAT Content in Bilinguals." *Journal of Abnormal and Social Psychology* 68 (1964): 500-507.

Festinger, L. *A Theory of Cognitive Dissonance.* Evanston, Ill.: Row, Peterson, 1957.

Hess, Eckhard H. "Ethology." In *New Directions in Psychology,* edited by R. Brown, E. Galanter, E. Hess, and G. Mandley, pp. 157-266. New York: Holt, Rinehart and Winston, 1962.

Hunt, J. McV. "Intrinsic Motivation and its Role in Psychological Development." In *Nebraska Symposium on Motivation* 8, edited by S. Levine, pp. 189-282. Lincoln, Neb.: University of Nebraska Press, 1965.

Lilly, J. C. "Mental Effects of Reduction of Ordinary Levels of Physical Stimuli on Intact, Healthy Persons." *Psychiatric Research Reports* no. 5 (1956): 1-9.

Maslow, A. H. "Toward a Humanistic Biology." *American Psychologist* 24 (1969): 724-35.

Olds, J., and Olds, M. "Drives, Rewards, and the Brain." In *New Directions in Psychology II*, New York: Holt, Rinehart and Winston, 1965.

Skinner, B. F. *Contingencies of Reinforcement.* New York: Appleton-Century-Crofts, 1969.

Vinacke, W. E. "Motivation as a Complex Problem." *Nebraska Symposium on Motivation* 10: 1-49. Lincoln, Neb.: University of Nebraska Press, 1962.

Douglas Murray McGregor

THE HUMAN SIDE OF ENTERPRISE

It has become trite to say that industry has the fundamental know-how to utilize physical science and technology for the material benefit of mankind, and that we must now learn how to utilize the social sciences to make our human organizations truly effective.

To a degree, the social sciences today are in a position like that of the physical sciences with respect to atomic energy in the thirties. We know that past conceptions of the nature of man are inadequate and, in many ways, incorrect. We are becoming quite certain that, under proper conditions, unimagined resources of creative human energy could become available within the organizational setting.

We cannot tell industrial management how to apply this new knowledge in simple, economic ways. We know it will require years of exploration, much costly development research, and a substantial amount of creative imagination on the part of management to discover how to apply this growing knowledge to the organization of human effort in industry.

MANAGEMENT'S TASK: THE CONVENTIONAL VIEW

The conventional conception of management's task in harnessing human energy to organizational requirements can be stated broadly in terms of three

Reprinted by permission of the publisher from *Management Review*, November 1957.

propositions. In order to avoid the complications introduced by a label, let us call this set of propositions "Theory X":

1. Management is responsible for organizing the elements of productive enterprise—money, materials, equipment, people—in the interest of economic ends.
2. With respect to people, this is a process of directing their efforts, motivating them, controlling their actions, modifying their behavior to fit the needs of the organization.
3. Without this active intervention by management, people would be passive—even resistant—to organizational needs. They must therefore be persuaded, rewarded, punished, controlled—their activities must be directed. This is management's task. We often sum it up by saying that management consists of getting things done through other people.

Behind this conventional theory there are several additional beliefs—less explicit, but widespread:

4. The average man is by nature indolent—he works as little as possible.
5. He lacks ambition, dislikes responsibility, prefers to be led.
6. He is inherently self-centered, indifferent to organizational needs.
7. He is by nature resistant to change.
8. He is gullible, not very bright, the ready dupe of the charlatan and the demagogue.

The human side of economic enterprise today is fashioned from propositions and beliefs such as these. Conventional organization structures and managerial policies, practices, and programs reflect these assumptions:

In accomplishing its task—with these assumptions as guides—management has conceived of a range of possibilities.

At one extreme, management can be "hard" or "strong." The methods for directing behavior involve coercion and threat (usually disguised), close supervision, tight controls over behavior. At the other extreme, management can be "soft" or "weak." The methods for directing behavior involve being permissive, satisfying people's demands, achieving harmony. Then they will be tractable, accept direction.

This range has been fairly completely explored during the past half century, and management has learned some things from the exploration. There are difficulties in the "hard" approach. Force breeds counter-forces: restriction of output, antagonism, militant unionism, subtle but effective sabotage of management objectives. This "hard" approach is especially difficult during times of full employment.

There are also difficulties in the "soft" approach. It leads frequently to the abdication of management—to harmony, perhaps, but to indifferent performance. People take advantage of the soft approach. They continually expect more, but they give less and less.

Currently, the popular theme is "firm but fair." This is an attempt to gain the advantages of both the hard and the soft approaches. It is reminiscent of Teddy Roosevelt's "speak softly and carry a big stick."

IS THE CONVENTIONAL VIEW CORRECT?

The findings which are beginning to emerge from the social sciences challenge this whole set of beliefs about man and human nature and about the task of management. The evidence is far from conclusive, certainly, but it is suggestive. It comes from the laboratory, the clinic, the schoolroom, the home, and even to a limited extent from industry itself.

The social scientist does not deny that human behavior in industrial organization today is approximately what management perceives it to be. He has, in fact, observed it and studied it fairly extensively. But he is pretty sure that this behavior is *not* a consequence of man's inherent nature. It is a consequence rather of the nature of industrial organizations, of management philosophy, policy, and practice. The conventional approach of Theory X is based on mistaken notions of what is cause and what is effect.

Perhaps the best way to indicate why the conventional approach of management is inadequate is to consider the subject of motivation.

PHYSIOLOGICAL NEEDS

Man is a wanting animal—as soon as one of his needs is satisfied, another appears in its place. This process is unending. It continues from birth to death.

Man's needs are organized in a series of levels—a hierarchy of importance. At the lowest level, but pre-eminent in importance when they are thwarted, are his *physiological needs.* Man lives for bread alone, when there is no bread. Unless the circumstances are unusual, his needs for love, for status, for recognition are inoperative when his stomach has been empty for a while. But when he eats regularly and adequately, hunger ceases to be an important motivation. The same is true of the other physiological needs of man—for rest, exercise, shelter, protection from the elements.

A satisfied need is not a motivator of behavior! This is a fact of profound significance that is regularly ignored in the conventional approach to the management of people. Consider your own need for air: Except as you are deprived of it, it has no appreciable motivating effect upon your behavior.

SAFETY NEEDS

When the physiological needs are reasonably satisfied, needs at the next higher level begin to dominate man's behavior—to motivate him. These are called *safety needs.* They are needs for protection against danger, threat, deprivation. Some people mistakenly refer to these as needs for security. However, unless man is in a dependent relationship where he fears arbitrary deprivation, he does not demand security. The need is for the "fairest possible break." When he is confident of this, he is more than willing to take risks. But when he feels threatened or dependent, his greatest need is for guarantees, for protection, for security.

The fact needs little emphasis that, since every industrial employee is in a dependent relationship, safety needs may assume considerable importance. Arbitrary management actions, behavior which arouses uncertainty with respect to continued employment or which reflects favoritism or discrimination, unpredictable administration of policy–these can be powerful motivators of the safety needs in the employment relationship *at every level,* from worker to vice president.

SOCIAL NEEDS

When man's physiological needs are satisfied and he is no longer fearful about his physical welfare, his *social needs* become important motivators of his behavior–needs for belonging, for association, for acceptance by his fellows, for giving and receiving friendship and love.

Management knows today of the existence of these needs, but it often assumes quite wrongly that they represent a threat to the organization. Many studies have demonstrated that the tightly knit, cohesive work group may, under proper conditions, be far more effective than an equal number of separate individuals in achieving organizational goals.

Yet management, fearing group hostility to its own objectives, often goes to considerable lengths to control and direct human efforts in ways that are inimical to the natural "groupiness" of human beings. When man's social needs–and perhaps his safety needs, too–are thus thwarted, he behaves in ways which tend to defeat organizational objectives. He becomes resistant, antagonistic, uncooperative. But this behavior is a consequence, not a cause.

EGO NEEDS

Above the social needs–in the sense that they do not become motivators until lower needs are reasonably satisfied–are the needs of greatest significance to management and to man himself. They are the *egoistic needs,* and they are of two kinds:

1. Those needs that relate to one's self-esteem–needs for self-confidence, for independence, for achievement, for competence, for knowledge.
2. Those needs that relate to one's reputation–needs for status, for recognition, for appreciation, for the deserved respect of one's fellows.

Unlike the lower needs, these are rarely satisfied; man seeks indefinitely for more satisfaction of these needs once they have become important to him. But they do not appear in any significant way until physiological, safety, and social needs are all reasonably satisfied.

The typical industrial organization offers few opportunities for the satisfaction of these egoistic needs to people at lower levels in the hierarchy. The conventional methods of organizing work, particularly in mass-production industries, give little heed to these aspects of human motivation. If the practices of scientific management were deliberately calculated to thwart these needs, they could hardly accomplish this purpose better than they do.

SELF-FULFILLMENT NEEDS

Finally—a capstone, as it were, on the hierarchy of man's needs—there are what we may call the *needs for self-fulfillment.* These are the needs for realizing one's own potentialities, for continued self-development, for being creative in the broadest sense of that term.

It is clear that the conditions of modern life give only limited opportunity for these relatively weak needs to obtain expression. The deprivation most people experience with respect to other lower-level needs diverts their energies into the struggle to satisfy *those* needs, and the needs for self-fulfillment remain dormant.

MANAGEMENT AND MOTIVATION

We recognize readily enough that a man suffering from a severe dietary deficiency is sick. The deprivation of physiological needs has behavioral consequences. The same is true—although less well recognized—of deprivation of higher-level needs. The man whose needs for safety, association, independence, or status are thwarted is sick just as surely as the man who has rickets. And his sickness will have behavioral consequences. We will be mistaken if we attribute his resultant passivity, his hostility, his refusal to accept responsibility to his inherent "human nature." These forms of behavior are *symptoms* of illness—of deprivation of his social and egoistic needs.

The man whose lower-level needs are satisfied is not motivated to satisfy those needs any longer. For practical purposes they exist no longer. Management often asks, "Why aren't people more productive? We pay good wages, provide good working conditions, have excellent fringe benefits and steady employment. Yet people do not seem to be willing to put forth more than minimum effort."

The fact that management has provided for these physiological and safety needs has shifted the motivational emphasis to the social and perhaps to the egoistic needs. Unless there are opportunities *at work* to satisfy these higher-level needs, people will be deprived; and their behavior will reflect this deprivation. Under such conditions, if management continues to focus its attention on physiological needs, its efforts are bound to be ineffective.

People *will* make insistent demands for more money under these conditions. It becomes more important than ever to buy the material goods and services which can provide limited satisfaction of the thwarted needs. Although money has only limited value in satisfying many higher-level needs, it can become the focus of interest if it is the *only* means available.

THE CARROT-AND-STICK APPROACH

The carrot-and-stick theory of motivation (like Newtonian physical theory) works reasonably well under certain circumstances. The *means* for satisfying man's physiological and (within limits) his safety needs can be provided or withheld by management. Employment itself is such a means, and so are wages, working conditions, and benefits. By these means the individual can be controlled so long as he is struggling for subsistence.

But the carrot-and-stick theory does not work at all once man has reached an adequate subsistence level and is motivated primarily by higher needs. Management cannot provide a man with self-respect, or with the respect of his fellows, or with the satisfaction of needs for self-fulfillment. It can create such conditions that he is encouraged and enabled to seek such satisfactions for *himself,* or it can thwart him by failing to create those conditions.

But this creation of conditions is not "control." It is not a good device for directing behavior. And so management finds itself in an odd position. The high standard of living created by our modern technological know-how provides quite adequately for the satisfaction of physiological and safety needs. The only significant exception is where management practices have not created confidence in a "fair break"—and thus where safety needs are thwarted. But by making possible the satisfaction of low-level needs, management has deprived itself of the ability to use as motivators the devices on which conventional theory has taught it to rely—rewards, promises, incentives, or threats and other coercive devices.

The philosophy of management by direction and control—*regardless of whether it is hard or soft*—is inadequate to motivate because the human needs on which this approach relies are today unimportant motivators of behavior. Direction and control are essentially useless in motivating people whose important needs are social and egoistic. Both the hard and the soft approach fail today because they are simply irrelevant to the situation.

People, deprived of opportunities to satisfy at work the needs which are now important to them, behave exactly as we might predict—with indolence, passivity, resistance to change, lack of responsibility, willingness to follow the demagogue, unreasonable demands for economic benefits. It would seem that we are caught in a web of our own weaving.

A NEW THEORY OF MANAGEMENT

For these and many other reasons, we require a different theory of the task of managing people based on more adequate assumptions about human nature and human motivation. I am going to be so bold as to suggest the broad dimensions of such a theory. Call it "Theory Y," if you will.

1. Management is responsible for organizing the elements of productive enterprise—money, materials, equipment, people—in the interest of economic ends.
2. People are *not* by nature passive or resistant to organizational needs. They have become so as a result of experience in organizations.
3. The motivation, the potential for development, the capacity for assuming responsibility, the readiness to direct behavior toward organizational goals are all present in people. Management does not put them there. It is a responsibility of management to make it possible for people to recognize and develop these human characteristics for themselves.

4. The essential task of management is to arrange organizational conditions and methods of operation so that people can achieve their own goals *best* by directing *their own* efforts toward organizational objectives.

This is a process primarily of creating opportunities, releasing potential, removing obstacles, encouraging growth, providing guidance. It is what Peter Drucker has called "management by objectives" in contrast to "management by control." It does *not* involve the abdication of management, the absence of leadership, the lowering of standards, or the other characteristics usually associated with the "soft" approach under Theory X.

SOME DIFFICULTIES

It is no more possible to create an organization today which will be a full, effective application of this theory than it was to build an atomic power plant in 1945. There are many formidable obstacles to overcome.

The conditions imposed by conventional organization theory and by the approach of scientific management for the past half century have tied men to limited jobs which do not utilize their capabilities, have discouraged the acceptance of responsibility, have encouraged passivity, have eliminated meaning from work. Man's habits, attitudes, expectations–his whole conception of membership in an industrial organization–have been conditioned by his experience under these circumstances.

People today are accustomed to being directed, manipulated, controlled in industrial organizations and to finding satisfaction for their social, egoistic, and self-fulfillment needs away from the job. This is true of much of management as well as of workers. Genuine "industrial citizenship"–to borrow again a term from Drucker–is a remote and unrealistic idea, the meaning of which has not even been considered by most members of industrial organizations.

Another way of saying this is that Theory X places exclusive reliance upon external control of human behavior, while Theory Y relies heavily on self-control and self-direction. It is worth noting that this difference is the difference between treating people as children and treating them as mature adults. After generations of the former, we cannot expect to shift to the latter overnight.

STEPS IN THE RIGHT DIRECTION

Before we are overwhelmed by the obstacles, let us remember that the application of theory is always slow. Progress is usually achieved in small steps. Some innovative ideas which are entirely consistent with Theory Y are today being applied with some success.

Decentralization and Delegation

These are ways of freeing people from the too-close control of conventional organization, giving them a degree of freedom to direct their own activities, to assume responsibility, and, importantly, to satisfy their egoistic needs. In this connection, the flat organization of Sears, Roebuck and Company provides an interesting example. It forces "management by objectives," since it enlarges the number of people reporting to a manager until he cannot direct and control them in the conventional manner.

Job Enlargement

This concept, pioneered by I.B.M. and Detroit Edison, is quite consistent with Theory Y. It encourages the acceptance of responsibility at the bottom of the organization; it provides opportunities for satisfying social and egoistic needs. In fact, the reorganization of work at the factory level offers one of the more challenging opportunities for innovation consistent with Theory Y.

Participation and Consultative Management

Under proper conditions, participation and consultative management provide encouragement to people to direct their creative energies toward organizational objectives, give them some voice in decisions that affect them, provide significant opportunities for the satisfaction of social and egoistic needs. The Scanlon Plan is the outstanding embodiment of these ideas in practice.

Performance Appraisal

Even a cursory examination of conventional programs of performance appraisal within the ranks of management will reveal how completely consistent they are with Theory X. In fact, most such programs tend to treat the individual as though he were a product under inspection on the assembly line.

A few companies—among them General Mills, Ansul Chemical, and General Electric—have been experimenting with approaches which involve the individual in setting "targets" or objectives *for himself* and in a *self*-evaluation of performance semiannually or annually. Of course, the superior plays an important leadership role in this process—one, in fact, which demands substantially more competence than the conventional approach. The role is, however, considerably more congenial to many managers than the role of "judge" or "inspector" which is usually forced upon them. Above all, the individual is encouraged to take a greater responsibility for planning and appraising his own contribution to organizational objectives; and the accompanying effects on egoistic and self-fulfillment needs are substantial.

APPLYING THE IDEAS

The not infrequent failure of such ideas as these to work as well as expected is often attributable to the fact that a management has "bought the idea" but applied it within the framework of Theory X and its assumptions.

Delegation is not an effective way of exercising management by control. Participation becomes a farce when it is applied as a sales gimmick or a device for kidding people into thinking they are important. Only the management that has confidence in human capacities and is itself directed toward organizational objectives rather than toward the preservation of personal power can grasp the implications of this emerging theory. Such management will find and apply successfully other innovative ideas as we move slowly toward the full implementation of a theory like Y.

THE HUMAN SIDE OF ENTERPRISE

It is quite possible for us to realize substantial improvements in the effectiveness of industrial organizations during the next decade or two. The social sciences can contribute much to such developments; we are only beginning to grasp the implications of the growing body of knowledge in these fields. But if this conviction is to become a reality instead of a pious hope, we will need to view the process much as we view the process of releasing the energy of the atom for constructive human ends—as a slow, costly, sometimes discouraging approach toward a goal which would seem to many to be quite unrealistic.

The ingenuity and the perseverance of industrial management in the pursuit of economic ends have changed many scientific and technological dreams into commonplace realities. It is now becoming clear that the application of these same talents to the human side of enterprise will not only enhance substantially these materialistic achievements, but will bring us one step closer to "the good society."

* * *

Frederick Herzberg

ONE MORE TIME: HOW DO YOU MOTIVATE EMPLOYEES?

How many articles, books, speeches, and workshops have pleaded plaintively, "How do I get an employee to do what I want him to do?"

The psychology of motivation is tremendously complex, and what has been unraveled with any degree of assurance is small indeed. But the dismal ratio of knowledge to speculation has not dampened the enthusiasm for new forms of

Herzberg, Frederick "One More Time: How Do You Motivate Employees?" *Harvard Business Review, 46,* (January-February, 1968): 53-62.

snake oil that are constantly coming on the market, many of them with academic testimonials. Doubtless this article will have no depressing impact on the market for snake oil, but since the ideas expressed in it have been tested in many corporations and other organizations, it will help—I hope—to redress the imbalance in the aforementioned ratio.

"MOTIVATING" WITH KITA

In lectures to industry on the problem, I have found that the audiences are anxious for quick and practical answers, so I will begin with a straightforward, practical formula for moving people.

What is the simplest, surest, and most direct way of getting someone to do something? Ask him? But if he responds that he does not want to do it, then that calls for a psychological consultation to determine the reason for his obstinacy. Tell him? His response shows that he does not understand you, and now an expert in communication methods has to be brought in to show you how to get through to him. Give him a monetary incentive? I do not need to remind the reader of the complexity and difficulty involved in setting up and administering an incentive system. Show him? This means a costly training program. We need a simple way.

Every audience contains the "direct action" manager who shouts, "Kick him!" And this type of manager is right. The surest and least circumlocuted way of getting someone to do something is to kick him in the pants—give him what might be called the KITA.

There are various forms of KITA, and here are some of them:

Negative physical KITA. This is a literal application of the term and was frequently used in the past. It has, however, three major drawbacks: (1) it is inelegant; (2) it contradicts the precious image of benevolence that most organizations cherish; and (3) since it is a physical attack, it directly stimulates the autonomic nervous system, and this often results in negative feedback—the employee may just kick you in return. These factors give rise to certain taboos against negative physical KITA.

The psychologist has come to the rescue of those who are no longer permitted to use negative physical KITA. He has uncovered infinite sources of psychological vulnerabilities and the appropriate methods to play tunes on them. "He took my rug away"; "I wonder what he meant by that"; "The boss is always going around me"—these symptomatic expressions of ego sores that have been rubbed raw are the result of application of:

Negative Psychological KITA. This has several advantages over negative physical KITA. First, the cruelty is not visible; the bleeding is internal and comes much later. Second, since it affects the higher cortical centers of the brain with its inhibitory powers, it reduces the possibility of physical backlash. Third, since the number of psychological pains that a person can feel is almost infinite, the direction and site possibilities of the KITA are increased many times. Fourth, the person administering the kick can manage to be above it all and let the system accomplish the dirty work. Fifth, those who practice it receive some ego satisfaction (one-upmanship), whereas they would find drawing blood abhorrent. Finally, if the employee does complain, he can always be accused of being paranoid, since there is no tangible evidence of an actual attack.

Now, what does negative KITA accomplish? If I kick you in the rear (physically or psychologically), who is motivated? I am motivated; you move! Negative KITA does not lead to motivation, but to movement. So:

Positive KITA. Let us consider motivation. If I say to you, "Do this for me or the company, and in return I will give you a reward, an incentive, more status, a promotion, all the quid pro quos that exist in the industrial organization," am I motivating you? The overwhelming opinion I receive from management people is, "Yes, this is motivation."

I have a year-old Schnauzer. When it was a small puppy and I wanted it to move, I kicked it in the rear and it moved. Now that I have finished its obedience training, I hold up a dog biscuit when I want the Schnauzer to move. In this instance, who is motivated—I or the dog? The dog wants the biscuit, but it is I who want it to move. Again, I am the one who is motivated, and the dog is the one who moves. In this instance all I did was apply KITA frontally; I exerted a pull instead of a push. When industry wishes to use such positive KITAs, it has available an incredible number and variety of dog biscuits (jelly beans for humans) to wave in front of the employee to get him to jump.

Why is it that managerial audiences are quick to see that negative KITA is *not* motivation, while they are almost unanimous in their judgment that positive KITA *is* motivation? It is because negative KITA is rape, and positive KITA is seduction. But it is infinitely worse to be seduced than to be raped; the latter is an unfortunate occurrence, while the former signifies that you were a party to your own downfall. This is why positive KITA is so popular: it is a tradition; it is in the American way. The organization does not have to kick you; you kick yourself.

Myths About Motivation

Why is KITA not motivation? If I kick my dog (from the front or the back), he will move. And when I want him to move again, what must I do? I must kick him again. Similarly, I can charge a man's battery, and then recharge it, and recharge it again. But it is only when he has his own generator that we can talk about motivation. He then needs no outside stimulation. He *wants* to do it.

With this in mind, we can review some positive KITA personnel practices that were developed as attempts to instill "motivation":

1. Reducing time spent at work. This represents a marvelous way of motivating people to work—getting them off the job! We have reduced (formally and informally) the time spent on a job over the last 50 or 60 years until we are finally on the way to the "6½-day weekend." An interesting variant of this approach is the development of off-hour recreation programs. The philosophy here seems to be that those who play together, work together. The fact is that motivated people seek more hours of work, not fewer.

2. **Spiraling wages.** Have these motivated people? Yes, to seek the next wage increase. Some medievalists still can be heard to say that a good depression will get employees moving. They feel that if rising wages don't or won't do the job, perhaps reducing them will.

3. **Fringe benefits.** Industry has outdone the most welfare-minded of welfare states in dispensing cradle-to-the-grave succor. One company I know of had an informal "fringe benefit of the month club" going for a while. The cost of fringe benefits in this country has reached approximately 25 percent of the wage dollar, and we still cry for motivation.

People spend less time working for more money and more security than ever before, and the trend cannot be reversed. These benefits are no longer rewards; they are rights. A six-day week is inhuman, a ten-hour day is exploitation, extended medical coverage is a basic decency, and stock options are the salvation of American initiative. Unless the ante is continuously raised, the psychological reaction of employees is that the company is turning back the clock.

When industry began to realize that both the economic nerve and the lazy nerve of their employees had insatiable appetites, it started to listen to the behavioral scientists who, more out of a humanist tradition than from scientific study, criticized management for not knowing how to deal with people. The next KITA easily followed.

4. **Human relations training.** Over 30 years of teaching and, in many instances, of practicing psychological approaches to handling people have resulted in costly human relations programs and, in the end, the same question: How do you motivate workers? Here, too, escalations have taken place. Thirty years ago it was necessary to request, "Please don't spit on the floor." Today the same admonition requires three "please"s before the employee feels that his superior has demonstrated the psychologically proper attitudes toward him.

The failure of human relations training to produce motivation led to the conclusion that the supervisor or manager himself was not psychologically true to himself in his practice of interpersonal decency. So an advanced form of human relations KITA, sensitivity training, was unfolded.

5. **Sensitivity training.** Do you really, really understand yourself? Do you really, really, really trust the other man? Do you really, really, really, really cooperate? The failure of sensitivity training is now being explained, by those who have become opportunistic exploiters of the technique, as a failure to really (five times) conduct proper sensitivity training courses.

With the realization that there are only temporary gains from comfort and economic and interpersonal KITA, personnel managers concluded that the fault lay not in what they were doing, but in the employee's failure to appreciate what they were doing. This opened up the field of communications, a whole new area of "scientifically" sanctioned KITA.

6. **Communications.** The professor of communications was invited to join the faculty of management training programs and help in making employees understand what management was doing for them. House organs, briefing

sessions, supervisory instruction on the importance of communication, and all sorts of propaganda have proliferated until today there is even an International Council of Industrial Editors. But no motivation resulted, and the obvious thought occured that perhaps management was not hearing what the employees were saying. That led to the next KITA.

7. **Two-way communication.** Management ordered morale surveys, suggestion plans, and group participation programs. Then both employees and management were communicating and listening to each other more than ever, but without much improvement in motivation.

The behavioral scientists began to take another look at their conceptions and their data, and they took human relations one step further. A glimmer of truth was beginning to show through in the writings of the so-called higher-order-need psychologists. People, so they said, want to actualize themselves. Unfortunately, the "actualizing" psychologists got mixed up with the human relations psychologists, and a new KITA emerged.

8. **Job participation.** Though it may not have been the theoretical intention, job participation often became a "give them the big picture" approach. For example, if a man is tightening 10,000 nuts a day on an assembly line with a torque wrench, tell him he is building a Chevrolet. Another approach had the goal of giving the employee a *feeling* that he is determining, in some measure, what he does on his job. The goal was to provide a *sense* of achievement rather than a substantive achievement in his task. Real achievement, of course, requires a task that makes it possible.

But still there was no motivation. This led to the inevitable conclusion that the employees must be sick, and therefore to the next KITA.

9. **Employee counseling.** The initial use of this form of KITA in a systematic fashion can be credited to the Hawthorne experiment of the Western Electric Company during the early 1930s. At that time, it was found that the employees harbored irrational feelings that were interfering with the rational operation of the factory. Counseling in this instance was a means of letting the employees unburden themselves by talking to someone about their problems. Although the counseling techniques were primitive, the program was large indeed.

The counseling approach suffered as a result of experiences during World War II, when the programs themselves were found to be interfering with the operation of the organizations; the counselors had forgotten their role of benevolent listeners and were attempting to do something about the problems that they heard about. Psychological counseling, however, has managed to survive the negative impact of World War II experiences and today is beginning to flourish with renewed sophistication. But, alas, many of these programs, like all the others, do not seem to have lessened the pressure of demands to find out how to motivate workers.

Since KITA results only in short-term movement, it is safe to predict that the cost of these programs will increase steadily and new varieties will be developed as old positive KITAs reach their satiation points.

HYGIENE VS. MOTIVATORS

Let me rephrase the perennial question this way: How do you install a generator in an employee? A brief review of my motivation-hygiene theory of job attitudes is required before theoretical and practical suggestions can be offered. The theory was first drawn from an examination of events in the lives of engineers and accountants. At least 16 other investigations, using a wide variety of populations (including some in the Communist countries), have since been completed, making the original research one of the most replicated studies in the field of job attitudes.

The findings of these studies, along with corroboration from many other investigations using different procedures, suggest that the factors involved in producing job satisfaction (and motivation) are separate and distinct from the factors that lead to job dissatisfaction. Since separate factors need to be considered, depending on whether job satisfaction or job dissatisfaction is being examined, it follows that these two feelings are not opposites of each other. The opposite of job satisfaction is not job dissatisfaction but, rather, *no* job satisfaction; and, similarly, the opposite of job dissatisfaction is not job satisfaction, but *no* job dissatisfaction.

Stating the concept presents a problem in semantics, for we normally think of satisfaction and dissatisfaction as opposites—i.e., what is not satisfying must be dissatisfying, and vice versa. But when it comes to understanding the behavior of people in their jobs, more than a play on words is involved.

Two different needs of man are involved here. One set of needs can be thought of as stemming from his animal nature—the built-in drive to avoid pain from the environment, plus all the learned drives which become conditioned to the basic biological needs. For example, hunger, a basic biological drive, makes it necessary to earn money, and then money becomes a specific drive. The other set of needs relates to that unique human characteristic, the ability to achieve and, through achievement, to experience psychological growth. The stimuli for the growth needs are tasks that induce growth; in the industrial setting, they are the *job content.* Contrariwise, the stimuli inducing pain-avoidance behavior are found in the *job environment.*

The growth or *motivator* factors that are intrinsic to the job are: achievement, recognition for achievement, the work itself, responsibility, and growth or advancement. The dissatisfaction-avoidance or *hygiene* (KITA) factors that are extrinsic to the job include: company policy and administration, supervision, interpersonal relationships, working conditions, salary, status, and security.

A composite of the factors that are involved in causing job satisfaction and job dissatisfaction, drawn from samples of 1,685 employees, is shown in Exhibit I. The results indicate that motivators were the primary cause of satisfaction, and hygiene factors the primary cause of unhappiness on the job. The employees, studied in 12 different investigations, included lower-level supervisors, professional women, agricultural administrators, men about to retire from management positions, hospital maintenance personnel, manufacturing

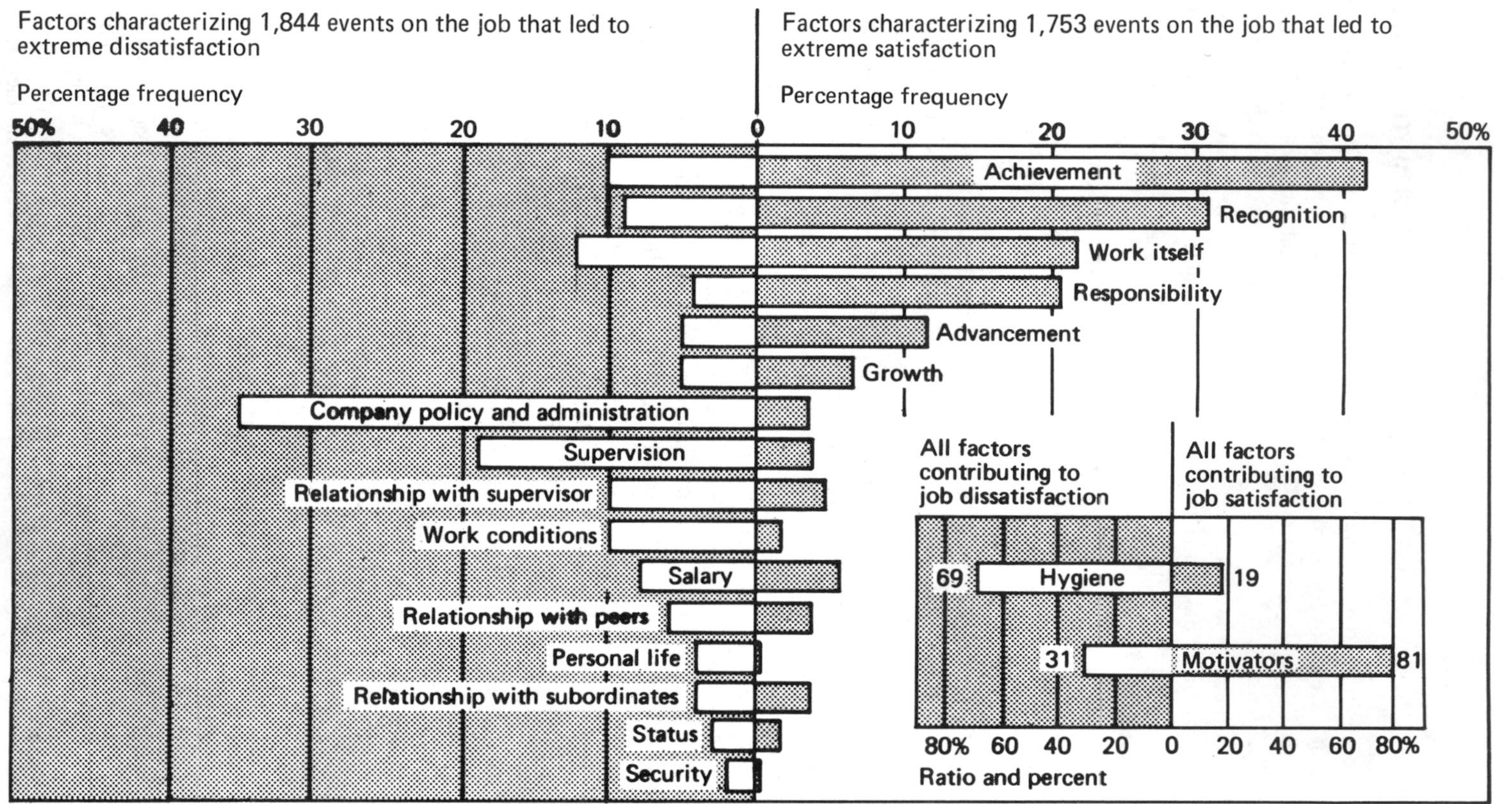

EXHIBIT 1. **Factors affecting job attitudes, as reported in 12 investigations**

supervisors, nurses, food handlers, military officers, engineers, scientists, housekeepers, teachers, technicians, female assemblers, accountants, Finnish foremen, and Hungarian engineers.

They were asked what job events had occurred in their work that had led to extreme satisfaction or extreme dissatisfaction on their part. Their responses are broken down in the exhibit into percentages of total "positive" job events and of total "negative" job events. (The figures total more than 100 percent on both the "hygiene" and "motivators" sides because often at least two factors can be attributed to a single event; advancement, for instance, often accompanies assumption of responsibility.)

To illustrate, a typical response involving achievement that had a negative effect for the employee was, "I was unhappy because I didn't do the job successfully." A typical response in the small number of positive job events in the Company Policy and Administration grouping was, "I was happy because the company reorganized the section so that I didn't report any longer to the guy I didn't get along with."

As the lower right-hand part of the exhibit shows, of all the factors contributing to job satisfaction, 81 percent were motivators. And of all the factors contributing to the employees' dissatisfaction over their work, 69 percent involved hygiene elements.

Eternal Triangle

There are three general philosophies of personnel management. The first is based on organizational theory, the second on industrial engineering, and the third on behavioral science.

The organizational theorist believes that human needs are either so irrational or so varied and adjustable to specific situations that the major function of personnel management is to be as pragmatic as the occasion demands. If jobs are organized in a proper manner, he reasons, the result will be the most efficient job structure, and the most favorable job attitudes will follow as a matter of course.

The industrial engineer holds that man is mechanistically oriented and economically motivated and his needs are best met by attuning the individual to the most efficient work process. The goal of personnel management therefore should be to concoct the most appropriate incentive system and to design the specific working conditions in a way that facilitates the most efficient use of the human machine. By structuring jobs in a manner that leads to the most efficient operation, the engineer believes that he can obtain the optimal organization of work and the proper work attitudes.

The behavioral scientist focuses on group sentiments, attitudes of individual employees, and the organization's social and psychological climate. According to his persuasion, he emphasizes one or more of the various hygiene and motivator needs. His approach to personnel management generally emphasizes some form of human relations education, in the hope of instilling healthy employee attitudes and an organizational climate which he considers to be felicitous to human values. He believes that proper attitudes will lead to efficient job and organizational structure.

There is always a lively debate as to the overall effectiveness of the approaches of the organizational theorist and the industrial engineer. Manifestly they have achieved much. But the nagging question for the behavioral scientist has been: What is the cost in human problems that eventually cause more expense to the organization—for instance, turnover, absenteeism, errors, violation of safety rules, strikes, restriction of output, higher wages, and greater fringe benefits? On the other hand, the behavioral scientist is hard put to document much manifest improvement in personnel management, using his approach.

The three philosophies can be depicted as a triangle, as is done in Exhibit II, with each persuasion claiming the apex angle. The motivation-hygiene theory claims the same angle as industrial engineering, but for opposite goals. Rather than rationalizing the work to increase efficiency, the theory suggests that work be *enriched* to bring about effective utilization of personnel. Such a systematic attempt to motivate employees by manipulating the motivator factors is just beginning.

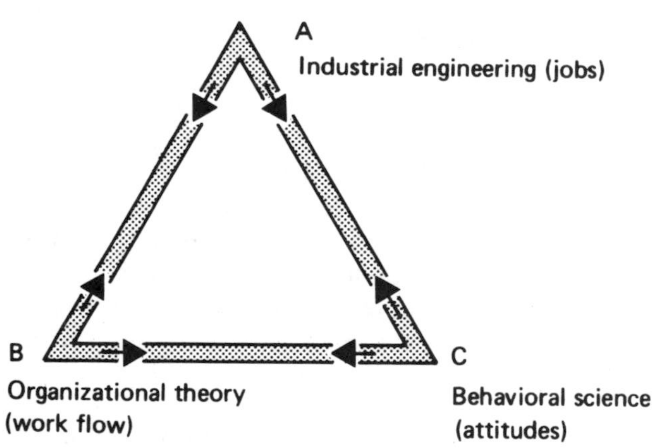

EXHIBIT II. 'Triangle' of philosophies of personnel management

The term *job enrichment* describes this embryonic movement. An older term, job enlargement, should be avoided because it is associated with past failures stemming from a misunderstanding of the problem. Job enrichment provides the opportunity for the employee's psychological growth, while job enlargement merely makes a job structurally bigger. Since scientific job enrichment is very new, this article only suggests the principles and practical steps that have recently emerged from several successful experiments in industry.

Job Loading

In attempting to enrich an employee's job, management often succeeds in reducing the man's personal contribution, rather than giving him an opportunity for growth in his accustomed job. Such an endeavor, which I shall call horizontal job loading (as opposed to vertical loading, or providing motivator factors), has been the problem of earlier job enlargement programs. This activity merely enlarges the meaninglessness of the job. Some examples of this approach, and their effect, are:

Challenging the employee by increasing the amount of production expected of him. If he tightens 10,000 bolts a day, see if he can tighten 20,000 bolts a day. The arithmetic involved shows that multiplying zero by zero still equals zero.

Adding another meaningless task to the existing one, usually some routine clerical activity. The arithmetic here is adding zero to zero.

Rotating the assignments of a number of jobs that need to be enriched. This means washing dishes for a while, then washing silverware. The arithmetic is substituting one zero for another zero.

Removing the most difficult parts of the assignment in order to free the worker to accomplish more of the less challenging assignments. This traditional industrial engineering approach amounts to subtraction in the hope of accomplishing addition.

These are common forms of horizontal loading that frequently come up in preliminary brainstorming sessions on job enrichment. The principles of vertical loading have not all been worked out as yet, and they remain rather general, but I have furnished seven useful starting points for consideration in Exhibit III.

A Successful Application

An example from a highly successful job enrichment experiment can illustrate the distinction between horizontal and vertical loading of a job. The subjects of this study were the stockholder correspondents employed by a very large corporation. Seemingly, the task required of these carefully selected and highly trained correspondents was quite complex and challenging. But almost all indexes of performance and job attitudes were low, and exit interviewing confirmed that the challenge of the job existed merely as words.

A job enrichment project was initiated in the form of an experiment with one group, designated as an achieving unit, having its job enriched by the principles described in Exhibit III. A control group continued to do its job in the traditional way. (There were also two "uncommitted" groups of correspondents formed to measure the so-called Hawthorne Effect—that is, to gauge whether productivity and attitudes toward the job changed artificially merely because employees sensed that the company was paying more attention to them in doing something different or novel. The results for these groups were substantially the same as for the control group, and for the sake of simplicity I do not deal with them in this summary.) No changes in hygiene were introduced for either group other than those that would have been made anyway, such as normal pay increases.

The changes for the achieving unit were introduced in the first two months, averaging one per week of the seven motivators listed in Exhibit III. At the end of six months the members of the achieving unit were found to be

EXHIBIT III. Principles of vertical job loading

	Principle	*Motivators involved*
A.	Removing some controls while retaining accountability	Responsibility and personal achievement
B.	Increasing the accountability of individuals for own work	Responsibility and recognition
C.	Giving a person a complete natural unit of work (module, division, area, and so on)	Responsibility, achievement, and recognition
D.	Granting additional authority to an employee in his activity; job freedom	Responsibility, achievement, and recognition
E.	Making periodic reports directly available to the worker himself rather than to the supervisor	Internal recognition
F.	Introducing new and more difficult tasks not previously handled	Growth and learning
G.	Assigning individuals specific or specialized tasks, enabling them to become experts	Responsibility, growth, and advancement

outperforming their counterparts in the control group, and in addition indicated a marked increase in their liking for their jobs. Other results showed that the achieving group had lower absenteeism and, subsequently, a much higher rate of promotion.

Exhibit IV illustrates the changes in performance, measured in February and March, before the study period began, and at the end of each month of the study period. The shareholder service index represents quality of letters, including accuracy of information, and speed of response to stockholders' letters of inquiry. The index of a current month was averaged into the average of the two prior months, which means that improvement was harder to obtain if the indexes of the previous months were low. The "achievers" were performing less well before the six-month period started, and their performance service index continued to decline after the introduction of the motivators, evidently because of uncertainty over their newly granted responsibilities. In the third month, however, performance improved, and soon the members of this group had reached a high level of accomplishment.

Exhibit V shows the two groups' attitudes toward their job, measured at the end of March, just before the first motivator was introduced, and again at the end of September. The correspondents were asked 16 questions, all involving motivation. A typical one was, "As you see it, how many opportunities do you feel that you have in your job for making worthwhile contributions?" The answers were scaled from one to five with 80 as the maximum possible score. The achievers became much more positive about their job, while the attitude of the control unit remained about the same (the drop is not statistically significant).

How was the job of these correspondents restructured? Exhibit VI lists the suggestions made that were deemed to be horizontal loading, and the actual

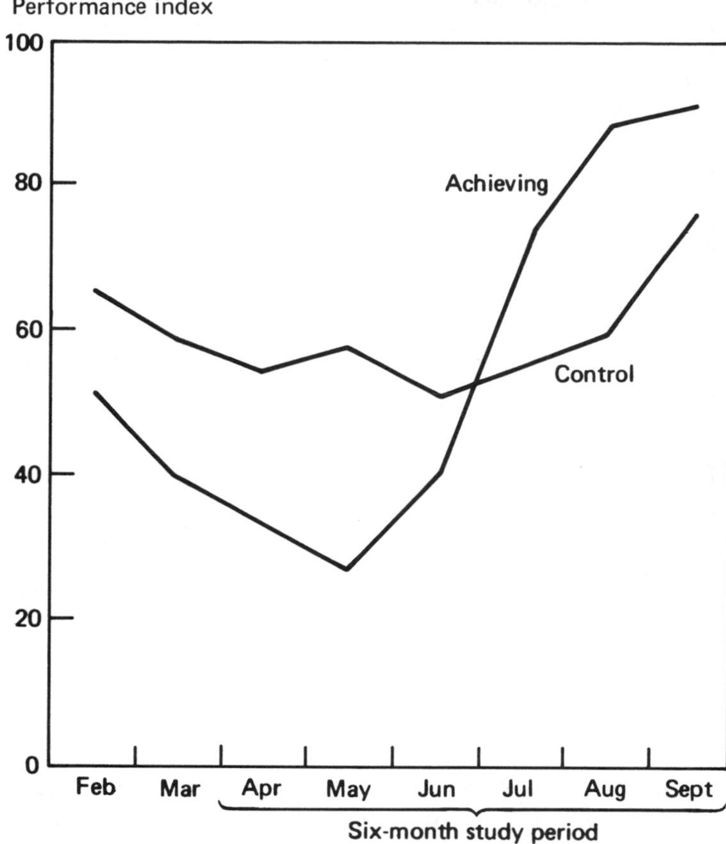

**EXHIBIT IV. Shareholder service index in company experiment–
[Three-month cumulative average]**

vertical loading changes that were incorporated in the job of the achieving unit. The capital letters under "Principle" after "Vertical loading" refer to the corresponding letters in Exhibit III. The reader will note that the rejected forms of horizontal loading correspond closely to the list of common manifestations of the phenomenon on page 76.

STEPS TO JOB ENRICHMENT

Now that the motivator idea has been described in practice, here are the steps that managers should take in instituting the principle with their employees:

(1) Select those jobs in which

a. the investment in industrial engineering does not make changes too costly,
b. attitudes are poor,
c. hygiene is becoming very costly, and
d. motivation will make a difference in performance.

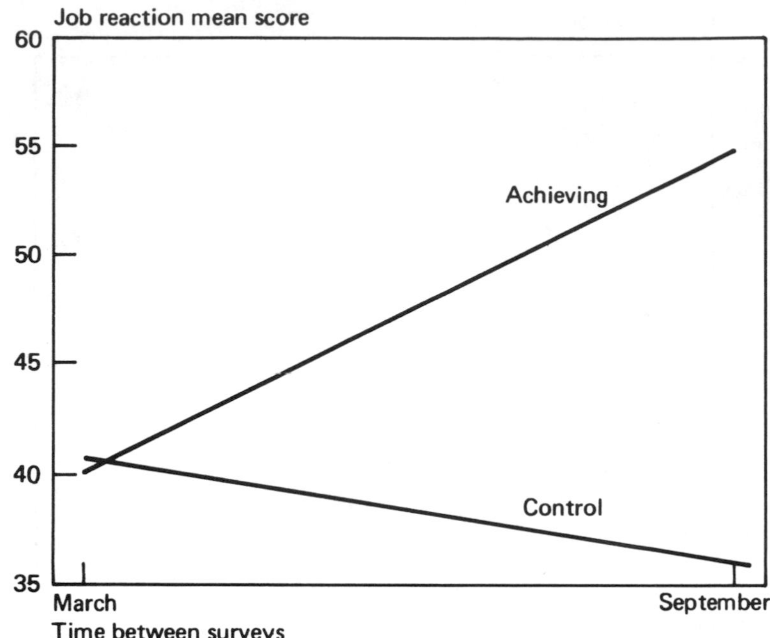

EXHIBIT V. Changes in attitudes toward tasks in company experiment [Changes in mean scores over six-month period]

(2) Approach these jobs with the conviction that they can be changed. Years of tradition have led managers to believe that the content of the jobs is sacrosanct and the only scope of action that they have is in ways of stimulating people.

(3) Brainstorm a list of changes that may enrich the jobs, without concern for their practicality.

(4) Screen the list to eliminate suggestions that involve hygiene, rather than actual motivation.

(5) Screen the list for generalities, such as "give them more responsibility," that are rarely followed in practice. This might seem obvious, but the motivator words have never left industry; the substance has just been rationalized and organized out. Words like "responsibility," "growth," "achievement," and "challenge," for example, have been elevated to the lyrics of the patriotic anthem for all organizations. It is the old problem typified by the pledge of allegiance to the flag being more important than contributions to the country—of following the form, rather than the substance.

(6) Screen the list to eliminate any *horizontal* loading suggestions.

(7) Avoid direct participation by the employees whose jobs are to be enriched. Ideas they have expressed previously certainly constitute a valuable source for recommended changes, but their direct involvement contaminates the process with human relations *hygiene* and, more specifically, gives them only a

Horizontal loading suggestions (rejected)	*Vertical loading suggestions (adopted)*	*Principle*
Firm quotas could be set for letters to be answered each day, using a rate which would be hard to reach.	Subject matter experts were appointed within each unit for other members of the unit to consult with before seeking supervisory help. (The supervisor had been answering all specialized and difficult questions.)	G
The women could type the letters themselves, as well as compose them, or take on any other clerical functions.	Correspondents signed their own names on letters. (The supervisor had been signing all letters.)	B
All difficult or complex inquiries could be channeled to a few women so that the remainder could achieve high rates of output. These jobs could be exchanged from time to time.	The work of the more experienced correspondents was proofread less frequently by supervisors and was done at the correspondents' desks, dropping verification from 100% to 10%. (Previously, all correspondents' letters had been checked by the supervisor.)	A
The women could be rotated through units handling different customers, and then sent back to their own units.	Production was discussed, but only in terms such as "a full day's work is expected." As time went on, this was no longer mentioned. (Before, the group had been constantly reminded of the number of letters that needed to be answered.)	D
	Outgoing mail went directly to the mailroom without going over supervisors' desks. (The letters had always been routed through the supervisors.)	A
	Correspondents were encouraged to answer letters in a more personalized way. (Reliance on the form-letter approach had been standard practice.)	C
	Each correspondent was held personally responsible for the quality and accuracy of letters. (This responsibility had been the province of the supervisor and the verifier.)	B,E

EXHIBIT VI. **Enlargement vs. enrichment of correspondents' tasks in company experiment**

sense of making a contribution. The job is to be changed, and it is the content that will produce the motivation, not attitudes about being involved or the challenge inherent in setting up a job. That process will be over shortly, and it is what the employees will be doing from then on that will determine their motivation. A sense of participation will result only in short-term movement.

(8) In the initial attempts at job enrichment, set up a controlled experiment. At least two equivalent groups should be chosen, one an experimental unit in which the motivators are systematically introduced over a period of time, and the other one a control group in which no changes are made. For both groups, hygiene should be allowed to follow its natural course for the duration of the experiment. Pre- and post-installation tests of performance and job attitudes are necessary to evaluate the effectiveness of the job enrichment program. The attitude test must be limited to motivator items in order to divorce the employee's view of the job he is given from all the surrounding hygiene feelings that he might have.

(9) Be prepared for a drop in performance in the experimental group the first few weeks. The changeover to a new job may lead to a temporary reduction in efficiency.

(10) Expect your first-line supervisors to experience some anxiety and hostility over the changes you are making. The anxiety comes from their fear that the changes will result in poorer performance for their unit. Hostility will arise when the employees start assuming what the supervisors regard as their own responsibility for performance. The supervisor without checking duties to perform may then be left with little to do.

After a successful experiment, however, the supervisor usually discovers the supervisory and managerial functions he has neglected, or which were never his because all his time was given over to checking the work of his subordinates. For example, in the R&D division of one large chemical company I know of, the supervisors of the laboratory assistants were theoretically responsible for their training and evaluation. These functions, however, had come to be performed in a routine, unsubstantial fashion. After the job enrichment program, during which the supervisors were not merely passive observers of the assistants' performance, the supervisors actually were devoting their time to reviewing performance and administering thorough training.

What has been called an employee-centered style of supervision will come about not through education of supervisors, but by changing the jobs that they do.

CONCLUDING NOTE

Job enrichment will not be a one-time proposition, but a continuous management function. The initial changes, however, should last for a very long period of time. There are a number of reasons for this:

The changes should bring the job up to the level of challenge commensurate with the skill that was hired.

Those who have still more ability eventually will be able to demonstrate it better and win promotion to higher-level jobs.

The very nature of motivators, as opposed to hygiene factors, is that they have a much longer-term effect on employees' attitudes. Perhaps the job will have to be enriched again, but this will not occur as frequently as the need for hygiene.

Not all jobs can be enriched, nor do all jobs need to be enriched. If only a small percentage of the time and money that is now devoted to hygiene, however, were given to job enrichment efforts, the return in human satisfaction and economic gain would be one of the largest dividends that industry and society have ever reaped through their efforts at better personnel management.

The argument for job enrichment can be summed up quite simply: If you have someone on a job, use him. If you can't use him on the job, get rid of him, either via automation or by selecting someone with lesser ability. If you can't use him and you can't get rid of him, you will have a motivation problem.

Karl W. Jackson
Dennis J. Shea

MOTIVATION TRAINING IN PERSPECTIVE

The naive psychology of everyday life is rich with an apparent understanding of human motivation (Heider, 1958; Schutz, 1963). Time after time we describe ourselves and others as being "motivated" or "unmotivated," and we frequently make sense out of motivated experiences and behavior by using motive-concepts. When we say things like "he's power-hungry," or "she has a strong need to be independent," we are attributing motives, thereby typifying the person by means of a causal shorthand that allows us to explain and predict his or her behavior. Yet with all of our personal knowledge of motivation, and with all of our skill in attributing motives, few psychological concepts have generated as much controversy as "motivation" and "motive." Some psychologists with a strong Behavioristic orientation (e.g., Skinner, 1964) argue that the concept of "motive" should be excluded from scientific psychology, while others (e.g., Koch, 1964) strongly urge that the concept is vital to an understanding of human behavior. Even among psychologists who espouse its value, there are vast differences in how they define the concept. For example, Hull's learning theory model (1943) defines a "motive" as a stimulating drive, while Tolman's (1959)

This article was prepared especially for this volume.

more cognitive approach to behavior defines motivation in terms of purposeful behavior. More recently, behavioral scientists have taken different approaches in attempts to increase human motivation. McClelland and Winter (1970) stress programs that emphasize individual change, while Herzberg's job enrichment approach (1968) suggests that a change in the environment leads to increased motivation.[1]

These controversies (and many more) are reflected in the theories, practices, and the effects of organizational psychologists. Nord (1969) and McGregor (1960), for example, disagree about whether the concept "motive" is needed at all. Nord's operant conditioning approach doesn't bother with the concept "motive," while McGregor's "theory" management depends on it. These approaches lead in turn to markedly different strategies for enhancing work productivity, and there is reason to believe that these different strategies will have different effects. For example, a sales manager who decided to apply operant conditioning principles to "motivate" his salesmen might employ a system of prizes or other extrinsic incentives as "motivators." If he decided to apply management based on "theory Y" assumptions, on the other hand, he would deemphasize the manipulation of extrinsic incentives and try to free his salesmen to set their own objectives and satisfy their own needs.

A study by Harlow (1950) suggests that these different strategies may lead to different motivational effects. He found that curiosity-motivated monkeys will manipulate puzzles ad infinitum without extrinsic reinforcers, but that when raisins were provided as reinforcers and were subsequently withdrawn the manipulative behavior stopped. This finding suggests that if a salesman is intrinsically motivated, he might suffer a decrement in sales after an incentive system is instituted and stopped, despite the fact that his sales performance may temporarily increase during the contest period. His performance may even decrease when the incentives are added.[2]

It is clear that different ways of resolving conceptual and theoretical controversies lead to different programs of action with potentially different effects. At the very time when organizations are turning more and more to social science for help, organizational psychology is fragmenting into a series of diverse schools, characterized by a proliferation of models and intervention strategies.

[1] These controversies in turn reflect more fundamental disagreements about the nature of man. Differing modes of resolving key philosophical problems have lead to different concepts and theories of motivation. See de Charms (1968) for a discussion of the philosophical issues revolving around (a) the mind-body problem, (b) the problem of causation, (c) the problem of hedonism, and (d) the problem posed by the subjective-objective dualities–and for a discussion of how these issues lead to different concepts and theories of motivation. Value differences also seem to play an important part in determining the way in which social scientists define and think about motivation. See Köhler (1928) and Polanyi (1958) for a discussion of values in the world of scientific theorizing.

[2] We know of another example of a situation where the introduction of an "extrinsic" reinforcer interfered with the behavior it was designed to enhance. A "motivated" graduate student was in the process of writing up an experiment he had been doing with one of his mentors. When the professor offered to pay him for writing up the article for publication, the "bribe" resulted in a great deal of negative feelings and the project was never completed.

These models and strategies in turn flow from different assumptions about motivation. Usually those assumptions are implicit, rather than explicit, so it is difficult for the student of organizational psychology (and for psychologists) to relate the approaches to each other in a systematic way and to evaluate and compare them in the light of the empirical support for their basic assumptions.

Our first major objective in this paper will be to share some key questions arising out of the study of motivation, show how answers to some of those questions have been translated into action with motivation training programs, and describe the effects of those kinds of training. Our second objective is to place the motivation training described here in perspective. We shall do so by presenting some of the problems associated with it and compare it to other programs and the problems associated with them. Finally, we shall suggest a broader approach to motivation training programs that would attempt to deal with the problems presented. We shall attempt to make our basic assumptions explicit so that they can be compared with those of other approaches.

KEY MOTIVATION CONCEPTS

What is it like to "be motivated?" When do we say of another that he is "motivated?" When do we attribute motives to another? How are motives related to experience? Answers to these questions will pave the way for a look at the basic motivation research which has led to motivation training.

What is it like to "be motivated?"

The words that we use in describing the state of "being motivated" are packed with energy–words like "drive," "desire," "concerned," and "engrossed." When we are motivated we are "turned on"–so actively concentrating on what we're doing that all else fades into the background. We are deeply committed to the task at hand, free of conflicting thoughts or preoccupations, polarized and unified toward a specific objective. Present thoughts are translated immediately and smoothly into action.

The contrasting condition of "being unmotivated" is a state of passivity or conflict. When we're unmotivated we're "turned off"–rather than being engrossed in anything or polarized toward a specific objective and free of conflicting thoughts, we tend to be inactive, or even if we're doing something, we have a difficult time concentrating on the task at hand. We are dull, uncreative, unspontaneous, or filled with anxiety. We hesitate about translating our thoughts into action.

"Being motivated" is a state characterized by three basic features not evident in "unmotivated" states. First, "being motivated" implies goal direction–a deep commitment toward some objective. In Heider's (1958) terms, a high level of *intention* is present. Second, when we're motivated we are energized, we are exerting ourselves. In other words (Heider), we're *trying*. Finally, we're conflict-free. We're not distracted by competing concerns.

When do we say of another, "He is really a motivated person"?

Let's take a look at John, a hypothetical worker who is employed at plant X as a lathe operator. We get out first view of him at midmorning. He is standing over his lathe concentrating intensely on the chair leg he is making. His body is alert, yet he seems relaxed. His eyes are glued to the leg he is carving as he deftly finishes the design. He moves quickly to the next block of wood and he begins to carve it without pause. The whistle for coffee break sounds but he doesn't seem to hear it. He is trying to finish the leg for the next shipment at noon and he continues to work quickly and effectively. He smiles as he works. He is achieving.

Our second view of John is at lunch. He is sitting at a corner table in the cafeteria talking with Laura, the sales manager's secretary. They are engrossed in a serious conversation. John is animated, alive, and obviously deeply pleased to be talking with Laura. He listens carefully to her and shares his reactions with her. Suddenly the whistle to end lunch blows but he continues to talk, oblivious to the sound. When his co-worker comes over to interrupt, John is momentarily startled and angry, but thanks his friend and continues his conversation. Finally, he and Laura get up together, he squeezes her hand, and they smile as they depart. He's been affiliating.

Later that evening we see John at a union meeting. He's caucusing with a group of workers who support him for the local presidency. His voice is loud as he tells the men what he will do for them if they support him. A man comes over and tells him that Laura is on the phone. He tells the men to wait for him. Once he reaches the telephone, he says, "Laura, I think I have them in the palm of my hand. They're doing everything that I want them to. I think you'll really be proud of me when I'm president. . .oh. . .sorry. . .I have to go. . .I see a guy and I need his vote." John wants power.

Based on our earlier description of individual motivation, it should be clear that in each of these three instances, John is highly motivated–he's intensely concerned, goal directed, committed to a specific task, and energetically pursuing it with little thought of anything else. In the first case his concern was with his work; in the second it was with his relationship with another person; in the third it was in reaching a position of high status, influence and power. In our terms his concern was with achievement, affiliation, and power, respectively.

We get knowledge of another person's level of motivation by observing the intensity of his behavior. The more actively he is pursuing an activity, the more we describe him as being motivated.[3] We attribute motivation (or concern,

[3] *When does a manager attribute motivation to a worker?* Organizations are polarized toward the attainment of specific objectives. "Motivated behavior," or "motivation" tend to be defined in terms of those objectives. Managers tend to attribute motivation to their workers when they are doing what they "ought" to be doing, i.e., when they are energetically pursuing the objectives of the organization. A manager looking at John in our three cases is likely to perceive him as "being motivated" in the first case, where his concern was with his work, but is much less likely to see him as being motivated in the other two (he may, in fact, accuse him of just "goofing off"). Managers (and teachers) in short, tend to

needs, desires, obsession. etc.) to him because we've known from personal experience that the intensity of *our* behavior is generally a function of the level of our motivation.

The specific motive that we attribute to another at any given time is a function of the direction in which we see him moving. If we see that a person is trying to make or repair a friendship we attribute to him a desire for that friendship. If we see him trying to dominate or impress another person we attribute to him a desire to have power over that person. We are able to make these attributions because of our own personal knowledge that our own motives lead us to particular kinds of activities.

When do we attribute motives to another?

It is one thing to say that a person is "motivated" at any given time and quite another to say that he's a highly motivated person. In one observation we can see that a person is "motivated," but it takes many observations for us to be sure that we can safely say, "He's really a motivated guy." Everyone is highly motivated from time to time, but only a few people will be highly motivated most of the time. We say that another is a motivated person when our experience with him indicates that he typically displays "motivated" behavior.

We use the same general procedure in attributing particular motives to people. Given that we have observed a person's motivated behavior several times, and that we have seen that he typically pursues objectives of a particular kind, we are able to categorize him with a particular motive concept. In the same way that everyone is "motivated" from time to time, but not everyone is a "motivated person"; everyone is concerned about a friendship from time to time, but not everyone is very frequently concerned about friendships. When we have the opportunity to observe another person several times, however, and when we have seen that he is frequently moved to establish and maintain friendships, then we summarize his behavior with a motive concept by saying, "He's really concerned with making friends," or "He's really an affiliative guy." We attribute particular motives to people, in short, when we see that they are *typically* motivated to reach a particular type of objective.

How are motives related to experience?

Human experience is a rich and varied stream of sights, sounds, smells, etc. Much of it is a representation of what is available to our direct perception at the moment. Night dreams, day dreams, and images of what was, will be, or could be available to perception, but is not, are all forms of fantasy. Our fantasy lives seem to reflect our obsessions and preoccupations. When we assign the "boy crazy" motive concept to a teenage girl we are implying not only that she typically engages in motivated behavior with respect to boys, but also that she is obsessed or preoccupied with thoughts of boys. Her fantasy life is filled with

---

define motivation and motivated behavior by answering the question, "Is the behavior consistent with the demands of the job?"

boys, and observations of that aspect of her experience would indicate a typical fantasy pattern of boy-concern which corresponds with her behavior. Typical fantasy patterns, in short, seem to correspond with typical behavior patterns; and a person's typical fantasy patterns correspond with his motives.

We all have vast fantasy lives. The intensity of a person's obsessions or motives should be reflected by how frequently he thinks about the particular class of incentives defining the motive, and by how vivid the fantasies are. If we could somehow sample a person's thoughts or fantasies, we could learn a great deal about his motives; and if we could somehow change a person's typical fantasy patterns we could affect his motivated behavior.

RESEARCH OF INDIVIDUAL MOTIVATION– THE WORK OF McCLELLAND, ET AL.

Can we measure individual motivation?

One of the major problems in the study of psychological variables is that of measurement. If we assume that "motivated behavior" is a function of thoughts or fantasies, the first problem becomes that of measuring a individual's thoughts. The second becomes that of relating those to measures of behavior. To go about that first task, Atkinson and McClelland (1948) provided some Navy men with a goal (to get something to eat) by creating a state of hunger. Some of the men had not eaten for an hour, some for four hours, and some had gone without food for 16 hours. The men were then asked to write some imaginative stories to picture cues that were flashed on a screen. To help them in the writing of their stories, they were given the following questions as guides:

1. What is happening? Who are the persons?
2. What has led up to this situation? What has happened in the past?
3. What is being thought? What is wanted? By whom?
4. What will happen? What will be done? By whom? (Atkinson, 1958, p. 48).

This technique of measurement, borrowed from Murray's (1943) thematic apperception test (TAT), is now called the method of thought sampling (de Charms, 1968).[4] The assumption behind the technique is that the writer "projects" his thoughts into the characters in his story. When the writer composes the story, he is giving us a sample of the way he thinks, i.e., a sample of his fantasy pattern. If he is concerned or obsessed about something, he should express that concern in his stories.

Once the story had been written, we may analyze the stories to see if their content fits our categories. Atkinson and McClelland analyzed the sailors' stories and they found the predicted relationship between the concern for food and the content of the stories. The more hungry the men, the more they wrote stories about characters being hungry, expressing a need for food, and taking part in

[4] See de Charms (1968) for an analysis and critique of this technique of measurement.

activity that was successful in overcoming their hunger (Atkinson, 1958, p. 62). Not only had they demonstrated that the "motivated" men wrote stories about "motivated" people, Atkinson and McClelland had performed the first step in the development of a general measure of motivation.

How do we define (differentiate) specific motives?

Hunger is a physiological need and it and other primary drives have been studied quite extensively by experimental psychologists. When we look at learned or secondary needs we find that the number of defined needs or motives (e.g., the need to be independent or dependent; to be aggressive or submissive, etc.) increases, while the research on each is quite minimal.

Following their hunger study, McClelland, Atkinson, and others set out to define and measure other motives in a similar manner. They confined their major efforts to the study of three motives, the needs for achievement, affiliation and power. In defining each, they had to answer two questions: (1) How do we define and measure the goal associated with each motive? and (2) How do we define and measure the intensity of the obsession associated with each motive?

After a great deal of research with the measurement instrument[5], the following definitions were derived for the three motives:

1. *Power motivation* (abbreviated "*n* Pow") was defined in terms of influence and control. A power goal is manifested in a story when a character shows concern about controlling, advising, or influencing another person (Winter, 1968).
2. *Affiliation motivation* (*n* Aff) is defined in terms of friendship. An affiliation goal is manifested in a story when one of the characters display concern about creating a friendly relationship with another or when he is concerned with losing a friend (Shipley & Veroff, 1958).
3. *Achievement motivation* (*n* Ach) is defined in terms of concern about success in competiton with some standard of excellence (McClelland, et al., 1953).

Comprehensive scoring manuals have been developed (Atkinson, 1958; Winter, 1968) for determining when a story contains a power, affiliation, or achievement goal. Because the majority of the research on individual motivation by the McClelland group has concentrated on the achievement motive, we shall elaborate on the recognition and measurement of that particular need.

A story is recognized as containing achievement imagery and receives a point in the scoring system if one or more characters in the story exhibits:

1. Concern with competing with some outside standard of excellence (e.g., doing better than another; surpassing a record)
2. Concern with competing with a self standard (e.g., improving one's performance)
3. Concern with engaging in a long-term effort
4. Concern with doing something unique

[5] See McClelland, et al., 1953 and Atkinson, 1958 for a detailed analysis of the development of the measure.

If an individual's story contains one or more of these concerns, we say that the story has an achievement goal, an indication of the writer's need for achievement. Once this has been indicated, we may look further at the story for an indication of the level of intensity of that concern. The more intense the concern, the more obsessed the writer is with achievement, the more he will write about the kinds of things that move him toward an achievement goal. A story is scored for the intensity of the obsession with achievement when a character:

1. Expresses a desire for excellence as a *need* (N)
2. Expresses some instrumental *activity* (ACT) that will move him toward his goal
3. Expresses hope that he will succeed in reaching his goal–*hope of success* (HOS)
4. Expresses a fear that he might fail, for he sets goals that require effort–*fear of failure* (FOF)
5. Expresses a feeling of success when he achieves his goal–*success feelings* (SF)
6. Expresses knowledge about things in the world that might keep him from reaching his goal–*world obstacles* (WO)
7. Express a feeling of failure when he fails to reach his goal–*failure feelings* (FF)
8. Expresses knowledge about personal inadequacies that might prevent him from reaching his goal–*personal obstacles* (PO)
9. Expresses the fact that he can get *help* (H) in reaching his goal
10. Expresses only a concern for achievement in his story (and not, e.g., affiliation, power, etc.)–*thema* (TH)

These scoring categories, then, define operationally an individual's level or intensity of achievement motivation. Using other categories we can also measure an individual's level of affiliation or power motivation. The more the individual is concerned (obsessed) with the thoughts reflected in those categories, the more we say that he has a particular level of motivation.

What do people with high achievement motivation do (i.e., what kind of motivated behavior do they emit) that distinguishes them from others?

In defining very specifically what we mean by an individual's "achievement motivation," as we have here, we have simply said that people who have high achievement motivation are those who are concerned about competing with some standard of excellence and that they write stories that manifest that concern. The test of the concept and the measure comes when we validate it by relating it to "behavior."[6] The data indicate that both in the laboratory and in the real world, people with high achievement motivation perform differently than those with low achievement motivation.

[6] See McClelland, et al., 1953; Atkinson, 1958; and de Charms, 1968 for an extended discussion and evaluation of the measure's reliability and other features.

First of all, in the laboratory, it has been demonstrated that in relation to those who score low on the measure, those who have high *n* Achievement do better at a number of activities–they complete more paper and pencil tasks, they solve more mathematical problems, and they solve more verbal problems (unscrambling words) in a given amount of time (de Charms, 1968).

While these results are interesting and provide support for the validity of the measure, other data from the field are more impressive, especially to those in the business community. For example, early in the development of the measure at Wesleyan University, McClelland collected stories from a group of males. He reports (1965b) that upon checking the alumni directory he found that 83 percent of the men who could be classified as entrepreneurs had high *n* Achievement scores as Sophomores in college. In contrast, only 21 percent of those classified as non-entrepreneurs had high *n* Achievement. These data indicate that men who have a high need to achieve actually go on to be successful in their careers, especially in the business world.

How do they do it? What are the characteristics of an "achiever"? In answering these questions, McClelland has developed the concept of the "achievement syndrome" (1961), a cluster of behavioral indices that distinguishes the individual with high *n* Achievement.

1. *To begin with, he likes situations in which he takes personal responsibility for finding solutions to problems* (McClelland, 1962, p. 104). The achiever, in setting his goals, likes to be in charge of his fate.
2. *Another characteristic of a man with a strong achievement concern is his tendency to set moderate achievement goals and to take calculated risks* (McClelland, 1962), p. 104). Probably the most replicated finding in the achievement motivation literature is that the high achiever avoids "sure things" by setting goals that require some effort (i.e., they are challenging) on his part, while he avoids "pie-in-the-sky" goals over which he has little control.[7]
3. *The man who has a strong concern for achievement also wants concrete feedback as to how well he is doing* (McClelland, 1962, p. 105). The high achiever plans his life very carefully. He sets goals that he can reach and he makes them quite specific. In doing so, he is constantly aware of his progress.

How is an individual's achievement motivation developed?

We view achievement motivation as a learned, rather than as an innate motive. The question that follows from this assumption is: How does one learn the motive? The answer to this question is important, for historically it opened the door to an enormous expansion in research interests. Roger Brown (1965) says that "probably the single research result that was most crucial in effecting the expansion of scope was Marian Winterbottom's study of the childhood origins of achievement motivation" (p. 446). What Winterbottom (1958) did was to find a relationship between childhood training and achievement motivation. Mothers of

[7] See Atkinson and Feather (1966) for an extensive review of the risk-taking literature.

boys with high *n* Achievement expected that their children should do more things independently at an earlier age than mothers of boys with low need achievement. In another similar study, Rosen and D'Andrade (1959) found that parents of high scorers tended to give their children more responsibility in a block stacking task. Both of these studies are important in that they stress the relationship between childhood experiences and the achievement motive.

Once McClelland and his co-workers had discovered the relationship between childhood independence training and achievement motivation, they looked at other sources that might influence the development of individuals with high achievement motivation. Since the reading that a child does may influence his fantasies, McClelland investigated that relationship.

In what Brown (1965) calls " . . . one of the more audacious investigations in the history of social science" (p. 450), McClelland (1961) assembled fourth and fifth grade readers for children from about 30 countries all over the world. Those stories (after they were translated into English) were then scored for *n* Achievement and those scores were related to indices of economic development. The results showed that those countries with high *n* Achievement present in their children's readers were more developed (in terms of per capita income and the amount of electricity produced) than those countries with low *n* Achievement. Later (1962), de Charms and Moeller found a similar relationship between *n* Achievement in children's readers in the United States and economic activity. The higher the *n* Achievement content in the children's readers, the more those children went on to increase the economic productivity in the country.

In summary, these data show that achievement motivation is developed by learning how to work independently (which assumes taking personal responsibility, planning, and learning from experience—the elements of the achievement syndrome) in a cultural milieu that stresses thoughts about achievement. When achievement motivation is developed in individuals, they perform relatively successfully, especially in entrepreneurial roles.

Can achievement motivation be increased?

What we have done here is to present evidence that indicates that individuals do differ along the dimension of motivation, and in particular achievement motivation, that we can measure the variable scientifically, and that we have some knowledge about how it is learned. In addition, we know from a great deal of research that people who have high achievement motivation are more "successful" in their endeavors (especially business endeavors) than those who have low *n* Achievement.

Over the last ten years, McClelland and his students have devoted a great deal of their efforts to attempts to increase achievement motivation by means of training courses, based on the assumption that *n* Ach is a learned motive. Burris (1958) presented the first data that indicated that *n* Achievement counseling of college underachievers improved their grades. Kolb (1965), in the summer of 1961, conducted the first full-scale achievement motivation training program. In the program, 57 underachieving high school boys (I. Q. 120, average grade D+)

attended a summer school instruction course. From these, Kolb randomly selected 20 boys from lower and middle classes, put them on one floor of a dormitory, acted as their counselor, and conducted a training course with them. At the end of the semester, the trained students had significantly improved their grades. The effect was especially true for those boys who initially had low *n* Achievement.

Aronoff and Litwin (1971) conducted an achievement motivation training course with 16 middle-level executives in business. They had a control group of 11 untrained men who took part in a management development course. The authors devised an advancement score for the two-year period prior to the training and the two-year period after the course. The men who were trained in achievement motivation showed significantly greater advancement than the men who took part in the corporation course.

McClelland (1969) presented data showing the effects of achievement motivation training with a group of 49 Black businessmen from the Washington, D. C. area. His results showed that on every index of performance (from new business starts to promotion to new capital invested) that the trained men were at least twice as successful as a comparable group of 63 untrained men after six months.

Finally, the training has been shown to be effective in other countries besides the United States. In 1963, 34 Indian businessmen from the Bombay area attended a training course. Data on 30 of the trained men and 11 untrained men were collected from two years prior to and two years after the training. They found the trained group had significantly increased their activity over their previous behavior and that they were significantly more active than the group which had not had the training.

In 1969, McClelland and Winter presented the results of still another motivation change study in their book, *Motivating Economic Achievement.* In the study presented there, over 70 businessmen in two cities in India were trained. After an extended and very complex analysis of the effects of the training, the results may be summarized as follows: The course participants

1. were more active after the course, while the untrained individuals stayed about the same,
2. became more vigorous in their activity (in terms of working longer and harder),
3. made more attempts to start new businesses and were more successful in starting new businesses,
4. invested more capital, and
5. showed a greater increase in gross income.

How is achievement motivation and "motivated behavior" increased in the training courses?

Some of the basic principles upon which the training courses are built are presented by McClelland in his paper: *Toward a theory of motive acquisition* (1965a). A careful description of the training itself may be found in Shea and

Jackson (1975). Basically, the training course employs four training principles:

1. Participants are trained to examine themselves carefully—their behavior, their needs, and their feelings.
2. Participants are trained to be aware of the thoughts and actions of "motivated" individuals and are helped to learn how to think and behave like those individuals.
3. Participants are trained to set realistic goals that they can responsibly achieve.
4. Participants, in a group setting, are supported in their attempt at personal change.

We have found that any attempt to describe the training without going into a great deal of detail is doomed to failure. The training course is composed of well over 20 "psychological inputs" (Shea and Jackson) that are designed to facilitate motivation change based on the four principles outlined above. The course as now developed is composed of a three to ten-day experiential workshop in a retreat setting. The training involves an intensive self-examination and change process in which the participants and trainers work for about 12 hours per day.

OTHER RESEARCH ON INDIVIDUAL MOTIVATION—THE WORK OF DE CHARMS, ET AL.

One of McClelland's former students, Richard de Charms, has recently developed a fresh approach to the study of individual motivation (1968), and an expanded form of motivation training (1975). De Charms' key concept is "person causation" which he defines as ". . . *the initiation by an individual of behavior intended to produce a change in his environment*" (1968, p. 6). He asserts that one of the first concepts that an individual learns is that he can be effective in producing (causing) changes in his life and that man's striving to be a causal agent is his primary motivational propensity.

De Charms uses two terms to represent the polar extremes of personal causation representing idealized personality types. A person who typically sees himself as powerless, at the mercy of external events and people, is called a *Pawn.* A person who usually sees himself as a potent master of his own destiny is called an *Origin.* A *Pawn* is constrained, his behavior is determined by external forces beyond his control. An *Origin* feels that the locus of control of his behavior lies within himself—he makes the choices, and the effects of his behavior are determined by him.

In studies based on his theory, de Charms found that we attribute "Origin" and "Pawn" behavior to others and that feeling like an Origin rather than a Pawn has marked effects on one's behavior. Individuals seen as Pawns are not seen as responsible for their behavior; those seen as Origins are seen to "own" their behavior and are responsible for its consequences. People feeling like Origins enjoy their behavior more than when they act as Pawns. When they choose to act, ráther than being forced to, they are more creative and more productive (de Charms, 1968).[8]

Plimpton (1970) has developed a scoring system for measuring the Origin-Pawn variable. Like the measure of *n* Achievement, the system is applied to the content analysis of TAT stories. It has the following six categories:

1. Internal control
2. Goal setting
3. Instrumental activity
4. Reality perception
5. Personal responsibility
6. Self confidence[9]

Can personal causation be increased?

De Charms does not define personal causation as a "motive"; however, he notes that the feeling that one can control his fate is primary to any experience of motivation and any motivated behavior that might accompany that experience. One must feel that his energy is "worth it"–that it will result in the desired consequences–before he will expend that energy. Over the past several years de Charms and his co-workers have been engaged in a long-term research program designed to investigate the question: Can we train individuals to act more like Origins?

Origin training attempts to allow the trainee to develop the ability and desire to be independent by gradually training him to take increasing responsibility for his behavior by setting his own goals and planning and structuring his own life. It does so by providing the trainee with the skills and personal characteristics required for such independence, i.e., a realistic, accepted, and accurate self-concept, a disposition to think like an Origin, and ability and desire to set realistic objectives, etc. In its objectives, the training is similar to achievement motivation and self-esteem training.[10]

De Charms (1975) describes the effects of the first extensive Origin-training program that was conducted with several hundred low-income, Black elementary school children. The program was designed as a two-step process in which teachers were given Origin training (in conjunction with achievement motivation training) in a small group setting and then designed with the investigators a training program that they used in the schools. They were trained to act as trainers in their classrooms.

The program resulted in significant positive effects on both the teachers and their students. More trained than untrained teachers either went on to graduate

[8] Readers familiar with Rotter's (1966) internal-external control of reinforcements variable will see striking similarities between it and personal causation (Origin-Pawn). See de Charms (1968) for a discussion of the differences between the concepts.

[9] See Plimpton (1970) for a description of the development, reliability, and validity of the measure.

[10] The Origin concept is very similar to prevailing conceptions of high self-esteem (Coopersmith, 1967) or a positive self-esteem (Wylie, 1961). Coopersmith is now developing self-esteem training programs which are quite similar to Origin-training.

work or advanced to more responsible positions. In addition, the program resulted in substantial and significant increases in achievement motivation, Origin fantasies, realistic and successful goal setting, and academic performance for those children who participated in the training program.[11]

PROBLEMS IN MOTIVATION TRAINING

Psychologists, educators, parents, and many others have struggled for years with the question, "How can we motivate people?" While the programs described here have been quite successful, they have not been without problems. By discussing some of those problems, we hope to shed additional light on this complex question.

The major problems that occur center around the issue of the relationship between the individual and his environment. Simply instituting individual motivation training does not necessarily mean that the individual will benefit completely in terms of maximizing his potential; nor does it mean that the organization will benefit from the training.

Addressing ourselves to the second of those issues, we know of instances where individual motivation training has actually interfered with the objectives of the organization. McCowan (personal communication) found that unskilled workers in achievement motivation training programs were quite likely to quit the job that they held in favor of another job that provided the opportunity for more advancement. As we noted earlier, de Charms and his co-workers have found that when motivation training courses have been conducted with teachers (with the assumed goal of increasing the ability of the teachers to "motivate" their students to learn), a good number of the teachers either leave the teaching profession or move to "more advanced" positions in the profession where they have little contact with children (de Charms, 1975). Finally, Jackson found that when he conducted a motivation training workshop in his education psychology course, his students became so "motivated" that they have moved in the direction of changing the educational system (Jackson, 1973). In each of these cases, while the training has appeared to have been "successful," the sponsoring organization has, in some way, suffered from its success.

At least two other examples indicated that when the newly acquired "motivation" is not supported by the environment, the program has not led to optimal results. Kolb (1965), in his study of motivation training with middle- and lower-class students, found that the performance of the lower-class children fell back to its earlier level when the trained students remained in their old environment. De Charms' data indicate that when trained children return to classes with untrained teachers, their accelerated learning drops off, although not to its earlier level. Trained children in a supportive environment continue to exhibit the accelerated effects of earlier training.

These problems are at least partially explained if we note that "motivated"

[11] See de Charms, Collins, Jackson and Shea (1968), Shea (1969), Plimpton (1970), and Coor (1970) for detailed analyses of the results of the program. De Charms (1975) presents a comprehensive analysis of the entire project.

people seem to perform most effectively in relatively free situations in which available acitvities allow them to satisfy their achievement or personal causation needs. When the worker (or the student) is given that freedom he can satisfy his needs by selecting his own objectives, designing his own procedures, and evaluating his own work. If organizational objectives provide the opportunity for that "motivated" behavior, the organization benefits from the training; if not, the effects of the training may be debilitating.

Most organizations are organized around objectives and procedural recipes that limit the freedom of individual members. However, organizations, and specific positions within them, vary in terms of how much these objectives limit individual member freedom (Likert, 1967). The specific objective-classes available to any given member also vary with respect to how much they are consistent with his motive-hierarchy. Some positions prescribe achievement-related objectives, while others (e.g., manager, supervisor, teacher, etc.) prescribe power or affiliation objectives.

Highly motivated people tend to gravitate toward positions in which they feel free and in which they may pursue objectives consistent with their most intense motive-related concerns.[12] If a worker in an achievement motivation training course comes back to a position which does not allow him to satisfy his need to achieve because it doesn't allow him the freedom of choice necessary for the fulfillment of that need, he will be likely to seek a position where there is a better fit or match between his needs and the structure of his environment. If the alternative of locomotion to another environment does not exist for the individual, it seems that he is left with one of two courses of action. He can attempt to change the organization by attempting to move it in the direction of opening up to the needs of its members. If the environment cannot be changed, then it is quite likely that the newly trained individual will exhibit little "motivated behavior" and the program will appear useless, both for the organization and the individual.

MOTIVATION TRAINING: DEMOCRATIC MANAGEMENT

The notion that behavior is a function of both the individual and his environment is far from being new. Kurt Lewin, one of the first social scientists to propose that psychologists could and even should study change or intervention tactics in organizations, described the relationship in his famous equation: $B = f(P,E)$ (1966, p. 12). As a function of the theory presented in that equation, Lewin predicted that individuals will be more productive and experience higher morale when they operate in an environment which allows them the freedom to participate in decisions that affect their behavior. The now

[12] This is probably why people with intense concerns with achievement tend to become entrepreneurs. As an entrepreneur one is in a position to establish one's own objectives and procedures, and to satisfy one's competetive needs, without being constrained by organizational objectives—unless, of course, the objectives of one's organization are a direct reflection of one's own needs.

classic studies by Lippitt and White (1943) and Coch and French (1948) lended great support to his theory. Marrow (1970) in his excellent biography of Lewin, cites those as he traces the development of the theory and research that led to contemporary programs which stress democratic (or participatory) management, "worker-centered" climate, etc., as techniques to facilitate the motivation of the individual.

We briefly mention this approach to training because it appears to us that it places emphasis on the environmental (e.g., situational climate) effects on individual motivation, while McClelland's approach emphasizes individual change. Where *n* Achievement training neglects the environment, the "job enrichment" (see Herzberg, 1968) type of training seems to neglect the individual.

The latter approach, like the former, results in problems for the individual and the organization. Some individuals ("theory-X" types?) appear to need structure and completely fall apart in a "democratic" environment. Anecdotal evidence from the de Charms project indicated that when teachers began their school year committed to treating their students like "Origins" and gave them complete freedom, the students reacted with a great deal of anxiety to the new responsibility. The teachers had to modify their leadership behavior in terms of returning to a more structured environment until the students were trained (motivated?) to respond to a more free climate. When the classroom was gradually transformed into an "Origin" atmosphere as the teachers "loosened the reins" (de Charms, 1975), the "motivated behavior" in terms of increased academic performance was enhanced. We would think that the same general phenomenon would occur in a work situation. An "unmotivated" individual who is accustomed to tight direction is likely to suffer greatly in a "democratic" climate.

MOTIVATION TRAINING IN PERSPECTIVE

Motivation trainers who espouse the "individual" approach in motivation training have implicitly assumed what we could call a "one-factor" theory of motivation. They have either considered the other factor (the environment or the situation) to be unimportant or they have assumed that it is a constant. This approach is captured in the equation: Motivated Behavior = f (Individual Motivation, K), where K is a constant describing the environment in which the individual resides. Motivation training derived out of this assumption (e.g., achievement motivation training) would predict that the higher the individual motivation, the greater the evidence of motivated behavior. Based on the problems we have outlined earlier, it seems clear that this kind of equation does not suffice to predict behavior.

It seems quite interesting to us that most "motivation training programs" that have been developed in the "democratic management" tradition are also "one-factor" theories. Such training seems to assume that the individual factor is either unimportant or is constant (e.g. McGregor (1966) assumes that all people are "highly motivated"). The motivation assumptions behind such programs seem to be captured in the equation: Motivated behavior = f (Environment, K), where K is again a constant, this time applying to individual characteristics.

This type of training, which predicts that a "more democatic" (more free?) climate leads to more responsibility, more motivation, and more productivity, appears, like the achievement motivation training, to be quite successful (Herzberg, 1968; Likert, 1967). As we mentioned before, however, not everyone responds to increased responsibility in a positive manner, and the programs are not without problems.

This evidence indicates to us that if we are to predict motivated behavior we must pay attention to both the motivation of the individual *and* to the properties of the environment. But it seems important to note from the evidence presented that an increase in either of these two "factors" will not necessarily result in an increase in "motivated behavior." Man's "life space" cannot be viewed as a cookbook where an addition of x bits of individual motivation and y bits of a free environment will result in an increase in motivated behavior. The best results in motivation training seem to occur when there is a good fit (match) between individual motives and environmental opportunity. "Motivated" individuals perform quite well in an open environment; "unmotivated" individuals do not. The converse relationship seems to hold for closed or restricted environments. As we continue our efforts in the area of motivation training, we must focus our attention on the match or mismatch between individual needs and environmental opportunity.

BIBLIOGRAPHY

Aronoff, J. and Litwin, G. H. *Achievement motivation training and executive advancement. Journal of Applied Behavioral Science,* 7, 2, 215-219.

Atkinson, J. W. *Motives in fantasy, action, and society.* Princeton: Van Nostrand, 1958.

Atkinson, J. W. and Feather, N. T. (eds.) *A theory of achievement motivation.* New York: John Wiley & Sons, 1966.

Atkinson, J. W. and McClelland, D. C. The projective expression of needs: II. The effect of differential intensities of the hunger drive on thematic apperception. *Journal of Experimental Psychology, 38,* 1948, 643-58.

Brown, R. *Social psychology.* New York: Free Press, 1965.

Burris, R. W. *The effect of counseling on achievement motivation.* Unpublished doctoral dissertation. University of Indiana, 1958.

Coch, L. and French, J. R. P. Overcoming resistance to change. *Human relations,* 11, 1948, 512-32.

Coopersmith, S. *The antecedents of self esteem.* San Francisco: W. H. Freeman, 1967.

Coor, Ina F. *The effects of grade level and motivation training on ego development.* Unpublished doctoral dissertation, Washington University, 1970.

de Charms, R. *Personal causation.* Reading, Mass: Addison-Wesley, 1968.

de Charms, R. From Pawns to Origins: Toward self motivation. In Lesser, G. S. (ed.) *Psychology and educational practice.* Glenview, Illinois: Scott, Foresman and Co., 1971.

de Charms, R. *Origins and pawns at school.* New York: Irvington Publishers, 1975.

de Charms, R. and Moeller, G. H. Values expressed in American children's readers: 1890-1950. *Journal of Abnormal and Social Psychology,* 64, 1962, 136-42.

de Charms, R., Collins, Janet, Jackson, K. W., and Shea, D. J. *Can the motives of low income Black children be changed?* Paper presented in a symposium at the American Educational Research Association meetings, February, 1969, Los Angeles.

Harlow, H. F., Harlow, M. K., and Meyer, D. R. Learning motivated by a manipulative drive. *Journal of Experimental Psychology, 40,* 1950, 228-34.

Heider, F. *The psychology of interpersonal relations.* New York: John Wiley & Sons, 1958.

Herzberg, F. One more time: How do you motivate employees? *Harvard Business Review,* Jan.-Feb., 1968, 53-62.

Hull, C. L. *Principles of behavior.* New York: Appleton-Century-Crofts, 1943.

Jackson, K. A coparticipative, experiential learning design for educational psychology. In Rosenberg, M. *Educational therapy,* Vol III. Seattle: Bernie Straub Publishing Co. and Special Child Publications, 1973, 209-84.

Koch, S. Psychology and emerging conceptions of knowledge as unitary. In T. W. Wann (ed.), *Behaviorism and phenomenology.* Chicago: University of Chicago Press, 1964.

Köhler, W. *The place of value in the world of facts.* New York: Liveright, 1928.

Kolb, D. A. Achievement motivation training for underachieving high school boys. *Journal of Personality and Social Psychology, 2,* 1965, 783-92.

Lewin, K. *Principles of topological psychology.* New York: McGraw-Hill Book Company, 1966.

Likert, R. *The human organization: Its management and value.* New York: McGraw-Hill Book Company, 1967.

Lippitt, R. and White, R. K. The "social climate" of children's groups. In Barker, R. G., Kennin, J. S., and Wright, H. F. (eds.), *Child behavior and development.* New York: McGraw-Hill Book Company, 1943, 485-508.

Marrow, A. J. *The practical theorist: The life and work of Kurt Lewin.* New York: Basic Books, 1970.

McClelland, D. C. *The achieving society.* Princeton, N. J.: Van Nostrand, 1961.

McClelland, D. C. Business drive and national achievement. *Harvard Business Review,* July-August, 1962, 99-112.

McClelland, D. C. Toward a theory of motive acquisition. *American Psychologist,* 20, 1965a, 321-33.

McClelland, D. C. *N* Achievement and entrepreneurship: A longitudinal study. *Journal of Personality and Social Psychology,* 1, 1965b, 389-92.

McClelland, D. C. Black capitalism: Making it work. In *Think* (an IBM publication). July-August, 1969, 6-11.

McClelland, D. C. Atkinson, J. W., Clark, R. A. and Lowell, E. L. *The achievement motive.* New York: Appleton-Century-Crofts, 1953.

McClelland, D. C. and Winter, D. G. *Motivating economic achievement.* New York: Free Press, 1969.

McGregor, D. The human side of enterprise. In *Leadership and motivation.* MIT Press, 1966, 3-20.

Murray, H. *Thematic apperception test manual.* Cambridge, Mass: Harvard University Press, 1943.

Nord, W. Beyond the teaching machine: The neglected area of operant condition in the theory and practice of management. *Organizational Behavior and Human Performance,* Vol. 4, 4, Nov., 1969.

Plimpton, Franziska H. *O-P manual: A content analysis coding system designed to assess the Origin Syndrome.* Unpublished paper: Washington University, 1970.

Polanyi, M. *Personal knowledge.* Chicago: University of Chicago Press, 1958.

Rosen, B. C. and D'Andrade, R. G. The psychosocial origin of achievement motivation. *Sociometry, 22,* 1959, 185-218.

Rotter, J. B. Generalized expectancies for internal versus external control of reinforcement. *Psychological Monographs 80* (1, Whole No. 609). 1966.

Schutz, A. *Collected papers, Vol. 1.* The Hague: Nijhoff, 1963.

Shea, D. J. *The effects of achievement motivation training on motivational and behavioral variables.* Unpublished doctoral dissertation, Washington University, 1969.

Shea, D. J. and Jackson, K. W. Motivation training with teachers—a description. In de Charms, R. *Origins and pawns at school.* New York: Irvington Publishers, 1975.

Shipley, T. E. and Veroff, J. A projective measure of need for affiliation. In Atkinson, R. W. (ed.), *Motives in fantasy, action, and society.* Princeton, N. J.: Van Nostrand, 1958.

Skinner, B. F. Behaviorism at fifty. In Wann, T. W. (ed.) *Behaviorism and phenomenology.* Chicago: The University of Chicago Press, 1964.

Tolman, E. C. Principles of purposive behavior. In Koch, S. (ed.) *Psychology: A study of a science.* Vol. 2. New York: McGraw-Hill Book Company, 1959, 92-157.

Winter, D. G. *Scoring manual for n power.* Unpublished paper, 1968.

Winterbottom, Marian R. The relation of need for achievement to learning experiences in independence and mastery. In Atkinson, J. W. (ed.) *Motives in fantasy, action, and society.* Princeton, N. J.: Van Nostrand, 1958.

Wylie, Ruth C. *The self concept: a critical survey of pertinent research literature.* Lincoln: University of Nebraska Press, 1961.

Abraham H. Maslow

MANAGEMENT AS A PSYCHOLOGICAL EXPERIMENT

There are enough data available, and enough industrial experiences, and also enough clinical-psychological data on human motivations, to warrant taking a chance on the experiment of Theory Y type of management. And yet it is well to keep in mind always that this will be a kind of a pilot experiment for the simple reason that the data which justify this experiment are definitely not final data, not clearly convincing beyond a shadow of a doubt. There is still plenty of room for doubt, as is evidenced by the fact that many academic people and many managers still do, in fact, doubt the validity of the whole line of thinking involved, and this is not entirely arbitrary. They do bring up evidence, experience, data against the new kind of management. We must certainly agree that there is plenty of doubt, and that the whole business is an experiment, and we must also be very aware of the fact that we need lots of data, lots of answers to a lot of questions yet to come.

For instance, the whole philosophy of this new kind of management may be taken as an expression of faith in the goodness of human beings, in trustworthiness, in enjoyment of efficiency, of knowledge, of respect, etc. But the truth is that we don't really have exact and quantitative information on the proportion of the human population which does in fact have some kind of feeling for workmanship, some kind of desire for all the facts and all the truth, some sort of desire for efficiency over against inefficiency, etc. We know certainly that some individual human beings have these needs, and we know a little about the conditions under which these needs will appear, but we don't have any mass surveys of large populations that would give us some quantitative indication of just how many people prefer to have somebody else do their thinking for them, for instance. We don't know the answers to the question: What proportion of the population is irreversibly authoritarian? We don't even know what proportion of the population are psychopaths or paranoiac characters or overdependent or safety-motivated, etc., etc.

These are all crucial kinds of information that we would need in order to be absolutely certain about enlightened management policy. We don't know how

Abridged from Abraham H. Maslow, *Eupsychian Management,* pp. 53-60. Reprinted by permission of Richard D. Irwin, Inc. © 1965.

many people or what proportion of the working population would actually prefer to participate in management decisions, and how many would prefer not to have anything to do with them. What proportion of the population take a job as simply any old kind of a job which they must do in order to earn a living, while their interests are very definitely centered elsewhere outside of the job.

An example is the woman who works only because she has to support her children. It's perfectly true that she'll prefer a nice and pleasant job to a rotten job, but just how does she define rotten job? How much involvement does she really want in the enterprise if the center of her life is definitely in her children rather than in her job? What proportion of the population prefer authoritarian bosses, prefer to be told what to do, don't want to bother thinking, etc.? What proportion of the population is reduced to the concrete and so finds planning for the future totally incomprehensible and boring? How many people prefer honesty and how strongly do they prefer it to dishonesty, how strong a tendency is there in people against being thieves? We know very little about physical inertia or psychic inertia. How lazy are people and under what circumstances and what makes them not lazy? We just don't know.

All of this then is an experiment (because of inadequate final data) in just about the same way that political democracy is an experiment which is based upon a scientifically unproven assumption: namely that human beings like to participate in their own fate, that given sufficient information they will make wise decisions about their own lives, and that they prefer freedom to being bossed, that they prefer to have a say in everything which affects their future, etc. None of these assumptions has been adequately enough proven so that we would call it scientific fact in about the same way that we would label biological fact scientific. We have to know more about these psychological factors than we do. Because this is so, we ought to again be very aware, very conscious, of the fact that these are articles of faith rather than articles of final knowledge, or perhaps better said that they are articles of faith with some grounding in fact though not yet enough to convince people who are characterologically against these articles of faith.

I suppose that the ultimate test of scientific fact is that those people who are by temperament and character unsympathetic to the conclusion must accept it as a fact anyway. We will know that our knowledge of the authoritarian character structure is truly scientific final fact when an average authoritarian character will be able to read the information on the subject and then regard his own authoritarian character as undesirable or sick or pathological and will go about trying to get rid of it. Just so long as an authoritarian character can wave aside all the evidence which indicates that he is sick, just so long are those facts not sufficient, not final enough.

After all, if we take the whole thing from McGregor's point of view of a contrast between a Theory X view of human nature, a good deal of the evidence upon which he bases his conclusions comes from my researches and my papers on motivations, self-actualization, etc. But I of all people should know just how shaky this foundation is as a final foundation. My work on motivations came from the clinic, from a study of neurotic people. The carry-over of this theory to the industrial situation has some support from industrial studies, but certainly I would like to see a lot more studies of this kind before feeling finally convinced that this carry-over from the study of neurosis to the study of labor in factories is legitimate.

The same thing is true of my studies of self-actualizing people–there is only this one study of mine available (1). There were many things wrong with the sampling, so many in fact that it must be considered to be, in the classical sense anyway, a bad or poor or inadequate experiment. I am quite willing to concede this–as a matter of fact, I am eager to concede it–because I'm a little worried about this stuff which I consider to be tentative being swallowed whole by all sorts of enthusiastic people, who really should be a little more tentative, in the way that I am. The experiment needs repeating and checking–it needs working over in other societies–it needs a lot of things which it doesn't yet have. The main support for this theory–and, of course, there's plenty of this support–has come mostly from psychotherapists like Rogers and Fromm.

This, of course, leaves the problem of carry-over from the therapeutic situation to the industrial situation still open to testing. It needs to be validated as a legitimate carry-over. I may say also that my paper on the need for knowledge (2), on curiosity in the human being, is also practically the only thing of its kind, and while I trust it and believe my own conclusions, I am still willing to admit like a cautious scientist that it ought to be checked by other people before being taken as final. As we become aware of the probable errors of the data, we must underscore the necessity for more research. Smugness and certainty tend to stop research rather than to stimulate it.

On the other hand, of course, I should make clear that the evidence upon which Theory X management is based is practically nil; that there is even less evidence for Theory X than there is for Theory Y. It rests entirely on habit and tradition. It's no use saying that it rests on long experience, as most of its proponents would say, because this experience is a kind of self, or at least *can* be a kind of self-fulfilling prophecy. That is to say that the people who support Theory X on nonscientific grounds then proceed to use it as a management philosophy, which brings about just that behavior in the workers which Theory X would predict. But with this kind of Theory X treatment of workers, no other kind of behavior would be possible as a result.

To sum this up I would say that there is insufficient grounding for a firm and final trust in Theory Y management philosophy; but then I would hastily add that there is even less firm evidence for Theory X. If one adds up all the researches that have actually been done under scientific auspices and in the industrial situation itself, practically all of them come out on the side of one or another version of Theory Y; practically none of them come out in favor of Theory X philosophy except in small and detailed and specific special circumstances.

The same is true for the studies of the authoritarian personality. These also come out generally in favor of the democratic personality. And yet there are a few specific special instances in which it is better to have an authoritarian personality, in which the authoritarian will get better results. For instance, an authoritarian personality will get better results for a transitional period as a teacher with authoritarian students than will a democratic and permissive Theory Y kind of teacher. This is the same order of evidence which indicates that practically *any* human being, however sick, can be used some place in a complex industrial civilization. I think, for instance, of Bob Holt's demonstration of the adaptive value even of the paranoid character; he showed that such people tend to make better detectives than do normal people – or at least that they do as well.

Another point here comes from my reading of the chapter by Scoutten in the book edited by Mason Haire called *Organization Theory in Industrial Practice.* Scoutten brings to mind that as soon as we take into account such factors as the long-range health of the business (instead of a merely short-range health), the duties to a democratic society, the need in an individualized situation for pretty highly developed human beings as workers and managers, etc., etc., *then* the necessity for Theory Y management becomes greater and greater. He speaks of production and sales as the only functions, the only goals, of the company with which he is connected, the Maytag Company. Everything else he considers unnecessary or subsidiary to these two functions. But it should be pointed out that this is a kind of isolated or encapsulated view of the situation, i.e., as if this company had no relationship with the community, the environment, or the society, nor any debt to it. He takes an awful lot for granted in a situation like this, including a democratic society with high levels of education, with great respect for law and property, etc., etc. He leaves these things out entirely. If you include them, then it becomes obvious also that the company or the enterprise has to give certain things to the society as well as receive certain things from the society, and this makes a different picture altogether. The picture that Scoutten gives of an enterprise might work perfectly well in a fascist economy, but it would not work at all if it were taken seriously in our democratic society, where any enterprise – as a matter of fact, any individual – has also its obligations to the whole society.

(At this point there should be a reference to my memorandum on the patriot, and on the enlightened industrialist as a patriot.)

More should be said on the relations between the enterprise and the society, especially if we take into account the ways to keep the organization healthy over a period of a hundred years. It then becomes most obvious about the mutual ties between the enterprise and the society – for one thing the healthy organization will need a steady supply of fairly well-matured and well-educated personalities (it cannot use delinquents, criminals, cynical kids, spoiled and indulged kids, hostile people, warmongers, destroyers, vandals, etc., but exactly these people are the products of a poor society). This is very much like saying that a poor society cannot support healthy enterprises, in the long run at least. (Although it probably is true that some kinds of products can be well made in the authoritarian society or the authoritarian enterprise, or under conditions of fear and starvation. I really should find out what kinds of exports for instance, can come from Spain today, or how good are Negro workers in South Africa? What kind of production do they have?)

It is also true that the healthy enterprise cannot function at all well under conditions of riots and civil war, of epidemics, of sabotage and murder, of class warfare, or caste warfare. The culture itself has to be healthy for this reason as well. Also there cannot be conditions of corruption, political corruption, nor can there be religious corruption or religious domination. The enterprise must be free to develop itself in all ways which do not interfere with the goodness and the health of the society. This means also that there ought not to be too much political domination either.

In effect any company that restricts its goals purely to its own profits, its own production, and its own sales is getting a kind of a free ride from me and other taxpayers. I help pay for the schools and the police departments and the fire departments and the health departments and everything else in order to keep the society healthy, which in turn supplies high-level workers and managers to such companies at little expense to them. I feel that they should, in order to be fair, make more returns to the society than they are making–that is, in terms of producing good citizens, people who because of their good work situation can themselves be benevolent, charitable, kind, altruistic, etc., etc., in the community.

I am impressed again with the necessity, however difficult the job may be, of working out some kind of moral or ethical accounting scheme. Under such a scheme tax credits would be given to the company that helps to improve the whole society, that helps to improve the local population, and helps to improve the democracy by helping to create more democratic individuals. Some sort of tax penalty should be assessed against enterprises that undo the effects of a political democracy, of good schools, etc., etc., and that make their people more paranoid, more hostile, more nasty, more malevolent, more destructive, etc. This is like sabotage against the whole society. And they should be made to pay for it.

Partly it must be put up to the accountants to try to figure out some way of turning into balance sheet terms the intangible personnel values that come from improving the personality level of the workers, making them more cooperative, better workers, less destructive, etc. It does cost money to hire this kind of personnel; it costs money to train and teach them and to build them into a good team, and there are all sorts of other costs involved in making the enterprise attractive to this kind of worker and this kind of engineer, etc. All these real expenditures of money and effort ought somehow to be translated into accounting terms so that the greater value of the enterprise that contributes to the improvement of the whole society can somehow be put on the balance sheets. We all know that such a company for instance, is a better credit risk and lending banks will take this into account. So will investors. The only ones who don't take these things into account are the accountants.

BIBLIOGRAPHY

1. *Motivation and Personality* (New York: Harper & Row, Publishers, 1954).
2. The Need to Know and the Fear of Knowing. *Journ. General Psychol.* 1963, *68,* 11-25.

Charles L. Hulin
Milton R. Blood

JOB ENLARGEMENT, INDIVIDUAL DIFFERENCES, AND WORKER RESPONSES

One of the most pervasive and dominant themes which exists in the attempts of industrial psychologists to provide guidelines and frameworks for the motivation of industrial workers is the notion of job enlargement. Job enlargement is a concerted attempt to stem and even reverse the current trends among industrial engineering programs toward job simplification and specialization. The attack on job specialization and job simplification has a long and impressive history going back nearly 200 years to the writings of Adam Smith. In 1776, Smith (reported in Lewis, 1963) stated that

> It [division of labor] corrupts even the activity of his body, and renders him incapable of exerting his strength with vigour and perseverance, in any other employment than that to which he has been bred. His dexterity at his own particular trade seems, in this manner, to be acquired at the expense of his intellectual, social, and martial virtues [p.237].

Further early support for this position has been found in the writings of Durkheim (1933). However, the support from Durkheim is more in the eye of the reader than in the writings since Durkheim did not attack the division of labor per se, only the anomic division of labor. He stated that normally the division of labor produces social solidarity and that there is nothing noble about a man doing a large job in a mediocre fashion nor nothing debasing about a man doing a small job well. Unfortunately, most of the references to Durkheim are to his discussion of the anomic division of labor, which he considered a pathological state of society. The problem in the discussion presented by Durkheim is to define that point at which the division of labor ceases to be beneficial and becomes pathological and produces anomie. We raise the question of whether such a point exists and is indeed definable. If it does exist, can it be considered a constant or does it vary from worker to worker with some workers regarding extremely specialized, short-time-cycle, simple jobs as good jobs?

Reprinted from the *Psychological Bulletin 69*, (1968): 41-55, by permission of the American Psychological Association.

Most modern writers (Argyris, 1957; Kornhauser, 1965; Likert, 1961; MacGregor, 1957; Whyte, 1955) regard nearly all division of labor, with the resulting job simplification and specialization, as leading almost inevitably to monotony, boredom, job dissatisfaction, and inappropriate (from the point of view of management) behavior patterns. The evidence on this point will be reviewed in this paper, along with an analysis of the effects of the individual differences of workers on their responses to job enlargement and job simplification. An attempt will also be made to specify a model based on the cultural differences of workers which can be used to resolve the contradictions in the literature and to predict responses to larger (or enlarged) jobs.

DEFINITION

For the purposes of this review, job enlargement has been considered as the process of allowing individual workers to determine their own working pace (within limits), to serve as their own inspectors by giving them responsibility for quality control, to repair their own mistakes, to be responsible for their own machine setup and repair, and to attain choice of method. In this sense, job enlargement is qualitatively different from *job extension,* which consists of merely adding similar elements to the job without altering job content (e.g., soldering the red wires as well as the black wires). However, changing from a line-paced job to a self-paced job would be regarded as job enlargement. It can also be seen that the process of job enlargement produces jobs at a higher level of skill, with varied work content and relative autonomy for the worker. On the other hand, the process of job simplification results in jobs requiring less skill which are more repetitive and have less autonomy. The process of job simplification has progressed much further with some jobs than with others. Thus, jobs at different points in the process of simplification exist contemporaneously. While we do not normally think of differences between jobs in such terms, it seems to be a veridical way of organizing thinking about job levels. Also, such categorizations of jobs enable us to consider both experimental and correlational methods of analyzing differences or changes in worker responses. That is, changes in workers' responses which correlate with the degree of job simplification should also be observed if changes in job specialization are made experimentally.

TRADITIONAL MODEL

According to the theorists, as jobs become increasingly specialized the monotony (perception of the *sameness* of the job from minute-to-minute, perception of the unchanging characteristic of the job) increases. That is, short-time-cycle, simplified jobs lead to monotony. Monotony is supposedly associated with feelings of boredom and job dissatisfaction. Boredom and job dissatisfaction lead to undesirable (from management's point of view) behavior. This reasoning could be diagrammed as follows:

Stimulus condition	*Perception*	*Affective response*	*Behavioral response*
Simplified, low skill level, short-cycle jobs	Monotony	Boredom, job dissatisfaction	Absenteeism, turnover, restriction of output

Several assumptions in this line of reasoning deserve discussion. Consider the assumption that repetitiveness leads to monotony and, conversely, that uniqueness and change lead to a lack of monotony. Smith (1955) has demonstrated that there are important individual differences in susceptibility to monotony among workers on the same job. Apparently, some workers do not report monotony even in the face of a job with an extremely short work cycle. Baldamus (1961) has pointed out that repetitive work can often have positively motivating characteristics (traction) which tend to "pull the worker along" and are pleasant. This notion has been experimentally verified by Smith and Lem (1955) using a sample of industrial workers. Thus the assumption of repetitiveness leading to monotony could be questioned on two grounds–effects of individual differences and positive motivational characteristics of repetition.

The second assumption is that monotony leads to boredom and job dissatisfaction. Even granting that the physical reality of short time cycles or repetition leads to monotony, can we assume that workers respond with negative affect to this perception? This assumption can be questioned on much the same grounds as the first. At the very least, we should allow the possibility that some workers prefer the safety of not being required to make decisions. Vroom (1960) has demonstrated that not all workers are satisfied when they are allowed to take part in the decision-making process about their jobs, and there are significant individual differences (F scale scores) between workers who respond positively to the opportunity to make decisions and those who do not. While not exactly to the point, these data at least indicate that some workers prefer routine, repetition, and specified work methods to change, variety, and decision making.

The final assumption is that boredom and job dissatisfaction are associated with undesirable behavior patterns. This assumption is probably the least crucial to the argument since trite as it may seem, a high level of job satisfaction among industrial workers may be an appropriate goal in itself. If job enlargement had no other result than decreased boredom and increased job satisfaction, it would be appropriate. Also, there is evidence (Hulin, 1966; Weitz & Nuckols, 1953) that in certain circumstances, job satisfaction is significantly related to individual decisions to quit. The relationship between satisfaction and productivity and other on-the-job behaviors is somewhat more elusive. The fact that this relationship has been so difficult to obtain indicates the weakness of the final assumption of the traditional model.

EVIDENCE

Empirical studies linking job satisfaction to job size have a long history but have generally been poorly controlled, and most of the authors have attempted to generalize from severely limited data. In an early study, Wyatt, Fraser, and Stock (1929a) reported that workers on a soap-wrapping job gave higher outputs when working conditions were uniform than when conditions were varied. Outputs were not different in the two conditions when the jobs were folding handkerchiefs and making bicycle chains. From this they concluded that varied conditions were better and they began studying optimum spacing of task changes! There are obvious problems with this study. The Ns were small and results did not reach statistical significance, most of the results do not support their conclusions, and they did not control for variations in output which may have been caused by the change per se as opposed to the particular variations of their hypotheses. Their writings also fail to distinguish among the effects of fatigue, inhibition, boredom, and monotony. In later studies, Wyatt, Fraser, and Stock (1929b) and Wyatt, Langdon, and Stock (1937) investigated the effects of jobs having short time cycles. Smith (1953) has pointed out "certain deviations from normally acceptable methods of scientific investigation . . . [p.69]." Part of their measure of boredom consisted of questions about slowing of output during the middle of the day. Those who reported such slowing were regarded as bored. Also, those who reported such slowing did indeed slow down at these times. Therefore, Wyatt et al. were able to obtain good matches between their measure of boredom and "typical" boredom output curves. The circularity is evident. The results relating boredom, IQ, and production cause concern. High-IQ workers were more bored and boredom reduced the rate of working, but high-IQ workers were more productive. Boredom was less likely to occur on fully automated work, and the experience of boredom was largely dependent on individual characteristics. The workers in all these studies were female, which serves as an additional restriction on generalization. All in all, both the measures and the conclusions of these studies are extremely suspect. Roethlisberger and Dickson (1941) and Smith (1953) were unable to replicate the original results of Wyatt et al. Generalizations from these data must, indeed, be cautious.

Walker (1950) presented a report of the benefits of a job-enlargement program which was undertaken at IBM. Though some might consider this article a heuristic success, it presented little in the way of data. There was no control for a Hawthorne effect, and no data were presented which concerned satisfaction, turnover, costs, etc.

Walker and Marriott (1951) provided data indicating that more than a third of the employees of mass production factories complained of boredom, but in rolling mills the proportion was only 8 percent. Boredom was more widespread among conveyor workers, and workers were less satisfied on such jobs if they had previously held a skilled job. Data came from interviews with 976 men from three large factories. This seems to be evidence supporting the traditional model which relates uniformity and repetition in work to dissatisfaction. While we have no disagreement with the results as presented, there are some problems associated with the generality of the conclusions. Individual differences in worker responses were considerable, and, in fact, "Many liked their work because it was simple, straightforward, and carried no responsibility."

Differences between factories were attributed to differences in production techniques rather than to differences between the persons making up the work forces of the factories. A subsequent interview study (Walker & Guest, 1952) related increased dissatisfaction, increased absences, and increased turnover to assembly line work. The basic conclusion was that very little could be said in favor of assembly line work.

While Walker and Guest were careful not to generalize beyond their sample, their conclusions and recommendations were stated in very general terms, and sound as if they are cures for ills everywhere. In light of the sample described by Walker and Guest and the findings of Blood and Hulin (1967) and Turner and Lawrence (1965), there is little doubt that Walker and Guest's results would be anticipated by the model to be presented in this paper. Typical descriptive statements given by Walker and Guest (1952) are: "The area from which [the workers] were recruited has few mass production factories [p. 4]." "Only two in our sample had ever worked in an automobile plant before [p. 19]," and "... 34.5 percent of all those [in the sample] with manual work experience were skilled persons. Considering the relatively unskilled nature of automobile assembly work, this high proportion of skilled workmen ... is of interest [p. 31]." While our model would predict negative responses to simplified, line-paced jobs from workers such as those described by Walker and Guest, we would not expect such negative responses to be a general characteristic of the United States work force. In subsequent papers (Guest, 1955, 1957; Walker, 1954), these investigators have extolled the virtues of job flexibility, job rotation, and job enlargement without contributing any additional data. Their claims are unjustifiable because of the peculiarities of their sample and their lack of acceptable experimental controls.

The Detroit Edison Electric Utility Company carried out a program of job enlargement among first-line supervisors and clerical workers (Elliott, 1953). Though there were no controls and no statistical information was provided, Elliott claimed that job enlargement reduced costs and increased production. He then assumed a positive relationship between productivity and morale. On the basis of this assumed relationship, he argued that satisfaction had increased! Cost reduction and production increase are more easily explained in this case as a result of the elimination of duplications in the work process. The report did include the recognition that some workers prefer repetitive jobs.

Marks (1954) reported a study of 29 female employees in the manufacturing department of a company on the West Coast. A similar department was monitored as a control. Production was poorer with enlarged jobs, but quality improved.[1] After experience with the enlarged job, some workers disliked the lack of personal responsibility of an assembly line design. The conclusion, however, which is normally drawn from this study is that enlarged jobs are better.

[1]Quality improvement would be expected in nearly all programs of job enlargement since the worker serves as his own inspector. If he makes a mistake and discovers it he can repair it on the spot. Such repairs on assembly line work are, of course, impossible since the worker cannot stop to make the repairs. This improvement in quality, however, should be

When assembly operations were enlarged in the Maytag Company plant in Newton, Iowa, there were quantity and quality improvements in production (Biganne & Stewart, 1963). These workers would be expected by the model to be presented in this paper to be more satisfied with enlarged jobs. No statistical evidence was presented, but it was reported that most of the workers came to like their new jobs and they seemed to become involved.

In a study of the attitudes of skilled and semiskilled workers to job enlargement, Davis and Werling (1960) surveyed a West Coast plant employing 400 operating and 250 clerical and administrative personnel. The interests of skilled workers, similar to those of management, included company success, improvement of self, and improvement of operations. Semiskilled workers, on the other hand, lacked concern for company goals and they attached little importance to job content. From this, Davis and Werling concluded that semiskilled jobs are insufficiently enlarged. Such a conclusion requires evidence that the size of the job determines attitude. Of course there is no evidence of this sort, and, indeed, attitudes toward company goals and job content may be as influenced by many subcultural and personal background factors as by one aspect of the task. Further, the inference that the workers *should* think job content important is an evaluative asumption not necessary for empirical analysis of the data.

Argyris (1959) provided information from content analysis of interviews with 34 employees from a department with high skill demands and 90 unskilled and semiskilled employees from another department. As compared with the skilled employees, those of lower skill expressed

a. less aspiration for high-quality work,
b. less need to learn more about their work,
c. more emphasis on money,
d. lower estimates of personal abilities,
e. less desire for variety and independence,
f. high work spoilage (subjectively judged since the tasks were different),
g. fewer lasting friendships formed on the job, and
h. less creative use of leisure time.

Also, the lower skilled employees expressed needs "to be left alone," "to be passive," and "to experience routine or sameness." According to the theories of Argyris, these differences are caused by the organization's stifling the maturity of individuals on the job. However, just as in the Davis and Werling study, there is no reason to believe that these differences were caused by the job rather than brought to the work situation.

In a study auspiciously titled "Job Enlargement: Antidote to Apathy," Reif and Schoderbek (1966) reported the results of a survey of companies regarding their use of job enlargement. Questionnaires were mailed to 276 companies.

regarded as a direct result of the technical changes in the jobs and not of changes in worker motivation or satisfaction. Kilbridge (1960b) has also pointed out that many of the positive results obtained in studies of job enlargement could be attributed to reductions in balance-delay time and nonproduction time and not to changes in worker motivations or satisfaction.

Replies were received from 210, and of these, 41 said they had used job enlargement. The most popular reasons for undertaking job enlargement were cost reduction and profit increase. Twenty-three respondents checked "increase in job satisfaction" as an advantage of job enlargement. It is significant that only 23 of the 41 companies which used job enlargement noted an increase in job satisfaction in spite of

a. the popularity of the traditional notion that workers want larger jobs, and
b. the opportunity for bias in this sample.

Reif and Schoderbek seemed unaware that their data may have been atypical even though the sample represented less than 15 percent of their initial population. Returns perhaps should not be expected from companies who have tried job enlargement unsuccessfully, and if an executive from such a company did reply he would probably be hesitant to admit that an executive policy of his firm had failed. Reif and Schoderbek's conclusions in favor of job enlargement and the proposal of job enlargement as an "antidote for apathy" are unjustified.

In a study of the effects of repetitive work on the mental health of industrial workers, Kornhauser (1965) found that many production workers from an urban area gave interview responses which he considered indicative of poor mental health. He showed that, in general, such indications of poor mental health increased as job level decreased (from skilled workers to semiskilled workers with repetitive tasks). He has gleaned a large amount of information from interviews with 655 men, and his data and his conclusions merit discussion. He convincingly showed that there are systematic differences in the interview responses of workers at different job levels. From the nature of the response differences he concluded that the persons in the lower skilled jobs were in poorer mental health and, furthermore, that their occupational situation caused this condition. He argued that job simplification is a cause of poor mental health. Before accepting these conclusions, some of the methods of his study must be examined.

First, all data were obtained from interview responses. Therefore, they are open to such biasing factors as social acceptability, interviewer bias, and bias of the coder who arranged the interview transcripts into quantitative material. Social acceptability bias would enter the situation and distort responses in the obtained direction if the interviewee shaped his answers to his expectations of the responses desired by his middle-class-oriented interviewer. That is, persons in repetitive jobs may feel hesitant to admit that they are not dissatisfied with their work if they feel that such admission will lead to an unfavorable judgment from the interviewer. If the interviewer or coder was familiar with the hypothesis of the study (either explicitly or implicitly), there is the additional possibility that responses were systematically interpreted in the manner most favorable to the hypothesis. Since no information was presented which would either confirm or disconfirm the existence of these biases, we must approach the results with proper caution and the realization that such distortions *might* have taken place.

Second, Kornhauser attempted to generalize from an urban blue-collar sample to all production workers. Recent studies by Turner and Lawrence (1965) and

Blood and Hulin (1967) have demonstrated that we cannot generalize from urban blue-collar workers to all blue-collar workers.

Further, Kornhauser chose to ignore differences in workers' personal backgrounds. Perhaps this is justified since he explained that these differences were not the point of his discussion. However, we should not overlook his data which show the relationship between personal background variables and the Mental Health Index score to be at least as strong as that between job level and the Mental Health Index score. He pointed to the relative independence of these influences, but his analytic techniques were such that they would not have been sensitive to interaction effects so this conclusion must be attributed to his personal judgment.

Finally, it is inevitable that the Mental Health Index depends on value judgments as to what constitutes good or poor health. In this case, good mental health seems to depend more on striving for personal betterment than on a realistic evaluation of the situation. For example, the interview response "There's such a thing as beating your brains against the wall. Some things you just can't change; might as well accept them and adjust yourself to them" was said by Kornhauser to "call attention to the very limited self-expectations, the degree of passivity, fatalism, and resignation that characterize many of the workers [p. 241]." Thus Kornhauser shows that he himself subscribes to what he considers to be a middle-class concept—that every person is responsible for his own situation rather than being influenced by forces beyond his control. He saw as evidence of poor mental health that members of a lower-class subculture do not hold middle-class ideals. What these data show most convincingly is that there are differences by job level among urban workers in the extent to which workers adhere to a middle-class value system. Another problem with the Mental Health Index results is that we are not able to compare them with any kind of base line. Some comparison data were provided from a small sample of low-ranking white-collar workers and a small sample of production workers from outside Detroit. Because of the sample sizes, these comparison data are less trustworthy than the experimental data. Statistical probabilities of the differences between these comparison samples and the larger, Detroit blue-collar sample were not provided and in many cases the results look similar.

In several ways Kornhauser's study demonstrates the dangers of trying to index a culture-bound concept such as mental health when using a research sample which may contain subcultural differences and may be culturally different from the investigators and persons who are judging the validity of the research instrument. Nonetheless, the study confirms that there are response differences between different job levels. This is not a new concept, but whereas blue-collar and white-collar differences have been discussed in the past, Kornhauser showed that within the gross blue-collar category finer discriminations will provide additional information. Porter (1961) has shown that such differentiation is profitable in the white-collar realm. Certainly job level is an influential dimension in the determination of workers' responses and the extent to which class ideals prevail. If we can find other useful dimensions, we will increase our ability to understand, and hence predict, workers' reactions to job enlargement and other aspects of their work situation.

Scott (1966) has generalized the activation theory of vigilance behavior to the area of task and job design. The activation theory of vigilance behavior is a physiological explanation of behavior in situations characterized by low levels of stimulation and has been found to summarize much of the literature on vigilance decrement (Frankmann & Adams, 1962). Briefly, this theory holds that stimuli impinging on the human receptor serve two purposes. One is a cue or information function which is accomplished when the stimulation travels directly to the appropriate cortical projection area. The other is an arousal or activation function and is accomplished when the neural stimulation also travels through the ascending reticular formation and is diffused over a wide area of the cortex. This pathway serves no cue or information function but does serve to maintain the organism at a high state of arousal or activation. Generalizing from the activation theory and the results of vigilance studies, Scott argued that amount and variety of stimulation serve to motivate the worker and enable him to maintain a high level of performance. In short, nonroutine, nonrepetitive jobs are likely to serve as positive motivators of behavior. Basing a theory of industrial motivation in physiology would, of course, tend to give it the appearance of being more basic, general, and valid.

While we have no disagreement with the efficacy of the activation theory when applied to vigilance data, we do feel there are a number of problems involved with generalizing the theory to the area of industrial task design. First, the similarity between the experimental settings where vigilance decrements are reliably obtained and even the most routine and repetitive of industrial jobs is slight. The presence of other people, random intermittant noise, illumination changes, multiple tasks, the opportunity to move about, stretch, talk to other workers, etc., all summate to produce a situation far removed from the usual vigilance situations. Considering the fact that vigilance decrements can be eliminated by the introduction of multiple tasks, other people in the room, etc., industrial tasks are so different from vigilance tasks that any generalizations are exceedingly dangerous. Second, whenever tasks are enlarged, several derived social motivation variables are changed along with the desired changes in amount and variety of the physical stimulation. When more elements are added to a task, a greater variety of skills is required and, at the extreme, greater involvement in the job is required. Whether all or even most workers are willing to make this investment in their jobs is a matter for investigation, not assumption. Finally, while not an inherent problem of the activation theory, there is the matter of individual differences in the optimal levels of stimulation. While parameters for individual differences could be built into the theory, there are at present no such parameters nor are there any indications in the activation theory as to the source of information for predicting such individual differences parameters. Considering the variance controlled by these ubiquitous individual differences in the behavior and motivation of industrial workers, such an omission amounts to a very serious gap in the theory.

In addition to the references cited above, Worthy (1950), Argyris (1957, 1964), Davis (1957a, 1957b), and Davis and Canter (1955) presented the traditional viewpoint that larger jobs are "better" jobs. Though the human relations approach has gained widespread popular support, the data are unconvincing. These supportive data present us with severe restrictions either because of methodological problems or because of the nature of the samples. Warren (1958) reviewed the traditional literature and the research data and called for the research-team approach to the evaluation of job enlargement. He concurred in some of the human relations concepts, but he made clear the difference between monotony and boredom. An approach to the problem of disatisfaction with repetitive work which is notable for its novelty was presented by Behling (1964). He began with the human relations assumption that repetitive work leads to dissatisfaction. He then invoked the Maslow hierarchy of needs to explain this dissatisfaction, saying it results from the fact that our present civilization is able to satisfy our lower level needs thus making our higher level needs more potent. Of course while the lower level needs of workers are unsatisfied, these higher level needs are not motivators of behavior. He concluded that many of the needs of workers would be more properly fulfilled outside of the work organization. MacKinney, Wernimont, and Galitz (1962) reviewed the studies relating job specialization and job satisfaction, and they concluded that the issue was not settled by the data at that time. We obviously feel that the issue is still not structured, and also agree with MacKinney et al.'s (1962) statement:

> The most compelling argument against specialization as a major cause of job dissatisfaction lies in the fact of individual differences. This is the central fact of life in the behavioral sciences, and yet the would-be reformers apparently believe that all people must react in exactly the same way to the same job. The observer says to himself, "That job would drive me nuts in half an hour." From this he somehow concludes that it must drive everyone else nuts as well. This simply is not so! (For that matter, it's highly probable that many of the workers interviewed by sympathetic social scientists privately regard their questioners' activities as a pretty terrible way to earn a living, too) [p. 17].

More recent data presented by Whyte (1955), Kennedy and O'Neill (1958), Kilbridge (1960a), Katzell, Barrett, and Parker (1961), Kendall (1963), Conant and Kilbridge (1965), Kornhauser (1965), and Blood and Hulin (1967) indicate that the general conclusion regarding the effects of job enlargement on job satisfaction and/or motivation is overstated and may be applicable to only certain segments of the working population. Further, it seems that each of the assumptions in the job-enlargement model can be seriously questioned by numerous other studies.

Perhaps the most dramatic of these studies was done by Turner and Lawrence (1965). Turner and Lawrence attempted a comprehensive study of the attitudinal and behavioral responses of workers to different aspects of their jobs. The original hypotheses were that workers respond favorably (high satisfaction and low absence rates) to jobs which are more complex, have more responsibility, more authority, more variety, etc. In short, "good" responses would accompany high-level jobs. The hypothesis concerning attendance was confirmed for a sample of 470 workers from 11 industries working on 47 different jobs. The hypothesized positive relationship between job level and satisfaction was *not* supported. This finding plus the presence of a number of curvilinear relationships led Turner and Lawrence to the conclusion that the workers in the sample had been drawn from two separate and distinct populations whose members responded in different ways to similar job characteristics. The investigators, by splitting their group of workers on a succession of variables and analyzing the relationship between task attributes and job satisfaction, were able to determine that workers from factories located in small towns responded dramatically differently from workers who came from more urban settings. The workers from small-town settings tended to respond to task attributes in the manner predicted by Turner and Lawrence. Workers from cities indicated no relationship between task attributes and attendance and responded with *low* job satisfaction to supposedly desirable job attributes and with high satisfaction to such "undesirable" attributes as repetitiveness. Turner and Lawrence posited an explanation based on a notion of alienation qua anomie. They argued that workers in large cities with their extremely heterogeneous social cultures would be more likely to be normless (anomic). They would fail to develop strong group or subcultural norms and values due to the extreme size and heterogeneity of the city population and would fail to respond positively to the white-collar-oriented values attached to larger, more autonomous, more skilled jobs. Rather than ignoring the effects of individual differences or attributing them to chance, Turner and Lawrence were able to determine that the unexpected results could not be attributed to chance or poor mental health but could be attributed to differences in cultural backgrounds.

Blood and Hulin (1967) argued that workers from large cities could not be considered as being anomic on the basis of the evidence but could be considered to be alienated from the "work" norms of the middle calss (positive affect for occupational achievement, a belief in the intrinsic value of hard work, a striving for the attainment of responsible positions, and a belief in the work-related aspects of Calvinism and the Protestant ethic) and integrated with the norms of their own particular subculture. Simply because blue-collar workers do not share the work norms and values of the middle classes does not mean they have no norms. In the case of the industrial workers sampled by Turner and Lawrence, there is no compelling reason to suspect that workers in large industrialized cities would adhere to the dominant work value systems of the white middle-class groups. In fact, it would be somewhat surprising if these workers whose grandfathers and fathers had (likely) worked as unskilled or semiskilled laborers and had failed to rise above their initial job or, even worse, had been replaced by a machine or a younger worker at age 50 would behave in the way demanded by the Protestant ethic. (Work hard and you will get ahead. You are responsible for your own destiny. Acceptance into the Kingdom of Heaven is dependent on hard work on this mortal earth.) Starting from this position, Blood and Hulin reanalyzed some data gathered by Patricia C. Smith. These data had been gathered from some 1,300 blue-collar workers employed in 21 plants located throughout the eastern half of the United States. Using results of Kendall's (1963) principal component analysis based on variables available in the census tracts, Blood and Hulin ordered the 21 plants along a number of dimensions which they felt would reflect the degree to which the blue-collar workers in the communities would feel alienated from middle-class work norms. Kendall (1963) labeled the principal components which were chosen for this analysis as extent of slums, urbanization, population density, standard of living, etc. (see Kendall, 1963, or Blood and Hulin, 1967, for a description of how these variates were constructed). These community variates were then used to predict a number of variables obtained from each of the 21 plants. These dependent variables included extent of preparation for retirement, correlation between pay satisfaction and overall job satisfaction, etc. The predictions made were that blue-collar workers in communities where one could expect integration with and acceptance of middle-class work norms (small community, low standard of living, few slums, etc.) would respond as the human relations theory or the striving type of motivation theory (Maslow, 1943) would expect. However, workers in communities where we would expect alienation from middle-class work norms (large, industrialized communities with large slum areas, etc.) would not respond as expected and, in some cases, would respond in an opposite manner from the counterparts in the "integrated" communities. These predictions were confirmed beyond the chance level. Of particular interest to the present review are their finding regarding job level and work satisfaction. In the most "alienated" community the correlation between job level and work satisfaction was approximately −.50, while among the workers drawn from the plant located in the most "integrated" community the correlation between these two variables was approximately .40. These results raise questions for the generality of the job-enlargement model.

Similar evidence regarding the importance of plant location has been presented by Kendall (1963). While his analysis was not designed to answer the questions crucial to this review, he did present canonical regression variates indicating the role played by community characteristics in predicting different combinations of specific job satisfaction and general job satisfaction.

Katzell et al. (1961) determined that among a sample of warehouse workers drawn from a number of locations there existed strong relationships between both satisfaction and productivity on the response side and community characteristics on the input side. They demonstrated that the location of the plant and hence the backgrounds of the workers, since these would seem to be correlated variables, play important roles in shaping the attitudes of the workers and influencing their behavior.

Whyte's (1955) descriptions of rate busters and quota restricters also indicate the importance of the workers' cultural backgrounds. In his analysis, based on a group of workers working under a piece-rate bonus system, he found that workers who were likely to be "rate busters" (produce above the group standards) were those workers with rural or small-town backgrounds, whose fathers had been entrepreneurs or farmers, who were Protestants, who were

Republicans, and who had tended to look "upward" toward their parents for authority sanctions rather than toward their peer group. Quota restricters were more likely to have been reared in large cities, have come from working-class families who were Catholic, have belonged to a boy's gang as a youth, and to be Democrats. It could be argued that the rate busters *rejected* the norms of their peer group and *accepted* the norms of management (middle-class norms). If this is true, then we can predict on the basis of background those workers who will be alienated from middle-class work norms and those who will be integrated with these norms.

Kilbridge (1960a) attacked the question of the preference of workers for larger versus smaller jobs and the issue of mechanical pacing versus self-pacing. Of a sample of 202 (141 females, 61 males) assembly line workers employed by a radio and television set factory in Chicago, 51 percent stated they would prefer a smaller job, 37 percent were indifferent, and only 12 percent preferred a larger job. Further, 84 percent stated they preferred mechanical pacing, 6 percent were indifferent, and only 10 percent preferred a self-paced job. Considering the location of this factory and the results of Turner and Lawrence (1965), Blood and Hulin (1967), and Whyte (1955), these results are not surprising.

Kennedy and O'Neill (1958) surveyed workers in four automotive production departments. They determined that assembly operators performing highly routine and repetitive tasks held opinions toward their supervisors or work situations no more negative than those held by utility men who were performing a much more varied set of tasks.

Finally, Turner and Miclette (1962) interviewed 115 female assembly workers from an electronics plant. Even though the work was extremely repetitive and routine, most of the workers expressed satisfaction with the work itself. The main sources of dissatisfaction came from the sense of being caught in a quantity-quality squeeze and the interruptions from staff and supervisory personnel. Object, batch, line, and process traction were discussed as sources of satisfaction (cf. Baldamus, 1961; Smith & Lem, 1955). Thus, repetition (job size) alone is a poor indicator of worker response and the various sources of positive motivations of repetitive work must be considered.

DISCUSSION

The studies reviewed appear to be of two types. Those which have used acceptable methodology, control groups, appropriate analysis, and multivariate designs have generally not yielded evidence which could be considered as supporting the job-enlargement thesis. Those studies which do appear to support such a thesis frequently contain a number of deviations from normally acceptable research practice. Unfortunately, the former studies are in the minority and the latter studies have generated the greatest fervor and have been accepted as gospel by a large number of psychologists and human relations theorists.

The case for job enlargement has been drastically overstated and overgeneralized. Further, the evidence of the simultaneous effects of plant location and job size (or job level) provides a means of summarizing the literature and resolving the contradictions. Specifically, the argument for larger jobs as a means of motivating workers, decreasing boredom and dissatisfaction, and increasing attendance and productivity is valid only when applied to certain segments of the work force—white-collar and supervisory workers and nonalienated blue-collar workers. That is, if we choose the urban-rural dimension of the location of the plant as a crude but useful index of the expected alienation of the blue-collar workers in the community we could construct Table 1.

TABLE 1. **Plant-Location Index of Expected Worker Alienation from Middle-Class Work Norms.**

Type of worker	*Urban location*	*Rural location*
Blue-collar	Alienated	Nonalienated
White-collar	Nonalienated	Nonalienated

We would expect the job-enlargement hypothesis to predict the behavior of the white-collar workers and the rural or small-town blue-collar workers. Such a hypothesis would not predict responses and behavior of the urban blue-collar workers. This interaction between job size, job satisfaction, and plant location could be further amplified by the following representation of a three-dimensional plot.

Figure 1 is based on data taken from Blood and Hulin (1967). The communities in which the 21 plants in their sample were located were ordered on one of the alienation indexes (or, more properly, dimensions of communities which may be used to index the extent of predicted alienation among the blue-collar workers), and the extremes of the alienation index were used to obtain the slopes of the front and back edge of the surface. In this instance, the back edge of the surface, which represents a community which should foster integration with middle-class work norms, has been drawn to indicate a correlation of .39 between job level and work satisfaction. The front edge of the surface, which represents a community which should develop feelings of alienation from middle-class norms among the blue-collar workers, has been drawn to indicate a correlation of –.52 between job level and work satisfaction.[2]

This response surface indicates that as we move from nonalienated to alienated communities, we should expect the relationship of job level to work satisfaction to change linearly from positive through zero to negative. It further indicates that if we hold job level constant at high-skill-level jobs, we would expect greater job satisfaction among nonalienated workers. However, if we look

[2] A very convenient property of a response surface of this type is that any slice taken parallel to either of the stimulus planes results in a linear function relating the other stimulus variable to job satisfaction. This of course means we need not be concerned with any other than first degree functions with this particular model.

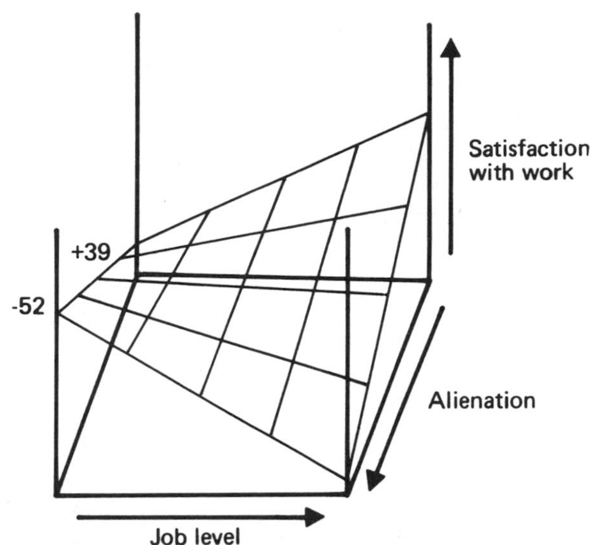

FIGURE 1. **Response surface depicting the interrelationship between job level, satisfaction with work, and alienation of blue-collar workers from middle-class work norms. (Based on data from Blood and Hulin, 1967.)**

only at low levels of blue-collar jobs, we would expect greater work satisfaction among the alienated workers.

This response surface summarizes a great deal of the literature on job enlargement, job level, and job satisfaction. It seems evident, for example, that the rural workers sampled by Turner and Lawrence would have been drawn from the nonalienated end of the continuum while the urban workers would have come from plants located at the alienated end of the continuum. Likewise, those workers Katzell et al. found to be the most satisfied and the most productive should have been drawn from the nonalienated end of the continuum since they were located in small towns with nonunionized work forces. The workers interviewed by Walker and Guest (1952) seem to have been drawn from a plant located in a community which would be described as having workers who were nonalienated since "The area from which [the workers] were recruited has few mass production factories [p. 4]," "Only two in our sample had ever worked in an automobile plant before [p. 8]," etc. Thus, the workers' negative responses to assembly line work would be predicted by the model. The workers in the Maytag study (Biganne & Stewart, 1963), being drawn from a small community, should have also responded positively to job enlargement. On the other hand, the workers studied by Kilbridge should have responded negatively to job enlargement since they were drawn from the Chicago metropolitan area (only 10 percent preferred a self-paced job and only 12 percent preferred a "larger" job). Whyte's (1955) descriptions of rate busters and quota restricters could also be explained by such a response surface. His rate busters appear to have been reared in an environment which would cause them to internalize the norms and value systems of the middle class. This was not true for the quota restricters. Also, this model would be expected to summarize the results of Blood and Hulin (1967) since these were the data used to verify the tenability of the response surface.

Finally, support for the part played by individual differences can be found even in those studies which make the strongest arguments for job enlargement. For example, Walker and Marriott reported that "many liked their [assembly line] work because it was simple, straightforward, and carried no responsibility." Argyris (1959) found lower skilled employees tending to express a desire "to experience routine or sameness." While these last two studies provide no direct support for such a model, they do indicate that the search for individual differences will be fruitful.

It would also seem that this response surface is reasonable from a theoretical point of view since it is consistent with most of the literature on anomie and alienation. Blue-collar workers living in small towns or rural areas would not be members of a work group large enough to develop and sustain its own work norms and values and would be more likely to be in closer contact with the dominant middle class. On the other hand, blue-collar workers living and working in large metropolitan areas would likely be members of a working-class population large enough to develop a set of norms particular to that culture. There is no compelling reason to believe that the norms developed by an urban working-class subculture would be the same or similar to those of the middle class.

If these arguments are correct, then we could expect that workers living in small towns would be more likely to be integrated with middle-class norms and workers in large cities would be more likely to feel alienated from the middle class and its norms and values. Turner and Lawrence (1965), provided discussion of the effects of heterogeneity and homogeneity of population on values and norms. However, it is not necessary to apply an argument based directly on number of blue-collar workers and social heterogeneity. One could argue that the dominant norms and values that all children learn in school and at home are those brought by the Anglo-Saxon Protestants from Europe in the seventeenth and eighteenth centuries. These norms and values have become the standard in American middle-class society. Children are taught these values in school by their middle-class teachers and attempt to reach goals defined in terms of these values by means of behavior consistent with these values. However, children raised in slums, where the cost of living is high, or where there is a great deal of migration are more likely to be frustrated in these attempts. Also, the lower-class American city dweller is less likely to be Anglo-Saxon Protestant (Turner & Lawrence, 1965) and less sympathetic to American middle-class values. Therefore, the acquisition by the lower-class city dweller of goals consistent with the Anglo-Saxon Protestant value system is likely to be met with criticism from his peer group (Whyte, 1955). Such frustration or negative reinforcement should extinguish behavior and beliefs consistent with American middle-class ideals.[3]

[3] The authors would like to thank Harry C. Triandis for pointing out this line of argument. We are, of course, fully responsible for its exposition.

While we have cast our explanation of these results into a static model which implies fixed values of alienation from middle-class work norms, this is not a necessary aspect of the response surface. It would be possible to postulate a second moderating variable related to length of time since the job was enlarged or changed. This second moderator effect would be expected to indicate initial strong rejection of the enlarged job and initial dissatisfaction. As time on the enlarged job increases, however, we would expect less rejection and less dissatisfaction. The extent of the moderating effect of this latter variable is open to empirical study, but it does indicate the possibility of this model fitting into the current emphasis on dynamic as opposed to static models of work behavior (Vroom, 1966).

Even though such a model appears to summarize a great deal of the published evidence on job size and job satisfaction and is consistent with much of the theorizing regarding alienation and anomie, there are a number of unanswered problems. Nearly all of the data which have been published regarding the joint effects of job size and cultural variables on job satisfaction have used the environmental characteristics of the plant as one of the stimulus conditions. The assumption is that the environmental setting of the plant serves to index certain psychological variables of the individual workers. We have no disagreement with the use of index variables per se. However, the environmental setting of the plant or office is thoroughly confounded with the cultural backgrounds of the workers. Plants located in rural areas are more likely to have a work force with rural backgrounds who are Protestants, third or fourth generation Americans, etc. On the basis of the data, we have no way of disentangling the effects of plant location from the effects of the backgrounds of the workers. To attribute the changes in the relationship between job size and satisfaction to differences in the norms and value systems of the workers, as we have done, may not be warranted. On the other hand, the description of rate busters and quota restricters provided by Whyte does indicate that cultural and background differences are important. It would be incredible if the location of the plant had such an effect without operating through an intervening psychological variable. There is also evidence (Bronfenbrenner, 1958) that with socioeconomic status held constant, rural mothers adhere to more rigid patterns of socialization in their child-rearing practices. The probable effect of such practices (as opposed to permissiveness) is to result in children who are more likely to adopt the values of those who are in positions of authority (the middle-class oriented foremen and plant managers).

Finally, the writings of Durkheim, Weber, and Marx on the values and behavior of the industrial proletariat all point in the direction we have taken in the explanation of these findings.

There are also a number of problems raised by the studies relating job level to job satisfaction. For example, Ash (1954), Hoppock (1935), Hulin and Smith (1965), Inlow (1951), Katz (1949), Mann (1953), Miller (1940), and Morse (1953) have all presented data which indicate that higher satisfaction levels are associated with higher job levels. However, most of these studies contained problems mitigating against their being regarded as evidence negative to the model presented in Fig. 1. Many of these studies used white-collar as well as blue-collar workers as subjects. Others did not specify the location of the plant from which the workers were drawn. Thus, there is no way of knowing whether the findings are consistent with the model. Further, Blood and Hulin (1967) reanalyzed the data originally presented by Hulin and Smith (1965) and concluded that Hulin and Smith's conclusions had to be modified to take plant location into account. Finally, many of these studies did not separate the effects of job size from the effects of salary or wages.

In addition to the problems already mentioned, we are making the assumption that well-designed correlational studies can provide evidence on effects of basically manipulative programs. That is, the job-enlargement thesis states that if jobs are reengineered to make them larger, then certain desirable consequences will take place–notably decreases in monotony, increases in satisfaction, and decreases in turnover and restriction in output. We have made several inferences regarding this thesis and have based these inferences to a great extent on information contained in studies which have *correlated* job level or job size with satisfaction. Being *placed* on a high-skill-level job may be qualitatively different than having a present job *enlarged.* However, predictions based on a model (Fig. 1) which has been generated by such correlations appear to be valid for several of the job-enlargement studies. Second, we would expect differences between skilled and unskilled blue-collar workers to operate against the hypotheses. Highly skilled workers who have gone through an extensive training period should be more likely to adopt the norms and values of the middle class. Yet, we find that the highly skilled blue-collar workers do not necessarily report the higher satisfaction levels expected of them.

In summary, studies bearing on the job-enlargement thesis have been received and analyzed. These studies do not support the hypothesis that job size or job level is positively correlated *in general* with job satisfaction. Such hypotheses must be modified to take into account the location of the plant and the cultural backgrounds of the workers.

BIBLIOGRAPHY

Argyris, C. *Personality and organization.* New York: Harper, 1957.

Argyris, C. The individual and organization: An empirical test. *Administrative Science Quarterly* 1959, 4(2), 145-67.

Argyris, C. *Integrating the individual and the organization.* New York: John Wiley & Sons, 1964.

Ash, P. The SRA employee inventory–A statistical analysis. *Personnel Psychology,* 1954, 7, 337-60.

Baldamus, W. *Efficiency and effort.* London: Tavistock, 1961.

Behling, O. C. The meaning of dissatisfaction with factory work. *Management of Personnel Quarterly* 1964, 3(2), 11-16.

Biganne, J. F., and Stewart, P. A. Job enlargement: A case study. Research Series No. 25, 1963, State University of Iowa, Bureau of Labor and Management.

Blood, M. R., and Hulin, C. L. Alienation, environmental characteristics, and worker responses. *Journal of Applied Psychology,* 1967, 51, 284-90.

Bronfenbrenner, U. Socialization and social class through space and time. In E. E. Maccoby, T. M. Newcomb, and E. L. Hartley (Eds.), *Readings in social psychology.* New York: Holt, Rinehart and Winston, 1958. Pp. 400-25.

Conant, E. H., and Kilbridge, M. D. An interdisciplinary analysis of job enlargement: Technology, costs, and behavioral implications. *Industrial and Labor Relations Review,* 1965, 18(3), 377-95.

Davis, L. E. Job design and productivity: A new approach. *Personnel,* 1957, 33, 418-30. (a)

Davis, L. E. Toward a theory of job design. *Journal of Industrial Engineering,* 1957, 8, 305-9. (b)

Davis, L. E., and Canter, R. R. Job design. *Journal of Industrial Engineering,* 1955, 6(1), 3-6, 20.

Davis, L., and Werling, R. Job design factors. *Occupational Psychology,* 1960, 34, 109-32.

Durkheim, E. *The division of labor.* Glencoe, Ill.: Free Press, 1933.

Elliott, J. D. Increasing office productivity through job enlargement. In, *The human side of the office manager's job.* (No. 134, Office Management Series) New York: American Management Association, 1953. Pp. 3-15.

Frankmann, J. P., and Adams, J. A. Theories of vigilance. *Psychological Bulletin,* 1962, 59, 257-72.

Guest, R. H. Men and Machines: An assembly-line worker looks at his job. *Personnel,* 1955, 31, 496-503.

Guest, R. H. Job enlargement–A revolution in job design. *Personnel Administration,* 1957, 20(2), 9-16.

Hoppock, R. *Job satisfaction.* New York: Harper & Row, Publishers, 1935.

Hulin, C. L. Job satisfaction and turnover in a female clerical population. *Journal of Applied Psychology,* 1966, 50, 280-85.

Hulin, C. L., and Smith, P. C. A linear model of job satisfaction. *Journal of Applied Psychology,* 1965, 49, 209-16.

Inlow, G. M. Job satisfaction of liberal arts graduates. *Journal of Applied Psychology,* 1951, 35, 175-81.

Katz, D. Morale and motivation in industry. In W. Dennis (Ed.), *Current trends in industrial psychology.* Pittsburgh: University of Pittsburgh Press, 1949. Pp.145-171.

Katzell, R. A., Barrett, R. S., and Parker, T. C. Job satisfaction, job performance, and situational characteristics. *Journal of Applied Psychology,* 1961, 45, 65-72.

Kendall, L. M. Canonical analysis of job satisfaction and behavioral, personal background, and situational data. Unpublished doctoral dissertation, Cornell University, 1963.

Kennedy, J. E., and O'Neill, H. E. Job content and worker's opinions. *Journal of Applied Psychology,* 1958, 42, 372-75.

Kilbridge, M. D. Do workers prefer larger jobs? *Personnel,* 1960, 37, 45-48. (a)

Kilbridge, M. D. Reduced costs through job enlargement. *Journal of Business* 1960, 33 (10), 357-62. (b)

Kornhauser, A. W. *Mental health of the industrial worker: A Detroit study.* New York: John Wiley & Sons, 1965.

Likert, R. *New patterns of management.* New York: McGraw-Hill Book Company, 1961.

MacGregor, D. M. Adventure in thought and action. In, *Proceedings of the fifth anniversary convocation of the school of industrial management.* Cambridge, Mass.: MIT Press, 1957.

MacKinney, A. C., Wernimont, P. F., and Galitz, W. O. Has specialization reduced job satisfaction? *Personnel,* 1962, 39(1), 8-17.

Mann, F. C. A study of work satisfaction as a function of the discrepancy between inferred aspirations and achievement. Unpublished doctoral disertation, University of Michigan, 1953.

Marks, A. R. N. An investigation of modifications of job design in an industrial situation and their effects on some measures of economic productivity. Unpublished doctoral dissertation, University of California, 1954. (Summarized in L. E. Davis & R. R. Canter, Job design research. *Journal of Industrial Engineering,* 1956, 7(6), 275-82.

Maslow, A. H. A theory of human motivation. *Psychological Review,* 1943, 50, 370-96.

Miller, D. C. Morale of college-trained adults. *American Sociological Review,* 1940, 5, 880-89.

Morse, N. C. *Satisfactions in the white-collar job.* Ann Arbor: University of Michigan, Institute for Social Research, Survey Research Center, 1953.

Porter, L. A study of perceived need satisfactions in bottom and middle management jobs. *Journal of Applied Psychology,* 1961, 45, 232-36.

Reif, W. E., and Schoderbek, P. P. Job enlargement: Antidote to apathy. *Management of Personnel Quarterly,* 1965, 5(1), 16-23.

Roethlisberger, F. J., and Dickson, W. J. *Management and the worker.* Cambridge: Harvard University Press, 1941.

Scott, W. E., Jr. Activation theory and task design. *Organizational Behavior and Human Performance,* 1966, 1, 3-30.

Smith, A. The education of the worker. (Orig. publ. 1776) Reported in A. O. Lewis (Ed.), *Of men and machines,* New York: Dutton, 1963. Pp. 236-39.

Smith, P. C. The curve of output as a criterion of boredom. *Journal of Applied Psychology,* 1953, 37; 69-74.

Smith, P. C. Individual differences in susceptibility to industrial monotony. *Journal of Applied Psychology,* 1955, 39, 322-29.

Smith, P. C., and Lem, C. Positive aspects of motivation in repetitive work: Effects of lot size upon spacing of voluntary rest periods. *Journal of Applied Psychology,* 1955, 39, 330-33.

Turner, A. N., and Lawrence, P. R. *Industrial jobs and the worker: An investigation of response to task attributes.* Boston: Harvard University, Graduate School of Business Administration, 1965.

Turner, A. N., and Miclette, A. L. Sources of satisfaction in repetitive work. *Occupational Psychology,* 1962, 36, 215-31.

Vroom, V. H. *Some personality determinants of the effects of participation.* Englewood Cliffs, N. J.: Prentice-Hall Inc., 1960.

Vroom, V. H. A comparison of static and dynamic correlational methods in the study of organization. *Organizational Behavior and Human Performance,* 1966, 1, 55-70.

Walker, C. R. The problem of the repetitive job. *Harvard Business Review,* 1950, 28 (3), 54-58.

Walker, C. R. Work methods, working conditions, and morale. In A. Kornhauser, R. Dubin, and A. M. Ross (Eds.), *Industrial conflict.* New York: McGraw-Hill Book Company, 1954. Pp. 345-58.

Walker, C. R., and Guest, R. H. *The man on the assembly line.* Cambridge: Harvard University Press, 1952.

Walker, C. R., and Marriott, R. A study of attitudes to factory work. *Occupational Psychology,* 1951, 25, 181-91.

Warren, N. D. Job simplification versus job enlargement. *Journal of Industrial Engineering,* 1958, 9(5), 435-39.

Weitz, J., and Nuckols, R. C. The validity of direct and indirect questions in measuring job satisfaction. *Personnel Psychology,* 1953, 6, 487-94.

Whyte, W. F. *Money and motivation: An analysis of incentives in industry.* New Yorker: Harper, 1955.

Worthy, J. C. Organizational structure and employee morale. *American Sociological Review,* 1950, 15, 169-79.

Wyatt, S., Fraser, J. A., and Stock, F. G. L. The comparative effects of variety and uniformity in work. Report No. 52, 1929, Industrial Fatigue Research Board. (a)

Wyatt, S., Fraser, J. A., and Stock, F. G. L. The effects of monotony in work. Report No. 56, 1929, Industrial Fatigue Research Board. (b)

Wyatt, S., Langdon, J. N., and Stock, F. G. L. Fatigue and boredom in repetitive work. Report No. 77, 1937, Industrial Fatigue Research Board.

chapter **4**

Personality

When an individual enters an organization, he brings with him his own unique ways of interpreting and responding to his environment. The process through which these characteristics evolve may be termed personality development. Why should we be concerned with this process? Why don't we just hire a psychologist to develop a personality test and select people for the organization who have the type of personality we want? The fact that so many people think that the implications of personality for organizations end with selection is itself a strong argument for exploring the concept at some depth.

Even if selection were the only issue, the concept of personality would still be important. First of all, we need to know what characteristics will be most helpful for the jobs we wish to fill now and in the future. We also need to know how to test for these characteristics. Therefore, we require a basic understanding of the characteristics themselves and of personality in general. Unfortunately, a truly adequate, overall concept of personality has not yet been formulated.

So far, we have been considering personality as it exists at one point in time. However, most students of personality would argue that one's personality is subject to constant change. Individuals are influenced by situational factors; they learn new ways and vary their behavior in many of their accustomed roles. Thus, the individual who enters an organization, even though he does bring with him a well-established pattern of responses to his environment, will be significantly influenced by the demands of the new environment. Different demands bring different responses, which may be either strengthened or weakened as a result of their consequences. Different consequences bring changes in self-perception and self-esteem. Thus the concept of personality and the process of personality development have continuing significance for management.

All explanations of personality are based on observations of the behavior of humans and other animals; proponents of the different theories disagree mainly on how the empirical data fit into a unified schema. One need not choose any one theory or set of theories but may use all of them as a basis for insights into himself and others.[1]

1. The reader can find an excellent example of a sophisticated eclectic conceptualization of personality in a paper by Mischel (1973). Mischel observed that students of person-

In the reading that follows, Lazarus summarizes and compares several important personality theories. For present purposes, little need be added to his discussion except for some attention to the definition of personality itself. Perhaps the most widely used definition comes from Gordon Allport (1937), who defined personality as ". . . the dynamic organization within the individual of those psycho-physical systems that determine his unique adjustments to his environment" (p. 48). Lazarus (1963) viewed personality in a similar way, ". . . as an organization of stable structures within a person that dispose him to act in certain ways" (p. 49). These definitions imply some underlying structure which an individual carries with him but also stress the role of the environment in determining or influencing the behavior which will occur. Thus, both the prior experiences in the individual and his current situation become co-determinants of his behavior. It is within this framework that Lazarus, in the following selection, examines the issues of personality theory.

The second selection in this chapter was written by the editor. This paper describes three concepts derived from the study of personality which can help managers to anticipate and diagnose organizational problems.

As you study the concept of personality, you may find it helpful if you keep a central theme of this book in mind. Individuals and organizations are considered as systems which interact with elements of their environments. The outcomes of these interactions are determined in part by the structure of the individual system and the nature of the environment. The behavior of many systems cannot be fully understood through study of either the internal or external properties alone. Rather, since the instrinsic and extrinsic factors affect each other, it is their dynamic interaction which must be studied.

REFERENCES

Allport, G. W. *Personality: A Psychological Interpretation.* New York: Holt, Rinehart and Winston, 1937.

Lazarus, R. S. *Personality and Adjustment.* Englewood Cliffs, N.J.: Prentice-Hall, Inc. 1963.

McGregor, D. *The Human Side of Enterprise.* New York: McGraw-Hill Book Company, 1960.

Mischel, W. Toward a Cognitive Social Learning Reconceptualization of Personality. *Psychological Review,* 80 (1973): 252-83.

---

ality have viewed their subject from one of three basic perspectives. Some scholars have focused primarily on the environmental conditions which influence an individual's behavior. Other writers have been more concerned with properties of the person himself which influence the individual's expectations, values and information processing. A third group of investigators have been most concerned with how an individual reports experiencing environmental events. These investigators take human thoughts, feelings, wishes and other subjective experiences as their major source of data. Mischel was able to integrate information from all three of these approaches through his Cognitive Social Learning model.

Richard S. Lazarus

PERSONALITY THEORY

THEORETICAL FRAMES OF REFERENCE

We must first consider the nature of a psychological event in order to identify some of the frames of reference in which it may be regarded. There are three components of any psychological event. The first is the *stimulus* to which a person responds. The last is his *response.* The other component is made up of the states and activities in the *organism* in between the first and last. We cannot directly observe these states and activities, which are sometimes called mediating structures and processes, but we assume that they intervene between stimulus and response. We have already seen examples of them in the form of motivation and control.

The exact definition of stimulus is a source of controversy. Some hold that we can identify a stimulus only by physical measurements, such as wave lengths of light or decibels of sound. Others hold that we must define a stimulus by the reactions it induces, such as the interpretations a person gives some physical object. The meaning of response is broad: It can include not only obvious actions like reaching for something, but also, what is more difficult to identify, the styles of action. We may include as a response even the internal physiological accompaniments of a psychological event, such as the changes in heart activity or respiration that are associated with emotional states such as fear or anger. Still, in spite of the ambiguity of these terms, psychologists in analyzing psychological events have found it useful to think in terms of stimulus, the intervening structures and processes of the organism, and response.

The S-O-R analysis also turns out to be an excellent way of distinguishing among different frames of reference in personality theory. A frame of reference in itself is not precisely a theory, rather it is the philosophic basis of a theory because it delineates assumptions and emphases. Some theorists, for instance, tend to focus on responses, others on the intervening processes (such as subjective interpretations of stimuli), and still others on the physical qualities of stimuli. Although these variations in assumption and emphasis are not, as we shall see, the only sources of disagreement among persons with differing theoretical orientations, they are fundamental and important. Sometimes, however, several specific theories can be grouped together because they agree in their basic S-O-R frame of reference.

Now we shall examine three frames of reference that diverge with respect to stimulus, organism, and response. The first, trait-and-type, falls on the response side of the S-O-R analysis; the second, the stimulus-response-associative-learning frame of reference, centers around physical stimuli and how habits of response are acquired; finally, the phenomenological approach, which defines the stimulus subjectively—that is, how a person apprehends it—focuses mainly on the intervening structures and processes. All current personality theories may in fact, be subsumed under these three basic frames of reference. Although a given theory may incorporate more than one frame of reference, any theory or part of a theory can be analyzed along these lines.

The Trait-and-Type Frame of Reference

The simplest and most traditional way of describing a person's personality is to identify his consistent patterns of behavior and label them with trait names. Every language contains large numbers of words that define traits of personality. We describe people as shy, aggressive, submissive, lazy, melancholy, easy-going, ambitious, and so on. But what do we mean when we use such terms? And how can this common sense approach to the description of personality become a systematic scientific enterprise?

The Trait Approach. If we observe a person in a variety of situations and note that he always allows someone else to take the initiative in deciding what to do, we have reason to think that this tendency is a consistent part of his personality. We have only to interpret it and to find a term that describes it—say, "submissiveness." If such a descriptive term applies to a person in a wide variety of situations, then we can fairly claim it as a trait. The more consistent the behavior and the more frequent its occurrence in dissimilar situations, the more clearly and importantly characteristic the trait. In the trait approach to personality, then, we identify the most important characteristics in human personality and analyze their organization.

We said earlier that the trait approach is largely oriented to response characteristics. Let us consider how this is so. We know that we identify traits by observing a person behave consistently in response to a variety of stimuli. Thus, to identify a trait we must observe characteristic responses occurring independently of the stimulus context (pattern of stimuli to which the person is exposed). For it is just those responses that are not governed by the stimulus context and therefore recur in a variety of circumstances that define a trait. The trait approach to personality requires, then, that stimuli be held constant or ruled out and that a person's responses be clearly attributes or dispositions that belong to him rather than the situation. To the degree that a trait theorist is interested in forces within personality that determine consistent patterns of behavior, he introduces intervening structures and processes into his system.

* * *

The Type Approach. Personality typologies are built on a response-oriented frame of reference that is very similar to that involved in traits. The difference is that whereas in the latter approach we assign a variety of traits to a person, as in a psychogram, in the type approach we adopt a much broader, unifying scheme of classification, or pigeonholing. The type approach, then, is an extension of the trait approach. By the pattern of his traits we can classify a person. If he shares a trait pattern with a large group of other individuals, we can simplify the description: Instead of listing each trait according to the extent he has it, we use a few categories for characteristic patterns. Thus, we observe that shyness tends to go with other qualities, such as an inclination to be introspective, easily hurt, and so on, and we can identify this grouping of traits by a single inclusive category called introversion. And we can identify a complementary type called extroversion. Having isolated these two categories, we can say that because such-and-such a person has such-and-such traits he is a member of one or the other type.

Just as the vocabulary of traits has existed for thousands of years, so have typologies. The best known typology in ancient Greece was that of Hippocrates, in the fifth century B.C. Conceiving that the body contained four fluids, or humors–yellow bile, black bile, phlegm, and blood–Hippocrates speculated that personality depended on which of these humors predominated in a person's constitution. Thus, yellow bile went with a choleric or irascible temperament, black bile with melancholy, phlegm with the sluggish, apathetic, or phlegmatic person, and blood with the cheerful, active, sanguine personality.

Among the best-known modern typologies of personality is that of Carl Jung, an early associate of Freud. Jung's typology includes two broad categories–the *extrovert,* who is oriented primarily toward others and the external world, and the *introvert,* who is more preoccupied with himself and his subjective world. Extroversion and introversion are expressed in a variety of functions, including thinking, feeling, sensing, and intuiting, so that, in actuality, Jung's typology is more complex than people usually realize. For example, one could be a thinking extrovert, but an introvert in the intuitive function. Another familiar personality typology is that of Freud himself, who conceived of types according to his theory of psychosexual development. In this theory Freud proposed that everyone passes through three infantile psychosexual stages distinguished according to the primary means of sexual gratification. In the oral stage erotic activity centers around the lips and mouth, in the anal stage on bowel activity and the stimulation of the mucous membranes of the anus, and in the phallic stage on the genital organs.

In the course of development some individuals, because of traumatic experiences at one or another stage, fail to progress normally to the next stage. When they are adults, the primitive psychosexual tendencies characteristic of the respective immature stages continue to remain active, governing their personalities and producing characteristic psychological traits. Thus, Freud identified three types: oral, anal, and phallic. The *oral type* is characterized by dependent attitudes toward others. He continues to seek sustenance, or feeding, from others, and, depending on when during the oral stage fixation occurred, is either optimistic, immature, and trusting, or pessimistic, suspicious, and sarcastic, about the prospects of continuing support. The *anal type* is also characterized by two substages, the first identified by outbursts of aggression, sloppiness, and petulance, the second associated with obstinacy, orderliness, and parsimoniousness. The *phallic type* is characterized by an adolescent immaturity in which the predominant conflicts are heterosexual, stemming from the Oedipus complex and the anxieties associated with it. The phallic period is stormy, with sharp emotional swings and preoccupation with love object choices. Adults with severe disturbances in childhood development can be classified into oral, anal, and phallic types according to when the psychosexual disturbance occurred and what types of behavior pattern they display as a result.

There are many other personality typologies. Usually, as with those of Jung and Freud, rather than being merely simple, independent classification schemes of behavior, they are also based on theoretical propositions about the structure, dynamics, and development of personality. The reader should consult the other sources listed at the end of the volume for elaboration of these systems.

From a practical standpoint, the trait-and-type approach is most useful when the pertinent behavior patterns are absolutely consistent—that is, characteristic of a person regardless of circumstances. What limits the usefulness of any trait or type system is the problem of degree of trait generality. The statement that a person has the trait of submissiveness is useful for prediction only insofar as he is submissive in all or most situations. If he is submissive only in certain circumstances, then we can predict his behavior accurately only if we know what those circumstances are.

This puts the finger on the most serious deficiency of the trait-and-type approach to personality, namely, that it largely ignores the dynamic interchange between a person and his environment. For the stimulus context normally limits the manifestations of trait characteristics.

The problem of prediction also suggests the weakness of typologies: They are likely to be so excessively broad that a classification will apply to a person only to a limited degree except in extreme instances. Identifying someone as anal, for example, is useful so long as it permits us to expect such characteristic behavior as obstinacy or orderliness. But few people are so inordinately typical that they are obstinate or orderly in every situation that may arise.

Thus, the trait-and-type approach is limited by focusing exclusively on responses and assuming that personality structures are static properties that can be inferred from consistencies of response, rather than adaptive transactions with the environment. Because of this critical limitation, psychologists have constructed other frames of reference that pay more attention to the stimulus context. Let us now turn to one of these, the stimulus-response-associative-learning approach, and examine how it handles this difficulty in the trait-and-type frame of reference.

Stimulus-Response-Associative-Learning Theory (SRAL)

The central concern of SRAL theorists is the problem of how organisms acquire habits of response. They have traditionally attempted to discover the details of the learning process, to find out how connections are established between stimuli and responses in juxtaposition (association) so that when a given stimulus, or one similar to it, recurs, it will induce the same, or similar, response. In their theories of learning they try to specify *how* these connections are made, strengthened, or broken.

Besides elevating the question of how habits or traits are acquired, the SRAL frame of reference stands on the physical stimulus side of the S-O-R sequence. Instead of being built around correlations among responses as the trait-and-type frame of reference is, associative-learning approaches rest on correlations between physical stimuli and responses.

Although SRAL theorists were originally concerned entirely with principles of learning, some came to recognize that their propositions might have general application to other fields, such as personality. Personality psychologists have, in fact, tended simply to accept the learning process as given, without much concern about its details, even though they usually assume that personality structure develops, in part, through learning. To fill the gap, therefore, learning theoreticians with broad concerns such as Edwin Guthrie in past years and John Dollard and Neal Miller in recent years have attempted to carry associative-learning theory into the realm of personality. But exactly how does personality become established through the learning process?

Dollard and Miller identify four concepts of prime importance in the learning process—drive, response, cue, and reinforcement. *Drive* is what initiates responses. It originates as tissue needs, which, when unsatisfied, produce internal discomforts that lead a person to activities that may or may not satisfy it. *Reinforcement* of a drive is the product of responses that do satisfy the need. Thus, if the need for food produces drive, the response of eating reinforces the hunger drive by fulfilling it and so terminates that behavior sequence. Learning, then, is the establishment of *responses* that reinforce under conditions of drive—that is, responses which reduce or eliminate the drive. Learning also requires the establishment of connections between such responses and certain *cues,* or stimuli, in the environment. Thus, if the reinforcing response is eating, a person must identify those stimuli to which the response is appropriate. These situations may involve the presence of food or environmental circumstances under which food may be found—for instance, a refrigerator can be an appropriate cue for obtaining food. In sum, under conditions of drive, and in the presence of cues, or stimuli, a person makes responses that reinforce the drive, and those responses that do are learned in association with those cues.

In addition to these fundamental factors, Dollard and Miller identify certain other characteristics of learning. The strengthening of connections between certain cues and drive-reinforcing responses implies the converse weakening of other connections and the elimination of inappropriate responses that may have been tried before. This elimination of previously learned responses is called *extinction.* This process is essential to learning, for learning could not take place unless, along with the establishment and strengthening of desired responses, unwanted acts were extinguished.

According to still another principle of SRAL theory, *stimulus generalization,* responses that have been learned in association with one specific cue may be transferred to other similar situations. If we have learned to be afraid of speaking up in one particular social situation, the response of fear is likely to be induced by other social situations as well. The greater the similarity between stimuli, the more the likelihood that a response that has been learned to one stimulus will generalize to the other; and conversely, the less the similarity, the less the likelihood. Since no two situations are ever precisely the same, consistency of behavior would never occur without stimulus generalization. The perception of stimulus similarity, it is generally thought, is based on the physical features of the stimuli. But actually specifying which physical quality is critical remains one of the most perplexing unsolved problems in learning theory, since we can respond similarly to stimuli on the basis of many physical dimensions. The cues of similarity to which a person responds or fails to respond are difficult, if not impossible, to predict without a knowledge of intervening structures and processes.

If responses learned to one stimulus tended to generalize indiscriminately to others, learning could not occur, since the same response could then be made to all. For adaptive behavior to develop, a person must learn to distinguish among stimuli so that he makes reinforcing responses to the correct one. To give a concrete example, he must learn to differentiate a refrigerator that contains food from a cabinet that contains material incapable of reducing his hunger drive. The process by which we differentiate appropriate from inappropriate cues is called *discrimination.* Just as stimulus generalization is required in order for a person to spread a given response to all members of a class of appropriate cues, so discrimination is required to permit him to select the proper class of cues that will produce drive reduction.

Finally, through *anticipation,* another process postulated by associative-learning theory, we identify the probable consequences of a stimulus or response; thereby we can learn to perform actions that will reduce a drive in the future and to avoid those that will have painful or dangerous consequences. Anticipation, which involves making a response earlier than it would normally occur, helps the individual react appropriately to an impending situation about which he has been alerted.

According to SRAL theory, complex social motives, such as the desire to achieve or to be liked, are learned in the same way as any other simpler type of response, such as tying a shoe or hitting a typewriter key. Rewards can also be learned. Thus, we learn to accept expressions of approval as rewards because the approval has become associated in childhood with the reinforcement, by parents or other adults, of primary drives like hunger and thirst. In other words, we have learned that approval is connected with desirable consequences even though social approval itself originally had no intrinsic value.

According to the principles of learning briefly sketched above, it is plain that we can learn complex patterns of response, including neurotic symptoms, such as phobias and hysterical paralyses characteristic of certain types of neurotic disorder as well as the defense mechanisms connected with these disorders. Defense mechanisms as responses—although they are maladjustments in the sense that, in using them, we distort reality in our perceptions and judgments—do reduce the drives of anxiety and fear. Clearly, then, any characteristic of personality–motives, control processes, defense mechanisms, and so on–is learned according to the same set of laws specified by learning theorists.

For *our* analysis of frames of reference, the important feature of SRAL theory is its emphasis on the physical stimulus. The point is that from this position the stimulus to a behavioral act can be defined in terms of physical dimensions (such as wave lengths, shape, weight, size, and distance) and completely independently of the person behaving–that is, responding. And since it is these objective characteristics to which the person presumably responds, we can construct behavioral laws by separately identifying the physical characteristics of environmental stimuli and the characteristics of responses made in association with these stimuli. The basic unit of description is the stimulus-response connection.

It is a direct attack on this emphasis on the physical stimulus that identifies the phenomenological point of view, the third major frame of reference in personality theory.

Personality from a Phenomenological Point of View

For a theorist in the phenomenological camp, defining a stimulus physically immediately poses a problem, namely, that our perception of objects is not necessarily identical with the objects themselves. Our senses do not directly transmit physical objects. Rather, we respond to representations of objects–that is, objects as mediated by our perceptual apparatuses and by our individual interpretations. In an effort to articulate the distinction, psychologists interested in perception have termed the physical object itself the "distal stimulus," and the the object as mediated by intervening mechanisms the "proximal stimulus." The phenomenologist argues that what determine responses are not physical objects themselves but the intervening structures and processes within a person that mediate the physical stimuli. He reconstructs the causes of action through inferences about these psychological representations of external stimuli. Thus, in phenomenological approaches to personality the stimulus in the S-O-R analysis is still significant, but as a psychological representation within a person, not as an external physical condition. Here the emphasis is on the O, and the psychological representation of a physical stimulus may deviate sharply from physical reality.

The essence of the phenomenological frame of reference to personality is this: The cause of action is the world as a person apprehends it privately. This privately apprehended world is the core construct of the theoretical systems of such phenomenologists as Kurt Lewin and Carl Rogers. In Lewin's system the term employed for the construct is *life space,* in Rogers' it is *phenomenal field.*

For Lewin the psychological representation of the world (the life space) consists of the person's needs and the potentialities of action available, as he apprehends them. Every aspect of a person's physical environment that is not part of the life space and to which he does not directly respond is the "foreign hull" of the life space. To understand his behavior at any point in time we must reconstruct and describe the life space, which means that we must understand the psychological forces in operation at that moment.

These forces are described by a Lewinian graphically in diagrams that include: goal regions (shown as enclosed places); positive and negative valences (designated by plus or minus signs), which identify desirable or undesirable aspects of the life space; vectors (arrows), which point out the directions to which a person is pulled; and barriers (lines separating the person from positive goals), which block or slow down a person's approach to any goal region. Many forces may affect the person, and his behavior at any time is a resultant of them. Not only can the total psychological field (called the life space) be thus represented diagrammatically, but the structure of the individual personality can also be diagrammed. . . .

The important elements in the Lewinian system are these: Psychological events are considered in terms of the construct of life space, which comprises subjective definitions of the environment, and some of the psychodynamic laws that pertain to it are identified diagrammatically. The system makes use of both motivational and cognitive structures in continual interplay. Inferences about a person's life space are always derived from systematic observation of his behavior in his environment. Yet the terms of the analysis of behavior and setting are not static traits and stationary objects but the person's own subjective apprehension of his environment and his relationship to it.

In contrast with Lewin's brand of phenomenology is the self theory of Rogers, whose concepts are also couched in the language of subjective experience (for example, what we want and how we think and feel). The Rogerian concept that is analogous to life space is phenomenal field, and the core (or most important aspect) of that field is the *self-concept* of the individual, that is, his notion of who he is in relation to his environment. It is this self-concept that determines his behavior. This phenomenal self is, for a person himself, reality. He does not respond to the objective environment but to what he perceives it to be, regardless of how distorted or personalized his perception may be. These subjective realities are tentative hypotheses that a person entertains about environmental situations.

Thus, one person will conceive of himself as a reformer with the mission of correcting certain worldly ills and helping others to "see the light." Another will view himself as a "realist," able to accept gracefully, and even benefit from the weaknesses of human nature and man's social institutions. Self-concepts are complex and variable and they determine how persons will react to and deal with a wide variety of situations. These conceptions of who and what one is not only comprise central values and belief systems, but also include images of oneself as physically strong or weak, attractive or unattractive, popular or unpopular, and so on, based partly on the reflected appraisals of other people with whom one has had contact. According to self theorists, this differentiated portion of the phenomenal field, the self-concept, determines all behavior. And most behavior, indeed, is organized around efforts to preserve and enhance this phenomenal self.

While Lewin goes about the task of reconstructing a person's life space, with its multiplicity of psychological forces, from observing how he acts in different situations, Rogers identifies the self-concept largely from introspection. That is, a Rogerian learns about someone's self-system by listening to his introspective report about himself and his perceptions of the world. Lewin systematically observed behavior in various naturalistic and experimental situations, but Rogers developed his theoretical constructions primarily from psychotherapy. He argued that to the degree that he could provide an environment of permissiveness and support, a patient's reports would validly reflect his whole phenomenal field and his narrower self-concept.

Regardless of the exact form of the phenomenological system, however, it is clear that it shifts theoretical attention from the physical stimulus itself to the way a person apprehends it and, therefore, to the properties of the person that mediate between the physical stimulus and behavior. Thus, to recapitulate, although trait-and-type theory is response-centered and associative-learning theory is stimulus-response-centered, phenomenological theory revolves around the properties of the person that intervene between the stimulus and the behavioral response.

All theories of personality are variations of one sort or another of the three main frames of reference derived from the stimulus, organism, and response sequence. Some theories, as we have seen, are in the main anchored to one or another of these three points of view. Other systems, such as that of Freud, are mixtures, in that they draw on features of all three frames of reference. For example, psychoanalysis contains features of the trait-and-type approach, yet its essential character does not fall in that category. The point to remember is that the frames of reference described do not specify individual theoretical systems, but rather orientations or emphases that vary among them.

* * *

Walter R. Nord

PERSONALITY AND ORGANIZATIONS[1]

Of the many concepts employed in the study of personality, three are especially important for understanding behavior of people in organizations. First, *psychological defense* is a term which helps a manager understand responses, of both himself and others, to psychological threat. The notion of self-concept is valuable as an aid to understanding how people see themselves and the consequences of attacks on this perception. Finally, in considering personality change,

[1] The personality vs. organization issue is treated in part 2.

a manager will obtain ideas which will help him to understand the relationship of the organizational context to personality and personnel development.

PSYCHOLOGICAL DEFENSE

Freud noted that the perception of threats produces anxiety. Typically, people attempt to defend themselves from anxiety by distorting, falsifying, or even denying reality. To the organizational observer, such behavior appears to be irrational. While these defenses do not directly help the individual to deal with external reality, they are adaptive, since they maintain the internal tension at a manageable level.

Most textbooks in introductory psychology include an extensive list of defense mechanisms. One commonly listed ego defense is *repression,* by which threatening information is forced out of consciousness without awareness. Another common defense, known as *projection,* is the attribution of one's own problems or motives to someone else. The third defense, called *denial,* is the failure to acknowledge that certain threats or feelings exist. There are many more defense mechanisms; most people employ a variety, though they tend to favor one defense or another as characteristic of themselves. In addition, the more intense the anxiety or threat experienced by the individual, the more likely it becomes that these defenses will play an important part in much of his behavior.[2] These defenses create problems for human interaction because they often seem irrational. Commonly, would-be helpers attempt to give aid on the rational level or respond with defenses of their own. Success is seldom achieved, and greater tensions often result.

Perhaps no psychological concept has more importance for administrators than psychological defense. Ideas and actions that appear to be rational and quite functional from the manager's point of view are often perceived as threats by other members of the organization. These participants attempt to reduce their anxiety through some type of ego defense. The manager often responds in turn by accusing the participants of being irrational. As a result, without realizing what he has done, the manager often increases the amount of anxiety and the operation of defense mechanisms. Of course, not all opposition to management actions takes the form of a psychological defense; however, much opposition may well do so. An understanding of personality theory may contribute to better management by providing means of anticipating, recognizing, and preventing the operation of costly defenses.

SELF-CONCEPT

A second major contribution of personality theory is the idea of self-concept, the individual's view of himself. The self-concept often takes the form of the "good me," the "bad me," and the "not me." The "good me" includes things about me for which I have been rewarded, the "bad me" includes things for

[2] This direct relation is probable at least within some range, until perhaps bodily harm or survival is involved.

which I have been punished, and the "not me" includes those things which are not part of me.

More recently, the self-concept has been applied to personality in some creative ways. For example, Rotter (1966) suggested that some people see themselves as able to control their environment (internal control), while others see themselves as controlled by the environment (external control). De Charms (1968) has developed a similar notion in distinguishing between "origins," those who can be expected to initiate change in the world, and "pawns," who are more apt to accept things as they are. These concepts, suggesting important differences in how people react to their surroundings, have important implications for selection and training in organizations.

Goffman (1967) has argued that the self-concept has important sociological as well as psychological importance. He noted that society sanctions elaborate rituals of behavior patterns which enable people to save face. For example, individuals employ jokes, politeness, and other ceremonies to prevent social offenses. Furthermore, people avoid discussing certain topics and avoid noticing or calling attention to certain embarrassing behaviors in order to allow others to maintain their role or the self which they expect to maintain. Thus, social mechanisms exist to protect the self-concept of individuals. These mechanisms may serve important social functions. Nevertheless, attempts to maintain self-esteem can also have negative consequences for organizations.

Bennis, Schein, Steele, and Berlew (1968) suggest that attempts to maintain self-esteem lead to three sets of outcomes which may be dysfunctional for organizations. First, people respond to threats to self-esteem by trying to hide those parts of themselves which they feel are less than totally acceptable. Secondly, attempts to maintain self-esteem lead individuals to pretend to be something that they are not. Finally, efforts to maintain self-esteem often result in cautious and ritualized behavior. Organizations which expect creative, innovative behavior may find they encourage caution instead by inadvertently threatening individuals.

An example of these consequences is found in the case of an organizational merger. The details of the problems in the merger of a company manufacturing high-status, expensive furniture with a company producing relatively inexpensive furniture were reported by Nord (1968). The workers from the former plant viewed themselves as craftsmen. They had been accustomed to working on prestigious furniture and making each piece individually in the manner of a traditional craft. One of the consequences of the merger was that these men were put on an assembly-line operation. Many workers expressed the feeling that they had lost a great deal of status. One worker commented that management had cheapened the furniture, and another mentioned that he had felt like a craftsman before but now was working on a job which required very little skill. Even the lower-skilled workers empathized with the threat to self-esteem felt by the more skilled group. Although this loss of status and esteem was not the sole cause of problems in the merger, it appeared to be an important contributing factor.

In general, people respond to threats to their self-concept in much the same way that they might respond to other psychological threats. An important variable for managers to consider is the way people think of themselves. Changes which threaten a person's perception of himself or of a group to which he belongs can produce defensive reactions. The manager's own self-perception, of course, is also of great import. His defenses may produce behavior which appears irrational to his subordinates and other co-workers; the result may be costly for the functioning of the organization.

THE SOCIAL NATURE OF PERSONALITY AND CHANGE

A third contribution of personality theory to management is derived from the social nature of personality and personality change. Kurt Lewin's description of the process of personal change as "unfreezing," "changing," and "refreezing," is especially important in recent thinking. Lewin hypothesized that, for change to occur, some forces had to be introduced that would encourage the individual to *want* a change. Then other forces were needed to produce the change. Finally, after the change had occurred, support was required for maintenance of the new behavior. This "refreezing" process is often neglected, because the social factors in change are not considered. Lewin's work, however, stressed the social environment which surrounds the change.

Often, personality and personality change are, to an important degree, interpersonal or social processes. Other people are important sources of an individual's identity and self-concept. It is widely recognized that other people's approval can have substantial effects on individual behavior. Many studies have demonstrated the pressures for conformity which a group can exert. Other studies have shown that an individual will seek out others for support of his own views or for definition of his own position by comparison with others. In addition, the particular features a person exhibits depend on others. Robert Tannenbaum has conceptualized this process through a "hooking" metaphor. He suggests that people have various facets of personality which are "hooked" or drawn out by certain facets of the personality of others.[3] Thus, a person is in part a product of the characteristics of those around him. Other people become a potential source of individual growth rather than conformity or inhibition. In any case, personality is in part a function of interpersonal relationships rather than a set of character traits.

Two important implications for organizational management stem from this perspective on personality: First, because the development and maintenance of individual behavior depends on other people, personality is not fixed. Second, attempts to change individuals require attention to the existing social environment, not just to individual behavior patterns in isolation. Selection procedures, training programs, and management policies that consider only the individual are doomed to very limited success.

[3] This model was presented by Robert Tannenbaum in an informal talk at an organizational development training group at UCLA in July, 1970.

REFERENCES

Bennis, W. G.; Schein, E. H.; Steele, F. I.; and Berlew, D. E. *Interpersonal Dynamics.* Homewood, Ill.: Dorsey Press, 1968.

DeCharms, R. *Personal Causation.* New York: Academic Press, 1968.

Goffman, E. *Interaction Ritual.* New York: Doubleday & Company, 1967.

Lazarus, R. S. *Personality and Adjustment.* Englewood Cliffs, N.J.: Prentice-Hall, Inc., 1963.

Nord, W. "Individual and Organizational Conflict in an Industrial Merger." In *Proceedings of the 11th Midwest Management Conference.* Pp. 50-66. Madison, Wisc.: Academy of Management, 1968.

Rotter, J. B. "Generalized Expectancies for Internal versus External Control of Reinforcement." *Psychological Monographs* 80 (1, whole no. 609), 1966.

chapter **5**

Learning and Behavior Change

Although there is no universally accepted definition of learning, most theorists would agree that learning involves actual and/or potential changes in behavior which result from the interaction of an individual with his environment. Generally, changes that result from fatigue and maturation are excluded.

Major differences within the field of learning occur over the basic question of how people learn to come to terms with their environment. Many psychologists rely heavily on conditioning processes, using the notion of reinforcement or reward and punishment as the explanation for behavior change. In this view, people learn by being rewarded or punished for their behavior. Another group of psychologists relies heavily on the mental apparatus of man to explain learning. These cognitive theorists employ inferred mental processes to explain changes in individual thought and behavior.

These are certainly not the only approaches to learning, but they do provide contrasting ways of understanding the issues on which major theories of learning diverge. The first selection in this section, by Bigge, highlights these contrasts by comparing conditioning and insight theories of learning.

Bigge's paper provides a theoretical background for the final two selections in this chapter. The first of these, by Nord, describes the potential value of conditioning procedures to the management of organizations. The next paper, by Gamboa and Petrock, is more balanced, in that these authors give more attention to cognitive perspectives by describing expectancy theory and comparing it with the conditioning approach. The expectancy approach directs our attention to the relationship between external events and psychological states of the individual. By contrast, the operant conditioning approach deals only with behavior and makes no assumptions about internal states.

Morris L. Bigge

DESCRIBING THE LEARNING PROCESS

WHAT ARE THE TWO MAJOR CONTEMPORARY VERSIONS OF THE NATURE OF LEARNING?

Whereas contemporary S-R associationists–the neobehaviorists–conceive of learning as *conditioning* or *reinforcement,* Gestalt-field psychologists think of it as *development of insight.*

Is learning conditioning-reinforcement?

In the eyes of neobehaviorists, learning is more or less permanent change of behavior which occurs as a result of practice. Thus, the learning process consists of impressions of new reaction patterns on pliable, passive organisms. Since learning arises, in some way, from an interplay of organisms and their environments, the key concepts of neobehaviorists are *stimulus* (that excitement which is provided by an environment) and *response* (that reaction which is made by an organism). Consequently, the problem of the nature of the learning process is centered in a study of the relationships of processions of stimuli and responses and what occurs between them. Since the focus always is upon behavior, in practical application, a neobehavioristically oriented teacher strives to change behaviors of his students in the desired direction by providing the right stimuli at the proper time.

Neobehaviorists use "conditioning" or "reinforcement" to describe the learning process as they understand and interpret it. "Conditioning" is so called because it results in formation of conditioned responses. A conditioned response is a response which is associated with, or evoked by, a new–conditioned–stimulus. Conditioning implies a principle of adhesion; one stimulus or response is attached to another stimulus or response so that revival of the first evokes the second.

Reinforcement is a special kind or aspect of conditioning within which the tendency for a stimulus to evoke a response on subsequent occasions is increased by reduction of a *need* or a *drive stimulus.* A "need," as used here, is an objective, biological requirement of an organism which must be met if the organism is to survive and grow. Examples of needs are an organism's requirement for food, sex, or escape from pain. A "drive stimulus" is an aroused state of an organism. It is closely related to the need which sets the organism into action, and may be defined as a strong, persistent stimulus which demands an adjustive response. When an organism is deprived of satisfaction of a need, drive stimuli occur.

What are the possible kinds of conditioning?

There are two kinds of positive conditioning–*classical* and *instrumental*–and a negative conditioning process–*extinction.* Through classical and instrumental conditioning, an organism *gains* responses or habits; through extinction it *loses* them.

Classical Conditioning. Classical conditioning usually is associated with such incidents as Pavlov's teaching a dog to salivate at the ringing of a bell; it is *stimulus substitution.* In Pavlov's conditioning experiment, the sound of a bell occurred prior to, or simultaneously with, the dog's salivation, which was caused by the presence of food. Then in the future the dog salivated at the ringing of the bell, even when the food was not present.

In classical conditioning a new stimulus is presented along with an already adequate, unconditioned stimulus–such as the smell of food–and just prior to the response, which is evoked by the unconditioned stimulus. The new stimulus becomes the conditioned stimulus, and the response which follows both stimuli becomes the conditioned response. Thus, in classical conditioning, an organism learns to respond to a new stimulus in the same, or similar, way it responds to the old, unconditioned stimulus. In Pavlov's experiment, the sound of the bell became the new, conditioned stimulus which evoked the old, unconditioned response–salivation. Then, salivation was a conditioned response.

Classically conditioned learning is revealed in the behavior of an organism by the increasing capacity of a previously neutral stimulus, with successive training trials to evoke a response which originally was evoked by some other (unconditioned) stimulus. A "neutral stimulus" is one whose first occurrence does nothing toward evoking or reinforcing the response which is under study.

Instrumental Conditioning. Just as classical conditioning theory derives from the early work of Pavlov, instrumental conditioning theory has emerged from the foundation built by Thorndike. Instrumental conditioning usually is equated with reinforcement; it is response modification or change. An animal first makes a response, then receives a "reward"; the response is instrumental in bringing about its reinforcement. There is a *feedback* from the "rewarding" stimulus which follows the response that the organism is learning; a dog is fed after he "speaks" and, thereby, the likelihood of his "speaking" in the future is increased.

Extinction. Extinction is the process whereby an organism gradually loses a response or habit through repeating the response a number of times while no reinforcing stimulus accompanies it. Any habits gained through either classical or instrumental conditioning may be lost through extinction.

How does reinforcement occur?

Neobehaviorists, who emphasize the importance of reinforcement in learning, assume that some psychological conclusions are fairly well established: (1) patterns of action and expectation develop through an organism's responses to repeated stimuli accompanied by "fumble and success" type of trial and error learning under conditions of positive or negative reinforcement; (2) reinforcement occurs through satisfaction of either basic biological needs like hunger or sex, or secondary needs such as a need for security, recognition, or aesthetic gratification; and (3) educational encouragement must take the form of positive and negative reinforcers. A positive reinforcer is a stimulus which strengthens a behavior; a negative one is a stimulus whose withdrawal strengthens a behavior. Note that negative reinforcement, psychologically, is different from punishment.

Primary Reinforcement. Reinforcement may be either *primary* or *secondary*. Primary reinforcement strengthens a certain behavior through the satisfaction of a basic biological need or drive. Secondary reinforcement sometimes is called high-order reinforcement. The reinforcers of secondary or high-order reinforcement have acquired their power of reinforcement indirectly through learning; poker chips for which a chimpanzee will work and money for which man will do almost anything are secondary reinforcers.

The drive reduction sequence of primary reinforcement proceeds as follows: (1) deprivation of satisfaction of a basic requirement, such as that for food, produces a state of need in an organism, (2) the need expresses itself as a tension state or drive stimulus which energizes the organism into action (a food-deprived animal shows the restless activity whose manifestation is called the hunger drive), (3) the activity achieves satisfaction of the need and relieves the tension state, and (4) the form of the activity which immediately preceded the satisfaction of the need or reduction of the drive is reinforced.

Within a drive reduction sequence, a response is closely associated with a drive stimulus and the stimulus-response conjunction is associated with a rapid decrease in the drive produced stimuli—hunger pangs. Thus the response is reinforced; the tendency for hunger to evoke it is increased. This, supposedly, is how we learn to like our various kinds of food.

Secondary Reinforcement. Secondary reinforcement is reinforcement which is brought about by occurrence of an originally neutral stimulus. When a neutral stimulus such as a sound or light is repeatedly paired with food in the presence of a food-deprived (hungry) animal, the formerly neutral stimulus becomes a secondary, conditioned reinforcer. Thus, secondary reinforcement results when originally neutral stimuli become closely associated with primary reinforcing stimuli and thereby become effective in reducing needs. In this way, neutral stimuli acquire the power of acting as reinforcing agents; a chimpanzee learns to accept poker chips as a "reward" just as readily as he accepts food. Consequently, actions of the chimpanzee are reinforced by his receiving poker chips when he performs them; this is secondary reinforcement.

How may we group S-R associationists?

On the basis of their position in regard to the associationistic nature of learning, we may divide neobehaviorists into three groups. One group makes conditioning the heart of the learning process but holds that reinforcement is not necessary for conditioning to occur. A second group is committed to reinforcement or law of effect theories. The third group consists of two-factor theorists who contend that there are two basically different learning processes—conditioning independent of reinforcement and conditioning governed by principles of reinforcement.

Edwin R. Guthrie's *contiguous conditioning* is most representative of the first—conditioning, nonreinforcement—group. The names of Clark L. Hull (1884-1952) and B. F. Skinner are most often associated with the *reinforcement* group. However, Hull and Skinner have differed sharply in regard to the nature of the reinforcement process. Three prominent *two-factor psychologies* are those of Kenneth W. Spence (1907-), Edward C. Tolman (1886-1959), and O. H. Mowrer (1907-). Hence, four representative neobehaviorisms are Guthrie's *contiguous conditioning,* Hull's *deductive behaviorism or reinforcement theory,* Skinner's *operant conditioning,* and Spence's *quantitative S-R theory.* All four are alike in their emphasis upon a mechanical treatment of stimuli and responses. They agree that at no time is purposiveness to be assumed. Problems of "purposes" must be explained by natural laws or principles whereby organisms mechanically develop "purposes." However, they differ in their interpretations of stimulus-response relationships in learning procedures. Guthrie is convinced that learning occurs when a stimulus and a response happen simultaneously; Hull centered the essence of learning in what occurs between the stimulus and the response; and Skinner places his emphasis upon the stimulus which follows a response. When we express these serial relationships symbolically, using S for stimulus, R for response, and O for organism, Guthrie holds to an S-R, Hull to an S-O-R, and Skinner to an R-S learning theory. Since Spence incorporates both contiguity and reinforcement into his theory, it cannot be categorized in this way.

Although there are clear-cut psychological theories of learning, neobehaviorists in education tend not to adhere rigidly to any one of the S-R patterns but to intermix them in applying psychology to teaching procedures. In this way they attempt to achieve an integration of the earlier works of Pavlov, Watson, and Thorndike with that of contemporary associationists. . . . Let us now examine very briefly three representative, systematic neobehavioristic theories of learning and see how each would color teaching procedures in a school learning situation.

Guthrie's Contiguous Conditioning. Guthrie's learning theory is classical conditioning, not reinforcement. Furthermore, it is a special kind of conditioning which we may identify as *simultaneous contiguous conditioning. Contiguity* means that stimuli acting *at the time* of a response, on their recurrence, tend to evoke that response. Furthermore, if a stimulus occurs contiguously with a response, the response to that stimulus will continue to occur with it until some other response becomes conditioned to that stimulus.

Strengthening of individual connections of stimuli and response—the actual conditioning—supposedly takes place with a single simultaneous occurrence of a stimulus and response. This does not mean that repetition has no place in learning, but that within repetition an increasing number of stimuli are made into conditioners; there is no strengthening of individual connections, but there is enlistment of more.

Guthrie thinks that, since association can occur with one connection and last for life, there is no need for anything like reward, pleasure, or need reduction to explain learning. Thus, there is no place for reinforcement in his contiguity theory. To Guthrie, scientific laws deal with observable phenomena only. In psychology these are physical stimuli, and responses in the form of contractions of muscles and secretions of glands, but there is no place for hypothetical intervening variables between stimuli and responses. We only need to know that "... a combination of stimuli which has accompanied a movement will on its recurrence tend to be followed by that movement."[1]

A proponent of contiguous conditioning in teaching people first gets them to perform in a certain way, then while they are doing so gives them the stimuli which he wants associated with that behavior. To teach that man is *Homo sapiens,* a Guthriean would induce his student to say *Homo sapiens* and while he was saying it stimulate him with *man* either spelled out, pictured, or both. The more "man" stimuli he could give the student while he was saying *Homo sapiens* the better it would be. In this teaching-learning process *man* is the conditioned stimulus and *Homo sapiens* is the conditioned response.

Hull's Reinforcement Theory. Hull's learning theory also is stimulus-response conditioning, but of a special kind, called *reinforcement.* In presenting his theory of learning Hull stated,

> Whenever a reaction (R) takes place in temporal contiguity with an afferent receptor impulse (s) resulting from the impact upon a receptor of a stimulus energy (S) and this conjunction is followed closely by the diminution in a need (and the associated diminution in the drive, D, and in the drive receptor discharge, s_D), there will result an increment Δ ($s \rightarrow R$), in the tendency for that stimulus on subsequent occasions to evoke that reaction.[2]

Within Hullian reinforcement, the stimulus and the response are not simultaneous; the stimulus precedes the response. Furthermore, learning does not take place with a single trial; it is stamped in through a process of repeated need or drive stimulus reductions.

Hull thought that learning occurs through biological adaptation of an organism to its environment in a way to promote survival. A state of need means

[1] Edwin R. Guthrie, *The Psychology of Learning,* rev. ed. (New York: Harper & Row, Publishers, 1952), p. 23.

[2] Clark L. Hull, *Principles of Behavior* (New York: Appleton-Century-Crofts, 1943), p. 71.

that survival of the organism is not being adequately served. Drive is a general condition of organic privation arising from lack of food, water, or air, from unhealthful temperatures, from tissue injury, from sex-linked conditions, or from other deficiencies. When needs or drive stimuli develop, the organism acts and the action brings reduction in needs or drive stimuli. Actions–responses–which lead to reduction of needs or drive stimuli are reinforced; thus reinforcement is centered in adaptation for survival. However, in life situations there are many reinforcers which do not contribute directly to biological adaptation of an organism. Through higher-order conditioning many things and actions come to have value and can serve as reinforcers. Higher-order conditioning is conditioning based upon previous conditioning; it more often is called secondary conditioning . . . .

A child is conditioned to think–say to himself "man" when he sees a man or a picture of a man. This conditioning could have been based upon reduction of drive stimuli. Perhaps he wanted a piece of candy and his parents withheld it from him until he said "man." Now, in ninth grade, "stimulus man" evokes *Homo sapiens,* perhaps through the satisfaction of curiosity, and curiosity is a product of higher-order conditioning; the youth previously had been conditioned to be curious.

Skinner's Operant, Instrumental Conditioning. The unique feature of operant conditioning is that the reinforcing stimulus occurs not simultaneously with or preceding the response but following the response. In operant conditioning, an organism must first make the desired response and then a "reward" is provided. The reward reinforces the response–makes it more likely to recur. The response is instrumental in bringing about its reinforcement. The essence of learning is not stimulus substitution but response modification. In learning, there is a feedback from the reinforcing stimulus to the previous response. To illustrate, in the training of pets a desired response is reinforced after it occurs–a dog is fed after it "speaks," and this increased the likelihood of its "speaking" in the future.

Note that in operant conditioning the stimulus which produced the response in the first place is not in any way involved in the learning process. The original response is a result of a stimulus, but the nature of this stimulation is irrelevant to operant conditioning. It is only necessary that some–any–stimulus elicit the response for operant conditioning to function. Emphasis is on reinforcing agents, not on original causative factors.

An operant-reinforcement approach to teaching a ninth-grader that man is *Homo sapiens* would be to show the student *man* along with several other more complicated words, one of which is *Homo sapiens.* If the student chooses *"non sequitur,"* or any expression other than *Homo sapiens,* nothing happens. If he chooses *"homo sapiens,"* the teacher says "wonderful." This is reinforcement, and they proceed to a new "problem."

Within neobehaviorism, learning is nonpurposive habit formation. Habits are formed through conditioning, which attaches desired responses to specific stimuli. A stimulus triggers an action or response, which can take only one form because of the nature of the stimulus, the condition of the organism, and the "laws of learning" involved. Teachers who adopt this mechanistic approach to learning decide specifically what behaviors they want their students, when finished products, to manifest, and they proceed to stimulate them in such a way as to evoke and fix those behaviors.

Is learning development of insight?

The key word of Gestalt-field psychologists in describing learning is *insight.* They regard learning as a process of developing new insights or modifying old ones. Insights occur when an individual, in pursuing his purposes, sees new ways of utilizing elements of his environment, including his own bodily structure. The noun *learning* connotes the new insights—or meanings—which are acquired.

Gestalt-field theorists attack two weaknesses in the theory that learning is conditioning: (1) the attempt of S-R associationists to explain complex interrelated organizations in terms of simpler elements, that is, to insist that learning consists of an accumulation of individual conditioned responses, each relatively simple in itself, but eventuating in a complicated pattern of habits; and (2) the tendency of S-R associationists to attribute learning to reduction of basic organic drives.

Gestalt-field psychologists view learning as a purposive, explorative, imaginative, and creative enterprise. This conception breaks completely with the idea that learning consists of linking one thing to another according to certain principles of association. Instead, the learning process is identified with thought or conceptualization; it is a nonmechanical development or change of insight.

S-R associationists also sometimes use the term *insight,* but when they do they mean something quite different from what a Gestalt-field theorist means. When used by associationists, the term describes a special and rare kind of learning. To use Woodworth's definition, insight is ". . . some penetration into the [absolutely] true nature of things."[3] But to Woodworth and other associationists, the ordinary form which learning takes is conditioning. The most systematic of the associationists would deny that there can be two entirely different kinds of learning; therefore they prefer to describe *all* learning as conditioning. Since insight obviously implies something very different from conditioning, many associationists do not use the term at all. To them it connotes something intuitive and mystical, something which cannot be described operationally. In contrast, Gestalt-field psychologists do not like to use the term *conditioning;* they regard *development of insight* as the most descriptive phrase available to describe the manner in which learning actually takes place.

The Gestalt-field definition of insight is a sense of, or feeling for, pattern or relationships. To state it differently, insight is the "sensed way through" or "solution" of a problematic situation. Insights often first appear as vague "hunches." We might say that an insight is a kind of "feel" we get about a situation which permits us to continue actively serving our purposes, or trying

[3] R. S. Woodworth, *Psychology* (New York: Holt, Rinehart & Winston, Inc., 1940), pp. 299-300.

to. When are insights verbalized? Perhaps at once; perhaps never. We probably know many things which we never manage to put into words. This is a problem on which animal experimentation sheds some light. Animals below man cannot talk; they can communicate, but not by putting sounds together in coherent subject-predicate sentences. Yet the evidence indicates beyond much doubt that they learn insightfully when confronted with what to them are problems.

If we define *hypothesis* broadly, we may refer to insights as hypotheses. However, a hypothesis usually is defined as a special kind of verbalized insight. It is a statement which takes the form of a declarative sentence, or in many cases an "if-then" sentence. For example, one might say, "Most redheaded girls have violent tempers" (a declarative statement), or one might say, "If most redheaded girls reach a certain frustration level, they then display a violent temper" (an if-then statement). Hypotheses, defined as verbal statements, are the only kind of insight which we can test in a strictly scientific fashion.

This brings us to a crucial question: Are insights necessarily true? Gestalt-field psychologists do not use the term "insights" in a way to imply that they are necessarily true. Granted, the term sometimes is used this way by others–Woodworth, for one. . . . But the relativistic orientation of Gestalt-field theorists necessarily leads them to think of insights as trial answers which may or may not help a person toward his goal; they may or may not be true. Truth, relativistically defined, "is that quality of an insight which enables its possessor to design behavior which is successful in that it achieves what it is designed to achieve."[4] Insights derive from a person's best interpretations of what comes to him; they may be deeply discerning or they may not. They may serve as dependable guides for action or they may prove ruinous. Sultan, one of Köhler's chimpanzees, held a box in the air beneath a hanging banana. He then suddenly released his hold on the box and attempted to jump on it to reach the food. Sultan had an insight, but not a true one.

Insights are to be considered, not as literal descriptions of objective physical-social situations, but as interpretations of one's perceived environment on the basis of which subsequent action can be designed. Although insights are not physicalistic descriptions of objects or processes in the environment, they necessarily take account of the physical environment. Their usability depends in part on how well this is done. Insights may misinterpret a physical environment so badly that they are useless as rules of action, in which case they are to be regarded as false.

It is important to understand that insights are always a learner's own. It is true, of course, that they may become his own through adoption. An insight is usable to a learner only if he can "fit it in." He must understand its significance–for him. A teacher cannot give an insight to a student as we serve a person meat on a platter. He may acquaint students with his insights, but they do not become insights for students until students see their meaning for themselves and adopt them as their own.

[4] Ernest E. Bayles, *Democratic Educational Theory* (New York: Harper & Row, Publishers, 1960), p. 80.

One objection frequently raised to the Gestalt-field tendency to construe all learning as insightful is that some learning tasks are performed successfully without apparent development of insight—as, for example, when a child memorizes the multiplication tables. A field psychologist concedes that some learning appears highly mechanical, but he goes on to say that it is not necessarily as mechanical as it appears. He argues that even though a child may repeat the multiplication tables until he appears to have memorized them by rote, what the child actually has done is to get the feel of some pattern which is present in the tables. The pattern may lie in the relationship of numbers or perhaps merely in the order in which the student placed the numbers to "memorize" them.

Insight does not imply that for a person to learn something he must understand all aspects of its use. Any degree of "feel for a pattern" is sufficient to constitute insightful learning. For example, in learning to extract the square root of a number, one might develop insight as to *why* the method works. Or the insight gained might be much more superficial; it might be merely a "feel" for the method—the pattern of steps—with no real understanding of the basic algebraic formula

$$(x + y)^2 = x^2 + 2xy + y^2$$

Some Examples of Insightful Learning

Before he can become a sharpshooter, a rifleman must get a "feel" for his rifle. Often a Tennessee squirrel hunter was slow in learning to be an army rifleman. He had an excellent feel for his squirrel gun, but a squirrel gun was not an army rifle. In his army training he had to change old insights as well as develop new ones. On his squirrel gun his sights were fixed immovably to the barrel. To hit a squirrel he had to take wind and distance into consideration and move the rifle away from a line on the target (windward and upward) to give "Tennessee windage" and "Kentucky elevation." He had developed insights to the point that he could behave intelligently without thinking; he could aim his gun and pull the trigger while giving very little attention to what he was doing.

Since his army rifle had movable sights which, prior to aiming, were to be adjusted to allow for windage and elevation, he was supposed to set his sights and then line them directly on his target. But under pressure of target practice he used his new insights to adjust his sights correctly, then when he began to fire he gave his rifle Tennessee windage and Kentucky elevation. In army terminology he got a "Maggie"—he missed the target completely. He had used two sets of incompatible insights. He could learn to shoot his army rifle accurately only by getting complete feel for his army rifle and leaving most of his squirrel-gun-aiming insights out of the picture.

What is the answer to $\sqrt{(\text{dog})^2}$=? How did you know it was "dog"? Had you ever before worked with square root and dog at the same time? If you knew the answer was "dog," you had an insight into the problem. Perhaps you had never put the insight into words, but you knew that $\sqrt{x^2}=x$ and $\sqrt{4^2}=4$. Your insight, when verbalized, would run something like, "The square root of anything squared is that thing." Conversely, you may have "learned"—memorized—"The square root of a quantity squared is that quantity" and still not know the answer to $\sqrt{(\text{dog})^2}=?$

How would students study spelling so as to develop insight? Teaching for insight has definite implications for methods in spelling. Groups or families of words might be studied in such a way that students develop feeling for a certain spelling pattern. Once a pattern is discovered other words will be sought which conform to it. *Cat, fat,* and *bat* are "at" words. Now what about *hat, mat, pat, rat,* and *sat?* As students, working cooperatively with their teacher, find other word families, they soon will encounter words which apparently should, but do not, fit a certain family—they find some limitations to an insight. They then seek other words with the same divergence from the "rule" and make a family of them. Or in case there is only one divergent word, they think of it as an exception. As the insights into patterns of spelling are put into words, a class can formulate rules. But now rules will be verbalizations of students' insight as contrasted with meaningless statements memorized at the beginning of study.

Insight and Generalization

Often when an insight is first "caught" it applies to a single case. Even so, a person is likely to assume that the insight may work in similar situations. Suppose, for example, that, after studying a particular situation, we hypothesize, "Mary became a shoplifter because she felt unwanted by her parents." The natural next step is to think, "Boys and girls who feel unwanted at home tend to become thieves." Of course, this generalization is only *suggested.* It is not *warranted* by evidence from a single case. Before generalizations become reliable it is usually necessary that they rest on a number of specific insights, all suggesting the same conclusion. In short, dependable generalizations are usually products of considerable experience. Further, they are prone to change in the course of experience, evolving continuously in the direction of greater usefulness as tools of thought.

A tested generalization is assumed to be valid in any future situation similar to the situations in which it was tested. Tested generalizations have the character of *rules, principles,* or *laws.* Syntactically, generalizations are frequently if-then statements: if we take a given action, then the probability is high that a given consequence will follow. We emphasize that tested generalizations should be regarded as *probabilities.* Although, to behave with foresight, we must assume that our generalizations have predictive value, the predictions are to some degree always based on probability.

As suggested earlier, if-then statements usually also may be expressed in present-tense declarative sentences. For example, when a person says, "An increase in the quantity of money is likely to produce a rise in prices," he may mean exactly the same as if he said, "If the quantity of money in circulation is increased, then prices are likely to rise." In using generalizations as hypotheses in scientific procedure, the if-then form often is preferable. It is more likely than is a simple declarative sentence to suggest operations to be performed, and therefore throw emphasis upon experimental tests.

WHAT IS THE RELATIONSHIP OF BEHAVIOR TO LEARNING?

Behavioristically defined, "*Behavior* is the publicly observable activity of muscles or glands of external secretion as manifested in movements of parts of the body or in the appearance of tears, sweat, saliva and so forth."[5] Gestalt-field psychology gives "behavior" a quite different meaning. It is any change in a person, his perceived environment, or the relation between the two which is subject to *psychological* principles or laws. Psychological behavior involves purpose and intelligence; hence it is not correlated with physical movement. From a Gestalt-field point of view, psychological behavior is not directly observable; it must be inferred.[6]

Learning and change in observable behavior usually occur side by side and obviously are interrelated in some way. Accordingly, S-R associationists contend that any change of behavior is learning, and conversely, that learning is a change of behavior. Thus, the current practice among many educators of defining learning as "change in behavior" usually reflects an associationist psychology.

Gestalt-field theorists counter that S-R associationists err in making synonymous the observable results of learning and the learning itself. They argue that a change in physiological behavior does not necessarily mean that learning has occurred. A person who is struck from behind and knocked down may gain from this experience a healthy respect for dark alleys, but the change in behavior—falling down—is not equivalent to a change in insight. Furthermore, a person may use insights he has had for some time as a basis for change in his present behavior. An author may know that too much coffee is not good for him but persist in drinking coffee until he completes a manuscript and then reduce the amount of coffee he drinks. Probably many changes in the behavior of school children do not reflect change of insight, or at least not the kind of change which the teacher assumes. Johnny may start saying "please" and "thank you" without an insightful grasp of the implications. He may labor hours every night over homework without having his work produce any change of mind about matters embraced in the homework itself. (Of course, the assignments may cause changes in his attitudes toward teachers and school.)

Gestalt-field psychologists maintain that not only may change in behavior occur without learning, but also learning may occur without observable changes in behavior. This is true in any of innumerable situations. There may be no opportunity or occasion for a change in behavior, as when a person decides it would be nice to give more to charity but doesn't have the money to do so. New insights may fail to change a person's behavior if they are competing with old insights which have a stronger hold. Thus, one may decide that racial discrimination is bad but continue to practice it. In summary, when a person

[5] D. O. Hebb, *A Textbook of Psychology* (Philadelphia: W. B. Saunders Company, 1958), p. 2.

[6] See Morton Deutsch, "Field Theory in Social Psychology," in Gardner Lindzey (ed.), *Handbook of Social Psychology* (Reading, Mass.: Addison-Wesley, 1954), p. 191.

learns, his behavior usually changes; but it does not follow that for learning to take place a change in observable behavior must take place at the same time, or that from a change in overt behavior we can always accurately infer the full nature of the insight behind it.

Many people with a behavioristic orientation think that doing something a number of times will necessarily affect future behavior. Thus, if one smokes a pack of cigarettes a day for a few weeks he is likely to become a habitual smoker. Gestalt-field theorists deny that this is the case. Doing a thing once or many times will affect subsequent behavior only in the degree to which doing it gives the doer a feeling for the act or insight into the consequences of its performance. It is the thought process, not the action, which is crucial. For this reason, Gestalt-field psychologists emphasize experience rather than behavior, with experience defined as an interactive event in which a person comes to see and feel the consequences of a given course of action, through acting and seeing what happens.

The emphasis of S-R associationists upon overt behavior has led to school practices designed to produce a desired kind of behavior and to methods of evaluation which measure overt behavior–and nothing else. Teachers, or other school authorities, decide which specific behaviors they want students to display. They then stimulate the students in such a way as to evoke the desired behaviors. The success of the process is judged by how dependably the behavior can be invoked in the future (usually on tests). Field psychologists protest this approach to education; they argue that a student may learn little more from it than the insights he gains about teachers and schools and about how to play the memory-work game successfully.

Walter R. Nord

BEYOND THE TEACHING MACHINE

The work of B. F. Skinner and the operant conditioners has been neglected in management and organizational literature. The present paper is an attempt to eliminate this lacuna. When most students of management and personnel think of Skinner's work, they begin and end with programmed instruction. Skinner's

From Walter R. Nord, "Beyond the Teaching Machine: The Neglected Area of Operant Conditioning in the Theory and Practice of Management," *Organizational Behavior and Human Performance,* Vol. 4, (1969), pp. 375-401. Reprinted by permission.

ideas, however, have far greater implications for the design and operation of social systems and organizations than just the teaching machine. These additional ideas could be of great practical value.

While neglecting conditioning, writers in the administrative, management, and personnel literature have given extensive attention to the work of other behavioral scientists. McGregor and Maslow are perhaps the behavioral scientists best known to practitioners and students in the area of business and management. Since the major concern of managers of human resources is the prediction and control of the behavior of organizational participants, it is curious to find that people with such a need are extremely conversant with McGregor and Maslow and totally ignorant of Skinner. This condition is not surprising since leading scholars in the field, of what might be termed the applied behavioral sciences, have turned out book after book, article after article, and anthology after anthology with scarcely a mention of Skinner's contributions to the design of social systems. While many writers who deal with the social psychology of organizations are guilty of the omission, this paper will focus primarily on the popular positions of Douglas McGregor, Abraham Maslow, and Frederick Herzberg to aid in exposition.

Almost every book in the field devotes considerable attention to Maslow and McGregor. These men have certainly contributed ideas which are easily understood and "make sense" to practitioners. Also, many practitioners have implemented some of these ideas successfully. However, the belief in the Maslow-McGregor creed is not based on a great deal of evidence. This conclusion is not mine alone, but in fact closely parallels Maslow's (1965) own thoughts. He wrote:

> After all, if we take the whole thing from McGregor's point of view of a contrast between a Theory *X* view of human nature, a good deal of the evidence upon which he bases his conclusions comes from my researches and my papers on motivations, self-actualization, etc. But I of all people should know just how shaky this foundation is as a final foundation. My work on motivations came from the clinic, from a study of neurotic people. The carry-over of this theory to the industrial situation has some support from industrial studies, but certainly I would like to see a lot more studies of this kind before feeling finally convinced that this carry-over from the study of neurosis to the study of labor in factories is legitimate. The same thing is true of my studies of self-actualizing people—there is only this one study of mine available. There were many things wrong with the sampling, so many in fact that it must be considered to be, in the classical sense anyway, a bad or poor or inadequate experiment. I am quite willing to concede this—as a matter of fact, I am eager to concede it—because I'm a little worried about this stuff which I consider to be tentative being swallowed whole by all sorts of enthusiastic people, who really should be a little more tentative in the way that I am (p. 55-56).

By contrast, the work of Skinner (1953) and his followers has been supported by millions of observations made on animals at all levels of the phylogenetic scale, including man. Over a wide variety of situations, behavior has been reliably predicted and controlled by operant and classical conditioning techniques.

Why then have the applied behavioral sciences followed the McGregor-Maslow approach and ignored Skinner? Several reasons can be suggested. First is the metaphysical issue. Modern Americans, especially of the managerial class, prefer to think of themselves and others as being self-actualizing creatures operating near the top of Maslow's need-hierarchy, rather than as animals being controlled and even "manipulated" by their environment. McGregor (1960) developed his argument in terms of Maslow's hierarchy. Skinner's position is unattractive in the same way the Corpernican theory was unattractive. Second, Skinner's work and stimulus-response psychology in general appear too limited to allow application to complex social situations. Certainly, this point has much merit. The application of S-R theory poses a terribly complex engineering problem, perhaps an insoluble one in some areas. Nevertheless, the designs of some experimental social systems, which will be discussed later in this paper, demonstrate the feasibility of the practical application of Skinnerian psychology to systems design. A third possible reason for the acceptance of the McGregor and Maslow school and rejection of Skinner may stem from the fact that the two approaches have considerable, although generally unrecognized overlap. As will be shown below, McGregor gave primary importance to the environment as the determinant of individual behavior. Similarly, although not as directly, so does Maslow's hierarchy of needs. The major issue between Skinner and McGregor-Maslow has to do with their models of man. Skinner focuses on man being totally shaped by his environment. Maslow-McGregor see man as having an essence or intrinsic nature which is only congruent with certain environments. The evidence for any one set of metaphysical assumptions is no better than for almost any other set. Empirically, little has been found which helps in choosing between Skinner's and McGregor's assumptions. Further, since most managers are concerned mainly with behavior, the sets of assumptions are of limited importance. It should be noted, however, that if McGregor's writings were stripped of Maslow's model of man, his conclusions on the descriptive and proscriptive levels would remain unchanged. Such a revision would also make McGregor's ideas almost identical with Skinner's. With more attention to contingencies of reinforcement and a broader view of the possibilities of administering reinforcement, the two sets of ideas as they apply to prediction and control of action would be virtually indistinguishable.

The remainder of this paper will be devoted to three areas. First, the similarities and differences between McGregor and Skinner will be discussed. Then, a summary of the Skinnerian position will be presented. Finally, the potential of the Skinnerian approach for modern organizations will be presented with supporting evidence from social systems in which it has already been applied.

McGREGOR AND SKINNER COMPARED

The importance of environmental factors in determining behavior is the crucial and dominant similarity between Skinner and McGregor. As will be shown below, environmental determination of behavior is central to both men.

McGregor (1960) gave central importance to environmental factors in determining how a person behaves. For example, he saw employee behavior as a consequence of organizational factors which are influenced by managerial strategy. In a sense, Theory *X* management leads to people behaving in a way which confirms Theory *X* assumptions, almost as a self-fulfilling prophecy. In addition, McGregor's statement of Theory *Y* assumptions places stress on "proper conditions," rewards and punishments, and other environmental factors. Further, he recognized the importance of immediate feedback in changing behavior. Also, he noted that failure to achieve results is often due to inappropriate methods of control. These are the very terms a behaviorist such as Skinner uses in discussing human actions. Finally, McGregor (1966) noted stimulus-response psychology as a possible model for considering organizational behavior. However, he discarded the reinforcement approach because it did not permit intrinsic rewards to be dealt with. Such a view not only led him to discard a model which describes, by his own admission, important behaviors, but is based on an incomplete view of reinforcement.

McGregor's basic arguments could have been based on Skinner rather than Maslow. The major difference would be the assumption of fewer givens about human nature. In view of this similarity one need not choose either Skinner or McGregor. Rather, there is considerable overlap in that both focus on changing the environmental conditions to produce changes in behavior. Further, both writers place substantial emphasis on the goals of prediction and control. Both are quite explicit in suggesting that we often get undesired results because we use inappropriate methods of control. In fact, the emphasis that McGregor's (1960) first chapter gives to the role of environment in controlling behavior seems to place him clearly in the behavioral camp.

Certainly there are important differences between Skinner and McGregor as well as the marked similarities noted above. For example, McGregor's (1960) use of Maslow's hierarchy of needs implies a series of inborn needs as a focus of the causal factors of behavior whereas Skinner (1953) views environmental factors as the causes of behavior. This difference does not, however, suggest an unresolvable conflict on the applied level. Skinner too allows for satiation on certain reinforcers which will be subject to species' and individual differences. Proceeding from this premise, Skinner focuses on the environmental control of behavior in a more rigorous and specific fashion than did McGregor. For example, McGregor (1960) advocated an agricultural approach to development which emphasizes the provision of the conditions for behavioral change as a management responsibility. He noted in a general way that features of the organization, such as a boss, will influence behavioral change. He added that the change would not be permanent unless the organizational environment reinforced the desired behavior pattern. Such a general approach is an assumed basis for Skinner, who proceeds to focus on the types of reinforcement, the details of the administration of reinforcement, and the outcomes which can be expected from the administration of various types of reinforcement. Thus, changes in behavior which are predicted and achieved by Skinnerian methods can be viewed as empirical support for the work of McGregor.

There are other commonalities in the thinking of the two men. Both assume that there are a wide number of desirable responses available to a person which he does not make, because the responses are not rewarded in the environment. Both suggest that many undesired responses are repeated because they are rewarded. Both are clearly advocating a search for alternatives to controlling behavior which will be more effective in developing desired responses.

At this same level of analysis, there seems to be one major difference which revolves around the issue of self-control. However, this difference may be more apparent than real. Skinner (1953) wrote "It appears, therefore, that society is responsible for the larger part of the behavior of self-control. If this is correct, little ultimate control remains with the individual (p. 240)." Continuing on self-control, Skinner adds: "But it is also behavior; and we account for it in terms of other variables in the environment and history of the individual. It is these variables which provide the ultimate control (p. 240)."

In apparent contrast, McGregor (1960) stated: "Theory *Y* assumes that people will exercise self-direction and self-control in the achievement of organizational objectives *to the degree that they are committed to those objectives* (p. 56)." Seemingly this statement contradicts Skinner in placing the locus of control inside the individual. However, this conflict is reduced a few sentences later when McGregor (1960) added "Managerial policies and practices materially affect this degree of commitment (p. 56)." Thus, both writers, Skinner far more unequivocally than McGregor, see the external environment as the primary factor in self-control. While McGregor polemicized against control by authority, he was not arguing that man is "free." Perhaps the more humanistic tone of McGregor's writing or his specific attention to managerial problems faced in business is responsible for his high esteem among students of management relative to that accorded Skinner. While metaphorically there is great difference, substantively there is little. It would seem, however, that metaphors have led practitioners and students of applied behavioral science to overlook some valuable data and some creative management possibilities.

One major substantive difference between the two approaches exists: it involves intrinsic rewards. McGregor (1960) saw a dicotomy in the effects of intrinsic and extrinsic rewards, noting research which has shown intrinsic ones to be more effective. He concludes the "mechanical" view (reinforcement theory) is inadequate, because it does not explain the superior outcomes of the use of "intrinsic" over "extrinsic" rewards. Here, as will be discussed in more detail later in connection with Herzberg, the problem is McGregor's failure to consider scheduling of reinforcement. "Intrinsic" rewards in existing organizations may be more effective because they occur on a more appropriate schedule for sustaining behavior than do "extrinsic" rewards. Intrinsic rewards are given by the environment for task completion or a similar achievement, and often occur on a ratio schedule. The implications of this crucial fact will be discussed shortly in considering Skinner's emphasis on the scheduling of rewards. For the present, it is suggested that McGregor gave little attention to reinforcement schedules and made a qualitative distinction between external and internal rewards. He seems to agree with Skinner that achievement, task completion, and control of the environment are reinforcers in themselves. Skinner's work suggests, however, that these rewards have the same consequences as "extrinsic" rewards, if they are given on the same schedule.

By way of summary to this point, it appears that more humanistic social scientists have been preferred by managers to behaviorists such as Skinner in their efforts to improve the management of human resources. Perhaps the oversight has been due to the congruence between their values and the metaphysics of people such as McGregor and Maslow. The differences between McGregor and Skinner do not appear to involve open conflict.

To the extent the two approaches agree, the major criterion in employing them would seem to be the degree to which they aid in predicting and controlling behavior toward organizational goals. The work of Skinner and his followers has much to offer in terms of the above criterion. In particular, McGregor's followers might find Skinner's work an asset in implementing Theory *Y*. The remainder of this paper will develop some of the major points of the Skinnerian approach and seek to explore their potential for industrial use.

CONDITIONING–A SYNTHESIS FOR ORGANIZATIONAL BEHAVIOR

The behavioral psychology of Skinner assumes, like Theory *Y* that rate of behavior is dependent on the external conditions in which the behavior takes place. Like Theory *X*, it stresses the importance of the administration of rewards and punishments. Unlike Theory *X*, Skinnerian psychology places emphasis on rewards. Like Theory *Y* it emphasizes the role of interdependence between people in a social relationship and thus views the administration of rewards and punishments as an exchange. For those who are unfamiliar with the work of Skinner and his followers, a brief summary follows. Like any summary of an extensive body of work, this review omits a lot of important material. A more detailed, yet simple, introduction to conditioning can be found in Bijou and Baer (1961) and Skinner (1953). Extensions of this work by social exchange theorists such as Homans (1961) suggest that the conditioning model can be extended to a systems approach, contrary to McGregor's (1966) belief.

Generally, conditioned responses can be divided into two classes. Each class is acquired in a different fashion. The first class, generally known as respondent or classically conditioned behavior, describes the responses which are controlled by prior stimulation. These responses, generally thought of as being involuntary or reflexive, are usually made by the "smooth muscles." Common ones are salivation and emotional responses. Initially, the presentation of an unconditioned stimulus will elicit a specific response. For example, food placed on one's tongue will generally cause salivation. If a bell is sounded and then food is placed on the tongue, and this process is repeated several times, the sound of the bell by itself will elicit salivation. By this process, stimuli which previously did not control behavior such as the bell, can become a source of behavior control. Many of our likes and dislikes, our anxieties, our feelings of patriotism, and other emotions can be thought of as such involuntary responses. The implications of emotional responses are of major importance to the management of human resources and more will be said about them later. However, the second class of responses, the operants, are of even greater importance.

The rate of operant responses is influenced by events which follow them. These events are considered to be the consequences of behavior. The responses, generally thought to be voluntary, are usually made by striped muscles. All that is necessary for the development of an operant response is that the desired response has a probability of occurring which is greater than zero for the individual involved. Most rapid conditioning results when the desired response is "reinforced" immediately (preferably about one-half second after the response). In other words, the desired response is followed directly by some consequence. In simple terms, if the outcome is pleasing to the individual, the probability of his repeating the response is apt to be increased. If the consequence is displeasing to the individual, the probability of his repeating the response is apt to be decreased. The process of inducing such change (usually an increase) in the response rate, is called operant conditioning. In general, the frequency of a behavior is said to be a function of its consequences.

The above description of operant conditioning is greatly simplified. The additional considerations which follow will only partially rectify this state. One crucial factor has to do with the frequency with which a given consequence follows a response. There are several possible patterns. Most obviously, the consequence can be continuous (for example, it follows the response every time the response is made). Alternatively a consequence might follow only some of the responses. There are two basic ways in which such partial reinforcement can be administered. First, the consequence can be made contingent on a certain number of responses. Two sub-patterns are possible. Every nth response may be reinforced or an average of 1/n of the responses may be reinforced in a random pattern. These two related patterns are called ratio schedules. The former is known as a fixed ratio and the latter is known as a variable ratio. Ratio schedules tend to generate a high rate of response, with the variable ratio schedule leading to a more durable response than both the fixed-ratio and continuous patterns. A second technique of partial reinforcement can be designed where the consequence follows the response only after a certain amount of time has elapsed. The first response made after a specified interval is then reinforced, but all other responses produce neutral stimulus outcomes. This pattern can also be either fixed or variable. Generally, interval schedules develop responses which are quite long lasting when reinforcement is no longer given, but do not yield as rapid a response rate as ratio schedules do. Obviously, mixed patterns of ratio and interval schedules can also be designed.

A second consideration about operant conditioning which deserves brief mention is the concept of a response hierarchy. All the responses which an individual could make under a given set of conditions can be placed in order according to probability that they will be made. In this view, there are two basic strategies for getting an individual to make the desired response. First, one could attempt to reduce the probability of all the more probable responses. Second, one could attempt to increase the probability of the desired response. Of course, some combination of these two approaches may often be used.

Strategies for changing the probability of a response can be implemented by punishment, extinction, and positive reinforcement. Generally punishment and extinction are used to decrease the occurrence of a response whereas positive reinforcement is used to increase its probability. An understanding of these three operations in behavior control is important, not only for knowing how to use them, but chiefly because of their unanticipated consequences or their side-effects.

Punishment is the most widely used technique in our society for behavior control. Perhaps, as Reese (1966) said, the widespread use of punishment is due to the immediate effects it has in stopping or preventing the undesired response. In this sense, the punisher is reinforced for punishing. Also, many of us seem to be influenced by some notion of what Homans (1961) called distributive justice. In order to reestablish what we believe to be equity, we may often be led to punish another person. This ancient assumption of "... an eye for an eye ..." has been widely practiced in man's quest for equity and behavior control.

Whatever the reason for punishing, it can be done in two ways, both of which have unfortunate side-effects. First, punishment can be administered in the form of some aversive stimulus such as physical pain or social disapproval. Secondly, it can be administered by withdrawing a desired stimulus. The immediate effect is often the rapid drop in frequency of the punished response. The full effects, unfortunately, are often not clearly recognized. Many of these consequences are crucial for managers of organizations.

Punishment may be an inefficient technique for controlling behavior for a number of reasons. First, the probability of the response may be reduced only when the threat of punishment is perceived to exist. Thus, when the punishing agent is away, the undesired response may occur at its initial rate. Secondly, punishment only serves to reduce the probability of the one response. This outcome does not necessarily produce the desired response, unless that response is the next most probable one in the response hierarchy. Really, what punishment does is to get the individual to do something other than what he has been punished for. A third effect is that the punishment may interfere with the response being made under desired circumstances. For example, if an organizational member attempts an innovation which is met with punishment by his superiors because they did not feel he had the authority to take the step, it is quite possible that his creative behavior will be reduced even in those areas where his superiors expect him to innovate.

In addition to these effects there are some other important by-products of punishment. Punishment may result in a person making responses which are incompatible with the punished response. Psychological tension, often manifested in emotional behavior such as fear or anxiety, is often the result. Secondly, punishment may lead to avoidance and dislike of the punishing agent. This effect can be especially important to managers who are attempting to build open, helping relationships with subordinates. The roles of punishing agent and helper are often incompatible. Many line-staff conflicts in organizations undoubtedly can be explained in these terms. Finally, punishment may generate counter-aggression. Either through a modeling effect or a justice effect, the punished person may respond with aggressive responses towards the punishing agent or towards some other stimulus.

The second technique for behavior change, commonly called extinction, also focuses primarily on reducing the probability of a response. Extinction arises from repeated trials where the response is followed by a neutral stimulus. This technique generates fewer by-products than punishment. However, like punishment, it does not lead to the desired response being developed. Furthermore, to the extent that one has built up an expectation of a reward for a certain response, a neutral consequence may be perceived as punishing. Thus, extinction may have some advantages over punishment, but has many of the same limitations.

Positive reinforcement is the final technique for changing behavior. Under conditions of positive reinforcement, the response produces a consequence that results in an increase in the frequency of the response. It is commonly stated that such a consequence is rewarding, pleasing, or drive-reducing for the individual. The operant conditioners, however, avoid such inferences and define positive reinforcers as stimuli which increase the probability of a preceding response. Positive reinforcement is efficient for several reasons. First, it increases the probable occurrence of the desired response. The process involves rewarding approximation of desired response itself immediately after it is made. The desired behavior is being directly developed as opposed to successive suppression of undesired acts. Secondly, the adverse emotional responses associated with punishment and extinction are apt to be reduced and in fact favorable emotions may be developed. Since people tend to develop positive affect to others who reward them, the "trainer" is apt to become positively valenced in the eyes of the "learner."

By way of summary, Skinner's (1953) approach suggested that the control of behavior change involves a reduction in the probability of the most prepotent response and/or an increase in the probability of some desired response. Punishment and extinction may be used. These means can only reduce the probability of the unwanted response being made. Also, they may have undesired side-effects. The third technique, positive reinforcement, has the important advantage of developing the desired response rather than merely reducing the chances of an undesired one. Also, positive reinforcement is apt to produce favorable rather than unfavorable "side-effects" on organizational relationships.

This approach seems to suggest that both or neither Theory *X* and Theory *Y* assumptions are useful. This section suggested that conditioning may be both Theory *X* and Theory *Y*. Perhaps since the operant view does not make either set of assumptions, it is neither Theory *X* nor Theory *Y*. Operant conditioning is consistent with Theory *Y* in suggesting that the limits on human beings are a function of the organizational setting, but like Theory *X*, implies something about human nature; namely that deprivation or threat of some sort of deprivation is a precondition for behavior to be controlled. From the managerial perspective, however, the nomonological question is of little significance. The important thing to managers is behavior and the major point of this approach is that behavior is a function of its consequences. Good management is that which leads to the desired behavior by organizational members. Management must see to it that the consequences of behavior are such as to increase the frequency of desired behavior and decrease the frequency of undesired behaviors. The question becomes, how can managers develop a social system which provides the appropriate consequences? In many ways the answer to this question is similar to what Theory *Y* advocates have suggested. However, there are some new possibilities.

APPLICATIONS OF CONDITIONING IN ORGANIZATIONS

The potential uses of the Skinnerian framework for social systems are increasing rapidly. The approach has far more applicability to complex social systems than has often been recognized. McGregor's rejection of the stimulus-response or the reward-punishment approach as inadequate for management because it does not allow for a systems approach is quite inconsistent with this general trend and his own environmentally based approach. Recent work in the field of behavioral control has begun to refute McGregor's position. The Skinnerian view can be and has been used to redesign social systems.

The most complete redesign was envisioned by Skinner (1948) in his novel, *Walden Two*. In this book, Skinner developed a society based on the use of positive reinforcement and experimental ethics geared to the goal of competition of a coordinated social unit with its environment. In other words, the system is designed to reward behaviors which are functional for the whole society. Social change is introduced on the basis of empirical data. As a result of the success of this system, man is enabled to pursue those activities which are rewarding in themselves. Although the book is a novel, it can be a valuable stimulus for thought about the design of social organization.

In addition, Skinner (1954) has taken a fresh look at teaching and learning in conventional educational systems. He noted that the school system depends heavily on aversive control or punishment. The use of low marks and ridicule have merely been substituted for the "stick." The teacher, in Skinner's view, is an out of date reinforcing mechanism. He suggested the need to examine the reinforcers which are available in the system and to apply them in a manner which is consistent with what is known about learning. For example, control over the environment itself may be rewarding. Perhaps grades reinforce the wrong behavior and are administered on a rather poor schedule. It would seem that a search for new reinforcers and better reinforcement schedules is appropriate for all modern organizations.

These speculations suggest the potential for great advances. *Walden Two* is in many ways an ideal society but has been a source of horror to many readers. The thoughts about changes in teaching methods are also a subject of controversy. However, the environment can be designed to aid in the attainment of desired ends. People resist the idea that they can be controlled by their environment. This resistance does not change the fact that they are under such control. Recently, evidence has begun to accumulate that the Skinnerian approach can be employed to design social systems.

Much of this evidence was collected in settings far removed from modern work organizations. The reader's initial response is apt to be, "What relevance do these studies have to my organization?" Obviously, the relationship is not direct. However, if, as the operant approach maintains, the conditioning process describes the acquisition and maintenance of behavior, the same principles can be applied to any social organization. The problem of application becomes merely that of engineering. The gains may well be limited only by an administrator's ingenuity and resources.

Much of the evidence comes from studies of hospitalized mental patients and autistic children, although some has been based on normal lower class children. A few examples from these studies will serve to document the great potential of the conditioning methods for social systems. Allyon and Azrin (1965) observed mental patients' behavior to determine what activities they engaged in when they had a chance. They then made tokens contingent on certain responses such as work on hospital tasks. These tokens could be exchanged for the activities the patients preferred to engage in. The results of this approach were amazing. In one experiment five schizophrenics and three mental defectives served as Ss. They did jobs regularly and adequately when tokens were given for the job. Such performance was reported to be in sharp contrast to the erratic and inconsistent behavior characteristic of such patients. When the tokens were no longer contingent on the work, the performance dropped almost to zero. In a second experiment, a whole ward of 44 patients served as Ss. A similar procedure was followed and 11 classes of tasks observed. When tokens were contingent upon the desired responses, the group spent an average of 45 hours on the tasks daily. When tokens were not contingent on responses, almost no time was spent on the tasks. The implications seem rather clear. When desired behavior is rewarded, it will be emitted, when it is not rewarded, it will not be emitted.

A great deal of related work has been reported. Allyon (1966) and Wolf, Risley, and Mees (1966) have shown how a reinforcement procedure can be effective in controlling the behavior of a psychotic patient and of an autistic child respectively. These are but a few of the many studies in a growing body of evidence.

More important for present purposes is the application of this approach in more complex social situations. The work of Hamblin et al. (1967) shows some of the interesting possibilities of the conditioning approach for school classes and aggressive children. A token system was used to shape desired behavior. Through the application of the conditioning approach to the school system, gains may be made in educating children from deprived backgrounds. Two examples will illustrate these possibilities.

The first example comes from a recent newspaper story. A record shop owner in a Negro area of Chicago reported seeing the report card of a Negro boy. The owner thought the boy was bright, but the report card showed mostly unsatisfactory performance. He told the boy he would give him $5 worth of free records if he got all "excellents" on the next report card. Ten weeks later the boy returned with such a card to collect his reward. The owner reported that similar offers to other children had a remarkable effect in getting them to study and do their homework. The anecdote demonstrates what everyone knows anyway: people will not work if rewards do not exist. The problems of education in the ghetto and motivation to work in general, may be overcome by appropriate reinforcement. Further support for this statement comes from the work of Montrose Wolf.

Wolf (1966) ran a school for children, most of whom were sixth graders, in a lower class Negro area of Kansas City. The children attended this school for several hours after school each day and on Saturday. Rewards were given in the form of tickets which could be saved and turned in for different kinds of things like toys, food, movies, shopping trips, and other activities. Tickets were made contingent on academic performance within the remedial school itself, and on performance in the regular school system. The results were remarkable. The average regular school grade of the students was raised to C from D. The results on standard achievement tests showed the remedial group progressed over twice as much in one year as they had done the previous year. They showed twice as much progress as a control group. Other gains were also noted. Wolf reported that a severe punishment was not to let the children attend school. They expressed strong discontent when school was not held because of a holiday. He further noted that when reading was no longer rewarded with tickets, the students still continued to read more than before the training. Arithmetic and English did not maintain these increments. Thus, to some extent, reading appeared to be intrinsically rewarding.

A final point concerns the transferability of skills learned in such a school to society at large. Will the tasks that are not rewarding in themselves be continued? The answer is probably not, unless other rewards are provided. The task then becomes to develop skills and behavior which society itself will reward. If this method is applied to develop behavior which is rewarded by society, the behavior is apt to be maintained. The same argument holds for organizational behavior. It will be fruitless to develop behavior which is not rewarded in the organization.

In summary, evidence has been presented to show the relevance of the Skinnerian approach to complex social systems. Certainly the evidence is only suggestive of future possibilities. The rest of this paper attempts to suggest some of these implications for organizational management.

MANAGEMENT THROUGH POSITIVE REINFORCEMENT

The implications of the systematic use of positive reinforcement for management range over many traditional areas. Some of the more important areas include training and personnel development, compensation and alternative rewards, supervision and leadership, job design, organizational design, and organizational change.

Training and Personnel Development

The area of training has been the first to benefit from the application of conditioning principles with the use of programmed learning and the teaching machine. An example of future potential comes from the Northern Systems Company Training Method for assembly line work. In this system, the program objectives are broken down into sub-objectives. The training employs a lattice which provides objective relationships between functions and objectives, indicates critical evaluation points, and presents a visual display of go-no-go functions. Progress through various steps is reinforced by rewards. To quote from a statement of the training method ". . . the trainee gains satisfaction only by demonstrated performance at the tool stations. Second, he quickly perceives that correct behaviors obtain for him the satisfaction of his needs, and that incorrect behaviors do not (p. 20)." Correct performance includes not only job skills, but also the performance of social interaction which is necessary in a factory setting. The skills taught are designed to allow for high mobility in the industrial world. The Northern System's method develops behavior which the economic and social system will normally reinforce and has been successful in training people in a wide variety of skills. Its potential in training such groups as the "hard-core" unemployed seems to be limited only by the resources and creativity of program designers.

The Skinnerian approach seems to have potential for all areas of personnel development, not only for highly programmed tasks. Reinforcement theory may be useful in the development of such behaviors as creativity. The work of Maltzman, Simon, Raskin, and Licht (1960) demonstrated this possibility. After a series of experiments employing a standard experimental training procedure with free association materials, these investigators concluded that a highly reliable increase in uncommon responses could be produced through the use of reinforcement. The similarity of their results to those of operant experiments with respect to the persistance of the responses and the effect of repetitions, led them to conclude that originality is a form of operant behavior. Positive reinforcement increased the rate at which original responses were emitted.

Support is also available for the efficacy of operant conditioning to more conventional personnel and leadership development. Three such contributions are discussed below. The first concerns the organizational environment as a shaper of behavior of which Fleishman's (1967) study is a case in point. He found that human relations training programs were only effective in producing on-the-job changes if the organizational climate was supportive of the content of the program. More generally it would appear that industrial behavior is a function of its consequences. Those responses which are rewarded will persist: those responses which are not rewarded or are punished will decrease in frequency. If the organizational environment does not reward responses developed in a training program, the program will be, at best, a total waste of time and money. As Sykes (1962) has shown, at worst, such a program may be highly disruptive. A second implication of operant conditioning concerns the content of personnel development programs in the area of human relations. If, as

Homans (1961) and others have suggested, social interaction is also influenced by the same operant principles, then people in interaction are constantly "shaping" or conditioning each other. The behavior of a subordinate is to some degree developed by his boss and vice-versa. What more sensible, practical point could be taught to organizational members than that they are teaching their fellow participants to behave in a certain manner? What more practical, sensible set of principles could be taught than that, due to latent dysfunctions generated, punishment and extinction procedures are less efficient ways to influence behavior than positive reinforcement? Clearly, the behavioral scientists who have contributed so greatly to organizational practice and personnel development have not put enough emphasis on these simple principles. The third implication for personnel development is added recognition that annual merit interviews and salary increments are very inefficient development techniques. The rewards or punishments are so delayed that they can be expected to have little feedback value for the employees involved. More frequent appraisals and distribution of rewards are apt to be far more effective, especially to the degree that they are related to specific tasks or units of work.

Job Design

Recently, behavioral scientists have emphasized the social psychological factors which need to be attended to in job design. McGregor and others have suggested job enlargement. Herzberg (1968) has argued that job enlargement just allows an individual to do a greater variety of boring jobs and suggests that "job enrichment" is needed. For present purposes, job enlargement and job enrichment will be lumped together. Both of these approaches are consistent with the conditioning view if two differences can be resolved. First, the definitions of motivation must be translated into common terms. Second, reinforcers operating in the newly designed jobs must be delineated and tested to see if the reinforcers postulated in the newly designed jobs are really responsible for behavioral changes or if there are other reinforcers operating.

With respect to the definitions of motivation, the two approaches are really similar in viewing the rate of behavior as the crucial factor. The major differences exist on the conceptual level. Both job enlargement and job enrichment are attempts to increase motivation. Conceptually, McGregor and Herzberg tend to view motivation as some internal state. The conditioning approach does not postulate internal states but rather deals with the manipulation of environmental factors which influence the rate of behavior. Actually, some combination of the two approaches may be most useful theoretically as Vinacke (1962) has suggested. However, if both approaches are viewed only at the operational level, it is quite probable that rates of behavior could be agreed on as an acceptable criterion. Certainly from the practitioner's viewpoint, behavior is the crucial variable. When a manager talks about a motivated worker, he often means one who frequently makes desired responses at a high rate without external prompting from the boss. The traditional view of motivation as an inner-drive is of limited practical and theoretical value.

If both approaches could agree on the behavioral criterion, at least on an operational level, the operant approach could be employed to help resolve some practical and theoretical problems suggested by the work of McGregor and Herzberg. Since, generally speaking, the external conditions are most easily manipulated in an organization, attention can be focused on designing an environment which increases the frequency of the wanted responses. As a result, practitioners and students of organization could deal with motivation without searching for man's essence. We can avoid the metaphysical assumptions of Maslow and McGregor until they are better documented. The issue of a two-factor theory of motivation proposed by Herzberg which recently has been severely challenged by Lindsay, Marks, and Gorlow (1967) and Hulin and Smith (1967) among others can also be avoided. Attention can be confined to developing systems which produce high rates of desired behavior. Thus the conceptual differences about motivation do not cause unresolvable conflict at the present time.

The second area of difference between McGregor-Herzberg and the operant explanation of the effects of job enrichment stems from the failure of Herzberg and McGregor to recognize the great variety of possible rewards available in job design. The Skinnerian approach leads to the development of a more comprehensive discussion of the rewards from enriched or enlarged jobs. In terms of the operant approach, both job enrichment and job enlargement are apt to lead to what would generally be called greater motivation or what we will call higher rates of desired behavior. McGregor and Herzberg suggest feelings of achievement and responsibility explain these results. The reinforcement approach leads to a search for specific rewards in these newly designed jobs.

Job enlargement can be viewed simply as increasing the variety of tasks a person does. Recent research on self-stimulation and sensory deprivation has suggested that stimulation itself is reinforcing, especially when one has been deprived of it. The increased variety of tasks due to job enlargement may thus be intrinsically rewarding due to a host of reinforcers in the work itself rather than to any greater feeling of responsibility or achievement. These feelings may be a cause of greater productivity or merely correlates of the receipt of these intrinsic rewards from stimulation. The evidence is not clear, but the effects of job enlargement can at least be partially explained in operant terms.

Some additional support from this idea comes from Schultz's (1964) work on spontaneous alternation of behavior. Schultz suggested that spontaneous alternation of human behavior is facilitated (1) when responses are not reinforced and/or are not subjected to knowledge of correctness, (2) by the amount of prior exercise of one response alternative, and (3) by a short intertrial interval. Low feedback and reinforcement, short intervals between responses, and the frequent repetition of one response are all characteristic of many jobs which need enlargement. Merely making different responses may be rewarding to a worker, thereby explaining some of the benefits noted from job enlargement. It has also been noted that people create variation for themselves in performing monotonous tasks. For example, ritualized social interaction in the form of social "games" is a form of such alternation workers developed noted by Roy (1964).

By way of summary, much of the current work on job enlargement and enrichment has attributed the effects to feelings of achievement or responsibility, without taking into account numerous other possible reinforcers which may be more basic. Further research to determine the efficacy of these various possibilities is needed before definite conclusions can be drawn. Do the feelings of achievement or responsibility operate as reinforcers in an operant manner? Do these feelings come from other more basic rewards as task variety? Present data do not permit answers to these questions.

With respect to the benefits noted from job enrichment, an operant model may provide further insights. Herzberg (1968) maintained that some jobs can not be "enriched" or made more motivating in themselves. It is the contention of this paper that it is not the tasks which are the problem, but it is the reinforcement schedules. For example, what could be more boring, have less potential for achievement and realization of Herzberg's satisfiers, than the game of bingo. Yet people will sit for hours at bingo, often under punishing conditions (since the house takes in more than it pays out) and place tokens on numbers. Similar behavior is exhibited at slot-machines and other gambling devices. Most operational definitions of motivation would agree that these players are highly motivated. The reason is clear from the operant viewpoint. The reinforcement schedule employed in games of chance, the variable ratio schedule, is a very powerful device for maintaining a rapid rate of response. With respect to job design, the important requirement is that rewards follow performance on an effective schedule.

The type of rewards Herzberg (1968) called satisfiers may be important motivators because they are distributed on a variable ratio schedule. Herzberg's data do not rule out this explanation. Take achievement, for example. If a person is doing a job from which it is possible to get a feeling of achievement, there must be a reasonably large probability that a person will not succeed on the task. Often times, this condition means that some noncontinuous schedule or reinforcement is operating. An individual will succeed only on some variable ratio schedule. In addition, successful completion of the task is often the most important reward. The reward is, of course, immediate. A similar statement could be made about tasks which are said to yield intrinsic satisfaction, such as crossword puzzles or enriched jobs. Thus the factors Herzberg called motivators may derive their potency from the manner in which the rewards are administered. The task is immediately and positively reinforced by the environment on a variable ratio schedule. Often the schedule is one which rewards a very small fraction of a large number of responses. Since behavior is a function of its consequences, if jobs can be designed to reinforce desired behavior in the appropriate manner, "motivated" workers are apt to result. Some of Herzberg's results may be explained without resort to a two-factor theory more parsimoniously in terms of schedules of reinforcement. Herzberg's (1966) finding that recognition is only a motivator if it is contingent on performance further documents the operant argument.

Another suggestion for job design from the operant tradition was suggested by Homans. He explored the relationship of the frequency of an activity and satisfaction to the amount of a reward. He concluded that satisfaction is generally positively related to the amount of reward whereas frequency of an activity is negatively related to the amount of reward the individual has received in the recent past. In order to have both high satisfaction and high activity, Homans (1961) suggested that tasks need to be designed in a manner such that repeated activities lead up to the accomplishment of some final result and get rewarded at a very low frequency until just before the final result is achieved. Then the reinforcement comes often. For example, consider the job of producing bottled soda. An optimal design would have the reward immediate on the completion of putting the caps on the bottles, but the task would be designed such that all the operations prior to capping were completed before any capping was done. Near the end of a work day, all the capping could be done. High output and satisfaction might then exist simultaneously. In general then, the operant approach suggests some interesting possibilities for designing jobs ir ways which would maximize the power of reinforcers in the job itself.

A similar argument can be applied to some problems faced in administration and management. For example, it is commonly recognized that programmed tasks tend to be attended to before unprogrammed ones. It is quite obvious that programmed functions produce a product which is often tangible. The product itself is a reinforcer. An unprogrammed task often requires behavior which has not been reinforced in the past and will not produce a reward in the near future. It may be beneficial to provide rewards relatively early for behavior on unprogrammed tasks. This suggestion will be difficult to put into practice because of the very nature of unprogrammed tasks. Perhaps the best that can be done is to reward the working on such tasks.

Compensation and Alternative Rewards

Although whether money is a true "generalized reinforcer" as Skinner suggests, has not been demonstrated conclusively, for years operant principles have been applied in the form of monetary incentive systems. Opsahl and Dunnette (1966) concluded that such programs generally do increase output. However, the restriction of output and other unanticipated consequences are associated with these programs. Many writers have attributed these consequences to social forces, such as the desire for approval from one's peers. Gewitz and Baer (1958), for example, have shown that social approval has the same effects as other reinforcers in an operant situation. Dalton's (1948) famous study on rate-busters may be interpreted to show that people who are more "group-oriented" may place a higher value on social approval and hence are more apt to abide by group production norms than are less "group-oriented" people. Thus, it is not that money in piece-rate systems is not a potential reinforcer, but rather other reinforcers are more effective, at least after a certain level of monetary reward.

The successful use of the Scanlon Plan demonstrates the value of combining both economic and social rewards. This plan rewards improved work with several types of reinforcers, and often more immediately and directly than many incentive systems. The Scanlon Plan combines economic rewards, often given monthly, with social rewards. The latter are given soon after an employee's idea has been submitted or used.

Related arguments can be made for other group incentive programs. Often jobs are interdependent. The appropriate reinforcement for such tasks should be contingent upon interdependent responses, not individual ones. Even if the jobs are independent, the workers are social-psychologically interdependent. Social rewards are often obtainable by restricting output. It is hardly surprising that individual incentive programs have produced the unanticipated consequences so often noted. Further, since rewards and punishments from the informal group are apt to be administered immediately and frequently they are apt to be very powerful in controlling behavior.

In general then, money and other rewards must be made contingent on the desired responses. Further, the importance of alternative rewards to money must be recognized and incorporated into the design of the work environment. The widely known path-goal to productivity model expresses a similar point.

Another problem of compensation in organizations is also apparent in an operant context. Often, means of compensation, especially fringe benefits, have the unanticipated consequence of reinforcing the wrong responses. Current programs of sick pay, recreation programs, employee lounges, work breaks, and numerous other personnel programs all have one point in common. They all reward the employee for not working or for staying away from the job. These programs are not "bad," since often they may act to reduce problems such as turnover. However, an employer who relies on them should realize what behavior he is developing by establishing these costly programs. Alternative expenditures must be considered. If some of the money that was allocated for these programs was used to redesign jobs so as to be more reinforcing in themselves, more productive effort could be obtained. This idea is certainly not new. A host of behavioral scientists have suggested that resources devoted to making performance of the job itself more attractive will pay social and/or economic dividends.

Another interesting application of conditioning principles has to do with the schedule on which pay is distributed. The conventional pay schedule is a fixed interval one. Further, pay often is not really contingent on one's performance. The response needed to be rewarded is often attending work on pay day. Not only is pay often not contingent upon performance, but the fixed interval schedule is not given to generating a high response rate. In a creative article, Aldis (1966) suggested an interesting compensation program employing a variable ratio schedule. Instead of an annual Christmas bonus or other types of such expected salary supplements, he suggested a lottery system. If an employee produced above an agreed-upon standard, his name would be placed in a hat. A drawing would be held. The name(s) drawn would receive an amount of money proportionate to the number of units produced during that period of time. This system would approximate the desired variable ratio schedule.

In addition to the prosperity of the owners of gambling establishments, there is some direct evidence that variable ratio schedules will be of use to those charged with predicting and controlling human behavior. A leading St. Louis hardware company,[1] although apparently unaware of the work of the operant conditioners, has applied an approximate variable ratio schedule of reinforcement to reduce absenteeism and tardiness. Although the complete data is not available, the personnel department has reported surprising success. A brief description of the system will be presented below and a more detailed study will be written in the near future.

Under the lottery system, if a person is on time (that is, not so much as a half minute late) for work at the start of his day and after his breaks, he is eligible for a drawing at the end of the month. Prizes worth approximately $20 to $25 are awarded to the winners. One prize is available for each 25 eligible employees. At the end of six months, people who have had perfect attendance for the entire period are eligible for a drawing for a color television set. The names of all the winners and of those eligible are also printed in the company paper, such that social reinforcement may also be a factor. The plan was introduced because tardiness and absenteeism had become a very serious problem. In the words of the personnel manager, absenteeism and tardiness ". . . were lousy before." Since the program was begun 16 months ago, conditions have improved greatly. Sick leave costs have been reduced about 62 percent. After the first month, 151 of approximately 530 employees were eligible for the drawing. This number has grown larger, although not at a steady rate to 219 for the most recent month. Although the comparable figures for the period before the program were unfortunately not available, management has noted great improvements. It would appear that desired behavior by organization participants in terms of tardiness and absenteeism can be readily and inexpensively developed by a variable ratio schedule of positive reinforcement. The possibilities for other areas are limited largely by the creativity of management.

The operant approach also has some additional implications for the use of money as a reward. First, many recent studies have shown money is not as important as other job factors in worker satisfaction. Herzberg, (1968) among others, has said explicitly that money will not promote worker satisfaction. Undoubtedly, in many situations, Herzberg is correct. However, crucial factors of reward contingencies and schedules have not been controlled in these studies. Again, it appears that the important dinstinction that can be made between Herzberg's motivators and hygiene factors is that the former set of rewards are contingent on an individual's responses and the latter are not. If a work situation were designed so that money was directly contingent on performance, the results might be different. A second point has to do with the perception of money as a reward. Opsahl and Dunnette (1966) have recently questioned pay secrecy policies. They maintained that pay secrecy leads to misperception of the amount of money that a promotion might mean. The value of the reinforcers are underestimated by the participants suggesting that they are less effective than they might otherwise be. Certainly, alternative rewards are likely to be "over chosen." By following policies of pay secrecy, organizations seem to be failing to utilize fully their available monetary rewards.

[1] The author wishes to thank Mr. C. for making this information available and one of his students, Richard Weis, for informing him about this program.

In addition to under utilization of money rewards, organizations seem to be almost totally unaware of alternative reinforcers, and in fact see punishment as the only viable method of control when existing reinforcers fail. What are some alternatives to a punishment centered bureaucracy? Some, such as job design, improved scheduling of reinforcement, and a search for new reinforcers have already been suggested. There are other possible reinforcers, a few of which are discussed below.

The important thing about reinforcers is that they be made immediately contingent on desired performance to the greatest degree possible. The potential reinforcers discussed here also require such a contingent relationship, although developing such relationships may be a severe test of an administrator's creativity. One of the more promising reinforcers is leisure. It would seem possible in many jobs to establish an agreed upon standard output for a day's work. This level could be higher than the current average. Once this amount is reached, the group or individual could be allowed the alternative of going home. The result of experiments in this direction would be interesting to all concerned. Quite possibly, this method might lead to a fuller utilization of our labor force. The individual may be able to hold two four-hour jobs, doubling his current contribution. Such a tremendous increase in output is quite possible as Stagner and Rosen (1966) have noted, when the situation possesses appropriate contingencies. Certainly, the problems of industrial discipline, absenteeism, and grievances which result in lower productivity might be ameliorated. Another possible reinforcer is information. Guetzkow (1965) noted that people have a strong desire to receive communication. Rewarding desired performance with communication or feedback may be a relatively inexpensive reinforcer. Graphs, charts, or even tokens which show immediate and cumulative results may serve this function. Some of the widely accepted benefits from participative management may be due to the reinforcing effect of communication. Certainly the "Hawthorne effect" can be described in these terms. In addition, social approval and status may be powerful reinforcers. Blau's classic study described by Homans (1961) on the exchange of approval and status for help is but one example. People will work for approval and status. If these are made contingent on a desired set of responses, the response rate can be increased. At present, often social approval is given by one's peers, but is contingent on behavior which is in conflict with organizational goals.

In addition to these reinforcers, there are certain social exchange concepts such as justice, equity, reciprocity, and indebtedness which deserve attention. Recent research has demonstrated that an unbalanced social exchange, such as one which is inequitable or leaves one person indebted to someone else, may be tension producing in such a way that individuals work to avoid them. In other words, unbalanced exchanges are a source of punishment. Relationships, such as those involving dependency, which result in such social imbalance can be expected to have the same latent consequences as punishment. Techniques which employ social imbalance to predict and control behavior can be expected to be less efficient in most respects than ones based on positive reinforcement.

The crucial variable in distributing any reward is contingency. Managers have been quick to point out that the problem with a "welfare-state" is that rewards do not depend on desired behavior. This point is well taken. It is surprising that the same point has not been recognized in current management practices.

Organizational Climate and Design

Important aspects of human behavior can be attributed to the immediate environment in which people function. The potential then exists to structure and restructure formal organizations in a manner to promote the desired behavior. Once this point is recognized and accepted by managers, progress can begin. The reaction of managers to this approach is often, "You mean my organization should reward people for what they ought to do anyway?" The answer is that people's behavior is largely determined by its outcomes. It is an empirical fact rather than a moral question. If you want a certain response and it does not occur, you had better change the reinforcement contingencies to increase its probable occurrence.

The first step in the direction of designing organizations on this basis involves defining explicitly the desired behaviors and the available reinforcers. The next step is to then make these rewards dependent on the emission of the desired responses. What are some of the implications of such reasoning for organizational design?

Already the importance of organizational climate has been discussed in connection with human development. Some additional implications merit brief consideration. A major one concerns conformity. Often today the degree to which people conform to a wide variety of norms is lamentably acknowledged and the question is asked, "Why do people do it?" The reasons in the operant view are quite clear: conformity is rewarded, deviance is punished. People conform in organizations because conformity is profitable in terms of the outcomes the individual achieves. In fact, Nord (in press) and Walker and Heyns (1962) presented considerable evidence that conformity has the same properties as other operant responses. If managers are really worried about the costs of conformity in terms of creativity and innovation, they must look for ways to reward deviance, to avoid punishing nonconformity, and to avoid rewarding conformity. Furthermore, the way in which rewards are administered is important. Generally, if rewards are given by a person or group of people, a dependency relationship is created, with hostility, fear, anxiety, and other emotional outcomes being probable. Dependence itself may be a discomforting condition. It is therefore desirable to make the rewards come from the environment. Rewards which have previously been established for reaching certain agreed-upon goals are one such means. Meaningful jobs, in which achievement in itself is rewarding are another way. In general, to the degree that competition is with the environment or forces outside the organization, and rewards come from achievement itself, the more effective the reinforcers are apt to be in achieving desired responses.

A final point concerns the actual operation of organizations. Increasingly it is recognized that a formal organization, which aims at the coordination of the efforts of its participants, is dependent on informal relationships for its operation. As Gross (1968) noted,

> In administration, also, "the play's the thing" and not the script. Many aspects of even the simplest operation can never be expressed in writing. They must be sensed and felt. . . . Daily action is the key channel of operational definition. In supplying cues and suggestions, in voicing praise and blame, in issuing verbal instructions, administrators define or clarify operational goals in real life. (p. 406)

More generally, what makes an organization "tick" is the exchange of reinforcers within it and between it and its environment. The nature of these exchanges involves both economic and social reinforcers. Many of these are given and received without explicit recognition or even awareness on the part of the participants. The operant approach, focuses attention on these exchange processes. As a result, it may prove to be an invaluable asset to both administrators and students of administration and organization.

A final advantage of the operant approach for current organizational theory and analysis may be the attention it focuses on planned and rational administration. Gouldner (1966) noted "Modern organizational analysis by sociologists is overpreoccupied with the spontaneous and unplanned responses which organizations make to stress, and too little concerned with patterns of planned and rational administration (p. 397)." The Skinnerian approach leads to rational planning in order to control outcomes previously viewed as spontaneous consequences. This approach could expand the area of planning and rational action in administration.

BIBLIOGRAPHY

Aldis, O. Of pigeons and men. In R. Ulrich, T. Stachnik and T. Mabry (Eds.), *Control of Human Behavior,* Glenview, Ill.: Scott, Foresman, 1966, 218-21.

Ayllon, T. Intensive treatment of psychotic behavior by stimulus satiation and food reinforcement. In R. Ulrich, T. Stachnik and T. Mabry (Eds.), *Control of Human Behavior,* Glenview, Ill.: Scott, Foresman, 1966, 170-76.

Ayllon, T., and Azrin, N. H. The measurement and reinforcement of behavior of psychotics. *Journal of Experimental Analysis of Behavior,* 1965, 8, 357-83.

Bijou S. W., and Baer, D. M. *Child Development.* Vol. 1. New York: Appleton-Century-Crofts, 1961.

Dalton M. The Industrial "rate-buster": a characterization. *Applied Anthropology* 1948, 7, 5-18.

Fleishman, E. A. Leadership climate, human relations training, and supervisory behavior. In *Studies in Personnel and Industrial Psychology,* Homewood, Ill.: Dorsey, 1967, 250-63.

Free records given for E's, pupils report cards improve. *St. Louis Post Dispatch,* December 3, 1967.

Gewirtz. J. L., and Baer, D. M. Deprivation and satiation of social reinforcers as drive conditions. *Journal of Abnormal and Social Psychology,* 1958, 57, 165-72.

Gouldner, A. W. Organizational analysis. In Bennis, W. G., Benne, K. D., and Chin, R. (Eds.), *The Planning of Change,* New York: Holt, Rinehart and Winston, 1966, 393-99.

Gross, B. M. *Organizations and their Managing.* New York: Free Press, 1968.

Guetzkow, H. Communications in Organizations. In March, J. G. (Ed.), *Handbook of Organizations,* Chicago: Rand McNally, 1965, 534-73.

Hamblin, R. L., Bushell, O. B., Buckholdt, D., Ellis D., Ferritor, D., Merritt, G., Pfeiffer, C., Shea, D., and Stoddard, D. Learning, problem children and a social exchange system. Annual Report of the Social Exchange Laboratories, Washington University, and Student Behavior Laboratory, Webster College, St. Louis, Mo. August, 1967.

Herzberg, F. One more time: How do you motivate employees? *Harvard Business Review,* January-February 1968, 53-62.

---*Work and the Nature of Man.* Cleveland: World, 1966.

Homans, G. C. *Social Behavior: Its Elementary Forms.* New York: Harcourt Brace Jovanovich, Inc., 1961.

Hulin, C. L., and Smith, P. A. An empirical investigation of two implications of the two-factor theory of job satisfaction. *Journal of Applied Psychology,* 1967, 51, 396-402.

Lindsay, C. A., Marks, E., and Gorlow, L. The Herzberg theory: a critique and reformulation. *Journal of Applied Psychology,* 1967, 51, 330-39.

Maltzman, I., Simon, S., Roskin, D., and Licht, L. Experimental studies in the training of originality. *Psychological Monographs: General and Applied,* 1960, 74 (6, Whole No. 493).

Maslow, A. *Eupsychian Management.* Homewood, Ill.: Dorsey, 1965.

McGregor, D. *The Human Side of Enterprise.* New York: McGraw-Hill Book Company, 1960.

---*Leadership and Motivation.* Cambridge, Mass.: M.I.T. Press, 1966.

Nord, W. R. Social exchange theory: an integrative approach to social conformity. *Psychological Bulletin,* (in press).

Northern Systems Company, A proposal to the department of labor for development of a prototype project for the new industries program. Part one.

Opsahl, R. L., and Dunnette, M. D. The role of financial compensation in industrial motivation. *Psychological Bulletin,* 1966, 66, 94-118.

Reese, E. P. *The Analysis of Human Operant Behavior.* Dubuque, Ia.: William C. Brown, 1966.

Roy, D. F. "Banana time"–job satisfaction and informal interaction. In Bennis, W. G., Schein, E. H., Berlew, D. E., and Steele, F. I. (Eds.), *Interpersonal Dynamics.* Homewood, Ill.: Dorsey, 1964, 583-600.

Schultz, D. P. Spontaneous alteration behavior in humans, implications for psychological research. *Psychological Bulletin,* 1964, 62, 394-400.

Skinner, B. F. *Science and Human Behavior.* New York: The MacMillan Company, 1953.

---The science of learning and the art of teaching. *Harvard Educational Review,* 1954, 24, 86-97.

---*Walden Two.* New York: The MacMillan Company, 1948.

Stagner, R., and Rosen, H. *Psychology of Union-Management Relations.* Belmont, Cal.: Wadsworth, 1966.

Sykes, A. J. M. The effect of a supervisory training course in changing supervisors' perceptions and expectations of the role of management. *Human Relations* 1962, 15, 227-43.

Vinacke, E.W. Motivation as a complex problem. *Nebraska Symposium on Motivation,* 1962, 10, 1-45.

Walker, E. L., and Heyns, R. W. *An Anatomy of Conformity.* Englewood Cliffs, N. J.: Prentice-Hall Inc., 1962.

Wolf, M. M., Risley, T., and Mees, H. Application of operant conditioning procedures to the behavior problems of an autistic child. In R. Ulrich, T. Stachnik and T. Mabry (Eds.), *Control of Human Behavior,* Glenview, Ill.: Scott, Foresman, 1966, 187-93.

Frank Petrock
Victor Gamboa

EXPECTANCY THEORY AND OPERANT CONDITIONING: A CONCEPTUAL COMPARISON

Operant conditioning and expectancy theory have become major perspectives in organizational behavior. Despite numerous parallels between the two approaches, they have evolved almost independently of each other. The major purpose of this paper is to examine the points of conflict and convergence of these two models as they apply to the behavior of people in organizations.

In the last few years numerous writers (e.g., Vroom, 1964; Atkinson, 1965; Rotter, 1966; Lawler, 1971) have employed expectancy theory as a model for understanding behavior in organizations at a particular moment in time and in a specific situation. Most expectancy theorists share a cognitive orientation; they seek to account for motivated behavior by understanding certain mental processes.

In contrast to expectancy theorists, operant conditioners have focused almost exclusively on the influence of environmental conditions on behavior. These researchers have reported thousands of observations on the behavior of animals and humans without resorting to theory (Skinner, 1950) or to the development of hypothetical constructs, such as expectancy, which cannot be measured directly using current methods of psyco-social research (Skinner, 1953). Our discussion of operant conditioning will be based on the work of Skinner, who is the acknowledged spokesman in this field.

REVIEW OF OPERANT CONDITIONING IN ORGANIZATIONAL LITERATURE

After a slow start, the increase in the use of operant conditioning techniques in organizational behavior has been rapid. While Aldis (1961) discussed the implications of various schedules of reinforcement for such things as the design of wage systems and company bonus schemes, these observations seemed to have had little impact for nearly a decade. Nord (1969) (see preceding article) pointed to operant conditioning as an untapped area in the organizational literature.

Recently several studies have applied the operant viewpoint to the study of organizations. For example, Yukl, Wexley, and Seymore (1972) experimentally

Prepared especially for this volume.

examined the effectiveness of pay incentives under various schedules of reinforcement. They found that pay incentives were more effective in motivating increased production when administered on an intermittent reinforcement schedule than on a continuous reinforcement schedule. Cherrington, Reitz, and Scott (1971), in a study of the satisfaction-productivity issue, concluded that "... by manipulating the contingencies of a reward system, one should be able to create conditions under which satisfaction and performance can be shown empirically to be either independent, positively related, or negatively related" (p. 531). Adam (1972) applied conditioning procedures to 160 individuals who were performing a routine repetitive task. The data revealed that conditioning procedures facilitated higher levels of performance and the maintenance of these higher levels over time. While a number of other studies could be cited, this brief review is adequate to demonstrate the viability of operant conditioning as a major perspective for organizational research and development.

Although rewards and punishments have been used to control human behavior for centuries, the work of Skinner and his followers has induced more systematic application of reinforcement to change human behavior. Most of these applications have been attempted in highly controlled settings (e.g., mental hospitals and prisons) or designed to accomplish only narrowly defined changes in behavior (e.g., programmed learning).

Recently the relevance of operant techniques for complex and open systems (e.g., corporations) has been recognized. Brethower (1972) discussed how these techniques could be used effectively in a variety of work organizations. Moreover, several major work organizations (e.g., Bell Telephone, Emery Air Freight, B. F. Goodrich, General Motors, Allied Foods, Questor Corporation) have conciously applied the principles of operant conditioning in a systematic way to their everyday operations for as long as ten years.

EXPECTANCY THEORY

Expectancy theorists attempt to account for the same behavior discussed by the operant conditioners. However, expectancy theorists explain behavior in terms which the operant conditioners regard as highly speculative. Consequently, these two paradigms seem to be on a collision course. However, since the two approaches may complement each other in important ways, careful study of the similarities and differences of the two perspectives may stimulate the development of a superior perspective than could be constructed from either approach taken alone. By reviewing expectancy theory and then contrasting it with operant conditioning, this paper seeks to begin this rapproachment.

Classes of Motivation Theory

We know that man behaves; we observe human behavior every day. However, in view of the large number of competing theories of motivation, there is less consensus about why man behaves.

In nearly all theories of motivation the unifying conceptual theme is that motivation is an agency, force, or factor that helps to explain why a particular behavior occurs (Bolles, 1967). However, as Bolles pointed out, motivation is an assumed or hypothetical cause of behavior. These agencies, forces, or factors that are assumed to cause behavior are not construed as having any objective reality that can be measured directly.

Depending on what the theorist assumes to be the predominant motivating factor or force, each of the various theories of motivation can be classified into one or more of four general categories. These categories are: instinct, drive, reinforcement, and incentive (Bindra, 1959; Bolles, 1967).

Modern expectancy theories belong in the incentive category. In most respects work of such contemporary expectancy theorists such as Atkinson (1964), Rotter (1966), Vroom (1964), and Lawler (1971, 1973) is clearly based on the central postulate of incentive theory which describes behavior as being consciously purposeful and goal-directed (Tolman, 1932; Bindra, 1959). They have assumed that organisms, especially man, are able to anticipate desirable outcomes and this anticipation or expectation of reward energizes or gets behavior started (Bolles, 1967). In contrast to the instinct, drive, or reinforcement theories of motivation which gave little place for man's behavior as conscious, rational, goal-directed and deliberate, the energizing factor or force for behavior in incentive theories of motivation is cognitive in nature.

Lawler's Expectancy Model

A number of expectancy theories about work behavior are available. Since the various expectancy theories have much in common, we have chosen to limit our discussion to one approach—Edward Lawler's. We selected Lawler's (1971, 1973) formulation for two reasons.

1. Lawler concentrates specifically on the work organization in developing and explaining the utility of his theory and,
2. His theoretical development attempts to be more inclusive than earlier formulations of expectancy theory.

Lawler (1973) summed up the main propositions of his expectancy theory in the following four statements.

(1) *"People have expectancies about the likelihood that certain outcomes will follow their behavior"* (p. 49). This prosposition is a central element of all formulations of expectancy theory. It suggests that people have momentary subjective beliefs about whether or not their behavior or performance will result in desired outcomes. To put it another way, in every situation where a person has an opportunity to behave, he or she has an expectation as to whether or not the behavior will have desirable consequences. These expectations, called Performance-Outcome (P→O) Expectancies, are subjective or perceived P→O Expectancies; they are not necessarily accurate or realistic judgments. They represent what the person believes will result from his performance. These beliefs, according to Lawler, are important in determining performance. If a person believes desirable outcomes will follow performance, then motivation to act will be high.

(2) *"People have a preference about the various outcomes that are poten-*

tially available to them" (p. 49). This is a commonsense notion; each person perceives potential outcomes as being desirable, neutral, or undesirable. In other words, outcomes have a Valence (V). The Valence may be either a positive, neutral or negative. Valence can be thought of as the perceived attractiveness value or worth of an outcome.

Most performances or behaviors usually lead to more than one outcome—each act has a variety of outcomes. More importantly, each outcome usually leads to other secondary outcomes. Consequently the Valence of an action is measured in terms of the perceived attractiveness of the first outcome combined with the perceived value of all the secondary outcomes.

Lawler (1973) hypothesized that motivation to act is a function of Valence associated with an outcome and Performance → Outcome expectancies summed over all possible outcomes. Lawler expressed this relationship in algebraic form as follows:

$$\text{Motivation to Act} = f(\Sigma[(P \rightarrow O)\ (V)]).$$

It is important to note that Lawler did not maintain that the sum of all the (P→O) (V) products is the sole determinant of motivation to act in a certain situation. An additional dimension is needed to account for motivation. Lawler discussed this factor in his third proposition.

(3) *"People have expectancies about the likelihood that an action (effort) on their part will lead to the behavior or performance needed to produce the outcomes"* (p. 49). It is this third proposition of Lawler's that completes his basic model and distinguishes it from other formulations of expectancy theory. He argued that people do not just have expectancies pertaining to P→O beliefs; they also have subjective Effort→Performance (E→P) expectancies about whether or not their Effort (E) will result in the level of Performance (P) required to obtain the desirable outcomes. A person may actually believe that performance will result in desirable outcomes [(P→O) (V)] and still not act, because the person does not believe that his or her effort will result in the level of performance needed to obtain the outcomes. In other words, the individual's (E→P) expectancy is low.

We have now discussed the core elements of Lawler's Expectancy Theory. In his complete model, motivation is viewed as a multiplicative function of the sum of the E→P expectancies and the sum of the [(P→O) (V)] products. Expressed algebraically,

$$\text{Motivation to Act} = \Sigma\left((E \rightarrow P) \times \Sigma[(P \rightarrow O)\ (V)]\right).$$

(4) *"In any situation, the actions a person chooses to take are determined by the expectancies and the preferences that the person has at the time"* (p. 49). This proposition states that a person's expectancies and valances may be subject to change. Thus, without changing the basic formula, Lawler was able to account for the fact that from time to time, within the same situation, an individual's behavior may vary. A person's behavior is influenced by his valences and expectations as they exist at a specific point in time.

To summarize, we have used Lawler's theory as an example of incentive theories of motivation. It is typical of many incentive theories in that it stresses the role of cognition; it maintains that people actively select the behaviors that they engage in and that this selection is influenced by the subjective expectancies and valences associated with particular behaviors.

COMPARISON OF EXPECTANCY THEORY AND OPERANT CONDITIONING

For the most part operant conditioning and expectancy theories have been viewed as competing perspectives. However, if the central postulates of the two approaches are compared and contrasted, and an effort is made to translate each model into the terms of the other, the two appear to be more overlapping and complementary than contradictory. We reached this conclusion by comparing the postulates of the two approaches on a variety of issues. Each of these issues is treated separately below.

Use of the Concept of Probability

While probability plays a major part in the thinking of Lawler and Skinner, each writer uses the term to refer to different things. Lawler (1971) focused on the subjective or perceived probabilities that "effort will result in a particular level of performance (E→P) and 2) this level of performance will result in desired outcomes (P→O)." Skinner, however, employed the concept of probability to refer to actual behavior—the likelihood that a particular response will be emitted. His measure is direct; it does not refer to cognitive or mentalistic beliefs.

While both writers agree that the probability of a response is affected by the performance-outcome relationship, they differ in their explanation of this process. Lawler sees the performance-outcome relationship as changing the subjective probabilities directly. These altered subjective probabilities, in turn, affect how the person will behave in the future. In contrast, Skinner does not resort to such internal events. He deals only with manifest actions on the basis that it is enough to know that contingent outcomes increase, decrease, or maintain the probability of a particular response.

These conceptual differences are associated with different research strategies. Due to its concern with subjective probabilities, Lawler's expectancy perspective leads the researcher to amass self-report protocols about internal conditions of organizational participants. Such self-report data provide operational measures of effort-performance (E→P) and performance-outcome (P→O) probabilities which are necessary for the computation of motivational scores.

By contrast, since operant conditioners apply the idea of probability to observable behavior, their data are not self-report protocols about internal conditions; they measure the frequency of rate of response. In Skinner's words:

> An organism possesses a habit to the extent that a certain form of behavior is observed with special frequency—attributable to the history of the individual. . . . These frequencies are the observable facts and must be studied

> as such rather than as evidence for the embodiment of probability in neural or psychic states. (1953a, p. 69)

In effect, behavior and the frequency of behavior are the major dependent variables for most Skinnerians; they deny the value of inferring the causes of these frequencies from internal expectancies. However some behavioristically inclined writers have proposed alternatives to the total exclusion of self-report data. For example, Bandura (1969) suggested that it might be better to treat self-report data (whether of valences, expectancies, attitudes, etc.) as simply another class of behavior. However, he was clear that these indices of an internal state should not be conceptualized as having special causal powers.

In sum, probability is an important concept in both the expectancy and operant perspectives. Researchers from both camps agree that the occurance of a behavior is a matter of likelihood rather than absolute definiteness. However, the operant conditioners deal primarily with the probability of actual behavior, whereas the expectancy theorists are more concerned with subjective probabilities.

Performance-Reward Relationship

A crucial and dominant similarity between Lawler and Skinner is the importance each gives to the relationship between rewards and the performance of desirable behavior. Lawler (1971) concluded,

> As we have seen, pay serves to motivate employees when it is closely tied to performance. As we have seen, the research evidence shows that people are most satisfied with their pay when they feel that it is based on performance. (p. 257)

Note that emphasis is placed on tying rewards "closely" to performance.

Similarly Skinner (1953) maintains that rewards have the greatest effect on performance when they are contingent on performance; the closer in time the reward follows the response, the more effect it has on the probability of the response occuring again. As Skinner (1958) wrote:

> A delay of even a fraction of a second is sometimes important, as we have found in designing equipment for the study of operant behavior in the pigeon. When the response studied is pecking a plastic disc, the controlling circuit must act so rapidly that the sound of the magazine, as a conditioned reinforcer, will coincide with striking the disc rather than pulling the head *away* from it. This is a matter of perhaps a twentieth of a second, but such a delay produces disturbing changes in the topography of the response. (p. 95)

Reward or Reinforcement

Lawler speaks of the importance of attaching rewards to performance; Skinner speaks of *reinforcements* following desired performance. What is the relationship between rewards and reinforcements?

The two are not synonymous. Ayllon and Azrin (1968) argued that to study human motivation effectively, a crucial distinction must be made between reward and reinforcement because the concept of reward directs attention to the relationship between behavior and the internal, psychic environment, which can be neither directly measured nor modified. In contrast, the concept of reinforcement directs the study of motivation to the interaction between behavior and the external environment, which is both directly measurable and modifiable. Studying motivation from a reward orientation leads primarily to the development of theory, whereas a reinforcement orientation leads to the development of technology to manage behavior.

The distinction between reward and reinforcement is related to the more general difference between mentalistic and behavioristic approaches. Reward is primarily a mentalistic concept. Rewards are typically understood or defined in terms of the subjective reactions they produce in the individual (Allyon, 1968) which act to reduce a physiological drive or to fulfill a psychological need. (Thibaut & Kelly, 1959). In contrast, a reinforcer is defined as any stimulus event or consummatory behavior that leads directly to an increase in the probability of a specific response (Ayllon, 1968). Reinforcement, unlike reward, is based on the direct effect it has on behavior rather than on some mental or physical state of the individual. Reinforcement is a concept that directs attention to behavior instead of to assumed internal cognitive or emotional states.[1]

Performance-Reward-Satisfaction Relationship

Satisfaction is a subjective state of the individual; it cannot be directly observed or measured. Consequently most operant conditioners have not taken satisfaction as problematic whereas it is a central concern of many expectancy theorists.

As shown in the diagram below, Lawler envisions a close relationship between performance, reward and satisfaction.

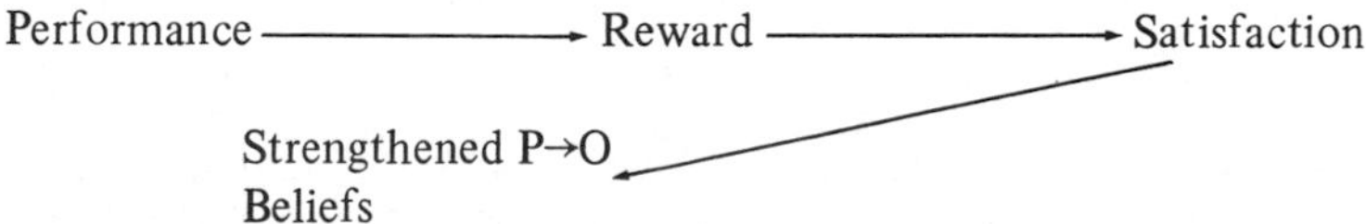

Lawler (1967) maintained that performance causes satisfaction because performance leads to rewards, which in turn lead to satisfaction. Furthermore, by strengthening a person's expectations that his or her performance will lead to desired outcomes in the future, rewards can act to increase an individual's motivation.

In contrast operant conditioners see no necessary cause and effect relationship between performance and satisfaction. Instead, to the extent they discuss satisfaction at all, they argue that the structure of performance-reinforcement

[1] Having recognized this difference, in the remainder of the paper we will attempt to maintain this distinction. We will use rewards when discussing expectancy theory and reinforcement when treating operant conditioning. When discussing an issue where we are treating both approaches together, we will use either "rewards" or "reinforcement."

contingencies influences satisfaction. As Cherrington, Reitz, and Scott (1971) have shown, satisfaction may be independent, positively, or negatively related to performance. This position is represented schematically below.

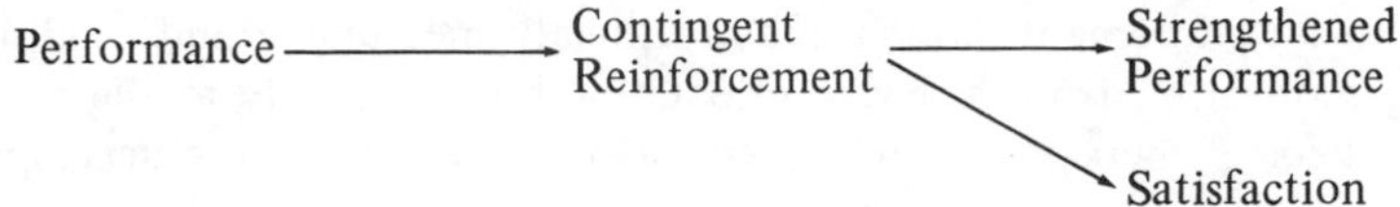

Thus, at least some behaviorists suggest that reinforcement made contingent on desired performance results in both an increase in the frequency of the desired performance and in satisfaction.

It appears that both expectancy theory and operant conditioning regard satisfaction as an outcome rather than as a causal variable. Neither perspective views satisfaction as strongly affecting performance or motivation. Instead, both focus on contingencies between performance and reward. Thus both approaches receive support from Cherrington *et al.*'s finding that such contingencies can actually determine the relationship between satisfaction and performance.

Schedules of "Reinforcement"

Expectancy theorists and operant conditioners agree that outcomes must be closely connected to performance to maximize their impact on future behavior. However, there is a great difference between the two approaches about how closely and through what patterns "rewards" should be related to performance. In other words, the two approaches disagree on the nature of optimal schedules of "reinforcement."

Expectancy theory maintains the need for a close connection between outcome and performance on a continuous schedule of reward. This means that after every act there should be an objective or subjective reward for the individual. Lawler (1971) reasons:

> If he receives them (rewards) for performing well, this should strengthen his P→O beliefs and thereby increase his motivation when he again finds himself in that situation. If he performs well and does not get the rewards, however, his P→O beliefs will be weakened and he will be less motivated next time around. (p. 270)

Thus, for Lawler, each actual performance-outcome cycle affects the subjective P→O expectancies. Rewarding contingencies strengthen the expectancies; nonrewarding expectancies weaken them and thereby reduce motivation. From this assumption it would appear that a reward for every desirable behavior–i.e., a continuous schedule of reward, is logically best for increasing the motivation to perform.

In contrast, based on data and not on theory, operant conditioners maintain that in order to increase and maintain high rates of behavior, intermittent schedules–where only some fraction of the responses are reinforced–are best.

While the data show that a continuous schedule is best when the person or organism is learning new behavior, once learning has occured, a gradual shift to an intermittent schedule of reinforcement produces more sustained changes in behavior.

A recent laboratory study by Yukl *et al.* (1972) on pay schedules dealt specifically with this source of disagreement between the operant conditioners and expectancy theorists. The expectancy theory prediction that production would be greater on a continuous schedule of pay was tested against the operant conditioning prediction that production (i.e., rates of response) would be greater under an intermittent schedule. The experimenters found ". . . that a variable ratio schedule of reinforcement is a more efficient way of using pay incentives than a continuous reinforcement schedule" (p. 19). This result is in sharp contrast to Lawler's present formulation of expectancy theory which suggests that continuous reinforcement contingencies are optimal.

These results cannot be interpreted to mean that expectations are not affected by outcomes, but do call into question the hypothesized linkage between expectancies and performance. It is perfectly logical that a person would be more definite about his or her expectations that outcomes will result from his or her performance under a continuous schedule of reinforcement than he or she would be under an intermittent schedule. What the expectancy theorists are saying is that expectancies determine or motivate behavior. The more consistent the outcomes, the stronger the expectancies; the stronger or more definite the P→O expectancies, the more likely is the behavior.

However, the data show that behavior is more likely and consistent under intermittent schedules. Perhaps rewards affect expectancies but expectancies have no causal affect upon behavior. Thus, under an intermittent schedule of reinforcement, the expectancy of reward may be low, but the rate of behavior may remain high. Under these conditions a person may be certain that outcomes will result from behavior but not be able to say exactly which response will produce the outcome. Therefore, if asked what is the likelihood of reinforcement occuring on the next response, the person may report a low perceived expectancy but still continue to respond.

Intrinsic vs. Extrinsic "Reinforcement"

Intrinsic "reinforcers" are internal consequences that a person experiences as a result of his or her performance. These consequences include such experiences as feelings of competence, satisfaction and pride. In contrast, extrinsic "reinforcement" stems from sources external to the person. They are also contingent upon behavior, but are usually presented by others in the environment who control the sources of "reward." (Of course this outcome can also lead to people's reporting feelings of competence, satisfaction and pride.)

Operant conditioners have given most of their attention to extrinsic reinforcement, because it can be directly observed, measured, and manipulated. When they do discuss internally mediated reinforcers, they prefer the term "self-reinforcement" (Katz, 1967) over intrinsic reinforcement. This preference is perhaps due their experimental framework. As Katz observed, the only way to study intrinsic reinforcement empirically is to literally give subjects opportunity to give themselves "rewards" for their performance. However, to deal with intrinsic reinforcement conceptually, operant conditioners have referred to a reinforcement hierarchy. As Zeigler and Kanzer (1962) noted, individual development is associated with changes in the value attached to various sources of reinforcement. As individuals develop, they often move from being responsive to primarily tangible rewards to being more responsive to social approval. At higher stages an individual becomes more responsive to self-reinforcement. For example, a person becomes more interested in giving a "right" answer than in whether or not the answer results in tangible rewards or social approval (Katz, 1967).

In summary, operant conditioners prefer to work with extrinsic rather than intrinsic sources of reinforcement because they can be observed, measured, and manipulated. However, self-reinforcement can be introduced into the operant framework by considering self-administered "rewards" and/or intrinsic feelings that are contingent upon performance.

On the other hand, expectancy theory is mainly concerned with intrinsic sources of reward. Lawler (1971) perceives intrinsic rewards as being crucial because they can be immediately and directly connected to performance. Even Horabin (1967), who is closely associated with the operant conditioning viewpoint, stresses the importance of intrinsic reinforcement because it can be immediately presented when warranted and withheld automatically when not warranted. Moreover, intrinsic rewards do not depend on other people who may misjudge or fail to reinforce.

Expectancy theorists have stressed that intrinsic rewards have a strong impact on behavior in a large number of circumstances, such as the work environment. For example, they hypothesize that work motivation is often low because jobs are not designed to be intrinsically rewarding. To increase motivation they point to the need to design jobs so that just doing them is rewarding.

The emphasis expectancy theorists give to intrinsic rewards is complemented in their discussions of extrinsic rewards. Porter and Lawler (1968), for example, assume that the effects of intrinsic and extrinsic rewards are additive—an interesting task combined with contingent pay produces better performance than either condition taken alone. Research, however, has given mixed support to this assumption. Deci (1972) found that contingent pay decreased workers' intrinsic motivation to perform. However, Foster and Hamner (1974) challenged Deci's findings; they reported that when contingent payments were not delayed, the effects of intrinsic and extrinsic rewards were additive.

Both Deci's and Foster and Hamner's studies are initial attempts to determine the effects of extrinsic and intrinsic rewards on job performance. In the future such research may provide a bridge for integrating the two approaches. However, at present, most people associate operant conditioners with extrinsic reinforcement and expectancy with intrinsic reinforcement. Lawler (1971) emphasized intrinsic rewards because they are by nature more directly and immediately connected to performance; the Skinnerians (Brethower, 1972) have focused on extrinsic reinforcers because they are directly measurable.

DISCUSSION AND IMPLICATIONS

This paper analyzed the conceptual similarities and differences between expectancy theory and operant conditioning. It is clear that the two positions parallel each other in a number of important ways. In fact, organizational behaviorists, particularly those with a pragmatic orientation, might find it useful to draw on both approaches simultaneously.

The major differences between the two approaches are often conceptual rather than pragmatic. Consequently, for many purposes these points of disagreement are unimportant. If the development of a technology to improve organizational performance is a major goal, then it may be relatively unimportant what motivational constructs (if any) we use, because both the expectancy and the operant perspectives lead to similar or at least parallel recommendations for the design of organizations.

Both approaches advocate similar changes in the work environment, even though the theoretical reasons for the changes differ. Expectancy theory as proposed by Lawler and operant conditioning in general share a fundamental premise —environment ought to be restructured to fit individuals. For example, consider job design. Regardless of which of the two models a manager adopts, he or she will be encouraged to adopt similar strategies. First, the manager will be led to consider a number of possible sources of both intrinsic and extrinsic "reinforcement." Second, the manager will be induced to design jobs so that these "rewards" are made contingent upon performance.

REFERENCES

Adam, E. E. "An Analysis of Changes in Performance Quality with Operant Conditioning Procedures." *Journal of Applied Psychology* 56 (1972): 480-486.

Aldis, O. "Of Pigeons and Men." *Harvard Business Review* (1961): 59-63.

Aronfreed, J. *Conduct and Conscience.* New York: Academic Press, 1968.

Atkinson, J. W. "Towards Experimental Analysis of Human Motivation in Terms of Motives, Expectancies and Incentives." In *Motives in Fantasy, Action, and Society,* edited by J. W. Atkinson. Princeton, N.J.: Van Nostrand Reinhold, 1964.

Atkinson, J. W., and Reitman, W. R. "Performance as a Function of Motive Strength and Expectance of Goal Attainment." *Journal of Abnormal and Social Psychology* 8 (1965): 357-383

Ayllon, T., and Azrin, N. *The Token Economy.* New York: Appleton-Century-Crofts, 1968.

Bandura, A. *Principles of Behavior Modification.* New York: Holt, Rinehart and Winston, 1969.

Bindra, D. *Motivation: A Systematic Reinterpretation.* New York: Ronald, 1959.

Bolles, R. C. *Theories of Motivation.* New York: Harper and Row, 1967.

Brethower, D. M. *Behavioral Analysis in Business and Industry: A Total Performance System.* Kalamazoo, Mich.: Behaviordelia, Inc., 1972.

Carpenter, F. *The Skinner Primer.* New York: The Free Press, 1974.

Cherrington, D. J., Reitz, H. J., and Scott, W. E. "Effects of Contingent and Non-contingent Reward on the Relationship Between Satisfaction and Task Performance." *Journal of Applied Psychology* 55 (1971): 531-536.

Deci, E. L. "The Effects of Contingent and Non-Contingent Rewards and Controls on Intrinsic Motivation." *Organizational Behavior and Human Performance* 8 (1972): 217-229.

Foster, L. W., and Hamner, W. C. "Are Intrinsic and Extrinsic Rewards Additive: A test of Deci's Cognitive Theory and Task Motivators." Paper presented at the Academy of Management Conference at Seattle, 1974.

Horabin, I. *Toward Greater Employee Productivity.* Summit Point, W. Va.: 1967.

Hull, C. L. *Principles of Behavior.* New York: Appleton-Century-Crofts, 1943.

Jenkins, W. O., and J. C. Stanley, Jr. "Partial Reinforcement: A Review and Critique." *Psychological Bulletin* 47 (1950): 193-234.

Jones, M. R., ed. *Nebraska Symposium on Motivation.* Lincoln: University of Nebraska Press, 1955.

Katz, I. "Socialization of Academic Motivation." In *Nebraska Symposium on Motivation,* edited by D. Levine. Lincoln: University of Nebraska Press, 1967.

Lawler, E. E. *Pay and Organizational Effectiveness: A Psychological View.* New York: McGraw-Hill Book Co., 1971.

Lawler, E. E. *Motivation in Work Organizations.* Monterey, Calif.: Brooks/Cole Publishing Co., 1973.

Lawler, E. E., and Porter, L. W. "The Effect of Performance on Job Satisfaction." *Industrial Relations* 7 (1967): 20-28.

Lewin, K. *A Dynamic Theory of Personality.* New York: McGraw-Hill Book Co., 1935.

Lewis, D. J. "Partial Reinforcement: A Selective Review of the Literature since 1950." *Psychological Bulletin* 57 (1960): 1-28.

Nord, W. R. "Beyond the Teaching Machine: The Neglected Area of Operant Conditioning in the Theory and Practice of Management." In *Concepts and Controversy in Organizational Behavior,* edited by W. R. Nord, pp. 145-168. Pacific Palisades, Calif.: Goodyear Publishing Co., 1972.

Porter, L. W. "Turning Work into Non-work: The Rewarding Environment." In *Work and Non-work in the Year 2001,* edited by M. D. Dunnette, pp. 113-133. Monterey, Calif.: Brooks/Cole Publishing Co., 1973.

Porter, L. W., and Lawler, E. E. *Managerial Attitudes and Performance.* Homewood, Ill.: Richard D. Irwin, Inc., 1968.

Rotter, J. B. "Generalized Expectancies for Internal versus External Control of Reinforcement." *Psychological Monographs* 80, 1 (1966): 1-28.

Skinner, B. F. "Are Theories of Learning Necessary?" *Psychological Review* 57 (1950): 193-216.

Skinner, B. F. *Science and Human Behavior.* New York: The Free Press, 1953.

Skinner, B. F. "Some Contributions of an Experimental Analysis of Behavior to Psychology as a Whole." *American Psychologist* 8 (1953): 69-78, (a).

Skinner, B. F. "Reinforcement Today." *American Psychologist* 13 (1958): 94-99.

Skinner, B. F. *Beyond Freedom and Dignity*. New York: Alfred A. Knopf, 1972.

Thibaut, J. W., and Kelly, H. H. *The Social Psychology of Groups.* New York: John Wiley and Sons, Inc., 1959.

Tolman, E. C. *Purposive Behavior in Animals and Men.* New York: Century Co., 1932.

Vroom, V. H. *Work and Motivation.* New York: John Wiley and Sons, Inc., 1964.

Watson, D. L., and Tharp, R. G. *Self-Directed Behavior.* Monterey, Calif.: Brooks/Cole Publishing Co., 1972.

Yukl, G., Wexley, K. N., and Seymore, J. D. "Effectiveness of Pay Incentives under Variable Ratio and Continuous Reinforcement Schedules." *Journal of Applied Psychology* 56 (1972): 19-23.

Zeigler, E., and Kanzer, P. "The Effectiveness of Two Classes of Verbal Reinforcement on the Performance of Middle-Class and Lower-Class Children." *Journal of Personality* 30 (1962): 157-165.

chapter **6**

Personality, Culture, and Management

Personality development is influenced by interaction among members of a society. This section explores the process by which values and behavioral tendencies are transmitted within a culture. Linton, in the first selection, describes the relationship between personality and culture. One of the major functions of culture, in Linton's view, is the preparation or training of people for social positions, such as work and organizational roles that they will occupy in the future. In this view, culture has broad implications for the management of people in organizations. Nord, in the next selection, explores some of the implications of culture for organizational behavior.

THE CONCEPT OF CULTURE

Linton's (1945) definition of culture as "... the configuration of learned behavior and results of behavior whose component elements are shared and transmitted by the members of a particular society" (p. 32) is widely accepted. Importantly, this definition refers only to learned behaviors organized into a patterned whole. In other words, the behaviors in question are acquired and are part of a series of acts that occur together frequently. Further, Linton used "behavior and results of behavior" broadly to include overt behavior (physical and muscular movements) and covert or psychological behavior (attitudes, values, and knowledge). Finally, this definition includes only transmitted behaviors which are "shared" (held in common by two or more members of society).

Transmission of Behavior

For Linton, imitation was an important source of socialization. Support for this view has come from recent studies which have shown that people learn responses by watching other people interacting with the environment. It is quite likely that much role behavior, such as appropriate work behavior, is learned from observation of the actions of people who play those roles. Thus, much cultural learning may occur vicariously and informally as a result of imitation.[1]

1. An excellent discussion of modeling and imitative learning can be found in Bandura (1969).

This mode of transmission is central in the view of Linton and other sociologically oriented approaches to personality development.

REFERENCES

Bandura, A. *Principles of Behavior Modification.* New York: Holt, Rinehart and Winston, 1969.

Linton, R. *The Cultural Background of Personality.* New York: Appleton-Century-Crofts, 1945.

Ralph Linton

CULTURE AND PERSONALITY FORMATION

* * *

Our discussion of the possible role of hereditary factors in determining the personality norms for various societies should have made it clear that these factors are quite inadequate to account for many of the observable differences. The only alternative is to assume that such differences are referable to the particular environments within which the members of various societies are reared. As has been pointed out elsewhere, the environmental factors which appear to be most important in connection with personality formation are people and things. The behavior of the members of any society and the forms of most of the objects which they use are largely stereotyped and can be described in terms of culture patterns. When we say that the developing individual's personality is shaped by culture, what we actually mean is that it is shaped by the experience which he derives from his contact with such stereotypes. That it actually is shaped by such contacts to a very large extent will hardly be doubted by anyone familiar with the evidence; however, the literature on the subject seems to have largely ignored one important aspect of the shaping process.

The influences which culture exerts on the developing personality are of two quite different sorts. On the one hand we have those influences which derive from the culturally patterned behavior of other individuals *toward* the child. These begin to operate from the moment of birth and are of paramount importance during infancy. On the other hand we have those influences which derive from the individual's observation of, or instruction in, the patterns of behavior characteristic of his society. Many of these patterns do not affect him directly, but they provide him with models for the development of his own habitual responses to various situations. These influences are unimportant in early infancy but continue to affect him throughout life. The failure to distinguish between these two types of cultural influence has led to a good deal of confusion.

It must be admitted at once that the two types of influence overlap at certain points. Culturally patterned behavior directed toward the child may serve as a model for the development of some of his own behavior patterns. This factor becomes operative as soon as the child is old enough to observe and remember what other people are doing. When, as an adult, he finds himself confronted by the innumerable problems involved in rearing his own children, he turns to these childhood memories for guidance. Thus in almost any American community we find parents sending their children to Sunday School because they themselves were sent to Sunday School. The fact that, as adults, they greatly prefer golf to church attendance does little to weaken the pattern. However, this aspect of any society's patterns for child-rearing is rather incidental to the influence which such patterns exert upon personality formation. At most it insures that children born into a particular society will be reared in much the same way generation after generation. The real importance of the patterns for early care and child training lies in their effects upon the deeper levels of the personalities of individuals reared according to them.

It is generally accepted that the first few years of the individual's life are crucial for the establishment of the highly generalized value-attitude systems which form the deeper levels of personality content. The first realization of this fact came from the study of atypical individuals in our own society and the discovery that certain of their peculiarities seemed to be rather consistently linked with certain sorts of atypical childhood experiences. The extension of personality studies to other societies in which both the normal patterns of child-rearing and the normal personality configurations for adults were different from our own only served to emphasize the importance of very early conditioning. Many of the "normal" aspects of European personalities which were accepted at first as due to instinctive factors are now recognized as results of our own particular patterns of child care. Although study of the relations between various societies' techniques for child-rearing and the basic personality types for adults in these societies has barely begun, we have already reached a point where certain correlations seem to be recognizable. Although a listing of all these correlations is impossible in a discussion as brief as the present one, a few examples may serve for illustration.

In societies in which the culture pattern prescribes absolute obedience from the child to the parent as a prerequisite for rewards of any sort, the normal adult will tend to be a submissive individual, dependent and lacking in initiative. Even though he has largely forgotten the childhood experiences which led to the establishment of these attitudes, his first reaction to any new situation will be to look to someone in authority for support and direction. It is worth noting in this connection that there are many societies in which the patterns of child-rearing are so effective in producing adult personalities of this type that special techniques have been developed for training a few selected individuals for leadership. Thus, among the Tanala of Madagascar, eldest sons are given differential treatment from birth, this treatment being designed to develop initiative and willingness to assume responsibility, while other children are systematically disciplined and repressed. Again, individuals who are reared in very small family groups of our own type have a tendency to focus their emotions and their anticipations of reward or punishment on a few other individuals. In this they are harking back unconsciously to a childhood in which all satisfactions and frustrations derived from their own fathers and mothers. In societies where the child is reared in an extended family environment, with numerous adults about, any one of whom may either reward or punish, the normal personality will tend in the opposite direction. In such societies the average individual is incapable of strong or lasting attachments or hatreds toward particular persons. All personal interactions embody an unconscious attitude of: "Oh well, another will be along presently." It is difficult to conceive of such a society embodying in its culture such patterns as our concepts of romantic love, or of the necessity for finding the one and only partner without whom life will be meaningless.

Such examples could be multiplied indefinitely, but the above will serve to show the sort of correlations which are now emerging from studies of personality and culture. These correlations reflect linkages of a simple and obvious sort, and it is already plain that such one-to-one relationships between cause and effect are in the minority. In most cases we have to deal with complex configurations of child-training patterns which, as a whole, produce complex personality configurations in the adult. Nevertheless, no one who is familiar with the results which have already been obtained can doubt that here lies the key to most of the differences in basic personality type which have hitherto been ascribed to hereditary factors. The "normal" members of different societies owe their varying personality configurations much less to their genes than to their nurseries.

While the culture of any society determines the deeper levels of its members' personalities through the particular techniques of child-rearing to which it subjects them, its influence does not end with this. It goes on to shape the rest of their personalities by providing models for their specific responses as well. This latter process continues throughout life. As the individual matures and then ages, he constantly has to unlearn patterns of response which have ceased to be effective and to learn new ones more appropriate to his current place in the society. At every step in this process, culture serves as a guide. It not only provides him with models for his changing roles but also insures that these roles shall be, on the whole, compatible with his deep seated value-attitude systems. All the patterns within a single culture tend to show a sort of psychological coherence quite aside from their functional interrelations. With rare exceptions, the "normal" individual who adheres to them will not be required to do anything which is incompatible with the deeper levels of his personality structure. Even when one society borrows patterns of behavior from another, these patterns will usually be modified and reworked until they become congruous with the basic personality type of the borrowers. Culture may compel the atypical individual to adhere to forms of behavior which are repugnant to him, but when such behavior is repugnant to the bulk of a society's members, it is culture which has to give way.

Turning to the other side of the picture, the acquisition of new behavior patterns which are congruous with the individual's generalized value-attitude systems tends to reinforce these systems and to establish them more firmly as time passes. The individual who spends his life in any society with a fairly stable culture finds his personality becoming more firmly integrated as he grows older. His adolescent doubts and questionings with respect to the attitudes implicit in his culture disappear as he reaffirms them in his adherence to the overt behavior which his culture prescribes. In time he emerges as a pillar of society, unable to understand how anyone can entertain such doubts. While this process may not make for progress, it certainly makes for individual contentment. The state of such a person is infinitely happier than that of one who finds himself compelled to adhere to patterns of overt behavior which are not congruous with the value-attitude systems established by his earliest experiences. The result of such incongruities can be seen in many individuals who have had to adapt to rapidly changing culture conditions such as those which obtain in our own society. It is even more evident in the case of those who, having begun life in one culture, are attempting to adjust to another. These are the "marginal men" whose plight is recognized by all who have worked with the phenomenon of acculturation. Lacking the reinforcement derived from constant expression in overt behavior, the early-established value-attitude systems of such individuals are weakened and overlaid. At the same time, it seems that they are rarely if ever eliminated, still less replaced by new systems congruous with the cultural milieu in which the individual has to operate. The acculturated individual can learn to act and even to think in terms of his new society's culture, but he cannot learn to feel in these terms. At each point where decision is required he finds himself adrift with no fixed points of reference.

In summary, the fact that personality norms differ for different societies can be explained on the basis of the different experience which the members of such societies acquire from contact with their cultures. In the case of a few small societies whose members have a homogeneous heredity, the influence of physiological factors in determining the psychological potentialities of the majority of these members cannot be ruled out, but the number of such cases is certainly small. Even when common hereditary factors may be present, they can affect only potentialities for response. They are never enough in themselves to account for the differing content and organization which we find in the basic personality types for different societies.

Early in this chapter I cited three conclusions which anthropologists had arrived at as a result of their studies of personality in a wide range of societies and cultures. That personality norms differ for different societies is only the first of these. It is still necessary to explain why the members of any society always show considerable individual variation in personality and also why much the same range of variation and much the same personality types seem to be present in all societies. The first of these problems presents few difficulties. No two individuals, even identical twins, are exactly alike. The members of any society, no matter how closely inbred it may be, differ in their genetically determined potentialities for growth and development. Moreover the working out of these potentialities is affected by all sorts of environmental factors. From the moment of birth on, individuals will differ in size and vigor, while a little later differences in intelligence and learning ability will become apparent. It has already been said that the process of personality formation seems to be mainly one of the integration of experience. This experience, in turn, derives from the interaction of the individual with his environment. It follows that even identical environments, if such things are conceivable, will provide different individuals with different experiences and result in their developing different personalities.

Actually, the situation is much more complicated than this. Even the best-integrated society and culture provides the individuals who are reared in it with environments which are far from uniform. Culture expresses itself to the individual in terms of the behavior of other people and of his contacts with the objects which members of his society habitually make and use. The latter aspect of the cultural environment may be fairly uniform in some of the simpler societies where a combination of general poverty and patterns of sharing prevents the development of marked differences in living standards, but such societies certainly are in the minority. In most communities the various households vary in their equipment and thus provide the children reared in them with somewhat different physical environments. We do not know in how far differences of this sort are significant in personality formation, but everything indicates that they are of rather secondary importance. People have an infinitely greater effect on the developing individual than do things. In particular, the close and continuous contact which the child has with members of his own family, whether parents or siblings, seems to be crucial in establishing his generalized value-attitude systems. Needless to say, the experience which he may derive from such contacts is as varied as the individuals themselves. Even the most rigid culture patterns allow a certain amount of latitude in individual behavior, while the patterns for family relationships can never be too rigid in practice. Someone has said, "Nothing is as continuous as marriage," and the same would apply to parent-child relations. Repeated personal interactions lead to the development of individual patterns of behavior whose range of variation is limited only by fear of what the neighbors may say. Even while acting within the limits imposed by culture, it is possible for parents in any society to be affectionate or indifferent, strict or permissive, sources of aid and security in the child's dealings with outsiders or additional dangers in a generally hostile world. Individual differences and environmental differences can enter into an almost infinite series of permutations and combinations, and the experience which different individuals may derive from these is equally varied. This fact is quite sufficient to account for the differences in personality content which are to be found among the members of any society.

Why much the same range of variation and much the same personality types seem to be present in all societies presents a more difficult problem. Anthropologists themselves are in much less complete agreement on these points than on the preceding ones. Most anthropologists who have had intimate contacts with a number of different societies believe that such is the case, but any real proof or disproof must await the development of much better techniques for personality diagnosis. It must also be understood that when anthropologists say that much the same personality types seem to be present in all societies, in spite of marked differences in their frequencies, the term *personality* is used in a special sense. Most of the specific responses of individuals always fall within the limits set by culture, and it would be too much to expect to find them duplicated in members of different societies. What the anthropologist means is that when one becomes sufficiently familiar with an alien culture and with the individuals who share it, one finds that these individuals are fundamentally the same as various people whom he has known in his own society. While the specific, culturally patterned responses of the two will differ, their abilities and their basic value-attitude systems will be very much the same. This sort of matching does not require any elaborate typing of personalities in technical terms. What it does require is an intimate and sympathetic knowledge of the individuals and cultures involved. One must become exceedingly familiar with the culture of another group before the differences between individual norms of behavior and cultural norms become sufficiently obvious to serve as a guide in judging the deeper levels of individual personalities.

Similarities in the ability levels of members of different societies are not difficult to explain. All human beings are, after all, members of a single species, and the potential range of variations in this respect must be much the same for all societies. Similarities in the generalized value-attitude systems of individuals reared in different cultural environments are more difficult to account for, but there can be no question that they do occur. In the light of our present knowledge the most probable explanation seems to be that they are primarily a result of similar family situations operating upon individuals with similar levels of ability. It has already been noted that culture patterns for the interactions of family members always permit a considerable range of individual variation. In all societies the personalities involved in family situations tend to arrange themselves in much the same orders of dominance and to develop much the same patterns of private, informal interaction. Thus even in the most strongly patriarchal societies one encounters a surprising number of families in which the wife and mother is the dominant member. She may accord her husband exaggerated respect in public, but neither he nor the children will have any doubt as to where real power lies. Again, there are a whole series of biologically conditioned situations which repeat themselves irrespective of the cultural setting. In every society there will be eldest children and youngest children, only children and those reared as members of a large sibling group, feeble, sickly children and strong, vigorous ones. The same thing holds for various sorts of parent-child relationships. There are favorite children, wanted or unwanted children, good sons and black sheep who are constantly subject to suspicion and discipline. Even while operating within the culturally established limits of parental authority, various parents may be affectionate and permissive or take a sadistic delight in exercising their disciplinary functions to the full. Each of these situations will result in a particular sort of early experience for the individual. When essentially similar individuals in different societies are exposed to similar family situations, the result will be a marked similarity in the deeper levels of their personality configurations.

Although the family situations just discussed operate at what might be termed a subcultural level, the frequency with which a particular situation arises in a particular society will be influenced by cultural factors. Thus it is much more difficult for a wife to establish control in a strongly patriarchal society than in a matriarchal one. In the former case she has to work counter to the accepted rules for the marital relationship and to brave all sorts of social pressures. Only a woman of very strong character, or one with a very weak husband, will be able to establish dominance. In the latter case any woman with ordinary strength of character can dominate her household with the aid of social pressures. In every society the bulk of the families will approximate the culturally established norms in their members' interpersonal relationships. It follows that most of the children reared in a particular society will be exposed to similar family situations and will emerge with many elements of even the deeper levels of their personalities in common. This conclusion seems to be borne out by the study of a wide range of societies. In every case numerous correlations can be established between the culture patterns for family organization and child-rearing and the basic personality type for adult members of the society.

In summary, culture must be considered the dominant factor in establishing the basic personality types for various societies and also in establishing the series of status personalities which are characteristic for each society. It must be remembered that basic personality types and status personalities, like culture construct patterns, represent the modes within certain ranges of variation. It is doubtful whether the actual personality of any individual will ever agree at all points with either of these abstractions. With respect to the formation of individual personalities, culture operates as one of a series of factors which also includes the physiologically determined potentialities of the individual and his relations with other individuals. There can be little doubt that in certain cases factors other than the cultural ones are primarily responsible for producing a particular personality configuration. However, it seems that in a majority of cases the cultural factors are dominant. We find that in all societies the personalities of the "average," "normal" individuals who keep the society operating in its accustomed ways can be accounted for in cultural terms. At the same time we find that all societies include atypical individuals whose personalities fall outside the normal range of variation for the society. The causes of such aberrant personalities are still imperfectly understood. They unquestionably derive in part from accidents of early environment and experience. In how far still other, genetically determined factors may be involved we are still unable to say.

In bringing this discussion to a close I am keenly conscious of the number of problems which I have indicated without being able to provide solutions. I am also conscious of the extent to which I have had to depend on techniques which will appear unscientific to those who regard science as something inseparably linked with the laboratory and slide rule. Those who are investigating culture, society and the individual and the complex interrelations of these phenomena are pioneers and, like all pioneers, they have to live by rough and ready methods. They are laboring in the lonely outposts which science has set up on the fringes of a new continent. Even their longest expeditions into the unknown have been mere traverses leaving great unexplored areas between. Those who come after them will be able to draw maps in the terms required by exact science and to exploit riches. The pioneers can only press on, sustained by the belief that somewhere in this vast territory there lies hidden the knowledge which will arm man for his greatest victory, the conquest of himself.

Walter R. Nord

CULTURE AND ORGANIZATIONAL BEHAVIOR[1]

Linton (1945), in describing the influence of culture on personality formation, emphasized that the shaping of personality promotes the stability of a social system by developing human beings who are compatible with the demands made on them by the role requirements of the social system. Since work rcles are an important part of most social systems, one major aspect of the socialization process is the preparation of individuals for functioning in work organizations. To some degree the nature and content of this process determines the types of organizational structure and management which can be effective in any given society.

Often, managers attribute organizational problems to individuals who do not behave in an expected manner. While some organizational difficulties do arise from individual personality differences, many others originate from differences between classes or large groups of people. The behavior of a member of a particular social class may appear deviant to a manager who is accustomed to dealing with members of a different group. Managers may benefit from concepts which direct their thinking toward behavior common to large groups of people in addition to behavior unique to one or a few individuals. The concepts of culture and subculture may serve this function by helping the manager to recognize as potential sources of problems the variations in social learning among societies or among subgroups within a society. Much training in organizational behavior and management focuses mainly on individuals and small groups. This paper attempts to increase the amount of attention given to larger groups in contemporary training in organizational behavior.

The relevance of culture to organizational behavior is treated in two parts. The first part of the paper reviews some of the effects of culture on the develop-

This paper was prepared especially for this volume.

[1] The helpful comments of Ken Runyon are gratefully acknowledged.

ment and abilities of people. Some implications of culture for international management are noted. The second portion of the paper seeks to show the relevance of cultural awareness for domestic management in our contemporary, complex society. Since the same processes which explain cross-cultural differences operate within our society, it is believed that many of our current problems can best be understood and dealt with in cultural terms.

I–CULTURAL FACTORS AND CROSS-CULTURAL MANAGEMENT

People with experience in international management can tell of many incidents documenting the cultural relativity of management practices. These managers find that the role behaviors which are shared and transmitted in our society to prepare people for complex organizations do not take the same form in other cultures. Often, however, problems resulting from cultural factors are not recognized as cultural.

Cultural problems are difficult to diagnose because so many crucial elements are hidden from the participants in the system itself. Often cultural patterns exist as unrecognized assumptions. Generally only when looking at other cultures do people become aware of having taken their own cultural patterns for granted.

Cultural patterns have many powerful but often subtle effects upon the behavior of people. Due to the subtle nature of these effects, many of them went unnoticed for centuries. However, recently social scientists have demonstrated a number of ways that cultural patterns influence human behavior.

Culture and Perception. Cultural patterns influence the perception of reality. Segall, Campbell, and Herskovits (1966) found that people in different societies are differentially susceptible to certain geometric illusions. For example, people from Western societies are more accustomed than non-Westerners to three-dimensional structures which have straight lines and precise right angles. As a result it could be predicted that Westerners would be more apt to see obtuse angles on a two-dimensional drawing as being extended in space and therefore would mis-estimate the length of lines embedded in such figures. Support for this prediction and similar findings concerning other geometric illusions suggest that different environmental factors may produce experiences and expectations which generate certain distortions in perception.

Other work has shown that language is also an important factor in perception. For example, Carroll and Casagrande (1958) found that language differences between Navajo-dominant and English-dominant Navajo children were associated with perceptual differences. They found that the children who responded in the Navajo language tended to classify objects on the basis of form, whereas the English-speaking Navajo children tended to classify by size and color. The researchers attributed this contrast to the central role played by form and material in the grammatical structure of the Navajo language. Similarly, Whorf (1947) noted the linguistic determination of conceptual processes. For example, Eskimo languages, which have a relatively large number of words for snow, facilitate the discrimination among types of snow. Similarly, Brown and Lenneberg (1958) concluded that ". . . languages of the world, like the professional vocabularies within one language, are so many different windows on reality" (p. 18). It seems clear that intercultural differences in perception are in part due to differences in how people see the world and which parts of the world they are exposed to.

Culture, Space, and Interaction. Culture also influences the way people use and feel about space. Hall (1959) argued convincingly that in the socialization process people learn many small cues which have significant meaning in a particular context.[2] These cues play the same role as any conditioned stimulus in a classical conditioning situation. They are culture bound, since the associations and feelings they elicit in one culture are not elicited in others.

The use of space affects interaction patterns. One of Hall's examples compared the arrangement of offices in France and the United States. Americans tend to divide space equally among people and to distribute their desks and positions around the wall, leaving the center open for group activities. In contrast, the French are apt to place the key figure in the center and to divide the remaining space unequally. As a result, a newcomer from another culture may perceive his new French peers as hostile, since they may give him a desk crowded in a corner and may not move to give him "equal space." This is but one example of how people coming from another culture may experience feelings of discomfort without awareness of the cultural cause.

Similar discomforts may result from cultural differences in interpersonal distances. For example, Hall noted that the common interaction distance is much smaller in Latin America than it is in the United States. People in Latin America stand closer to each other for a particular type of conversation. Someone from the U.S. may be very uncomfortable talking to Latin Americans, because he may feel that Latin Americans stand "too close" when talking.

Culture and Time. The complex organizations of modern America depend on adherence to precise time schedules. In fact, some observers have suggested that the clock is the most important machine for the existence of complex organizations and industrial societies.

Americans are socialized, usually by their families and school systems, to be very sensitive to time. Such norms about time are not shared by other cultures. Again Hall reported that members of many cultures do not plan or schedule events very far in advance and are much less precise in meeting deadlines. For example, many people of the Middle East tend to lump all time beyond a week into one undifferentiated category, the future. As a result, they are apt not to keep appointments set too far ahead, much to the dismay of Americans who attempt to plan with them. Similarly, Americans tend to arrive very promptly (i.e., within a few minutes of the hour agreed upon) for an appointment. In other cultures it may not be considered impolite to keep someone waiting for hours.

[2] Shulman's discussion of channels of communication in part 3 of this book treats these cues in more depth.

Culture and Authority. Differences in perception and attitudes about authority are other important sources of intercultural variation. The magnitude of these differences can be demonstrated by two examples. First, the Japanese organizations members of management are permitted and, in fact, expected to play an active role in the personal life of employees. Obviously, Americans have a narrower definition of appropriate behavior for their organizational superiors.

A second example comes from Miller (1955), who noted that in European cultural traditions power and formal authority tend to be associated with height or elevation. Such associations are related to European religious conceptions, which place supernatural beings above people. Early European visitors to America were struck by what appeared to them to be the lack of authority among Indians known as the Central Algonkians. The deities of these Indians were thought to be on the same level as humans, at the corners of the universe. This religious symbolism was paralleled by an authority structure which differed radically from the European model. In fact, there appeared to be almost no authority structure in the traditional European sense. Miller noted that power in Algonkian society did not descend from a hierarchy but was perceived as being everywhere and equally accessible to all. Furthermore, the possession of power was temporary, being gained and lost through performance. In Algonkian society effort was coordinated without a hierarchy as we know it. Miller observed that coordination was achieved by people doing what was needed without being told, recalling what they had done the year before.

Culture, Organizational Structure, and Process. Differences in attitudes toward authority are often paralleled by contrasts in organizational structure and processes of decision making and communication. Japan provides a useful example. Although Prasad (1968) argued that the Japanese system of industrial organization is becoming somewhat more like our own, the fact remains that Japan developed and maintains a complex industrial system based on management practices which most American managers would brand as inefficient. For example, an employee of a Japanese firm can expect lifetime tenure, wages based on seniority, a great deal of emphasis on loyalty to his employer, and vaguely defined lines of authority and job responsibility. Nevertheless, the success of Japan in building a mighty industrial system in a very short time is undisputed. In its cultural context the Japanese style or organization has been an instrument of progress rather than inefficiency.

Emphasis again must be placed on cultural context. As Brown (1969) has pointed out, a variety of factors make the Japanese system functional. For example, the potential costs of incompetence as a result of the permanent employment system are dealt with by a very careful selection system and a relatively early retirement age–55. Furthermore, Brown argued that the communication system, which appears chaotic by our standards, in essence places the decision making in the hands of a qualified few. The real decision making is carried on by an informal process which distributes responsibility almost automatically to employees in proportion to their relevant expertise.[3] The people in the system

[3] Contemporary management theorists in the U.S. find it necessary to stress allocation

are acutely sensitive to the behavior and feelings of others, and a very smooth-running, yet informal, system is maintained. To quote Brown,

> To the westerner, the lack of work rules, job analysis, lack of definition of responsibility, etc., are evidence of the Oriental's lack of a sense of individualism. The Japanese approach to the work situation is not only an illustration of a certain degree of individualism but a means of preserving it and developing it. The executives of companies are instinctively aware of this trait. On paper all authority appears to be in their hands, but . . . the trust and approbation of subordinates' collective good sense of initiative is the most accurate delegation of authority possible. (p. 441)

The process through which decisions are communicated in Japanese organizations has also been baffling to many Western managers. For instance, one American manager in Japan found that many of his Japanese colleagues were so polite in saying "No" that he often thought they were saying "Yes."[4] In this case, the absence of formal procedures and misunderstood personal communication resulted in significant organizational problems. Probably better than any other society, Japan provides a radical demonstration of the relativity of management practices. The European examples which follow, however, show the importance of the relativity concept in more homogeneous cultures.

Widely varied practices of administration and management can thrive in different cultural contexts. From the cross-cultural study of organizations, we may be able to discern some of the essentials of coordination of effort which are hidden from us in our own culture. The writing of Levinson (1968) is extremely informative in this context.

Arguing from a psychoanalytical perspective, Levinson discussed the relationship of organizational and cultural practices. He noted that participants' expectations about organizations parallel their early experiences with such power figures as their parents. For example, he observed that there are national commonalities between patterns of parental behavior and attitudes and managerial practices of organizations. Levinson demonstrated this point by comparing the child-rearing practices and typical managerial behavior in Germany, England, and the United States. In Germany, the father is the primary source of socialization. He is generally viewed as being authoritative and directive. Paralleling this parental behavior are authoritarian and directive management practices. In contrast to Germany, in England, where the mother plays a more important role in socialization, management practices are more "feminine." For example, protective arrangements which prevent open competition are more characteristic of industry in Britain than in other countries.

Levinson extended his analysis to the United States. Socialization practices in the United States are highly child-centered. American children have considerable freedom, and the parental role is often at least partially that of "servant" to the child. American views of government and attitudes toward organizational

---

of responsibility according to function. In some ways, perhaps we have much to learn from the Japanese system.

[4] The author is indebted to Ken Runyon for this example.

authority are consistent with such parental relationships. Levinson noted that the American government is symbolized by a "benign Uncle Sam," who helps people help themselves. Similarly, other organizations are primarily seen as serving individual interests. This view of organizations, which stresses the value of the individual, helps to explain the emphasis on decentralization and the rapid growth of the human-relations movement in American organizations. Since helping the child grow toward independence is a major objective of the parent, the executive is similarly expected to help the individual grow.

Although Levinson warns that these analogies are only suggestive, they do imply that parental relationships develop attitudes and expectations about a person's future interaction with organizations and sources of power. Observation of family structure may provide valuable insights into the expectations people have of organizations and hence may be a useful guide to people in international management. In fact, a worthwhile training vehicle for managers assigned to posts abroad might be experience with families of the culture to which they will be moving.

So far our discussion has suggested that the nature of organizations is dependent on the cultures in which they are embedded. While there is much evidence to support such a relativistic statement, a recent study by England and Lee (1974) reported both similarities and differences across cultures.

England and Lee studied the relationship between personal values and managerial success for a sample of managers from Australia, India, Japan, and the United States. Some of their data supported a relativistic position; they found that certain personal values are more strongly associated with managerial success in some countries than in others. For example, the concept of loyalty was positively related to success for Japanese managers but negatively related to success for managers in the other three countries. However, overall results indicated that a number of values were associated with managerial success in all four nations. Most importantly, many of these values held in common were related to motivation. As England and Lee concluded,

> The general pattern emerging from the study indicates that more successful managers appear to favor pragmatic, dynamic, achievement-oriented values, while less successful managers prefer more static and passive values, the latter forming a framework descriptive of organization stasis rather than organizational and environmental flux. More successful managers favor an achievement orientation and prefer an active role in interaction with other individuals instrumental to achievement of the managers' organizational goals. Less successful managers have values associated with a static and protected environment in which they take relatively passive roles. (pp. 418-419)

The importance of such values has been reported in a number of studies which have confronted the relationship of managerial motivation and culture directly.

Culture and Motivation. One of the most important effects of culture is its influence on individual motivation. Earlier in this book Jackson and Shea discussed achievement motivation and its relationship to behavior in organizations.

McClelland (1962) argued that differences in socialization practice between cultures produce national differences in achievement orientation which have consequences for economic growth. He found that increasing themes of achievement motivation in a nation's popular literature are often followed by increases in economic growth.

McClelland's thesis suggests that socialization practices of the family and other institutions differ in the emphases given to independence training. The resulting differences in achievement motivation are in turn reflected in industrial growth rates. People who have a strong need for achievement tend to exhibit an affinity for taking personal responsibility for solutions to problems, a desire for concrete feedback, and a tendency to set moderate goals and take calculated risks. These are entrepreneurial characteristics, important ingredients for successful industrialization. Other writers have postulated similar relationships between economic growth and cultural motivation patterns. Best known is Weber's (1930) explanation for the rise of capitalism. He maintained that the value orientation of Protestantism was instrumental in producing behavior conducive to the accumulation of capital necessary for industrial development.

Whyte and Braun (1966) approached the relationship of the socialization process and industrial growth empirically. On the basis of case observations, Whyte and Braun concluded that the school system in nonindustrialized nations produced behavioral characteristics and attitudes incompatible with industrial growth. First of all, the heroes in the texts were military men whose behavior did not provide a model of sustained effort for the achievement of long-range goals. Second, successful industrial leaders and entrepreneurs were not considered worthy of respect, much less heroic. Third, Whyte and Braun reported that the schools were characterized by autocratic teachers and submissive children. The children were only infrequently rewarded for taking risks. Furthermore, the teachers were reluctant to have the students confront novel situations. In McClelland's terms, independence training was low. The teachers felt that it was unfair to ask students to attempt problems that had not first been explained in depth by the teacher.[5] Finally, the authors found that the teachers used group members to maintain discipline by rewarding the "squealer." One consequence was the students' failure to develop the trust of other people that is so necessary to coordinated effort. In general, Whyte and Braun's data suggested that the models and processes used in education influence the potential for economic growth.

To here, our discussion of cultural effects on motivation has revealed that subtle socialization practices have important consequences for industrial development and organization. Many of these consequences are unintended side effects, some consistent with industrialization as we know it and others making economic development very difficult. In addition, there is some evidence concerning the influence of culture on the motivation patterns of organizational participants.

[5] Whyte and Braun seem to be on the side of many critics of contemporary American education, who contend that, while content is important, it is the way people are taught, the process, the way they "learn how to learn" that influences their ability to deal with problems in the future.

One of the most widely known studies of the effects of culture on managerial motivation was reported by Haire, Ghiselli, and Porter (1963). Questionnaires were distributed in eleven countries[6] to 2800 managers to survey their views on leadership, management roles and practices, and their own job satisfaction. When asked what they wanted from their jobs, the respondents exhibited marked uniformity across cultural lines. In every case self-actualization needs were deemed the most important. Furthermore, in almost all countries the need for autonomy was second in importance, the need for security was generally third, social needs were generally fourth, and the need for esteem was generally fifth.

These managers from different cultures varied widely, however, in what they thought they were getting from their jobs. Whereas Maslow's hierarchy of needs fits the data quite well for satisfaction in England and the United States, it did not describe the results for other countries. The authors concluded:

> This suggests, perhaps, that the theoretical formulation is especially relevant to the cultural conditions existing in these two English-speaking countries. It also may suggest that industrial and business firms in these two countries have succeeded in satisfying basic needs first and are currently in a position where employees, at least managerial employees, are directing their efforts increasingly to each higher step on the scale of need prepotency. In other countries but these two, past conditions in business organizations may not have led to such a systematic, step-by-step fulfillment of needs from most basic to the least basic. In essence, then, this part of the findings for need satisfaction indicates either that the theory of prepotency of needs is particularly well adapted to organizational behavior in the U.S. and England, or that industrial firms in these countries have created conditions to fit the theory. (p. 116)

The authors further noted that the similarity in estimates of importance and the wide differences in the degree of need satisfaction suggest that human nature gives rise to universal needs, the satisfaction of which is influenced by the situation. They stated:

> There is little evidence here to suggest that the basic motivational equipment with which the manager approaches his job varies from country to country. What does vary is what he finds there. (p. 117)[7]

The Haire *et al.* study reiterates the point that a psychology of individual behavior is not, by itself, an adequate guide for management practice. Each manager must be concerned with situational and cultural variables, which will influence such factors as the degree to which individual needs are satisfied. It is useful, then, to consider management—domestic as well as international—in a cultural context.

[6] The nations included were Belgium, Denmark, England, France, Germany, Italy, Japan, Norway, Spain, Sweden, and the United States.

[7] While this statement may appear somewhat inconsistent with McClelland's data, it should be remembered that the study of Haire *et al.* deals with managers in highly industrialized nations, where as McClelland seems to be most concerned with distinguishing industrial from nonindustrial nations.

IMPLICATIONS OF STUDY OF SUBCULTURES FOR DOMESTIC MANAGEMENT

The study of subcultures may help domestic managers by directing their attention to behavior which is shared and transmitted by large groups of people within a complex culture. The term "culture" was advanced by early anthropologists, who dealt primarily with social systems far less complex than contemporary industrialized societies. In the United States it would be very difficult to discover many patterns shared throughout the society. "Modal" personality would be hard to define. Rather, there are many attitudes, values, and behavioral characteristics which are shared within subgroups of our society. The term "subculture" (a culture within a larger culture) provides the advantages of the concept of culture but allows the unit of social analysis to be smaller than the general society. In our society many important subcultural distinctions can be made which have direct implications for organizational behavior. A few of these distinctions are treated below, including those based on regional, ethnic, religious, sexual, and occupational differences.[8]

Age and Correlates of Age. One of the major divisions in our society today appears to be along age lines. Many younger people share values and behaviors more closely with each other than they do with older people, even their parents. These subcultural differences between age groups are a major source of social tension.

Although the reasons for the "generation gap" are much more complex than those mentioned here, the scope of this paper permits only brief comments. Some writers have attributed the gap to such technological changes as the advent of television, which communicates very quickly, making the individual aware of his interdependence with almost all areas of the world. Others, such as Berrelson and Steiner (1967), suggest that differences between generations may result from an interaction of physiological and institutional factors. They quote Washburn as noting,

> Modern medicine and diet have accelerated puberty by about three years over what it was at the beginning of the nineteenth century. On the other hand, social developments have tended to postpone the age at which people take responsible positions. For example, if puberty is at fifteen and a girl is married at seventeen, there is a minimum delay between biology and society. However, if puberty is at twelve and marriage at twenty, the situation is radically different. In terms of college entrance, people tend to enter older but to have grown up younger than formerly and nothing in our system takes account of these facts. . . . (p. 130)

Generational differences are providing strong challenges to organizations. College administrators and professors are being asked (even coerced) to redefine the substance and process of education. Businessmen are prompted to ask, "Why

[8] This list is not intended to be comprehensive. Missing are some obvious distinctions which exist on economic, occupational, and other related dimensions commonly considered in studies of social stratification.

are young people's feelings about business so different from mine?"[9]

Some of the implications of these differences in attitudes toward business were noted by Webber (1969). Webber's data revealed that contemporary college students admired a person most for his commitment to a cause. In contrast, contemporary executives were most apt to admire a person for his decisiveness. Furthermore, the students wanted business to be more involved in the community, more personal, and interested in societal improvement rather than just personal advancement. Incidentally, these views are not representative of a "radical fringe"; Webber reported that they are shared by master's degree candidates at the Wharton School of Finance and Commerce.

Many observers have noted that today's young people are typically more concerned with personal experience, authentic interpersonal relationships, and the development and enjoyment of their feelings than were youths 10 or 20 years ago. These are important differences. Such values are more apt to produce conflict with than commitment to traditional bureaucratic organizations.

Employees' lack of commitment to organizational goals seems to be a growing problem for management. Part of this problem is attributable to the generational differences under consideration. Managers may find it useful to view the problem in cultural terms. To some degree today's human input comes from a sharply different culture than that of even a few years ago.

Rural vs. Urban Backgrounds. Subcultures resulting from regional differences, such as rural vs. urban backgrounds, have also been shown to have important consequences for organizations. For example, Dalton (1948) noted certain characteristics of the industrial "rate-buster." Often people who violated group norms against high productivity were from rural backgrounds. By contrast, the non-rate-busters were more apt to have come from urban backgrounds. This cultural interpretation was supported by Turner and Lawrence's (1965) finding that sharply different reactions to job characteristics occurred as a function of the rural-urban variable. Satisfaction for rural workers was associated with more complex or "enriched" jobs, whereas satisfaction for urban workers was more positively related to such job characteristics as repetitiveness. These findings suggest that different types of technology and management strategies might be called for, depending on whether the work force has a predominantly "town" or "city" orientation.

Employing the Culturally Different. Another implication of culture for modern organizations involves the so-called "hard-core unemployed" or "the culturally different." The latter term is preferable for several reasons. First, it is more general. Second, it is less value laden. Third, and most significantly, it implies that we must examine the behaviors and values expected of people in modern organizations and compare them with behavior and value patterns of the groups which we are trying to integrate into the work force. Rather than leading into value judgments, such an approach leads to a focus on both what is desired and

[9] Of course, for many the question is phrased in more evaluative terms: "What's wrong with today's youth?"

what is—and, beyond that, to more fruitful diagnosis and therapy, since it implies accommodation rather than a molding of people.

There are two polar types of therapy: One type emphasizes changing organizational structures; the other stresses changing the people who participate. Often the second approach has been blindly taken, under the assumption that the organization is fixed and that the only therapy is therefore a change in the people. A more viable approach is to develop systems which achieve coordination of effort through means which are compatible with the cultural system.

Recently a great deal of attention has been focused on speeding the entry of the culturally different into the work force. Many of these people are known to suffer from disease and deficient nutrition and to have a long history of failure in organizational situations. Further, their socialization experiences have not included contacts with models of "good" work habits and attitudes. In fact, many have a long history of reward for nonwork activities and punishment for attempts to better themselves by conventional means.

Heims (1964), talking particularly of Negroes, suggested some cultural "deprivations"[10] which account for many work-related problems. For example, he noted that Negroes were often said to be uncouth, to be improperly dressed, to have limited knowledge, to be unsophisticated, and so forth. In other words, they differed significantly in their normal behavior from the generally accepted standard of the mainstream of society. In addition, they were handicapped by a lack of such basic skills as reading. Heims also suggested some other culturally determined, work-related deprivations. He noted that the social contacts of many Negroes exclude them from the work ethos. As a result they do not learn the work values which the typical American is assumed to acquire in the socialization process. Many black youths may be alienated from certain distinctive ways that factories and offices operate because they do not have the childhood experiences which give them the general atmosphere of daily work and occupational routines. In general, they lack the socialization assumed for most employees.

Staats and Staats (1963) presented a similar argument about reinforcement. They suggested that certain common achievement stimuli are far less reinforcing for lower-class boys than for middle-class boys. Rewards that ordinarily can be counted on to reinforce such achievement behavior as acquiring formal education among middle-class boys may not be effective for lower-class boys. Staats and Staats used an operant perspective to provide an additional way of dealing with problems of the culturally different. The factors which constitute effective reward systems differ among cultures. The combination of a cultural perspective and the operant view leads directly to a search for variables in the social system which function as reinforcers.

The cultural view also focuses attention on criteria for entry into organizations. The problems of selection and promotion of culturally different people go far beyond deliberate discrimination. Although intentional discrimination is

[10] The quotation marks indicate that these deprivations were not absolute but rather are relative to what members of the mainstream of the culture would consider normal.

still an important problem, a great deal of discrimination is very subtle and often may be unrecognized by the organizations involved. The selection process may often screen out valuable human assets on the basis of irrelevant cultural factors.

Selection procedures must be reconsidered in the light of subcultural differences. It is commonly recognized that psychological tests and other selection devices are valid only for populations on which they have been validated. Tests developed for measuring individual mental and psychological differences are apt to be culture bound. Since there are cultural differences within our society, we risk widespread underutilization of human resources unless we follow selection procedures validated on the relevant populations.[11] The potential loss from such discrimination against many minority groups, the sum of unused human resources, is great. However, the potential loss from discrimination against a majority group—women—may be even greater.

Cultural Definition of the Role of Women. In most cultures roles are allocated at least partially on the basis of sex. In our society, despite our rhetoric of equal opportunity and laws against job discrimination on the basis of sex,[12] few managers would maintain that women in fact have equal opportunity for advancement at all levels. In many organizations a remark like this is common: "Sally surely is an intelligent, capable woman. If she were only a man, she'd be vice president by now." Further, hidden cultural assumptions about what roles and role behaviors are appropriate for females influence the actions of nearly everyone and the consequences of those actions for females.

In a paper entitled "The Myth and the Reality," the Women's Bureau of the U.S. Department of Labor listed a number of these assumptions and compared them with certain statistical data. Portions of this comparison are quoted below.

The Myth	*The Reality*
A woman's place is in the home.	Homemaking in itself is no longer a full-time job for most people. . . . (p. 1)
Women aren't seriously attached to the labor force; they work only for extra pocket money.	Of the nearly 34 million women in the labor force in March 1973, nearly half were working beacuse of pressing economic need. They were either single, widowed, divorced, or separated or had husbands whose incomes were less than $3,000 a year. . . . (p. 1)
Women should stick to "women's jobs" and shouldn't compete for "men's jobs."	Job requirements, with extremely rare exceptions, are unrelated to sex. Tradition rather than job content has led to labeling certain jobs as women's and others as men's. In measuring 22 inherent aptitudes and knowledge areas,

[11] An excellent discussion of job testing and the disadvantaged was prepared by the APA Task Force on Employment Testing of Minority Groups (1969).

[12] The first federal government suit aimed at giving women job rights equal to those of men, in compliance with the 1964 Civil Rights Act, was not filed until July, 1970.

The Myth	*The Reality*
	a research laboratory found that there is no sex difference in 14, women excel in 6, and men excel in 2. (p. 2)
Women don't want responsibility on the job; they don't want promotions or job changes which add to their load.	Relatively few women have been offered positions of responsibility. But when given these opportunities, women, like men, do cope with job responsibilities in addition to personal or family responsibilities. In 1973, 4.7 million women held professional and technical jobs, another 1.6 million worked as nonfarm managers and administrators. Many others held supervisory jobs at all levels in offices and factories. . . . (p. 3)
Men don't like to work for women supervisors.	Most men who complain about women supervisors have never worked for a woman. In one study where at least three-fourths of both the male and female respondents (all executives) had worked with women managers, their evaluation of women in management was favorable. . . . in another survey in which 41 percent of the reporting firms indicated that they hired women executives, none rated their performance as unsatisfactory; 50 percent rated them adequate; 42 percent rated them the same as their predecessors; and 8 percent rated them better than their predecessors. (p. 3)

The women's movement has been successful in exposing the extent to which these and related assumptions have pervaded many American work organizations.

Women comprise an increasing proportion of the work force and a majority of the population. One of the criteria of effectiveness for any social organization is its ability to utilize its resources (human included) to carry on profitable exchanges with its environment. As long as socio-cultural factors cause underutilization of the potential of over half of society's human assets, the social system cannot operate at full effectiveness. Furthermore, such a system can be questioned on moral grounds and is certainly prone to latent social tension and mental health problems.

The changing role of women may well turn out to be the most vital social issue of our lifetime. Truly equal job opportunities for women could mean changes in our cultural patterns of childrearing, family structure, power distribution, and organizational management. The concept of culture may be valuable, both to society as a whole and to managers of organizations in particular, for dealing with this cultural change. If nothing else, viewing the role of women in cultural terms may help us to develop an awareness of the assumptions which have heretofore been unrecognized but have had dysfunctional consequences.

CONCLUSIONS

A cultural perspective is a valuable asset to management of human resources. The concept of culture may help a manager to diagnose and deal with classes of human differences both among and within social systems. People differ in important ways as a result of their culture.

The more that managers are aware of the widely shared cultural backgrounds, values, sets of assumptions, and ways of viewing reality which distinguish members of their organizations, the better they are apt to manage. Better management may involve two complementary strategies. In some cases resocialization may be possible to fit people into organizations as they now exist. However, in the future, an alternative strategy may be demanded. Organizations may need to change to accommodate members from a variety of cultural backgrounds.

REFERENCES

Allport, G. W. *Personality: A Psychological Interpretation.* New York: Holt, Rinehart & Winston, 1937.

APA Task Force on Employment Testing of Minority Groups, "Job Testing and the Disadvantaged." *American Psychologist* 24 (1969): 637-50.

Berrelson, B., and Steiner, G. A. *Human Behavior: Shorter Edition.* New York: Harcourt Brace Jovanovich, Inc., 1967.

Brown, W. "Japanese Management: The Cultural Background." *Monumenta Nipponica–Studies in Japanese Culture,* 21:47-60. R. A. Webber, ed., *Culture and Management.* Homewood, Ill.: Richard D. Irwin, Inc., 1969. pp. 428-42.

Brown, R. W., and Lenneberg, E. H. "The Function of Language Classifications in Behavior." In *Readings in Social Psychology.* 3rd ed., edited by E. E. Maccoby, T. M. Newcomb, and E. L. Hartley. New York: Holt, Rinehart & Winston, 1958. pp. 9-18.

Carroll, J. B., and Casagrande, J. B. "The Function of Language Classifications in Behavior." In *Readings in Social Psychology.* 3rd ed., edited by E. E. Maccoby, T. M. Newcomb, and E. L. Harteley. New York: Holt, Rinehart & Winston, 1958. pp. 62-112.

Dalton, M. "The Industrial 'Rate-Buster': A Characterization." *Applied Anthropology* 7 (1948): 5-18.

DeCharms, R. *Personal Causation.* New York: Academic Press, 1968.

England, G. W., and Lee, R. "The Relationship between Managerial Values and Managerial Success in the United States, Japan, India, and Australia." *Journal of Applied Psychology* 59 (1974): 411-19.

Goffman, E. *Interaction Ritual.* New York: Doubleday & Company, Inc., 1967.

Haire, M., Ghiselli, E., and Porter, L. "Cultural Patterns in the Role of the Manager." *Industrial Relations* 2 (1963): 95-117.

Himes, J. S. "Some Work-Related Cultural Deprivations of Lower-Class Negro Youths." In *Negroes and Jobs,* edited by L. A. Ferman, J. L. Kornbluh, and J. A. Miller. Ann Arbor: University of Michigan Press, 1968. pp. 187-93.

Lazarus, R. S. *Personality and Adjustment.* Englewood Cliffs, N.J.: Prentice-Hall, Inc., 1963.

Levinson, H. *The Exceptional Executive: a Psychological Conception.* Cambridge, Mass.: Harvard University Press, 1968.

Linton, R. *The Cultural Background of Personality.* New York: Appleton-Century-Crofts, 1945.

McClelland, D. "Business Drive and National Achievement." *Harvard Business Review* 40 (July-August, 1962): 99-112.

McGregor, D. *The Human Side of Enterprise.* New York: McGraw-Hill Book Company, 1960.

Miller, W. B. "Two Concepts of Authority." *The American Anthropologist.* April, 1955. In *Readings in Managerial Psychology,* edited by N. J. Leavitt and L. R. Pondy. Homewood, Ill.: Richard D. Irwin, Inc., 1964. Pp. 557-76.

Nord, W. "Industrial and Organizational Conflict in an Industrial Merger." *Midwest Management Conference.* Madison, Wisc.: Academy of Management, 1968. pp. 50-66.

Prasad, S. B. "A New System of Authority in Japanese Management." *Journal of Asian and African Studies* 3 (1968): 216-25.

Rotter, J. B. "Generalized Expectancies for Internal versus External Control of Reinforcement." *Psychological Monographs* 80 (1966) no. 1.

Segall, M. H., Campbell, D. T., and Herskovits, M. J. *The Influence of Culture on Visual Perception.* Indianapolis: Bobbs-Merrill, 1966.

Staats, A. W., and Staats, C. K. *Complex Human Behavior.* New York: Holt, Rinehart & Winston, 1963.

"The Myth and the Reality." U.S. Department of Labor Employment Standards. Administration–Women's Bureau. May, 1974 (revised), 1-3.

Turner, A. N., and Lawrence, P. R. *Industrial Jobs and the Worker.* Boston: Harvard University Press, 1965.

Webber, R. A., ed., *Culture and Management,* Homewood, Ill.: Richard D. Irwin, 1969.

Weber, M. *The Protestant Ethic and the Spirit of Capitalism.* London: George Allen & Unwin Ltd., 1930.

Whorf, B. L. "Science and Linguistics." *Technology Review* 44 (1940): 229-31, 247, 248.

Whyte, W. F., and Braun, R. R. "Heroes, Homework, and Industrial Growth." *Columbia Journal of World Business* 1 (Spring, 1966): 51-57. In *Culture and Management,* edited by R. A. Webber. Homewood, Ill.: Richard D. Irwin, 1969. pp. 286-94.

Walter R. Nord

SOCIAL STRUCTURE AND MANAGEMENT: AN INTRODUCTION TO WHYTE'S PAPER

In one of the most comprehensive discussions of how organizations are affected by their social settings, Stinchcombe (1965) defined social structure broadly; in his view it embodied ". . . any variables which are stable characteristics of society outside the organization" (p. 142). Major elements of social structure ". . . include groups, institutions, laws, population characteristics, and sets of social relations . . ." (p. 142).

Clearly Stinchcombe's concept of social structure is more comprehensive than Linton's definition of culture. Consequently, our earlier discussion of the relationship of organizations to culture dealt with only a few of the effects of social settings on organizations. In the paper which follows, Whyte analyzes some of these additional effects by comparing strategies for managing organizations in China and the West.

Whyte's paper is most significant for organizational behavior, because it demonstrates the cultural relativity of our own discipline. For example, recall the discussions by McGregor and Herzberg on motivation; they pointed to job redesign as a necessary step for providing people with meaningful, motivating work. Whyte's paper should make clear that the ideas which American organizational behaviorists have offered management have been heavily influenced by a particular social context–post-capitalist America in the mid-1900s. Associated with this context are a number of institutions and values which stress individualism and private enterprise. These institutions and values are very different from those Whyte found in contemporary China. The differences have produced sharply contrasting approaches to the management of organizations and the motivation of people.

Once we recognize the close relationship between organizational strategies and the cultural and social context in which they have developed, a major question must be considered. Has our thinking been limited by our social context? For example, has our emphasis on individual autonomy rather than group orientation led us to focus on only a limited set of ways to provide meaningful work for people?

Whyte's paper was included in this anthology to stimulate discussion of this issue. Whyte examines the Maoist approach to organizing and motivating people for work. He finds that while many of the aims and problems are similar to those of Western organizations, the ways in which organizations are designed and managed to achieve these goals differ; these differences are related to the social structures and cultures of the two social systems.

REFERENCES

Stinchcombe, A. L. "Social Structure and Organizations." In *Handbook of Organizations,* edited by J. G. March, pp. 142-43. Chicago: Rand McNally, 1965.

Martin King Whyte

BUREAUCRACY AND MODERNIZATION IN CHINA: THE MAOIST CRITIQUE

In the West the term bureaucracy has an ambivalent heritage. Max Weber stressed that bureaucracy, in particular the rational bureaucracy of capitalist societies, could more efficiently coordinate the diverse activities of large numbers of individuals than organizational forms based on such things as kinship and personal loyalty. He foresaw that with growing trends toward rationality, mass democracy, and complex divisions of labor, the increasing dominance of the bureaucratic form of organization could not be avoided. At the same time Weber was very aware of the features of real bureaucracies (impersonality, red tape, etc.) which have given the term its negative connotation in common speech. Weber also predicted that future socialist societies would require an even higher degree of formal bureaucratization than capitalist societies (Weber, 1968:225). The evolution of Soviet society has given us no grounds for rejecting this prediction, and has in fact reinforced the conviction of Western social scientists that bureaucratization is an inevitable concomitant of economic development, whether socialist or capitalist.

Recent events in China, however, direct renewed attention to the relationship between bureaucratization and modernization. The Cultural Revolution (1966-1969) witnessed a broad attack on the growing bureaucratization of Chinese society in terms which sometimes parallel, but in other cases differ from, Western

From M. K. Whyte, "Bureaucracy and Modernization in China: the Maoist Critique" *American Sociological Review,* Vol. 38, No. 2, April, 1973, pp. 149-163. ©Reprinted by permission of The American Sociological Association.

critiques of bureaucracy. The Cultural Revolution was portrayed in Chinese media as a struggle between two roads, one toward Soviet-style bureaucratic development, and one toward a new Maoist style of non-bureaucratic development. The Cultural Revolution debates have produced reverberations in the West, with some saying that the "Maoist model" is more suited to the needs and problems of today's developing societies than Western or Soviet-style development (Gurley, 1971; Andors, 1971); while others view Maoism as a romantic and irrational approach, incompatible with the demands of modernization (Lewis, 1968; Loewenthal, 1970).[1]

The present article is an attempt to deal with some of the issues raised in these debates, while relating them to theoretical concerns of those studying organizations outside of the Chinese context. First it will be necessary to specify what the nature of the Maoist critique of bureaucracy is, and what the features of the alternative Maoist organizational ideal are. How thorough is the Maoist critique of bureaucracy? How non- or anti-bureaucratic is the Maoist alternative? Our tactic will be to compare various features of the emerging Maoist organizational conception with traits from Western organizational models—many, but not all of them, stemming from the Weberian tradition. After we have clarified somewhat the nature of the Maoist organizational ideal, we will try to deal with the more difficult question of its appropriateness to the needs and problems of China and other developing societies. Throughout this article we will concentrate on bureaucracy and Maoism within organizations, rather than in national political and economic institutions.

The term bureaucracy has connotations to Mao and his followers beyond those, good and bad, which are attached to the term in the West. While to some Westerners the traditional Chinese bureaucracy, with its emphasis on philosophical and literary training for service, seemed close to the Platonic ideal of rule by philosopher kings, the Chinese Communists have always held a very different view. They argue that the traditional bureaucratic system allowed the educated to set themselves apart from the rest of the population and to advance themselves and their relatives at the expense of the common man. Thus to the Chinese Communists bureaucracy entails not only ritualism and red tape, but a selfish quest for power and office obtained through education and perpetuated by emphasizing the distinctive status of the office-holders. While Weber stressed the ways in which the traditional Chinese bureaucracy differed from the rational bureaucracy emerging in capitalist societies, the Chinese Communists tend to emphasize the similarities, and the evils, of both.

Although our knowledge of internal Chinese politics prevents us from being very precise about just what constitutes a "Maoist," and whether Mao Tse-tung would give full blessing to all who use his name, it is clear that throughout his political career Mao has held a sharply critical view of bureaucracy and bureaucrats. As early as 1933, when the Chinese Communists controlled a relatively isolated area of China with a population of only three million, Mao Tse-tung was

[1] Here the Maoist ideal for organizations is seen as part of a more general Maoist model for economic development, which is discussed most specifically by Gurley (1971).

already railing, "This great evil, bureaucracy, must be thrown into the cesspool" (quoted in Meisner, 1971:29). After assuming power in 1949 the Chinese Communists increasingly followed the Soviet model of economic development; but in the late 1950's they became dissatisfied with the results and, in 1958, launched the Great Leap Forward. The Great Leap was a frenetic attempt to apply the Maoist model of economic development, and it was a dismal failure. While some other Chinese leaders took this experience as evidence of the superiority of rational bureaucratic development. Mao Tse-tung did not. In the Cultural Revolution he launched another attempt to get his anti-bureaucratic model adopted as the ideal for China's future development. Mao's 1967 "Twenty Manifestations of Bureaucracy" is surely one of the most damning critiques ever written on the subject (translated in Joint Publications Research Service, 1970:40-3). From Mao's writings, from the policies of the Great Leap Forward and the Cultural Revolution, and from the descriptions in the Chinese press of model organizations, we can piece together the Maoist alternative to rational bureaucracy.

One basic aspect of the Weberian ideal type that is modified by the Chinese Communists is the notion that bureaucracies contain a hierarchy of specialized posts to which people are appointed and promoted according to criteria of technical competence. The Chinese do not argue for organizations without hierarchy or without specialized offices, but they do object to the emphasis on technical competence. They do not ignore questions of education and skills, but they also place strong weight on political purity. In practice this means considering social class origins, Party membership, level of political enthusiasm, and performance in past political campaigns. The Chinese Communists also resist the tendency toward a high degree of specialization and the development of professionalism. During the Great Leap and the Cultural Revolution periods in particular, the press was full of examples of highly trained specialists who could not solve the simplest work problems, and of unskilled personnel who, using common sense and political inspiration, were able to come up with vital work innovations. "Specialists in command," a slogan not out of keeping with the Weberian bureaucratic model, has come to signify an ideological deviation in China. Thus personnel allocation schemes in China are supposed to favor the politically pure generalist more than the apolitical technical specialist.

One can argue that this emphasis on the generalist and the politically pure represents an effort by those who made the revolution to hold on to power and control the technocrats, even if modernization be impeded. But the Maoists feel that there are good economic, rather than simply political, reasons for this emphasis. An exclusive stress on technical competence would not only promote elitism among China's limited number of specialists, but would also, so the argument goes, dull the spirit and initiative of the ordinary members of organizations, the "masses" upon whose efforts the Maoist model depends so heavily. The masses would feel incapable of contributing to the decisions affecting their lives due to their ignorance, and pessimistic about their abilities to compete for higher places and positions. The result, according to the argument, would be passivity and lack of dedication on the part of subordinates, phenomena which would undermine whatever decisions their superiors would make. On the other hand if generalists and the politically pure hold sway, they should be less concerned about establishing their professional prerogatives and more concerned about forging close ties with, and mobilizing the full energy and initiative of, their subordinates.

Perhaps on re-examination, this personnel policy is not such a departure from the bureaucratic ideal type. Hiring in Chinese organizations is supposed to be based on universalistic standards, and vigorous measures are taken to prevent personal ties and favoritism from interfering. But the specialized offices in Chinese organizations are somewhat broader in conception than in the rational-bureaucratic type, in each case including the obligation to work with and mobilize the ideologically-based enthusiasm of subordinates. So political criteria for hiring are seen as required in order to get personnel with the suitable technical *and* political skills. If all officers in the organization (cadres in the Chinese terminology) are to have political as well as technical duties, then from the point of the view of the Chinese it would be irrational to rely solely on technical criteria in allocating personnel. From this perspective the departure from the bureaucratic ideal type comes more in the conception of the duties of the offices than in the hiring criteria per se.

The Chinese Communists also challenge the Weberian emphasis on the autonomy of bureaucratic organizations. It is generally assumed in most Western writings that organizations need a certain autonomy from, or control over, their environment if they are to operate well (cf. Udy, 1970, Chap. 3). Outside demands and interference are seen as diverting the organization from the most rational and efficient pursuit of its goals. The Chinese Communists fundamentally reject this notion of the need for organizational autonomy, and a large number of colorful epithets—"departmentalism," "localism," "mountaintop stronghold mentality"—are used for organizations which try to assert such autonomy. The proposed alternative emphasis is signified by the slogan "politics takes command." What this means is that all organizational decisions and actions are seen as having political implications which extend beyond organizational boundaries. Ideally this means that every action is supposed to be based not only on the desire to maximize internal efficiency, but on its effect on the pursuit of revolutionary social goals. When the two are in conflict, the latter should take precedence. Since the Chinese Communist Party and the authorities in Peking are the arbiters of revolutionary social goals, this means that all organizations throughout society are supposed to be open to continuous direction from these sources. The use of political criteria in personnel allocation is supposed to ensure this openness, by promoting people who are especially responsive to outside political authority. The Chinese Communists claim to have good economic as well as political justification for arguing for both lack of autonomy and the use of political criteria in personnel matters. Political authorities within and outside the organization are not seen as meddlers in affairs better left to experts, but as both the people who make sure that decisions do not have undesirable social consequences, and as those who play central roles in getting organizational participants to keep on their toes and avoid mistakes and inefficiency. By relating every organizational activity to national social goals, they may deem some actions and programs unacceptable. But the argument is that those activities which are approved will be pursued with greater dedication because of the politicization involved. Organizational participants should become convinced that their most mundane daily activities have some ultimate impact on the future of socialism and communism, and this realization is supposed to promote high quality work and diligence in avoiding waste and inefficiency. The method used is somewhat different, but the rationale is similar to that of Western advocates of job enlargement and enrichment: if a man finds more meaning in his work, he will work better.

It should be clear by now that the Chinese Communists do not subscribe to the notions of authority contained in the bureaucratic ideal type. They are fundamentally ambivalent toward rational-legal justifications of authority and toward the hierarchy and obedience entailed in large, complex organizations. Individuals are not supposed to obey because they are subordinates in a legitimate organization, or because they have less technical knowledge than their superiors. As mentioned previously, this sort of obedience would be classified as "dulling the initiative of the masses." In Weberian terms, the kind of authority relations desired would probably be classified as charismatic; but this pigeonholing misses the spirit of the Maoist ideal. Unquestioned obedience to superiors because they are portrayed as carrying out the wishes of Chairman Mao and the Party is also labelled dulling the initiative of the masses. The Maoists idealize a more participatory style of leadership, and it is this emphasis that has occasioned the most interest in the West.

The term "mass line" stands for a large number of procedures organizations are supposed to use to ameliorate the effects of hierarchy. Cadres are required to establish regular schedules for spending part of their time out of their offices and down working with their hands alongside their subordinates. While to the Western mind this may seem like a poor use of time for skilled personnel, again the Maoists see economic benefits. Sending administrators and technical personnel down to the basic levels is seen as fostering organizational cohesion, while increasing the information superiors have about concrete problems and how subordinates are reacting to work situations. The emphasis on getting cadres to go down and participate in labor is only one side of the "two participations." The other is that subordinates are supposed to be systematically organized to participate in decision making. In industry one of the most common forms advocated is the "triple combination" in which technical problems are attacked by ad hoc groups composed of cadres, technicians, and ordinary workers. The "revolutionary committees" which now administer post-Cultural Revolution Chinese organizations are similarly supposed to include representatives not only of administrators, but of subordinates and even janitorial personnel.

Even when decisions do originate from organizational superiors (or authorities outside the organization), they are not supposed to be simply announced and obeyed. Rather there are elaborate procedures for mobilizing support for decisions made at higher levels. This, too, reflects the mass line approach. A new policy is announced and explained, and then subordinates break into regular discussion groups to go over each point in detail. In these groups efforts are made to convince everyone of the need for a change in routine, to elicit suggestions and ideas, and to get "activists" to encourage their co-workers to support the change. This kind of communication process is supposed to take place not only in technical matters, but in basic political decisions as well. All things affecting the lives of members of an organization are supposed to include those members in some way in their resolution. The extent of actual influence of subordinates over policy decisions may not be great, but they should not be left out of the process completely. The aim here is similar to the goals of "participative management" in the West: subordinates, by taking an active although perhaps secondary part in decisions affecting them, will identify more with the organization and contribute more to it.

The thoroughness with which subordinate participation is supposed to be pursued in China, however, goes much further than the Western thought (and also Soviet thought) along these lines. In Western organizations subordinates may or may not respond to higher requests for ideas and suggestions, depending in part on the influence of informal social groupings and norms. In Chinese organizations subordinate participation is not to be just solicited, but guaranteed; and to this end active efforts are made to formalize and mobilize the informal social groupings of subordinates. The basic vehicle is the discussion group already mentioned. The factory work group, school row, office section, and military squad all constitute groups which are to maintain their form outside the activities and hours of formal organizational life (cf. also Schurmann, 1959); Whyte, 1970). These groups, numbering generally eight to fifteen members, elect officers, arrange joint recreation, hold outside political study meetings, and engage in group criticism and self-criticism rituals. Notes are taken by a designated "recorder" at discussion and criticism meetings, and these are used to report group ideas and morale to superiors. The group leader will cultivate within the group certain "activists" whom he can count on to help him steer discussion and criticism meetings along proper channels. It is in these groups that subordinates not only discuss new pronouncements, but criticize their own ideological shortcomings and poor work performance, and promise improvement to their peers. Just as the organization itself is supposed to be permeated by outside political demands, so primary groups within that organization are to be formalized and politicized, and made unable to pursue autonomous objectives. Obviously there are problems in implementing this ideal, since participation which is mandatory and organized from above may not be enthusiastic, and views expressed in the group may not come from the heart. But the procedure does illustrate the ideal conception of the leader-led relationship within Chinese organizations in which leaders will be in close contact with and solicitous of the views of the led, but the led will be unable to resist or be uninvolved.

By a number of other devices the Chinese Communists strive to minimize the importance and effects of organizational hierarchy. The similarity of dress of people high and low tends to downplay status distinctions, and this egalitarianism was given its most noted application in the elimination of ranks and insignia of rank in the Chinese armed forces in 1965. Here it should be noted that absolute equality is not being pursued, and is in fact denounced as a deviation. The commanders of companies and regiments are still the commanders of companies and regiments, with much more authority than the ordinary soldier; but they now have less in the way of visible symbols of their distinctiveness. Similarly, the Chinese do not reject the basic bureaucratic feature of higher remuneration for those holding higher posts. In fact both wages and perquisities such as apartments are distributed according to rank. But at the same time efforts are made to downplay the differences. Wage differentials are kept within limits narrower than are common in the United States, Russia, or developing societies; and the relatively more spacious apartment of an administrator may be in the same apartment complex where his unit's janitor lives (cf. Richman, 1969:804-8). In general it is felt that the higher performance that might result from those favored by wider differentials and status distinctions would be more than offset by lowered organizational cohesion and poorer morale among those at the lower end of the scale. In a variety of ways, then, the hierarchy that exists in Chinese organizations is supposed to be de-emphasized, with efforts made to form close ties and communications across hierarchical divisions.

At the same time alternative forms of rewards and recognition are provided which are not dependent on rank or productivity. In industry, piece rates have been largely discarded since the Cultural Revolution; and the differentiated wage levels which remain are supplemented by selections of honorary workers based not only on work performance, but on criteria of political enthusiasm and willingness to help other workers. In rural communes the pegging of rewards to individual work tasks has been replaced by wages set in public discussion meetings, where the criteria include not only work performance, but labor attitudes and political enthusiasm. While in the West we should expect a weakening of the link between performance and remuneration to lead to poorer performance, Chinese authorities argue the reverse: weakening this link makes it more possible to avoid the calculative involvement and lack of initiative that comes from a strong emphasis on material incentives. Or, to put the matter in the light of our earlier discussion, if organizational roles are defined more broadly to include not only immediate work tasks but political contributions, then perhaps rewards should be based on such broader criteria. But keep in mind that the Maoists argue that by such a strategy organizational performance will be enhanced even if we consider only work output, and the Chinese media are full of examples of organizations which improved their production after they scaled down their systems of material incentives and replaced them with increased political mobilization.

If the drive to blur hierarchical divisions and eliminate the autonomy of informal primary groups could be successful, then a number of assumptions of Western organizational thought would have to be modified. One basic empirical generalization is that varying means of securing compliance are required in different organizations, depending in part on the orientation of subordinates (Etzioni, 1961).[2] If you expect sullen and antagonistic subordinates, as in a prison, then

[2] Etzioni specifically states in his introduction that his empirical generalizations may not hold for non-Western, non-democratic societies. Skinner and Winckler (1969) have found,

you had better be willing to use coercion. If you expect relative indifference or calculative involvement, then material incentives are more appropriate; while if you expect enthusiasm and commitment you can rely more on persuasion and the manipulation of symbols. In China, while coercion and material incentives remain important (cf. Skinner and Winckler, 1969), there is a constant effort to get people to respond more to what Etzioni calls normative and social power. The organizational elements we have already described (the mass line, politics in command, the small group) are supposed to make this possible. If these techniques can be successfully applied, subordinates should respond more and more to social pressure and patriotic appeals; and there should be less need for coercion and material incentives, no matter what the type or goal of the organization involved. In other words, the Maoist ideal is supposed to be appropriate and beneficial not in special sorts of organizations, but in everything from the Party itself to the forced labor camps which form the core of the Chinese penal system. In the latter case, an inmate should feel surrounded not by an inmate subculture exerting pressure to subvert labor camp rules, but by other inmates urging him to reform and confess any thoughts he may have of escaping.

The emphases on close organizational ties and on relating every activity to national goals alert us to another Maoist deviation from the rational bureaucratic ideal type. The Maoist ideal does not entail formalistic impersonality. The Chinese Communists do want their organizations to be impersonal in the sense that individual friendships and rivalries are not supposed to influence activities and decisions. The ideal is comradeship rather than formalistic impersonality. This means that everyone is supposed to show a high degree of personalistic concern and solicitude for everyone else. People are expected to treat each other not just as holders of narrow roles, but as whole individuals with problems and private lives which may affect organizational performance. Within a small group it is supposed to work like this: Members are not simply to criticize each others' failings constantly. Rather they should engage in a variety of joint activities, helping each other to solve personal problems, while at the same time criticizing those who depart from the official line. The same kind of personal concern matched by criticism is supposed to extend across hierarchical divisions within the organization. This ethic of comradeship is seen as contributing to organizational loyalties in a way an ethic of impersonality could not, and we have already seen that the effort to build strong organizational loyalties occupies a central place in the Maoist ideal.

Emotions are also regarded somewhat differently in Chinese organizations. Individuals are not to let personal emotions interfere with their performance, but the ideal is not unemotionality. Rather a high degree of passion and zeal should be generated for even the most mundane tasks. Much of the effort of Party cadres and propagandists goes into proclaiming slogans, organizing group competitions and mass meetings, and so forth, in the effort to mobilize the proper spirit. Individuals are advised to regard taking school quizzes, selling

---

however, that Etzioni's scheme helps them to interpret patterns of change in rural organizations in China.

pork, or spreading manure as objects of revolutionary struggle which must be overcome with the same zeal that characterized the guerrilla struggle against Japan of an earlier era.

These basic notions of coopting primary groups, comradeship, and zeal are all related to the fact that Chinese organizations make greater claims on their participants than do their Western (or Soviet) counterparts. The "partial inclusion" and limited contractual obligations of officeholders which in the bureaucratic ideal type protect participants from undue exploitation are not basic features of the Maoist ideal. No aspect of the life of an individual is regarded as completely irrelevant to his organizational performance. Informal contacts within the organization, outside recreation with friends, marital relationships, and many other factors are seen as affecting the performance of individuals. The leaders of a Maoist organization are to try to make sure that all these influences support, rather than undermine, organizational goals. Internal activities are highly organized, spare time recreation is arranged, evening political study sessions are run, and at times efforts are even made to organize families and outside friends for organizational purposes. During the political campaigns which periodically sweep across Chinese society, work days may be extended; and in some cases individuals will have to remain within the organization for days or even weeks without returning home. These efforts tend to make Chinese organizations more total in scope and more pervasive than their Western counterparts (i.e., their members engage in more joint activities and there are more activities inside and outside the organization for which the organization sets norms—cf. Etzioni, 1961:160-3). While partial inclusion is seen in Western organizational thought as freeing officials from nonrational obligations and interference so that they can apply their expertise to their job, in Maoist organizations the more nearly total inclusion is seen as promoting organizational involvement and commitment, which is supposed to lead to more diligent and efficient work.

A few further contrasts round out our picture. The Chinese Communists also do not accept the bureaucratic notions of contractually based job security and office-holding as a career. In the Weberian ideal type these features are seen as encouraging the acquisition of high level skills and their optimal use, and eliminating the need to bend to pressures and toady to superiors. In Chinese organizations many people do serve in one post for long periods, and do ascend the ladder of ranks; but the official ideal is that individuals serve at the will of the state. "Careerism," the desire to acquire skills and use them to rise in a bureaucratic hierarchy, is seen as a traditional political evil. Instead, skilled personnel are supposed to be willing to leave comfortable and familiar posts for terms in manual labor or work for which they have not been trained. There are a number of reasons for this emphasis, including the desire to undermine bureaucratic elitism; but probably the major justification is the effort to prevent rigidities in the national personnel allocation system. (State control over employment and job changes is more nearly total in China than in, say, the Soviet Union.) Officeholders who have outlived their usefulness do not have to be "kicked upstairs," but can be "sent down" or shifted to some other work to meet the rapidly changing demands of the developing economy.

Maoists are also suspicious of the bureaucratic assumption that organizations should be rule-bound and possess stable routines so that participants will have the security and calculability needed for rational action. In China the notion of stable routines conflicts with the desire to maintain a spirit of revolutionary change. Rules and work procedures are looked on with suspicion as things bureaucrats use to control subordinates so that they can maximize their own successes, without necessarily maximizing the successes of their organizations. Routines and rules fall again into the familar category of "dampening the enthusiasm of the masses." According to the Maoists, organizations should strive to minimize their rules and procedures so that members (particularly subordinates) who have new ideas and innovations that will improve work will feel free to carry them out. Periodically special campaigns are launched to "shake up" organizations and "break through" unnecessary rules and procedures.

The Maoists also reject the notion of unity of command, prominent in classical organizational theory and in Weber's monocratic bureaucracy and Soviet one-man-management. With unity of command everyone has only one immediate superior to deal with, and this is usually seen as avoiding confusion and conflict while making it easy to specify responsibility and accountability for decisions. The Chinese, who followed Soviet one-man-management ideas in the early 1950's, have since shifted more to the diffusion of decision-making both vertically and horizontally within organizations. Horizontally this means collective decision making by Party committees in consultation with administrators, technicians, and workers. Vertically this means referring many kinds of decisions up and down various levels of the administrative hierarchy, often several times, for ideas, reactions, and approval. This procedure may lead to delays in decision making, and may make it difficult to individualize responsibility; but the Chinese feel that it will contribute to the desired general involvement in organizational goals and activities.

We have now reviewed a large number of ways in which the Chinese Communists (or at least the Maoists among them) either specifically reject or modify basic features of Western organizational models. These contrasts should not blind us to the similarities between Maoist and Western organizational conceptions. Chinese organizations do have specific goals, and they do employ a division of labor entailing a hierarchy of specialized offices in pursuit of these goals. Those at the top of organizations have authority over those lower down; and in general they have more training and experience, and receive greater rewards, than do their subordinates. Universalistic criteria are to be used in allocating personnel; and files, rules and written communications are basic facts of life in Chinese organizations. Offices are separated from office-holders, who can be replaced. Perhaps a brief list at this point will highlight the similarities and the contrasts.

CONTRASTS

Western conceptions	*Maoist conceptions*
1. Use criteria of technical competence in personnel allocation	1. Use both political purity and technical competence

2. Promote organizational autonomy	2. Politics takes command, and openness to outside political demands
3. Legal-rational authority	3. Mass line participative-charismatic authority
4. Informal social groups unavoidably occur	4. Informal groups can and should be fully coopted
5. Differentiated rewards to office and performance encouraged	5. Differentiated rewards to office and performance deemphasized
6. Varied compliance strategies needed, depending on the organization	6. Normative and social compliance should play the main role everywhere
7. Formalistic impersonality	7. Comradeship
8. Unemotionality	8. Political zeal encouraged
9. Partial inclusion and limited contractual obligations of officeholders	9. Near total inclusion and theoretically unlimited obligations
10. Job security encouraged	10. Job security not valued, and career orientations not encouraged
11. Calculability through rules and established procedures	11. Flexibility and rapid change valued, rules and procedures looked on with suspicion
12. Unity of command and strict heirarchy of communications	12. Collective leadership and flexible consultation

SIMILARITIES

1. Organizations have specific goals	1. Same
2. Organizations utilize a hierarchy of specialized offices	2. Same
3. Authority and rewards greater at the top of an organization	3. Same, although efforts to deemphasize
4. Universalistic hiring and promotion criteria	4. Same, although criteria differ
5. Files, rules, and written communications regulate organizational life	5. Same, although not always viewed positively
6. Offices separated from officeholders	6. Same

Admittedly this listing is something of a hodge-podge. We have compared features of the Maoist ideal with characteristics drawn from various Western sources: the Weberian ideal type of rational bureaucracy, basic assumptions of other schools of thought, and empirical generalizations from Western organizational research. It has also been mentioned that the prescriptions of the Maoist ideal have some parallels not listed here with the thinking of some other Western organizational theorists, most particularly with what is known as participative management (cf. McGregor, 1960; Likert, 1961; Tannenbaum, 1968). Weber himself was, of course, not unaware of the economic potential, but perhaps limited applicability, of organizations departing from the rational bureaucratic ideal type in the direction of value infusion and collective commitment. His writings on monastic and congregational forms of organization are particularly relevant here (cf. Weber, 1968:1168-70, 1204-10).

Clearly underlying all the contrasts listed is a general disagreement over the ways organizations are conceived. In the rational bureaucratic conception, the central concern is with achieving internal efficiency through the maximum use of technical knowledge. In the Maoist ideal the predominant emphasis is instead on finding ways to maximize the involvement and commitment of organizational participants, particularly the "masses" at the bottom of organizations. While Weber focussed most of his attention on the administrators within bureaucracies, rather than on the entire personnel, the Maoists focus most of their attention on how subordinates are tied into the organization. To oversimplify, the primary concern of Maoists is with maximizing (human) inputs rather than with getting the most return from limited inputs. It can be argued that there is some sense to this approach in China's case given her relatively low level of economic development and abundance of unskilled labor. But the Maoists make a more general case for the value of their organizational ideal, one that says it should be used in organizations of all types, no matter what the mix of backgrounds and skills of participants. Again the parallels with participative management are suggestive. Advocates of the Maoist ideal claim that its implementation will produce greater involvement in organizations among participants, thus producing more diligent, careful, and creative work. Thus much of the poor performance which occurs when the ideal type of rational bureaucracy is translated into practice[3] (ritualism, restriction of output, etc.) is seen as avoidable if the Maoist ideal is followed. In other words the major emphasis on involvement rather than on internal efficiency is seen as producing, as a byproduct, greater actual efficiency. This line of thinking is the basis for the argument that the Maoist ideal, far from being incompatible with economic development, can actually make a contribution. The Maoists do not feel that they have to sacrifice economic progress to remain true to their ideology; they feel they can be Maoists and also modernize Chinese society.

At this point we might return to the question of how non or anti-bureaucratic the Maoist ideal is. The answer depends on what we take as the defining attributes of bureaucracy. The Maoists have not dismantled large-scale organizations and introduced participatory democracy. As we have seen, the critique of bureaucracy is broad but not total; and organizations with multiple levels of specialized offices continue to exist. Individual organizations are controlled and coordinated by national state administrative, army, and party hierarchies.[4] If

[3] Rational bureaucracy as an ideal type has no direct normative implications. However, because of the efficiency which is claimed for rational bureaucracy, the ideal type easily becomes an ideal for those wishing to construct more efficient organization.

[4] During the Cultural Revolution the Chinese Communist Party was attacked and immobilized. The more recent reconstruction of the Party seems to have brought in new members, but the structure is largely as before.

we take size, hierarchy, and division of labor as our criteria, then, rather than other traits on our list, we can say that the Maoists, like the advocates or participative management, are not rejecting bureaucracy, but are trying to build more responsive and efficient bureaucracies.

However bureaucratic or non-bureaucratic we regard the Maoist ideal, it is clear that what is advocated is different in many ways from Western organizational experience. How do we evaluate the claims made for this organizational ideal? There seem to be two alternatives. We can examine the available evidence on whether the Maoist ideal, when implemented in real organizations, has the favorable results (both political and economic) which are claimed for it. Or we can consider the logic of the Maoist ideal—in other words consider it as an ideal type comparable to the Weberian rational-bureaucratic type, and deal with its adequacy at that level. We will discuss both approaches briefly in the pages to follow.

The problem in using the available empirical evidence is, of course, that there isn't much; and what there is doesn't bear directly on our question. To illustrate: The Chinese press regularly carries stories about how, during the Cultural Revolution, organizations scaled down material incentives, increased participation from below, etc.—with the result that everyone felt much more ideologically correct, and the organization in question broke all previous production records. But how representative are these articles of the experience of all organizations? May there not be organizations which achieved negative results from the same procedures? Are the production increases mentioned the result of improved involvement and commitment, or perhaps of other changes, such as technological improvements, improved supply of raw materials, and so forth?

We have similar problems with the negative evidence. The Maoist organizational ideal was espoused earlier, during the Great Leap Forward (1958-1960); and the Great Leap was a disaster, leading to economic depression and famine. But what role did following the Maoist organizational ideal play in this failure? How much was due instead to bad weather, poor national economic planning and coordination, the withdrawal of Soviet economic aid, the overly hasty introduction of new structural reforms, perhaps even an insufficient explanation of what the Maoist organizational ideal was? The economic recovery which occurred after the Great Leap Forward was abandoned has indicated to many China scholars the economic superiority of rational bureaucratic as opposed to Maoist tactics. But does the current record of post-Cultural Revolution economic progress indicate that the Maoist ideal, if properly implemented, does work? Or does it mean that the proper Maoist slogans and external forms are being observed, while underneath rational bureaucratic tactics are responsible for any favorable results? Nothing much of a definitive sort can be said using this sort of crude evidence.

There are some data from visitors to Chinese enterprises and from refugee interview studies of Chinese organizations, but even these do not get us much closer to understanding the consequences of pursuing the Maoist ideal. Barry Richman (1969) spent two months in China in 1966, just as the Cultural Revolution was getting under way, and collected a wealth of data on thirty-eight industrial enterprises. His report on these enterprises contains detailed comparisons with similar enterprises in India, Japan, the Soviet Union, and America. His conclusion is that enterprises in China operate more efficiently than their counterparts in India, although not so well as those in the other countries. But much of the credit for this superiority over India Richman assigns to China's coming closer to the rational bureaucratic ideal, rather than to being more Maoist. In general Richman feels, more on the basis of the Great Leap experience than on his own survey, that Maoism in small doses makes a positive contribution to work motivation, but in large doses is produces serious irrationalities in management. The actual data he collected in the thirty-eight enterprises doesn't tell us much about how Maoist or non-Maoist these organizations were. Below we reproduce selected data Richmond collected on two types of enterprises, machinery producing and chemical and pharmaceutical enterprises, ranked by Richman's rating (out of thirty-eight) of their managerial know-how and general efficiency given the physical technology available.

There seems to be a slight tendency among the machinery enterprises for some standard indicators of bureaucratization, such as the number of employees, the percentage of administrative and technical personnel, and the ratio of maximum pay to average pay, to correlate positively with Richman's subjective rating of enterprise efficiency; but among the chemical and pharmaceutical enterprises no such relationships are visible. But Richman's figures tell us relatively little about whether trying to implement the Maoist ideal helps or hurts organizational efficiency. There are no good indicators of closeness to the Maoist ideal in Richman's data, and we can't assume that where there is no bonus fund or where differentials are low there is a compensating use of political mobilization and participatory approaches. About such things as the proportion of Party membership, the frequency of organized political study and group recreation, and so forth, Richman provides no information. And since his ranking of efficiency is a subjective one based on his own conceptions of managerial effectiveness, we cannot be sure that it is independent of the other data it is ranged against, such as the proportion of personnel with specialized education.

Studies of Chinese organizations based on refugee interviews, provide some additional information (George, 1967; Barnett and Vogel, 1967; Whyte, 1970, 1973). These studies yield several generalizations. First, vigorous efforts have been made in organizations of widely varying types to implement the Maoist ideal. Second, when efforts are made to implement this ideal, various problems tend to produce an operating reality which is often rather distant from the ideal. The Maoist ideal does not seem to grow naturally, but has to be fostered and pushed through campaigns launched from Peking (cf. here also Skinner and Winckler, 1969). When this is not done, what seems to develop naturally is bureaucracy in the Western sense, which does not need central encouragement. But in those organizations which do approximate the Maoist ideal, the predicted effects of a heightened sense of community, willingness to work longer and harder, and strong identification with organizational and national goals do seem to result. And even when an organization does not closely approach the Maoist ideal, the communication and participation procedures may have beneficial effects from the point of view of administrators, which keep them from being abandoned. Let us elaborate briefly on these points.

Visitors to China bring back information about officials laboring with their hands, subordinates participating in decision making, regular group political study routines in organizations of all types, and so forth. Yet the fact remains that periodically campaigns are launched to revive these Maoist procedures; and officials are charged with not encouraging political rituals in their organizations, and with arrogantly ignoring ideas and criticisms from below.

This failure to approximate the Maoist ideal is not due solely to the bureaucratic mentality of Chinese administrators, but to a variety of problems which arise in real organizations when the ideal is applied. If organizational participants are not very committed or cohesive to start with (as in, say, a forced labor camp), they are unlikely to apply the kind of group social pressure necessary to achieve general involvement. Even when organizations try to maximize the inclusion of participants, individuals who have relatives who have suffered in past campaigns, who are worried about the illness of a spouse or who are hoping the clock will speed up so that they can resume yesterday's basketball game, are unlikely to respond to political appeals with the desired enthusiasm. In spite of vigorous efforts there are parts of the organizational environment over which administrators in China, as in other societies, have little control; and these may interfere with the creation of the desired atmosphere. Also in the Maoist ideal, as in participative management schemes, there is the problem of what happens when subordinate initiative is stimulated; and the result is ideas and demands that superiors do not wish to follow. In other words the participation in Chinese organizations is stimulated from above rather than below, and can also be managed and turned off from above; but in doing so the chances of maintaining valued participation are jeopardized. On the other hand the emphasis on subordinate participation can sometimes interfere with using the ideas and experience of subordinates. If superiors concentrate on mobilizing enthusiasm for, and eliminating anxieties about some new activity (such as building backyard steel furnaces during the Great Leap Forward), they may suppress valuable and rational objections. So much effort is given in the Maoist ideal to overcoming organizational inertia, which is seen as stemming from bad political views, individualism, and bureaucratic ritualism, that inertia stemming from rational sources may be overlooked.

Further problems could be cited, but this brief discussion should make clear a not very surprising fact: When trying to implement the Maoist ideal, as when trying to implement other ideals, reality intrudes to produce unanticipated non-ideal results. Given the great effort expended on political and participatory rituals in Chinese organizations, the question remains whether there is a commensurate pay-off. Or perhaps do administrators follow Maoist procedures because Peking demands them, although they create more problems than they solve? This may sometimes be the case, but the available evidence points to the value of the Maoist procedures in some circumstances even when they are not fully implemented.

Alexander George (1967), after extensive interviews with captured Chinese

TABLE 1. **Richman's Subjective Rating of Know-how and Efficiency Given the Available Technology by Selected Other Indicators, for Machinery and Chemical and Pharmaceutical Enterprises.**

Richman's[a] Rank (of 38)	*Name*	*No. of[b] Employees*	*Age of Firm[c]*	*Average[d] Pay (yüan/month)*	*Max. Pay[e]/Ave. Pay*	*Max.[f] Bonus Fund (% of Wage Fund)*	*Admin. &[g] Technical Personnel (% of Employed)*	*Percentage of Employees[h] with Higher or Specialized Secondary Education*
	Machinery enterprises:							
5	Shanghai Machine Tool	6,000	20+	70	3.0	10	20	8.3
6	Wuhan Heavy Machinery	7,000	8	66	2.27	Ceased 1966	36.5	25.5
13	Peking 1st Mach. Tool	4,000	16+	52	3.46	8-9	27.5	17.5
14	Shanghai Machine Tool #3	1,000	8+	75	1.68	15	20	7
19	Canton Mach. Tool	3,100	8 (app.)	67	2.09	Ceased 1966	n.a.	8.5
20	Wusih Machinery	300	8	48	1.81	7	13	2
22	Shanghai Forg. & Press	405	6+	75	1.53	10	12	2
31	Nanking Machinery	1,300	12 (app.)	60	2.0	Ceased 1965	n.a.	15
32	Tientsin N. Lake Instr.	165	8	47.5	2.02	4	6	0
37	Hangchow Mach. Tool	1,000	14 (app.)	61	1.77	8	20	11
	Chemical and pharmaceutical enterprises:							
1	Peking Coke & Chem.	2,100	7	61	2.46	6	20	11
16	Peking Pharmaceutical	3,000	11	60	2.3	7	18	10
17	Nanking Chem. Fertil.	10,000	30 (app.)	62	2.74	Ceased	27	6.9
18	Canton Chem. Fertil.	2,400	3	65	3.08	7	23	11
25	Shanghai Pharmaceutical	1,200	13	66	2.64	5	13	13

Key: n.a. = not available; app. = approximate
[a]Richman, 1969, 792-794.
[b]Richman, 1969, 792-794.
[c]Richman, 1969, 726-737
[d]Richman, 1969, 800-802 (pay scales follow a national scale, but with regional variations to accommodate varying cost of living standards).
[e]Computed from Richman, 1969, 800-802 (these figures are for total enterprise personnel, not just for the workers).
[f]Richman, 1969, 800-802.
[g]Richman, 1969, 754-756.
[h]Richman, 1969, 154-156.

soldiers during the Korean War, concluded that much of the impressive performance of the Chinese Army against the more heavily armed U.N. forces could be attributed to the skillful use of the Maoist ideal: the encapsulation of soldiers in small groups with regular political rituals and group criticism, the maintenance of comradely relations and mutual consultation between officers and men, the penetration of political cadres to the lowest levels, and the politicizing of every military activity. U.S. military observers had been sufficiently impressed by the cohesiveness and fighting spirit of the Chinese Communist Army of an earlier period, during the 1930's, to adapt the cohesive small group concept into what became the U.S. Marine Corps fire teams (George, 1967:52-3).

To pick another organizational example, the Maoist model would seem to be singularly inappropriate for penal institutions, where we could hardly expect the desired kind of enthusiasm and involvement to develop among incarcerated inmates. Interview materials (Whyte, 1973) suggest that this is true, but that even in forced labor camps the Maoist precedures have contributions to make. Even though inmates do not identify with their guards or sense devotion to the camp that confines them, their encapsulation in small groups led by activists, groups which engage in political study and mutual criticism rituals of inmate failings, does hinder the development of the kind of deviant inmate subculture which is a familiar feature of penal institutions in other societies. As a result the inmates are not enthusiastically reforming themselves, but they are easier to control; and this is reason enough for Chinese penal officials to continue to stress the coopting of informal groups even when they are not following other "mass line" procedures.

The admittedly sketchy evidence available suggests that it is difficult for organizations to approach the Maoist ideal, that when they try they often deviate in unexpected ways, but that in at least some circumstances organizations benefit from applying Maoist procedures. Where does this leave us in our analysis of the Maoist ideal? Let us conclude by considering the Maoist ideal not in practice, but as an ideal type, and compare its adequacy relative to the Weberian ideal type of rational bureaucracy. Weber's ideal types were constructs of abstracted elements forming a unified pattern which were to serve as conceptual tools to highlight certain features of organizations, even though no concrete organization would be a perfect fit on all the given characteristics. (Weber, 1968:20-1; Goode, 1947:473-5; Mouzelis, 1967, Chapter II). While it is not valid to criticize an ideal type because no real organization fits the type, or because it leaves out characteristics real organizations possess, it is legitimate to consider whether the traits specified are objectively possible, and whether they are coherent and adequate at the level of meaning, i.e. whether, taken together, they have the logical implications claimed for them. In the case of rational bureaucracy, this means whether Weber's list of traits contradicts known laws of nature, and if, taken together, the traits suggest a coherent model which, if realizable, would lead to maximum rationality and internal efficiency. Even on these grounds Weber's ideal type of rational bureaucracy is not immune from criticism (cf. Mouzelis, 1967:47-8), since, for example, there is an inherent contradiction between offices bound by rules and procedures and offices with incumbents free to make maximal use of their knowledge. And more recent theorizing has suggested that the maximum efficiency predicted for rational bureaucracy would only result in limited organizational situations, generally those of stable and routine technology (Perrow, 1970, 1972).

Considered in comparable terms the Maoist organizational ideal type does not fare badly. In spite of the criticism of some that Maoism represents utopianism and unrealizable objectives, it is not clear that the Maoist organizational traits discussed earlier violate known laws of nature. And the traits do seem to form a relatively coherent pattern organized around the concern for maximizing organizational involvement, even though internal contradictions (e.g. between getting perfect information on subordinate opinions and getting perfect subordinate consensus) are detectable here as well. What is less clear is that the Maoist ideal type should logically lead not only to a maximization of involvement, but also to an equal or higher degree of internal efficiency than the Weberian ideal type. Efficiency would seem to depend on both maximizing the application of knowledge and maximizing the motivation of participants, and a high degree of zeal in wasteful directions is possible within the framework of the Maoist ideal type.

The reasoning suggests a conclusion somewhere between the supporters and the critics of the Maoist ideal. The Maoist ideal does not seem to be totally irrational or contrary to human nature or the demands of industrialization. Activities which seem irrational to Western eyes may have a rational justification. For example, weekly sessions for the study of Mao's thought for factory workers may not simply interfere with production by tiring people out. Insofar as this activity strengthens a sense of organizational cohesion and identification, it may contribute to production. At the same time, it is not clear that the Maoist ideal is a panacea for all organizational problems, or that it can even be very easily applied. In real Chinese organizations its application may result in some cases in both political involvement and internal efficiency, in others in political involvement without greater efficiency, or perhaps in failure in both areas. It would take much better information than we have available now to specify the conditions required for successful application of the Maoist ideal. The suggestion that this ideal is appropriate for all circumstances may be just as dubious as the suggestion that organizations modeled after Weber's ideal type will be the most efficient in all circumstances. Thus claims that China has found a route to modernization without bureaucratization, or that the Maoist ideal solves the problem of how to modernize without sacrificing revolutionary social goals, must continue to be treated skeptically. But this skepticism should not blind us to the opportunity to broaden our understanding of organizational dynamics by a closer scrutiny of Chinese organizational innovations.

REFERENCES

Andors, Stephen, 1971. "Revolution and modernization: man and machine in industrializing societies, the Chinese case." Pp. 393-444 in Edward Friedman and Mark Selden (eds.), American's Asia. New York: Vintage.

Barnett, A. Doak and Ezra F. Vogel, 1967. Cadres, Bureaucracy and Political Power in Communist China. New York: Columbia University Press.

Etzioni, Amitai, 1961. A Comparative Analysis of Complex Organizations. New York: Free Press.

George, Alexander L., 1967. The Chinese Communist Army in Action. New York: Columbia University Press.

Goode, William J., 1947. "A note on the ideal type." American Sociological Review 12 (August): 473-5.

Gurley, John G., 1971. "Capitalist and Maoist economic development." Pp. 324-56, in Edward Friedman and Mark Selden (eds.), America's Asia. New York: Vintage.

Joint Publications Research Service, 1970. "Chairman Mao discusses twenty manifestations of bureaucracy." Pp. 40-3 in Translations on Communist China No. 90, Washington, D.C., February 12.

Lewis, John W., 1968. "Leader, commissar and bureaucrat: The Chinese political system in the last days of the revolution." Pp. 449-81, in Ping-ti Ho and Tang Tsou (eds.), China in Crisis. Chicago: University of Chicago Press, Vol. I, Book 2.

Likert, Rensis, 1961. New Patterns of Management, New York: McGraw-Hill.

Loewenthal, Richard, 1970. "Development vs. utopia in communist policy." Pp. 33-116, in Chalmers Johnson (ed.), Change in Communist Systems. Stanford: Stanford University Press.

McGregor, Douglas, 1960. The Human Side of Enterprise. New York: McGraw-Hill.

Meisner, Maurice, 1971. "Leninism and Maoism: Some populist perspectives on Marxism-Leninism in China." China Quarterly 45 (January/March): 2-36.

Mouzelis, Nicos P., 1968. Organization and Bureaucracy. Chicago: Aldine.

Perrow, Charles, 1970. Organizational Analysis: A Sociological View. Belmont, Calif.: Wadsworth Publishing.

Perrow, Charles, 1972. "A framework for the comparative analysis of organizations." Pp. 48-67, in Merlin B. Brinkerhoff and Phillip R. Kunz (eds.), Complex Organizations and Their Environments. Dubuque, Iowa: Wm. Brown.

Richman, Barry M., 1969. Industrial Society in Communist China. New York: Random House.

Schurmann, H.F., 1959. "Organization and response in Communist China." Annals of the American Academy of Political and Social Science 321 (January):51-61.

Skinner, G. William and Edwin A. Winckler, 1969. "Compliance succession in rural Communist China: A cyclical theory." Pp. 410-38, in Amitai Etzioni (ed.), A Sociological Reader on Complex Organizations, 2nd edition. New York: Holt, Rinehart and Winston.

Tannenbaum, Arnold S., 1968. Control in Organizations. New York: McGraw-Hill.

Udy, Jr., Stanley M., 1970. Work in Traditional and Modern Society. Englewood Cliffs, N.J.: Prentice-Hall.

Weber, Max, 1968. Economy and Society. Guenther Roth and Claus Wittich (eds.). New York: Bedminster Press.

Whyte, Martin K., 1970. Small Groups and Political Rituals in Communist China. Unpublished Ph.D. thesis, Harvard University.

Whyte, Martin K., 1970. "Corrective labor camps in the People's Republic of China." Asian Survey (March).

chapter 7

Freedom and Power: Value Dilemmas in Applied Behavioral Science

While the scientific method is used to test theories and propositions in organizational behavior, value judgments nevertheless influence knowledge in this field, as in any other. Every author has certain metaphysics that influences what he will write and perhaps even whether he will write. The earlier papers on perception support the idea that "facts" and data do not describe reality absolutely. Rather, what the viewer brings to the situation contributes a great deal of variance to what he "actually sees." Students of organizational behavior are no exception.

Earlier it was argued that operant conditioning differs from the more humanistic approaches to organizational behavior primarily in its underlying values. One of the most frequently voiced objections to the operant approach is, "It denies individual freedom." This statement reveals some of the metaphysical assumptions of the speaker. He holds a value position, shared by many in our culture, which stresses the dignity and freedom of the individual. This section addresses the issue of human dignity vs. applied science. It begins with a debate between two of the foremost contemporary psychologists, B. F. Skinner and Carl Rogers, concerning the issue of control.

Skinner and Rogers confront some of the basic philosophical issues in the control of human behavior in general. While the importance of their arguments goes far beyond the primary focus of this book, these issues have been raised repeatedly in the history of the application of scientific knowledge to organizations and people. The issue, simply stated, is, "When do influence and coordination of effort toward common goals become manipulation that violates human dignity?" Closely related is the question, "What is the role of behavioral science in the control of behavior?" Similarly, physical scientists are asked, "What is the responsibility of the scientist for the use of his data?" All of these questions raise important metaphysical issues.

The influence of metaphysics on social science was convincingly argued by Gouldner (1965). He suggested that metaphysics involves a person's ". . . most primitive beliefs and feelings and most general hypotheses about the world" (p. 349). These assumptions influence our theories without our realizing it. Furthermore, since these assumptions about the total universe were not derived from a systematic sampling of the universe itself, they often introduce unrecognized error. In this sense, metaphysics, like other cultural elements, makes it difficult for a scientist to see and report objectively. To quote Gouldner, metaphysical assumptions ". . . are all-purpose cognitive tools with which a scholar selects from and creates the particular tools of his specialized craft" (p. 350). Since values and science are inseparably interwoven, the nature of this relationship must be studied. Even though many scientists maintain that their work is "value-free," this notion is now commonly recognized as a myth.

The atomic bomb brought into sharp focus the notion of the social responsibility of the physical scientist. Many have taken the position that science is objective and that the scientist's role is to study reality and not be any more responsible than any other citizen for how his data are used. Other scientists, such as Bridgman (1948), have argued strongly that scientists are responsible for the uses of scientific discoveries. He states, ". . . I believe . . . that each and every scientist has a moral obligation to see to it that the uses society makes of scientific discoveries are beneficent" (p. 69). As the social sciences develop, the issue of values and science is apt to be vital, since the subject matter is man himself.

Those who apply social science to organizational behavior have run into the value question head-on. For example, the Hawthorne studies, which will be dealt with in depth in part 2, are an important landmark in the development of current thought. As Landsberger (1958) pointed out, these studies have been widely criticized because of value judgments made by the researchers in their other writings. Critics have charged that the researchers were anti-union, guilty of introducing manipulation of people into industry, biased in accepting primarily a management view of the worker, and callous in treating the individual more as an object than as a human.

A more comprehensive indictment of the whole field of industrial social science was provided by Baritz (1960). He contended that industrial social scientists, particularly psychologists, have accepted the norms of American managers. Baritz charged that as a consequence social scientists in industry have almost universally avoided dealing with the political and ethical implications of their work. Furthermore, psychologists have at least implicitly, by refusing to take a value stance concerning the uses of their work, accepted management's ends. Baritz charged that most firms have employed social scientists specifically in order to increase management's control over people. To him, the types of controls offered by psychologists were extremely dangerous, resulting in the manipulation of people without their awareness. Baritz's fear was heightened because, in his view, social scientists were devising increasingly effective means of controlling conduct. Certainly, Baritz is not alone in his fear of such power placed in the hands of managers.

These charges are inconsistent with the explicit aims of many behavioral scientists, who see their work as promoting individual growth. Most of the authors cited in this book share a commitment to the democratic values and the respect for individuals which characterize our cultural values. Herzberg, Maslow, McGregor, Maier, Likert, and others are centrally concerned with the individual as a human being, not as a tool for manipulation. Most of them have argued strongly that their techniques and ideas are quite the opposite of manipulation and in fact depend for their success on commitment to a positive view of human nature. Nevertheless, the issue of human dignity and control remains.

Questions relating to behavior control and the role of the social scientist in organizations are apt to become more important in the future. As more managers acquire sophisticated knowledge of behavioral techniques and as more powerful behavioral techniques are developed, the issues will become even more serious. What should be the role of the behavioral scientist in society and in organizations? What is the relationship of applied behavioral science to individual freedom? What is freedom? These are some of the issues that Skinner and Rogers wrestle with in the selection which follows.

In the final paper of this chapter Lefcourt goes beyond the philosophical and moral issues discussed by Rogers and Skinner. After studying a broad spectrum of empirical research, Lefcourt has developed a new perspective on the freedom-control issue. He has concluded that feelings of being free and feelings of being controlled have important effects on how humans and other animals behave.

The implications of Lefcourt's work for the design of work and organizations should be clear. Organizations, tasks, and work groups are major contributors to the people's feelings of being controlled or being controlling. These two sets of feelings will produce very different types of behavior. Consequently, managers may need to be concerned with the effects of their actions on what Lefcourt calls the "illusions of control and freedom" held by their subordinates.

REFERENCES

Baritz, L. *The Servants of Power.* Middletown, Conn.: Wesleyan University, 1960.

Bridgman, P. W. "Scientists and Social Responsibility." *Bulletin of the Atomic Scientists,* 4 (March 1948): 69-72.

Gouldner, A. W. *Enter Plato.* New York: Basic Books, 1965.

Landsberger, H. A. *Hawthorne Revisited.* Ithaca, N. Y.: Cornell University, 1958.

Carl R. Rogers
B. F. Skinner

SOME ISSUES CONCERNING THE CONTROL OF HUMAN BEHAVIOR: A SYMPOSIUM

I [SKINNER]

Science is steadily increasing our power to influence, change, mold–in a word, control–human behavior. It has extended our "understanding" (whatever that may be) so that we deal more successfully with people in nonscientific ways, but it has also identified conditions or variables which can be used to predict and control behavior in a new, and increasingly rigorous, technology. The broad disciplines of government and economics offer examples of this, but there is special cogency in those contributions of anthropology, sociology, and psychology which deal with individual behavior. Carl Rogers has listed some of the achievements to date in a recent paper. (1). Those of his examples which show or imply the control of the single organism are primarily due, as we should expect, to psychology. It is the experimental study of behavior which carries us beyond awkward or inaccessible "principles," "factors," and so on, to variables which can be directly manipulated.

It is also, and for more or less the same reasons, the conception of human behavior emerging from an experimental analysis which most directly challenges traditional views. Psychologists themselves often do not seem to be aware of how far they have moved in this direction. But the change is not passing unnoticed by others. Until only recently it was customary to deny the possibility of a rigorous science of human behavior by arguing, either that a lawful science was impossible because man was a free agent, or that merely statistical predictions would always leave room for personal freedom. But those who used to take this line have become most vociferous in expressing their alarm at the way these obstacles are being surmounted.

Now, the control of human behavior has always been unpopular. Any undisguised effort to control usually arouses emotional reactions. We hesitate to admit, even to ourselves, that we are engaged in control, and we may refuse to control, even when this would be helpful, for fear of criticism. Those who have explicitly avowed an interest in control have been roughly treated by history. Machiavelli is the great prototype. As Macaulay said of him, "Out of his surname

"Some Issues Concerning the Control of Human Behavior: A Symposium," Rogers, C. R. and Skinner, B. F. *Science* 124: 1057-66, 30 November 1956.

they coined an epithet for a knave and out of his Christian name a synonym for the devil." There were obvious reasons. The control that Machiavelli analyzed and recommended, like most political control, used techniques that were aversive to the controllee. The threats and punishments of the bully, like those of the government operating on the same plan, are not designed—whatever their success—to endear themselves to those who are controlled. Even when the techniques themselves are not aversive, control is usually exercised for the selfish purposes of the controller and, hence, has indirectly punishing effects upon others.

Man's natural inclination to revolt against selfish control has been exploited to good purpose in what we call the philosophy and literature of democracy. The doctrine of the rights of man has been effective in arousing individuals to concerted action against governmental and religious tyranny. The literature which has had this effect has greatly extended the number of terms in our language which express reactions to the control of men. But the ubiquity and ease of expression of this attitude spells trouble for any science which may give birth to a powerful technology of behavior. Intelligent men and women, dominated by the humanistic philosophy of the past two centuries, cannot view with equanimity what Andrew Hacker was called "the specter of predictable man" (2). Even the statistical or actuarial prediction of human events, such as the number of fatalities to be expected on a holiday weekend, strikes many people as uncanny and evil, while the prediction and control of individual behavior is regarded as little less than the work of the devil. I am not so much concerned here with the political or economic consequences for psychology, although research following certain channels may well suffer harmful effects. We ourselves, as intelligent men and women, and as exponents of Western thought, share these attitudes. They have already interfered with the free exercise of a scientific analysis, and their influence threatens to assume more serious proportions

Three broad areas of human behavior supply good examples. The first of these—*personal control*—may be taken to include person-to-person relationships in the family, among friends, in social and work groups, and in counseling and psychotherapy. Other fields are *education* and *government.* A few examples from each will show how nonscientific preconceptions are affecting our current thinking about human behavior.

Personal Control

People living together in groups come to control one another with a technique which is not inappropriately called "ethical." When an individual behaves in a fashion acceptable to the group, he receives admiration, approval, affection, and many other reinforcements which increase the likelihood that he will continue to behave in that fashion. When his behavior is not acceptable, he is criticized, censured, blamed, or otherwise punished. In the first case the group calls him "good"; in the second, "bad." This practice is so thoroughly ingrained in our culture that we often fail to see that it is a technique of control. Yet we are almost always engaged in such control, even though the reinforcements and punishments are often subtle.

The practice of admiration is an important part of a culture, because behavior which is otherwise inclined to be weak can be set up and maintained with its help. The individual is especially likely to be praised, admired, or loved when he acts for the group in the face of great danger, for example, or sacrifices himself or his possessions, or submits to prolonged hardship, or suffers martyrdom. These actions are not admirable in any absolute sense, but they require admiration if they are to be strong. Similarly, we admire people who behave in original or exceptional ways, not because such behavior is itself admirable, but because we do not know how to encourage original or exceptional behavior in any other way. The group acclaims independent, unaided behavior in part because it is easier to reinforce than to help.

As long as this technique of control is misunderstood, we cannot judge correctly an environment in which there is less need for heroism, hardship, or independent action. We are likely to argue that such an environment is itself less admirable or produces less admirable people. In the old days, for example, young scholars often lived in undesirable quarters, ate unappetizing or inadequate food, performed unprofitable tasks for a living or to pay for necessary books and materials or publication. Older scholars and other members of the group offered compensating reinforcement in the form of approval and admiration for these sacrifices. When the modern graduate student receives a generous scholarship, enjoys good living conditions, and has his research and publication subsidized, the grounds for evaluation seem to be pulled from under us. Such a student no longer *needs* admiration to carry him over a series of obstacles (no matter how much he may need it for other reasons), and, in missing certain familiar objects of admiration, we are likely to conclude that such *conditions* are less admirable. Obstacles to scholarly work may serve as a useful measure of motivation–and we may go wrong unless some substitute is found–but we can scarcely defend a deliberate harassment of the student for this purpose. The productivity of any set of conditions can be evaluated only when we have freed ourselves of the attitudes which have been generated in us as members of an ethical group.

A similar difficulty arises from our use of punishment in the form of censure or blame. The concept of responsibility and the related concepts of foreknowledge and choice are used to justify techniques of control using punishment. Was So-and-So aware of the probable consequences of his action, and was the action deliberate? If so, we are justified in punishing him. But what does this mean? It appears to be a question concerning the efficacy of the contingent relations between behavior and punishing consequences. We punish behavior because it is objectionable to us or the group, but in a minor refinement of rather recent origin we have come to withhold punishment when it cannot be expected to have any effect. If the objectionable consequences of an act were accidental and not likely to occur again, there is no point in punishing. We say that the individual was not "aware of the consequences of his action" or that the consequences were not "intentional." If the action could not have been avoided–if the individual "had no choice"–punishment is also withheld if the individual is incapable of being changed by punishment because he is of "unsound mind." In all of these cases—different as they are—the individual is held "not responsible" and goes unpunished.

Just as we say that it is "not fair" to punish a man for something he could not help doing, so we call it "unfair" when one is rewarded beyond his due or for something he could not help doing. In other words, we also object to wasting *reinforcers* where they are not needed or will do no good. We make the same point with the words *just* and *right.* Thus we have no right to punish the irresponsible, and a man has no right to reinforcers he does not earn or deserve. But concepts of choice, responsibility, justice, and so on, provide a most inadequate analysis of efficient reinforcing and punishing contingencies because they carry a heavy semantic cargo of quite different sort, which obscures any attempt to clarify controlling practices or to improve techniques. In particular, they fail to prepare us for techniques based on other than aversive techniques of control. Most people would object to forcing prisoners to serve as subjects of dangerous medical experiments, but few object when they are induced to serve by the offer of return privileges—even when the reinforcing effect of these privileges has been created by forcible deprivation. In the traditional scheme the right to refuse guarantees the individual against coercion or an unfair bargain. But to what extent *can* a prisoner refuse under such circumstances?

We need not go so far afield to make the point. We can observe our own attitude toward personal freedom in the way we resent any interference with what we want to do. Suppose we want to buy a car of a particular sort. Then we may object, for example, if our wife urges us to buy a less expensive model and to put the difference into a new refrigerator. Or we may resent it if our neighbor questions our need for such a car or our ability to pay for it. We would certainly resent it if it were illegal to buy such a car (remember Prohibition); and if we find we cannot actually afford it, we may resent governmental control of the price through tariffs and taxes. We resent it if we discover that we cannot get the car because the manufacturer is holding the model in deliberately short supply in order to push a model we do not want. In all this we assert our democratic right to buy the car of our choice. We are well prepared to do so and to resent any restriction on our freedom.

But why do we not ask *why* it is the car of our choice and resent the forces which made it so? Perhaps our favorite toy as a child was a car, of a very different model, but nevertheless bearing the name of the car we now want. Perhaps our favorite TV program is sponsored by the manufacturer of that car. Perhaps we have seen pictures of many beautiful or prestigeful persons driving it—in pleasant or glamorous places. Perhaps the car has been designed with respect to our motivational patterns: the device on the hood is a phallic symbol; or the horsepower has been stepped up to please our competitive spirit in enabling us to pass other cars swiftly (or, as the advertisements say, "safely"). The concept of freedom that has emerged as part of the cultural practice of our group makes little or no provision for recognizing or dealing with these kinds of control. Concepts like "responsibility" and "rights" are scarcely applicable. We are prepared to deal with coercive measures, but we have no traditional recourse with respect to other measures which in the long run (and especially with the help of science) may be much more powerful and dangerous.

Education

The techniques of education were once frankly aversive. The teacher was usually older and stronger than his pupils and was able to "make them learn." This meant that they were not actually taught but were surrounded by a threatening world from which they could escape only by learning. Usually they were left to their own resources in discovering how to do so. Claude Coleman has published a grimly amusing reminder of these older practices (3). He tells of a schoolteacher who published a careful account of his services during 51 years of teaching, during which he administered: ". . . 911,527 blows with a cane; 124,010 with a rod; 20,989 with a ruler; 136,715 with the hand; 10,295 over the mouth; 7,905 boxes on the ear; [and] 1,115,800 slaps on the head. . ."

Progressive education was a humanitarian effort to substitute positive reinforcement for such aversive measures, but in the search for useful human values in the classroom it has never fully replaced the variables it abandoned. Viewed as a branch of behavioral technology, education remains relatively inefficient. We supplement it, and rationalize it, by admiring the pupil who learns for himself; and we often attribute the learning process, or knowledge itself, to something inside the individual. We admire behavior which seems to have inner sources. Thus we admire one who *recites* a poem more than one who simply *reads* it. We admire one who *knows* the answer more than one who *knows where to look it up.* We admire the *writer* rather than the *reader.* We admire the arithmetician who can do a problem in his head rather than with a slide rule or calculating machine, or in "original" ways rather than by a strict application of rules. In general we feel that any aid or "crutch"–except those aids to which we are now thoroughly accustomed–reduces the credit due. In Plato's *Phaedrus,* Thamus, the king, attacks the invention of the alphabet on similar grounds! He is afraid "it will produce forgetfulness in the minds of those who learn to use it, because they will not practice their memories. . ." In other words, he holds it more admirable to remember than to use a memorandum. He also objects that pupils "will read many things without instruction. . .[and] will therefore seem to know many things when they are for the most part ignorant." In the same vein we are today sometimes contemptuous of book learning, but, as educators, we can scarcely afford to adopt this view without reservation.

By admiring the student for knowledge and blaming him for ignorance, we escape some of the responsibility of teaching him. We resist any analysis of the educational process which threatens the notion of inner wisdom or questions the contention that the fault of ignorance lies with the student. More powerful techniques which bring about the same changes in behavior by manipulating *external* variables are decried as brainwashing or thought control. We are quite unprepared to judge *effective* educational measures. As long as only a few pupils learn much of what is taught, we do not worry about uniformity or regimentation. We do not fear the feeble technique; but we should view with dismay a system under which every student learned everything listed in a syllabus–although such a condition is far from unthinkable. Similarly, we do not fear a system which is so defective that the student must *work* for an education; but we are loath to give credit for anything learned without effort–although this could well be taken as an ideal result–and we flatly refuse to give credit if the student already knows what a school teaches.

A world in which people are wise and good without trying, without "having to be," without "choosing to be," could conceivably be a far better world for everyone. In such a world we should not have to "give anyone credit"–we should not need to admire anyone–for being wise and good. From our present point of view we cannot believe that such a world would be admirable. We do not even permit ourselves to imagine what it would be like.

Government

Government has always been the special field of aversive control. The state is frequently defined in terms of the power to punish and jurisprudence leans heavily upon the associated notion of personal responsibility. Yet it is becoming increasingly difficult to reconcile current practice and theory with these earlier views. In criminology, for example, there is a strong tendency to drop the notion of responsibility in favor of some such alternative as capacity or controllability. But no matter how strongly the facts, or even practical expedience, support such a change, it is difficult to make the change in a legal system designed on a different plan. When governments resort to other techniques (for example, positive reinforcement), the concept of responsibility is no longer relevant and the theory of government is no longer applicable.

The conflict is illustrated by two decisions of the Supreme Court in the 1930's which dealt with, and disagreed on, the definition of control or coercion (4, p. 233). The Agricultural Adjustment Act proposed that the Secretary of Agriculture make "rental or benefit payments" to those farmers who agreed to reduce production. The government agreed that the Act would be unconstitutional if the farmer had been *compelled* to reduce production but was not, since he was merely *invited* to do so. Justice Roberts (4) expressed the contrary majority view of the court that "The power to confer or withhold unlimited benefits is the power to coerce or destroy." This recognition of positive reinforcement was withdrawn a few years later in another case in which Justice Cardozo (4, p. 244) wrote "To hold that motive or temptation is equivalent to coercion is to plunge the law in endless difficulties." We may agree with him, without implying that the proposition is therefore wrong. Sooner or later the law must be prepared to deal with all possible techniques of governmental control.

The uneasiness with which we view government (in the broadest possible sense) when it does not use punishment is shown by the reception of my utopian novel, *Walden Two* (4a). This was essentially a proposal to apply a behavioral technology to the construction of a workable, effective, and productive pattern of government. It was greeted with wrathful violence. Life magazine called it "a travesty on the good life," and "a menace . . . a triumph of mortmain or the dead hand not envisaged since the days of Sparta . . . a slur upon a name, a corruption of an impulse." Joseph Wood Krutch devoted a substantial part of his book, *The Measure of Man* (5), to attacking my views and those of the protagonist, Frazier, in the same vein, and Morris Viteles has recently criticized the book in a similar manner in *Science* (6). Perhaps the reaction is best expressed in a quotation from *The Quest for Utopia* by Negley and Patrick (7):

> Halfway through this contemporary utopia, the reader may feel sure, as we did, that this is a beautifully ironic satire on what has been called 'behavioral engineering.' The longer one stays in this better world of the psychologist, however, the plainer it becomes that the inspiration is not satiric, but messianic. This is indeed the behaviorally engineered society, and while it was to be expected that sooner or later the principle of psychological conditioning would be made the basis of a serious construction of utopia–Brown anticipated it in *Limanora*– yet not even the effective satire of Huxley is adequate preparation for the shocking horror of the idea when positively presented. Of all the dictatorships espoused by utopists, this is the most profound, and incipient dictators might well find in this utopia a guidebook of political practice.

One would scarcely guess that the authors are talking about a world in which there is food, clothing, and shelter for all, where everyone chooses his own work and works on the average only four hours a day, where music and the arts flourish, where personal relationships develop under the most favorable circumstances, where education prepares every child for the social and intellectual life which lies before him, where–in short–people are truly happy, secure, productive, creative, and forward-looking. What is wrong with it? Only one thing: someone "planned it that way." If these critics had come upon a society in some remote corner of the world which boasted similar advantages, they would undoubtedly have hailed it as providing a pattern we all might well follow–provided that it was clearly the result of a natural process of cultural evolution. Any evidence that intelligence had been used in arriving at this version of the good life would, in their eyes, be a serious flaw. No matter if the planner of *Walden Two* diverts none of the proceeds of the community to his own use, no matter if he has no current control or is, indeed, unknown to most of the other members of the community (he planned that, too), somewhere back of it all he occupies the position of prime mover. And this, to the child of the democratic tradition, spoils it all.

The dangers inherent in the control of human behavior are very real. The possibility of the misuse of scientific knowledge must always be faced. We cannot escape by denying the power of a science of behavior or arresting its development. It is no help to cling to familiar philosophies of human behavior simply because they are more reassuring. As I have pointed out elsewhere (8), the new techniques emerging from a science of behavior must be subject to the explicit countercontrol which has already been applied to earlier and cruder forms. Brute force and deception, for example, are now fairly generally suppressed by ethical practices and by explicit governmental and religious agencies. A similar countercontrol of scientific knowledge in the interests of the group is a feasible and promising possibility. Although we cannot say how devious the course of its evolution may be, a cultural pattern of control and countercontrol will presumably emerge which will be most widely supported because it is most widely reinforcing.

If we cannot forsee all the details of this (as we obviously cannot), it is important to remember that this is true of the critics of science as well. The dire consequences of new techniques of control, the hidden menace in original cultural designs—these need some proof. It is only another example of my present point that the need for proof is so often overlooked. Man has got himself into some pretty fixes, and it is easy to believe that he will do so again. But there is a more optimistic possibility. The slow growth of the methods of science, now for the first time being applied to human affairs, *may* mean a new and exciting phase of human life to which historical analogies will not apply and in which earlier political slogans will not be appropriate. If we are to use the knowledge that a science of behavior is now making available with any hope of success, we must look at human nature as it is brought into focus through the methods of science rather than as it has been presented to us in a series of historical accidents.

If the advent of a powerful science of behavior causes trouble, it will not be because science itself is inimical to human welfare but because older conceptions have not yielded easily or gracefully. We expect resistance to new techniques of control from those who have heavy investments in the old, but we have no reason to help them preserve a series of principles that are not ends in themselves but rather outmoded means to an end. What is needed is a new conception of human behavior which is compatible with the implications of a scientific analysis. All men control and are controlled. The question of government in the broadest possible sense is not how freedom is to be preserved but what kinds of control are to be used and to what ends. Control must be analyzed and considered in its proper proportions. No one, I am sure, wishes to develop new master-slave relationships or bend the will of the people to despotic rulers in new ways. These are patterns of control appropriate to a world without science. They may well be the first to go when the experimental analysis of behavior comes into its own in the design of cultural practices.

II [ROGERS]

There are, I believe, a number of matters in connection with this important topic on which the authors of this article, and probably a large majority of psychologists, are in agreement. These matters then are not issues as far as we are concerned, and I should like to mention them briefly in order to put them to one side.

Points of Agreement

I am sure we agree that men—as individuals and as societies—have always endeavored to understand, predict, influence, and control human behavior—their own behavior and that of others.

I believe we agree that the behavioral sciences are making and will continue to make increasingly rapid progress in the understanding of behavior, and that as a consequence the capacity to predict and to control behavior is developing with equal rapidity.

I believe we agree that to deny these advances, or to claim that man's behavior cannot be a field of science, is unrealistic. Even though this is not an issue for us, we should recognize that many intelligent men still hold strongly to the view that the actions of men are free in some sense such that scientific knowledge of man's behavior is impossible. Thus Reinhold Niebuhr, the noted theologian, heaps scorn on the concept of psychology as a science of man's behavior and even says, "In any event, no scientific investigation of past behavior can become the basis of predictions of future behavior" (9). So, while this is not an issue for psychologists, we should at least notice in passing that it is an issue for many people.

I believe we are in agreement that the tremendous potential power of a science which permits the prediction and control of behavior may be misused, and that the possibility of such misuse constitutes a serious threat.

Consequently Skinner and I are in agreement that the whole question of the scientific control of human behavior is a matter with which psychologists and the general public should concern themselves. As Robert Oppenheimer told the American Psychological Association last year (10) the problems that psychologists will pose for society by their growing ability to control behavior will be much more grave than the problems posed by the ability of physicists to control the reactions of matter. I am not sure whether psychologists generally recognize this. My impression is that by and large they hold a laissez-faire attitude. Obviously Skinner and I do not hold this laissez-faire view, or we would not have written this article.

Points at Issue

With these several points of basic and important agreement, are there then any issues that remain on which there are differences? I believe there are. They can be stated very briefly: Who will be controlled? Who will exercise control? What type of control will be exercised? Most important of all, toward what end or what purpose, or in the pursuit of what value, will control be exercised?

It is on questions of this sort that there exist ambiguities, misunderstandings, and probably deep differences. These differences exist among psychologists, among members of the general public in this country, and among various world cultures. Without any hope of achieving a final resolution of these questions, we can, I believe, put these issues in clearer form.

Some Meanings

To avoid ambiguity and faulty communication, I would like to clarify the meanings of some of the terms we are using.

Behavioral science is a term that might be defined from several angles but in the context of this discussion it refers primarily to knowledge that the existence of certain describable conditions in the layman being and/or in his environment is followed by certain describable consequences in his actions.

Prediction means the prior identification of behaviors which then occur. Because it is important in some things I wish to say later, I would point out that one may predict a highly specific behavior, such as an eye blink, or one may predict a class of behaviors. One might correctly predict "avoidant behavior," for example, without being able to specify whether the individual will run away or simply close his eyes.

The word *control* is a very slippery one which can be used with any one of several meanings. I would like to specify three that seem most important for our present purposes. *Control* may mean: (i) The setting of conditions by *B* for *A, A* having no voice in the matter, such that certain predictable behaviors then occur in *A.* I refer to this as external control. (ii)The setting of conditions by *B* for *A, A* giving some degree of consent to these conditions, such that certain predictable behaviors then occur in *A.* I refer to this as the influence of *B* on *A.* (iii) The setting of conditions by *A* such that certain predictable behaviors then occur in himself. I refer to this as internal control. It will be noted that Skinner lumps together the first two meanings, external control and influence, under the concept of control. I find this confusing.

Usual Concept of Control of Human Behavior

With the underbrush thus cleared away (I hope), let us review very briefly the various elements that are involved in the usual concept of the control of human behavior as mediated by the behavioral sciences. I am drawing here on the previous writings of Skinner, on his present statements, on the writings of others who have considered in either friendly or antagonistic fashion the meanings that would be involved in such control. I have not excluded the science fiction writers, as reported recently by Vandenburg (11), since they often show an awareness of the issues involved, even though the methods described are as yet fictional. These then are the elements that seem common to these different concepts of the application of science to human behavior.

(1) There must first be some sort of decision about goals. Usually desirable goals are assumed, but sometimes, as in George Orwell's book *1984,* the goal that is selected is an aggrandizement of individual power with which most of us would disagree. In a recent paper Skinner suggests that one possible set of goals to be assigned to the behavioral technology is this: "Let men be happy, informed, skillful, well-behaved and productive" (12). In the first draft of his part of this article, which he was kind enough to show me, he did not mention such definite goals as these, but desired "improved" educational practices, "wider" use of knowledge in government, and the like. In the final version of his article he avoids even these value-laden terms, and his implicit goal is the very general one that scientific control of behavior is desirable, because it would perhaps bring "a far better world for everyone."

Thus the first step in thinking about the control of human behavior is the choice of goals, whether specific or general. It is necessary to come to terms in some way with the issue, "For what purpose?"

(2) A second element is that, whether the end selected is highly specific or is a very general one such as wanting "a better world," we proceed by the methods of science to discover the means to these ends. We continue through further experimentation and investigation to discover more effective means. The method of science is self-correcting in thus arriving at increasingly effective ways of achieving the purpose we have in mind.

(3) The third aspect of such control is that as the conditions or methods are discovered by which to reach the goal, some person or some group establishes these conditions and uses these methods, having in one way or another obtained the power to do so.

(4) The fourth element is the exposure of individuals to the prescribed conditions, and this leads, with a high degree of probability, to behavior which is in line with the goals desired. Individuals are now happy, if that has been the goal, or well-behaved, or submissive, or whatever it has been decided to make them.

(5) The fifth element is that if the process I have described is put in motion then there is a continuing social organization which will continue to produce the types of behavior that have been valued.

Some Flaws

Are there any flaws in this way of viewing the control of human behavior? I believe there are. In fact the only element in this description with which I find myself in agreement is the second. It seems to me quite incontrovertibly true that the scientific method is an excellent way to discover the means by which to achieve our goals. Beyond that, I feel many sharp differences, which I will try to spell out.

I believe that in Skinner's presentation here and in his previous writings, there is a serious underestimation of the problem of power. To hope that the power which is being made available by the behavioral sciences will be exercised by the scientists, or by a benevolent group, seems to me a hope little supported by either recent or distant history. It seems far more likely that behavioral scientists, holding their present attitudes, will be in the position of the German rocket scientists specializing in guided missiles. First they worked devotedly for Hitler to destroy the U.S.S.R. and the United States. Now, depending on who captured them, they work devotedly for the U.S.S.R. in the interest of destroying the United States, or devotedly for the United States in the interest of destroying the U.S.S.R. If behavioral scientists are concerned solely with advancing their science, it seems most probable that they will serve the purposes of whatever individual or group has the power.

But the major flaw I see in this review of what is involved in the scientific control of human behavior is the denial, misunderstanding, or gross underestimation of the place of ends, goals or values in their relationship to science. This error (as it seems to me) has so many implications that I would like to devote some space to it.

Ends and Values in Relation to Science

In sharp contradiction to some views that have been advanced, I would like to propose a two-pronged thesis: (i) In any scientific endeavor–whether "pure" or applied science–there is a prior subjective choice of the purpose or value which that scientific work is perceived as serving. (ii) This subjective value choice which brings the scientific endeavor into being must always lie outside of that endeavor and can never become a part of the science involved in that endeavor.

Let me illustrate the first point from Skinner himself. It is clear that in his earlier writing (12) it is recognized that a prior value choice is necessary, and it is specified as the goal that men are to become happy, well-behaved, productive, and so on. I am pleased that Skinner has retreated from the goals he then chose, because to me they seem to be stultifying values. I can only feel that he was choosing these goals for others, not for himself. I would hate to see Skinner become "well-behaved," as that term would be defined for him by behavioral scientists. His recent article in the *American Psychologist* (13) shows that he certainly does not want to be "productive" as that value is defined by most psychologists. And the most awful fate I can imagine for him would be to have him constantly "happy." It is the fact that he is very unhappy about many things which makes me prize him.

In the first draft of his part of this article, he also included such prior value choices, saying for example, "We must decide how we are to use the knowledge which a science of human behavior is now making available." Now he has dropped all mention of such choices, and if I understand him correctly, he believes that science can proceed without them. He has suggested this view in another recent paper, stating that "We must continue to experiment in cultural design . . . testing the consequences as we go. Eventually the practices which make for the greatest biological and psychological strength of the group will presumably survive" (8, p. 549).

I would point out, however, that to choose to experiment is a value choice. Even to move in the direction of perfectly random experimentation is a value choice. To test the consequences of an experiment is possible only if we have first made a subjective choice of a criterion value. And implicit in his statement is a valuing of biological and psychological strength. So even when trying to avoid such choice, it seems inescapable that a prior subjective value choice is necessary for any scientific endeavor, or for any application of scientific knowledge.

I wish to make it clear that I am not saying that values cannot be included as a subject of science. It is not true that science deals only with certain classes of "facts" and that these classes do not include values. It is a bit more complex than that, as a simple illustration or two may make clear.

If I value knowledge of the "three R's" as a goal of education, the methods of science can give me increasingly accurate information on how this goal may be achieved. If I value problem-solving ability as a goal of education, the scientific method can give me the same kind of help.

Now, if I wish to determine whether problem-solving ability is "better" than knowledge of the three R's, then scientific method can also study those two values but *only*—and this is very important—in terms of some other value which I have subjectively chosen. I may value college success. Then I can determine whether problem-solving ability or knowledge of the three R's is most closely associated with that value. I may value personal integration or vocational success or responsible citizenship. I can determine whether problems-solving ability or knowledge of the three R's is "better" for achieving any one of these values. But the value or purpose that gives meaning to a particular scientific endeavor must always lie outside of that endeavor.

Although our concern in this symposium is largely with applied science, what I have been saying seems equally true of so-called "pure" science. In pure science the usual prior subjective value choice is the discovery of truth. But this is a subjective choice, and science can never say whether it is the best choice, save in the light of some other value. Geneticists in the U.S.S.R., for example, had to make a subjective choice of whether it was better to pursue truth or to discover facts which upheld a governmental dogma. Which choice is "better"? We could make a scientific investigation of those alternatives but only in the light of some other subjectively chosen value. If, for example, we value the survival of a culture, then we could begin to investigate with the methods of science the question of whether pursuit of truth or support of governmental dogma is most closely associated with cultural survival.

My point then is that any endeavor in science, pure or applied, is carried on in the pursuit of a purpose or value that is subjectively chosen by persons. It is important that this choice be made explicit, since the particular value which is being sought can never be tested or evaluated, confirmed or denied, by the scientific endeavor to which it gives birth. The initial purpose or value always and necessarily lies outside the scope of the scientific effort which it sets in motion.

Among other things this means that if we choose some particular goal or series of goals for human beings and then set out on a large scale to control human behavior to the end of achieving those goals, we are locked in the rigidity of our initial choice, because such a scientific endeavor can never transcend itself to select new goals. Only subjective human persons can do that. Thus if we chose as our goal the state of happiness for human beings (a goal deservedly ridiculed by Aldous Huxley in *Brave New World*), and if we involved all of society in a successful scientific program by which people became happy, we would be locked in a colossal rigidity in which no one would be free to question this goal, because our scientific operations could not transcend themselves to question their guiding purposes. And without laboring this point, I would remark that colossal rigidity, whether in dinosaurs or dictatorships, has a very poor record of evolutionary survival.

If, however, a part of our scheme is to set free some "planners" who do not have to be happy, who are not controlled, and who are therefore free to choose other values, this has several meanings. It means that the purpose we have chosen as our goal is not a sufficient and a satisfying one for human beings but must be supplemented. It also means that if it is necessary to set up an elite group which is free, then this shows all too clearly that the great majority are only the slaves—no matter by what high-sounding name we call them—of those who select the goals.

Perhaps, however, the thought is that a continuing scientific endeavor will evolve its own goals; that the initial findings will alter the directions, and subsequent findings will alter them still further, and that science somehow develops its own purpose. Although he does not clearly say so, this appears to be the pattern Skinner has in mind. It is surely a reasonable description, but it overlooks one element in this continuing development, which is that subjective personal choice enters in at every point at which the direction changes. The findings of a science, the results of an experiment, do not and never can tell us what next scientific purpose to pursue. Even in the purest of science, the scientist must decide what the findings mean and must subjectively choose what next step will be most profitable in the pursuit of his purpose. And if we are speaking of the application of scientific knowledge, then it is distressingly clear that the increasing scientific knowledge of the structure of the atom carries with it no necessary choice as to the purpose to which this knowledge will be put. This is a subjective personal choice which must be made by many individuals.

Thus I return to the proposition with which I began this section of my remarks—and which I now repeat in different words. Science has its meaning as the objective pursuit of a purpose which has been subjectively chosen by a person or persons. This purpose or value can never be investigated by the particular scientific experiment or investigation to which it has given birth and meaning. Consequently, any discussion of the control of human beings by the behavioral sciences must first and most deeply concern itself with the subjectively chosen purposes which such an application of science is intended to implement.

Is the Situation Hopeless?

The thoughtful reader may recognize that, although my remarks up to this point have introduced some modifications in the conception of the processes by which human behavior will be controlled, these remarks may have made such control seem, if anything, even more inevitable. We might sum it up this way: Behavioral science is clearly moving forward; the increasing power for control which it gives will be held by someone or some group; such an individual or group will surely choose the values or goals to be achieved; and most of us will then be increasingly controlled by means so subtle that we will not even be aware of them as controls. Thus, whether a council of wise psychologists (if this is not a contradiction in terms), or a Stalin or a Big Brother has the power, and whether the goal is happiness, or productivity, or resolution of the Oedipus complex, or submission, or love of Big Brother, we will inevitably find ourselves moving toward the chosen goal and probably thinking that we ourselves desire it.

Thus, if this line of reasoning is correct, it appears that some form of *Walden Two* or of *1984* (and at a deep philosophic level they seem indistinguishable) is coming. The fact that it would surely arrive piecemeal, rather than all at once does not greatly change the fundamental issues. In any event, as Skinner has indicated in his writings, we would then look back upon the concepts of human freedom, the capacity for choice, the responsibility for choice, and the worth of the human individual as historical curiosities which once existed by cultural accident as values in a prescientific civilization.

I believe that any person observant of trends must regard something like the foregoing sequence as a real possibility. It is not simply a fantasy. Something of that sort may even be the most likely future. But is it an inevitable future? I want to devote the remainder of my remarks to an alternative possibility.

Alternative Set of Values

Suppose we start with a set of ends, values, purposes, quite different from the type of goals we have been considering. Suppose we do this quite openly, setting them forth as a possible value choice to be accepted or rejected. Suppose we select a set of values that focuses on fluid elements of process rather than static attributes. We might then value: man as a process of becoming, as a process of achieving worth and dignity through the development of his potentialities; the individual human being as a self-actualizing process, moving on to more challenging and enriching experiences; the process by which the individual creatively adapts to an ever-new and changing world; the process by which knowledge transcends itself, as, for example, the theory of relativity transcended Newtonian physics, itself to be transcended in some future day by a new perception.

If we select values such as these we turn to our science and technology of behavior with a very different set of questions. We will want to know such things as these: Can science aid in the discovery of new modes of richly rewarding living? more meaningful and satisfying modes of interpersonal relationships? Can science inform us on how the human race can become a more intelligent participant in its own evolution—its physical, psychological and social evolution? Can science inform us on ways of releasing the creative capacity of individuals, which seem so necessary if we are to survive in this fantastically expanding atomic age? Oppenheimer has pointed out (14) that knowledge, which used to double in millenia or centuries, now doubles in a generation or a decade. It appears that we must discover the utmost in release of creativity if we are to be able to adapt effectively. In short, can science discover the methods by which man can most readily become a continually developing and self-transcending process, in his behavior, his thinking, his knowledge? Can science predict and release an essentially "unpredictable" freedom?

It is one of the virtues of science as a method that it is as able to advance and implement goals and purposes of this sort as it is to serve static values, such as states of being well-informed, happy, obedient. Indeed we have some evidence of this.

Small Example

I will perhaps be forgiven if I document some of the possibilities along this line by turning to psychotherapy, the field I know best.

Psychotherapy, as Meerloo (15) and others have pointed out, can be one of the most subtle tools for the control of *A* by *B.* The therapist can subtly mold individuals in imitation of himself. He can cause an individual to become a submissive and conforming being. When certain therapeutic principles are used in extreme fashion, we call it brainwashing, an instance of the disintegration of the personality and a reformulation of the person along lines desired by the controlling individual. So the principles of therapy can be used as an effective means of external control of human personality and behavior. Can psychotherapy be anything else?

Here I find the developments going on in client-centered psychotherapy (16) an exciting hint of what a behavioral science can do in achieving the kinds of values I have stated. Quite aside from being a somewhat new orientation in psychotherapy, this development has important implications regarding the relation of a behavioral science to the control of human behavior. Let me describe our experience as it relates to the issues of this discussion.

In client-centered therapy, we are deeply engaged in the prediction and influencing of behavior, or even the control of behavior. As therapists, we institute certain attitudinal conditions, and the client has relatively little voice in the establishment of these conditions. We predict that if these conditions are instituted, certain behavioral consequences will ensue in the client. Up to this point this is largely external control, no different from what Skinner has described, and no different from what I have discussed in the preceding sections of this article. But here any similarity ceases.

The conditions we have chosen to establish predict such behavioral consequences as these: that the client will become self-directing, less rigid, more open to the evidence of his senses, better organized and integrated, more similar to the ideal which he has chosen for himself. In other words, we have established by external control conditions which we predict will be followed by internal control by the individual, in pursuit of internally chosen goals. We have set the conditions which predict various classes of behaviors—self-directing behaviors, sensitivity to realities within and without, flexible adaptiveness—which are by their very nature unpredictable in their specifics. Our recent research (17) indicates that our predictions are to a significant degree corroborated, and our commitment to the scientific method causes us to believe that more effective means of achieving these goals may be realized.

Research exists in other fields—industry, education, group dynamics—which seems to support our own findings. I believe it may be conservatively stated that scientific progress has been made in identifying those conditions in an interpersonal relationship which, if they exist in *B,* are followed in *A* by greater maturity in behavior, less dependence on others, an increase in expressiveness as a person, an increase in variability, flexibility and effectiveness of adaptation, an increase in self-responsibility and self-direction. And, quite in contrast to the concern expressed by some, we do not find that the creatively adaptive behavior which results from such self-directed variability of expression is a "happy accident" which occurs in "chaos." Rather, the individual who is open to his experience, and self-directing, is harmonious not chaotic, ingenious rather than random, as he orders his responses imaginatively toward the achievement of his own purposes. His creative actions are no more a "happy accident" than was Einstein's development of the theory of relativity.

Thus we find ourselves in fundamental agreement with John Dewey's statement: "Science has made its way by releasing, not by suppressing, the elements of variation, of invention and innovation, of novel creation in individuals" (18). Progress in personal life and in group living is, we believe, made in the same way.

Possible Concept of the Control of Human Behavior

It is quite clear that the point of view I am expressing is in sharp contrast to the usual conception of the relationship of the behavioral sciences to the control of human behavior. In order to make this contrast even more blunt, I will state this possibility in paragraphs parallel to those used before.

(1) It is possible for us to choose to value man as a self-actualizing process of becoming–to value creativity, and the process by which knowledge becomes self-transcending.

(2) We can proceed, by the methods of science, to discover the conditions which necessarily precede these processes and, through continuing experimentation, to discover better means of achieving these purposes.

(3) It is possible for individuals or groups to set these conditions, with a minimum of power or control. According to present knowledge, the only authority necessary is the authority to establish certain qualities of interpersonal relationship.

(4) Exposed to these conditions, present knowledge suggests that individuals become more self-responsible, make progress in self-actualization, become more flexible, and become more creatively adaptive.

(5) Thus such an initial choice would inaugurate the beginnings of a social system or subsystem in which values, knowledge, adaptive skills, and even the concept of science would be continually changing and self-transcending. The emphasis would be upon man as a process of becoming.

I believe it is clear that such a view as I have been describing does not lead to any definable utopia. It would be impossible to predict its final outcome. It involves a step-by-step development, based on a continuing subjective choice of purposes, which are implemented by the behavioral sciences. It is in the direction of the "open society," as that term has been defined by Popper (19), where individuals carry responsibility for personal decisions. It is at the opposite pole from his concept of the closed society, of which *Walden Two* would be an example.

I trust it is also evident that the whole emphasis is on process, not on end-states of being. I am suggesting that it is by choosing to value certain qualitative elements of the process of becoming that we can find a pathway toward the open society.

The Choice

It is my hope that we have helped to clarify the range of choice which will lie before us and our children in regard to the behavioral sciences. We can choose to use our growing knowledge to enslave people in ways never dreamed of before, depersonalizing them, controlling them by means so carefully selected that they will perhaps never be aware of their loss of personhood. We can choose to utilize our scientific knowledge to make men happy, well-behaved, and productive, as Skinner earlier suggested. Or we can insure that each person learns all the syllabus which we select and set before him, as Skinner now suggests. Or at the other end of the spectrum of choice we can choose to use the behavioral sciences in ways which will free, not control; which will bring about constructive variability, not conformity; which will develop creativity, not contentment; which will facilitate each person in his self-directed process of becoming; which will aid individuals, groups, and even the concept of science to become self-transcending in freshly adaptive ways of meeting life and its problems. The choice is up to us, and, the human race being what it is, we are likely to stumble about, making at times some nearly disastrous value choices and at other times highly constructive ones.

I am aware that to some, this setting forth of a choice is unrealistic, because a choice of values is regarded as not possible. Skinner has stated:

> Man's vaunted creative powers . . . his capacity to choose and our right to hold him responsible for his choice—none of these is conspicuous in this new self-portrait (provided by science). Man, we once believed, was free to express himself in art, music, and literature, to inquire into nature, to seek salvation in his own way. He could initiate action and make spontaneous and capricious changes of course. . . . But science insists that action is initiated by forces impinging upon the individual, and that caprice is only another name for behavior for which we have not yet found a cause. (12, pp. 52-53)

I can understand this point of view, but I believe that it avoids looking at the great paradox of behavioral science. Behavior, when it is examined scientifically, is surely best understood as determined by prior causation. This is one great fact of science. But responsible personal choice, which is the most essential element in being a person, which is the core experience in psychotherapy, which exists prior to any scientific endeavor, is an equally prominent fact in our lives. To deny the experience of responsible choice is, to me, as restricted a view as to deny the possibility of a behavioral science. That these two important elements of our experience appear to be in contradiction has perhaps the same significance as the contradiction between the wave theory and the corpuscular theory of light, both of which can be shown to be true, even though incompatible. We cannot profitably deny our subjective life, any more than we can deny the objective description of that life.

In conclusion then, it is my contention that science cannot come into being without a personal choice of the values we wish to achieve. And these values we choose to implement will forever lie outside of the science which implements them; the goals we select, the purposes we wish to follow, must always be outside of the science which achieves them. To me this has the encouraging meaning that the human person, with his capacity of subjective choice, can and will always exist, separate from and prior to any of his scientific undertakings. Unless as individuals and groups we choose to relinquish our capacity of subjective choice, we will always remain persons, not simply pawns of a self-created science.

III [SKINNER]

I cannot quite agree that the practice of science *requires* a prior decision about goals or a prior choice of values. The metallurgist can study the properties of steel and the engineer can design a bridge without raising the question of whether a bridge is to be built. But such questions are certainly frequently raised and tentatively answered. Rogers wants to call the answers "subjective choices of values." To me, such an expression suggests that we have had to abandon more rigorous scientific practices in order to talk about our own behavior. In the experimental analysis of other organisms I would use other terms, and I shall try to do so here. Any list of values is a list of reinforcers—conditioned or otherwise. We are so constituted that under certain circumstances food, water, sexual contact, and so on, will make any behavior which produces them more likely to occur again. Other things may acquire this power. We do not need to say that an organism chooses to eat rather than to starve. If you answer that it is a very different thing when a man chooses to starve, I am only too happy to agree. If it were not so, we should have cleared up the question of choice long ago. An organism can be reinforced by—can be made to "choose"—almost any given state of affairs.

Rogers is concerned with choices that involve multiple and usually conflicting consequences. I have dealt with some of these elsewhere (20) in an analysis of self-control. Shall I eat these delicious strawberries today if I will then suffer an annoying rash tomorrow? The decision I am to make used to be assigned to the province of ethics. But we are now studying similar combinations of positive and negative consequences, as well as collateral conditions which affect the result in the laboratory. Even a pigeon can be taught some measure of self-control! And this work helps us to understand the operation of certain formulas—among them value judgments—which folk-wisdom, religion, and psychotherapy have advanced in the interests of self-discipline. The observable effect of any statement of value is to alter the relative effectiveness of reinforcers. We may no longer enjoy the strawberries for thinking about the rash. If rashes are made sufficiently shameful, illegal, sinful, maladjusted, or unwise, we may glow with satisfaction as we push the strawberries aside in a grandiose avoidance response which would bring a smile to the lips of Murray Sidman.

People behave in ways which, as we say, conform to ethical, governmental, or religious patterns because they are reinforced for doing so. The resulting behavior may have far-reaching consequences for the survival of the pattern to which it conforms. And whether we like it or not, survival is the ultimate criterion. This is where, it seems to me, science can help—not in choosing a goal, but in enabling us to predict the survival of mankind. Do not ask me why I want mankind to survive. I can tell you why only in the sense in which the physiologist can tell you why I want to breathe. Once the relation between a given step and the survival of my group has been pointed out, I will take that step. And it is the business of science to point out just such relations.

The values I have occasionally recommended (and Rogers has not led me to recant) are transitional. Other things being equal, I am betting on the group whose practices make for healthy, happy, secure, productive, and creative people. And I insist that the values recommended by Rogers are transitional, too, for I can ask him the same kind of question. Man as a process of becoming—*what?* Self-actualization—for what? Inner control is no more a goal than external.

What Rogers seems to me to be proposing, both here and elsewhere (1), is this: Let us use our increasing power of control to create individuals who will not need and perhaps will no longer respond to control. Let us solve the problem of our power by renouncing it. At first blush this seems as implausible as a benevolent despot. Yet power has occasionally been foresworn. A nation has burned its Reichstag, rich men have given away their wealth, beautiful women have become ugly hermits in the desert, and psychotherapists have become nondirective. When this happens, I look to other possible reinforcements for a plausible explanation. A people relinquish democratic power when a tyrant promises them the earth. Rich men give away wealth to escape the accusing finger of their fellowmen. A woman destroys her beauty in the hope of salvation. And a psychotherapist relinquishes control because he can thus help his client more effectively.

The solution that Rogers is suggesting is thus understandable. But is he correctly interpreting the result? What evidence is there that a client ever becomes truly *self*-directing? What evidence is there that he ever makes a truly *inner* choice of ideal or goal? Even though the therapist does not do the choosing, even though he encourages "self-actualization"—he is not out of control as long as he holds himself ready to step in when occasion demands—when, for example, the client chooses the goal of becoming a more accomplished liar or murdering his boss. But supposing the therapist does withdraw completely or is no longer necessary—what about all the other forces acting upon the client? Is the self-chosen goal independent of his early ethical and religious training? of the folk-wisdom of his group? of the opinions and attitudes of others who are important to him? Surely not. The therapeutic situation is only a small part of the world of the client. From the therapist's point of view it may appear to be possible to relinquish control. But the control passes, not to a "self," but to forces in other parts of the client's world. The solution of the therapist's problem of power cannot be *our* solution, for we must consider *all* the forces acting upon the individual.

The child who must be prodded and nagged is something less than a fully developed human being. We want to see him hurrying to his appointment, not because each step is taken in response to verbal reminders from his mother, but because certain temporal contigencies, in which dawdling has been punished and hurrying reinforced, have worked a change in his behavior. Call this a state of better organization, a greater sensitivity to reality, or what you will. The plain fact is that the child passes from a temporary verbal control exercised by his parents to control by certain inexorable features of the environment. I should suppose that something of the same sort happens in successful psychotherapy. Rogers seems to me to be saying this: Let us put an end, as quickly as possible, to any pattern of master-and-slave, to any direct obedience to command, to the submissive following of suggestions. Let the individual be free to adjust himself to more rewarding features of the world about him. In the end, let his teachers and counselors "wither away," like the Marxist state. I not only agree with this as a useful ideal, I have constructed a fanciful world to demonstrate its advantages. It saddens me to hear Rogers say that "at a deep philosophic level" *Walden Two* and George Orwell's *1984* "seem indistinguishable." They could scarcely be more unlike—at any level. The book *1984* is a picture of immediate aversive control for vicious selfish purposes. The founder of *Walden Two,* on the other hand, has built a community in which neither he nor any other person exerts any *current* control. His achievement lay in his original *plan,* and when he boasts of this ("It is enough to satisfy the thirstiest tyrant") we do not fear him but only pity him for his weakness.

Another critic of *Walden Two,* Andrew Hacker (21), has discussed this point in considering the bearing of mass conditioning upon the liberal notion of autonomous man. In drawing certain parallels between the Grand Inquisition passage in Dostoevsky's *Brothers Karamazov,* Huxley's *Brave New World,* and *Walden Two,* he attempts to set up a distinction to be drawn in any society between conditioners and conditioned. He assumes that "the conditioner can be said to be autonomous in the traditional liberal sense." But then he notes: "Of course the conditioner has been conditioned. But he has not been conditioned by the conscious manipulation of another *person.*" But how does this affect the resulting behavior? Can we not soon forget the origins of the "artificial" diamond which is identical with the real thing? Whether it is an "accidental" cultural pattern, such as is said to have produced the founder of *Walden Two,* or the engineered environment which is about to produce his successors, we are dealing with sets of conditions generating human behavior which will ultimately be measured by their contribution to the future, not the past, for the test of "goodness" or acceptability.

If we are worthy of our democratic heritage we shall, of course, be ready to resist any tyrannical use of science for immediate or selfish purposes. But if we value the achievements and goals of democracy we must not refuse to apply science to the design and construction of cultural patterns, even though we may then find ourselves in some sense in the position of controllers. Fear of control, generalized beyond any warrant, has led to a misinterpretation of valid practices and the blind rejection of intelligent planning for a better way of life. In terms which I trust Rogers will approve, in conquering this fear we shall become more mature and better organized and shall, thus, more fully actualize ourselves as human beings.

BIBLIOGRAPHY

1. C.R. Rogers, *Teachers College Record 57,* 316. (1956).
2. A. Hacker, *Antioch Rev.* 14, 195 (1954).
3. C. Coleman, *Bull. Am. Assoc. Univ. Professors* 39, 457, (1953).
4. P. A. Freund *et al., Constitutional Law: Cases and Other Problems,* vol. 1 (Little, Brown, Boston, 1954).

4a. B. F. Skinner, *Walden Two,* (Macmillan, New York, 1948).

5. J. W. Krutch, *The Measure of Man* (Bobbs-Merrill, Indianapolis, 1953).
6. M. Viteles, *Science* 122 1167 (1955).
7. G. Negley and J. M. Patrick, *The Quest for Utopia* (Schuman, New York, 1952).
8. B.F. Skinner, *Trans. N. Y. Acad. Sci.* 17, 547 (1955).
9. R. Niebuhr, *The Self and the Dramas of History* (Scribner, New York: 1955), p. 47.
10. R. Oppenheimer, *Am. Psychol. 11, 127 (1956).*
11. S.G. Vandenberg, *ibid* 11, 339 (1956).
12. B.F. Skinner, *Am. Scholar* 25, 47 (1955-56).
13. —— *Am. Psychol.* 11, 221 (1956).
14. R. Oppenheimer, *Roosevelt University Occasional Papers* 2 (1956).
15. J.A.M. Meerloo, *J. Nervous Mental Disease* 122, 353 (1955).
16. C.R. Rogers, *Client-Centered Therapy* (Houghton-Mifflin, Boston, 1951).
17. —— and R. Dymond, Eds. *Psychotherapy and Personality Change* (Univ. of Chicago Press, Chicago, 1954).
18. J. Ratner, Ed., *Intelligence in the Modern World: John Dewey's Philosophy* (Modern Library, New York, 1939), p. 359.
19. K. R. Popper, *The Open Society and Its Enemies* (Rutledge and Kegan Paul, London, 1945).
20. B. F. Skinner, *Science and Human Behavior* (Macmillan, New York, 1953).
21. A Hacker, *J. Politics* 17, 590 (1955).

Herbert M. Lefcourt

THE FUNCTION OF THE ILLUSIONS OF CONTROL AND FREEDOM

Since the publication of B.F. Skinner's (1971) book *Beyond Freedom and Dignity,* the public has witnessed an extensive number of debates regarding the virtues and faults of Skinner's reasoning. While Skinner's arguments about the illusions of freedom and will are decent correctives for those who too easily espouse Protestant ethics and Horatio Alger fantasies, there seems to be a great imbalance in his discussions.

As the term *freedom* is an illusion or a construction of events that is independent of a man's actions, so too is *control* a construction or illusion. Whether people perceive themselves as free or controlled in their actions is a constructive process and not a "given." It is possible for one person to view himself as having freely chosen to stand in line for a glimpse of a popular politician. A cynic could easily counter that individual's vision of free choice by referring to the effects of public relations, mass media, and man's susceptibility to the influence of others. On the other hand, clinical psychologists often encounter individuals who believe that they are helpless pawns of fate or other persons. To the clinician, this illusion of control is often judged to be inappropriate and obstructive.

The point to be made in this article is that while freedom and control are both illusions, inventions of man to make sense of his experience, they do have consequences. To believe that one's freedom is a false myth and that one should submit to wiser or better controls contains the assumption that beliefs or illusions have no immediate consequences. It will be contended here that this assumption is specious. Illusions do have consequences, and as the research evidence presented in this article indicates, the loss of the illusion of freedom may have untoward consequences for the way men live.

Herbert M. Lefcourt, "The Function of the Illusions of Control & Freedom," *American Psychologist,* 1973, Vol. 28, No. 5, pp. 417-425. ©Reprinted with permission.

RESEARCH ON MAN'S ACCOMMODATION TO URBAN STRESSES

David Glass, Jerome E. Singer, and their colleagues (Glass, Reim, & Singer, 1971; Glass & Singer, 1972; Glass, Singer, & Friedman, 1969; Reim, Glass, & Singer, 1971) conducted a series of investigations concerned with the effects of noise on tasks requiring persistence and attention to details. In several of these experiments, subjects had to complete a set of simple tasks: number comparisons, addition, and letter finding. In the first of the above-named tasks, subjects were asked to indicate whether the multidigit numbers in each set of a series of pairs were the same or different. The addition task simply required subjects to add sets of one- and two-digit numbers. The letter-finding task required that subjects find the letter A in 5 words out of a column of 41 words. These tasks, simple enough in themselves, were administered under four conditions of noise distraction in one study (Glass et al., 1969). The investigators had combined the sounds of two people speaking Spanish, one person speaking Armenian, a mimeograph machine, a desk calculator, and a typewriter to produce a composite, nondistinguishable roar that served as an aversive noise. No doubt the roar was a good replica of general urban mayhem. The authors were all New York residents, well experienced with such stimuli. However, it was not simply the fact of noise and its impact on persons working at simple tasks that was of interest to these experimenters. Rather, the concern was with the effects of the predictability and controllability of the noise. In this study, each of four groups received a different combination of stimuli. One group was subjected to the noise at 110 decibels (loud noise) for nine seconds at the end of every minute of the session. Another group received the loud noise but at random intervals and for random lengths of time. Two other groups received fixed and random noise but at a softer volume (56 decibels).

As might have been expected, the initial bursts of noise were effective in distracting most subjects. However, as the session progressed, subjects adapted to the noise, improving in performance on the simple tasks and exhibiting lesser responsivity as assessed by physiological measurements. After this session, subjects were engaged in two further tasks during which there was no noise or like interference. One task was designed to evoke frustration. The other task, while routine, required caution and attentiveness. The frustration task consisted of design copying in which subjects had to trace over all lines in each of four designs with certain restrictions: subjects were not to lift the pencil from the paper at any time and were not to trace over any line twice. Several copies of each design were available so that a subject could make as many attempts to succeed as he desired. As it was, two of the diagrams were insoluble. Therefore, as many times as the subject attempted to succeed, he failed.

The second task was a proofreading job. Ten errors were included on each of seven pages of an essay. Misspellings, grammatical errors, etc., were to be located during a 15-minute period.

The dependent variable measured in the tracing task was the number of times that subjects attempted to solve the insoluble designs. Subjects who had received noise at fixed intervals did not differ from a control group that had not been subjected to noise at all. Those subjects who had suffered the noise on a random schedule made considerably fewer attempts, and this was most pronounced when the random noise had been of the higher intensity.

The proofreading task was measured in terms of the percentage of omitted errors. While the results of this task were somewhat less significant than those of the tracing task, subjects who had experienced random noise made more omissions than those who had received fixed-interval noise. Loud, random noise was associated with the highest percentage of omitted errors, whereas the softer, fixed-interval noise was associated with the best proofreading performance.

While the intensity of noise had some effect, it paled in comparison to the effects of predictability. The implications of these results regarding predictability deserve some close attention. If noise, or any aversive stimulus for that matter, were unanticipated, the shock value of that stimulus would no doubt be augmented. Who has not found himself startled in response to even soft but unexplainable sounds occurring in the night? The state of alertness and arousal thus engendered in the individual would probably be continuous if one were in a strange place where the meaning of noises and the inferences to be drawn from them were uncertain. In other words, if we do not know the significance of a noise, it will become arousing; the perceiver will feel a need to become ready for anything, the limits of which depend on that person's imagination.

It is now fitting to discuss the relationship between the meaning of a noise and the predictability of that noise. If we "know" a sound such as the starting of a furnace motor, we know from where it originates and what will result from that sound. The sequence is predictable; nothing untoward is anticipated. The sound will not change in pitch or intensity. If unusual changes do occur, we would become suspicious of the working of that furnace and summon a repairman. In short, predictability is a major facet of knowing something. An overly predictable person generates little arousal or interest and more likely creates boredom in others. The consistency and reliability of noise in the investigation described above instruct the subject that subsequent changes in volume and timing of the noise are unlikely: there need be little apprehension of a sudden increased intensity. As regularity is perceived, the subject can also ready himself, slowing down in his work efforts when he anticipates the onset of noise. He can, therefore, avoid interruptions by not letting himself be caught unawares and distracted in the midst of an activity.

Implicit in this discussion regarding predictability is the element of control. If we know the ordinary sounds of the furnace, then we know what must be done to it and when. If another person is predictable, then we have a good idea of how one must act with him to cause certain effects. In each instance, predictability allows us some sense of confidence that we can act to create desirable effects. In being forced to hear predictable noise, we may stop work and wait until it ceases, or steel ourselves for the onset, minimizing our own responses to the noise. We are not as helpless as we might otherwise be since we can do something to minimize the impact of predictable noise. It is in the perception of this ability "to do something" that we arrive at the concept of perceived control.

In a second investigation reported in the same article by Glass et al. (1969), the effect of perceived control was examined more directly. All of the subjects received loud, randomly occurring noise, the most aversive and debilitating combination found in the first study. The major difference between the first and second studies was that in the second investigation, half of the subjects were provided with a button that would enable them to terminate the noise. These subjects were instructed as to the use of the button but were encouraged to use it only if the noise became too much for them to bear. In essence, subjects were provided with the best modern analog of control—the off switch. As the authors had predicted, subjects with access to the off switch tried almost five times the number of insoluble puzzles and made significantly fewer omissions in proofreading than did their counterparts who were given no such option to control the aversive stimulation. These differences were obtained despite the fact that subjects who had potential control did not actually exercise it. The mere knowledge that one can exert control, then, serves to mitigate the debilitating effects of aversive stimuli.

From the investigations reported by Glass et al. (1969), it is possible to conclude that when an aversive event is predictable, its effects are minimized, possibly through the opportunity that regularity creates for us to schedule our efforts so as to avoid interruption, or to prepare our sensory apparatus so as to be less sensitive to the disturbing event. Second, the control of termination of the aversive stimulus diminishes the impact of that stimulus, perhaps by eliminating the fear that "things can get worse" and even beyond endurance. Conceivably, it is the *fear of unendurable pain* that is debilitating to the cognitive processes of individuals undergoing the experience of unpredictable and uncontrollable yet lesser levels of pain and irritation.

If an extrapolation is made from the above conclusions and conjectures regarding fear of pain to the suffering of anxiety, some explanation of well-known clinical phenomena may be forthcoming. One may ask whether an individual would experience anxiety if he had ways of avoiding events that offered a threat to him. Perhaps, *la belle indifférence,* the beautiful indifference of hysterical women toward their functional disabilities during the Victorian era, derived from a sense of inner content. Conversion reactions, through which neurologically impossible paralyses would occur, often created "secondary gains" for patients in that they would be allowed to avoid "aversive experiences" such as sexual intercourse. It is tempting to suggest that for the hysterical patients who frequented psychoanalysts' offices during the first decades of this century, symptoms were a "button," a device by which it became possible to terminate threatening events; likewise, therapy as it is practiced today often seems directed toward helping a patient find a better "button," one that enables him to more comfortably approach and cope with threats.

Such conjecturing as the above would seem premature if it were not for the reliability of findings with perceived control. Glass et al. (1971) were able to replicate the "access to a button" phenomenon described above when subjects themselves were not in direct control, but could ask a partner-collaborator to press the button and terminate the noise for them. With shock as the aversive stimulus, Staub, Tursky, and Schwartz (1971) found that subjects who were allowed to administer shock to themselves and to select the level of intensity of that shock reported less discomfort at higher levels of shock and endured stronger shocks than did paired subjects to whom shock was administered passively. However, when all of the subjects were engaged in a second series of shock trials administered without subject control, the group that had previously experienced control declined in their tolerance for the shocks, rating lower intensity levels as being more uncomfortable and enduring less shock than previously. On the other hand, no changes were found among subjects who had not experienced control.

Where the Glass and Singer experiments exhibit the effects of control on task performance under aversive conditions, the investigation by Staub et al. reveals similar shifts in self-reports. The reported aversive quality of a stimulus decreases when subjects exercise control over that stimulus. These findings are congruent with those reported by Pervin (1963), who found that subjects expressed a preference for predictable and self-controlled shock administration to unpredictable and experimenter-controlled conditions. Parallel findings with regard to acknowledged anxiety in each condition were obtained. Other investigators (Corah & Boffa, 1970; Haggard, 1943) have found that stress, as measured by physiological changes, was reduced when subjects could control the onset and termination of aversive stimulation.

It seems evident, then, that the exercise of control and the ability to predict the occurrence of aversive stimuli have an ameliorating affect on the recipient. Pain-producing stimuli prove less painful and disruptive to individuals who can predict and control those stimuli, and these findings are obtained with different types of data, that is, performance, self-report, and physiological indexes. To further illustrate the pervasiveness of the effects of perceived control, research literature with similar implications among other species is presented next.

PERCEIVED CONTROL AND THE RESPONSE TO AVERSIVE STIMULATION AMONG NONHUMANS

The classic study concerned with the ramifications of control is undoubtedly that by Mowrer and Viek (1948). In that seminal and theoretically prophetic experiment, Mowrer and Viek were able to show that rats exhibited less fear of an aversive stimulus when they could exercise control in terminating it. For each of 15 days, 20 food-deprived rats were offered a bit of food after they had been placed in an experimental cage. Ten seconds after the food was taken by the rat, a shock was delivered through a grid at the floor of the cage. For half of the sample the shock was left on until the rat leaped into the air. If the rat did not eat within 10 seconds after food was presented, it was regarded as an inhibition. The food was subsequently withdrawn, and the shock was applied 10 seconds later. Whereas one group of 10 animals could terminate the shock through leaping, a second group of 10 were passively yoked to the first group. That is, each member of what was referred to as the "shock-uncontrollable" group was paired with one rat from the shock-controllable group and received shock for whatever length of time his controlling partner had received it on each respective day.

The crucial dependent variable consisted of the number of inhibitions recorded in each group, for each of the 15 successive days. The 10 rats of the shock-controlling group produced an overall total of only 16 inhibitions (M = 1.6) throughout the experiment in contrast to the shock-noncontrolling or helpless animals who produced 85 inhibitions (M = 8.5), a difference that was strongly significant. In addition, the helpless group notably increased in the incidence of inhibition from the first three days (0, 1, 3) to the last three days (8, 8, 8). In contrast, the shock-controlling group did not inhibit at all until the third day, at which time only one inhibition was noted. On only four later days did more than one inhibition occur, and on three of those days there were but two inhibitions, while three were obtained on the other day. The helpless group, on the other hand, produced less than five inhibitions on only 3 of the 15 days.

These results support the hypothesized effect of control rather well. When rats could terminate shock they exhibited less fear-related behavior. Since all of the animals were hungry, shock-controlling rats can be said to have been acting more in their own interests in continuing to eat the proffered food. The inhibition of eating by helpless rats, on the other hand, can be construed as a maladaptive response in that the animal, frozen with fear, was unable to eat despite its hunger. One might say that the helpless rats "lost their will" or the active response of defending their self-interests. Although such terms can inspire a facetious response, constructs such as hope, helplessness, and will have been resurrected recently in a number of works to help account for the persistence of human activity despite sometimes overwhelming adversity (May, 1969; Menninger, 1963).

Mowrer (1950) himself seemed keenly aware of some of the far-reaching ramifications of his work:

> Perhaps we have isolated here, in prototype, one of the central reasons why human beings so universally prize freedom and why threats to freedom, under a totalitarian regime, are anxiety-producing. [p. 472]

In addition, Mowrer extrapolated from his results to the rather mundane but human experience of concern with illness:

> One is ill and suffering from pain and inconvenience. The physician arrives, diagnoses the difficulty, prescribes treatment, and intimates that in a day or two one will be quite hale again. It is unlikely that the examination or the ensuing exchange of words has altered the physical condition of the patient in the least; yet he is likely to "feel a lot better" as a result of the doctor's call. What obviously happens in such instances is that initially the patient's physical suffering is complicated by concern lest his suffering continue indefinitely or perhaps grow worse. After a reassuring diagnosis, this concern abates; and if, subsequently, the same ailment recurs, one can predict that it will arouse less apprehension than it did originally. [p. 473]

Never to be caught anthropomorphizing, Mowrer attempted to explain the rat's relief with control as deriving from anticipatory motoric movements associated with leaping, the shock-terminating response. Later investigators examining the effect of control among animals have been less hesitant in employing such concepts as hopelessness and futility in discussing their animals' behavior.

Among the more dramatic investigations concerned with the loss of control among infrahumans is that of Curt Richter (1959). Richter had observed some unanticipated sudden deaths among his laboratory rats as they underwent different procedures. After whisker cutting, an occasional animal would display a strange corkscrewing motion that eventually ended in death. Richter did not initially draw any inferences from the strange occurrences until unexplained deaths became more frequent in later experimentation. In a study primarily concerned with swimming endurance at varying water temperatures, Richter found that a few animals whose whiskers had been trimmed would swim around excitedly for a few seconds in a turbulent bath, dive to the bottom apparently in search of escape, and then, after swimming around for a short time below the surface, would suddenly stop and die. Most fascinating was the fact that autopsies revealed no signs that the animal had drowned. Rats can swim for great lengths of time. Richter himself had found rats capable of swimming for up to 81 consecutive hours under ideal conditions. Consequently, the short-lived attempt at swimming and sudden death presented a mysterious challenge for a curious investigator. Up to this point Richter had found whisker trimming to be a major determinant of this sudden-death phenomenon. While whisker trimming produced sudden death among all wild rats (street and farm bred), it seemed less deleterious to the tame, laboratory-bred variety. Additionally, several wild rats whose whiskers were not trimmed also died suddenly after being placed in the swimming jars, so whisker trimming was obviously not the *sine qua non* determinant of this strange occurrence. Ultimately, Richter concluded that handling per se seemed to be the primary cause of death among wild rats. Handling, while producing arousal among wild rats, also prevented any instrumental activity that could result in escape from the aversive experience. If, on the other hand, rats were allowed to escape just once, the sudden-death phenomenon was eliminated. Richter (1959) observed:

> Interesting evidence showing that the phenomenon of sudden death may depend on emotional reactions to restraint or confinement in glass jars comes from the observation that after elimination of hopelessness the rats do not die. On several occasions we have immersed rats in water and promptly removed them. The animals quickly learned that the situation was not actually hopeless and so became aggressive and tried to free themselves or escape and showed no signs of giving up. Such conditioned rats swam on the average 40 to 60 hours or more. Once freed from restraint in the hand or confinement in the glass jar, speed of recovery is remarkable. A rat that would certainly have died in another minute or two becomes normally active and aggressive in only a few minutes. [p. 309]

Richter then concluded that neither restraint alone nor whisker trimming often kills a rat. Rather, death results from a combination of responses to various stresses occurring in rapid succession which generates a sense of hopelessness in the animal. Richter expressed this in the following manner:

> This sudden-death phenomenon may however be considered also as a reaction at a much higher level of integration. The situation of these rats is not one that can be resolved by either fight or flight—it is rather one of hopelessness: being restrained in the hand or in the swimming jar with no chance of escape is a situation against which the rat has no defense. Actually, such a reaction of apparent hopelessness is shown by some wild rats very soon after being grasped in the hand and prevented from moving. They seem literally to give up. [pp. 308-309]

In other words, the wild animal whose repertoire of behavior consists of rapid movements such as biting, running, and jumping is suddenly bereft of any adequate and ready response for coping with stressful demands. And yet, if rescued once, the animal, as it were, seemed to learn that if it only persevered all was not hopeless—torture was not infinite. Richter's rats did not learn an instrumental response. When rescued, it was a fortuitous event. The animal could not really have learned what it could do to prevent a recurrence of its good fortune. Some learning theorists such as Guthrie might suggest that removal from the jar would be a reward for the last response made at the time of rescue. Expectancy theorists, on the other hand, might contend that the animal enjoyed a revival of hope, through learning that indeed there was an end and a limit to the aversive stimulation. Consequently, if the rat were able to persist in swimming for rather lengthy periods of time, survival was possible. However, the swimming itself could not terminate their duress so that the animals may simply be said to have learned to endure while waiting for the end of confinement.

This endurance through hope of relief is familiar to medical settings. Patients must often wait as wounds heal, sometimes with little or no certainty that therapeutic healing will actually occur. While waiting for recovery, patients must amuse themselves and keep actively engaged enough so that the desire to regain health is maintained. Deaths have been ascribed to a "lessened will to live" or a giving up in the face of improbably recovery.

This writer witnessed one such case of death due to a loss of will within a psychiatric hospital. A female patient who had remained in a mute state for nearly 10 years was shifted to a different floor of her building along with her floor mates, while her unit was being redecorated. The third floor of this psychiatric unit where the patient in question had been living was known among the patients as the chronic, hopeless floor. In contrast, the first floor was most commonly occupied by patients who held privileges, including the freedom to come and go on the hospital grounds and to the surrounding streets. In short, the first floor was an exit ward from which patients could anticipate discharge fairly rapidly.

All patients who were temporarily moved from the third floor were given medical examinations prior to the move, and the patient in question was judged to be in excellent medical health though still mute and withdrawn. Shortly after moving to the first floor, this chronic psychiatric patient surprised the ward staff by becoming socially responsive such that within a two-week period she ceased being mute and was actually becoming gregarious. As fate would have it, the redecoration of the third-floor unit was soon completed and all previous residents were returned to it. Within a week after she had been returned to the "hopeless" unit, this patient, who like the legendary Snow White had been aroused from a living torpor, collapsed and died. The subsequent autopsy revealed no pathology of note, and it was whimsically suggested at the time that the patient had died of dispair.

Such stories as these could be cast aside as selected and unrepresentative anecdotes if they were not so commonplace. Richter cited a variety of determinants of sudden, unexplained death which have included voodoo, hexes, fright, the sight of blood, and hypodermic injections. Unaccountable deaths have been reported among persons in good health who have attempted to commit suicide although they had barely scratched the surface of their skin or had only ingested a few aspirin tablets.

As Richter (1959) concluded: "Some of these instances seem best described in terms of hopelessness–literally a giving up when all avenues of escape appeared to be closed and the future holds no hope [p. 311]." Likewise, Kobler and Stotland (1964) have reported on the outbreak of a series of suicides within a psychiatric hospital in which staff conflicts had resulted in the patients losing hope that they could ever improve. While this latter example consists of a more instrumental response terminating a hopeless situation, the assumedly more "passive" surrender of chronically ill patients may likewise represent a determined act. The patient concedes to what he sees as his inevitable decline and becomes apathetic, which then results in a lesser responsiveness to his felt needs. The positive contribution of self-participation and involvement in medical healing has been examined with some success by Rue Cromwell (1968) and his colleagues.

I would like now to draw your attention to two other groups of investigations that have implicated the importance of control among other nonhuman primates.

Seligman, Maier, and Solomon (1969) have summarized their findings from a series of studies in which they had investigated the effects of inescapable shock on the subsequent escape behavior of dogs. In most of the experiments conducted by these investigators (Overmier & Seligman, 1967; Seligman, 1968; Seligman & Maier, 1967; Seligman, Maier, & Geer, 1968), inescapable shock was administered by placing the dog in a cloth hammock so that the dog's legs hung below his body through four holes. A shock source was applied to the dog through brass plate electrodes that were taped to the footpads of the dog's hind feet. In this unit, dogs were given a series of shocks, varying in duration and frequency of administration with each experiment. Next, dogs were placed in a two-way shuttle box in which escape or avoidance responding could be observed. In this unit the animal was exposed to a conditioned stimulus (often light dimming) after which an unconditioned stimulus (an electric shock) would be administered through the grid floor. Whenever the animal crossed the shoulder-high barrier in the center of the box, the shock would terminate. In other words, where the first unit administered an aversive stimulus before which the animal could do nothing that would alter the situation, the latter unit offered immediate control in that the animal's movements could eliminate the shock experience altogether if he responded to the conditioned stimulus or warning signal.

In the study by Overmier and Seligman (1967), three groups of dogs that had received inescapable shock of varying frequency and duration were compared with a group receiving no such treatment before entering the shuttle box unit. Comparisons between groups were made in latency of escape responses, the number of failures to escape shock, and the overall percentage of subjects that never escaped shock. The authors summarized their data as follows:

> Not only do statistical differences appear between the performances of *S*s exposed to inescapable shock and those of unshocked *S*s during subsequent instrumental avoidance training 24 hr. later, but large qualitative differences also appear which are dramatic to observe. Whenever *S*, which was not treated with inescapable shock, first received shock in the course of instrumental training, it typically barked, yelped, ran, and jumped until it escaped. An *S* previously exposed to inescapable shock *initially* [italics added] reacted to the first shock during instrumental training in much the same way. In contrast, however, it soon typically stopped vocalizing and moving in an agitated fashion and would remain silent until shock terminated. On succeeding trials, *S* would typically continue in a maladaptive pattern of behavior—not necessarily the same on each trial—and passively "accept" the severe pulsating shock. [p. 30]

After experimenting with other relevant conditions, the authors posited that the source of interference in learning to escape from the shock in the shuttle box derived from a helplessness learned in experiencing the inescapable shock.

Subsequent experiments have replicated the finding that inescapable shock interferes with the learning of instrumental behavior for eliminating shock in the shuttle box unit and have offered some clues as to how learned helplessness may be overcome. For one, Seligman and Maier (1967) reported that prior experience with escapable shock immunizes dogs against the negative effects of later inescapable shock. That is, a group of dogs that received a sequence of escapable shock trials behaved very similarly in the shuttle box unit to the group of animals that had only received escapable shock. In contrast, both of these groups differed greatly from those animals that received only inescapable shock. As Seligman and Maier described it:

> Subjects which have had prior experience with escapable shock in the shuttlebox show more energetic behavior in response to inescapable shock in the harness. This contrasts with the interference effect produced by inescapable shock in *S*s which have had no prior experience with shock or in *S*s which have had prior experience with inescapable shock. Thus, if an animal first learns that its responding produces shock termination and then faces a situation in which reinforcement is independent of its responding, it is more persistent in its attempts to escape shock than is a naive animal. [pp. 7-8]

In other words, the passivity-engendering effect of inescapable shock was eliminated if the animal had previously had some successful experience of controlling shock. In a later quasi-therapy experiment, Seligman et al. (1968) attempted to overcome the interference effect of inescapable shock by encouraging successful behavior in the shuttle box. The barrier between sections of the shuttle box was removed, and the experimenter called out "here boy" to the dog through an open window on the side of the box opposite the side on which the dog sat. If the dog responded to the call and crossed the lowered barrier, the shock would terminate and the dog would therefore have "fortuitously" learned of the escape route. One of the four subjects did respond to this treatment and began to escape shock in the shuttle box. The other three, however, had to be subjected to more strenuous approaches. With leashes attached to the dogs' collars, the animals were pulled across to the "safe side" on each trial of shock. The rationale was, of course, to force the subject to be exposed to the response reinforcement contingency. The dog that responded to the simpler calling procedure began to escape reliably after 20 such trials. Those that had to be pulled across the barrier required 20, 35, and 50 such trials, respectively, before escape became a reliable phenomenon. In short, the resistance to learning the simple contingencies of the shuttle box was marked.

These authors concluded that the inappropriate passive acceptance of aversive stimuli among their canine subjects could be construed in terms of perceived lack of control over reinforcements.

Among all of the investigations cited thus far, the phenomenon of perceived control of aversive stimuli would seem to be a central determinant of the manner in which one responds to those stimuli. Among humans, rats, and dogs, to have some instrumental response at one's disposal and to be able to perceive contingency between one's actions and the termination of an aversive stimulus seems to be a good and necessary thing. It serves us well then to refer to one investigation in which perceived effective control proved harmful for the subject, whereas the passive recipient of aversive stimuli seemed to survive experimental treatment more adequately.

In an investigation concerned with the development of ulcers, Brady, Porter, Conrad, and Mason (1958) found that monkeys pressing levers at a fast rate to avoid shocks developed ulcers. During these experiments Brady devised a procedure whereby monkeys were yoked in an apparatus. One, euphemistically called the "executive" monkey, was trained to press a lever that would terminate a shock delivered to the animal's feet. Another monkey was connected electrically in series with the executive so that any shock received by one would also be received by the other. The executive could exercise control, whereas the latter was a passive recipient. In this way, both animals of a pair were subjected to the same shocks but one had "the button" and the other did not. After a number of days in this procedure, death occurred to each of four executives, whose autopsies revealed extensive gastrointestinal lesions with ulceration. Sacrificed partners did not reveal any indications of such gastrointestinal complications. This latter study would encourage us to be a bit more temperate in judging the value of perceived control. However, in an elaborate replication of the executive monkey study, Weiss (1971) has found evidence indicating that ulcers are both more common and the ulcerous lesions more extensive among animals that have been deprived of control. Although Weiss used a different species (rats), the major reason for the reversal in findings was attributed to the method of selection of executive and yoked subjects. In the study by Brady et al., subjects were not randomly selected for each role. Rather, each pair of monkeys was administered a two- to four-hour avoidance pretest, and the monkey responding at the higher rate was always chosen as the executive. The Weiss investigation was an improvement on the Brady study in several ways. Where the latter employed a subject sample of only four pairs of monkeys, Weiss used 180 male rats. In addition, Weiss varied the manner in which the rats were to be cued in to the onset of shock. From his overall findings, Weiss (1971) was able to conclude as follows:

> The present experiment showed that regardless of whether electric shock was preceded by a warning signal, by a series of warning signals forming, so to speak, an external clock, or by no signal at all, rats that could perform coping responses to postpone, avoid, or escape shock developed less severe gastric ulceration than matched subjects which received the same shocks but could not affect shock by their behavior . . . the present results, in combination with earlier experiments, serve to establish that the beneficial effect of coping behavior in stressful situations is of considerable generality. [p. 8]

CONCLUSION

It is possible to conclude, then that with respect to the response to aversive stimulation, perceived control makes a great difference. Pain- or anxiety-arousing stimuli are not simply to be found in the stimuli impinging on our senses. Our responses are evidently shaped and molded by our perceptions of those stimuli and by our perception of ourselves vis-à-vis those stimuli. These conclusions are far from unique. What is remarkable, however, is the fact that the findings appear similar across species with different devices and different aversive stimuli. Where behaviorists have often attempted to reduce differences between species through invoking universal principles such as reinforcement, it is possible to conclude thus far that there are remarkable similarities among diverse species without reducing complex cognitive-perceptual systems to simple reinforcement assimilators. The perception of control would seem to be a common predictor of the response to aversive events regardless of species. Although this review has focused solely on the response to aversive stimulation, it was not due to a lack of data implicating the perception of freedom and control as major determinants of other sorts of behavior. The point is already clear from this narrow review, however, that the sense of control, the illusion that one can exercise personal choice, has a definite and a positive role in sustaining life. The illusion of freedom is not to be easily dismissed without anticipating undesirable consequences. To submit to however wise a master planner is to surrender an illusion that may be the bedrock on which life flourishes.

REFERENCES

Brady, J. V., Porter, R. W., Conrad, D. G., & Mason, J. W. Avoidance behavior and the development of gastroduodenal ulcers. *Journal of the Experimental Analysis of Behavior,* 1958, 1, 69-72.

Corah, J. L., & Boffa, J. Perceived control, self-observation and response to aversive stimulation. *Journal of Personality and Social Psychology,* 1970, 16, 1-14.

Cromwell, R. Stress, personality and nursing care in myocardial infarction. Unpublished progress report, National Institute of Mental Health, Bethesda, Maryland, 1968. (Mimeo)

Glass, D. C., Reim, B., & Singer, J. E. Behavioral consequences of adaptation to controllable and uncontrollable noise. *Journal of Experimental Social Psychology,* 1971, 7, 244-257.

Glass, D. C., & Singer, J. E. *Stress and adaptation: Experimental studies of behavioral effects of exposure to aversive events.* New York: Academic Press, 1972.

Glass, D. C., Singer, J. E., & Friedman, L. N. Psychic cost of adaptation to an environmental stressor. *Journal of Personality and Social Psychology,* 1969, 12, 200-210.

Haggard, E. S. Experimental studies in affective processes: I. Some aspects of cognitive structure and active participation on certain autonomic reactions during and following experimentally induced stress. *Journal of Experimental Psychology,* 1943, 33, 257-284.

Kobler, A. L., & Stotland, E. *The end of hope.* Toronto: Free Press, 1964.

May, R. *Love and will.* New York: Norton, 1969.

Menninger, K. *The vital balance.* New York: Viking, 1963.

Mowrer, O. H. *Learning theory and personality dynamics.* New York: Ronald, 1950.

Mowrer, O. H., & Viek, P. An experimental analogue of fear from a sense of helplessness. *Journal of Abnormal and Social Psychology,* 1943, 43, 193-200.

Overmier, J. B., & Seligman, M. E. P. Effects of inescapable shock upon subsequent escape and avoidance responding. *Journal of Comparative and Physiological Psychology,* 1967, 63, 28-33.

Pervin, L. A. The need to predict and control under conditions of threat. *Journal of Personality,* 1963, 31, 570-585.

Reim, B., Glass, D. C., & Singer, J. E. Behavioral consequences of exposure to uncontrollable and unpredictable noise. *Journal of Applied Social Psychology,* 1971, 1, 44-56.

Richter, C. P. The phenomenon of unexplained sudden death in animals and man. In H. Feifel (Ed.), *The meaning of death.* New York: McGraw-Hill, 1959.

Seligman, M. E. P. Chronic fear produced by unpredictable shock. *Journal of Comparative and Physiological Psychology,* 1968, 66, 402-411.

Seligman, M. E. P., & Maier, S. F. Failure to escape traumatic shock. *Journal of Experimental Psychology,* 1967, 74, 1-9.

Seligman, M. E. P., Maier, S. F., & Geer, J. The alleviation of learned helplessness in the dog. *Journal of Abnormal and Social Psychology,* 1968, 73, 256-262.

Seligman, M. E. P., Maier, S. F., & Solomon, R. R. Unpredictable and uncontrollable aversive events. In F. R. Brush (Ed.), *Aversive conditioning and learning.* New York: Academic Press, 1969.

Skinner, B. F. *Beyond freedom and dignity.* New York: Knopf, 1971.

Staub, E., Tursky, B., & Schwartz, G. E. Self-control and predictability: Their effects on reactions to aversive stimulation. *Journal of Personality and Social Psychology*, 1971, 18, 157-162.

Weiss, J. M. Effects of coping behavior in different warning signal conditions on stress pathology in rats. *Journal of Comparative and Physiological Psychology*, 1971, 1, 1-14.

part 2

FORMAL ORGANIZATIONS IN THEORY AND PRACTICE

C. Wright Mills in *The Power Elite* quotes a statement by Mr. John L. McCaffrey, the chief executive of International Harvester, "The biggest trouble with industry is that it is full of human beings . . ." (p. 135). Part 1 of this book centered around what is known about how and why individuals behave. Most of the selections agreed that a significant portion of the variance in individual behavior is attributable to environmental factors.

Formal organizations create a multitude of environmental conditions which have important consequences for individual participants. As Mr. McCaffrey's statement implies, the behavior of participants is often detrimental to the realization of organizational goals. His diagnosis is basically psychological, directing attention to changes in individuals that might improve organizational effectiveness. However, a second view must be noted. An alternative, sociological diagnosis directs attention to properties of a social system that evoke various behavior patterns. It states, "The trouble with individuals is that they must function in formal organizations." Perrow (1970) introduces his exposition of the sociological view by noting certain "prejudices" in the field of organizational behavior.

> The most important prejudice . . . is that organizational problems are people problems and that good leadership is the answer. The second, minor prejudice is that current work in psychology, social psychology, and sociology has demolished classical management theory and replaced it with new and true principles. I try to show that many people problems and leadership problems are really due to organizational structure and that, while classical management theory is quite deficient, it does deal with important problems that the other approaches neglect. (pp. viii-ix)

The psychological and sociological diagnoses are complementary rather than mutually exclusive. Individuals, in attempting to satisfy their needs, often follow paths other than those expected by the organization's planners and directors. The readings in part 1 suggest that the choice of paths is "psychologically lawful" and, to some degree, can be predicted and controlled by environmental forces. Part 2 focuses on formal organization as a means for coordination of individual behavior.

An organization's performance is affected by the complex interaction of many forces originating inside and outside its boundaries. Economic, cultural, psychological, sociological, technological, and historical factors form only a partial list of the variables. The only way for both managers and students of organizations to deal adequately with this complexity is to view organizations as social systems.

THE STUDY OF FORMAL ORGANIZATIONS PAST AND PRESENT

Formal organizations hold a position of central importance in the life of almost every American. Our society has long been characterized as stressing formal organizations, and Americans have pioneered in the theory and practice of management. Most members of our society are familiar with many concepts and principles of organization management. Line-staff, organization charts, authority, job descriptions, and span of control are almost everyday phrases to many organizational participants.

The foregoing terms are characteristic of classical management or organization theory, which emphasizes "action-oriented" principles appropriate for structuring and administering an organization. As numerous writers have pointed out, a major shortcoming of classical theory is its tendency to deal with the human factor only through implicit assumptions. Recent work has attempted to compensate for this lacuna in classical thought by stressing social and psychological variables. However, the newer approach may have made an equally serious omission. The so-called "human relations school," in stressing the human factor, makes implicit, simplified assumptions about technological and structural considerations. More recently, integrative approaches have evolved which seek to encompass the dynamic interaction of people, culture, structure, technology, and tasks.

Unfortunately, popular knowledge about organization theory seems to be derived mostly from classical theory and only to a limited extent from the more recent trends. The thinking of beginning students in organizational behavior often reflects these popular notions. Therefore, as Gross (1968) has suggested, the training of administrators often needs to begin with unlearning.

The modern view is well summarized by Leavitt (1972), who suggested that an organization can be understood in terms of the interaction of its people, structure, technology, and tasks with each other and with the environment. The characteristics and variations in the characteristics of each of these five elements have potential consequences for the other four. This model is a useful framework for understanding the nature of the dynamic interaction of the various elements of an organization. Moreover, by focusing attention on the interaction of each of these elements with the environment, Leavitt's model calls our attention to the fact that, as we said in part 1, organizations are open systems. As open systems they constantly restructure themselves in order to survive and grow in the environment in which they exist. Moreover, in order to achieve their goals of survival and growth, organizations often attempt to change their environments.

The role of goals deserves more specific attention than is suggested by a simple summary of Leavitt's model. Perrow (1970) demonstrated how goals can be an important independent variable. For example, envision two companies in the textile business. Company A places heavy emphasis on maximizing profit, whereas Company B places considerable importance on being a leader in introducing new fabrics. This difference in goals is apt to be associated with—and maybe causative of—important differences between the two organizations. If the original goals are subsequently modified, vestiges of the differences can still be observed long afterward.

Formal organizations, having a deliberately planned structure and specifically stated goals, foster relatively homogeneous and predictable behavior on the part of their participants. Researchers have taken advantage of these fortunate circumstances and have published a substantial amount of empirical data about the behavior of people in formal organizations. This research is practically and theoretically important. The study of organizations is both a part of general social and psychological theory and a distinct field in and of itself.

The readings that follow introduce the student to the rapidly growing literature of formal organizations. Emphasis is given to the sociological view; the major focus is on properties of social systems as independent variables. However, as will be seen in the readings themselves, the nature of the topic requires the use of knowledge from a number of disciplines.

Part 2 is divided into two chapters. The first reviews the development of organizational study from the early mechanistic approaches through the contemporary view of organizations as complex, organic systems. The selections in the second chapter describe some of the internal dynamics of formal organizations. These selections stress some of the unanticipated consequences which an organization generates as its members attempt to achieve their own goals and the organization's goals simultaneously.

REFERENCES

Gross, B. M. *Organizations and Their Managing.* New York: Free Press, 1968.

Leavitt, H. J. *Managerial Psychology.* Rev. ed. Chicago: University of Chicago Press, 1972.

Perrow, C. *Organizational Analysis: A Sociological View.* Belmont, Calif.: Wadsworth, 1970.

chapter **8**

Formal Organizations: Introduction and Theory

This chapter introduces some of the major trends in the study of organizations. Some of the conflicts among approaches have their roots in what has been taken as problematic and what has been assumed by various scholars.

In the first selection Tausky explores some of these diverse approaches and describes how the various quests for the "one best way" led to the modern view of organizations as complex "open systems." Here we see how some of the early controversies resulted in an integration of competing approaches rather than the victory of one viewpoint over another.

The next selection, by Magnusen, summarizes the most important work supporting the systemic view of organizations. Taken together, the research trends discussed by Magnusen reveal that, while organizational behaviorists do not have a comprehensive theory of organizations, their domain is not as chaotic as some critics have charged. While we are a long way from having settled all the ideological differences in the field, Magnusen demonstrates that significant progress has been made in the understanding and management of organizations.

Tausky and Magnusen both view organizations as complex social systems. The final three papers in this chapter demonstrate some of the advantages and disadvantages of this perspective.

Gross and Terreberry use systems theory as a framework for understanding the complex set of internal and external processes that influence organizations. Gross discusses the internal dynamics. He suggests that we can best understand and manage organizations if we realize that their operations reflect a variety of purposes. The goals of the organization reflect the interests of some participants but are in conflict with the interests of others. Gross implies that organizations, being more like coalitions than teams, require a multidisciplinary approach. Certainly if classical economics, classical organization theory, or the human-relations view is taken alone as a basis for describing organizations, the picture will be distorted.

Terreberry uses a systemic approach to analyze the relationship between organizations and their environments. Organizational behaviorists have devoted far less study to organizational-environmental relationships than intra-organizational processes. This neglect, taken together with our growing sensitivity to the constraints placed on organizations by their environments, suggests that the interactions of organizations with their environments will become a major subject of study for organizational behaviorists in the next few years. By increasing our awareness that organizations are really subsystems of larger systems, Terreberry's article provides a firm foundation for understanding the need for more study of this relationship.

In the final selection in this chapter Scott suggests some new directions for organizational theory dictated by changes in the environment. It is instructive to compare this article with one Scott published nearly 15 years earlier, in which he described enthusiastically the merits of general systems theory as a framework for organization theory. In the paper reprinted here, however, Scott notes that he has been convinced of the need to reexamine his position on systems theory. He suggests that changes in the economic and social environment in which firms operate may necessitate the development of a new, more radical paradigm for management theory. Thus we are left with the provocative thought that, while the systems approach appears to provide a means of integrating previous knowledge, once we begin to appreciate the full impact of the dynamic environments in which organizations operate we may find it necessary to change some of our basic assumptions about the role of organizations in our social system.

Curt Tausky

THEORIES OF ORGANIZATION

In this chapter we draw from the diverse approaches to organization theory the major themes of several key theories of formal organization. The sequence of discussion will approximately reflect their order of development. As a guide, the theories and some of their contributors are listed in Chart 1.

It is important at the outset to remark, first, that the term "theory" is used here quite loosely. No arrangement of theorems and propositions will be encountered, since the materials we deal with are mainly discursive. Second, to gain an overall perspective on the discussion it is useful to make a distinction between *prescriptive* and *descriptive* "theory."

From *Work Organizations: Major Theoretical Perspectives,* pp. 24-68, by Curt Tausky, Copyright F. E. Peacock Publishers, Inc., 1970, Itasca, Illinois.

Prescriptive theory is concerned with how things should be, whereas descriptive theory centers on how things are. Classical theory is, for the most part, prescriptive; structuralism is descriptive; and human relations has elements of both prescription and description. Both types of theory can be empirically based, and neither is inherently better. They simply represent different approaches to the subject matter for somewhat different purposes. Prescriptive theory is "advice" to the practitioner, such as a manager, whereas descriptive theory explains to the interested observer, such as a social scientist, what the situation looks like. From sound description useful prescriptions can be derived, and familiarity with descriptive analyses can help to uncover untenable prescriptions.

CHART 1

Theories	*Contributors*
Classical	
(a) Physiology and organization of work	Frederick W. Taylor
	Frank B. Gilbreth
	Henry L. Gantt
(b) Organizational structure	Max Weber
	Henri Fayol
	Lyndall F. Urwick
Human Relations	Elton Mayo
	Rensis Likert
	Chris Argyris
Structuralism	Amitai Etzioni
	Robert Dubin
	Wilbert E. Moore

CLASSICAL THEORY

Physiology and Organization of Work

Industrial life was never again to be the same after this branch of classical theory—often referred to as scientific management—gained momentum. The core ideas took shape under the influence of the applied studies and writings of Frederick W. Taylor[1] at the turn of the 20th century, a bustling time of population growth and industrial expansion. Managements were faced with the problem of bringing large numbers of men—many industrially inexperienced—together into a cooperative system. Within this situation scientific management attempted to increase productivity through better utilization of manpower.

Industrial organizations of the early 1900's were chaotic by modern standards. In the workplace men frequently used their own tools which were purchased to suit individual tastes. Machine speeds were often determined by the operator's preference. Learning on the job was haphazard and frequently accomplished by having the opportunity to watch a more skilled workman. To the then powerful position of foreman was delegated the discretion to decide upon

[1] An excellent collection of Taylor's ideas is in Frederick W. Taylor, *Scientific Management* (New York: Harper and Row, 1947).

personnel selection, worker layoff, and rest periods: arbitrary decisions executed in heavy-handed fashion were common practice.

Thus, the way tasks were accomplished and coordinated with related tasks was thought out in large part on the shop floor; thinking and doing were fused. Into this situation Taylor's ideas entered. Before he was through, the separation between doing and thinking was firmly implanted in management thought and, where possible, in practice. Scientific management placed heavy emphasis on manipulation of the division of labor through detailed planning as the means to increase productivity. This requires, as a necessary first step, the separation of the functions of management and labor as distinct activities. Then, after careful studies and detailed administrative planning, management can divide work tasks into small, quickly learned and routinized operations, with quantity, quality, and time standards for each operation. Thus, by the systematic division of whole tasks into their component operations, the total work process from start to completion can be more quickly and economically accomplished and the need for skilled workmen decreased.

The studies Taylor and his followers carried out were designed to facilitate planning. He gave much attention to the physiological aspects of workmen on routine operations, especially their *capacity*. This refers to the factors of work speed and muscle fatigue. By selecting a worker whom Taylor felt was suited to the task the workman was to perform, and instructing him to work at various speeds, the average speed for performing a task was calculated and the most physically useful rest periods determined. Taylor utilized time and motion studies, holding that they were scientific means to set standard times for work tasks and to determine the "one best way" to perform in the most efficient manner possible the motions necessary to a task.

A theory of motivation and "mutuality of interests" interlocks with time and motion analyses to provide the foundation for the application of these "scientific" tools. Taylor urged that a man's pay should be related to his productivity because effort to raise output can be increased by providing a financial incentive. Time study determines how many units a good workman operating at a strenuous but not physically harmful pace can produce in a day. With the aid of this information is calculated the base daily wage—which should be 30 to 60 percent higher than the industry average for that job because the output standard is set at 50 to 300 percent higher than the industry average—and productivity beyond the standard receives additional incentive earnings. The incentives of high-base pay, and allowance for additional incentive earnings, are the means to motivate men to increased effort. Taylor felt that the fundamental desire of the worker was to obtain the highest possible wage; hence, among rational men the upper limit to effort would be determined by their physiological capacity. (As we will see later, these motivational views are strongly challenged by human relations.) Because the worker is motivated by wages, and management by profit, increased productivity is a *mutual interest* of both since greater productivity reduces labor costs, increases profits, and makes possible higher wages.

Management, for its part, must commit itself to scientific determination of the best way to perform tasks, production standards, and pay rates, and under no condition reduce incentive earnings by raising the standard production rate. Given this commitment, conflict between management and labor can only be the result of mistrust and misunderstanding and can be overcome by adherence to scientific management principles. Thus, labor unions are unnecessary since the science of time and motion study replaces conflicting opinions about fair work standards and pay with objective facts.

Taylor's views on ordering the workplace can be summarized as consisting of four prescribed techniques: (1) For each task use a time and motion study to determine the one best way of task performance which permits the largest average amount of production over the day. (2) Provide the worker with a financial incentive to perform in the best way at a good pace. (3) Use from four to eight specialized experts–functional foremen–to instruct and supervise the workers on the different aspects of their work: methods, speeds, tools, task priorities, discipline, quality, machine maintenance. And (4), adhere absolutely to the principle that the standard production rate must not be arbitrarily changed.

Let us flesh out these prescriptions with two examples drawn from Taylor's applied studies in the physiology of work. First we look at the famous pig-iron experiment conducted at the Bethlehem Steel Company.

A pig-iron handler lifted from the ground a 92 pound pig, carried it up an inclined plank and dropped it in a railroad car. When Taylor came upon the scene, pig iron was loaded on the railroad cars at the rate of 12.5 tons per man per day. Although the work looked deceptively simple, Taylor noted that "the science of handling pig iron is so great and amounts to so much that it is impossible for the man who is best suited to this type of work to understand the principles of this science. . . . The task which faced us as managers under the modern scientific plan was clearly before us."[2] After a detailed time, motion and fatigue study, it was calculated that pig iron should be loaded at the rate of 47 tons per man per day, rather than the current 12.5 tons. To demonstrate that it could be done, one man was selected–the renowned Schmidt who weighed 130 pounds. After close instruction on motions, pace and rest, Schmidt indeed loaded over 106,000 pounds of pig iron per day, and steadily continued to do so. His wages were raised from $1.15 to $1.85 per day. Other workers soon asked to participate in the new method and incentive pay scale.

The second illustration deals with the "science of shoveling," again at the Bethlehem Steel Company. Inspection showed that each yard laborer had purchased one shovel. Taylor found that to perform more efficiently, the company would have to provide 10 different kinds of shovels, each appropriate to a given material. It was determined that the optimum weight a shoveler should handle was 21 pounds. Thus, the differently shaped shovels the company purchased each had to load 21 pounds: a small shovel for heavy ores and a very large scoop for light materials. Next, each laborer was instructed on how to shovel and when to rest: "Press the forearm hard against the right leg just below the thigh . . . , instead of using the muscular effort of your arms . . . throw the weight of your

[2] *Ibid.*, "The Principles of Scientific Management," pp. 40 and 42.

body on the shovel. . . ."[3] With these methods, the company was soon ahead by more than 50 percent over the previous labor cost for handling a ton of material. The wage of laborers rose by 60 percent over previous earnings, but less than half as many laborers were needed.

Scientific management promised much, and to a large extent delivered on the promise. Yet the success of its influence also brought problems. Although Taylor believed that his methods were "neutral," that they benefited both management and labor, it appeared to many that they could readily be misused. By claiming scientific objectivity, it was feared that managements with scant concern for the workers' benefit had a lever to raise productivity. The ideas of scientific management had a revolutionary impact on managerial thought and industrial practice but did not usher in harmony between management and labor. Despite Taylor's belief that collective bargaining was beside the point when scientific management principles were employed, labor organizations did not wither but grew larger and stronger. Labor wished to share in the benefits of productivity increases but also desired a voice in influencing the conditions of work and determination of wages since "scientific managers" were, after all was said and done, managers. By formalizing labor representation, management's definition of beneficial and equitable practices could, it was hoped, be nudged by the need to consider labor views of fair play.

In the wake of the newer, more productive methods, mistrust continued to exist and was joined by another serious human problem. The emphasis by scientific management on small, quickly learned and routinized tasks increased output but had negative consequences for many workers performing such tasks. The problem is still very much alive. The evidence suggests that among men employed on repetitive tasks, a large majority–as high as 90 percent according to some studies[4]–dislike their work tasks. To lessen the impact of this feature of the division of labor, *job enlargement* has been introduced in some organizations. Job enlargement recombines short, fragmented tasks into lengthier and larger tasks. Thus, one man performs the tasks previously allocated among several men. This has in certain cases proven possible without decreases in output and with an increase in work satisfaction.[5] Although broad conclusions are as yet not warranted on the basis of the available evidence,[6] job enlargement is not

[3] *Ibid.*, "Testimony," p. 60.

[4] See Charles R. Walker and Robert Guest, *The Man on the Assembly Line* (Cambridge, Mass.: Harvard University Press, 1952), p. 141, and a later study with similar conclusions noted in *Toward the Automatic Factory* (New Haven, Conn.: Yale University Press, 1957), p. 193; also, Ely Chinoy, *Automobile Workers and the American Dream* (Garden City, N.Y.: Doubleday & Co., 1955). For contradictory views, see J. E. Kennedy and H. E. O'Neill, "Job Content and Workers' Opinions," *Journal of Applied Psychology*, Vol. 42 (1958), pp. 372-75; and A. C. MacKinney, P. F. Wernimont, and W. O. Galitz, "Has Specialization Reduced Job Satisfaction," *Personnel*, Vol. 39 (1962), pp. 8-17.

[5] For example, Robert H. Guest, "Job Enlargement–A Revolution in Job Design," *Personnel Administration*, 20 (1957), pp. 9-16; and Charles R. Walker, "The Problem of the Repetitive Job," *Harvard Business Review*, Vol. 28 (1950), pp. 54-58.

[6] For a recent review of relevant studies, see Charles L. Hulin and Milton R. Blood, "Job Enlargement, Individual Differences, and Worker Responses," *Psychological Bulletin*, Vol. 69 (1968), pp. 41-55; Milton R. Blood and Charles L. Hulin, "Alienation, Environmental

likely to be a panacea. It appears that although satisfaction with tasks does increase with a program of job enlargement, the outcome for productivity is so questionable that it is not likely that mass-production industries will undertake *extensive* redesign of methods of product assembly. We repeat an earlier comment: What is good for technological effectiveness is not necessarily that which is best for people. If it should turn out that satisfaction with task and higher income cannot be had simultaneously, what is best for people? There is no compelling reason to assume that the man on the assembly line does not prefer the higher income.[7]

Organizational Structure

This branch of classical theory deals with how to organize. One important facet of this branch received attention from the great German sociologist, Max Weber (1864-1920). His studies in this area were focused on the structure of the administrative component of organization and stimulated extensive sociological research on bureaucracy. Weber's analytical effort was essentially descriptive, and thus differs from the more directly practitioner-oriented prescriptions of classical theory.

Weber worked with *ideal types.* An ideal type is a conceptual construction of a phenomenon in terms of its essential properties. Further, the properties included must be adequate to explain the operation of the phenomenon. Although no given member of the class of that phenomenon for which an ideal type has been constructed may exhibit characteristics identical to those included in the ideal type, all members will tend to resemble it. The properties included in an ideal type may be viewed as central tendencies around which variation occurs in the empirical cases to which the ideal type refers.

On the basis of empirical study, Weber developed an ideal type of the bureaucratic component of modern large-scale organizations whether public or private. The essential components of the type are:[8] (1) The duties of each office are clearly specified, with the result that the division of labor is determinate. (2) An official hierarchy of authority exists. Each office is subject to discipline from a superordinate office, but only in regard to the duties of the office—the private life of the official is free from organizational authority. (3) The officeholder is an employee. The "means of administration" are attached to the office, not the officeholder, and there are no ways whereby to gain personal rights to the office. (4) Membership in the bureaucracy constitutes a career with distinct ladders of career progression. (5) Hiring and promotion are governed by competence, as

---

Characteristics, and Worker Responses," *Journal of Applied Psychology,* Vol. 51 (1967), pp. 284-90; and Paul Blumberg, *Industrial Democracy: The Sociology of Participation* (New York: Schocken Books Inc., 1969), pp. 66-69.

[7] Walker and Guest, op. cit., chap. 6; also, Elizabeth Lyman, "Occupational Differences in the Value Attached to Work," *American Journal of Sociology,* Vol. 61 (1955), pp. 138-44.

[8] This discussion is drawn from H. H. Gerth and C. Wright Mills (eds. and trans.), *From Max Weber* (New York: Oxford University Press, 1958), pp. 196-204; A. M. Henderson and Talcott Parsons (eds. and trans.), *Max Weber: The Theory of Social and Economic Organization* (New York: The Free Press, 1964), pp. 329-41; and Reinhard Bendix, *Max Weber: An Intellectual Portrait* (Garden City, N.Y.: Doubleday & Co., 1960), pp. 418-25.

measured by certificated training or performance in office. (6) Impersonality, as contrasted to personal relationships, regulates activity. The body of specific and general rules regarding dealings with subordinates, peers, rank and file members and clients are binding.

These characteristics may be recognized as a mechanistic model of administrative organization. It is not that Weber felt other characteristics did not occur, but that the mechanistic model was the most penetrating characterization. However, a good deal of valid criticism has been directed to it for disregarding the spontaneous, nonformal aspects of behavior without which things would grind to a halt. Thus, Weber's ideal type is less than adequate to explain the operation of bureaucracy.

This is neatly shown in Peter Blau's study of a federal agency.[9] The agency was one of several district agencies of a bureau with headquarters in Washington, D.C. Sixteen agents and a supervisor comprised the district agency which was responsible for enforcing compliance with specific federal laws. This required the agents to inspect the records of business establishments to obtain information on whether or not a violation had occurred. The agents were guided in their work by a thousand-page manual of regulations and two shelves of volumes on court opinions and administrative rulings. Yet is was often extremely difficult to determine how the regulations applied to a specific case. In ambiguous cases, the agent was to consult with the supervisor, and only the supervisor, since the records of the inspected firms were confidential.

Note that the formal conditions of operation of this agency fit well Weber's characterization of bureaucracy. But clues as to why operations will not proceed as officially specified are already present in our summary. Consider the rule regarding the source of aid to an agent with a difficult case. The rule requires an agent to expose his ignorance. The agent can consult with his superior to some extent before he feels uneasy, but not too much and not too often. The benefits of aid are soon outweighed by the costs of showing uncertainty and indecision.[10] This is exactly what happened. The practice of mutual consultation between recurrent pairs of agents about difficult cases was common. This pattern of help was useful to the agent and avoided the potentially negative judgment about an agent's competence by the supervisor. Since the supervisor was responsible for officially evaluating the performance of each agent, the agents' careers were at stake. Let us now see what happened to a case after the agent completed it.

The federal agency took careful precautions to determine the correctness of the disposition of each case. After a case was completed, the supervisor examined the agent's finding, and then sent it to a "review section" for more detailed scrutiny. The review section consisted of four men who reviewed the cases of inside departments, located in the same building as the reviewers, and

[9] Peter M. Blau, *The Dynamics of Bureaucracy* (Chicago: University of Chicago Press, 1955), Part 2.

[10] For a detailed analysis of behavior as an "exchange" process, with emphasis on the self-interest elements of exchange, see Peter M. Blau, *Exchange and Power in Social Life* (New York: John Wiley & Sons, Inc., 1967); and George C. Homans, *Social Behavior: Its Elementary Forms* (New York: Harcourt, Brace & World, Inc., 1961).

outside departments, which were located upstate. On a rotating basis, agents served six months as reviewers. When review of a case disclosed an error, great or small, the reviewer was to file a rejection slip which was taken into account in the performance rating of the agent who prepared the case. The reviewers took their work seriously, and cases were indeed carefully examined. Thus, the system worked, at least in terms of results. But the process which led to the results was not as formally planned.

Since the reviewers served on a rotating basis, they were agents before reviewing and became agents again after reviewing, frequently rejoining their former colleagues. The reviewers were very aware of the negative impact on an agent colleague when he received rejection on a case. In response to this situation, the practice developed of "walking back" cases. The reviewer, instead of filing a formal notice of rejection, directly took the case to the agent for the necessary corrections. Recall that the cases of both inside and outside departments were reviewed in the same location, but walking back a case to an upstate agent was impossible. The reviewers officially rejected 15 percent of the cases of outside departments, but only 5 percent of the cases of inside departments. Despite the fact that each reviewer was partly evaluated on the number of cases he officially rejected, the preference was to maintain cordial relations with the agents by walking back cases. This practice sacrificed a high rating while serving temporarily as reviewer, while as agent in the long run it would raise the rating by minimizing official rejection of cases by colleagues performing as reviewers.

Thus, the rules and control system intended to regulate the review process, as well as the rule prohibiting an agent from consulting about a case with another agent, were highly unlikely to operate as planned. In both instances we should note that the reward system itself almost guaranteed that the rules would be violated. In order to receive a high rating, agents did not want to appear ignorant in front of their supervisor in the disposition of cases. And, in addition to desiring the maintenance of cordial relations with agents by walking back cases while serving as reviewers, the reviewer could hope for reciprocity from the agents when they rotated to the review section and he became an agent, thereby raising his rating over the long run by receiving fewer rejections of cases.[11]

Within this situation of prescribed rules and actual behavior patterns which we have described, the distinction between the rationally designed organization and the natural system comes alive. The two systems interact, but the rational design, especially the reward system, shapes and constrains the spontaneous patterns of behavior which emerge in the ongoing situation.

Indeed, an understanding of the achievements for which an organization rewards participants is highly useful in predicting what the members of that organization will emphasize in their behavior. As we saw in the law enforcement agency, the agents violated the no consultation rule, but meticulously disposed of cases since performance was judged on accurate disposition rather than the

[11] Excellent descriptions of rule evasion are found in Melville Dalton's, *Men Who Manage* (New York: John Wiley & Sons, Inc., 1959); and Joseph S. Berliner, *Factory and Manager in the USSR* (Cambridge, Mass.: Harvard University Press, 1957).

means used to achieve accuracy. One more example should drive home the general point. We draw here again on the work of Blau, this time in a state employment agency.[12] The goal of the employment agency was, of course, the placement of applicants in suitable jobs. To determine the effectiveness of employment interviewers, the agency initially kept records only of the number of interviews by each interviewer. It gradually became apparent that this form of evaluation had led interviewers to the practice of trying to interview as many job seekers as possible, but putting less emphasis on actual job placement. To overcome this unexpected negative consequence of the evaluation procedure, several other measures of performance were initiated. Among these was a record of job placements. This did have the effect of increasing job placements, but at the cost to the clients of placement in jobs which frequently were not matched to their prior experience and training.

It seems, then, that the manner in which the members of an organization budget their time is constrained by the operation of the reward system, sometimes to the detriment of the goals which the organization is designed to accomplish. One of the problems of a new man on a job is, in fact, to discern the relative reward weights of the elements of his task. The actual weights may differ from official weights, but interaction with more experienced co-workers ordinarily clarifies the rank order of importance among task elements. Clearly, socialization into the "private culture" of the workplace is as important to a man on a new job as it is for a youth to learn the patterns of culture extant in his society. As with other interpersonal aspects of work in Weber's model, the nonformal relationships through which criteria of evaluation are clarified drop out of sight.

Weber's ideal type is an analytical description of the essential elements of bureaucracy as he perceived them. We turn now to prescriptions which, unlike Weber's ideal type, were intentionally formulated as guides for ordering an administrative organization.

The principles of classical theory elaborate the view that for effective operation (*a*) coordination and (*b*) specialization must be carefully designed into the structure of an organization.[13] We are referring to coordination broadly as control activities which integrate the flow of segmented events into a unified whole. Specialization refers broadly to the allocation of activities among positions and groupings of positions. It is evident why with specialization, even of a rudimentary sort, coordination is necessarily a fundamental problem.

Generated by concern with coordination and specialization, principles in-

[12] Blau, *The Dynamics of Bureaucracy, op. cit.,* Part I; also the follow-up study by Harry Cohen, *The Demonics of Bureaucracy* (Ames, Ia.: University of Iowa Press, 1965). A good description of an attempt to shift evaluations from goals to means, following public disclosure of the use of illegitimate means, is Clarence W. Walton and Frederick W. Cleveland, Jr.'s *Corporations on Trial: The Electric Cases* (Belmont, Calif.: Wadsworth Publishing Co., Inc., 1964).

[13] See Henri Fayol, *General and Industrial Management,* trans. by Constance Stours (London: Pitman & Sons, Ltd., 1949); Lyndall F. Urwick, *The Elements of Administration* (New York: Harper Bros., 1943); James D. Mooney and Alan C. Reiley, *The Principles of Organization* (New York: Harper Bros., 1939).

tended to aid in the adequate handling of these matters were advanced.[14] Among the principles that were addressed to coordination is (*A*) the scalar principle. Essential here is the idea of clear-cut areas of responsibility and hierarchy of authority: directives should flow downward from the highest position in the chain of command to the lowest in a determinate, unbroken manner. The scalar principle is recognizable in the boxes and connecting lines of authority drawn on organization charts. (*B*) The unity of command principle: this specifies that in order to avoid conflicting orders and evasion of duties, no member of an organization should receive orders from more than one superior. (*C*) The span of control principle: since the time and energy of any manager is limited, no superior should have more subordinates than can be effectively overseen. (*D*) The exception principle: to save the time resources of higher executives, they must deal only with exceptional matters. Recurrent decisions should be routinized and delegated to subordinates.

Three important principles dealt with specialization. (*A*) The departmentalization or aggregation principle maintains that duties should be distributed in a manner that combines homogeneous or related activities within organization units and heterogeneous activities should be separated among units and organization levels. The basic idea centers on the advantages of specialization for increasing proficiency at a particular task by reducing the diversity of activities to which any one person or organization unit must give attention. Also, departmentalization simplifies the problem of coordination since each department is essentially a small organization whose chief executive is by delegation responsible for "his" unit's operations, but he is in turn subordinate to another office which supervises several aggregated department heads. The bases suggested for the departmentalization of organization units are: (*a*) major purpose, e.g., a vocational high school within a secondary school system; (*b*) process, as in the body paint unit of an automobile assembly plant; (*c*) clientele, such as the seriously sick patients in an intensive care unit of a hospital; and (*d*) place, which basically aggregates tasks by the geographical areas to be served.

(*B*) The second principle of specialization deals with the line-staff distribution of functions. Line activities are those directly concerned with "doing" what the organization is set up to accomplish. The line offices are arranged according to the scalar principle: staff units provide advice and services to the line departments, for example, research, machine maintenance, or personnel services in an industrial firm. As formally specified, staff units do not have authority in line matters, which means that they do not fit vertically into the pyramidal structure of line command but are restricted, as we noted, to advice and services. (*C*) The profit center concept: Particularly among firms with diversified products or geographically dispersed markets, this concept gained attention in large part be-

[14] For discussion of classical principles, see Joseph L. Massie, "Management Theory," in James G. March (ed.), *Handbook of Organizations* (Chicago: Rand McNally & Co., 1965), pp. 387-422; also, William G. Scott, *Organization Theory* (Homewood, Ill.; Richard D. Irwin, Inc., 1967), pp. 102-19; James G. March and Herbert A. Simon, *Organizations* (New York: John Wiley & Sons, Inc., 1958), pp. 22-23; and Herbert A. Simon, *Administrative Behavior* (New York: The Free Press, 1965), pp. 20-44.

cause of its successful implementation in the 1920's in the General Motors Corporation, Du Pont, Sears, Roebuck, and Standard Oil Company. Essentially, the concept is built around a motivational assumption and elaborates organization by major purpose. Structurally, self-contained product divisions are aggregated, each with its own production facilities and line and staff personnel; each division competes with the others and is financially accountable for profits and losses. This form of organization discloses the profitability of each product division, and the competition between divisions for profitability is assumed to motivate the management of each division to greater effectiveness, thereby increasing profitability for the overall organization. Further, these administrative arrangements provide a testing ground and command experience at a relatively early career stage for the senior managers in the semiautonomous divisions. The profit center, or semiautonomous division, as a form of organization which allowed administration of diversified products was in fact a significant breakthrough in organization design.[15]

The "principles" of organization presented above were, and continue to be, important guides. However, critics aptly note that these prescriptions are at best crude rules of thumb, and at worst, confusing and contradictory.

Part of the confusion regarding these principles stems from the diversity of workable patterns of interaction in different types of organizations. Consider the scalar principle. Should it be rigidly applied? It may be recalled that some organizations rather closely conform to the pattern of mechanistic organization, while others more nearly approximate the organic form of organization. Woodward's work lays bare the hazards of generalizing a "rule" of organization to all organizations. From a descriptive viewpoint, we have noted that a lattice of lateral nonformal communication is necessary to tie together the specialized units of organization and rapidly coordinate ongoing activities. These channels of communication supplement but do not supplant the official scalar means of coordination. A highly rigid emphasis on the scalar principle is unlikely to be useful for very long in any organization, and particularly not in those with many nonrepetitive tasks or those which require a potential for instantaneous response to disruptions in operations.

The scalar and unity of command principles are intended to decrease problems of coordination and control: every task in its place, and a place for every necessary task, including supervision. But everything cannot be foreseen. Positions expand or contract as the necessary tasks change, and the men in organizational positions bring to their jobs greater or less ability, and develop their skills over time. Thus, neither a position nor the man in it is necessarily a constant. Many managers administer a subtly changing organization of elastic tasks and changeful men, a feature which influences the delegation or drift of responsibility to subordinates. As they change, so may the responsibilities the boss feels they can handle.[16] Furthermore, particularly the organizations which face a

[15] See Alfred D. Chandler, Jr., *Strategy and Structure* (Garden City, N.Y.: Doubleday & Co., 1966).

[16] For an insightful approach to responsibility, see Elliott Jaques, *The Measurement of Responsibility* (Cambridge, Mass.: Harvard University Press, 1956).

changing environment require a coordinated administrative response that a mechanistic pattern of organization does not yield.

Moreover, the scalar and unity of command principles do not come to grips with how to combine these principles with the advantages of specialization without blurring the clear-cut delineation of lines of authority. The advantage of specialization to organization is that it concentrates specialized decisions at those locations in the organization with the relevant information and skill to expertly make decisions. But here is the rub. The specialized expert may not be in a command office over the position which uses his services. This means either that the expert's opinion is only advisory and can be ignored, or that the expert's opinion is not advice but more in the nature of a directive which must be followed although no official lines of authority link the specialized expert and the recipient of the directive. Notice that to officially link the expert and recipient would require that staff "advisory" positions have authority over line matters thus diluting the line-staff distinction, and that line positions would be open to directives from several superordinates including a line boss and several staff officers whose expertise has a bearing on line responsibilities, thus muddying the scalar and unity of command principles. The root of the problem is that the principles, as they stand, simply do not furnish guidelines which inform the administrator how to choose between the principles. To maximize the scalar and unity of command organization pattern diminishes the value of expert services. But to transform expert advice into a directive introduces a confusion which classical theory, with its emphasis on unity of command and the line-staff distinction, carefully tried to avoid, i.e., subjecting a subordinate to the potentially conflicting directives of several superiors. A conflict of this sort can of course be resolved by both subordinates carrying their case to a common superior. However, his decision then settles a "specialized" question by an administrative fiat, thereby still not wringing maximum use from an expert opinion.

Let us glance at a few illustrations of these problems. Conceive of two departments in a factory, production and maintenance, each responsible for its major functions and each with a separate budget. The production department is rewarded for productivity, whereas maintenance is rewarded for, among other factors, minimizing downtime on machinery and keeping its repair operations within the budgetary allotment. The interest in productivity may interfere with proper periodic maintenance, whereas maintenance activities may interfere with meeting tight production schedules. Should maintenance be subordinate to the production department, or the other way around, or should they be on an equal footing? The "resolution" of this dilemma can take almost any conceivable form.

These problems do not respect national boundaries. A highly interesting case is found in Russian industry.[17] In the typical state-owned factory, the plant manager and chief maintenance engineer both have line authority: the plant

[17] Berliner, *op. cit.* For some American examples, see Dalton, *op. cit.;* Frank J. Jasinski, "Use and Misuse of Efficiency Controls," *Harvard Business Review,* Vol. 34 (1956), pp. 105-12; and Chris Argyris, *The Impact of Budgets on People* (New York: Controllership Institute, 1952).

manager is responsible for meeting production quotas and standards, while the maintenance engineer is responsible for the upkeep of machinery and has the authority to issue directives to line officers regarding machine maintenance. This appears to be a reasonable arrangement. The evasion of strict compliance with maintenance schedules by all parties nevertheless is very common because all personnel—including the maintenance engineer—receive a bonus if the production quotas set for the factory by government officials are fulfilled, with an additional bonus for exceeding the quota. Usually the quota is "stormed" toward the end of an accounting period: the machinery is mercilessly operated to meet and exceed quotas, with maintenance postponed until after the accounting. The transition to rewarding management officials on the basis of factory profits earned by manufacturing goods of sufficient quality and style to be marketable may well not resolve this sticky organizational problem.

The principles so far discussed are, it turns out, rather ambiguous guidelines. Much the same can be said of the departmentalization principles. The distinction between purpose and process is not at all clear. For example, is a pool of typists a purpose or process arrangement? Does the intensive care unit of a hospital represent organization by purpose or process? Organization by clientele or place is easier to visualize as a basis of departmentalization, but requires that the organizational segments specialized by clientele or place must each include the necessary purpose and process departments, thereby duplicating many functions although some services may be supplied by specialized units serving all clientele or place segments.

Many such combinations of patterns are possible. A choice between the combinations inevitably requires anticipating the advantages and disadvantages of each pattern which is considered and reaching a satisfactory, never perfect, compromise solution between the gains and losses in organizational effectiveness which are likely to occur.

The span of control principle is similarly difficult to pin down. There is scant evidence on which to argue that, say, five subordinates rather than eight should be supervised. It is clear that a small span of control increases the number of hierarchical levels, and a larger span decreases levels. But the question remains as to which is preferable, a tall or flat organization? A flat organization, with a necessarily large span of control, virtually compels supervisors to delegate authority since they have more subordinates than can be closely supervised, whereas a tall organization allows for close supervision, but requires more personnel and potentially incorporates communication lags since communications must descend and ascend through longer vertical channels.

Finally, a direct look at the unity of command principle. It has become clear that unity of command has not existed in any organization and probably cannot. For example, consider the relationships between an accounting department and other organizational departments. In practically all such relationships the accounting department is in effect exercising the authority to specify the types of budget forms and records that are to be used throughout the organization. We will say that an authority relationship exists when a subordinate willingly conforms his behavior to a decision reached by another, regardless of his own judgment as to the correctness of that decision.[18] In our example, other departments act as if they were subordinate to the accounting department, and expect to so act. This means that authority is in actuality not likely to be found in a unified form exercised by one superior over a subordinate. Rather, spheres of authority embedded in different organizational offices exercise the "right" to regulate functions related to the major purpose of the regulating office. This situation is strikingly similar to the functional foremen splitting of authority suggested by Frederick Taylor.

Classical theory falls short of specifying with precision how to organize. It does not resolve fundamental problems of organizational structure because, as we saw, to implement one principle may undercut another. Classical theory nevertheless does deal with basic questions of structure. Although the answers are not adequate, they help to point out the important structural variables which must be considered in the design of organization. The classical attempt to provide answers has contributed to clarification of those problems to which an ongoing organization must devise workable solutions.

Classical theory offered prescriptions bearing on the design of effective organization. In the following section the emphasis shifts to efficiency. This was not a major focus of attention in classical theory, but is a central concern of human relations theorists.

HUMAN RELATIONS

Human relations as a distinct school of thought has its roots in research initiated in the late 1920's by Elton Mayo in the Western Electric Company's Hawthorne plant in Chicago. This was followed by another major contribution to human relations thought which emerged during the war years of the 1940's from the research of Kurt Lewin and his associates. We will describe several of these studies later.

Classical theory was concerned with how to arrange the relationships among an aggregation of men and positions. Human relations also focuses on the ordering of relationships, but the approach differs in that it emphasizes men in contrast to positions. This is another way of saying that human relations is deeply concerned with attitudes, values, and emotional responses, or more generally, the social psychology of men and groups.

Before turning to the founding research of human relations, several of the assumptions which underlie human relations merit attention. First, the stress on attitudes. This emphasis shifts the explanatory factors of behavior away from positional constraints to subjective states. If you want to know why, say, a manager behaves as he does, it is necessary to understand his attitudinal and emotional makeup. Behavior, thus is seen to arise, in part, from within the person

[18] Simon, *Administrative Behavior, op. cit.,* p. 22. The application of this definition of authority to relations between organizational units not formally in a superior-subordinate relationship is clearly illustrated in Charles A. Myers and John G. Turnbull, "Line and Staff in Industrial Relations," *Harvard Business Review,* Vol. 34 (1956), pp. 113-24. See also Robert T. Golembiewski, "Toward the New Organization Theories: Some Notes on Staff," *Midwest Journal of Political Science,* Vol. 5 (1961), pp. 237-46.

rather than determined from without. This is a very great shift, indeed, away from the scientific management and classical assumptions which regarded effective control as operating chiefly by means of administering positive and negative financial and career-relevant rewards.

Human relations, thus, sees man as only superficially controllable by administration of the carrot and stick; truly effective control, rather, is viewed as emanating from inside the individual. This view of control is joined with assumptions about types of control arrangements. Since external control will not motivate men to apply their intelligence and enthusiasm in behalf of organizational goals, it is advisable to control men by social-psychological methods. Hence, the emphasis is on nonauthoritarian leadership style, group participation in decision making, and jobs which capture the participant's interest. The compatibility of this view of control with democratic values has quite likely much enhanced its appeal. Also, changes in the composition of the work force since the time of Frederick Taylor have made the crude manipulation of rewards and costs less feasible. The unskilled, low-educated immigrant, available in ample numbers in Taylor's day, readily tolerated coarse supervision. However, as the education and standard of living of the work force rose, the differences between superior and subordinate declined. Organizational "hands" became personnel with an admitted right to dignified treatment. Harshly repressive means of control have declined throughout American society, in schools, military life, prisons, and parent-child relations, for example. The ideas of human relations are at ease within this social trend.

Embedded in human relations theory is the additional assumption that there is one best way to organize relationships—this follows from the assumptions we have discussed. There is not agreement as to what precisely constitutes the best way, but we can broadly say that it is that form of organization which permits individual autonomy, thereby maximizing task involvement and motivation from within. Further, the individual's needs and organizational goals do not inherently conflict. When they do, something is wrong—but this can be rectified. Again, full agreement as to the precise means to accomplish this does not occur. But that it is possible is important to the human relations perspective.

The "one best way" and "no inherent conflict" assumptions are similar to the views of Taylor. Another interesting but less obvious similarity is the promise of increased productivity. Like Taylor, human relations theorists have argued that if particular human relations practices were followed, productivity would rise. . . . For now, we anticipate slightly by saying that this view in an overall sense has not proven accurate.

The Hawthorne Studies

When research began in 1927, it centered on questions following from the scientific management view of man: the physical conditions of work and physiological capacity of the worker, coupled with monetary incentives, were held to be the primary influences on productivity. These views were soon modified and finally rejected by the time the last study ended in 1932.[19]

The first study dealt with illumination and productivity in three departments. Lighting was increased and decreased in these departments, but no consistent relationship to productivity was found. One of the departments was then selected for further experimentation. This department was divided into a test group and control group, each in a separate building. The illumination in the control group was kept nearly constant but was varied in the test group. Productivity increased in the test group as illumination increased but, surprisingly, productivity rose equally in the control group. Another control and test group were then set up. Lighting in the control group was again kept constant. This time, lighting in the test group was decreased from an initially high level of illumination. Again productivity in both the control and test groups increased. Clearly, some unexpected factors were interfering with the expected illumination-productivity relationship. This stimulated the researchers to devise a further study to uncover the human factors which began to look very important. One study then led to another in the attempt to pin down the individual and group influences on work behavior. We will look at three of these studies.

The Relay Assembly Test Room. Two women who were friendly with one another were asked to select four others for this study. This they did, and the six women were placed in a separate room off the main shop floor. An observer was placed in the room to keep records and "maintain a friendly atmosphere." Better lighting was installed and fans were placed in the room.

Each day's output was recorded for each of the women, as were the temperature and humidity of the test room. Additionally, the women were given physical examinations at six-week intervals. Some of the women participants were hesitant about the medical examinations, so they went as a group. Ice cream and cake were served to them on these occasions.

After a period of several months a new wage incentive plan was applied in the test room: pay was to be determined by the group output of the Relay Test Room. Following this, rest periods were lengthened and shorter work hours introduced. Additionally, the test room observer assumed the functions of a supervisor and, it should be added, numerous company officials and academic scholars came frequently to the room to observe the experiment. These events took place over a span of two years, during which the productivity of the test

[19] Materials dealing with the Hawthorne data are reported in F. J. Roethlisberger and William J. Dickson, *Management and the Worker* (Cambridge, Mass.: Harvard University Press, 1939); T. North Whitehead, *The Industrial Worker* (Cambridge, Mass.: Harvard University Press, 1938): Elton Mayo, *The Human Problems of an Industrial Civilization* (New York: The Macmillan Co., 1933). For commentary on the Hawthorne research, see, for example, Henry A. Landsberger, *Hawthorne Revisited* (Ithaca, N.Y.: Cornell University Press, 1958), especially pp. 28-29 for a listing of critical articles: Reinhard Bendix and Lloyd Fisher, "The Perspectives of Elton Mayo," in Amitai Etzioni (ed.), *Complex Organizations: A Sociological Reader* (New York: Holt, Rinehart & Winston, Inc., 1962), pp. 113-26; and George C. Homans "Some Corrections to the 'Perspectives of Elton Mayo,' " in Amitai Etzioni (ed.), *Complex Organizations: A Sociological Reader* (New York: Holt, Rinehart & Winston, Inc., 1962), pp. 127-29; also, George C. Homans, *The Human Group* (New York: Harcourt, Brace & World, Inc., 1950), chaps. 3-6.

room rose over that of the base period before the first experimental change in wage payment began.

The Second Relay Assembly Test Group. An experiment with five women, selected as in the first test room, was set up to isolate the impact of the group wage incentive scheme. Other conditions of work were similar to those on the larger shop floor. When the group wage plan was applied to the five operators productivity went up. But when the small group wage plan was later eliminated, and the women were paid on the basis of the productivity of their entire department in the main shop, productivity sharply decreased.

What do these interesting findings mean? It depends, it seems, on who answers this question. The Hawthorne researchers saw in these data a refutation of the scientific management assumptions about motivation. Conditions of work, fatigue, and pay were secondary factors in comparison to the human elements of work. This view stems from an emphasis on the friendly relations that developed among the women in the various experimental groups. They enjoyed each other's company which in turn made of work a pleasant experience. Also, the easy, nonauthoritarian supervision which developed in the First Relay Assembly Test Room was considered a critical factor. In short, considerate treatment by superiors, and the formation of a friendly work group, were seen as the elements underlying increased productivity. The results of the Second Relay Assembly Test Room were judged to be equivocal rather than contradictory to the ideas being developed.

One could, of course, conclude from the research that the physical conditions of work and the pay envelope were chiefly responsible for increases in output. Also, the now famous "Hawthorne effect" might be viewed as a major factor. This term refers to the unintended effect produced by means of the special attention given to the research subjects by the researchers and unintentionally involved persons or conditions. (Recall the special treatment the women in the First Relay Assembly Test Room received, for example, medical examinations and attention by the many visitors to the test room.) This was not, however, the interpretation made by the original researchers.

The Bank Wiring Room. We turn now to the final study conducted in the Hawthorne plant. This, incidentally, was the only experimental research in which the subjects were men. Fourteen men volunteered for assignment to the Bank Wiring Room in which would be assembled electrical switches. Although the entire group was to be paid on a group piecework basis, the actual work units involved three distinct groups of three "wiremen" and one "solderman" who soldered the connections made by "his" three wiremen. Two additional men inspected the switches assembled by each of the three work groups. An observer was stationed in the back of the room.

It soon became clear that the wage incentive plan was not working as planned by management.[20] The physical ability of the workers to produce substantially

[20] This point is among the most firmly established findings of industrial human relations. Study after study has reached similar conclusions. For example, see William F. Whyte,

more than they did was apparent, yet despite potentially higher earnings output was on a "straight line" of about 6,000 connections a day or two switches per man. Thus emerged the now universally recognized phenomenon of output restriction as a group norm. The man who deviated too far below or above the "fair day's work" was in no uncertain terms made aware of the opinions of his fellow workers about rate-busting or loafing.

But why? The Bank Wiring Room operatives said that "something" would happen if output went much above the current level. The workers perhaps feared that the piece rate would be cut if higher output was consistently maintained. This, of course, is an economic argument to explain output restriction. It was not the interpretation of the Hawthorne researchers. They felt that the excellent record of the company for fair dealings with employees could not account for the expressed mistrust of the men toward the company's intentions. The interpretation, rather, was that the stated fears which justified output restriction were a rationalization for maintaining the existing relationships based on the existing productivity of each man and thereby maintain the present social ranking among the men in the group. Therefore, economic interest was rejected as the explanation of output restriction of the Bank Wiring Room. The "economic man" of scientific management, who rationally pursued the largest possible pay envelope, had been replaced by the "social man" whose on-the-job behavior could not be controlled by the size of the pay envelope.

Let us summarize now the major conclusions which emerged from the Hawthorne studies. (1) An organization must be viewed as a social system, an entity with interdependent parts. A change in one part inevitably ripples out and influences other parts which in turn affect yet more removed parts. (2) An organization performs two functions: (*a*) creating a service or product and (*b*) distributing satisfactions among its members. Therefore, two classes of problems must be continuously dealt with: (*a*) surviving as an economic unit by performing adequately in the production and marketing process—or what we have earlier referred to as effectiveness—and (*b*) maintaining the allocation of satisfactions at a level which induces cooperation and sustains morale—which we previously referred to as efficiency. (3) In the organization, as in any social system, the process of social evaluation is a constant feature. Distinctions of superior and inferior emerge on the basis of organization members' values. (4) Every person in the organization, whether in a high or low position, regards those real or imagined occurrences which tend to reduce his status as unjust. Every conceivable object or event thus provides a basis for invidious comparisons. Material surroundings, physical events, wages or hours of work cannot be considered in isolation from their "value" in relating a person to the status hierarchy of the workplace. (5) No person's behavior in the organization, from top to bottom, should be viewed as motivated strictly by economic or rational considerations. Values, beliefs and emotions are inextricably involved in each member's behavior.

Money and Motivation (New York: Harper Bros., 1955); Orvis Collins, Melville Dalton, and Donald Roy, "Restriction of Output and Social Cleavage in Industry," *Applied Anthropology,* Vol. 5 (1946), pp. 1-14; and Donald Roy, "Quota Restriction and Goldbricking in a Machine Shop," *American Journal of Sociology,* Vol. 57 (1952), pp. 427-42.

(6) An organization is in part formally organized—this includes the policies, rules, and regulations which define what the relations between persons are supposed to be—and informally organized. People in associating with one another spontaneously develop personal relationships. Informal groups form which are the carriers of values, beliefs, and norms. Thus, because membership in such groups is valued, they exert powerful influences on behavior.

Three Founding Studies in Human Relations

Three important studies are briefly described in the following paragraphs. These studies strongly influenced the human relations view regarding the "best way" to gain members' cooperation and to achieve organizational goals. Their conclusions are similar to, and reinforce, the emphasis on the "social man" which emerged from the Hawthorne research.

We will look first at a study which dealt with leadership style and reactions to the manner in which leadership was exercised. The human relations concern with the "quality" of superior-subordinate relations is found in the Hawthorne studies and has continued to be a hotly debated issue between advocates of human relations and their critics. In the 1939 study by Lippit, White and Lewin,[21] four school clubs of 11-year-old boys were closely observed under conditions of varying leadership patterns. The leadership patterns were (*a*) authoritarian: the adult leader of the club determined all policies and procedures for the meetings of the club; (*b*) democratic: policies and activities were a matter for group discussion and decision, with the active guidance of the adult leader; and (*c*) laissez-faire: the adult "leader" adopted a passive attitude, with complete freedom of choice of policy and activity determined by the club members. Each of the four groups of boys operated at different times during the study under two leadership conditions.

The results showed that virtually all the boys were more satisfied with the democratic leadership, but were almost equally divided as to whether they preferred authoritarian or laissez-faire leadership. The laissez-faire groups spent much of their time trying to decide what to do, and little in the way of actual activity was accomplished. The democratic and authoritarian-led groups were able to complete more activities, but with a difference. The leader in the authoritarian-led groups had to be physically present in the room in order for the club members to begin or complete an activity. The democratic groups, however, were much less dependent on the presence of the leader. The activities, having been previously decided upon in open discussion, were carried out whether the adult leader was present or absent. Thus, more was accomplished in the democratic and authoritarian-led groups than in the talkative but inactive laissez-faire

[21] Ronald Lippit and Ralph K. White, "An Experimental Study of Leadership and Group Life," in Eleanor E. Maccoby, Theodore M. Newcomb, and Eugene L. Hartley (eds.), *Readings in Social Psychology* (3rd ed.; New York: Henry Holt, 1958), pp. 496-511; and the more complete report by Kurt Lewin, Ronald Lippit, and Ralph K. White, "Patterns of Aggressive Behavior in Experimentally Created 'Social Climates,' " *Journal of Social Psychology,* Vol. 10 (1939), pp. 271-99.

groups. However, to maintain activity under conditions of authoritarian leadership required the watchful presence of a formal leader.

This study among boys, then, suggested that commitment to a task is far more likely if the participants have a voice in determining the task. In short, motivational advantages accrue to democratic leadership. This line of thought received support from the following study conducted among women by Lewin and his associates in the early 1940's.[22]

Six Red Cross groups of volunteer home nurses were exposed to two methods for changing attitudes. Three groups of these volunteer nurses were presented with lectures, and three engaged in group discussions. The objective, in line with war needs, was to alter food-buying habits so that the women would buy and serve to their families beef hearts, sweetbreads, and kidneys.

The underlying theory was that existing attitudes must be "unfrozen," changed to the new attitude, and then the new attitude must be "frozen." The results from the Red Cross volunteers indicated that lectures could unfreeze an attitude and change it, but not permanently. That is, the new attitude is not "frozen" and backsliding occurs. With group discussion, however, the situation is different. The act of participating, and voicing an opinion in behalf of the new activity, tends to freeze the new attitude and thus result in a commitment to the new activity. Through the mechanism of active participation in group deliberations, the "converted" individual is less likely to backslide because he will act as a group member and less on the basis of personal preferences. As it turned out, only 3 percent of the women who received lectures on the nutritional and cost advantages of the kidneys and other exotic meats actually served them, whereas over 30 percent of the women who participated in the group discussions and a show of hands decision to serve these foods did serve at least one of these meats at a family meal.

The final study we will describe was conducted by Coch and French in a pajama factory among women workers.[23] The management of this factory had experienced difficulty with labor turnover shortly after each time a new method of production was introduced. Also after changes, the production rate was very slow to recover to the pre-change level, indicating a strong resistance to change among the workers. The researchers attempted to demonstrate a method whereby to reduce the turnover which accompanied changes, and to speed up the recovery rate of production.

Each of four groups of workers was observed in order to determine the effects of varying methods of introducing change. (*a*) One group, the *no-participation* group, was simply told by a management official in a group meeting that an alteration in production methods would take place and a new piece rate would

22 Kurt Lewin, "Group Decision and Social Change," in Eleanor E. Maccoby, Theodore M. Newcomb, and Eugene L. Hartley, *Readings in Social Psychology* (3rd ed.; New York: Henry Holt, 1958), pp. 197-211.

23 Lester Coch and John R. P. French, Jr., "Overcoming Resistance to Change," *Human Relations*, Vol. 1 (1947), pp. 512-32; also see the replication study, John R. P. French, Jr., Joachim Israel, and Dagfin As, "An Experiment in Participation in a Norwegian Factory," *Human Relations*, Vol. 13 (1960), pp. 3-19. This latter study did not confirm the original findings.

be instituted. (*b*) The *participation through representation* group met as a group, and a management representative explained the need to change methods. Questions were asked and answered to everyone's satisfaction. The group then chose representatives who were to be trained in the new methods. The new piece rate was to be determined by a time study of the group representatives. After these events had taken place, a second meeting was called and the new piece rate was explained. The representatives of the group then trained the other group members in the new method. (*c*) The two *total participation* groups each met separately as a group. The need for change was explained and discussed in detail. This time, however, *all* the members of each group worked under the new methods and made suggestions. Each person was then studied by the time study man to determine the new piece rate.

The results showed that the production rate of the no-participation group improved only slightly over time as experience with the new methods was gained. Their quit rate was 17 percent in the first 40 days after the change. The participation through representation group quickly recovered the old production rate after the change, and in less than a month exceeded the previous rate. This group had no quits for the first 40 days. The two total participation groups quickly recovered their previous production rate, exhibited no labor turnover, and went on to produce at a higher rate than either of the other two experimental groups. Satisfaction with the work situation was markedly higher among the total participation and participation through representation groups than among the no-participation group.

The "founding" research of the late 1930's and 1940's presented here should help to provide a feel for the human relations viewpoint. We might repeat the earlier comment that at least part of the attraction of the human relations program for "the best way" of organizing human relationships lies in its compatibility with democratic values. But a curious point emerges here. A large-scale study of managers in 14 countries, including the United States, found that the majority of managers in each country believe that participative-democratic methods of leadership are desirable and effective.[24] Yet these same managers, representing a variety of countries, simultaneously hold a low opinion of the abilities of the average organization member. These managers are essentially saying, "it would be nice, but. . . ." At the risk of repetition, we should note that the organic form of organization indeed does occur when it has to, but runs into resistance stemming, in part, from the views of each level in the organization about the capacities and motivation of the men in the level below. Advocates of human relations practices are of course sensitive to this situation and have attempted to make management aware of how the unspoken assumptions held about people influence the relationships between organization members.[25] Apparently, a jaundiced view of others is widespread, here and abroad, and is one of the factors impeding participative patterns of organization.

[24] Mason Haire, Edwin E. Ghiselli, and Lyman W. Porter, *Managerial Thinking: An International Study* (New York: John Wiley & Sons, Inc., 1966).

[25] An excellent statement is that of Douglas McGregor, *The Human Side of Enterprise* (New York: McGraw-Hill Book Co., 1960).

STRUCTURALISM

It must be admitted that we are using the term *structuralism* somewhat as a large basket in which to place certain moderate human relations theory as well as some ideas not associated with the human relations viewpoint. Since Max Weber has somewhere cautioned us that social scientists avoid using other men's terminology like they avoid using their toothbrushes, we will stick to the imperfect term structuralism and try to make clear the major content of this viewpoint.[26]

Fusion of Classical and Human Relations Perspectives

It has been shown that the "economic man" of scientific management was replaced by human relations with the "social man." We do more than play with words by noting that "socioeconomic man" inhabits the changing, technologically constrained organizations of structuralism. In this more complicated view of organizational behavior, the central idea is that classical theory and human relations must somehow be meshed since both contain partial insights. "Somehow" is, of course, a vague way to make the point, but the precise nature of the meshing is yet unclear although the necessity of such theory is clear.

Socioeconomic man is a complex bundle of social needs and economic self-interest. He is responsive to group influences on behavior: his ego needs are such that he wants the companionship, respect, and approval of his fellows. Yet the social influences on behavior are weakened if and when self-interest would suffer, and are heightened when self-interest is served by immersion in group activities and adhesion to group norms. In short, the "fit" between social demands and self-wants is an important consideration.

Recall the Bank Wiring Room experiment. The Hawthorne researchers found that the men were restricting output to what they considered to be a fair day's work. Something would happen to the piece rate, the workers claimed, if output went beyond the group standard. The researchers believed this to be a rationalization. The structuralist, however, would argue that group pressures indeed restricted output, but the group norm of output restriction was effectively binding because it interlocked with the workers' real fears that they would have to produce more for the same wage if productivity increased.

The social man of human relations by no means disappears in this view—but he is endowed with a more egoistic nature. The cohesion between man and group may be strong, but when the advantages of adhesion to group norms wane, so too will the cohesion.[27] Thus, the potential for tension between the demands of a social group and self-needs is assumed, as is an inherent potential for conflict

[26] This term is used by Etzioni. Rather than coin a new term, we will use Etzioni's label and lean somewhat on his discussion. See Amitai Etzioni, *Modern Organizations* (Englewood Cliffs, N.J.: Prentice-Hall, Inc., 1964), chap. 3. Scott's term *industrial humanism* was considered, but his view of the theoretical thrust of industrial humanism was too heavily weighted in the direction of human relations: William G. Scott, *Organization Theory, op. cit.*, especially p. 420.

[27] See, for example, George C. Homans, *Social Behavior: Its Elementary Forms, op. cit.*, especially p. 382; also, Peter M. Blau, *Exchange and Power in Social Life, op. cit.*, chap. 4.

between levels in an organization and between organizational goals and goals of individuals.[28]

Scientific management and human relations view conflict between individual and organizational goals as solvable, whereas to the structuralist friction is an inherent feature of organization. The basis for this view is that top management is of necessity more sensitive to, and concerned with, the productivity and profitability of the organization than with satisfying the varied wants of organization members. Moreover, wants are not satisfiable for all time. By satisfying the wants of one subgroup in the organization, a previously satisfied group may feel that justice demands that it then receive more.

If effectiveness and efficiency truly went hand in hand, a rational management course of action would be to devote as much resources and attention to members' satisfaction as to getting the work done. The traditional human relations view suggests this is indeed the best strategy for management to pursue. The structuralist is skeptical about this and leans toward the view that getting the work done in the most effective way and satisfying the participants are often not wholly compatible goals. A dramatic and sad illustration of this dilemma can be seen in the history of the Studebaker Corporation. Its operations in South Bend, Indiana, stretch back to carriage making in the 1850's. In 1954, a human relations theorist wrote: "An example of high worker satisfaction is found in the Studebaker company, which has an enviable record with respect to overt conflict. . . . At the Studebaker company the union contract gives the stewards and the workers a real measure of control and power which the factory manager, the personnel manager, and the top foremen have in other plants. . . . Yet this small company continues to compete successfully in the market with the giants of the automobile industry, and its workers are probably more involved and identified with the company than is true of most industrial organizations."[29] We may agree that the workers were more satisfied at the Studebaker plant than in other car manufacturing firms; nevertheless, the other companies still produce cars whereas Studebaker closed its gates at the South Bend plant in 1963.

Additionally in the structuralist viewpoint, the formal structure of organization reemerges to the foreground. The nonformal social influences on members' behavior are seen as partial influences. The official job requirements are at least equally important, especially those elements of the formal requirements which are visible to superiors and provide a basis for evaluation by superiors. Thus, the evaluation and reward system is held to be an important determinant of behavior, although it may be partially evaded. As Wilbert Moore put it, "in an argument

[28] For insightful discussion of this view, see Arthur Kornhauser, Robert Dubin, and Arthur M. Ross (eds.), *Industrial Conflict* (New York: McGraw-Hill Book Co., 1954), pp. 37-62; Walter Buckley, *Sociology and Modern Systems Theory* (Englewood Cliffs, N.J.: Prentice-Hall, Inc., 1967), chap. 5; Gerhard E. Lenski, *Power and Privilege* (New York: McGraw-Hill Book Co., 1966), chaps. 2-3; Wilbert E. Moore, *The Conduct of the Corporation* (New York: Random House, Inc., 1962), chap. 9; and Anthony Downs, *Inside Bureaucracy* (Boston: Little, Brown & Co., 1967), pp. 83-87.

[29] Daniel Katz, "Worker Satisfactions and Deprivations in Industrial Life," in Arthur Kornhauser, Robert Dubin, and Arthur M. Ross (eds.), *Industrial Conflict* (New York: McGraw-Hill Book Co., 1954), pp. 104-05.

with a fellow scholar also interested in industrial organization, but more fascinated by informal groups than I, I proposed a wager. . . . I offered to lay out on a table all sorts of bits of information about workers' private lives, their informal associations, even their personality traits. But one bit of information would be the answer to the question, 'What are they supposed to be doing?' That information . . . I would choose and bet against the field, expecting to win on the average."[30]

Technology

Few organizational researchers, of whatever persuasion, would today quarrel over the importance of the technology variable. This means that a shift toward a view of work as taking place in a sociotechnical system has occurred. The concept of a sociotechnical system refers to the interdependence of the social elements in group effort, personal values and attitudes, and the technical processes whereby work is accomplished.[31]

Thus, work satisfaction is seen as the outcome of the interpersonal relations between work colleagues, superior-subordinate relations and working conditions, as well as the technical nature of the task. It has become clear that if the technical demands of the task are unpleasant, neither the social elements nor pay envelope can wholly make up for a dissatisfying task. The company and workmates may be liked, but not the job.

The structuralist, however, emphasizes the technology of work as a primary factor. The degree of work autonomy, the closeness of supervision, and the chance for satisfying interpersonal relationships are seen to lie in the influences of work techniques on patterns of organization. This was discussed . . . in looking at the organic and mechanical forms of organizations. The human relations advocate would say that everyone's job should be of a nature that allowed him to "see his role as difficult, important, and meaningful. . . . When jobs do not meet this specification they should be reorganized so that they do."[32] But this requires assumptions about the efficacy in all respects of the "one best way" to organize that the structuralist would question.

Organization as an Open System

The term system refers to an entity with interdependent parts. The parts or units in a system, then, are linked together in such a manner that a change in one part affects other parts, with all the activity taking place within an integument which bounds the system. A closed system is wholly comprehensible and predictable by understanding the inner workings of the bounded system; an open

[30] Moore, *op. cit.*, p. 106.

[31] See, for example, E. L. Trist and K. W. Bamforth, "Some Social and Psychological Consequences of the Longwall Method of Coal-Getting," *Human Relations*, Vol. 4 (1951), pp. 3-38; also E. L. Trist, *et al., Organizational Choice* (London: Tavistock Publications, Ltd., 1963).

[32] Rensis Likert, *New Patterns of Management* (New York: McGraw-Hill Book Co., 1961), p. 103.

system is not.[33] The workings of the open system are as they are in part because of responses to the external environment within which the system exists.

The notion of closed and open system is not an either-or matter; there are degrees of openness. Take the clock as an example of a closed system: the mechanical operation of the clock, once it is wound, is a totally closed system, completely understandable and predictable if you have the appropriate knowledge. The motor in your car, however, is somewhat more open, since its operation is affected by temperature and humidity. If we take the motor out of your car and encase it in a box with an unchanging temperature, humidity, and fuel mixture, then we are back to a closed system, like the clock, in which we need not know anything about the environment in order to understand and predict the operation of the motor. Another example of a different type of open system is a burning fire which wanes and rages in response to the amount of oxygen in its environment. The reasoning may perhaps be easily grasped by considering the different effects of environmental air pollution on the internal state of a tree and a rock.

An open system is "open" in two senses. (*A*) The materials necessary for the maintenance of the system must be obtained from the environment, for example, oxygen for fire or food for the human body. Also, "something" is extruded into the environment as a useful product or waste material. This differs from the closed system of the clock in that the mechanical clock is not engaged in a continual interchange with its environment, so too for a variety of mechanical devices. (*B*) A second sense in which openness may be used, in addition to the passive interchange with the environment as in our illustration of fire and oxygen, is an active response. This requires sensing devices which enable a system to "actively" adjust its responses to stimuli. The extent of adjustment may be limited only by the complexity of the variety of responses of which the system is capable. The sensing devices on the human body, for example, enable the organism to locate paths to food while warning of pitfalls. Finally we note that, within limits, a human organization has the potential to alter its internal state in response to external stimuli, e.g., alter a product the environment does not readily absorb.

More often than not, organizations have been studied as closed systems: entities which are understandable and predictable by knowledge of the units of the system and their linkages. However, the emphasis has more recently changed to a conception of organizations as adaptive open systems, dependent on a continual interchange with the environment for maintenance. The interchange occurs on two "sides" of the organization. First on the input side–the capital, personnel, and materials which the system needs in order to operate in the

[33] See Kenneth E. Boulding, "General Systems Theory–The Skeleton of a Science," *Management Science,* Vol. 2 (1956), pp. 197-208; Stafford Beer, *Cybernetics and Management* (New York: John Wiley & Sons, Inc., 1959); Stanley Young, *Management: A Systems Analysis* (Glenview, Ill.: Scott, Foresman & Co., 1966), chap. 2; Daniel Katz and Robert Kahn, *The Social Psychology of Organizations* (New York: John Wiley & Sons, Inc., 1966), chaps. 1-2; and F. E. Emery and E. L. Trist, "The Causal Texture of Organizational Environments," *Human Relations,* Vol. 18 (1963), pp. 20-26.

throughput stage (which is internal to the organization), and on the output side—disposing of the product or service operated on in the throughput stage in order to replenish the "materials" for another cycle of input-throughput-output.

Further, at the boundaries of the organization are positions which act as sensing devices. The boundaries face outward from the organization in two directions: to the environment which supplies the inputs, and to the environment which must absorb the outputs. The boundary positions are critical, since changes in the environment of either inputs or outputs may require alerting the throughput system to changed conditions.

Let us look at some implications of this view, but reserve fuller discussion for the following section on reduction of uncertainty. Consider the "quality" of the available labor force, whether it is skilled or unskilled. If it is determined that low skill is dominant, the production process (throughput) can be structured, by job fragmentation, to turn out a very complicated product with a very low proportion of skilled workers.[34] Obviously, a misreading of the labor input could be disastrous. At the output boundary in a firm, a gauging of consumer tastes and purchasing power in the economy are vital. The ill-fated Edsel car is a grim reminder to the Ford Motor Company of misjudged consumer preferences.

The open system, then, must establish positions at the input and output boundaries. The number of such positions is related to the complexity of the environment with which the organization must cope, or put another way, to which it must adapt. The greater the variety of factors in the environment which critically bear upon the maintenance and growth of the organization, the greater must be the variety of positions which take readings on these environmental elements. The boundary positions, without which survival would be impossible, are the eyes and ears of the organization.

Reduction of Uncertainty

When the outcome of an event is certain, it is predictable without risk of error. However, if the outcome is uncertain it may be either highly unpredictable on the basis of available information or partially predictable, that is, enough is known to say that the *probability* is high or low that a given outcome will occur. Top management abhors unpredictability. This is a very important notion.

Organizations, internally in the throughput process, are designed to operate predictably. Rules, regulations, chain of command, division of labor, and so forth are means to stabilize certainty of throughput. Boundary positions unscramble and interpret the environment in order to render the unpredictability of the environment into partial predictability, or, as is sometimes possible if the environment can be controlled, into certainty.

Since, ordinarily, only the throughput segments operate under conditions of certainty—because the inner workings of the organization are relatively controllable, whereas the environment is not—the boundary positions are intended to

[34] William J. Goode, "The Protection of the Inept," *American Sociological Review,* Vol. 32 (1967), pp. 5-18.

protect the throughput process from fluctuations in the environment.[35] There are four basic ways of accomplishing this. (*a*) Buffering: on the input side, for example, the stockpiling of materials so that they are available as a steady input into the production process; also, the recruitment and training of personnel. On the output side, the maintaining of inventories in warehouses or by distributors so that the throughput can operate at a steady rate. (*b*) Leveling: smoothing out fluctuations in the environment. For example, gas or electric utility firms may offer reduced rates to consumers if they use the utility during the "slow" period of the day. Airlines offer reduced fares during the "light" part of the week and in the "off-season"; fire departments advise homeowners on fire prevention in order to protect against the possibility of multiple fires which exceed fire-fighting capacity. (*c*) Forecasting: in addition to the "absorption" function of buffering and the "manipulation" function of leveling, which as far as possible seal off the throughput process from environmental fluctuations, forecasting or anticipating environmental alterations allows the throughput to respond adaptively while there is still time, thus reducing the potential for internal crisis in the organization. Forecasting may involve anticipating consumer preferences, peak periods of customer use, regulatory standards for product safety, raw material supply, labor supply, competitors' pricing policy, and so on.

These several ways of reducing uncertainty may be viewed as passive. Thus, we must add the notion of active control. When possible, organizations try to control, that is, make predictable what would otherwise remain unpredictably threatening to the throughput process without control. Vertical and horizontal merger may be understood in this light apart from organizational growth interests on the part of management. For example, if unreliability of quality or quantity of raw materials occurs on the input side, or inadequate and mismanaged distribution channels on the output side, then vertical merger may be a solution. In this manner, the grossly fluctuating environment is smoothed out and made predictable by enveloping and controlling it. If several firms with a similar product reduce profitability by price competition, horizontal merger may be a viable solution; or perhaps, although illegal, agreement between competitors may result.[36] If regulatory action by a governmental body appears threatening to existing operations, influence will likely be exerted to minimize the unfavorable aspects of impending regulation.

If, then, there is a way to reduce the uncertainty of environmental factors, it is a good bet that the attempt will be made to do so in order to protect the throughput from disruptive fluctuation. The boundary positions which deal with important uncertainties in the environment are by this fact influential offices.[37] Conversely, positions with duties that are standardized and repetitive are less influential because they are more easily replaceable by other men, or

35 Thompson, *op. cit.*, chap. 2. We are indebted to his insightful discussion.

36 A fascinating and detailed case history of this "solution" is presented in Walton and Cleveland, *op. cit.*

37 For a fuller discussion see Michael Crozier, *The Bureaucratic Phenomenon* (Chicago: University of Chicago Press, 1964), especially chap. 7.

even by a computer,[38] since standardized procedures can be transmitted and learned. Not so, however, with the ways of gauging, interpreting, and responding to novel situations which inherently require unstandardized procedures. The man who has demonstrated the ability to assess or control nonrecurrent events is indeed valuable to the organization. He must be respectfully treated and appropriately compensated for his ability to reduce potential disturbances from the environment to predictable events which will not violently upset the routinized procedures of the throughput process.

The extent of environmental fluctuations is of obvious importance. An organization which has a stable environment depends less on boundary positions for maintenance of the organization. On the other hand, if critical elements in the environment oscillate broadly, the positions dealing with these elements rise to prominence. For example, if market demand drops, the advertising and sales managers are in a position to increase their value to the organization or diminish it; if the labor market is tight, the personnel manager's actions become highly visible, if a raw material becomes scarce, the ability of the purchasing function to obtain supplies assumes prominence. These sorts of fortuitous situations can make or break careers since the stability of the organization, at least temporarily, rests on the boundary positions' anticipation of, and response to, environmental fluctuations.

The importance of an organizational position thus partly depends on situational factors, regardless of rank on an organization chart. A boundary position responsible for an organizationally critical element in a changing environment is of necessity an essential and exclusive function.[39] Let us put it more broadly this way: the person whose duties call for behavior which is highly predictable has less influence in the organization than the person whose duties at times require unpredictable actions to which others must adapt if the organization, or a component of it, is to remain viable. We see then that those positions which deal with uncertainty are potentially in a more "powerful" position than those which deal more exclusively with certainty of operation.

Let us now briefly go back to the classification of organizational types and tie the discussion into it. The mechanistic form of organization can only exist if the throughput is well insulated from disturbances on both the input and output sides. This is characteristic of mass production or large-batch in Woodward's scheme. The highly elaborated division of labor, clear-cut tasks, military-like chain of command, strict scheduling, and coordination of tasks, is indeed a rational system for accomplishing tasks under the conditions of a closed system. These conditions exist for the large-batch throughput process, which can operate as if it were a closed system since the boundary mechanisms of buffering, leveling, and so forth seal it off from the major disruptions with which the overall open system may have to cope. The organic form of organization, however—such as the small-batch or job shop in Woodward's typology—is as it is because

[38] See Herbert A. Simon, *The New Science of Management Decision* (New York: Harper & Row, Publishers 1960).

[39] Robert Dubin, "Power, Function, and Organization," *Pacific Sociological Review,* Vol. 6 (1963), pp. 16-24.

the "seal" between input-throughput-output is leaky. There is a high degree of continual interdependence between sales, design, production, testing, and the customer's wishes. The job shop is in a highly fluctuating environment which cannot be smoothed out. This requires continuous adaptation by the organization and therefore does not permit the highly predictable performance associated with the closed system throughput of a mechanistic system.

Let us now see what decentralization means in this framework. Decentralization permits a component of an organization, such as a product division or profit center, to operate autonomously within broad limits. But why decentralize? The conventional answer is that decisions concerning a problem should be nearest to that point where the problem arose, since more is known about the problem at that point. In our terms, uncertainty can most effectively be reduced to partial predictability at the location where the problem exists. We get a bit further by asking, Where are the locations in the organization which are likely to have autonomy of operations? It would seem that the answer is that autonomy for an organizational component hinges on whether or not that component can effectively be sealed off by its own input-output boundary positions from environmental fluctuations, including other organizational components. If buffering, leveling, and so forth are applicable, then that component may operate its throughput in a predictable manner at a steady rate. Units that cannot be effectively sealed off at the boundaries are likely to remain as subordinate components within a larger grouping of units with common input-output boundary positions.

Decentralization is thus one way to respond to the problem of uncertainty in the throughput process. By creating autonomous units, sealed off at the boundaries, a mechanistic, highly predictable form of organization can be devised for the throughput process. Decentralization from this point of view indeed makes sense.

The product divisions of General Motors are prime examples of separate mechanistic systems, each with its own boundary positions. What happens is something like this. An organization expands its product line. The existing, initial boundary positions are inadequate to cope with the many elements of the environment as they diversely affect the separate products. The existing boundary positions are faced with the awesome task of unscrambling the diverse environmental fluctuations and relating each of the environmental elements to the particular product on which it bears. Rather than cut back the diversity of products in order to regain a stable throughput, it is possible to fashion separate decentralized units which can, as it were, cast a protective net around their throughput processes. In this manner, predictability of operations is regained.[40]

We began this section by noting that organizations abhor uncertainty. The mechanistic form of organization provides the greatest certainty of results. On this basis it appears reasonable to hold that, when possible, a mechanistic pattern

[40] See Alfred D. Chandler, Jr., *op. cit.;* also Lawrence E. Fouraker and John M. Stopford, "Organizational Structure and the Multinational Strategy," *Administrative Science Quarterly*, Vol. 13 (1968), pp. 47-64.

of organization will be devised. This, of course, is not always possible, and we have shown under what conditions it is not. But when the mechanistic form is possible, it is a good bet that it will in fact exist.

In any event, there is an interesting parallel between societal and organizational change. It has been suggested that one of the most persistent characteristics of societal change is an increasingly comprehensive network of laws to regulate conduct.[41] Similarly, this is so in organizations. Even though a fully mechanistic system may not emerge, the organizational quest for predictability generates a growing set of rules, regulations, and standard operating procedures.

We have stressed the reduction of uncertainty as a central managerial interest. The structure of organization is in large part a result of the assessment of how certainty of operations can best be achieved in the throughput component. There is not, as we have tried to show, a one best way of organizing which is applicable across the board.[42] The nature of the external environment, skills and expectations of personnel, and technology are basic elements which constrain the design of organization. Structuralism attempts to mesh classical theory and human relations, as well as to incorporate what appear to be highly promising insights concerning the reduction of uncertainty. It has been said that classical theory has concerned itself with "organizations without people," whereas human relations theory has revolved around "people without organization."[43] Although the two have not as yet been adequately joined, such a union is underway with the continuing abandonment of the "one best way" mode of thought.

[41] Wilbert E. Moore, *Social Change* (Englewood Cliffs, N.J.: Prentice-Hall, Inc., 1963), p. 26.

[42] See the excellent discussion by Raymond A. Katzell, "Contrasting Systems of Work Organization," *American Psychologist*, Vol. 17 (1962), pp. 102-08.

[43] Warren G. Bennis, "Leadership Theory and Administrative Behavior," *Administrative Science Quarterly*, Vol. 4 (1959/1960), pp. 259-301.

Karl O. Magnusen

A COMPARATIVE ANALYSIS OF ORGANIZATIONS–A CRITICAL REVIEW:

"Organizational behavior," according to George Strauss, "is an orphan among fields," possessing no professional society, no leading journal, and characterized by a flourishing but disorganized labor market. The area's subject matter is eclectic at best, and theoretical development lags behind empirical research. Contradictory propositions abound in the literature. As examples: task specialization and job enrichment increase productivity; bureaucratic and nonbureaucratic structures maximize work coordination; monetary and self-actualization needs increase motivation; and stability and conflict promote organizational effectiveness. To properly assess these competing prescriptions, managers must learn how to diagnose their respective organizations–a task made easier through an awareness of organization theory and research.

Chronologically, we can identify four major approaches to the study of organizational behavior. The earliest phase, scientific management, emphasized shop-level production activities and assumed that human motivation occurs primarily from economic incentives. Later, classical administrative theory, complementary to scientific management, focused on the bureaucratic aspects of organizations and sought universal principles of management. The human relations movement, a reaction to classical theory, produced a welter of findings that reflected both economic and human dimensions, but it provided no systematic theory of organizations. Finally, and most recently, attempts have been made to develop frameworks for the comparative analysis of organizations. Leading efforts here have emphasized the importance of technology-environment variables as primary determinants of organizational behavior.

It is this last approach that will be discussed in this article, especially the three theoretical perspectives developed by Woodward, Perrow, and Lawrence and Lorsch. Although no single framework presents a total solution to the complex problems of organizational design, their critical review should provoke thought

From Karl Magnusen, "A Comparative Analysis of Organizations: A Critical Review." Reprinted by permission of the publisher from *Organizational Dynamics,* Summer 1973, and discussion. As Landsberger once noted, "Gems in isolation are worth far less than when they are strung together as a necklace. They all gain greatly by being compared and contrasted in an orderly fashion, even if we cannot yet weld them together by means of a single, overarching theory."

THE TECHNOLOGICAL IMPERATIVE

Early in this century, F. W. Taylor had related technology to productivity, yet attention was subsequently directed away from the technological aspects of work by ensuing debates over the relative importance of classical and human relations theory. Yet impressive, but scattered, evidence throughout the 1940s and 1950s supported the importance of technology as a determinant of organizational behavior.

By the early 1960s, more systematic attention was devoted to technological aspects of work, and research took a comparative approach. For example, in a study of 20 British firms, Burns and Stalker found that different rates of technical innovation were associated with different kinds of organizational structures. Innovation was low in firms with "mechanistic" systems, which were characterized by distinct functional specialisms, precise definitions of duties and responsibilities, and a well-defined command hierarchy. Rapid and major technical innovation, by contrast, was more evident in firms with "organic" systems, where structures were more flexible, jobs less rigorously specified, and communication resembled consultation rather than order-giving.

The most widely acknowledged research into technology, however, was produced in the mid-1960s. While the major impetus was British in origin (discussed in the next section), receptiveness to the approach in the United States was sparked by Blauner's study of employee alienation in four industries with different technologies: printing, automobiles, textiles, and chemicals. Results indicated that levels of alienation were unevenly distributed among the work forces considered, being highest in auto production and substantially lower in the other three industries. (The study provides an interesting contrast to the recent and controversial HEW study on *Work in America,* which found alienation to be more pervasive).

THE SOUTH ESSEX STUDIES

For purposes of comparative analysis, the most extensive and influential study to date of technology and its impact on organizational design was published in 1965 by Joan Woodward. Her research into 100 manufacturing firms in the South Essex area of England disclosed that organizational differences were not accounted for by company size, type of industry, or personality factors among executives. Further, conformity with the classical principles of organization had no relation to business success in the firms studied. Some of the most successful firms were the most conspicuous deviates.

However, when the firms were classified according to a scale of technical complexity based on nine systems of production grouped into three major categories (unit, mass, and process production–in increasing order of complexity), the data concerning organization structures fell into clear patterns. Not only were specific structures associated with each technological grouping, but within each category, companies that most nearly conformed to the median figure for each structural characteristic were most successful–success being defined in terms of profits and growth rates. High-performing firms with mass-production technologies tended to have mechanistic management systems, while high-performing firms with unit- or process-production technologies tended to have organic systems. Unit and process firms did not have identical structures, however, and neither grouping displayed the variety found among mass-production companies in the way production operations were planned and controlled.

Acknowledging that her research did not produce a general law about the relationship of technology to organizational behavior, Woodward suggested that classical management writers apparently had mass-production firms in mind when they formulated their principles of organization. She further noted that while there seems to be no "one best way" to organize manufacturing firms, there does seem to be "a particular form of organization most appropriate to each technical situation."

Woodward also found that the relative importance of different functional groups and their interrelationships varied within each type of production system. Each type of technology had a "critical" function, and firms above average in success not only had status systems that adequately rewarded the importance of this function, but also tended to have a chief executive who had been associated with it earlier in his career.

These results stemmed from an analysis of manufacturing cycles and require further discussion. In unit firms, for example, the manufacturing cycle began with marketing–finding a customer by convincing him that the company could produce whatever he needs. Development, however–creating a custom product –was the critical activity, because demands for product quality outweighed considerations of cost or customer service. Production came last in the cycle. Interdepartmental relationships were "good" in unit firms because the manufacturing task required the close integration of functions, which, in turn, required high levels of interpersonal interaction. As Woodward noted, "In unit production, the network of relationships required to bring coordination about is also conducive to the development of satisfactory social relationships. What is best for production seems also to be best for people."

In mass-production systems, the cycle started with development and long-range planning, necessitated by the considerable expenditures involved in product changes. Production was the critical function because, at least in the short run, success depended on operating efficiency, especially the reduction of unit costs. Marketing came last in the cycle, because the need for the product was known and any competitive edge was based on price and prompt deliveries. In contrast to unit firms, the functions composing the manufacturing cycle here were more self-contained. Because end results did not depend on the formation of close operational relationships between development, production, and marketing, management did not have a homogeneous view of the company–instead there were sectional interests, exaggerated departmental loyalties, and mutual suspicion. Technical and social ends apparently conflict in mass-production firms, yet the conflict seemed to contribute to results. A measure of unhappiness and mutual animosity among the staff appeared necessary for commercial success.

In process production, development also was the first phase in the manufacturing cycle, because basic research was needed to expose potential new markets. Unlike either unit or mass-production firms, the critical function was marketing. Markets had to be assured, not only because of heavy capital expenditures for plant construction, but also because efficient operations depended on the continuous demand for products. As in unit production, however, production was the final phase of the cycle; but, unlike unit production, process operations—once established—were expected to run for years in a highly controlled, predictable manner.

Although the tasks of process production were more independent of each other than in either of the other production categories, the result was not a fragmented, competing structure but a two-dimensional structure with considerable intergroup harmony. The process plant may be viewed as forming an inner ring, with the research laboratories and marketing departments forming an outer ring. Minimum coordination is required between departments or "rings," and within the plant itself, controls are built into the technological system. Consequently, Woodward observed that "As far as commercial success is concerned, the form of organization is comparatively unimportant. There is therefore no reason why the organization planner should not concentrate on building an organizational structure which meets the needs of the people employed."

To summarize: Woodward related technology not only to organizational structures but also to power relationships. Engineering predominated in unit firms, production in mass-production firms, and marketing in process firms. Technical and social functions of management were thoroughly meshed in unit firms, partially meshed in mass-production companies, and totally separated in continuous-process firms. Conflict levels were highest in mass-production firms and seemed related to successful operations. (This implies that traditional human relations techniques that emphasize improved communications may only antagonize legitimately conflicting groups in mass-production firms and may be unnecessary in unit or process firms where the work system itself insures the necessary interactions.)

SOUTH ESSEX: LATER STUDIES

Although Woodward found specific organizational characteristics associated with different manufacturing technologies, her research did not explain why unit and process firms, at opposite ends of the technical complexity scale, sometimes resembled each other; nor did it explain why the link between technology and structure was least predictable in the mass-production category. She speculated that either the classification of technology was inadequate to deal with technical differences between mass-production firms or some other variable was an intervening influence between technology and structure.

Attempts to refine measures of operations technology have either met with little success or tended to question the "technology causes structure" hypothesis. For example, a study of a stratified sample of 46 diverse organizations, including 31 manufacturing firms, concluded that "variables of operations technology will be related only to those structural variables that are centered on the workflow . . . size and dependence and similar factors make the greater overall impact."

Woodward, herself, had recognized earlier that the "technological imperative" might be too sweeping a generalization, and that organizational structure might be less a function of technology than of the managerial control system. To examine this possibility, she first had to develop a means to classify controls. Her fieldwork experience suggested a four-fold classification based on whether one or more control systems were used (single vs. multiple controls) and whether the controls were of a personal or mechanical nature.

When she cross-tabulated her sample of South Essex firms by the technology and control categories, she obtained the results given in Figure 1. Similarities between unit and process production firms occurred because single system control processes predominated in both groups. Differences were due to personal control processes predominating in unit production and mechanical control systems in process production. The weak link between technology and structure in the mass-production category was the result of firms being spread across all control categories. Mass-production firms with personal controls structurally resembled unit firms, however, and mass-production firms with impersonal controls resembled continuous-process companies. Woodward concluded that managers of mass-production firms had more choice in the selection of control systems than their counterparts in unit or process technologies. Precisely why and how these managers decided on particular controls, however, was not answered by the research.

Reflecting on the difficulties associated with using technology and controls to predict organizational variations, Woodward and her staff decided that the

	Control System			
Technology	*Unitary-Personal*	*Multiple-Personal*	*Multiple-Mechanical*	*Unitary Mechanical*
Unit/Small Batch	75%	25%	–	–
Large Batch/Mass	15	35	40	10
Process	–	–	5	95
Total Firms	28	21	18	33

FIGURE 1. **Technology and control**

common thread underlying her attempts to measure technical characteristics was the amount of "variety." This variety might depend on the nature of the product, the nature of the market, or the nature of the manufacturing processes themselves in the systems of production.

In continuous-process firms, for example, there was little uncertainty in the production task, and the managerial control system was designed to handle whatever existed. In unit-production firms, by contrast, the high degree of variety could not be handled by either mechanical or administrative control devices, and this created the need for a social system able to deal with continuing unpredictability. In mass production, product and process standardization deal in part with the variety factor, yet the elaborateness of these controls itself sometimes injected additional sources of variety into the system. Woodward commented: "If, as the work done so far suggests, the causal link between technology and organizational behavior is the degree of uncertainty and predictability in the production task, it might be more profitable to find a way of classifying technical systems by identifying the types and degree of variety within them rather than by detailed measurement of particular technical characteristics."

TOWARD A BROADER FRAMEWORK

A theoretical approach envisioned by Woodward already exists in the literature. Recognizing that not all organizations have a machine-based technology, Charles Perrow sought a more generic foundation for analyzing organizations—one that uses the concepts of variability and analyzability to predict organizational structures.

But, a word of caution. Perrow terms his independent variable "technology," but it is not the same production technology referred to in the South Essex studies. Instead, he is talking about knowledge technology—the characteristics of information used in work processes.

In Perrow's view, the technology of an organization can be determined by examining (1) the number of exceptional cases that the organizational system must deal with, and (2) the extent to which these exceptions are analyzable. By dichotomizing and cross-classifying these two dimensions, four technology quadrants can be identified, as indicated in Figure 2.

In an organization with routine operations (cell 4) few problems occur and those that do are readily analyzed. Product variety by itself may have little to do with uncertainty. For example: "Automobile firms produce an amazing variety of models and a staggering variety of parts, but these are not novel situations requiring search behavior (except in the design and engineering of model changes)." By contrast, organizations with nonroutine technologies (cell 2) must deal with numerous exceptional cases that are not readily analyzed. Solutions to system crises depend on intuition, guesswork, and change. Examples of this kind of nonroutineness include aerospace firms, manufacturers of exotic metals or nuclear fuels, certain kinds of advertising agencies, and noncustodial psychiatric units.

The dotted line in Figure 2 suggests a one-dimensional scale of organizational nonroutineness; yet the Perrow framework offers two additional variants. Engineering technologies (cell 3) are similar to routinized operations in that exceptional cases can be readily understood and analyzed; but they differ in the frequency with which exceptions occur—rarely in routine firms and often in engineering firms, which must continually modify designs to meet customer needs. Craft organizations (cell 1), such as those making specialty glassware, are confronted with relatively few deviant cases requiring unique solutions but, when

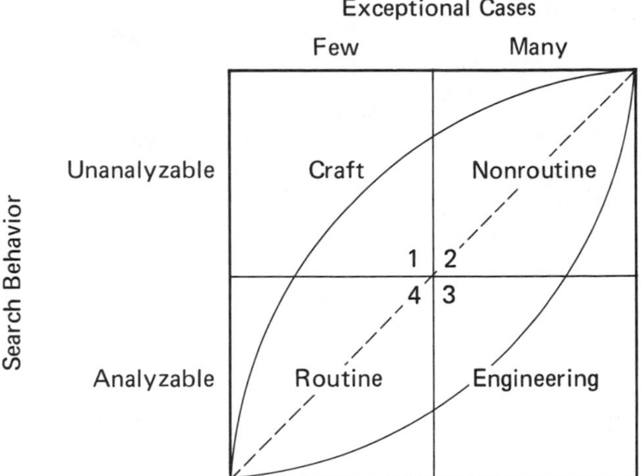

FIGURE 2. **Technology variable**

these exceptions occur, the intuitive search process typical of non-routine organizations is required.

While the conceptualization given in Figure 2 may appear static, movement between cells is likely: "One may move from cell 2 to cell 1 with increasing production runs, clients served, accounts handled, research projects underway, agency programs administered and so forth, since this allows more experience to be gained and thus reduces the number of stimuli seen as exceptions. If technical knowledge increases, increasing the reliability of search procedures, one may move from cell 2 to cell 3. If both things happen—and this is the aim of most organizations—one may move from cell 2 to cell 4." To permit more routinized programs and procedures, the variability of inputs must be reduced and knowledge about them increased.

Having developed a classification system, Perrow states that certain organizational structures and goal patterns will be associated with each basic technological setting. These relationships are summarized in Figure 3. No claim is made that technology always must be an independent variable; nor is there certainty about goals being dependent variables. As Perrow notes, "occasions can be readily cited where changes in goals, for example those brought about by changes in the marketplace or the personalities of top executives, have brought about changes in the technology utilized."

According to the theory, routine organizations will possess centralized mechanistic management systems where members will be especially concerned about matters such as pay, job security, and protection from arbitrary authority. Goals emphasized will include system stability, high profits, and quantity output. Little risk or innovation is likely, and organizational power will be used to promote conservative attitudes and philosophies. Nonroutine organizations, by comparison, will have decentralized, organic management structures, where coordination within and between groups is based on spontaneous interactions.

Craft Organizations

TASK STRUCTURE

	Discretion	*Power*	*Coord. w/in Groups*	*Group Interdependence*
MM*	Low	Low	Planning	Low
LM**	High	High	Feedback	
	(Decentralized)			

SOCIAL STRUCTURE

Social Identity: Based on Friendship

GOALS

System	*Product*	*Derived*
Stability	Quality	Conservative
Low Risk	No Innovations	
Moderate Profit Emphasis		

Nonroutine Organizations

TASK STRUCTURE

	Discretion	*Power*	*Coord. w/in Groups*	*Group Interdependence*
MM*	High	High	Feedback	High
LM**	High	High	Feedback	
	(Decentralized)			

SOCIAL STRUCTURE

Goal Identity: Based on a Sense of Mission

GOALS

System	*Product*	*Derived*
High Growth	High Quality	Liberal
High Risk	Innovative	
Low Profit Emphasis		

Routine Organizations

TASK STRUCTURE

	Discretion	*Power*	*Coord. w/in Groups*	*Group Interdependence*
MM*	Low	High	Planning	Low
LM**	Low	Low	Planning	
	(Centralized)			

SOCIAL STRUCTURE

Instrumental Identity: Based on Pay, Job Security Protection from Arbitrary Authority

GOALS

System	*Product*	*Derived*
Stability	Quantity	Conservative
Low Risk	No Innovations	
High Profit Emphasis		

Engineering Organizations

TASK STRUCTURE

	Discretion	*Power*	*Coord. w/in Groups*	*Group Interdependence*
MM*	High	High	Feedback	Low
LM**	Low	Low	Planning	
	(Centralized)			

SOCIAL STRUCTURE

Task Identity: Based on Technical Satisfactions

GOALS

System	*Product*	*Derived*
Moderate Growth	Quantity	Liberal
Moderate Risk	Moderate Innovations	
Moderate Profit Emphasis		

*Middle Management
**Lower Management

FIGURE 3. **Structural and goal patterns**

Members will be more concerned with the organization's mission and special competences than with pay and security, and goals emphasized will include risk and innovation over stability, growth and quality over profits, and liberal orientations toward the use of organizational power.

Craft and engineering organizations have "mixed" characteristics. Craft firms are less decentralized than nonroutine companies, members emphasize friendship patterns, and goal orientations resemble routine companies—except for a somewhat greater emphasis on matters of quality. Finally, engineering firms are less centralized than their "routine" counterparts, technical satisfactions based in the work process become important to members, and with the exception of a somewhat higher concern for quantity output, goal patterns are similar to those found in nonroutine organizations.

IMPLICATIONS

If this reasoning is persuasive, then a number of implications follow. First, a relationship found in one organization may not be found in another, unless the organizations have similar technologies. Second, "some schools, hospitals, banks, and steel companies may have more in common," because of their routine character, than nonroutine organizations in the same areas of activity. Third, the highly structured bureaucratic form of organization with its emphasis on rules, hierarchy, close division of labor, and clear lines of authority, probably works best where the underlying technology is routine and predictable.

Finally, prescriptions for certain management techniques may be more relevant in some situations than others. Consider, for example, two "steady-state" systems—one routine, the other nonroutine. The routine system, seeking greater order and control, might selectively emphasize: (1) PERT networks, (2) value analysis, (3) long-range planning, (4) system design, (5) operations research, (6) cost-effectiveness analysis, (7) decision theory, and (8) human factors engineering. By contrast, the nonroutine system, seeking flexibility and expansion of personal initiative, might selectively use: (9) business gaming, (10) sensitivity training, (11) decentralization, including profit center and unit management, 12) creativity training, (13) management grid training, (14) profit sharing, (15) motivation laboratories, and (16) job enrichment. If these system states change, of course, the relative applicability of the listed techniques would also change

A CRITIQUE OF PERROW

An exploratory study by Magnusen sought empirical support for the Perrow framework. Managers in 14 medium-sized manufacturing corporations in two geographical parts of the country were given questionnaires that asked about their work and organizations. Of 2841 forms distributed, 93 percent were completed and returned.

By examining managerial perceptions about the variability and analyzability of their jobs, a modal "technology" score for each organization was determined and used to classify the respective firms into Perrow's "technology" quadrants. When this was done, however, the data showed that the companies were more homogeneous than anticipated and could be categorized only as routine or nonroutine. The craft and engineering models were eliminated from further consideration as a result. Despite this reduction in theoretical scope, the differences between the routine and nonroutine clusters of organizations were in the directions predicted for the task structure and goals sections of the theory (little support was found for social structure aspects). The magnitudes of these differences were not great, but they remained when functional groups and managerial levels of authority were held constant.

Although this study reinforces the apparent utility of the Perrow framework as a guide to organizational analysis, a number of vexing issues remain. For example, because the theory understates the importance of organizational environment, it offers few insights into the subject of change. Institutional growth and time-lags between a change in technology and subsequent change in structure are not discussed—nor is the question of whether level of technology or rate of technological change has the greater impact on organizational behavior.

The greatest challenge to the Perrow theory, however, is that it ignores the existence of multiple technologies within organizations. When Magnusen applied a nonroutineness index to functional groups, he found distinct differences both within and between these subunits. As shown in Figure 4, production and research and development tended to be at technological extremes, with sales and finance/administration groups taking intermediate positions but tending to cluster in the routine category.

The functional subsystems also had varied task structures but, with the exception of production, which was highly structured, they did not follow patterns expected on the basis of technology alone. Research and development units, for example, despite their relative nonroutineness, had structural features similar to the production groups. They also were the greatest source of organizational criticism. While this criticism could result from having structures incongruent with technological requirements, more likely it resulted from the limited power of the research and development units studied. In general, sales departments were dominant, followed by production, finance/administration, and research and development. The critical point, in any case, is that Perrow seems preoccu-

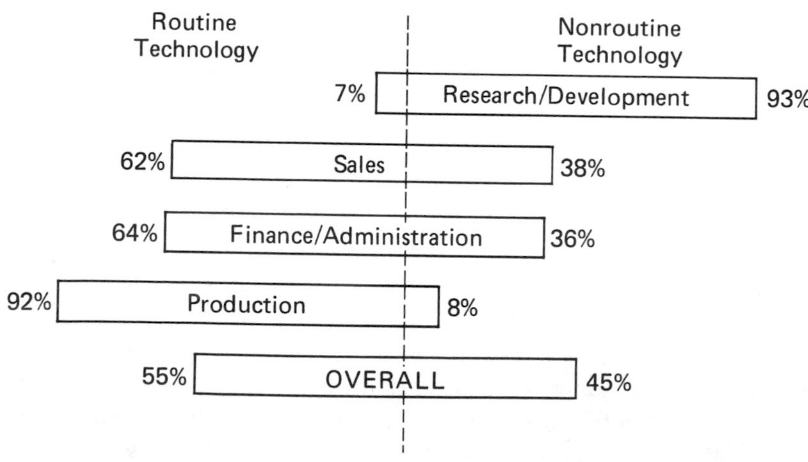

FIGURE 4. **Percentage of functional groups having routine and nonroutine technologies**

pied with differences between organizations to the neglect of variations within them.

The Perrow framework, in sum, has conceptual appeal and some empirical support. It is one-sided in emphasis—as other theories have been—but this is not so much an emphasis on technology (in the sense of machine operations) as it is a focus on system uncertainty. Although Perrow makes no claim that his approach is a "magical package" for organizational design, he regards his theories as part of the base from which, he hopes, "more subtle models of types of organizations will emerge."

THE ENVIRONMENTAL IMPERATIVE

The comparative frameworks of Woodward and Perrow assume that organizational structures and processes are contingent upon the demands of technology (variously defined). Another approach has been taken by Lawrence and Lorsch, who examined the relationships of organization to environment in three industrial settings chosen primarily for their different rates of technological change in both products and processes. These settings or "environments" included plastics (high change), packaged foods (moderate change), and containers (low change). A total of ten organizations were studied, six plastics firms and two companies each in the other two industries. All firms used continuous-process technologies.

Observing that organizations design their subsystems to cope with different parts of the total environment, Lawrence and Lorsch first sought measures of environmental uncertainty for the marketing, production, and scientific sectors in each industry grouping. This was done by considering rates of information change, uncertainties over causal relationships, and time spans of feedback about results.

Results confirmed the researchers' expectations about the role of environment. In plastics, where pressures for innovation were greatest, the total environment was most highly diversified and uncertain. By contrast, the container environment was more predictable and stable, no doubt because innovation was less of an issue—being superseded by competitive demands for consistent, routine operations and reliable delivery services. The foods environment was intermediate in diversity.

Next, Lawrence and Lorsch measured the actual degree of differentiation among functional units as well as differences in problems of integration (coordination). Differentiation was measured along four dimensions: (1) formality of structure, e.g., formal rules and procedures vs. fewer rules and procedures; (2) time orientation, e.g., short vs. long; (3) interpersonal orientation, e.g., concern for task vs. concern for people; and (4) goal orientation, e.g., concern with market competition and customer problems vs. output, and efficiency vs. scientific advancements. Integration was examined in terms of which units needed tightest linking, the organizational level at which this linking was required, and the kinds of devices used to implement coordination.

A major finding in the study was that effective organizations (effectiveness was defined in terms of growth in profits, sales volume, and return on investment) had structures and member orientations that were congruent with ("fit") the demands of their respective environments. Thus, in plastics, and to a slightly lesser extent in foods, managers had heterogeneous outlooks. Structure was considered high in production, medium in sales, and low in research. Time horizons were short in production and sales but long in research. Interpersonal relations were more formal and task-oriented in production and more permissive in sales and research. Managers in container firms, however, had more homogeneous orientations and each tended to view the organization as having high structure, short time horizons, and a task emphasis in interpersonal relations.

High-performing organizations also achieved high levels or integration (defined as "the quality of the state of collaboration that exists among departments that are required to achieve unity of effort by the demands of the environment"). Although the degree (or "tightness") of integration was high in all three industries, there were differences accounted for by the dominant competitive issue in each environment. Where customer service was critical (containers), tightest integration was required between production and sales (to handle scheduling). Where innovation was more important (plastics and foods), interdependence had to be greatest between sales and research and research and production (to handle new products and technological changes).

The means of accomplishing this integration varied, and a comparison of all high-performing organizations revealed both differences and similarities in effective conflict resolution procedures and practices. Differences tended to be structural in nature, while similarities related to managerial attitudes and behavior.

Successful firms in each industry, for example, used different integrating devices, with diverse environments requiring more complex mechanisms. Container firms (low differentiation) achieved integration primarily through the management hierarchy, direct managerial contacts, and paperwork systems (plans, schedules, and budgets). These methods also were used in the foods and plastics environments, but they were less important than other kinds of devices. Food organizations (moderate differentiation) relied on individual integrators, e.g., functional managers assigned to integrating roles and on temporary cross-functional teams. Plastics firms (high differentiation), however, used formal integrating departments and permanent cross-functional teams at three levels of management.

Effective companies also differed in the relative influence of various departments and the location of influence within the management hierarchy. Decision power had to be placed in units and levels where there was requisite knowledge of existing problems. Units requiring high influence were: sales in container firms (to implement customer service); sales and research in foods (to handle market and food science demands); and a separate integrating unit in plastics (to handle change). Further, in container firms, decision making power was centralized in upper management, whereas in foods and plastics this influence was distributed more equally throughout the organization.

There were similarities among all high-performing companies as well—similarities of style in managing conflict. To begin with, managers centrally involved in achieving integration dealt with conflict by open confrontation (problem solving), instead of compromise (splitting differences), "smoothing" (trying to keep everybody happy), or "forcing" (resorting to unilateral power plays). Interestingly, Lawrence and Lorsch found that, while managers in general considered confrontation to be the most desirable mode of conflict resolution, relatively few practiced it.

Two other similarities in conflict management were important when special integrating devices were used. First, integrators felt that they were rewarded for achieving unified efforts; and second, integrators and integrating units in high-performing firms developed "balanced orientations"; i.e., they had scores on the structural, time, interpersonal, and goal dimensions that were intermediate to those of the managers and units being linked. If coordinators adopted attitudes and behavior either too similar or too dissimilar to any given department, they typically were charged with either favoritism or nonresponsiveness–the result being ineffective integration.

To summarize: Lawrence and Lorsch found that successful organizations were able to diagnose and meet environmental requirements for differentiation and integration. (The classical writers also dealt with these concepts, but failed to understand how different systems produce different working styles that, in turn, necessitate different methods for achieving unified effort). These requirements were explored within and among organizations, and common errors in organizational design were identified, including: (1) combining two different major tasks in the same unit, (2) placing similar tasks in separate units, with consequent conflict and redundancy of effort, (3) using the management hierarchy as the major integrating device in highly differentiated organizations, (4) using integrating devices between mildly differentiated units, which merely adds "noise" to the system, and (5) structuring and orienting an integrating unit so much like one of the sections being linked that it loses contact with the other.

As a final point, Lawrence and Lorsch focused on the organization's *present* relationship to its environment. While this leaves in question the *future* viability of organizational characteristics should environmental demands or goals change, the theoretical framework can be used to analyze the possible impact of such changes.

IMPLICATIONS AND RELATED RESEARCH

Efforts to systematically explain variations in organization design, termed "contingency" theory, have provided at least partial guides for designing organizations according to the tasks they are trying to perform. Research based on the organization-environment model has led to additional insights as well. Three such studies are closely tied to the Lawrence and Lorsch framework and deserve a brief review.

First, Walker and Lorsch examined the managerial dilemma of whether an organization should be structured by product or by function. The basic problem has been recognized for decades, but it continues to be difficult below the divisional level. Based on research in two consumer foods manufacturing plants. Walker and Lorsch concluded that "the functional organization seems to lead to better results in a situation where stable performance of a routine task is desired, while the product organization leads to better results in situations where the task is less predictable and requires innovative problem solving." Compromises between product and functional bases might be necessary, of course, involving forms such as cross-functional teams, product or project management, and matrix organization (which overlays product and functional forms), but these are difficult to administer and make complex demands on interpersonal skills. While there is no easy solution to the product-function dilemma, an accurate assessment of the organization's basic task demands should assist greatly in making some "proper" choice.

Second, Morse examined the relationship between organization design and individual motivation. His results challenge the widespread humanist notion that formalized organizations cannot motivate people, whereas less formalized units always do. The study centered on four organizational units: two manufactured standardized containers (certain task) and two performed research and development work in communication technology (uncertain task). Each pairing belonged to the same company and included a high and low-performing unit, as rated by management.

Both effective units had different structures, but in each case there was a congruence between these structures and task demands. The high-performing container section had highly structured duties, rules, procedures, and controls. By contrast, the high-performing research laboratory had a low degree of structure and more flexible control procedures. Ineffective units also had different structures, but these were inappropriate to their task demands. The low-performing container section resembled the effective research laboratory, and the low-performing laboratory resembled the successful container unit.

Most interesting, however, was the finding that managers and professionals in the two effective units had higher feelings of competence than those in the two ineffective units. According to Morse, the "fit" between task demands and organizational structures produced effective task performance and a sense of competence. Both structured and unstructured settings, then, can lead to personal motivation, a conclusion that casts further doubt on "either-or" preferences for classical or human relations theory. Morse's study emphasizes the need to consider multiple interactions among task, organization, and human variables and not to give exclusive attention to some single factor, whether it be the individual (as in McClelland's work on achievement training) or the environment (as in Herzberg's work on job enrichment).

The third and final example of research related to the organization-environment model deals with conglomerates (highly diversified, multi-divisional firms). This corporate form has been given little systematic attention by organization theorists, even though the failure rate of mergers is nearly 25 percent. Some insights, however, have been provided by Allen's study of two "typical" conglomerates. Both operated in the areas of producers' and consumers' durables, had annual sales between \$300 and \$500 million, and were composed of ten or more product divisions operating as profit centers.

Because no significant technological or market links existed between the divisions in either firm, the main area of management interdependence occurred between the product divisions and corporate headquarters (CHQ). Consequently, and in contrast to Lawrence and Lorsch's hypothesis that subunit diversity requires complex integrating devices, both firms coordinated their numerous subunits (divisions) through comparatively simple paperwork systems (plans, budgets, and routine funds requests).

Ease of integration occurred, however, only when profit performance was on target. When a division did not meet its profit commitments or made unusual or unanticipated requests for funds, integration problems immediately became more complicated as the "felt need" for joint decision making increased between corporate and divisional executives. As expected, this greater involvement produced effective results only when certain partial determinants of conflict resolution were met (such a direct confrontation to resolve the conflict, a balance of influence between the parties involved, and the presence of integrating personnel with time and goal orientations intermediate to those of corporate headquarters and the executives of the problem division.

While low performance alone could explain the need for increased integrative efforts, another possible explanation involved top management views about the achievement of synergy. Both firms studied had secured financial synergy and some managerial synergy, but neither had obtained any real results with operating synergy (despite substantial efforts in this direction by executives in the low-performing firm). Allen noted that the organizational arrangements of conglomerates may be such that financial and operating synergy are mutually antagonistic goals. If so, headquarters' emphasis on operating synergy could inappropriately reduce corporate-divisional differentiation by involving the corporate office too heavily in divisional operations. This would not only increase integration efforts and problems but also hinder overall performance by causing the CHQ unit to lose "the detachment and discipline that its role of evaluating division plans and allocating funds requires."

To summarize: Allen's work on conglomerates, Morse's study of structure and motivation, and Walker and Lorsch's research into the product-function dilemma further indicate the usefulness of the organization-environment model as a means to guide empirical investigations and management practice. Although the research above has focused on industrial firms, the underlying conceptual perspective seems applicable to other organizations as well. This should not imply, of course, that use of the differentiation-integration concepts will produce indisputable analyses about organizational design. As Etzioni has commented, "Designing an organization is somewhat like planning a forest, and generally not like designing a building."

CONCLUSION

Comparative organizational analysis should assist managers in diagnosing system demands, developing appropriate structures, and selectively applying behavioral concepts and techniques. While the technology-environment models discussed in this article are empirically based, they hardly represent "final" solutions to problems of organizational design and development.

Each approach has distinct limitations. Woodward's research is based on production systems, yet not all firms have machine-based production units. Perrow's work seeks a more generic definition of technology, yet does not deal adequately with the question of multiple technologies within the same system. Lawrence and Lorsch deal with organizational environments instead of technology, yet the concept of environment is handled only in very general terms.

Further, most organizational research has been done in industrial firms. This suggests a need for empirical ventures into private-public sector complexes where planning and control techniques face more iterative settings, where multiple dependency relationships require executives to become project monitors and decision influencers instead of order givers and decision makers, and where effective linkages must be developed among diverse groups of professionals.

Overall, however, organizational behavior has made substantial recent progress, even while being an "orphan among fields." Comparative research has offered insights into organizational structure, patterns of integration, conflict management, motivation, and system effectiveness. Despite a residue of old issues and the generation of many new ones, a spirit of cautious optimism about the area seems warranted. As some authors have noted, "We feel we are as confused as ever. But we think we are confused on a higher level and about more important things."

SELECTED BIBLIOGRAPHY

This article has emphasized the impact of technology and environment as major determinants or organizational design. For additional detail regarding the "technological imperative," see Robert Blauner's *Alienation and Freedom* (University of Chicago Press, 1964), two books by Joan Woodward–*Industrial Organization: Theory and Practice* (Oxford University, 1965) and *Industrial Organization: Behavior and Control* (Oxford University, 1970), Charles Perrow's *Organizational Analysis* (Wadsworth, Belmont, California, 1970), and Karl Magnusen's *Technology and Organizational Differentiation: A Field Study of Manufacturing Corporations* (unpublished doctoral dissertation, University of Wisconsin-Madison, 1970). For an extended discussion of the "environmental imperative," see Paul Lawrence and Jay Lorsch's *Organization and Environment* (Harvard University, 1967) and their subsequent *Studies in Organization Design* (Irwin-Dorsey, Homewood, Illinois, 1970).

Bertram M. Gross

WHAT ARE YOUR ORGANIZATION'S OBJECTIVES?

A General-Systems Approach to Planning

There is nothing that managers and management theorists are more solidly agreed on than the vital role of objectives in the managing of organizations. The daily life of executives is full of such exhortations as:

"Let's plan where we want to go . . . ."
"You'd better clarify your goals . . . ."
"Get those fellows down (or up) there to understand what our (or their) purposes really are . . . ."

Formal definitions of management invariably give central emphasis to the formulation or attainment of objectives. Peter Drucker's (1954) idea of "managing by objectives" gave expression to a rising current in administrative theory. Any serious discussion of planning, whether by business enterprises or government agencies, deals with the objectives of an organization.

Yet there is nothing better calculated to embarrass the average executive than the direct query: "Just what are your organization's objectives?" The typical reply is incomplete or tortured, given with a feeling of obvious discomfort. The more skillful response is apt to be a glib evasion or a glittering generality.

To some extent, of course, objectives cannot be openly stated. Confidential objectives cannot be revealed to outsiders. Tacit objectives may not bear discussion among insiders. The art of bluff and deception with respect to goals is part of the art of administration.

But the biggest reason for embarrassment is the lack of a well-developed language of organizational purposefulness. Such a language may best be supplied by a general-systems model that provides the framework for "general-systems accounting," or "managerial accounting" in the sense of a truly generalist

From Bertram M. Gross, "What Are Your Organization's Objectives? A General Systems Approach to Planning," *Human Relations* 18 (Aug. 1965): 195-215. Reprinted by permission.

approach to all major dimensions of an organization. It is now possible to set forth-even if only in suggestive form—a general-systems model that provides the basis for clearly formulating the performance and structural objectives of any organization.

Let us now deal with these points separately—and conclude with some realistic observations on the strategy of planning.

THE NEED FOR A LANGUAGE OF PURPOSEFULNESS

Many managers are still too much the prisoners of outworn, single-purpose models erected by defunct economists, engineers, and public administration experts. Although they know better, they are apt to pay verbal obeisance to some single purpose: profitability in the case of the business executive, efficiency in the case of the public executive.

If profitability is not the sole objective of a business—and even the more tradition-ridden economists will usually accept other objectives in the form of constraints or instrumental purposes—just what are these other types? If efficiency is not the only objective of a government agency—and most political scientists will maintain that it cannot be—what are the other categories? No adequate answers to these questions are provided by the traditional approaches to economics, business administration, or public administration. Most treatises on planning—for which purpose formulation is indispensable—catalogue purposes by such abstract and nonsubstantive categories as short-range and long-range, instrumental and strategic (or ultimate), general and specific. One book on planning sets forth 13 dimensions whithout mentioning anything so mundane as profitability or efficiency (LeBreton & Henning, 1961). Indeed, in his initial writings on management by objectives, Drucker never came to grips with the great multiplicity of business objectives. In his more recent work Drucker (1964) deals with objectives in terms of three "result areas": product, distribution channels, and markets. But this hardly goes far enough to illuminate the complexities of purpose multiplicity.

Thus far, the most systematic approach to organizational purposes is provided by budget experts and accountants. A budget projection is a model that helps to specify the financial aspects of future performance. A balance sheet is a model that helps to specify objectives for future structure of assets and liabilities. Yet financial analysis—even when dignified by the misleading label 'managerial accounting'—deals only with a narrow slice of real-life activities. Although it provides a way of reflecting many objectives, it cannot by itself deal with the substantive activities underlying monetary data. Indeed, concentration upon budgets has led many organizations to neglect technological and other problems that cannot be expressed in budgetary terms. Overconcentration on the enlargement of balance-sheet assets has led many companies to a dangerous neglect of human and organizational assets.

The great value of financial analysis is to provide a doorway through which one can enter the whole complex domain of organizational objectives. To explore this domain, however, one needs a model capable of dealing more fully with the multiple dimensions of an organization's performance and structure. To facilitate the development of purposefulness in each of an organization's subordinate units, the model should also be applicable to internal units. To help executives to deal with the complexities of their environment, it should also be applicable to external competitors or controllers.

THE GENERAL-SYSTEMS APPROACH

As a result of the emerging work in systems analysis, it is now possible to meet these needs by developing a "general-systems model" of an organization. A general systems model is one that brings together in an ordered fashion information on all dimensions of an organization. It integrates concepts from all relevant disciplines. It can help to expand financial planning to full-bodied planning in as many dimensions as may be relevant. With it, executives may move from financial accounting to "systems accounting." It can provide the basis for "managerial accounting" in the sense of the managerial use not only of financial data (which is the way the term has been recently used) but of all ideas and data needed to appraise the state of a system and guide it towards the attainment of desirable future system states.[1]

Before outlining a general-systems model, it is important to set aside the idea that a system is necessarily something that is fully predictable or tightly controlled. This impression is created whenever anyone tries to apply to a human organization the closed or nonhuman models used by physicists and engineers. A human organization is much more complicated.

Specifically, when viewed in general-systems terms, a formal organization (whether a business enterprise or a government agency) is

1. a man-resource system in space and time,
2. open, with various transactions between it and its environment,
3. characterized by internal and external relations of conflict as well as cooperation,
4. a system for developing and using power, with varying degrees of authority and responsibility, both within the organization and in the external environment,
5. a "feedback" system, with information on results of past performance activities feeding back through multiple channels to influence future performance,
6. changing, with static concepts derived from dynamic concepts rather than serving as a preliminary to them,
7. complex, that is, containing many subsystems, being contained in larger systems, and being criss-crossed by overlapping systems,

[1] "General-systems theory" often refers to theories dealing broadly with similarities among all kinds of systems–from atoms and cells to personalities, formal organizations, and populations. In this context the term refers to a special application of general systems theory to formal organizations–an application that deals not merely with a few aspects but generally with all aspects of formal organizations.

8. loose, with many components that may be imperfectly coordinated, partially autonomous, and only partially controllable,
9. only partially knowable, with many areas of uncertainty, with "black regions" as well as "black boxes" and with many variables that cannot be clearly defined and must be described in qualitative terms, and
10. subject to considerable uncertainty with respect to current information, future environmental conditions, and the consequences of its own actions.

THE PERFORMANCE-STRUCTURE MODEL

The starting-point of modern systems analysis is the input-output concept. The flow of inputs and outputs portrays the system's performance. To apply the output concept to a formal organization, it is helpful to distinguish between two kinds of performance: producing outputs of services or goods and satisfying (or dissatisfying) various interests. To apply the input concept, a three-way breakdown is helpful: acquiring resources to be used as inputs, using inputs for investment in the system, and making efficient use of resources. In addition, we may note that organizational performance includes efforts to conform with certain behaviour codes and concepts of technical and administrative rationality.

These seven kinds of performance objective may be put together in the following proposition:

> The performance of any organization or unit thereof consists of activities to (1) satisfy the varying interests of people and groups by (2) producing outputs of services or goods, (3) making efficient use of inputs relative to outputs, (4) investing in the system, (5) acquiring resources, and (6) doing all these things, in a manner that conforms with various codes of behaviour and (7) varying conceptions of technical and administrative rationality.

In simplified form, the relations between these categories of performance may be visualized as follows:

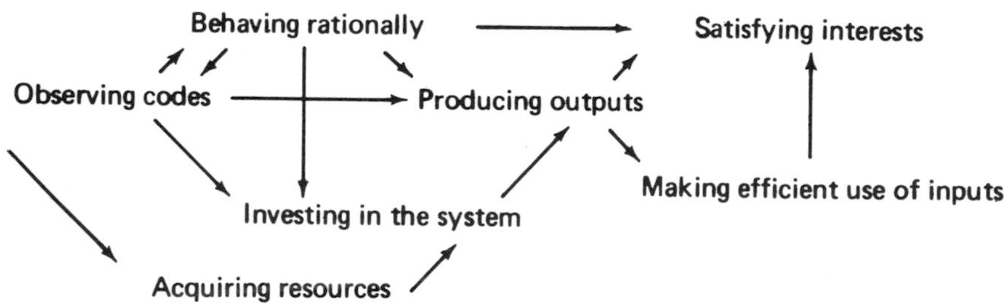

Let us now turn to system structure. The minimum elements in a machine system are certain physical components, including a "governor" (or "selector"), an "effector," a "detector," and lines of communication between them and the environment. For a formal organization these may be spelled out more specifically as subsystems in general, a central guidance subsystem, internal relations among the subsystems, and relations with the external environment. It is helpful at times to consider separately the people and the physical assets grouped together in the subsystems. It may also be helpful to give separate attention to the values held by individuals and the various subsystems.

These seven sets of structural objectives may be put together in the following proposition:

> The structure of any organization or unit thereof consists of (1) people and (2) nonhuman resources, (3) grouped together in differentiated subsystems that (4) interrelate among themselves and (5) with the external environment, (6) and are subject to various values and (7) to such central guidance as may help to provide the capacity for future performance.

In the language of matrix algebra, one can bring the two elements of system performance and system structure together into a 2 X 1 "nested" vector which may be called the "system state vector." Let *P* symbolize system performance and *S* system structure. Then the following sequence of vectors may symbolize changing system states over a period of time:

$$\begin{bmatrix} \underline{P} \\ \underline{S} \end{bmatrix}^1 \quad \begin{bmatrix} \underline{P} \\ \underline{S} \end{bmatrix}^2 \quad \begin{bmatrix} \underline{P} \\ \underline{S} \end{bmatrix}^n$$

The vector is "nested" because both the performance element and the structure element consist of seven subelements and are themselves 7 X 1 vectors. Each subelement, in turn, is a multidimensional matrix.

The performance vector, it should be noted, includes among its many components the basic elements in income statements and revenue-expenditure budgets. The structure vector includes all the assets (and claims against them) measured in a balance sheet. Indeed, the former may be regarded as a greatly enlarged performance budget, the latter a balance sheet that includes human and institutional assets as well as financial assets. The relations between the two are even closer than those between an income statement and a balance sheet. Almost any aspect of system performance will have some effect on system structure. Any important plans for future performance inevitably require significant changes in system structure. Changes in system structure, in turn, are invariably dependent upon some types of system performance. In everyday affairs, of course, executives often make the mistake of

- –planning for major improvements in performance without giving attention to the structural prerequisites, and
- –planning for major changes in structure (sometimes because of outworn or unduly abstract doctrines of formal organization) without considering their presumed connection with performance.

The skillful use of a performance-structure model may help to avoid these errors.[2]

[2] This performance-structure model represents a major adaptation of what has long been known as "structural-functional" analysis. It is more dynamic than traditional structural-functional analysis, however, since it starts with action (performance) and works back to structure as the more regularized aspect of action. Also, instead of assuming a single function such as "system maintenance," it broadens the idea of function to cover the major dimensions of performance.

The first elements in both structure and performance, let it be noted, are human: people and the satisfaction of people's interests. All the other elements and their many decisions—both financial and technological—are ways of thinking about people and their behaviour. An organization's plans for the future are always plans made by people for people—for their future behaviour and for their future relations with resources and other people. Financial and technological planners may easily lose sight of these human elements. Another virtue of general-systems analysis, therefore, is that it helps to bring together the "soft" information of human relations people with the "hard" data of accountants and engineers.

PERFORMANCE OBJECTIVES

Any one of the seven elements of system performance, as baldly stated above, may be used in a statement of "where we want to go" or as a criterion of "doing an effective job." But none of them is meaningful unless broken down into its subelements. When this is done, indeed, the basic subelements may be rearranged in many ways. There is no magic in any one ordering.

Within the present space limits I shall merely touch upon some of the major dimensions of each element and subelement. Additional details are available in *The Managing of Organizations* (Gross, 1964, Pt. V. Chs. 20-29).

Some random illustrations for both an organization (an aircraft company) and a unit thereof (its personnel office) are provided in Table 1. Tables 2 and 3 provide more detailed illustrations in two areas of special complexity: output objectives and input-output objectives. In these tables "goal" refers to a specific type of subelement and "norm" to a more specific formulation of a goal. To save space, reference to the tables will not be made in the text.

1. Satisfying Interests

Although the satisfaction of human interests is the highest purpose of any organization, interest-satisfaction objectives (often referred to as *benefits, welfare, utility, value,* or *payoff*) are the most difficult to formulate.

First of all, such objectives always involve a multiplicity of parties at interest—or "interesteds." These include the members of the organization, the organization's "clientele network," and other external groups and individuals. They vary considerably in visibility and in the extent to which their interests are affected by an organization's performance.

Second, their interests are usually multiple, often hard to identify, always divergent, and sometimes sharply conflicting. In psychological terms these interests may be described in terms of the human needs for security, belonging, status, prestige, power, and self-development. Many of these needs are expressed in terms of services and goods designed to meet them and the monetary income which, in a market economy, is necessary to provide such services and goods. They may also be expressed in terms of the needs for both employment and leisure. The terms "public interest" or "national interest" are ways of referring

TABLE 1. **Performance Objectives: Some General Illustrations.**

Performance Objectives	Aircraft Company: Goals	Aircraft Company: Norms	Personnel Unit: Goals	Personnel Unit: Norms
1. *Satisfying Interests*				
(a) Members	Higher morale	Reducing labour turnover to 6%	Professional prestige	Leadership in professional organizations
(b) Clientele network	Meeting airlines' needs	5% rise in total sales	Meeting needs of line	Fewer complaints
(c) Others	Investors	Maintaining 3% yield on common stock	Serving all employees	Reducing labour turnover to 10%
2. *Producing Output*				
(a) Output mix	Adding short-range jets	End-product production schedule	New management training programme	End-product services
(b) Quantity	Increased market penetration	15% of industry sales	Greater coverage	150 "trainees" per year
(c) Quality	Safer planes	Wing improvements	Better designed courses	Better consultants
(d) Output flow	Work-flow	Detailed schedules	Work-flow	Detailed schedules
3. *Making Efficient Use of Inputs*				
(a) Profitability	Higher profits on net worth (or total assets)	20% on net worth	–	–
(b) Costs per unit	Lower engine costs	8% reduction	Total costs per trainee	$200 per week
(c) Partial input ratios	More output per man-hour	10% increase	Teacher costs	$150 per training-hour
(d) Portion of potential used	Reducing idle equipment-time	5% reduction	Full participation in training programme	No vacancies
4. *Investing in the Organization*				
(a) Hard goods	Re-equipment programme	Detailed specifications	New files	No vacancies
(b) People	Management training programme	50 trainees per year	"Retooling" of old-timers	Participation in "refresher" courses
(c) Internal units	Reorganization of personnel unit	Higher status for training section	Maintenance of existing organization	Maintaining present status for training section
(d) External relations	More support in Congress	Support by specific senators	More support from "line" executives	Support by specific executives
5. *Acquiring Resources*				
(a) Money	More equity	Selling securities	Larger budget	5% increase
(b) People	Better managers	Recruitment programme	More professional staff	Recruitment programme
(c) Goods	New machines	Procurement programme	New files	Procurement programme
6. *Observing Codes*				
(a) External codes	Obeying anti-trust laws	Competition within limits	Living within budgets	Controls on commitments
(b) Internal codes	Obeying company regs.	Control of deviations	Loyalty to unit	Social exclusiveness
7. *Behaving Rationally*				
(a) Technical rationality	Aeronautical research	Specific studies	Personnel research	Specific studies
(b) Administrative rationality	Formal reorganization	More decentralization	More "democracy"	Monthly staff meetings

TABLE 2. **Output Performance Objectives: Some Detailed Illustrations.**

Output Production Objectives	Aircraft Company: Goals	Aircraft Company: Norms	Personnel Unit: Goals	Personnel Unit: Norms
A. *Output Mix*	Continued output of long-range jets New short-range jet Parts production Research for government Advisory services for users	Detailed production schedule	Maintaining personnel records Recruitment services Classification system Job analysis and evaluation Training programme	Operating programme
B. *Output Quality*				
1. Client satisfactions	Planes:		Training programme:	
(a) Presumed results	Faster, safer flights	Specific speed and safety standards	Better managers	Subsequent performance of trainees
(b) Choices made	Popularity among passengers	Prosperity of airline customers	Popularity of programme	Backlog of applications
(c) Payments given	Rising volume of airline sales	15% of industry sales	Budgets allocated	Specific budget figures
(d) Opinions expressed	Low complaint level	Decline in pilots' complaints	Trainees' opinions	Specific statements
2. Product characteristics	Conformance with specifications	Detailed specifications	Improved curriculum	Emphasis on decision-making skills
3. Production processes	Careful testing	Specific tests	Improved teaching methods	Use of field studies
4. Input quality	Outstanding productive personnel	Acquiring best designers	Outstanding teachers	Acquiring teachers of high repute
C. *Output Quantity*				
1. Monetary value	Planes:			
(a) Total sales value	15% of industry sales	X million dollars	–	–
(b) Value added	Lower proportion of value added with more sub-contracting	$\frac{X}{3}$	–	–
(c) Value added adjusted for price changes	20% beyond 1960	$\frac{X^9}{3}$ (price deflator)	–	–
(d) Imputed value of nonmarketed output	Advisory services: Input value	Specific cost figures	Input value	Specific cost figures
2. Physical volume	Planes:		Training programme:	
(a) Tangible units	Number to be produced	Detailed production schedule		–
(b) Surrogates for intangible services	Advisory services:		–	
(i) clients	More clients	Specific figures	More trainees	Specific figures
(ii) duration	Longer periods		Longer courses	
(iii) intermediate or subsequent products	Memoranda produced		Field studies undertaken	
(iv) input value	Total costs		Total costs	

TABLE 3. **Input-Output Performance Objectives: Some Detailed Illustrations.**

Efficiency (Input-Output) Objectives	*Aircraft Company* *Goals*	*Norms*	*Personnel Unit* *Goals*	*Norms*
A. *Profitability*				
1. Unit profits	Short-range jet: higher profits with rising volume	Specific figures	–	–
2. Total profits				
Before taxes	Higher profits	10% increase	–	–
After taxes	Higher profits	12% increase		
Total profits				
3. Net worth	Lower (with replacement of debt by equity)	10% decrease	–	–
4. Total assets	Higher	10% increase	–	–
5. Sales	Lower (with higher volume of sales)	10% decrease	–	–
B. *Costs per unit*	New short-range jets: Declining total costs with rising volume	10% decline per unit over first year	Training programme: Rising costs with longer duration and higher quality	20% more per trainee
C. *Partial Input-Output Relations*				
1. Labour-output ratios	For a specific output unit:			
(a) Labour time	More output per direct man-hour	10% increase	More teacher-time per trainee	10% more per trainee
(b) Labour cost	No increase in direct costs	Same	Higher teacher fees	20% more per trainee
	Small increase in direct plus indirect labour costs	5% increase	Higher overhead costs	5% increase
(c) Output per \$1 of labour cost	Lower total value	–6%	–	–
	Lower added value	–29%	–	–
2. Capital output ratio	For specific machines: fuller use of rated capacity	Specific figures	Low-cost residential facilities	Specific figures
D. *Portion of Output Potential Used*				
1. Waste	Less scrap material		Less waste	Elimination of unnecessary paperwork
	Better utilization of scrap	Specific figures		
2. Gap between actual and potential	Fuller use of capacity	Reaching 80% in 2 shifts	Fuller use of computers (on personnel records)	Reaching 35% of capacity
	Higher fulfilment of profit potential	8% on total assets	Higher fulfilment of service potential	Specific data on quality and quantity of end-products

to the great multiplicity of interests that many people and groups throughout a society have in common. There are always conflicting views concerning the nature of "public interests."

Third, it is immensely difficult to specify the extent of satisfactions desired or attained. Satisfactions themselves are locked in the hearts and minds of the people whose interests are presumed to be satisfied. They are inextricably associated with dissatisfactions and frustration. The most we can do is use certain indirect indicators expressed in terms of the observable behaviour of the "interesteds." Two of the most immediate forms of behaviour are the choices they make (in participating in the organization or using its product) and the money they are willing to pay (in the form of consumer purchases, taxes, or dues). Other indicators are their expressed opinions (complaints or praise) and their subsequent behaviour as a presumed result of the satisfactions obtained. Such indicators with respect to clientele satisfactions provide the most important measures of output quality.

2. Producing Output

Output production objectives are much easier to formulate. They may best be expressed in terms of an "output mix" listing the types of services or goods supplied to the organization's (or unit's) clientele. For each type quality and quantity objectives may then be set.

Yet there are at least five major problems in this area. First of all, output quality has many dimensions. As already indicated, clientele satisfaction, the most important dimension of output quality, is exceedingly difficult to measure. Less direct indicators–such as product specifications, production processes, and the quality of input factors–may also be needed. The objective of higher quality often conflicts with the objective of higher quantity.

Second, although monetary aggregates are the only way of measuring total output, they must be used with considerable care. Important distinctions may be needed between the total value of output and value added, between marginal value and total or average value, between different ways of allocating value to time periods. For comparisons over time, adjustments for price changes may be needed; for international comparisons, adjustments in the value of international currencies.

Third, in the case of services and goods that are not sold (and this includes most of the intermediate output within business organizations) the only direct measure of output quantity is physical units. In most instances this means that there is no common denominator for the total quantity of different kinds of unit. All that can be done to aggregate quantity objectives is to use input costs or some administratively determined "price" (as in internal pricing systems) as an indirect quantity indicator.

Fourth, in the case of intangible services there are no physical units that can readily be identified. Here one can set objectives only in terms of such indirect indicators as the number of clients, the duration of services, certain intermediate products that are more tangible, and the volume or value of input factors.

Fifth, considerable confusion may develop between intermediate products and the end-products supplied to an organization's clientele. This readily happens with intangible end-product services that are provided on a nonsale basis to an intangible, unorganized, or reluctant clientele. More tangible intermediate products—particularly when supplied by hard-driving, ambitious units—may then receive disproportionate attention. One remedy is to formulate objectives in terms of work flow—that is, a series of intermediate outputs leading to the production of the organization's end products.

3. Making Efficient Use of Inputs

When resources available for use as inputs are perceived as scarce, an organization or unit usually becomes interested in making efficient use of inputs relative to outputs. Since there are many ways of calculating input and output and of relating the two, there are many varieties of input-output performance.

Profitability is the most useful input-output relation, since it provides a common measure of value for both input and output. Profitability measures may be used in many ways, however, depending upon whether one (1) relates profits to net worth, total assets, or sales, (2) focuses on unit profits or total profits, or (3) thinks in short- or long-range terms. Depending upon a variety of techniques for handling difficult accounting problems, they are subject to considerable statistical manipulation. They may also reflect an organization's monopoly power and its ability to obtain subsidies, as well as its efficiency. Nevertheless, in many circumstances—particularly over a long time period—profitability is the best single measure of efficiency, output quantity and quality, and interest satisfaction.

The most generally applicable efficiency objective is attaining the lowest possible total costs for a given unit of output. This cost-accounting measure is an essential instrument in attaining—even in formulating—profitability objectives. It is relevant to non-marketed products as well. In developing cost-accounting goals, however, it is essential not to neglect the quality dimensions of output. In the case of intangible services, as already indicated, the identification of the unit is extremely difficult. Where capital and material inputs are involved, it is necessary to make difficult—and sometimes arbitrary—decisions with respect to depreciation, the distinction between current and capital expenditures, and the value of withdrawals from inventories.

Partial input-output ratios are those relating some measure of input—usually either labour or capital—to some measure of total output. Such a ratio is particularly meaningful when the volume of other input factors may be presumed to remain unchanged. It will be very misleading, however, whenever there is any significant change in any other input factor—as when increased output per employee is counterbalanced, and in fact caused, by increased capital per unit of output.

Another efficiency measure is the proportion of potential actually used. This may be expressed in terms of a reduction in waste, a higher utilization of capacity (potential output), or profits in relation to potential profitability.

4. Investing in the System

In addition to producing current output, an organization must invest in its capacity for future production. Investment objectives involve the expansion, replacement, conservation, or development of assets. They are essential not only for survival, but to prevent decline or promote growth.

The most obvious investment objectives relate to hard goods and monetary reserves. The hard goods may include land, buildings, equipment and machinery, and stocks of materials. The monetary reserves may include cash, deposits, securities, receivables, and any other funds that can be drawn upon.

Less obvious, although equally important, is investment in people, subsystems, subsystem relations, external relations, and the development of values. Investment in the guidance subsystem itself—that is, in the management structure—is particularly important.

In other words, investment performance may deal directly with any element of system structure. Accordingly, the specifics of investment objectives may be presented in the subsequent discussion of system structure.

In general, however, it should be pointed out that investment objectives often mean a diversion of resources from use in current output. Thus there are often important conflicts not only among different forms of investment but between investment and output production.

5. Acquiring Resources

Neither output production nor investment is possible without resources that can be used as inputs. These must be obtained from the external environment or from within the organization. Under conditions of scarcity and competition this requires considerable effort. Thus resource-acquisition objectives usually receive high priority. Indeed, long-range planning is often oriented much more to acquiring resources than to utilizing them.

Organizations that sell their output may acquire external resources from the consumer market (through sales revenue), the capital market (through investment), and banks (through loans). Their sales, investment, and borrowing objectives are closely related to the extent of clientele satisfactions. Organizations and units that do not sell their output must depend mainly upon budgetary allocations.

In both cases monetary terms provide the most general expression of resource-mobilization objectives. But the monetary objectives are meaningful only when they reflect the specific resources to be acquired with money—people, information, facilities, goods, or organizations. In many circumstances it is also necessary to include (1) specifications for the resources desired, (2) specific terms and conditions, (3) selection methods, (4) the maintenance of supply lines, and (5) inspection of resources received.

The logical justification of an organization's "requirements" for additional resources is best provided by a set of objectives that moves back from (1) interest satisfactions and (2) output mix to (3) efficiency and (4) investment. In the budget-allocation process "acquisition logic" also requires efforts to appeal to the interests of those with most influence in the allocation decisions.

6. Observing Codes

Every organization aims at doing things in the "right" way. To some extent the "right" way is set forth in external codes–laws, regulations, moral and ethical prohibitions and prescriptions, and professional principles. It is also determined by the codes of the organization–its written and unwritten rules and rituals.

Some may prefer to think of code observance as a restraint upon efforts to attain other objectives. Nonetheless, a considerable amount of purposeful activity in organizations is involved in containing inevitable tendencies towards code deviation.

The greatest attention is usually given to internal codes. In the case of external codes that are not "internalized," the organization will often tolerate deviation. Indeed, the deception of external inspectors may itself become part of the internal code. Similarly, the deception of the organization's code-enforcement efforts may become part of the internal code of various units. These tendencies towards deviation are facilitated by the difficulty of understanding–or even keeping up with–complex regulations. They are promoted by recurring code conflicts.

These difficulties may be handled only in part by formal enforcement measures. Successful code observance also requires widespread internalization of codes and the continuing adjustment of conflicting and confusing codes.

7. Behaving Rationally

An organization or unit also aims at doing things "rationally." This means the selection of the most satisfactory means of attaining a given set of objectives–from interest satisfaction and output production down to rational behaviour itself. Thus rationality is an all-pervasive instrumental objective.

Perfect rationality is an impossible objective. The instruments of rational calculation–information, knowledge, and skill–are always imperfect. The dimensions of rational behaviour–desirability, feasibility, and consistency–are themselves frequently conflicting. The more desirable objective will frequently be less feasible, the more feasible objective less consistent with other goals, the more consistent objective less desirable.

Technical rationality involves the use of the best methods devised by science and technology. With rapid scientific and technological progress, it is constantly changing. On the one hand, the rational methods of a few years ago may be irrational today. On the other hand, new techniques are often adapted on the basis of "technological faddism" rather than truly rational choice. In either case, there are usually serious disputes among technicians, disputes that cannot be entirely settled within the confines of technical rationality.

Administrative rationality is a much broader type of rationality. It involves the use of the best methods of guiding or managing organizations. This involves the interrelated processes of planning, activating, and evaluating with respect to all significant dimensions of both performance and structure. It provides the framework for resolving technical disputes. Yet administrative rationality, although highly developed on an intuitive basis, still awaits systematic scientific formulation. Many so-called "principles" of administration neglect the major dimensions of performance, deal formalistically with structure, and ignore the relation between the two. Management theory has not yet gone far enough in encouraging managers to think and communicate explicitly in connection with such delicate subjects as the development and use of power and the management of internal and external conflict.

STRUCTURE OBJECTIVES

In thinking of system structure we should beware of images derived from the "nonhuman" structure of a building. The structure of an organization is based upon the expectations and behaviour of people and human groups. It has informal as well as formal aspects. It can never be understood (not even in its formal aspects) from an inspection of written decisions alone. It is never free from internal conflicts and inconsistencies. Unlike the frame of a building, it is always changing in many ways. Indeed, structure is merely the more stabilized aspect of activity. It consists of interrelations that provide the capacity for future performance and that can be understood only in terms of performance objectives. Some random illustrations of objectives for structural change are provided in Table 4.

1. People

The people in an organization are the first element in an organization's structure. Thus structural objectives may be formulated in terms of the types of personnel, their quality, and their quantity.

Personnel may be classified in terms of specific positions with such-and-such titles, salaries, and perquisites; abilities, knowledge, and interests; experience; educational background; health; and various personality characteristics. Other characteristics relate to age, sex, race, religion, geographical origins. Some combination of these dimensions is usually employed in objectives for recruitment, replacement, and promotion.

The formulation of quality objectives involves consideration of the place of various people within a specific subsystem. Without reference to any subsystem, however, it also involves attention to people's capacity for learning and self-development. It involves objectives for promoting the utilization of such capacity.

The number of people in an organization is one of the simplest measures of its size. Larger numbers are often sought as a prelude to obtaining other assets, as a substitute for them, or as a compensation for the lack of quality. Even with high-quality personnel and an adequate complement of non-human resources, larger numbers are often needed to supply essential reserves or the basis of major output expansion.

TABLE 4. **Structural Objectives: Some General Illustrations.**

Structural Objectives	Aircraft Company Goals	Aircraft Company Norms	Personnel Unit Goals	Personnel Unit Norms
1. *People*				
(a) Types	Fewer "blue-collars"	Specific manning tables	More professionals	Specific manning tables
(b) Quantity	No overall increase	Specific manning tables	Larger staff	4 new positions
(c) Quality	Better-educated staff	90% college graduates above supervisory level	Better educational background	All college graduates with a few PhDs
2. *Nonhuman Resources*				
(a) Physical assets	More modern plant	Specific re-equipment programme	More adequate space	5 more rooms
(b) Monetary assets	More liquid position	2 : 1 current ratio	Larger reserves	More transferable budget items
(c) Claims against assets	Higher ratio of equity to long-term debt	$10 million equity increase		
3. *Subsystems*				
(a) Units	Improved divisional structure	Stronger jet-plane divisions	Improved internal structure	Stronger training group
(b) Committees	Improved committee structure	Inter-divisional task force on new jets	Better representation on committees	Participation in jet-plane task force
4. *Subsystem Relations*				
(a) Cooperation-conflict	Settlement of inter-divisional disputes	Compromise on jet-plane design	Settlement of inter-unit disputes	Compromise on location of training division
(b) Hierarchy	Stronger central control	Fewer levels	Stronger unit position	Direct line to top manager
(c) Polyarchy	Dispersed responsibility	New clearance procedures	Dispersed responsibility	New clearance procedures
(d) Communication	Better communication among divisions	Weekly paper	Better communication with line executives	Liaison units in line divisions
5. *External Relations*				
(a) Clients and suppliers	Better distribution channels for parts	Relations with specific distributors	More support from line executives	Support by specific executives
(b) Controllers and controllees	More support in Congress	Support by specific senators	More support by budget unit	Support for 4 new positions
(c) Associates and adversaries	Limits on completion	"Understandings" on division of markets	Rivalry with budget unit	Less budget opposition to training programme funds
6. *Values*				
(a) Internal-external orientation	Public service	Safer planes	Professionalism in personnel management	Advancement of unit's interests
(b) Conformity and individualism	Initiative	Proposing of company policy by divisions	Loyalty to unit	Subordination of external interests
(c) Activism-passivity	Progress	Faster planes	Progress	All-round improvement
7. *System Management*				
(a) Higher level	More "professional" approach	Specific planning and control methods	More "human" approach	More emphasis on personnel management
(b) Lower level	More effective supervision	Participatory activation methods	More effective supervision	Better check of supervisors

2. Non-human Resources

With advancing science and technology, non-human resources become increasingly essential as instruments of human activity.

Certain natural resources—if only a piece of land—are an essential foundation of human activity. Physical facilities provide the necessary housing for human activity. Equipment and machinery, particularly when driven by electrical energy, make it possible for people to move or process things with little expenditure of human energy. Data processing machinery replaces human labour in the processing of information. Thus investment objectives must deal with the structure of these physical assets.

As indicated in the discussion of investment performance, they may also include objectives with respect to monetary assets and—where balance-sheet accounting is used—to the structure of claims against them (liabilities).

3. Subsystems

Within any organization people and non-human resources are grouped together in various subsystems. Each subsystem, in turn, is often subdivided still further. The smallest subdivision is the individual person.

Each subsystem is identifiable mainly by its role or function. The major element in role definition is the output expected from the subsystem. In larger organizations, particularly those based upon advancing technology, role differentiation tends to become increasingly specific and detailed. It also tends to undergo change—but at uneven and varying rates in response to recurring new environmental conditions, new technology, and adjustments in the quantity and quality of the organization's output mix. This means an internal restructuring of the subsystems. With growth of the organization as a whole, the subsystems change in a disproportional manner. Some expand, some decline, and some must be liquidated.

Important distinctions must be made between individuals and roles. People may come and go, while a role remains. Moreover, one person may play a number of roles—that is, "wear many hats." Some roles are substantially developed by the people who play them. Most people are substantially affected by the roles they play.

There are many kinds of subsystems. Some are hierarchically organized units; others are committees. Some are organized to perform functions peculiar to a specific organization; others provide certain kinds of services (personnel, budgeting, accounting, procurement, methods analysis, public relations) that are widely used by many organizations. Some are called "line," others "staff." Some are informal only. The most important subsystem is the management or guidance subsystem (discussed separately under 7 below).

4. Internal Relations

By itself subsystem differentiation is divisive. The system as a whole exists only to the extent that the parts are brought together in a network of internal relations.

The first element in internal relations is cooperation among and within the subsystems. This cooperation must be based upon certain commonly accepted objectives for future performance. Otherwise work flows will not mesh. A large part of this cooperation may consist of routinized, habitual expectations and activity. At the same time cooperation is always associated with conflict relations within and among subsystems. If carried too far, conflict and tension may impair—even destroy—the internal structure. Within limits they may help to invigorate it.

Hierarchic relations are an indispensable element in the cooperation-conflict nexus. These consist of superior-subordinate relations, usually confined to certain spheres of behaviour. The lines of hierarchic authority provide formal channels of internal communication and ladders for career advancement. The upper positions in a hierarchy provide valuable points for conflict settlement and important symbols of organizational unity. At the same time, the growing role differentiation in modern organizations leads inevitably towards the subdivision of hierarchic authority and the growth of multiple hierarchy (see Gross, 1964, pp. 377-9).

Hierarchy is always accompanied by polyarchy—sometimes referred to as "lateral relations." One form of polyarchy is "joint authority." Thus committee members (often representing different units) may operate together as equals rather than as superiors and subordinates. Another is "dispersed authority." In budget procedures various units negotiate and bargain with each other—at least up to the point where hierarchic authority may be brought into play.

The communication network is an all-pervasive part of internal relations. A critical role in this network is always played by the various lines of hierarchic authority. But many other multi-directional channels and media—some of them informal—are also needed.

5. External Relations

The immediate environment of any organization includes not only individuals but also various groups that may be classified as enterprises, government agencies, and various types of association. The relations between an organization and this immediate environment may be expressed in terms of the roles played by such individuals and groups:

a. *Clients and suppliers*
The clients are those who receive, or are supposed to benefit from, an organization's output. The suppliers those who supply the goods, services, information, or money acquired by the organization.

b. *Controllers and controllees*
The controllers are the external regulators or "superiors." The controllees are the organization's regulatees or "subordinates."

c. *Associates and adversaries*
The associates are partners or allies engaged in joint or cooperative undertakings. The adversaries include rivals for the same resources, competitors in producing similar outputs, and outright enemies interested in limiting or destroying the organization's performance or structure.

The same external organization often plays many—at times even all—of these roles. In so doing it will use many forms of external persuasion, pressure, or penetration.

Resistance to external influence usually involves an organization in preventive or counter measures of persuasion, pressure, or penetration. A more positive approach to external relations involves efforts to isolate, neutralize, or win over opponents and build up a farflung structure of external support through coalitions, alliances, and "deals." Such efforts may be facilitated by persuasive efforts aimed at unorganized publics.

6. Values

The individuals and subsystems in any organization are always guided by some pattern of values—that is, general attitudes towards what is desirable or undesirable and general ways of looking at the world. Some of the most important elements in this value structure may be defined in terms of the continua between:

a. Internal and external orientation
Internal orientation emphasizes the interests of members—in terms of their income, status, power, or self-development. External orientation emphasizes the interests of nonmembers; these may range from investors (owners) to clients to the society as a whole. Some organizations aim at integrating the two sets of values.

b. Conformity and individualism
In many organizations conformity is a high value—sometimes to the point of the complete subordination of individual initiative. Nevertheless, highly individualistic values may be hidden behind a façade of superficial conformism.

c. Passivity and activism
Among many members or organizations passivity is a highly cherished value. It leads to "playing it safe," "taking it easy," "following the book," and waiting for orders. Activist values, in contrast, lead to risk-taking, initiative, and innovation. Although apparently conflicting, the two are often intertwined.

Other values relate to freedom and control, authoritarianism and democracy, material and nonmaterial interests, equity and equality, impersonality and particularism, and ascription and achievement.

7. Guidance Subsystem

Some amount of coordinated action is always provided by the autonomous action—both routinized and spontaneous—of an organization's subsystems. But sufficient capacity for effective performance is not possible without the coordinating and promotional functions of a special subsystem with the responsibility for system guidance, or management. This guidance subsystem is composed of a network extending from a general directorate and top executives down through the middle and lower levels of managerial or supervisory personnel. At any level the members of this subsystem play various roles in decision making and communication with respect to the making of plans, the activating of people and groups, and the evaluating of plans made and action taken. The interrelation among these roles helps to determine the structure of the guidance subsystem.

An important aspect of management structure is the balance between centralization and decentralization. Both centralization and decentralization may be thought of in terms of the distribution of responsibility and authority by (a) vertical levels, (b) horizontal levels, and (c) geographical location. The extent of centralization or decentralization in any of these dimensions can best be specified with reference to specific roles or functions. The prerequisite for effective decentralization of some functions is the centralization of other functions. With increasing size and complexity, it usually becomes necessary to delegate greater responsibility and authority to lower levels and to field offices. This, in turn, requires the strengthening of certain planning, activating, and evaluating functions *of* the "centre," as well as various horizontal shifts in the centralization-decentralization balance *in* the centre.

Another vital aspect of management structure is its power base. This includes the resources at its disposal. It includes the support it obtains from the membership and major points of internal influence. It includes the support obtained externally–from associates, from clients and suppliers, and from controllers and controllees. Top business executives need support from their boards of directors and banks; government executives from President or Governor, legislators, and external interest groups.

Other important dimensions of management structure relate to managerial personnel and tenure. Admission to the upper ranks of management may be dependent upon a combination of such factors as sponsorship, ability, education, personality characteristics, and social origins. Some top managers seek a self-perpetuating oligarchy, with little or no provision made for inevitable replacement. Others set as major objectives the development of career and recruitment systems that make for high mobility within managerial ranks.

THE STRATEGY OF PLANNING

Planning is the process of developing commitments to some pattern of objectives.

The preceding section set forth the major categories of objectives.

Let us now turn to some of the strategic considerations involved in deriving a pattern from these categories.

1. The Selectivity Paradox

As specialists develop comprehensive ways of looking at systems, they often tend to overemphasize the role of comprehensive objectives in planning. Thus economists often give the false impression that national aggregates of income, product, investment, and consumption are the major goals in national policy-making. In the process of "selling their wares," budgeteers and accountants often give the impression that comprehensive projections of budgets, income statements, or balance sheets can define an organization's major goals. If this approach should be automatically transferred to general-systems accounting, we should then find ourselves recommending that an organization's planners should formulate comprehensive objectives for all the elements of system performance and system structure.

Yet this would be a misleading position. The essence of planning is the *selection of strategic objectives in the form of specific sequences of action to be taken by the organization.* These critical variables must be selected in terms of:

a. The major interest satisfactions that must be "promised" to obtain external and internal support.
b. Present, imminent, or foreseeable crises or emergencies. These may require "contingency plans."
c. Their decisive impact upon preceding, coordinate, or subsequent events.
d. The long-range implications of action in the present or the immediate future. These are the critical considerations with respect to the "sunk costs" of investment programmes and the immediate steps in extended production processes (such as the building of houses, ships, or aircraft).

With these strategic elements selected, many elements of performance and structure may be detailed in subsystem plans or handled on the basis of current improvisation. A passion for comprehensive detail by either the organization or its subsystems may undermine selectivity. It may easily result in a loss of perspective, in document-orientation instead of action-orientation, and in an information supply that overloads communication channels and processing capacity. It may thus lead to serious waste of resources.

But—and here is the paradox of selectivity—strategic objectives can be selected rationally *only if the planners are aware of the broad spectrum of possible objectives.* Otherwise, objectives may be set in a routinized, arbitrary, or superficial fashion. The very concept of selection implies the scanning of a broad range of possibilities.

The solution to this paradox may be found in the use of general-systems accounting to provide *a comprehensive background for the selection of strategic objectives.*

2. The Clarity-Vagueness Balance

There is no need to labour the need for clarity in the formulation of an organization's objectives. Precise formulations are necessary for delicate operations. They provide the indispensable framework for coordinating complex activity. They often have great symbolic significance.

Yet in the wide enthusiasm for "crystal-clear goals," one may easily lose sight of the need for a fruitful balance between clarity and vagueness. The following quotation is an effort to contribute to this balance through a "crystal-clear" statement on the virtues of vagueness:

> If all the points on a set of interrelated purpose chains were to be set forth with precise clarity, the result would be to destroy the subordination of one element to another which is essential to an operating purpose pattern. The proper focusing of attention on some goals for any particular moment

or period in time means that other goals must be left vague. This is even more true for different periods of time. We must be very clear about many things we aim to do today and tomorrow. It might be dangerously misleading to seek similar clarity for our long-range goals.

Apart from its role in helping provide focus, vagueness in goal formation has many positive virtues. It leaves room for others to fill in the details and even modify the general pattern; over-precise goals stifle initiative. Vagueness may make it easier to adapt to changing conditions; ultraprecision can destroy flexibility. Vagueness may make it possible to work towards many goals that can only be attained by indirection. Some of the deepest personal satisfactions from work and cooperation come as by-products of other things. If pursued too directly, they may slip through one's fingers; the happiest people in the world are never those who set out to do the things that will make them happy. There is something inhuman and terrifying about ultrapurposeful action proceeding according to blueprint and schedule. Only vagueness can restore the precious element of humanity.

Above all, vagueness is an essential part of all agreements resulting from compromise. When a dispute is resolved, some degree of ambiguity enters into the terms of settlement. Hence the wide-open language often used in the final language of statutory law. Similar ambiguities are found in most constitutions, charters, declarations of purpose, policy manifestos, and collective bargaining agreements. Certain anticipated situations are always referred to in terms that mean different things to different people, and are valuable because of, not despite, this characteristic. (Gross, 1964, p. 497.)

3. *Whose Objectives?*

Whose objectives are an organization's objectives?

The crystal-clear answers to this question point to (1) the people who wrote the charter (law or articles of incorporation) under which the organization operates, (2) the holders of formal authority over the organization (legislators or stockholders), (3) the members of the organization as a whole, (4) the organization's specialized planning people, or (5) the organization's top managers.

Yet each of these answers is incomplete. The charter-writers and the holders of formal authority can deal with only a small portion of an organization's objectives. The members, the subsystems, and the specialized planners have or propose many objectives that the organization never accepts. The managers' objectives may be accepted only in part by the rest of the organization. All of these groups have many conflicting objectives.

A better, although vaguer, answer is one that defines an organization's objectives as those widely accepted by its members. These objectives may (to some extent, they *must*) reflect the objectives of charter-writers, the holders of formal authority, and other external groups. They must represent a common area of acceptance on the part of the organization's subsystems and members, albeit within a matrix of divergent and conflicting purposes. The technical planners play a major role in helping to formulate planning decisions. The top managers make (or legitimate) the decisions and play a major role in winning their acceptance throughout the organization. Whether recognized in formal planning procedures or not, the entire management structure is involved *de facto* in the daily operation of formulating and winning commitment to objectives for future performance and structure.

4. Conflict Resolving and Creating

As already indicated, the process of organizational planning involves dealing with many conflicting objectives and with divergent or conflicting parties at interest both inside and outside an organization.

Hence planning—rather than involving nothing but the sober application of technical rationality—is an exercise in conflict management. In this exercise systematic technical calculations are exceedingly valuable as a means both of narrowing areas of conflict and of revealing possibilities for conflict resolution. Yet technical calculations are never enough. Overreliance upon them can lead to administrative irrationality.

Rational planning, in contrast, requires realistic attention to the power for and against alternative plans. It requires the resolution of conflicts through the use of power in various combinations of persuasion and pressure. It also requires the building of a power base through various methods of conflict resolution.

The most widespread mode of conflict resolution is compromise, through which some interests are sacrificed. A more creative—but more difficult—method is integration. This involves a creative readjustment of interests so that all parties may gain and none lose. In some cases, total victory may be obtained for one point of view, with consequent defeat for its opposition. To prevent defeat on some objectives, it is often necessary to tolerate deadlock or avoid an issue entirely. Any real-life planning process may be characterized as *a stream of successive compromises punctuated by frequent occasions of deadlock or avoidance and occasional victories, defeats, and integrations.* All these outcomes lead to new conflicts to be handled by the planners and managers.

Successful planning is often possible only when the key members of an organization see themselves threatened by an imminent crisis. In noncrisis conditions the subsystems tend to move in their own directions. They will most readily accept common objectives when the alternative is perceived as an onslaught of acute dissatisfactions, that is, a crisis. With crisis as the alternative, conflicts may be more quickly and effectively resolved. This is particularly relevant to subsystem resistance against plans for significant structural change.

In developing an organization's purposes, therefore, managers are frequently involved in crisis management. They try to anticipate crises around the corner. They try to respond promptly to crises that emerge. They may even try to create crises by setting high aspirations and accentuating fears of failure. These are delicate activities. For managers without a broad perspective on an organization's performance, structure, and environmental relations, they are dangerous undertakings—with much to be lost on one front as the price of victory on another. Even with such a broad perspective, they involve considerations that may not always be publicly discussed with complete frankness.

Hence a better-developed language of organizational purposefulness will not provide an outsider with a satisfactory answer when he asks a manager, "Just what are your organization's purposes?" The most it can do is help the managers themselves in the difficult and unending process of asking the question and finding workable answers.

BIBLIOGRAPHY

Drucker, Peter F. *The practice of management.* New York: Harper & Row, Publishers, 1954.

Drucker, Peter F. *Managing for results.* New York: Harper & Row, Publishers, 1964.

Gross, Bertram M. *The managing of organizations.* 2 vols. New York: Free Press, 1964.

LeBreton, Preston P. and Henning, Dale A. *Planning theory.* Englewood Cliffs, N.J.: Prentice-Hall, Inc., 1961.

Shirley Terreberry

THE EVOLUTION OF ORGANIZATIONAL ENVIRONMENTS

Darwin published *The Origin of Species by Means of Natural Selection* in 1859. Modern genetics has vastly altered our understanding of the variance upon which natural selection operates. But there has been no conceptual breakthrough in understanding *environmental* evolution which, alone, shapes the direction of change. Even today most theorists of change still focus on internal interdependencies of systems–biological, psychological, or social–although the external environments of these systems are changing more rapidly than ever before.

From Shirley Terreberry, "The Evolution of Organizational Environments," *Administrative Science Quarterly,* 1968, *12,* 590-613.

INTRODUCTION

Von Bertalanffy was the first to reveal fully the importance of a system being open or closed to the environment in distinguishing living from inanimate systems.[1] Although von Bertalanffy's formulation makes it possible to deal with a system's exchange processes in a new perspective, it does not deal at all with those processes in the environment *itself* that are among the determining conditions of exchange.

Emery and Trist have argued the need for one additional concept, "the causal texture of the environment."[2] Writing in the context of formal organizations, they offer the following general proposition:

> That a comprehensive understanding of organizational behavior requires some knowledge of each member of the following set, where L indicates some potentially lawful connection, and the suffix 1 refers to the organization and the suffix 2 to the environment:
>
> $$\begin{matrix} L_{11} & L_{12} \\ L_{21} & L_{22} \end{matrix}$$
>
> L_{11} here refers to processes within the organization—the area of internal interdependencies; L_{12} and L_{21} to exchanges between the organization and its environment—the area of transactional interdependencies, from either direction; and L_{22} to processes through which parts of the environment become related to each other—i.e., its causal texture—the area of interdependencies that belong within the environment itself.[3]

We have reproduced the above paragraph in its entirety because, in the balance of this paper, we will use Emery and Trist's symbols (i.e., L_{11}, L_{21}, L_{12}, and L_{22}) to denote intra-, input, output, and extra-system interdependencies, respectively. Our purpose in doing so is to avoid the misleading connotations of conventional terminology.

Purpose

The theses here are: (*1*) that contemporary changes in organizational environments are such as to increase the ratio of externally induced change to internally induced change; and (*2*) that *other* formal organizations are, increasingly, the important components in the environment of any focal organization. Furthermore, the evolution of environments is accompanied—among viable systems—by an increase in the system's ability to learn and to perform according to changing contingencies in its environment. An integrative framework is outlined for the concurrent analysis of an organization, its transactions with environmental units, and interdependencies among those units. Lastly, two hypotheses are presented, one about organizational *change* and the other about organizational

[1] Ludwig von Bertalanffy, General System Theory, *General Systems,* 1 (1956), 1-10.

[2] F. E. Emery and E. L. Trist, The Causal Texture of Organizational Environments, *Human Relations,* 18 (1965), 21-31.

[3] *Ibid.,* 22.

adaptability; and some problems in any empirical test of these hypotheses are discussed.[4]

Concepts of Organizational Environments

In Emery and Trist's terms, L_{22} relations (i.e., interdependencies within the environment itself) comprise the "causal texture" of the field. This causal texture of the environment is treated as a quasi-independent domain, since the environment cannot be conceptualized except with respect to some focal organization. The components of the environment are identified in terms of that system's actual and *potential* transactional interdependencies, both input (L_{21}) and output (L_{12}).

Emery and Trist postulate four "ideal types" of environment, which can be ordered according to the degree of *system connectedness* that exists among the components of the environment (L_{22}). The first of these is a "placid, randomized" environment: goods and bads are relatively unchanging in themselves and are randomly distributed (e.g., the environments of an amoeba, a human foetus, a nomadic tribe). The second is a "placid, clustered" environment: goods and bads are relatively unchanging in themselves but clustered (e.g., the environments of plants that are subjected to the cycle of seasons, of human infants, of extractive industries). The third ideal type is "disturbed-reactive" environment and constitutes a significant qualitative change over simpler types of environments: an environment characterized by similar systems in the field. The extinction of dinosaurs can be traced to the emergence of more complex environments on the biological level. Human beings, beyond infancy, live in disturbed-reactive environments in relation to one another. The theory of oligopoly in economics is a theory of this type of environment.[5]

These three types of environment have been identified and described in the literature of biology, economics, and mathematics.[6] "The fourth type, however, is new, at least to us, and is the one that for some time we have been endeavouring to identify."[7] This fourth ideal type of environment is called a "turbulent field." Dynamic processes "arise from the *field itself*" and not merely from the interactions of components; the actions of component organizations and linked

[4] I am particularly grateful to Kenneth Boulding for inspiration and to Eugene Litwak, Rosemary Sarri, and Robert Vinter for helpful criticisms. A Special Research Fellowship from the National Institutes of Health has supported my doctoral studies and, therefore, has made possible the development of this paper.

[5] The concepts of ideal types of environment, and one of the examples in this paragraph, are from Emery and Trist, *op. cit.,* 24-26.

[6] The following illustrations are taken from Emery and Trist, *ibid.:* For random-placid environment see Herbert A. Simon, *Models of Man* (New York: John Wiley, 1957), p. 137; W. Ross Ashby, *Design for a Brain* (2nd ed.; London: Chapman and Hall, 1960), Sec. 15/4; the mathematical concept of random field; and the economic concept of classical market.

For random-clustered environment see Edward C. Tolman and Egon Brunswick, The Organism and the Causal Texture of the Environment, *Psychological Review,* 42 (1935), 43-72; Ashby, *op. cit.,* sec. 15/8; and the economic concept of imperfect competition.

For disturbed-reactive environment see Ashby, *op. cit.,* sec. 7; the concept of "imbrication" from I. Chein, Personality and Typology, *Journal of Social Psychology,* 18 (1943), 89-101; and the concept of oligopoly.

[7] Emery and Trist, *op. cit.,* 24.

sets of them "are both persistent and strong enough to induce autochthonous processes in the environment."[8]

An alternate description of a turbulent field is that the accelerating rate and complexity of interactive effects exceeds the component systems' capacities for prediction and, hence, control of the compounding consequences of their actions.

Turbulence is characterized by complexity as well as rapidity of change in causal interconnections in the environment. Emery and Trist illustrate the transition from a disturbed-reactive to a turbulent-field environment for a company that had maintained a steady 65 percent of the market for its main product—a canned vegetable—over many years. At the end of World War II, the firm made an enormous investment in a new automated factory that was set up exclusively for the traditional product and technology. At the same time postwar controls on steel strip and tin were removed, so that cheaper cans were available; surplus crops were more cheaply obtained by importers; diversity increased in available products, including substitutes for the staple; the quick-freeze technology was developed; home buyers became more affluent; supermarkets emerged and placed bulk orders with small firms for retail under supermarket names. These changes in technology, international trade, and affluence of buyers gradually interacted (L_{22}) and ultimately had a pronounced effect on the company: its market dwindled rapidly. "The changed texture of the environment was not recognized by an able but traditional management until it was too late."[9]

Sociological, social psychological, and business management theorists often still treat formal organizations as closed systems. In recent years, however, this perspective seems to be changing. Etzioni asserts that interorganizational relations need intensive empirical study.[10] Blau and Scott present a rich but unconceptualized discussion of the "social context of organizational life."[11] Parsons distinguishes three distinct levels of organizational responsibility and control: technical, managerial, and institutional.[12] His categories can be construed to parallel the intraorganizational (i.e., technical or L_{11}), the interorganizational (i.e., managerial or L_{21} and L_{12}), and the extra-organizational levels of analysis (i.e., the institutional or L_{22} areas). Perhaps in the normal developmental course of a science, intrasystem analysis necessarily precedes the intersystem focus. On the other hand, increasing attention to interorganizational relations may reflect a real change in the phenomenon being studied. The first question to consider is whether there is evidence that the environments of formal organizations are evolving toward turbulent-field conditions.

[8] *Ibid.*, 26.

[9] *Ibid.*, 24.

[10] Amitai Etzioni, New Directions in the Study of Organizations and Society, *Social Research*, 27 (1960), 223-228.

[11] Peter M. Blau and Richard Scott, *Formal Organizations* (San Francisco: Chandler, 1962), pp. 194-221.

[12] Talcott Parsons, *Structure and Process in Modern Socieites* (New York: Free Press, 1960), pp. 63-64.

Evidence for Turbulence

Ohlin argues that the sheer rapidity of social change today requires greater organizational adaptability.[13] Hood points to the increasing complexity, as well as the accelerating rate of change, in organizational environments.[14] In business circles there is growing conviction that the future is unpredictable. Drucker[15] and Gardner[16] both assert that the kind and extent of present-day change precludes prediction of the future. Increasingly, the rational strategies of planned-innovation and long-range planning are being undermined by unpredictable changes. McNulty found no association between organization adaptation and the introduction of purposeful change in a study of 30 companies in fast-growing markets.[17] He suggests that built-in flexibility may be more efficient than the explicit reorganization implicit in the quasi-rational model. *Dun's Review* questions the effectiveness of long-range planning in the light of frequent failures, and suggests that error may be attributable to forecasting the future by extrapolation of a noncomparable past. The conclusion is that the rapidity and complexity of change may increasingly preclude effective long-range planning.[18] These examples clearly suggest the emergence of a change in the environment that is suggestive of turbulence.

Some writers with this open-system perspective derive implications for interorganizational relations from this changing environment. Blau and Scott argue that the success of a firm increasingly depends upon its ability to establish symbiotic relations with other organizations, in which extensive advantageous exchange takes place.[19] Lee Adler proposes "symbiotic marketing."[20] Dill found that the task environments of two Norwegian firms comprised four major sectors: *customers,* including both distributors and users; *suppliers* of materials, labor, capital, equipment, and work space; *competitors* for both markets and resources; and *regulatory groups,* including governmental agencies, unions, and interfirm associations.[21] Not only does Dill's list include many more components than are accommodated by present theories, but all components are themselves evolving into formal organizations. In his recent book, Thompson discusses "task environments," which comprise the units with which an organization has input and out-

[13] Lloyd E. Ohlin, Conformity in American Society Today, *Social Work,* 3 (1958), 63.

[14] Robert C. Hood, Business Organization as a Cross Product of Its Purposes and of Its Environment," in Mason Haire (ed.), *Organizational Theory in Industrial Practice* (New York: John Wiley, 1962), p. 73.

[15] Peter F. Drucker, The Big Power of Little Ideas, *Harvard Business Review,* 42 (May 1964), 6-8.

[16] John W. Gardner, *Self-Renewal* (New York: Harper & Row, 1963), p. 107.

[17] James E. McNulty, Organizational Change in Growing Enterprises, *Administrative Science Quarterly,* 7 (1962), 1-21.

[18] Long Range Planning and Cloudy Horizons, *Dun's Review,* 81 (Jan. 1963), 42.

[19] Blau and Scott, *op. cit.,* p. 217.

[20] Lee Adler, Symbiotic Marketing, *Harvard Business Review,* 44 (November 1966), 59-71.

[21] W. R. Dill, Environment as an Influence on Managerial Autonomy, *Administrative Science Quarterly,* 2 (1958), 409-443.

put transactions (L_{21} and L_{12}), and postulates two dimensions of such environments: homogeneous-heterogeneous, and stable-dynamic. When the task environment is *both* heterogeneous and dynamic (i.e., probably turbulent), he expects an organization's boundary-spanning units to be functionally differentiated to correspond to segments of the task environment and each to operate on a decentralized basis to monitor and plan responses to fluctuations in its sector of the task environment.[22] He does not focus on other organizations as components of the environment, but he provides a novel perspective on structural implications (L_{11}) for organizations in turbulent fields.

Selznick's work on TVA appears to be the first organizational case study to emphasize transactional interdependencies.[23] The next study was Ridgway's 1957 study of manufacturer-dealer relationships.[24] Within the following few years the study by Dill[25] and others by Levine and White,[26] Litwak and Hylton,[27] and Elling and Halebsky[28] appeared, and in recent years, the publication of such studies has accelerated.

The following are examples from two volumes of the *Administrative Science Quarterly* alone. Rubington argues that structural changes in organizations that seek to change the behavior of "prisoners, drug addicts, juvenile delinquents, parolees, alcoholics [are] . . . the result of a social movement whose own organizational history has yet to be written."[29] Rosengren reports a similar phenomenon in the mental health field whose origin he finds hard to explain: "In any event, a more symbiotic relationship has come to characterize the relations between the [mental] hospitals and other agencies, professions, and establishments in the community."[30] He ascribes changes in organizational goals and technology to this interorganizational evolution. In the field of education, Clark outlines the increasing influence of private foundations, national associations, and divisions of the federal government. He, too, is not clear as to how these changes have come about, but he traces numerous changes in the behavior of educational organizations to interorganizational influences.[31] Maniha and Perrow analyze the origins and development of a city youth commission. The agency had little reason to be formed, no goals to guide it, and was staffed by people who sought

22 James D. Thompson, *Organizations in Action* (New York: McGraw-Hill, 1967), pp. 27-28.

23 Philip Selznick, *TVA and the Grass Roots* (Berkeley: University of California, 1949).

24 V. F. Ridgway, Administration of Manufacturer-Dealer Systems, *Administrative Science Quarterly,* 2 (1957), 464-483.

25 Dill, *op. cit.*

26 Sol Levine and Paul E. White, Exchange as a Conceptual Framework for the Study of Interorganizational Relationships, *Administrative Science Quarterly,* 5 (1961), 583-601.

27 Eugene Litwak and Lydia Hylton, Interorganizational Analysis: A Hypothesis on Coordinating Agencies, *Administrative Science Quarterly,* 6 (1962), 395-420.

28 R. H. Elling and S. Halebsky, Organizational Differentiation and Support: A Conceptual Framework, *Administrative Science Quarterly,* 6 (1961), 185-209.

29 Earl Rubington, Organizational Strain and Key Roles, *Administrative Science Quarterly,* 9 (1965), 350-369.

30 William R. Rosengren, Communication, Organization, and Conduct in the Therapeutic Milieu," *Administrative Science Quarterly,* 9 (1964), 70-90.

31 Burton R. Clark, Interorganizational Patterns in Education, *Administrative Science Quarterly,* 10 (1965), 224-237.

a minimal, no-action role in the community. By virtue of its existence and broad province, however, it was seized upon as a valuable weapon by other organizations for the pursuit of their own goals. "But in this very process it became an organization with a mission of its own, in spite of itself."[32]

Since uncertainty is the dominant characteristic of turbulent fields, it is not surprising that emphasis in recent literature is away from algorithmic and toward heuristic problem-solving models;[33] that optimizing models are giving way to satisficing models;[34] and that rational decision making is replaced by "disjointed incrementalism."[35] These trends reflect *not* the ignorance of the authors of earlier models, but a change in the causal texture of organizational environments and, therefore, of appropriate strategies for coping with the environment. Cyert and March state that "so long as the environment of the firm is unstable–and predictably unstable–the heart of the theory [of the firm] must be the process of short-run adaptive reactions."[36]

In summary, both the theoretical and case study literature on organizations suggests that these systems are increasingly finding themselves in environments where the complexity and rapidity of change in external interconnectedness (L_{22}) gives rise to increasingly unpredictable change in their transactional interdependencies (L_{21} and L_{12}). This seems to be good evidence for the emergence of turbulence in the environments of many formal organizations.

INTERORGANIZATIONAL ENVIRONMENT

Evidence for Increasing Dependence on Environment

Elsewhere the author has argued that Emery and Trist's concepts can be extended to *all* living systems; furthermore, that this evolutionary process gives rise to conditions–biological, psychological, and social–in which the rate of evolution of environments exceeds the rate of evolution of component systems.[37]

In the short run, the openness of a living system to its environment enables it to take in ingredients from the environment for conversion into energy or information that allows it to maintain a steady state and, hence, to violate the dismal second law of thermodynamics (i.e., of entropy). In the long run, "the characteristic of living systems which most clearly distinguishes them from the nonliving is their property of progressing by the process which is called evolution

32 John Maniha and Charles Perrow, The Reluctant Organization and the Aggressive Environment, *Administrative Science Quarterly*, 10 (1965), 238-257.

33 Donald W. Taylor, "Decision Making and Problem Solving," in James G. March (ed.), *Handbook of Organizations* (Chicago: Rand McNally, 1965), pp. 48-82.

34 James G. March and Herbert A. Simon, *Organizations* (New York: John Wiley, 1958), pp. 140-141.

35 David Braybrooke and C. E. Lindblom, *A Strategy of Decision* (Glencoe: The Free Press, 1963), especially ch. 3, 5.

36 Richard M. Cyert and James G. March, *A Behavioral Theory of the Firm* (Englewood Cliffs, N.J.: Prentice-Hall, 1963), p. 100.

37 Shirley Terreberry, "The Evolution of Environments" (mimeographed course paper, 1967), pp. 1-37.

from less to more complex states of organization."[38] It then follows that to the extent that the environment of some living system X is comprised *of other living systems,* the environment of X is *itself* evolving from less to more complex states of organization. A major corollary is that the evolution of environments is characterized by an increase in the ratio of externally induced change over internally induced change in a system's transactional interdependencies (L_{21} and L_{12}).

For illustration, let us assume that at some given time, each system in some set of interdependent systems is equally likely to experience an internal (L_{11}) change that is functional for survival (i.e., improves its L_{21} or L_{12} transactions). The greater the number of other systems in that set, the greater the probability that some system other than X will experience that change. Since we posit interdependence among members of the set, X's viability over time depends upon X's capacity (L_{11}) for adaptation to environmentally induced (L_{22}) changes in its transactive position, or else upon control over these external relations.

In the case of formal organizations, disturbed-reactive or oligopolistic environments require some form of accommodation between like but competitive organizations whose fates are negatively correlated to some degree. A change in the transactional position of one system in an oligopolistic set, whether for better or worse, automatically affects the transactional position of all other members of the set, and in the opposite direction (i.e., for worse or better, as the case may be).[39] On the other hand, turbulent environments require relationships between dissimilar organizations whose fates are independent or, perhaps, positively correlated.[40] A testable hypothesis that derives from the formal argument is that the evolution of environments is accompanied, in viable systems, by an increase in ability to learn and to perform according to changing contingencies in the environment.

The evolution of organizational environments is characterized by a change in the important constituents of the environment. The earliest formal organizations to appear in the United States (e.g., in agriculture, retail trade, construction, mining)[41] operated largely under placid-clustered conditions. Important inputs, such as natural resources and labor, as well as consumers, comprised an environment in which strategies of optimal location and distinctive competence were critical organizational responses.[42] Two important attributes of placid-clustered environments are: (1) the environment is itself *not* formally organized; and (2) transactions are largely initiated and controlled by the organization (i.e., L_{12}).

Later developments, such as transport technology and derivative overlap in loss of strength gradients, and communication and automation technologies that increased economies of scale, gave rise to disturbed reactive (oligopolistic) conditions in which similar formal organizations become the important actors in an

38 J. W. S. Pringle, On the Parallel Between Learning and Evolution, *General Systems,* 1 (1956), 90.

39 Assuming a nonexpanding economy, in the ideal instance.

40 Emery and Trist argue that fates, here, are positively correlated. This writer agrees if an expanding economy is assumed.

41 Arthur L. Stinchcombe, "Social Structure and Organizations," in March (ed.), *op. cit.,* p. 156.

42 Emery and Trist, *op. cit.,* 29.

organization's field. They are responsive to its acts (L_{12}) *and* it must be responsive to theirs (L_{21}). The critical organizational response now involves complex operations, requiring sequential choices based on the calculated actions of others, and counteractions.[43]

When the environment becomes turbulent, however, its constituents are a multitude of other formal organizations. Increasingly, an organization's markets consist of other organizations; suppliers of material, labor, and capital are increasingly organized, and regulatory groups are more numerous and powerful. The critical response of organizations under these conditions will be discussed later. It should be noted that *real* environments are often mixtures of these ideal types.

The evolution from placid-clustered environments to turbulent environments[44] can be summarized as a process in which formal organizations evolve: (*1*) *from* the status of systems within environments not formally organized; (*2*) *through* intermediate phases (e.g., Weberian bureaucracy); and (*3*) *to* the status of subsystems of a larger social system.

Clark Kerr traces this evolution for the university in the United States.[45] In modern industrial societies, this evolutionary process has resulted in the replacement of individuals and informal groups by organizations as *actors* in the social system. Functions that were once the sole responsibility of families and communities are increasingly allocated to formal organizations; child-rearing, work, recreation, education, health, and so on. Events which were long a matter of chance are increasingly subject to organizational control, such as population growth, business cycles, and even the weather. One wonders whether Durkheim, if he could observe the current scene, might speculate that the evolution from "mechanical solidarity" to "organic solidarity" is now occurring on the *organizational level,* where the common values of organizations in oligopolies are replaced by functional interdependencies among specialized organizations.[46]

Interorganizational Analysis

It was noted that survival in disturbed-reactive environments depends upon the ability of the organization to anticipate and counteract the behavior of similar systems. The analysis of interorganizational behavior, therefore, becomes meaningful only in these and more complex environments. The interdependence of organizations, or any kind of living systems, at less complex environmental levels is more appropriately studied by means of ecological, competitive market, or other similar models.

The only systematic conceptual approach to interorganizational analysis has been the theory of oligopoly in economics. This theory clearly addresses only disturbed-reactive environments. Many economists admit that the theory, which

[43] *Ibid.,* 25-26.

[44] The author does not agree with Emery and Trist, that *formal* (as distinct from social) organization will emerge in placid-random environments.

[45] Clark Kerr, *The Uses of the University* (New York: Harper Torchbooks, 1963).

[46] Emile Durkheim, *The Division of Labor in Society,* trans. George Simpson (Glencoe: The Free Press, 1947).

assumes maximization of profit and perfect knowledge, is increasingly at odds with empirical evidence that organizational behavior is characterized by satisficing and bounded rationality. Boulding comments that "it is surprisingly hard to make a really intelligent conflict move in the economic area simply because of the complexity of the system and the enormous importance of side effects and dynamic effects."[47] A fairly comprehensive search of the literature has revealed only four conceptual frameworks for the analysis of interorganizational relations outside the field of economics. These are briefly reviewed, particular attention being given to assumptions about organization environments, and to the utility of these assumptions in the analysis of interorganizational relations in turbulent fields.

William Evan has introduced the concept of "organization-set" after Merton's "role-set."[48] Relations between a focal organization and members of its organization-set are mediated by the role-sets of boundary personnel. "Relations" are conceived as the flow of information, products or services, and personnel.[49] Presumably, monetary, and legal, and other transactions can be accommodated in the conceptual system. In general, Evan offers a conceptual tool for identifying transactions at a given time. He makes no explicit assumptions about the nature of environmental dynamics, nor does he imply that they are changing. The relative neglect of interorganizational relations, which he finds surprising, is ascribed instead to the traditional intraorganizational focus, which derives from Weber, Taylor, and Barnard.[50] His concepts, however, go considerably beyond those of conventional organization and economic theory (e.g., comparative versus reference organizations and overlap in goals and values). If a temporal dimension were added to Evan's conceptual scheme, then, it would be a very useful tool for describing the "structural" aspects of transactional interdependencies (L_{21} and L_{12} relations) in turbulent fields.

Another approach is taken by Levine and White who focus specifically on relations among community health and welfare agencies. This local set of organizations "may be seen as a system with individual organizations or system parts varying in the kinds and frequencies of their relationships with one another."[51] The authors admit that interdependence exists among these local parts only to the extent that relevant resources are not available from *outside* the local region, which lies beyond their conceptual domain. Nor do we find here any suggestion of turbulence in these local environments. If such local sets of agencies are increasingly interdependent with other components of the local community and with organizations outside the locality, as the evidence suggests, then the utility of Levine and White's approach is both limited and shrinking.

Litwak and Hylton provide a third perspective. They too are concerned with

47 Kenneth E. Boulding, "The Economies of Human Conflict," in Elton B. McNeil (ed.), *The Nature of Human Conflict* (Englewood Cliffs, N.J.: Prentice-Hall, 1965), p. 189.

48 William M. Evan, "The Organization-Set: Toward a Theory of Interorganizational Relations," in James D. Thompson (ed.), *Approaches to Organizational Design* (Pittsburgh, Pa.: University of Pittsburgh Press, 1966), pp. 177-180.

49 *Ibid.*, pp. 175-176.

50 *Ibid.*

51 Levine and White, *op. cit.*, 586.

health and welfare organizations, but their major emphasis is on coordination.[52] The degree of interdependence among organizations is a major variable; low interdependence leads to *no* coordination and high interdependence leads to merger, therefore they deal only with conditions of moderate interdependence. The type of coordinating mechanism that emerges under conditions of moderate interdependence is hypothesized to result from the interaction of three trichotomized variables: the *number* of interdependent organizations; the degree of their *awareness* of their interdependence; and the extent of *standardization* in their transactions. The attractive feature of the Litwak and Hylton scheme is the possibility it offers of making different predictions for a great variety of environments. Their model also seems to have predictive power beyond the class of organizations to which they specifically address themselves. If environments are becoming turbulent, however, then increasingly fewer of the model's cells (a 3 x 3 x 3 space) are relevant. In the one-cell turbulent corner of their model, where a large number of organizations have low awareness of their complex and unstandardized interdependence, "There is little chance of coordination,"[53] according to Litwak and Hylton. If the level of awareness of interdependence increases, the model predicts that some process of arbitration will emerge. Thus the model anticipates the interorganizational implications of turbulent fields, but tells us little about the emerging processes that will enable organizations to adapt to turbulence.

The fourth conceptual framework available in the literature is by Thompson and McEwen.[54] They emphasize the interdependence of organizations with the larger society and discuss the consequences that this has for goal setting. "Because the setting of goals is essentially a problem of defining desired relationships between an organization and its environment, change in either requires review and perhaps alteration of goals."[55] They do not argue that such changes are more frequent today, but they do assert that reappraisal of goals is "a more constant problem in an unstable environment than in a stable one," and also "more difficult as the 'product' of the enterprise becomes less tangible."[56]

Thompson and McEwen outline four organizational strategies for dealing with the environment. One is competition; the other three are subtypes of a cooperative strategy: bargaining, co-optation, and coalition. These cooperative strategies all require direct interaction among organizations and this, they argue, increases the environment's potential control over the focal organization.[57] In bargaining, to the extent that the second party's support is necessary, that party is in a position to exercise a veto over the final choice of alternative goals, and thus takes part in the decision. The co-optation strategy makes still further inroads into the goal-setting process. From the standpoint of society, however, co-optation, by providing overlapping memberships, is an important social device

52 Litwak and Hylton, *op. cit.*

53 *Ibid.*, 417.

54 James D. Thompson and William J. McEwen, Organizational Goals and Environment, *American Sociological Review*, 23 (1958), 23-31.

55 *Ibid.*, 23.

56 *Ibid.*, 24.

57 *Ibid.*, 27.

for increasing the likelihood that organizations related to each other in complicated ways will in fact find compatible goals. Co-optation thus aids in the integration of heterogeneous parts of a complex social system. Coalition refers to a combination of two or more organizations for a common purpose and is viewed by these authors as the ultimate form of environmental conditioning of organization goals.[58]

The conceptual approaches of Levine and White and of Litwak and Hylton therefore appear to be designed for nonturbulent conditions. Indeed, it may well be that coordination *per se,* in the static sense usually implied by that term is dysfunctional for adaptation to turbulent fields. (This criticism has often been leveled at local "councils of social agencies."[59]) On the other hand, Evan's concept of organization-set seems useful for describing static aspects of interorganizational relations in either disturbed-reactive *or* turbulent-field environments. Its application in longitudinal rather than static studies might yield data on the relationship between structural aspects of transactional relations and organizational adaptability. Lastly, Thompson and McEwen make a unique contribution by distinguishing different *kinds* of interorganizational relations.

As an aside, note that Evan's extension of the role-set concept to organizations suggests still further analogies, which may be heuristically useful. A role is a set of acts prescribed for the occupant of some position. The role accrues to the position; its occupants are interchangeable. If formal organizations are treated as social actors, then one can conceive of organizations as occupants of positions in the larger social system. Each organization has one or more roles in its behavioral repertoire (these are more commonly called functions or goals). The organization occupants of these social positions, however, are also interchangeable.

INTEGRATIVE FRAMEWORK

Model

It is assumed that the foregoing arguments are valid: (*1*) that organizational environments are increasingly turbulent; (*2*) that organizations are increasingly less autonomous; and (*3*) that other formal organizations are increasingly important components of organizational environments. Some conceptual perspective is now needed, which will make it possible to view any formal organization, its transactional interdependencies, and the environment itself within a common conceptual framework. The intent of this section is to outline the beginnings of such a framework.

A formal organization is a system primarily oriented to the attainment of a

58 *Ibid.,* 25-28.

59 Examples include: Robert Morris and Ollie A. Randall, Planning and Organization of Community Services for the Elderly, *Social Work,* 10 (1965), 96-103; Frank W. Harris, A Modern Council Point of View, *Social Work,* 9 (1964), 34-41; Harold L. Wilensky and Charles N. Lebeaux, *Industrial Society and Social Welfare* (New York: Russell Sage Foundation, 1958), especially pp. 263-265.

specific goal, which constitutes an output of the system and which is an input for some other system.[60] Needless to say, the output of any living system is dependent upon input into it. Figure 1 schematically illustrates the skeletal structure of a living system. The input and output regions are partially permeable with respect to the environment, which is the region outside the system boundary. Arrows coming into a system represent input and arrows going out of a system represent output. In Figure 2, rectangles represent formal organizations and circles represent individuals and *non*formal social organizations. Figure 2 represents the statics of a system *X* and its turbulent environment. Three-dimensional illustration would be necessary to show the *dynamics* of a turbulent

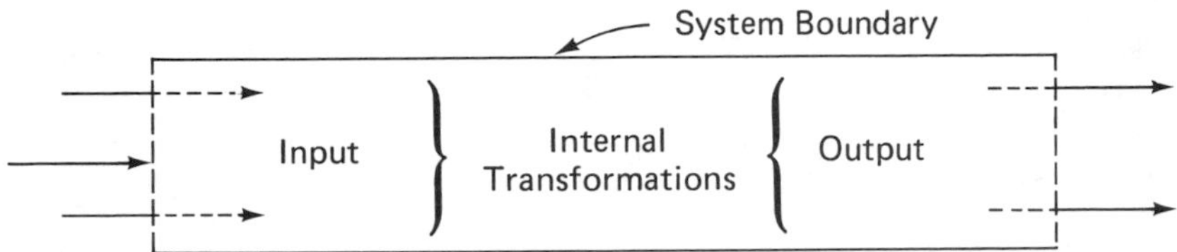

FIGURE 1. **Structure of living systems such as a formal organization**

environment schematically. Assume that a third, temporal dimension is imposed on Figure 2 and that this reveals an increasing number of elements and an increasing rate and complexity of change in their interdependencies over time. To do full justice to the concept of turbulence we should add other sets of elements even in Figure 2 above, although these are not yet linked to *X's* set. A notion that is integral to Emery and Trist's conception of turbulence is that changes outside of *X's* set, and hence difficult for *X* to predict and impossible for *X* to control, will have impact on *X's* transactional interdependencies in the future. The addition of just one link at some future time may not affect the supersystem but may constitute a system break for *X*.

This schematization shows only one-way directionality and is meant to depict energic inputs (e.g., personnel and material) and output (e.g., product). The organization provides something in exchange for the inputs it receives, of course, and this is usually informational in nature—money, most commonly. Similarly the organization receives money for its product from those systems for whom its product is an input. Nor does our framework distinguish different kinds of inputs, although the analysis of interorganizational exchange requires this kind of taxonomic device. It seems important to distinguish energic inputs and outputs from informational ones. Energic inputs include machinery, personnel, clientele in the case of service organizations, electric power, and so on. Informational inputs are not well conceptualized although there is no doubt of their increasing importance in environments which are more complex and changeable. Special

[60] Talcott Parsons, "Suggestions for a Sociological Approach to the Theory of Organizations," in Amitai Etzioni (ed.), *Complex Organizations* (New York: Holt, Rinehart, and Winston, 1962), p. 33.

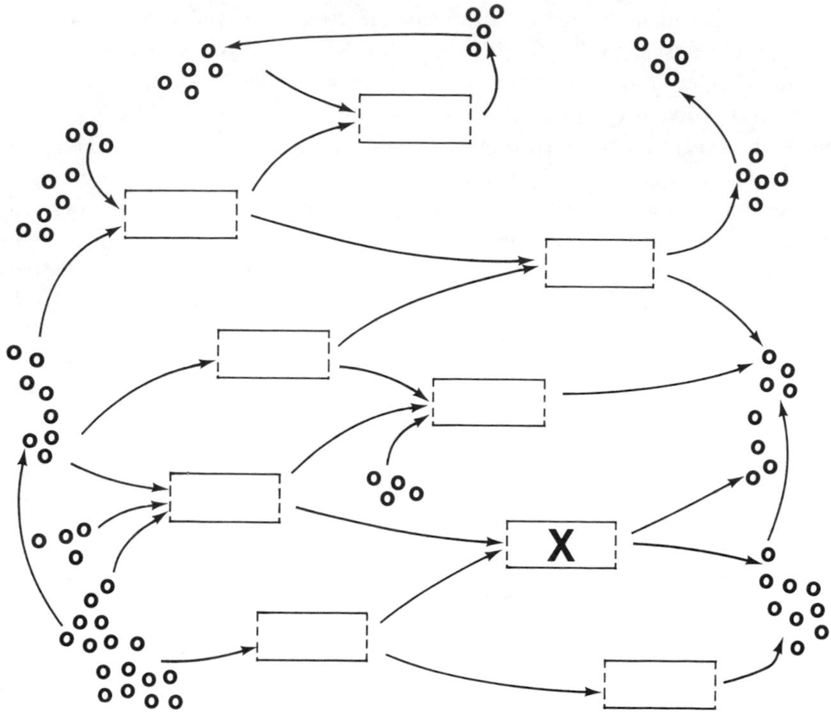

FIGURE 2. **Illustration of system X in turbulent environment**

divisions of organizations and whole firms devoted to information collecting, processing, and distributing are also rapidly proliferating (e.g., research organizations, accounting firms, the Central Intelligence Agency).

An input called "legitimacy" is popular in sociological circles but highly resistant to empirical specification. The view taken here is that legitimacy is mediated by the exchange of other resources. Thus the willingness of firm *A* to contribute capital to *X*, and of agency *B* to refer personnel to *X* and firm *C* to buy *X's* product testifies to the legitimacy of *X*. This "willingness" on the part of organizations *A, B,* and *C,* however, can best be understood in terms of informational exchange. For example, *A* provides *X* with capital on the basis of *A's* information about the market for *X's* product. Or *B* refuses to refer skilled workmen to *X* since *B* has information on *X's* discriminatory employment practices and also knows of consequences to itself from elsewhere if it is party to *X's* practice. Technology is also sometimes treated as an input to organizations. We use the term, however, to refer to the complex set of interactions among inputs which takes place in the internal region shown in Figure 1. It is technology which transforms the inputs of the system into the output of the system. Transportation and communication technologies, however, are of a uniquely different order; the former constitutes an energic and the latter an informational transcendence of space-time that enabled the evolution of the more complex environments (L_{22}) which concern us here. Automation and computer technologies are roughly equivalent (i.e., energic and informational, respectively) but on an intra-organizational (L_{11}) level.

Our attention to "legitimacy" and "technology" was tangential to our main theme, to which we now return. Our simplistic approach to an integrative framework for the study of organizations (L_{11}), their transactional interdependencies (L_{21} and L_{12}), and the connectedness within their environments (L_{22}), gives the following conceptual ingredients: (*1*) units that are mainly formal organizations, and (*2*) relationships between them that are the directed flow[61] of (*3*) energy and information. The enormous and increasing importance of informational transaction has not been matched by conceptual developments in organization theory. The importance of information is frequently cited in a general way, however, especially in the context of organizational change or innovation. Dill has made a cogent argument on the need for more attention to this dimension.[62]

The importance of communication for organizational change has been stressed by Ohlin, March and Simon, Benne, Lippitt, and others.[63] Diversity of informational input has been used to explain the creativity of individuals as well as of social systems.[64] The importance of boundary positions as primary sources of innovative inputs from the environment has been stressed by March and Simon[65] and by Kahn *et al.*[66] James Miller hypothesizes that up to a maximum, which no living system has yet reached, the more energy a system devotes to information processing (as opposed to productive and maintenance activity), the more likely the system is to survive.[67]

Evolution on the biological level is accompanied by improvement in the ability of systems to discover and perform according to contingencies in their environments. The random walk which suffices in a placid-randomized environment must be replaced by stochastic processes under placid-clustered conditions, and by cybernetic processes in disturbed-reactive fields. Among biological/psychological systems, only man appears to have the capacity for the purposeful behavior that may permit adaptation to or control of turbulent environments.

[61] Dorwin Cartwright, "The Potential Contribution of Graph Theory to Organization Theory," in Mason Haire (ed.), *Modern Organization Theory* (New York: John Wiley, 1959), pp. 254-271.

[62] William R. Dill, "The Impact of Environment in Organizational Development," in Sidney Mailick and Edward H. Van Ness (eds.), *Concepts and Issues in Administrative Behavior* (Englewood Cliffs, N.J.: Prentice-Hall, 1962), pp. 94-109.

[63] Ohlin, *op. cit.*, 63; March and Simon, *op. cit.*, pp. 173-183; Kenneth D. Benne, "Deliberate Changing as the Facilitation of Growth," in Warren G. Bennis *et al.* (eds.), *The Planning of Change* (New York: Holt, Rinehart, and Winston, 1962), p. 232; Ronald Lippitt, *The Dynamics of Planned Change* (New York: Harcourt, Brace, and World, 1958), p. 52.

[64] For example: Floyd H. Allport, *Theories of Perception and the Concept of Structure* (New York: John Wiley, 1955), p. 76; William F. Ogburn and Meyer F. Nimkoff, *Sociology* (4th ed.; Boston: Houghton Mifflin, 1964), pp. 662-670.

[65] March and Simon, *op. cit.*, pp. 165-166, 189.

[66] Robert L. Kahn *et al.*, *Organizational Stress* (New York: John Wiley, 1964), pp. 101-126.

[67] James G. Miller, Toward a General Theory for the Behavioral Sciences, *The American Psychologist*, 10 (1955), 530.

There is some question, of course, as to whether man actually *has* the capacity to cope with the turbulence that he has introduced into the environment.

Analogous concepts are equally applicable to the evolution of social systems in general and to formal organizations in particular. The capacity of *any* system for adapting to changing contingencies in its environment is inversely related to its dependence upon instinct, habit, or tradition. Adaptability exists, by definition, to the extent that a system (L_{11}) can survive externally induced (L_{22}) change in its transactional interdependencies (L_{21} and L_{12}); therefore viability equals adaptability.

Hypotheses

Hypothesis 1. Organizational change is largely externally induced.

Any particular change may be adaptive or maladaptive, and it may be one of these in the short run and the other in the long run. There is *no* systematic empirical evidence on the relative influence of internal versus environmental antecedents to organizational change. The empirical task here is to identify organizational changes, and the internal or external origins of each change.

It is crucial to distinguish change on the organizational level from the multitude of changes that may occur in or among subsystems, only some of which give rise to change on the system level. Many social psychologists, for example, study change in individuals and groups *within* organizations, but with no reference to variables of organizational level. Likert's book is one noteworthy exception.[68] The important point is that change on the organizational level is analytically distinct from change on other levels.

Organizational change means any change in the kind or quantity of output. Ideally, output is treated as a function of inputs and of transfer functions (i.e., intraorganizational change is inferred from change in input-output relations). Haberstroth illustrates the use of these general system concepts in the organization context.[69] An excellent discussion of the efficiency and effectiveness of organizations, in an open-systems framework, is given in Katz and Kahn.[70]

However, the input-output functions in diversified industries and the outputs of many service organizations are resistant to objective specification and measurement. An empirical test of this hypothesis, with presently available tools, may have to settle for some set of input and internal change that seems to be reasonably antecedent to output change.

The identification of the origin of change is also beset by difficulties. An input change may indeed have external antecedents, but external events may also be responses to some prior internal change in the focal organization. And internal change may be internally generated, but it may also be the result of an informational input from external sources. Novel informational inputs, as well as novel

68 Rensis Likert, *New Patterns of Management* (New York: McGraw-Hill, 1961).

69 Chadwick J. Haberstroth, "Organization Design and Systems Analysis," in March (ed.), *op. cit.*, pp. 1171-1211.

70 Daniel Katz and Robert L. Kahn, *The Social Psychology of Organizations* (New York: John Wiley, 1966), especially pp. 149-170.

communication channels, often derive from change in personnel inputs. Increasingly, organizations seek personnel who bring specialized information rather than "manpower" to the organization. The presence of first, second, and higher order causation poses a problem for any empirical test of this hypothesis.

Hypothesis 2. System adaptability (e.g., organizational) is a function of ability to learn and to perform according to changing environmental contingencies.

Adaptability exists, by definition, to the extent that a system can survive externally induced change in its transactional interdependencies in the long run. Diversity in a system's input (L_{21}) and output (L_{12}) interdependencies will increase adaptability. The recent and rapid diversification in major industries illustrates this strategy. Flexible structure (L_{11}, e.g., decentralized decision making) will facilitate adaptation. Beyond this, however, adaptability would seem to be largely a function of a system's perceptual and information-processing capacities.[71] The following variables appear crucial: (1) *advance information* of impending externally induced (L_{22}) change in L_{21} or L_{12} transactions; (2) *active search* for, and activation of, more advantageous input and output transactions; and (3) *available memory store* (L_{11}) of interchangeable input and output components in the environment.

Advance information and active search might be empirically handled with Evan's concept of the role-sets of boundary personnel, along with notions of channel efficiency. For example, overlapping memberships (e.g., on boards) would constitute a particularly efficient channel. Likewise, direct communication between members of separate organizations, while less effective than overlapping memberships, would be a more efficient channel between agencies *A* and *B* than instances where their messages must be mediated by a third agency, *C*. Efficiency of interorganizational communication channels should be positively associated with access to advance information, and be facilitative of search, for example. The members of an organization's informational set may become increasingly differentiated from its energic set. Communication channels to research and marketing firms, universities, governmental agencies and other important information producing and distributing agencies would be expected to increase long-run viability. The third variable, memory store, is probably a function of the efficiency of past and present informational channels, but it involves internal (L_{11}) information processing as well.

Lastly, *any* internal change that improves an organization's transactional advantage (e.g., improved technology) will also be conducive to adaptability. Since organizational innovation is more often imitation than invention,[72] these changes are usually also the product of informational input and can be handled within the same integrative framework.

[71] Igor Ansoff speaks of the "wide-open windows of perception" required of tomorrow's firms, and offers a perspective on the future that is fully compatible with that presented here; see The Firm of the Future, *Harvard Business Review*, 43 (September 1965), 162.

[72] Theodore Levitt, Innovative Imitation, *Harvard Business Review*, 44 (September 1966), 63-70.

SUMMARY

The lag between evolution in the real world and evolution in theorists' ability to comprehend it is vast, but hopefully shrinking. It was only a little over one hundred years ago that Darwin identified natural selection as the mechanism of evolutionary process. Despite Darwin's enduring insight, theorists of change, including biologists, have continued to focus largely on internal aspects of systems.

It is our thesis that the selective advantage of one intra- or inter-organizational configuration over another cannot be assessed apart from an understanding of the dynamics of the environment itself. It is the environment which exerts selective pressure. "Survival of the fittest" is a function of the fitness of the environment. The dinosaurs *were* impressive creatures, in their day.

William G. Scott

ORGANIZATION THEORY: A REASSESSMENT

This author's first organization theory paper (33), which appeared in the *Academy of Management Journal* in 1961, had a certain immediate acceptance and remained remarkedly durable in the following years. One reason for the popularity of this article was the emphasis which it placed on systems theory. However, another more important reason for its continued success was that it demonstrated that systems theory was an elaboration of the management "paradigm." The term paradigm is used throughout this essay to refer to a composite of values, premises, models, and techniques in management. The paradigm represents the core of the field as it has developed through the refinement of theory, research, and practice over 75 years. The usefulness of paradigmatic analysis has been shown by Thomas S. Kuhn (19) and by Petro Georgiou (14).

Presently, systems theory provides the field of management with concepts imputed to every single important movement to appear since 1960, including organizational development, contingency theory, organization behavior, socio-technical systems, industrial dynamics, operations research, management information systems, and human resource systems. Even the venerable fields of

William G. Scott, "Organizational Theory: A Reassessment," *Academy of Management Journal,* Vol. 17, No. 2, June 1974, pp. 242-254. ©Reprinted by permission.

business policy and management principles are yielding to a systems approach. A distinction must be made between systems theory and systems analysis, however. Systems analysis provides a mathematical, computer-based technology that, like a taxicab, can take you almost anywhere without regard to ends. Systems theory, following the traditions of Ludwig von Bertalanffy, is paradigmatic in nature and embodies a world view of values, methodology, and technique (40).

The systems model now is so widely accepted that to hold its "promise is unfulfilled" brings accusations of heresy from protectors of the established management paradigm. Therefore, one cannot help admiring the courage of Peery (28), Phillips (29), and Thayer (38) in providing critical evaluations of systems theory. Communications with these scholars have convinced this writer that he should reexamine his earlier position on systems theory.

The one fact which stands out clearly, after some years of experience and with hindsight, is that in 1960 major changes in American values, politics, and resources were unanticipated by management scholars and practitioners. American industry during the 1950s had reached extraordinary levels of productivity and earnings, which were, in measure, the result of 8 years of peace and benign guidance under the Eisenhower administration. The Eisenhower years gave way to the presidency of John F. Kennedy, whose administration promised continued abundance from its devotion to instrumental rationality (15).

In 1960, Americans expected that the technological and educational trends of the previous decade would continue. In the 1950s changes in organizations were fostered by the fact that graduates of the G.I. Bill were filling the labor market, the first commercial computer was developed and marketed, Sputnik was launched, the National Defense Education Act was implemented, the national space exploration policy was announced by President Kennedy, and the Polaris Missile System was developed. Among these events, Polaris has a special place in the hearts of management theorists, partly because the PERT technique was first used in this project, but mainly because Polaris stands for something of a pinnacle of management achievement. Rational management practices combined many scientific breakthroughs and coordinated the efforts of a huge number of subcontractors, permitting the Polaris system to become operational a decade before it was originally thought possible (17, pp. 67-68).

During simpler times, the classical model of bureaucracy had served management theory and practice well. However, due to the need to respond to the military and the consumer, to the demands of national policy, and to internal imperatives, some organizations were becoming not only complex, but of gigantic size as well during the 1950s. These organizations contained highly trained people devoted to the development, financing, production, and distribution of advanced products and processes. Such organizations were theoretical anomalies —they fell outside limits of the classical model and required a new model which projected different types of organization structures and styles of management practice. The systems model seemed to fill this need, and as a result the age of systems thinking began for management in the late 1950s.

The 1960s began with a certitude that national achievement would follow trends of the previous decade, although at an accelerated pace. Many people believed that the pace would be set by an elite of enlightened politicians, managers, and technologists. This belief was fed by the typical American optimism regarding the future. While the sources of this optimism remain murky, they appear to lie in our social, political, and economic institutions; in our science and technology; in our abundance of resources; in the instrumental and pragmatic powers of our educational institutions; and in the rectitude of our cause in world affairs (16).

The author's original paper was written against this background of national events and conventional optimism. For its time (more than 10 years ago) the article was a reasonable statement of the *technical* elements of organization theory in the management paradigm. But what was its strength proved also to be its weakness, *the emphasis on the technical aspects of organization theory shrouded the values upon which the theory itself rested.* Failure to discern these values caused two related errors in the analysis: (a) ignoring the ambience in which organization theory existed, and (b) treating classical and systems theory as essentially different models of organization. Actually, the two models are not different in their ultimate values; rather, differences lie in their operational premises, nothing more.

THE CONSERVATISM OF CLASSICAL AND SYSTEMS MODELS

Classical and systems models are conservative because they belong to the dominant paradigm of management thought and practice. Rationality is the common medium shared by both models within this paradigm. Management rationality has been defined in other places as being indistinguishable from the notion of efficiency, the ratio of $E = 0/I$ (34). The purpose of management, and hence the purpose of organization theory, is to increase the value of E by adjusting the relative values of outputs over inputs.

While one can quibble about definitions and become confused by pseudohumanistic rhetoric, the major implications of this proposition must be accepted because otherwise it would not be possible to explain management's role in organizations. The role of management has been socially and legally defined as the stewardship of resources: if the stewardship function is executed successfully, the wealth of an organization is protected and increased; the welfare of the clients and constituents is improved; and the fortunes of the management are advanced.

Organization theory contributes to the science and art of the managerial process that is implicit in the concept of stewardship. An organization theory that works counter to the stewardship notion is simply inconceivable within the value framework of management thought that has developed over the last 75 years.

Values of the Conservative Models

The values of conservative theory correspond to American utilitarian beliefs that hold material *growth* to be efficacious, material *abundance* to be limitless, and *consensus* to be the natural manner of human relationships. Heilbroner discusses American optimism as rooted in the faith in economic growth, which in turn is based on a bountiful natural environment (16). Dahrendorf discusses consensus as it is woven into the fabric of management theory (9). Both the classical and systems models assume these beliefs because they are the ultimate *a priori* values of conservative organization theory.

These values are interlaced through the paradigmatic structure of contemporary management theory and practice in that organization growth creates organizational abundance, or surplus, which is used by management to buy off internal consensus from the potentially conflicting interest group segments that compete for resources in organizations (28). This aspect of the management paradigm is so fundamental that it is easily overlooked; yet it is the basic historical continuity that links contemporary theory and practice with the past. The concept of internal consensus is found as early as Charles Babbage in 1835 (2). It was reaffirmed subsequently by Frederick W. Taylor (36), mutuality of interests; Elton Mayo (25) and F. J. Roethlisberger (32), equilibrium for the maximization of efficiency and collaboration; Chester I. Barnard (3) and James G. March and Herbert A. Simon (23), inducement-contribution analysis as a form of equilibrium theory; Peter Drucker (10), twin allegiance; P. R. Lawrence and J. W. Lorsch (20), managing integration and differentiation; Douglas McGregor (26), unity of purpose; Rensis Likert (21), linking-pin mediation between individual and organization; and Chris Argyris (1), personality and organization integration.

Finally, French and Bell in their major work on organizational development ask, "Will OD be a passing fad?" They answer no, observing that "OD is partially a response to the needs of both individuals and organizations for improvement strategies that will bring individual aspirations and organization objectives together. There will always be that need" (13, p. 198). This last source, which documents to date, is clearly in the paradigmatic tradition of management. This tradition presumes that consensus is part of the natural order of values, but that it relies on science financed from organizational surpluses to achieve it.

Although these scholars represent a major segment of management thought, Taylor deserves credit for recognizing that internal consensus is the outcome of *growth*-created surplus distributed by a scientifically enlightened management as a side payment for harmony of interests. While this point lacks the clarity it once had in the management paradigm, it is still true that the level of consensus depends upon management's success in creating organizational surpluses through growth.

Thus, growth, abundance, and consensus are the paradigmatic values that control the classical and systems models. These values supply the criteria for acceptable social, economic, and technological policies. They define the nature of the problems to be solved by management theory and practice and establish the parameters of research in management and allied fields. They influence the curricula to be studied in courses of learning in management. They determine the content of communication between managers of organizations and the people served by them; and they control the expectations that people have of the managers of organizations. As such, these *a priori* values are the ruling forces of the paradigm.

Operational Premises in Classical and Systems Models

Operational premises reflect the implied governance mode of the model and provide the foundations upon which managerial techniques are built. When classical and systems models are compared, such as in Kast's and Rosenzweig's treatment of contingency theory (18, pp. 315-318), differences are drawn between their operational premises. The shorthand for categorizing these differences often is expressed in terms of autocratic or democratic modes of organizational governance.

For example, the classical model is considered to be deterministic, closed, mechanistic, inflexible, narrowly adaptable to change, and oriented toward hierarchy as the means of coordination and control. Alternatively, the systems model is considered to be probabilistic, open, organic, flexible, broadly adaptable to change, and oriented toward lateral and diagonal organizational interfaces as the source of coordination and control.

The key to understanding these differences lies in the fact that operational premises are addressed to the rational, pragmatic issue of how management can best proceed to achieve the values of growth, abundance, and consensus through the medium of organization. The classicists have one set of premises; the system theorists have another. The former believe in the minimization of interaction, viewed as autocracy in governance terms, while the latter believe in democratic governance for the maximization of interaction. However, the level of discourse concerns means rather than ends. The focus of debate is on the operational techniques used by management, not on the values sought.

THE EROSION OF OLD VALUES

The attention that management gives to operational premises results in the disappearance of *a priori* values. When we debate the relative merits of operational premises, we think we are discussing values. In reality we are doing no such thing. But why this concern with the values of growth, abundance, and consensus? They have served admirably in the past. Indeed, the belief in them has been justified.

A single nation never had such a friendly environment, such abundant resources, and such a vital, innovative people. These factors, coupled with a strong work ethic and an insatiable desire for material well-being, made growth appear as a limitless possibility. These are the factors that Heilbroner attributes to the "special circumstances" of American history (16).

American management had a large part in reinforcing these beliefs. "Faith without good works is hollow." Management supplied the good works through an enviable record of achievement. So impressive is the evidence in the form of goods and services that growth has become the basis of public and private policy for economic development, technological change, and social uplift both domestically and internationally.

Contemporary management scholars and practitioners have a vested interest in the established models. As protectors of the conservative paradigm, they defend the barricades against assaults from those who may have different values that lead to different models. The basic and advanced textbook is the primary means for the propagation of the management paradigm and its chief line of defense. The successful textbooks in management, particularly in basic courses like principles, personnel, and operation systems, do not depart at all from the paradigmatic line. But textbooks are not the basis of paradigmatic change. A book is widely adopted because professors think that it will help them teach the youth most effectively the "vocabulary and syntax" of the field (19, pp. 10, 135-142).

What politician, public administrator, or business executive in practice supports overtly to his constituents policies of economic contraction, reduction of agency services, or stabilization of sales volume and corporate earnings? How many university courses are offered in "How to Shrink a Business"? How frequently do articles appear in the professional literature about management strategies of organizational stability or decay? These things seldom happen because they reflect values that are foreign to American expectations and, thereby, are foreign to the mainstream of management thought and practice. However, lately there is some doubt—but more, there is cynicism—about these values and the management practices that achieve them.

Many factors have contributed to the erosion of old values in our society, with Watergate and the Vietnam war among the most prominent. However, there are more proximate sources of strain on the management paradigm—for example, the declining reserves of natural resources, growing resistance to environmental contamination, changes in work expectations, and crises in confidence.

Declining Reserves of Natural Resources

The Club of Rome studies of world resources are well known (27). They conclude that world resources will not sustain present levels of population growth and consumption. These studies project resource crises by 1990. Similar projections are also made by the English study, *Blueprint for Survival.* Recently the U.S. Geological Survey added the weight of its authority to the impending crises by identifying American deficiencies in its natural resource base (6).

As of this writing, America is in the midst of a shortage atmosphere that includes many basic commodities such as gasoline, oil, natural gas, lumber, and agricultural feed grains. In addition, embargoes on several commodities have been either imposed or contemplated. The present crises in these commodities may be the result of short term dislocations brought on by government economic and foreign policy; nevertheless, they have focused public attention on shortage. The consequences, although unforeseeable, may be to create a national "scarcity mentality." Shortages, coupled with inflation, could well force the American public to scale down consumption expectations.

Agriculture, energy, and mineral resources are the foundation of an industrial society. Thus, shortages of any of these can influence the state of mind of the citizens, causing a reevaluation of priorities and a shifting of values. Indeed, if consumption patterns do change, management in the basic institutions of our society will have to respond with organizational strategies that rest on nongrowth assumptions.

Resistance to Environmental Contamination

That we have gone through some significant cultural changes in our thinking about the environment is indisputable. For example, there was rejoicing during the depression on the southside of Chicago when smoke poured from the stacks of the steel mills. At that time, the smoke meant that people were at work. Now that same smoke is accepted at best as a mixed blessing. As another example, not too long ago an industrialist said, "We always believed God gave us Puget Sound to dump waste into." Such an observation now sounds as curious as a defense of the Divine Right of Kings.

It is obvious that the preservation and nonabuse of our environment is of great concern and of urgent importance. The environment is a resource, and how this resource is used depends upon present-day values. Historically, we have leaned toward exploitation of the environment, but now attitudes are moving toward conservation. If this is more than a passing trend (and who can say now?), then attitudes governing the use of those resources which are essential to the technology of society will change toward a vision of scarcity that is consistent with the conservationist mentality.

Changes in Work Expectations

Attitudes about the environment are not the only facet of value change. A theme of some persistence is that man should rediscover humanism, which in contemporary argot is translated as a quest for innerpersonal and interpersonal satisfaction–Consciousness III, so to speak. There is no point in reviewing here the enormous amount of literature from Maslow (24) to Reich (31) pertaining to this subject, except to examine one subtlety of the modern humanistic movement as it bears on management.

Whether deservedly or not, humanism adapted to the management process has the taint of manipulation. It is difficult to imagine management using techniques like organizational development, sensitivity training, or job enrichment out of a pure "milk of human kindness." Certainly management expects the goal of rationality to be promoted if people find their work more rewarding in humanistic terms. This must be one reason for paying humanist-type change agents consulting fees. They create and apply behavioral technologies that management thinks are valuable for raising the efficiency of human resources–humanist technologies and technologists serve materialistic ends.

The difficulty of applying humanism in this manner is that personal satisfaction and organizational efficiency are compatible only at a most superficial level. The kinds of satisfaction sought for man by true humanists are nonmaterialistic. Hence, any attempt to mold humanism to the goals of organizations (as we know them) either will pervert the humanistic values or erode organizational rationality. We cannot have it both ways.

Humanism has a multitude of forms (4, 8, 12, 22, 30, 37). It suggests alternatives for inner moral growth, expanded emotional experiences, or more intense communion with God. While some aspect of humanism deals with "this" or "that" condition of man's existence (the ethical, the intellectual, the transcendental, and the emotional), humanism is not a comfortable partner with materialism. The most ardent organizational humanists, such as Argyris, Bennis, and Likert, seem to sense this but are unwilling to accept the idea that the true handmaiden of humanism is materialistic asceticism. In order to move in this nonmaterialistic direction, they must abandon the extant management paradigm.

Declining Confidences

Public opinion polls for the last six years show continuously declining faith in the time-honored institutions and their representatives in American society. Currently, the process of deterioration has reached an all-time low. It includes not only government, church, business, and labor, but also the professions which have been insulated in the past—law, medicine, and education.

The implications of and reasons for this are a matter for those such as Toynbee to address. However, along with the loss of faith in institutions, certain basic American confidences seem to be failing. There are two reasons for taking note of this: (a) old confidences are intimately related to values of the established management paradigm, and (b) old confidences are being replaced with new confidences. What effect the new confidences will have on the paradigm is indeterminate, other than that they are contributing to the destruction of the old value base. The shift from old to new confidences seems to be occurring along these dimensions:

1. Declining confidence in individuality, rising confidence in group processes
2. As a corollary, declining confidence in the individual's inherent value to a community or to an organization, and a rising confidence in the individual's dispensability
3. Declining confidence in some absolute, unassailable moral nature of man and a rising nihilism which expresses a confidence in the malleability of man and the contingency approach to organizations
4. Declining confidence in the spontaneity of behavior and a rising confidence in the efficacy of planning
5. As a corollary, declining confidence that somehow the future will yield to individual strivings and a rising confidence in the goodwill and kindly ministrations of organizational leadership to provide for the individual's future

Obviously this shifting of confidences will strain the management paradigm because the values of growth, abundance, and consensus ultimately have to do with the more conventional norms of individual welfare. Paradoxes probably will appear that cannot be resolved by traditional management wisdom as regards individual autonomy, freedom, creativity, and organizational stewardship. These changing confidences, along with dwindling resources, changing work expectations, and environmental use attitudes, are eroding the paradigmatic structure of contemporary management. A fair question to ask now is, "What might be the shape of the future?"

THE RADICAL MODEL

Paradigmatic thinking restricts us to those models and values that are already sanctioned. However, thoughtful people must explore alternatives for management that lie outside the boundaries of the paradigm if for no other reasons than:

1. There are limits to growth, and
2. Other than the restricted usefulness of utilitarian economic models, we do not understand the implications for management should the belief and the reality of growth, abundance, and consensus diminish in our world view.

But where can a discussion that will move further than the limits of conventional management thinking be introduced? As a *beginning,* it is possible to start with values that are opposite to those of the conservative models and see where they lead in terms of organizational governance and operational premises. The model may be called "radical" because it does affect vital principles.

A small disclaimer is necessary. One should not be so naive as to imagine that the radical model, whatever its final form, will be fulfilled completely any more than the conservative models have reached full realization. These models–the conservative and the radical–are analytical types that represent present, and perhaps future, directions in management theory and practice.

Values

The values of the radical model are stability or decay, scarcity, and conflict. Analysis of the interrelationships among these values has substantially different results as they are polar to the conservative models' values. Thus, organizations in mature industrial societies confronting a nongrowth future might expect that their sources of surplus may disappear. If so, one of the chief means for securing consensus will vanish or become attenuated. As a result, instead of expecting to participate in an ever-expanding largess, people will find it necessary to compete for the *relative size* of their share of fixed organizational resources. These conditions can do nothing but emphasize the conflictual nature of relationships among organizational interest groups.

The values of scarcity, stability, and conflict are alien to the traditionally optimistic American world view. Therefore, few people would disagree that associating these values with models of management is paradigmatic treason. Yet, if there is any truth in what was said previously about the erosion of old values, it may be that a vision of new values is coming into focus. Why not the values of the radical model? Perhaps, but we should not leave this subject without raising one important objection.

The form in which the radical values are presented depicts a static future.

Such a future is not foreseeable within 5, 10, or even 15 years. Organizations are in fluid, turbulent states; therefore, one would need considerable hubris to disregard the arguments of those who speak of "future shock," changing organizations, and contingency theory. Knowledgeable observers of the contemporary management scene such as Bennis and Slater (5), Kast and Rosenzweig (18), and Toffler (39) try to show a moving picture of organizations. The change and dynamism inherent therein probably is the best current representation of the organizational condition with which management must contend.

Another form of radical values is needed to account for organizational turbulence during this period of rapid change. One possibility is to represent the value structure of the radical model as movement either forward or backward along three continua:

1. Growth ⟷ Stability or decay
2. Abundance ⟷ Scarcity
3. Consensus ⟷ Conflict

In certain ways, this form of the radical model is a closer approximation to what contemporary economic models of development or stability attempt to portray for emerging nations and mature nations. Such a general framework of analysis may not be inappropriate for organizations. The difficulty with this interpretation of radical values is that it leaves management grappling with the problems of randomness, indeterminacy, and ambiguity. However, these conditions, which arise from value oscillations, may be precisely what are responsible for throwing the present management paradigm out of gear.

Operational Premises

Various government modes are implicit in the radical model. The first form of the model suggests two alternatives–federalism and totalitarianism. If we look to a future of federalism we might expect premises to emerge that will legitimatize politicization of structure and behavior, competing class interests, confrontation of interest groups, pluralism of instrumental ends, and functional decentralization. If the future holds totalitarianism for organizations, then such premises may appear to legitimatize elitism, mass homogenization, medicobehavioral technology, elaboration of control technique, and the propaganda of integration.

Traces of totalitarian and federal operational premises are found presently in organization theory. For example, the matrix structure requires the politicization of structure and behavior in order to work. The use of techniques to acquire greater power of predictability and control of process is as old as organization theory itself. This is not a surprising discovery since totalitarianism and federalism are in direct lineage from the traditional autocratic and democratic governance modes. However, the former two differ from the latter two in several crucial ways. Totalitarianism and federalism pertain to more complex organizational environments, rest upon much more advanced technology and, of course, are derived from different values.

Finding a word to label the governmental mode of the second version of the radical values is difficult because there are no equivalents in political science. Burnham (7) realized that the locus of sovereignty has shifted away from traditional forms of government and property. The result is to create a managerial society in which primary modules of government and economic management are administrative in nature. Therefore, we have to offer as a label the graceless word "managementocracy."

The indeterminate nature of the second form of the radical model is likely to cause a progressive enhancement of this equally graceless occupation for the next decade or two. Management in this period of value oscillation should take comfort governing organizations with operational premises that will legitimatize contingency, planning, group decision making, scientism, and uncertainty. Whatever premises emerge in support of these concepts and processes will be useful for management regardless of where the organization is on the value continua and in spite of the direction the organization is moving on the continua.

CONCLUSION

The changing circumstances in America relating to resources, environment, expectations, and confidences may cause significant value shifts. If these shifts occur, they will alter the management paradigm by bringing into serious question the pertinence of its cherished values—growth, abundance, consensus. With different values, like no-growth, either the operational premises of theory and practice will change or new connotations will be given to old premises. This reasoning explains the contention that the extant management paradigm is loaded with anomalies and why it is necessary to start thinking about alternative values, models, and premises.

Some will say that a chic form of pessimism has been adopted by this author in order to establish a brief in behalf of the case. True, it is currently fashionable to make gloomy predictions about the future. Therefore, if this whim was succumbed to, it was in part to provide a foil for contrasting the simple-minded optimism that is so much the essence of management theory and practice. But, beyond this, the present pessimism rests on a much more substantial foundation than mere journalistic artifice.

It is also possible, as others may argue, that technology will be able to solve the problems that man and technology combined have produced. For example, the energy crisis, caused by diminishing availability of crude petroleum, may be overcome by converting the vast Montana coal reserves into oil or by developing an economical means for hydrogen or lithium fusion.

However, these technological solutions to the energy crisis must first face environmental objections. These objections notwithstanding, the process of continuously seeking technical solutions to technical problems drops us into the Ellulian trap of *La Technique* (11). This trap threatening human dignity creates even greater dilemmas in the metaphysical domain.

The real challenge to the management paradigm lies, perhaps, between the fashionably pessimistic and the simple-minded optimistic forecasts of the shape of the future. Even if this compromise is accepted as a reasonable assessment of the future, it still means that the extant paradigm will change. No doubt this experience will be excruciating for many, because it will be the first time that such a change has occurred in the management field. The test of our maturity as scholars and practitioners will come from our ability to rethink our values, reorder our priorities, relinquish our models, and reconsider our premises.

REFERENCES

1. Argyris, Chris. "Personality and Organization Theory Revisited," *Administrative Science Quarterly,* Vol. 18 (1973), 141-167.
2. Babbage, Charles. *On the Economy of Machinery and Manufacturers* (London: Charles Knight, 1835).
3. Barnard, Chester I. *The Functions of the Executive* (Cambridge: Harvard University Press, 1938).
4. Barzun, Jacques. *The House of Intellect* (New York: Harper, 1959).
5. Bennis, Warren G., and Philip E. Slater. *Temporary Society* (New York: Harper and Row, 1968).
6. Brobst, Donald A., and Walden P. Pratt (Eds.). *United States Mineral Resources,* Geological Survey Professional Paper 820 (Washington: U.S. Government Printing Office, 1973).
7. Burnham, James. *The Managerial Revolution* (New York: John Day, 1941).
8. Cassier, Ernst. *An Essay on Man* (New York: Doubleday, 1953).
9. Dahrendorf, Ralf. *Class and Class Conflict in Industrial Society* (Stanford: Stanford University Press, 1959).
10. Drucker, P. F. *The New Society: The Anatomy of the Industrial Order* (New York: Harper, 1950).
11. Ellul, Jacques. *The Technological Society* (New York: Knopf, 1964).
12. Ellul, Jacques. *The Presence of the Kingdom* (New York: Seabury Press, 1967).
13. French, Wendell L., and Cecil H. Bell, Jr. *Organization Development* (Englewood Cliffs: Prentice-Hall, 1973).
14. Georgiou, Petro. "The Goal Paradigm and Notes Toward a Counter Paradigm," *Administrative Science Quarterly,* Vol. 18 (1973), 291-310.
15. Halberstam, David. *The Best and the Brightest* (New York: Random House, 1972).
16. Heilbroner, Robert L. *The Future as History* (New York: Harper, 1959).
17. Kahn, Herman, and Anthony J. Wiener. *The Year 2000* (New York: Macmillan, 1967).
18. Kast, Fremont E., and James E. Rosenzweig. *Contingency Views of Organization and Management* (Chicago: Science Research Associates, 1973).
19. Kuhn, Thomas S. *The Structure of Scientific Revolutions* (Chicago: University of Chicago Press, 1962).
20. Lawrence, P. R., and J. W. Lorsch. *Organization and Environment: Managing Differentiation and Integration* (Boston: Division of Research, Harvard Business School, 1967).
21. Likert, Rensis. *New Patterns of Management* (New York: McGraw-Hill, 1961).

22. Lubac, Henri de. *The Drama of Atheistic Humanism* (New York: World, 1963).
23. March, James G., and Herbert A. Simon. *Organizations* (New York: Wiley, 1958).
24. Maslow, Abraham. *Motivation and Personality* (New York: Harper and Row, 1964).
25. Mayo, Elton. *The Human Problems of an Industrial Civilization* (Boston: Graduate School of Business Administration, Harvard University, 1933).
26. McGregor, Douglas. *The Human Side of Enterprise* (New York: McGraw-Hill, 1960).
27. Meadows, Donella H., Dennis L. Meadows, Jorgen Randers, and William W. Behrens, III. *The Limits to Growth* (New York: Universe Books, 1972).
28. Peery, Newman S., Jr. "General Systems Theory: An Inquiry Into Its Social Philosophy," *Academy of Management Journal,* Vol. 15 (1972), 495-510.
29. Phillips, D. C. "The Methodological Basis of Systems Theory," *Academy of Management Journal,* Vol. 15 (1972), 469-477.
30. Rawls, John. *A Theory of Justice* (Cambridge: Harvard University Press, 1971).
31. Reich, Charles A. *The Greening of America* (New York: Random House, 1970).
32. Roethlisberger, F. J. *Management and Morale* (Cambridge: Harvard University Press, 1956).
33. Scott, William G. "Organization Theory: An Overview and an Appraisal," *Academy of Management Journal,* Vol. 4 (1961), 7-26.
34. Scott, William G., and Terence R. Mitchell. *Organization Theory: A Structural and Behavioral Analysis,* rev. ed. (Homewood: Irwin-Dorsey, 1972).
35. Sutton, Francis X., Seymour E. Harris, Carl Kaysen, and James Tobin. *The American Business Creed* (Cambridge: Harvard University Press, 1956).
36. Taylor, Frederick W. *Shop Management* (New York: Harper, 1911).
37. Teilhard de Chardin, Pierre. *The Phenomenon of Man* (New York: Harper and Row, 1961).
38. Thayer, Frederick. "General System(s) Theory: The Promise that Could Not be Kept," *Academy of Management Journal,* Vol. 15 (1972), 481-493.
39. Toffler, Alvin. *Future Shock* (New York: Random House, 1970).
40. Von Bertalanffy, Ludwig. *Problems of Life* (London: Watts, 1952).

chapter **9**

Unanticipated Consequences and Dysfunctions in Formal Organizations

To be successful, organizations must somehow elicit from their participants a commitment to the organization's goals. Methods of evoking commitment range from extreme coercion to laissez-faire. Almost every strategy has worked well in some situations, adequately in many, and not at all in others. Generally success (functional outcomes) is mixed with dysfunctional consequences, those which run counter to organizational objectives.

FUNCTIONAL ANALYSIS AND UNANTICIPATED CONSEQUENCES

Many sociologists have classified consequences in another way, following Merton's distinction between manifest and latent consequences (Loomis and Loomis, 1965). Manifest outcomes are intended and recognized by participants in the system, while latent consequences are unintended and unrecognized.[1] Many organizational problems can be described as latent consequences of actions taken to produce functional outcomes. The division of labor is a classic example. As jobs have been broken down into small operations, the nature of work has changed. Many people have argued that, while productivity has increased, the commitment, self-esteem, and mental health of workers have been damaged.[2]

Most organizations attempt to achieve their goals not only by the division of labor but also by the establishment of rules, procedures, hierarchies, and other formal mechanisms. These steps generally contribute to organizational success as measured by certain criteria. At the same time, there generally are unanticipated consequences which are dysfunctional from the organization's viewpoint.[3]

Many of the dysfunctional consequences seem to result from attempts by participants to protect themselves or to satisfy their individual needs. Mathewson (1931), in a book written before the publication of the Hawthorne studies, dis-

1. For our purposes latent and unanticipated consequences are used synonymously.

2. The issue of personality vs. the organization is discussed further by Argyris and Strauss in this section.

3. It is important to specify for what system a consequence is functional or dysfunctional. For example, many outcomes which are functional for an organization may be dysfunctional for some other unit, such as society.

cussed how workers developed an informal social system to protect themselves and their group from other individuals and other groups in the organization. In addition, Mathewson showed that often supervisors' informal behavior was inconsistent with the formal goals of the organization. More recently, Orth (1963) found that graduate business students at Harvard engaged in similar restrictive behavior. The cross-cultural nature of this behavior was shown by Ryapolov's (1966) discussion of how informal relationships in the Soviet Union served to protect organizational participants from managers and planners.

These examples, in addition to the "soldiering" noted by Taylor, the behavior of the groups in the Hawthorne plant, and numerous other reported experiences, illustrate one set of latent consequences which occur in formal organizations. Planners and managers set up a formal system to coordinate effort for the achievement of organizational goals. The system does not permit the satisfaction of many participant needs. In fact, often the organization generates new needs and tensions. Lower-level participants can often best satisfy these needs through behavior which conflicts directly with the formal goals of the organization.

It is important to recall that the examples cited above included workers, supervisors, managers from different cultures, and even future organizational leaders. Not just a particular class, but people in a variety of positions respond with protective and restrictive practices under conditions of distrust and fear. Defensive responses by individuals to complex organizations are pervasive.

Unions are associated with another latent dysfunction of formal organizations for managers. Often, members of one organization will join or form another organization for protection or enhancement of their position. In this manner, unionization shares important features with the development of informal groups in organizations and serves similar purposes for lower-level participants and even management. Managers tend to stress the dysfunctional consequences of unions and overlook some of the important ways in which unions help the firm. In fact, many scholars have argued that on balance unions have more functional consequences than dysfunctional ones for many business organizations. For example, unions may serve as valuable means for conflict resolution, communication, and industrial discipline. While this topic requires another book, the parallels between the formation of unions and other responses of participants to formal organizations should be recognized.[4]

In addition to restrictive practices, the activities of informal groups, and unionization, latent dysfunctions of formal organizations may take other forms. Jasinski (1956) documented some of the latent dysfunctions of efficiency controls. He reported that people in organizations strive to do well according to the criteria by which they are evaluated. For example, if monthly productivity

4. Unions, like other formal organizations, experience their own unanticipated consequences. For example, many unions are formally structured to be democratic and to satisfy the interests of their members. However, often the union leaders develop sets of personal needs and organizational interests at variance with the needs of the union membership. As a result, the behavior of many unions runs counter to the needs of the members whom they are presumed to represent.

ratings are all-important and productivity is down toward the end of the month, individuals in the system will often turn to some of the easier jobs before attending to the more difficult ones. However, it may well be that satisfaction of the organization's best client requires immediate attention to the unattended, more difficult job. Under the existing reward systems, the individuals are rewarded for attending to the easier job and, in effect, punished for attending to the most organizationally relevant task. Maintenance, quality control, planning, and many other crucial activities may be rewarded insufficiently or not at all because they are difficult to measure. The results of misdirecting the efforts of organizational participants may be increased costs, reduced quality, unmet production schedules, and overdue orders.

Ridgway (1956) presented supporting data on the latent consequences of performance measurements. He reported that many rating systems are based on a single criterion which does not fully represent the behavior that the organization really needs from the person. Under such conditions, an individual can maximize his own benefit by performing well the tasks on which he is evaluated and failing to attend to the rest. Thus an organization may fail simply because each person is performing his job "well." Further, Ridgway noted that applying pressure to achieve certain goals, such as improved performance, may have costly side effects: tensions, conflicts, and lower morale. Short-run gains may be paid for by unanticipated outcomes apparent only later or not at all. Often, the costly outcomes are difficult to diagnose, because they are not evident.

Argyris (1964) and Ryapolov (1966) showed how certain types of evaluation procedures may result in hardly noticeable but wasteful managerial behavior. For example, Argyris noted that many managers maintained "JIC" files, collections of documents kept "Just In Case" their bosses should ask. The cost of such defensive behavior is great in many organizations. Similarly, Ryapolov noted that Soviet managers sent a multitude of formal directives as a tactic to protect themselves from the planners, who evaluated the actions of the managers more vigorously than the outcomes. These Soviet managers found it far more advantageous to document their actions than to display goal-oriented behavior. Again, attempts by organizations to coordinate the efforts of participants to reach goals often produce quite different results. The same outcomes also occur in non-profit organizations.

Rogers (1968) argued that the evaluation of students interferes with the realization of the educational goals of universities. Rather than encouraging students to generate creative and innovative ideas and research, the current allocation of rewards develops individuals who are prone to memorize, deviate little from the mainstream, and agree with the professor or other authority. By their evaluation procedures, even organizations relatively free from the short-run pressures of the market mechanism generate forces in opposition to their own goals.

No discussion of the latent dysfunctions of bureaucratic structure would be complete without mention of the work of Robert Merton (1957). He pointed out, for example, that, when organizations develop specialists for a certain job, they are implicitly training those people to ignore other ways of doing the job and to ignore changed conditions. This "trained incapacity" is one source of inflexibility in bureaucratic organizations. Another source of latent dysfunctions in organizations is the rules which bureaucracies develop to increase the reliability of responses from participants. Pressure for strict adherence to rules tends to make the rules absolute and thereby interferes with the ability of people to adapt to new situations. Devotion to rules produces results similar to what Merton called "goal displacement"; evaluation procedures or particular techniques of goal achievement become ends for the organizational participants. It is through goal displacement that bureaucratic "red tape" is generated. Organizational participants are rewarded and safe if they follow certain procedures, even though these procedures may actually conflict with organizational efficiency and success.

In a sense, a great deal of the literature in organizational behavior attempts merely to recognize, prevent, and overcome the latent dysfunctions of formal organizational procedures. Recently, the latent consequences of organizational structure have been seen to affect the actual organizational goals themselves. In other words, the way organizational resources are actually allocated in business indicates that many goals are being pursued which are, at most, only partially consistent with the assumed goal of profit maximization.

PROFIT MAXIMIZATION AS A GOAL

While an organization may have one overriding stated goal, such as profit maximization, the behavior of the people in the system cannot be accurately described or understood in terms of this one goal. Those people pursue many other goals, including status, esteem, security, power, knowledge, approval, and the means of satisfying other human wants. And, although it may be assumed that each individual and each department within an organization does attempt to maximize profit in some way, it is doubtful whether the sum of these efforts yields maximization for the total organization.

Allocation of an organization's resources is political as well as economic. In many ways, the size of a departmental budget is used as a measure of status or value.[5] For a variety of organizationally relevant and irrelevant reasons, an individual may be able to "oversell" his function to the budgeting panel beyond the best economic interest of the organization.

It may be to a manager's advantage to maximize the size of his staff or the funds available for his favorite projects, but it may not be consistent with profit maximization. For example, Galbraith (1967) has argued that the various elements within organizations achieve their own individual ends at the expense of the organization's economic objectives, seeking only enough profit to keep top management and stockholders content. If Galbraith's description is correct, organizations can hardly be described as maximizing their profits. While his

5. An advertising executive once confided his disappointment that his budget had not been increased despite general agreement about the success of his division. He had overlooked the possibility that his superiors might have allocated scarce financial resources elsewhere precisely because they recognized how much he could accomplish on a limited budget.

argument has been rejected as polemical and unscholarly by many economists, the related arguments of two other social scientists are not so easily discarded.

Cyert and March (1963) questioned the contemporary economic view of organizational decision making by attacking the economic assumptions that firms seek to maximize profits and operate with perfect knowledge. They concurred with our earlier statement that individuals have a host of personal as well as purely economic ends. Furthermore, they noted that business decision makers seek satisfactory rather than maximum profits. The level which is considered satisfactory is determined by the organization's past goals and performance and by the past performance of comparable organizations. Cyert and March argued that, in addition to seeking satisfactory profit, decision makers also attempt to avoid uncertainty. Moreover, in gathering information for making decisions, organizational participants engage in only limited search behavior often guided by factors other than rational profit maximization. For example, search behavior is stimulated by a problem or a crisis rather than an overall strategy aimed at maximum utility. Second, the search tends to be concentrated in the vicinity of the symptom and current practice. When causes are sought, efforts focus on vulnerable parts of the organization rather than on the more powerful elements. In addition, the search reflects the special training of the searchers and their hopes and expectations. Further, unresolved conflict in the organization affects communication patterns, which bias the search process. As a result, actual decisions made by organizations are not rational in the purely economic sense.[6] While space does not permit a complete summary of the Cyert and March position, it is hoped that this treatment stimulates exploration and discussion of their important argument.

Since individuals appear to pursue psychological as well as economic goals, it may be that organizations cannot maximize profit in the economic sense. The issue of social responsibility of business may be an important case in point. Concern for community problems may or may not be in the best economic interests of the organization. However, increasingly the social and moral pressures felt by organizational participants may dictate that an organization devote some of its resources to certain social problems. When individual psychological needs require organizations to behave "uneconomically," this behavior may be rationalized as having long-run public relations value but in fact may be unavoidable even if it has no economic payoff.

THE READINGS

The readings in this section challenge the classical view of organizations. For the most part, the authors are questioning whether our traditional models of hierarchical organization and bureaucracy produce viable forms of organization.

6. Perhaps the ultimate blow to the rational economic model of organizational decision making can be found in the "garbage can" model proposed by Cohen, March and Olsen (1972). These writers suggested that often it may be less appropriate to think of organizations as devising solutions to problems than to think of organizations as containing a number of solutions which their advocates are seeking to attach to problems.

The brief selection by Townsend sets the stage for much of what follows. Townsend suggests that organization charts can be useful but that their misuse, which occurs frequently, leads people to behave in ways which conflict with the real purposes of the organization. The other papers in this chapter provide a number of examples supporting Townsend's general point.

The paper by Rosenhan provides one of the most interesting accounts of how an organization's internal functioning creates conditions which are in direct conflict with achievement of its goals. At first glance the setting of Rosenhan's study, mental hospitals, may seem far removed from typical business organizations; a closer look, however, reveals some parallels. Rosenhan notes how depersonalization and stereotypic thinking prevent organizational participants from carrying out their tasks effectively. He observes how people with the most power to correct the dysfunctional processes have lost touch with the small, day-to-day events which subtly determine an organization's success.

The next three papers deal with the relationship between individuals and the organization. Many managers have learned the hard way that individuals at all organizational levels—even the lowest one—have enough power to resist and defeat unpopular rules, policies, and directives. The delightful short story by Barrett, based on a real series of incidents, shows one way in which lower-level participants can respond to organizational rules. The responses described by Barrett are benign compared to the sabotage, destruction, and violence frequently observed.

The papers by Argyris and Strauss deal with the consequences of formal organization for the psychological state of man. The issues they discuss underlie many of the controversies in the entire field. Argyris has been a leading exponent of the view that formal organizations are in conflict with the potential of man. This view is challenged by Strauss, co-author of one of the leading personnel books in the field, which stresses the human relations approach. While the Argyris-Strauss controversy may be resolved only at the metaphysical level or by a definitive answer to the nature-nurture controversy, its implications are vast. The relationship of the current structure of organizations to mental health and the possible alienation of individuals from the general social system as a result of the organization of work are vital concerns. Significant social problems—including mental illness, alcoholism, drug addiction, social unrest, and others—may in fact be partially described as latent consequences of the way that work is organized.

In the final paper Bennis examines how exogenous changes create problems for bureaucratic structures. He describes and summarizes the traditional arguments for bureaucracy and questions the viability of such organizations in modern society. In many ways Bennis's views parallel Terreberry's discussion in the previous chapter. Bennis suggests that yesterday's rigid bureaucratic organizations are poorly equipped to operate in the dynamic environments of today and tomorrow.

REFERENCES

Argyris, C. *Integrating the Individual and the Organization.* New York: John Wiley & Sons, 1964.

Cohen, M. D., March, J. G., and Olsen, J. P. "A Garbage Can Model of Organizational Choice." *Administrative Science Quarterly,* 17 (1972): 1-25.

Cyert, R. M., and March, J. G. *A Behavioral Theory of the Firm.* Englewood Cliffs, N.J.: Prentice-Hall, Inc., 1963.

Galbraith, J. K. *The New Industrial State.* Boston: Houghton-Mifflin, 1967.

Jasinski, F. J. "Use and Misuse of Efficiency Controls." *Harvard Business Review* 34, (July-Aug. 1956): 105-12.

Loomis, C. P., and Loomis, Z. K. *Modern Social Theories.* Princeton, N.J.: Van Nostrand, 1965.

Mathewson, S. B. *Restriction of Output Among Unorganized Workers.* New York: Viking Press, 1931.

Merton, R. K. *Social Theory and Social Structure.* Rev. ed. New York: Free Press, 1957.

Orth, Charles D., III, *Social Structure and Learning Climate: The First Year at the Harvard Business School.* Boston: Harvard University, 1963

Ridgway, V. F. "Dysfunctional Consequences of Performance Measurements." *Administrative Science Quarterly* 1 (1956): 240-47.

Rogers, C. "Graduate Education in Psychology: A Passionate Statement." In *Interpersonal Dynamics,* Rev. ed., edited by W. G. Bennis, E. H. Schein, F. I. Steele, and D. E. Berlew. Homewood, Ill.: Dorsey, 1968, pp. 687-703.

Ryapolov, G. "I Was a Soviet Manager." *Harvard Business Review* 44 (June-Feb. 1966): 117-25.

Robert Townsend

ORGANIZATION CHARTS: RIGOR MORTIS

They have uses: for the annual salary review; for educating investors on how the organization works and who does what.

But draw them in pencil. Never formalize, print, and circulate them. Good organizations are living bodies that grow new muscles to meet challenges. A chart demoralizes people. Nobody thinks of himself as *below* other people. And in a good company he isn't. Yet on paper there it is. If you have to circulate something, use a loose-leaf table of organization (like a magazine masthead) instead of a diagram with the people in little boxes. Use alphabetical order by name and by function wherever possible.

In the best organizations people see themselves working in a circle as if around one table. One of the positions is designated chief executive officer, because somebody has to make all those tactical decisions that enable an organization to keep working. In this circular organization, leadership passes from one to another depending on the particular task being attacked—without any hang-ups.

This is as it should be. In the hierarchical organization, it is difficult to imagine leadership anywhere but at the top of the various pyramids. And it's hard to visualize the leader of a small pyramid becoming temporarily the leader of a group of larger pyramid-leaders which includes the chief executive officer.

The traditional organization chart has one dead giveaway. Any dotted line indicates a troublemaker and/or a seriously troubled relationship. It also generally means that an unsatisfactory compromise has been worked out and the direct solution has been avoided.

D. L. Rosenhan

ON BEING SANE IN INSANE PLACES

If sanity and insanity exist, how shall we know them?

The question is neither capricious nor itself insane. However much we may be personally convinced that we can tell the normal from the abnormal, the evidence is simply not compelling. It is commonplace, for example, to read about murder trials wherein eminent psychiatrists for the defense are contradicted by equally eminent psychiatrists for the prosecution on the matter of the defendant's sanity. More generally, there are a great deal of conflicting data on the reliability, utility, and meaning of such terms as "sanity," "insanity," "mental illness," and "schizophrenia" (*1*). Finally, as early as 1934, Benedict suggested that normality and abnormality are not universal (*2*). What is viewed as normal in one culture may be seen as quite aberrant in another. Thus, notions of normality and abnormality may not be quite as accurate as people believe they are.

To raise questions regarding normality and abnormality is in no way to question the fact that some behaviors are deviant or odd. Murder is deviant. So, too, are hallucinations. Nor does raising such questions deny the existence of the personal anguish that is often associated with "mental illness." Anxiety and depression exist. Psychological suffering exists. But normality and abnormality, sanity and insanity, and the diagnoses that flow from them may be less substantive than many believe them to be.

At its heart, the question of whether the sane can be distinguished from the insane (and whether degrees of insanity can be distinguished from each other) is a simple matter: do the salient characteristics that lead to diagnoses reside in the patients themselves or in the environments and contexts in which observers find them? From Bleuler, through Kretchmer, through the formulators of the recently revised *Diagnostic and Statistical Manual* of the American Psychiatric Association, the belief has been strong that patients present symptoms, that those symptoms can be categorized, and, implicitly, that the sane are distinguishable from the insane. More recently, however, this belief has been questioned. Based in part on the theoretical and anthropological considerations, but also on philosophical, legal, and therapeutic ones, the view has grown that psychological categorization of mental illness is useless at best and downright harmful, misleading, and pejorative at worst. Psychiatric diagnoses, in this view, are in the minds of the observers and are not valid summaries of characteristics displayed by the observed (*3-5*).

Gains can be made in deciding which of these is more nearly accurate by getting normal people (that is, people who do not have, and have never suffered, symptoms of serious psychiatric disorders) admitted to psychiatric hospitals and then determining whether they were discovered to be sane and, if so, how. If the sanity of such pseudo-patients were always detected, there would be prima facie evidence that a sane individual can be distinguished from the insane context in which he is found. Normality (and presumably abnormality) is distinct enough that it can be recognized wherever it occurs, for it is carried within the person. If, on the other hand, the sanity of the pseudopatients were never discovered, serious difficulties would arise for those who support traditional modes of psychiatric diagnosis. Given that the hospital staff was not incompetent, that the pseudopatient had been behaving as sanely as he had been outside of the hospital, and that it had never been previously suggested that he belonged in a psychiatric hospital, such an unlikely outcome would support the view that psychiatric diagnosis betrays little about the patient but much about the environment in which an observer finds him.

This article describes such an experiment. Eight sane people gained secret admission to 12 different hospitals (*6*). Their diagnostic experiences constitute the data of the first part of this article; the remainder is devoted to a description of their experiences in psychiatric institutions. Too few psychiatrists and psychologists, even those who have worked in such hospitals, know what the experience is like. They rarely talk about it with former patients, perhaps because they distrust information coming from the previously insane. Those who have worked in psychiatric hospitals are likely to have adapted so thoroughly to the settings that they are insensitive to the impact of that experience. And while there have been occasional reports of researchers who submitted themselves to psychiatric hospitalization (*7*), these researchers have commonly remained in the hospitals for short periods of time, often with the knowledge of the hospital staff. It is difficult to know the extent to which they were treated like patients or like research colleagues. Nevertheless, their reports about the inside of the psychiatric hospital have been valuable. This article extends those efforts.

PSEUDOPATIENTS AND THEIR SETTINGS

The eight pseudopatients were a varied group. One was a psychology graduate students in his 20's. The remaining seven were older and "established." Among them were three psychologists, a pediatrician, a psychiatrist, a painter, and a housewife. Three pseudopatients were women, five were men. All of them employed pseudonyms, lest their alleged diagnoses embarrass them later. Those who were in mental health professions alleged another occupation in order to avoid the special attentions that might be accorded by staff, as a matter of courtesy or caution, to ailing colleagues (*8*). With the exception of myself (I was the first pseudopatient and my presence was known to the hospital administrator and chief psychologist and, so far as I can tell, to them alone), the presence of pseudopatients and the nature of the research program was not known to the hospital staffs (*9*).

The settings were similarly varied. In order to generalize the findings, admission into a variety of hospitals was sought. The 12 hospitals in the sample were located in five different states on the East and West coasts. Some were old and shabby, some were quite new. Some were research-oriented, others not. Some had good staff-patient ratios, others were quite understaffed. Only one was a strictly private hospital. All of the others were supported by state or federal funds or, in one instance, by university funds.

After calling the hospital for an appointment, the pseudopatient arrived at the admissions office complaining that he had been hearing voices. Asked what the voices said, he replied that they were often unclear, but as far as he could tell they said "empty," "hollow," and "thud." The voices were unfamiliar and were of the same sex as the pseudopatient. The choice of these symptoms was occasioned by their apparent similarity to existential symptoms. Such symptoms are alleged to arise from painful concerns about the perceived meaninglessness of one's life. It is as if the hallucinating person were saying, "My life is empty and hollow." The choice of these symptoms was also determined by the *absence* of a single report of existential psychoses in the literature.

Beyond alleging the symptoms and falsifying name, vocation, and employment, no further alterations of person, history, or circumstances were made. The significant events of the pseudopatient's life history were presented as they had actually occurred. Relationships with parents and siblings, with spouse and children, with people at work and in school, consistent with the aforementioned exceptions, were described as they were or had been. Frustrations and upsets were described along with joys and satisfactions. These facts are important to remember. If anything, they strongly biased the subsequent results in favor of detecting sanity, since none of their histories or current behaviors were seriously pathological in any way.

Immediately upon admission to the psychiatric ward, the pseudopatient ceased simulating any symptoms of abnormality. In some cases, there was a brief period of mild nervousness and anxiety since none of the pseudopatients really believed that they would be admitted so easily. Indeed, their shared fear was that they would be immediately exposed as frauds and greatly embarrassed. Moreover, many of them had never visited a psychiatric ward; even those who had, nevertheless had some genuine fears about what might happen to them. Their nervousness, then, was quite appropriate to the novelty of the hospital setting, and it abated rapidly.

Apart from that short-lived nervousness, the pseudopatient behaved on the ward as he "normally" behaved. The pseudopatient spoke to patients and staff as he might ordinarily. Because there is uncommonly little to do on a psychiatric ward, he attempted to engage others in conversation. When asked by staff how he was feeling, he indicated that he was fine, that he no longer experienced symptoms. He responded to instructions from attendants, to calls for medication (which was not swallowed), and to dining-hall instructions. Beyond such activities as were available to him on the admissions ward, he spent his time writing down his observations about the ward, its patients, and the staff. Initially these notes were written "secretly," but as it soon became clear that no one much cared, they were subsequently written on standard tablets of paper in such public places as the dayroom. No secret was made of these activities.

The pseudopatient, very much as a true psychiatric patient, entered a hospital with no foreknowledge of when he would be discharged. Each was told that he would have to get out by his own devices, essentially by convincing the staff that he was sane. The psychological stresses associated with hospitalization were considerable, and all but one of the pseudopatients desired to be discharged almost immediately after being admitted. They were, therefore, motivated not only to behave sanely, but to be paragons of cooperation. That their behavior was in no way disruptive is confirmed by nursing reports, which have been obtained on most of the patients. These reports uniformly indicate that the patients were "friendly," "cooperative," and "exhibited no abnormal indications."

THE NORMAL ARE NOT DETECTABLY SANE

Despite their public "show" of sanity, the pseudopatients were never detected. Admitted, except in one case, with a diagnosis of schizophrenia (*10*), each was discharged with a diagnosis of schizophrenia "in remission." The label "in remission" should in no way be dismissed as a formality, for at no time during any hospitalization had any question been raised about any pseudopatient's simulation. Nor are there any indications in the hospital records that the pseudopatient's status was suspect. Rather, the evidence is strong that, once labeled schizophrenic, the pseudopatient was stuck with that label. If the pseudopatient was to be discharged, he must naturally be "in remission"; but he was not sane, nor, in the institution's view, had he ever been sane.

The uniform failure to recognize sanity cannot be attributed to the quality of the hospitals, for, although there were considerable variations among them, several are considered excellent. Nor can it be alleged that there was simply not enough time to observe the pseudopatients. Length of hospitalization ranged from 7 to 52 days, with an everage of 19 days. The pseudopatients were not, in fact, carefully observed, but this failure clearly speaks more to traditions within psychiatric hospitals than to lack of opportunity.

Finally, it cannot be said that the failure to recognize the pseudopatients' sanity was due to the fact that they were not behaving sanely. While there was clearly some tension present in all of them, their daily visitors could detect no serious behavioral consequences—nor, indeed, could other patients. It was quite common for the patients to "detect" the pseudopatients' sanity. During the first three hospitalizations, when accurate counts were kept, 35 of a total of 118 patients on the admissions ward voiced their suspicions, some vigorously. "You're not crazy. You're a journalist, or a professor [referring to the continual note-taking]. You're checking up on the hospital." While most of the patients were reassured by the pseudopatient's insistence that he had been sick before he came in but was fine now, some continued to believe that the pseudopatient was sane throughout his hospitalization (*11*). The fact that the patients often recognized normality when staff did not raises important questions.

Failure to detect sanity during the course of hospitalization may be due to the fact that physicians operate with a strong bias toward what statisticians call the type 2 error (*5*). This is to say that physicians are more inclined to call a healthy person sick (a false positive, type 2) than a sick person healthy (a false negative, type 1). The reasons for this are not hard to find: it is clearly more dangerous to misdiagnose illness than health. Better to err on the side of caution, to suspect illness even among the healthy.

But what holds for medicine does not hold equally well for psychiatry. Medical illnesses, while unfortunate, are not commonly pejorative. Psychiatric diagnoses, on the contrary, carry with them personal, legal, and social stigmas (*12*). It was therefore important to see whether the tendency toward diagnosing the sane insane could be reversed. The following experiment was arranged at a research and teaching hospital whose staff had heard these findings but doubted that such an error could occur in their hospital. The staff was informed that at some time during the following 3 months, one or more pseudopatients would attempt to be admitted into the psychiatric hospital. Each staff member was asked to rate each patient who presented himself at admissions or on the ward according to the likelihood that the patient was a pseudopatient. A 10-point scale was used, with a 1 and 2 reflecting high confidence that the patient was a pseudopatient.

Judgments were obtained on 193 patients who were admitted for psychiatric treatment. All staff who had had sustained contact with or primary responsibility for the patient—attendants, nurses, psychiatrists, physicians, and psychologists—were asked to make judgments. Forty-one patients were alleged, with high confidence, to be pseudopatients by at least one member of the staff. Twenty-three were considered suspect by at least one psychiatrist. Nineteen were suspected by one psychiatrist *and* one other staff member. Actually, no genuine pseudopatient (at least from my group) presented himself during this period.

The experiment is instructive. It indicates that the tendency to designate sane people as insane can be reversed when the stakes (in this case, prestige and diagnostic acumen) are high. But what can be said of the 19 people who were suspected of being "sane" by one psychiatrist and another staff member? Were these people truly "sane," or was it rather the case that in the course of avoiding the type 2 error the staff tended to make more errors of the first sort—calling the crazy "sane"? There is no way of knowing. But one thing is certain: any diagnostic process that lends itself so readily to massive errors of this sort cannot be a very reliable one.

THE STICKINESS OF PSYCHODIAGNOSTIC LABELS

Beyond the tendency to call the healthy sick—a tendency that accounts better for diagnostic behavior on admission than it does for such behavior after a lengthy period of exposure—the data speak to the massive role of labeling in psychiatric assessment. Having once been labeled schizophrenic, there is nothing the pseudopatient can do to overcome the tag. The tag profoundly colors others' perceptions of him and his behavior.

From one viewpoint, these data are hardly surprising, for it has long been known that elements are given meaning by the context in which they occur. Gestalt psychology made this point vigorously, and Asch (*13*) demonstrated that there are "central" personality traits (such as "warm" versus "cold") which are so powerful that they markedly color the meaning of other information in forming an impression of a given personality (*14*). "Insane," "schizophrenic," "manic-depressive," and "crazy" are probably among the most powerful of such central traits. Once a person is designated abnormal, all of his other behaviors and characteristics are colored by that label. Indeed, that label is so powerful that many of the pseudopatients' normal behaviors were overlooked entirely or profoundly misinterpreted. Some examples may clarify this issue.

Earlier I indicated that there were no changes in the pseudopatient's personal history and current status beyond those of name, employment, and, where necessary, vocation. Otherwise, a veridical description of personal history and circumstances were not psychotic. How were they made consonant with the diagnosis of psychosis? Or were those diagnoses modified in such a way as to bring them into accord with the circumstances of the pseudopatient's life, as described by him?

As far as I can determine, diagnoses were in no way affected by the relative health of the circumstances of a pseudopatient's life. Rather, the reverse occurred: the perception of his circumstances was shaped entirely by the diagnosis. A clear example of such translation is found in the case of a pseudopatient who had had a close relationship with his mother but was rather remote from his father during his early childhood. During adolescence and beyond, however, his father became a close friend, while his relationship with his mother cooled. His present relationship with his wife was characteristically close and warm. Apart from occasional angry exchanges, friction was minimal. The children had rarely been spanked. Surely there is nothing especially pathological about such a history. Indeed, many readers may see a similar pattern in their own experiences, with no markedly deleterious consequences. Observe, however, how such a history was translated in the psychopathological context, this from the case summary prepared after the patient was discharged.

> This white 39-year-old male . . . manifests a long history of considerable ambivalence in close relationships, which begins in early childhood. A warm relationship with his mother cools during his adolescence. A distant relationship to his father is described as becoming very intense. Affective stability is absent. His attempts to control emotionality with his wife and children are punctuated by angry outbursts and, in the case of the children, spankings. And while he says that he has several good friends, one senses considerable ambivalence embedded in those relationships also . . .

The facts of the case were unintentionally distorted by the staff to achieve consistency with a popular theory of the dynamics of a schizophrenic reaction (*15*). Nothing of an ambivalent nature had been described in relations with parents, spouse, or friends. To the extent that ambivalence could be inferred, it was probably not greater than is found in all human relationships. It is true the pseudopatient's relationships with his parents changed over time, but in the ordinary context that would hardly be remarkable—indeed, it might very well be expected. Clearly, the meaning ascribed to his verbalizations (that is, ambivalence, affective instability) was determined by the diagnosis: schizophrenia. An entirely different meaning would have been ascribed if it were known that the man was "normal."

All pseudopatients took extensive notes publicly. Under ordinary circumstances, such behavior would have raised questions in the minds of observers, as, in fact, it did among patients. Indeed, it seemed so certain that the notes would elicit suspicion that elaborate precautions were taken to remove them from the ward each day. But the precautions proved needless. The closest any staff member came to questioning these notes occurred when one pseudopatient asked his physician what kind of medication he was receiving and began to write down the response. "You needn't write it," he was told gently. "If you have trouble remembering, just ask me again."

If no questions were asked of the pseudopatients, how was their writing interpreted? Nursing records for three patients indicate that the writing was seen as an aspect of their pathological behavior. "Patient engages in writing behavior" was the daily nursing comment on one of the pseudopatients who was never questioned about his writing. Given that the patient is in the hospital, he must be psychologically disturbed. And given that he is disturbed, continuous writing must be a behavioral manifestation of that disturbance, perhaps a subset of the compulsive behaviors that are sometimes correlated with schizophrenia.

One tacit characteristic of psychiatric diagnosis is that it locates the sources of aberration within the individual and only rarely within the complex of stimuli that surrounds him. Consequently, behaviors that are stimulated by the environment are commonly misattributed to the patient's disorder. For example, one kindly nurse found a pseudopatient pacing the long hospital corridors. "Nervous, Mr. X?" she asked. "No, bored," he said.

The notes kept by pseudopatients are full of patient behaviors that were misinterpreted by well-intentioned staff. Often enough, a patient would go "berserk" because he had, wittingly or unwittingly, been mistreated by, say, an attendant. A nurse coming upon the scene would rarely inquire even cursorily into the environmental stimuli of the patient's behavior. Rather, she assumed that his upset derived from his pathology, not from his present interactions with other staff members. Occasionally, the staff might assume that the patient's family (especially when they had recently visited) or other patients had stimulated the outburst. But never were the staff found to assume that one of themselves or the structure of the hospital had anything to do with a patient's behavior. One psychiatrist pointed to a group of patients who were sitting outside the cafeteria entrance half an hour before lunchtime. To a group of young residents he indicated that such behavior was characteristic of the oral-acquisitive nature of the syndrome. It seemed not to occur to him that there were very few things to anticipate in a psychiatric hospital besides eating.

A psychiatric label has a life and an influence of its own. Once the impression has been formed that the patient is schizophrenic, the expectation is that he will continue to be schizophrenic. When a sufficient amount of time has passed, during which the patient has done nothing bizarre, he is considered to be in remission and available for discharge. But the label endures beyond discharge, with the unconfirmed expectation that he will behave as a schizophrenic again. Such labels, conferred by mental health professionals, are as influential on the patient as they are on his relatives and friends, and it should not surprise anyone that the diagnosis acts on all of them as a self-fulfilling prophecy. Eventually, the patient himself accepts the diagnosis, with all of its surplus meanings and expectations, and behaves accordingly (*5*).

The inferences to be made from these matters are quite simple. Much as Zigler and Phillips have demonstrated that there is enormous overlap in the symptoms presented by patients who have been variously diagnosed (*16*), so there is enormous overlap in the behaviors of the sane and the insane. The sane are not "sane" all of the time. We lose our tempers "for no good reason." We are occasionally depressed or anxious, again for no good reason. And we may find it difficult to get along with one or another person–again for no reason that we can specify. Similarly, the insane are not always insane. Indeed, it was the impression of the pseudopatients while living with them that they were sane for long periods of time–that the bizarre behaviors upon which their diagnoses were allegedly predicated constituted only a small fraction of their total behavior. If it makes no sense to label ourselves permanently depressed on the basis of an occasional depression, then it takes better evidence than is presently available to label all patients insane or schizophrenic on the basis of bizarre behaviors or cognitions. It seems more useful, as Mischel (*17*) has pointed out, to limit our discussions to *behaviors,* the stimuli that provoke them, and their correlates.

It is not known why powerful impressions of personality traits, such as "crazy" or "insane," arise. Conceivably, when the origins of and stimuli that give rise to a behavior are remote or unknown, or when the behavior strikes us as immutable, trait labels regarding the *behaver* arise. When, on the other hand, the origins and stimuli are known and available, discourse is limited to the behavior itself. Thus, I may hallucinate because I am sleeping, or I may hallucinate because I have ingested a peculiar drug. These are termed sleep-induced hallucinations, or dreams, and drug-induced hallucinations, respectively. But when the stimuli to my hallucinations are unknown, that is called craziness, or schizophrenia–as if that inference were somehow as illuminating as the others.

THE EXPERIENCE OF PSYCHIATRIC HOSPITALIZATION

The term "mental illness" is of recent origin. It was coined by people who were humane in their inclinations and who wanted very much to raise the station of (and the public's sympathies toward) the psychologically disturbed from that of witches and "crazies" to one that was akin to the physically ill. And they were at least partially successful, for the treatment of the mentally ill *has* improved considerably over the years. But while treatment has improved, it is doubtful that people really regard the mentally ill in the same way that they view the physically ill. A broken leg is something one recovers from, but mental illness allegedly endures forever (*18*). A broken leg does not threaten the observer, but a crazy schizophrenic? There is by now a host of evidence that attitudes toward the mentally ill are characterized by fear, hostility, aloofness, suspicion, and dread (*19*). The mentally ill are society's lepers.

That such attitudes infect the general population is perhaps not surprising, only upsetting. But that they affect the professionals–attendants, nurses, physicians, psychologists, and social workers–who treat and deal with the mentally ill is more disconcerting, both because such attitudes are self-evidently pernicious and because they are unwitting. Most mental health professionals would insist that they are sympathetic toward the mentally ill, that they are neither avoidant nor hostile. But it is more likely that an exquisite ambivalence characterizes their relations with psychiatric patients, such that their avowed impulses are only part of their entire attitude. Negative attitudes are there too and can easily be detected. Such attitudes should not surprise us. They are the natural offspring of the labels patients wear and the places in which they are found.

Consider the structure of the typical psychiatric hospital. Staff and patients are strictly segregated. Staff have their own living space, including their dining facilities, bathrooms, and assembly places. The glassed quarters that contain the professional staff, which the pseudopatients came to call "the cage," sit out on every dayroom. The staff emerge primarily for caretaking purposes–to give medication, to conduct a therapy or group meeting, to instruct or reprimand a patient. Otherwise, staff keep to themselves, almost as if the disorder that afflicts their charges is somehow catching.

So much is patient-staff segregation the rule that, for four public hospitals in which an attempt was made to measure the degree to which staff and patients mingle, it was necessary to use "time out of the staff cage" as the operational measure. While it was not the case that all time spent out of the cage was spent mingling with patients (attendants, for example, would occasionally emerge to watch television in the dayroom), it was the only way in which one could gather reliable data on time for measuring.

The average amount of time spent by attendants outside of the cage was 11.3 percent (range, 3 to 52 percent). This figure does not represent only time spent mingling with patients, but also includes time spent on such chores as folding laundry, supervising patients while they shave, directing ward clean-up, and sending patients to off-ward activities. It was the relatively rare attendant who spent time talking with patients or playing games with them. It proved impossible to obtain a "percent mingling time" for nurses, since the amount of time they spent out of the cage was too brief. Rather, we counted instances of emergence from the cage. On the average, daytime nurses emerged from the cage 11.5 times per shift, including instances when they left the ward entirely (range, 4 to 39 times). Late afternoon and night nurses were even less available, emerging on the average 9.4 times per shift (range, 4 to 41 times). Data on early morning nurses, who arrived usually after midnight and departed at 8 a.m., are not available because patients were asleep during most of this period.

Physicians, especially psychiatrists, were even less available. They were rarely seen on the wards. Quite commonly, they would be seen only when they arrived and departed, with the remaining time being spent in their offices or in the cage. On the average, physicians emerged on the ward 6.7 times per day (range, 1 to 17 times). It proved difficult to make an accurate estimate in this regard, since physicians often maintained hours that allowed them to come and go at different times.

The hierarchical organization of the psychiatric hospital has been commented on before (*20*), but the latent meaning of that kind of organization is worth noting again. Those with the most power have least to do with patients, and those with the least power are most involved with them. Recall, however, that the acquisition of role-appropriate behaviors occurs mainly through the observation of others, with the most powerful having the most influence. Consequently, it is understandable that attendants not only spend more time with patients than do any other members of the staff—that is required by their station in the hierarchy—but also, insofar as they learn from their superiors' behavior, spend as little time with patients as they can. Attendants are seen mainly in the cage, which is where the models, the action, and the power are.

I turn now to a different set of studies, these dealing with staff response to patient-initiated contact. It has long been known that the amount of time a person spends with you can be an index of your significance to him. If he initiates and maintains eye contact, there is reason to believe that he is considering your requests and needs. If he pauses to chat or actually stops and talks, there is added reason to infer that he is individuating you. In four hospitals, the pseudopatient approached the staff member with a request which took the following form: "Pardon me, Mr. [or Dr. or Mrs.] X, could you tell me when I will be eligible for grounds privileges?" (or ". . . when I will be presented at the staff meeting?" or ". . . when I am likely to be discharged?"). While the content the question varied according to the appropriateness of the target and the pseudopatient's (apparent) current needs the form was always a courteous and relevant request for information. Care was taken never to approach a particular member of the staff more than once a day, lest the staff member become suspicious or irritated. In examining these data, remember that the behavior of the pseudopatients was neither bizarre nor disruptive. One could indeed engage in good conversation with them.

The data for these experiments are shown in Table 1, separately for physicians (column 1) and for nurses and attendants (column 2). Minor differences between these four institutions were overwhelmed by the degree to which staff avoided continuing contacts that patients had initiated. By far, their most common response consisted of either a brief response to the question, offered while they were "on the move" and with head averted, or no response at all.

The encounter frequently took the following bizarre form: (pseudopatient) "Pardon me, Dr. X. Could you tell me when I am eligible for grounds privileges?"

(physician) "Good morning, Dave. How are you today?" (Moves off without waiting for a response.)

TABLE 1. **Self-initiated Contact by Pseudopatients with Psychiatrists and Nurses and Attendants, Compared to Contact with Other Groups.**

	Psychiatric hospitals		*University campus (nonmedical)*	*University medical center*		
				Physicians		
	(1)	*(2)*	*(3)*	*(4)*	*(5)*	*(6)*
Contact	*Psychiatrists*	*Nurses and attendants*	*Faculty*	*"Looking for a psychiatrist"*	*"Looking for an internist"*	*No additional comment*
Responses						
Moves on, head averted (%)	71	88	0	0	0	0
Makes eye contact (%)	23	10	0	11	0	0
Pauses and chats (%)	2	2	0	11	0	10
Stops and talks (%)	4	0.5	100	78	100	90
Mean number of questions answered (out of 6)	*	*	6	3.8	4.8	4.5
Respondents (No.)	13	47	14	18	15	10
Attempts (No.)	185	1283	14	18	15	10

*Not applicable.

It is instructive to compare these data with data recently obtained at Stanford University. It has been alleged that large and eminent universities are characterized by faculty who are so busy that they have no time for students. For this comparison, a young lady approached individual faculty members who seemed to be walking purposefully to some meeting or teaching engagement and asked them the following six questions.

1) "Pardon me, could you direct me to Encina Hall?" (at the medical school: ". . . to the Clinical Research Center?").

2) "Do you know where Fish Annex is?" (there is no Fish Annex at Stanford).

3) "Do you teach here?"

4) "How does one apply for admission to the college?" (at the medical school: ". . . to the medical school?").

5) "Is it difficult to get in?"

6) "Is there financial aid?"

Without exception, as can be seen in Table 1 (column 3), all of the questions were answered. No matter how rushed they were, all respondents not only maintained eye contact, but stopped to talk. Indeed, many of the respondents went out of their way to direct or take the questioner to the office she was seeking, to try to locate "Fish Annex," or to discuss with her the possibilities of being admitted to the university.

Similar data, also shown in Table 1 (columns 4, 5, and 6), were obtained in the hospital. Here too, the young lady came prepared with six questions. After the first question, however, she remarked to 18 of her respondents (column 4), "I'm looking for a psychiatrist," and to 15 others (column 5), "I'm looking for an internist." Ten other respondents received no inserted comment (column 6). The general degree of cooperative responses is considerably higher for these university groups than it was for pseudopatients in psychiatric hospitals. Even so, differences are apparent within the medical school setting. Once having indicated that she was looking for a psychiatrist, the degree of cooperation elicited was less than when she sought an internist.

POWERLESSNESS AND DEPERSONALIZATION

Eye contact and verbal contact reflect concern and individuation; their absence, avoidance and depersonalization. The data I have presented do not do justice to the rich daily encounters that grew up around matters of depersonalization and avoidance. I have records of patients who were beaten by staff for the sin of having initiated verbal contact. During my own experience, for example, one patient was beaten in the presence of other patients for having approached an attendant and told him, "I like you." Occasionally, punishment meted out to patients for misdemeanors seemed so excessive that it could not be justified by the most radical interpretations of psychiatric canon. Nevertheless, they appeared to go unquestioned. Tempers were often short. A patient who had not heard a call for medication would be roundly excoriated, and the morning attendants would often wake patients with, "Come on, you m-----f-----s, out of bed!"

Neither anecdotal nor "hard" data can convey the overwhelming sense of powerlessness which invades the individual as he is continually exposed to the depersonalization of the psychiatric hospital. It hardly matters *which* psychiatric hospital—the excellent public ones and the very plush private hospital were better than the rural and shabby ones in this regard, but, again, the features that psychiatric hospitals had in common overwhelmed by far their apparent differences.

Powerlessness was evident everywhere. The patient is deprived of many of his legal rights by dint of his psychiatric commitment (*21*). He is shorn of credibility by virtue of his psychiatric label. His freedom of movement is restricted. He cannot initiate contact with the staff, but may only respond to such overtures as they make. Personal privacy is minimal. Patient quarters and possessions can be entered and examined by any staff member, for whatever reason. His personal history and anguish is available to any staff member (often including the "grey lady" and "candy striper" volunteer) who chooses to read his folder, regardless of their therapeutic relationship to him. His personal hygiene and waste evacuation are often monitored. The water closets may have no doors.

At times, depersonalization reached such proportions that pseudopatients had the sense that they were invisible, or at least unworthy of account. Upon being admitted, I and other pseudopatients took the initial physical examinations in a semipublic room, where staff members went about their own business as if we were not there.

On the ward, attendants delivered verbal and occasionally serious physical abuse to patients in the presence of other observing patients, some of whom (the pseudopatients) were writing it all down. Abusive behavior, on the other hand, terminated quite abruptly when other staff members were known to be coming. Staff are credible witnesses. Patients are not.

A nurse unbuttoned her uniform to adjust her brassiere in the presence of an entire ward of viewing men. One did not have the sense that she was being seductive. Rather, she didn't notice us. A group of staff persons might point to a patient in the dayroom and discuss him animatedly, as if he were not there.

One illuminating instance of depersonalization and invisibility occurred with regard to medications. All told, the pseudopatients were administered nearly 2100 pills, including Elavil, Stelazine, Compazine, and Thorazine, to name but a few. (That such a variety of medications should have been administered to patients presenting identical symptoms is itself worthy of note.) Only two were swallowed. The rest were either pocketed or deposited in the toilet. The pseudopatients were not alone in this. Although I have no precise records on how many patients rejected their medications, the pseudopatients frequently found the medications of other patients in the toilet before they deposited their own. As long as they were cooperative, their behavior and the pseudopatients' own in this matter, as in other important matters, went unnoticed throughout.

Reactions to such depersonalization among pseudopatients were intense. Although they had come to the hospital as participant observers and were fully aware that they did not "belong," they nevertheless found themselves caught up in and fighting the process of depersonalization. Some examples: a graduate student in psychology asked his wife to bring his textbooks to the hospital so he could "catch up on his homework"–this despite the elaborate precautions taken to conceal his professional association. The same student, who had trained for quite some time to get into the hospital, and who had looked forward to the experience, "remembered" some drag races that he had wanted to see on the weekend and insisted that he be discharged by that time. Another pseudopatient attempted a romance with a nurse. Subsequently, he informed the staff that he was applying for admission to graduate school in psychology and was very likely to be admitted, since a graduate professor was one of his regular hospital visitors. The same person began to engage in psychotherapy with other patients–all of this as a way of becoming a person in an impersonal environment.

THE SOURCES OF DEPERSONALIZATION

What are the origins of depersonalization? I have already mentioned two. First are attitudes held by all of us toward the mentally ill–including those who treat them–attitudes characterized by fear, distrust, and horrible expectations on the one hand, and benevolent intentions on the other. Our ambivalence leads, in this instance as in others, to avoidance.

Second, and not entirely separate, the hierarchical structure of the psychiatric hospital facilitates depersonalization. Those who are at the top have least to do with patients, and their behavior inspires the rest of the staff. Average daily contact with psychiatrists, psychologists, residents, and physicians combined ranged from 3.9 to 25.1 minutes, with an overall mean of 6.8 (six pseudopatients over a total of 129 days of hospitalization). Included in this average are time spent in the admissions interview, ward meetings in the presence of a senior staff member, group and individual psychotherapy contacts, case presentation conferences, and discharge meetings. Clearly, patients do not spend much time in interpersonal contact with doctoral staff. And doctoral staff serve as models for nurses and attendants.

There are probably other sources. Psychiatric installations are presently in serious financial straits. Staff shortages are pervasive, staff time at a premium. Something has to give, and that something is patient contact. Yet, while financial stresses are realities, too much can be made of them. I have the impression that the psychological forces that result in depersonalization are much stronger than the fiscal ones and that the addition of more staff would not correspondingly improve patient care in this regard. The incidence of staff meetings and the enormous amount of record-keeping on patients, for example, have not been as substantially reduced as has patient contact. Priorities exist, even during hard times. Patient contact is not a significant priority in the traditional psychiatric hospital, and fiscal pressures do not account for this. Avoidance and depersonalization may.

Heavy reliance upon psychotropic medication tacitly contributes to depersonalization by convincing staff that treatment is indeed being conducted and that further patient contact may not be necessary. Even here, however, caution needs to be exercised in understanding the role of psychotropic drugs. If patients were powerful rather than powerless, if they were viewed as interesting individuals rather than diagnostic entities, if they were socially significant rather than social lepers, if their anguish truly and wholly compelled our sympathies and concerns, would we not *seek* contact with them, despite the availability of medications? Perhaps for the pleasure of it all?

THE CONSEQUENCES OF LABELING AND DEPERSONALIZATION

Whenever the ratio of what is known to what needs to be known approaches zero, we tend to invent "knowledge" and assume that we understand more than we actually do. We seem unable to acknowledge that we simply don't know. The needs for diagnosis and remediation of behavioral and emotional problems are enormous. But rather than acknowledge that we are just embarking on understanding, we continue to label patients "schizophrenic," "manic-depressive," and "insane," as if in those words we had captured the essence of understanding. The facts of the matter are that we have known for a long time that diagnoses are often not useful or reliable, but we have nevertheless continued to use them. We now know that we cannot distinguish insanity from sanity. It is depressing to consider how that information will be used.

Not merely depressing, but frightening. How many people, one wonders, are sane but not recognized as such in our psychiatric institutions? How many have been needlessly stripped of their privileges of citizenship, from the right to vote and drive to that of handling their own accounts? How many have feigned insanity in order to avoid the criminal consequences of their behavior, and, conversely, how many would rather stand trial than live interminably in a psychiatric hospital—but are wrongly thought to be mentally ill? How many have been stigmatized by well-intentioned, but nevertheless erroneous, diagnoses? On the last point, recall again that a "type 2 error" in psychiatric diagnosis does not have the same consequences it does in medical diagnosis. A diagnosis of cancer that has been found to be in error is cause for celebration. But psychiatric diagnoses are rarely found to be in error. The label sticks, a mark of inadequacy forever.

Finally, how many patients might be "sane" outside the psychiatric hospital but seem insane in it—not because craziness resides in them, as it were, but because they are responding to a bizarre setting, one that may be unique to institutions which harbor nether people? Goffman (*4*) calls the process of socialization to such institutions "mortification"—an apt metaphor that includes the processes of depersonalization that have been described here. And while it is impossible to know whether the pseudopatients' responses to these processes are characteristic of all inmates—they were, after all, not real patients—it is difficult to believe that these processes of socialization to a psychiatric hospital provide useful attitudes or habits of response for living in the "real world."

SUMMARY AND CONCLUSIONS

It is clear that we cannot distinguish the sane from the insane in psychiatric hospitals. The hospital itself imposes a special environment in which the meanings of behavior can easily be misunderstood. The consequences to patients hospitalized in such an environment—the powerlessness, depersonalization, segregation, mortification, and self-labeling—seem undoubtedly countertherapeutic.

I do not, even now, understand this problem well enough to perceive solutions. But two matters seem to have some promise. The first concerns the proliferation of community mental health facilities, of crisis intervention centers, of the human potential movement, and of behavior therapies that, for all of their own problems, tend to avoid psychiatric labels, to focus on specific problems and behaviors, and to retain the individual in a relatively nonpejorative environment. Clearly, to the extent that we refrain from sending the distressed to insane places, our impressions of them are less likely to be distorted. (The risk of distorted perceptions, it seems to me, is always present, since we are much more sensitive to an individual's behaviors and verbalizations than we are to the subtle contextual stimuli that often promote them. At issue here is a matter of magnitude. And, as I have shown, the magnitude of distortion is exceedingly high in the extreme context that is a psychiatric hospital.)

The second matter that might prove promising speaks to the need to increase the sensitivity of mental health workers and researchers to the *Catch 22* position of psychiatric patients. Simply reading materials in this area will be of help to some such workers and researchers. For others, directly experiencing the impact of psychiatric hospitalization will be of enormous use. Clearly, further research into the social psychology of such total institutions will both facilitate treatment and deepen understanding.

I and the other pseudopatients in the psychiatric setting had distinctly negative reactions. We do not pretend to describe the subjective experiences of true patients. Theirs may be different from ours, particularly with the passage of time and the necessary process of adaptation to one's environment. But we can and do speak to the relatively more objective indices of treatment within the hospital. It could be a mistake, and a very unfortunate one, to consider that what happened to us derived from malice or stupidity on the part of the staff. Quite the contrary, our overwhelming impression of them was of people who really cared, who were committed and who were uncommonly intelligent. Where they failed, as they sometimes did painfully, it would be more accurate to attribute those failures to the environment in which they, too, found themselves than to personal callousness. Their perceptions and behavior were controlled by the situation, rather than being motivated by a malicious disposition. In a more benign environment, one that was less attached to global diagnosis, their behaviors and judgments might have been more benign and effective.

REFERENCES

1. P. Ash, *J. Abnorm. Soc. Psychol.* 44, 272 (1949); A. T. Beck, *Amer. J. Psychiat.* 119, 210 (1962); A. T. Boisen, *Psychiatry* 2, 233 (1938); N. Kreitman, *J. Ment. Sci.* 107, 876 (1961); N. Kreitman, P. Sainsbury, J. Morrisey, J. Towers, J. Scrivener, *ibid.*, p. 887; H. O. Schmitt and C. P. Fonda, *J. Abnorm. Soc. Psychol.* 52, 262 (1956); W. Seeman, *J. Nerv. Ment. Dis.* 118, 541 (1953). For an analysis of these artifacts and summaries of the disputes, see J. Zubin, *Annu. Rev. Psychol.* 18, 373 (1967); L. Phillips and J. G. Draguns, *ibid.*, 22, 447 (1971).
2. R. Benedict, *J. Gen. Psychol.* 10, 59 (1934).
3. See in this regard H. Becker, *Outsiders' Studies in the Sociology of Deviance* (Free Press, New York, 1963); B. M. Braginsky, D. D. Braginsky, K. Ring, *Methods of Madness: The Mental Hospital as a Last Resort* (Holt, Rinehart & Winston, New York, 1969); G. M. Crocetti and P. V. Lemkau, *Amer. Sociol. Rev.* 30, 577 (1965); E. Goffman, *Behavior in Public Places* (Free Press, New York, 1964); R. D. Laing, *The Divided Self: A Study of Sanity and Madness* (Quadrange, Chicago, 1960); D. L. Phillips, *Amer. Sociol. Rev.* 28, 963 (1963); T. R. Sarbin, *Psychol. Today* 6, 18 (1972); F. Schur, *Amer. J. Sociol.* 75, 309 (1969); T. Szasz, *Law, Liberty and Psychiatry* (Macmillan, New York, 1963); *The Myth of Mental Illness: Foundations of a Theory of Mental Illness* (Hoeber-Harper, New York, 1963). For a critique of some of these views, see W. R. Gove, *Amer. Sociol. Rev.* 35, 873 (1970).
4. E. Goffman, *Asylums* (Doubleday, Garden City, N. Y., 1961).
5. T. J. Scheff, *Being Mentally Ill: A Sociological Theory* (Aldine, Chicago, 1966).
6. Data from a ninth pseudopatient are not incorporated in this report because, although his sanity went undetected, he falsified aspects of his personal history, including his marital status and parental relationships. His experimental behaviors therefore were not identical to those of the other pseudopatients.
7. A. Barry, *Bellevue Is a State of Mind* (Harcourt Brace Jovanovich, New York, 1971); J. Belknap, *Human Problems of a State Mental Hospital*

(McGraw-Hill, New York, 1956); W. Caudill, F. C. Redlich, H. R. Gilmore, E. B. Brody, *Amer. J. Orthopsychiat.* 22, 314 (1952); A. R. Goldman, R. H. Bohr, T. A. Steinberg, *Prof. Psychol.* 1, 427 (1970); unauthored, *Roche Report* 1 (No. 13), 8 (1971).

8. Beyond the personal difficulties that the pseudopatient is likely to experience in the hospital, there are legal and social ones that, combined, require considerable attention before entry. For example, once admitted to a psychiatric institution, it is difficult, if not impossible, to be discharged on short notice, state law to the contrary notwithstanding. I was not sensitive to these difficulties at the outset of the project, nor to the personal and situational emergencies that can arise, but later a writ of habeas corpus was prepared for each of the entering pseudopatients and an attorney was kept "on call" during every hospitalization. I am grateful to John Kaplan and Robert Bartels for legal advice and assistance in these matters.
9. However distasteful such concealment is, it was a necessary first step to examining these questions. Without concealment, there would have been no way to know how valid these experiences were; nor was there any way of knowing whether whatever detections occurred were a tribute to the diagnostic acumen of the staff or to the hospital's rumor network. Obviously, since my concerns are general ones that cut across individual hospitals and staffs, I have respected their anonymity and have eliminated clues that might lead to their identification.
10. Interestingly, of the 12 admissions, 11 were diagnosed as schizophrenic and one, with the identical symptomatology, as manic-depressive psychosis. This diagnosis has a more favorable prognosis, and it was given by the only private hospital in our sample. On the relations between social class and psychiatric diagnosis, see A. deB. Hollingshead and F. C. Redlich, *Social Class and Mental Illness: A Community Study* (Wiley, New York, 1958).
11. It is possible, of course, that patients have quite broad latitudes in diagnosis and therefore are inclined to call many people sane, even those whose behavior is patently aberrant. However, although we have no hard data on this matter, it was our distinct impression that this was not the case. In many instances, patients not only singled us out for attention, but came to imitate our behaviors and styles.
12. J. Cumming and E. Cumming, *Community Ment. Health* 1, 135 (1965); A. Farina and K. Ring. *J. Abnorm. Psychol.* 70, 47 (1965); H. E. Freeman and O. G. Simmons, *The Mental Patient Comes Home* (Wiley, New York, 1963); W. J. Johannsen, *Ment. Hygiene* 53, 218 (1969); A. S. Linsky, *Soc. Psychiat.* 5, 166 (1970).
13. S. E. Asch, *J. Abnorm. Soc. Psychol.* 41, 258 (1946); *Social Psychology* (Prentice-Hall, New York, 1952).
14. See also I. N. Mensh and J. Wishner, *J. Personality* 16, 188 (1947); J. Wishner, *Psychol. Rev.* 67, 96 (1960); J. S. Bruner and R. Tagiuri, in *Handbook of Social Psychology,* G. Lindzey, Ed. (Addison-Wesley, Cambridge, Mass., 1954), vol. 2, pp. 634-654; J. S. Bruner, D. Shapiro, R. Tagiuri, in *Person Perception and Interpersonal Behavior,* R. Tagiuri and L. Petrullo, Eds. (Stanford Univ. Press, Stanford, Calif., 1958), pp. 277-288.
15. For an example of a similar self-fulfilling prophecy, in this instance dealing with the "central" trait of intelligence, see R. Rosenthal and L. Jacob-

son, *Pygmalion in the Classroom* (Holt, Rinehart & Winston, New York, 1968).

16. E. Zigler and L. Phillips, *J. Abnorm. Soc. Psychol.* 63, 69 (1961). See also R. K. Freudenberg and J. P. Robertson, *A.M.A. Arch. Neurol. Psychiatr.* 76, 14 (1956).
17. W. Mischel, *Personality and Assessment* (Wiley, New York, 1968).
18. The most recent and unfortunate instance of this tenet is that of Senator Thomas Eagleton.
19. T. R. Sarbin and J. C. Mancuso, *J. Clin. Consult. Psychol.* 35, 159 (1970); T. R. Sarbin, *ibid.* 31, 447 (1967); J. C. Nunnally, Jr., *Popular Conceptions of Mental Health* (Holt, Rinehart & Winston, New York, 1961).
20. A. H. Stanton and M. S. Schwartz, *The Mental Hospital: A Study of Institutional Participation in Psychiatric Illness and Treatment* (Basic, New York, 1954).
21. D. B. Wexler and S. E. Scoville, *Ariz. Law Rev.* 13, 1 (1971).
22. I thank W. Mischel, E. Orne, and M. S. Rosenhan for comments on an earlier draft of this manuscript.

William E. Barrett

SEÑOR PAYROLL

Larry and I were Junior Engineers in the gas plant, which means that we were clerks. Anything that could be classified as paper work came to the flat double desk across which we faced each other. The Main Office downtown sent us a bewildering array of orders and rules that were to be put into effect.

Junior Engineers were beneath the notice of everyone except the Mexican laborers at the plant. To them we were the visible form of a distant, unknowable paymaster. We were Señor Payroll.

Those Mexicans were great workmen; the aristocrats among them were the stokers, big men who worked Herculean eight-hour shifts in the fierce heat of the retorts. They scooped coal with huge shovels and hurled it with uncanny aim at tiny doors. The coal streamed out from the shovels like black water from a high pressure nozzle, and never missed the narrow opening. The stokers worked stripped to the waist, and there was pride and dignity in them. Few men could do such work, and they were the few.

The Company paid its men only twice a month, on the fifth and on the

From William E. Barrett, Señor Payroll. *Southwest Review* 29 (Autumn, 1943): 25-29. Reprinted by permission of Harold Ober Associates, Inc.

twentieth. To a Mexican, this was absurd. What man with money will make it last 15 days? If he hoarded money beyond the spending of three days, he was a miser—and when, Señor, did the blood of Spain flow in the veins of misers? Hence it was the custom for our stokers to appear every third or fourth day to draw the money due to them.

There was a certain elasticity in the Company rules, and Larry and I sent the necessary forms to the Main Office and received an "advance" against a man's pay check. Then, one day, Downtown favored us with a memorandum:

"There have been too many abuses of the advance-against-wages privilege. Hereafter, no advance against wages will be made to any employee except in a case of genuine emergency."

We had no sooner posted the notice when in came stoker Juan Garcia. He asked for an advance. I pointed to the notice. He spelled it through slowly, then said, "What does this mean, this 'genuine emergency'?"

I explained to him patiently that the Company was kind and sympathetic, but that it was a great nuisance to have to pay wages every few days. If someone was ill or if money was urgently needed for some other good reason, then the Company would make an exception to the rule.

Juan Garcia turned his hat over and over slowly in his big hands. "I do not get my money?"

"Next payday, Juan. On the 20th."

He went out silently and I felt a little ashamed of myself. I looked across the desk at Larry. He avoided my eyes.

In the next hour two other stokers came in, looked at the notice, had it explained and walked solemnly out; then no more came. What we did not know was that Juan Garcia, Pete Mendoza and Francisco Gonzalez had spread the word and that every Mexican in the plant was explaining the order to every other Mexican. "To get the money now, the wife must be sick. There must be medicine for the baby."

The next morning Juan Garcia's wife was practically dying, Pete Mendoza's mother would hardly last the day, there was a veritable epidemic among children and, just for variety, there was one sick father. We always suspected that the old man was really sick; no Mexican would otherwise have thought of him. At any rate, nobody paid Larry and me to examine private lives; we made out our forms with an added line describing the "genuine emergency." Our people got paid.

That went on for a week. Then came a new order, curt and to the point: "Hereafter, employes will be paid ONLY on the fifth and the 20th of the month. No exceptions will be made except in the cases of employes leaving the service of the Company."

The notice went up on the board and we explained its significance gravely. "No, Juan Garcia, we cannot advance your wages. It is too bad about your wife and your cousins and your aunts, but there is a new rule."

Juan Garcia went out and thought it over. He thought out loud with Mendoza and Gonzalez and Ayala, then, in the morning, he was back. "I am quitting this company for different job. You pay me now?"

We argued that it was a good company and that it loved its employes like children, but in the end we paid off, because Juan Garcia quit. And so did Gonzalez, Mendoza, Obregon, Alaya and Ortez, the best stokers, men who could not be replaced.

Larry and I looked at each other; we knew what was coming in about three days. One of our duties was to sit on the hiring line early each morning, engaging transient workers for the handy gangs. Any man was accepted who could walk up and ask for a job without falling down. Never before had we been called upon to hire such skilled virtuosos as stokers for handy gang work, but we were called upon to hire them now.

The day foreman was wringing his hands and asking the Almighty if he was personally supposed to shovel this condemned coal, while there in a stolid, patient line were skilled men–Garcia, Mendoza and others–waiting to be hired. We hired them, of course. There was nothing else to do.

Every day we had a line of resigning stokers, and another line of stokers seeking work. Our paper work became very complicated. At the Main Office they were jumping up and down. The procession of forms showing Juan Garcia's resigning and being hired over and over again was too much for them. Sometimes Downtown had Garcia on the payroll twice at the same time when someone down there was slow in entering a resignation. Our phone rang early and often.

Tolerantly and patiently we explained: "There's nothing we can do if a man wants to quit, and if there are stokers available when the plant needs stokers, we hire them."

Out of chaos, Downtown issued another order. I read it and whistled. Larry looked at it and said, "It is going to be very quiet around here."

The order read: "Hereafter, no employee who resigns may be rehired within a period of 30 days."

Juan Garcia was due for another resignation, and when he came in we showed him the order and explained that standing in line the next day would do him no good if he resigned today. "Thirty days is a long time, Juan."

It was a grave matter and he took time to reflect on it. So did Gonzalez, Mendoza, Ayala and Ortez. Ultimately, however, they were all back–and all resigned.

We did our best to dissuade them and we were sad about the parting. This time it was for keeps and they shook hands with us solemnly. It was very nice knowing us. Larry and I looked at each other when they were gone and we both knew that neither of us had been pulling for Downtown to win this duel. It was a blue day.

In the morning, however, they were all back in line. With the utmost gravity, Juan Garcia informed me that he was a stoker looking for a job.

"No dice, Juan," I said. "Come back in 30 days. I warned you."

His eyes looked straight into mine without a flicker. "There is some mistake, Señor," he said. "I am Manuel Hernandez. I work as the stoker in Pueblo, in Santa Fe, in many places."

I stared back at him, remembering the sick wife and the babies without medicine, the mother-in-law in the hospital, the many resignations and the rehirings. I knew that there was a gas plant in Pueblo, and that there wasn't any in Santa Fe; but who was I to argue with a man about his own name? A stoker is a stoker.

So I hired him. I hired Gonzalez, too, who swore that his name was Carrera, and Ayala, who had shamelessly become Smith.

Three days later, the resigning started.

Within a week our payroll read like a history of Latin America. Everyone was on it: Lopez and Obregon, Villa, Diaz, Batista, Gomez, and even San Martin and Bolivar. Finally Larry and I, growing weary of staring at familiar faces and writing unfamiliar names, went to the Superintendent and told him the whole story. He tried not to grin, and said, "Damned nonsense!"

The next day the orders were taken down. We called our most prominent stokers into the office and pointed to the board. No rules any more.

"The next time we hire you *hombres,*" Larry said grimly, "come in under the names you like best, because, that's the way you are going to stay on the books."

They looked at us and they looked at the board; then for the first time in the long duel, their teeth flashed white. *"Si, Señores,"* they said.

And so it was.

Chris Argyris

HUMAN BEHAVIOR IN ORGANIZATIONS

In this article, a discussion of some of the basic properties of personality will be followed by a similar discussion regarding formal organization, from which an attempt will be made to derive some of the basic characteristics of the relationship that will tend to arise when these two initial components are "married" to form the beginning of a social organization.[1]

The self, in this culture, tends to develop along specific developmental trends or dimensions which are operationally definable and empirically observable. The basic developmental trends may be described as follows. Human beings, in our culture:

Abridged from Chris Argyris, "Personal vs. Organizational Goals," *Yale Scientific,* (February, 1960), pp. 40-50. Reprinted by permission.

[1] This discussion is a short summary of the detailed analysis to be found in the report, *Personality and Organizations,* published by Harper & Bros., 1958.

(1). Tend to develop from a state of being passive as an infant to a state of increasing activity as an adult.

(2). Tend to develop from a state of dependence on others as an infant to a state of relative independence as an adult. Relative independence is the ability to "stand on one's own two feet" and simultaneously to acknowledge healthy dependencies.[2] It is characterized by the individual's freeing himself from his childhood determiners of behavior (e.g., family) and developing his own set of behavioral determiners. This individual does not tend to react to others (e.g., the boss) in terms of patterns learned during childhood. (1)

(3). Tend to develop from being capable of behaving in only a few ways as an infant to being capable of behaving in many different ways as an adult.[3]

(4). Tend to develop from having erratic, casual, shallow, quickly dropped interests as an infant to a deepening of interests as an adult. The mature state is characterized by an endless series of challenges in which the reward comes from doing something for its own sake. The tendency is to analyze and study phenomena in their full-blown wholeness, complexity and depth. (2)

(5). Tend to develop from having a short time perspective (i.e., the present largely determines behavior) as an infant to a much longer time perspective as an adult (i.e., behavior is more affected by the past and the future). (3,4)

(6). Tend to develop from being in a subordinate position in the family and society as an infant to aspiring to occupy a more equal and/or superordinate position relative to one's peers as an adult.

(7). Tend to develop from a lack of awareness of the self as an infant to an awareness of and control over one's self as an adult. The adult who tends to experience adequate and successful control over his own behavior tends to develop a sense of integrity (Erikson) and feelings of self-worth.

These dimensions are postulated as being descriptive of a basic multi-dimensional developmental process along which the growth of individuals in our culture may be measured. Presumably, every individual, at any given moment in time, could have his degree of development plotted along these dimensions. The exact location on each dimension will probably vary with each individual and even with the same individual at different times. Self-actualization may now be defined more precisely as the individual's plotted scores (or profile) along the above dimensions.[4]

A few words of explanation concerning these dimensions of personality development:

(1). The dimensions are continua in which the growth to be measured is assumed to be continuously changing in degree. An individual is presumed to

[2] This is similar to Erikson's sense of autonomy and Bronfenbrenner's state of creative interdependence.

[3] Lewin and Kounin believe that as the individual develops needs and abilities, the boundaries between them become more rigid. This explains why an adult is better able than a child to be frustrated in one activity and behave constructively in another.

[4] Another related but discrete set of developmental dimensions may be constructed to measure the protective (defense) mechanisms which individuals tend to create as they develop from infant to adulthood. Exactly how these would be related to the above model is not clear.

develop continuously in degree from the infant end to the adult end of each continuum.

(2). It is postulated that as long as one develops in a particular culture, one will never obtain maximum expression of these developmental trends. Clearly, all individuals cannot be maximally independent, active, and so forth, all the time and still maintain an organized society. It is the function of culture (e.g., norms, mores, etc.) to inhibit *maximum* expressions and to help an individual adjust and adapt by finding his *optimum* expression.

A second factor that prevents maximum expression and fosters optimum expression is the individual's own finite limits set by his personality. For example, some people fear the same amount of independence and activity that others desire. Also, it is commonplace to find some people who do not have the necessary abilities to perform specific tasks. No individual is known to have developed all known abilities to their full maturity.

Finally, defense mechanisms also are important factors operating to help an individual to deviate from the basic developmental trends.

(3). The dimensions described above are constructed in terms of latent or genotypical characteristics. If one states that an individual needs to be dependent, this need will probably be ascertained by clinical inference because it is one that individuals are not usually aware of. Thus, if one observes an employee acting as if he were independent, it is possible that if one goes below the behavioral surface, the individual may be quite dependent. The obvious example is the employee who seems to behave always in a manner contrary to that desired by management. Although this behavior may look as if he is independent, his contrariness may be due to his great need to be dependent on management, which he dislikes to admit to himself and to others.

One might say that an independent person is one whose behavior is not caused by the influence others have over him. Of course, no individual is completely independent. All of us have our healthy dependencies, i.e., those which help us to maintain our discreteness, to be creative, and to develop.

One operational criterion to ascertain whether an individual's desire to be, let us say, independent and active is a true manifestation is to ascertain the extent to which he permits others to express the same needs. Thus, an autocratic leader may say that he needs to be active and independent; he may also say that he wants subordinates who are the same; however, there is ample research to suggest that his leadership pattern only makes him and his subordinates more dependence ridden.

SOME BASIC PROPERTIES OF FORMAL ORGANIZATION

The next step is to focus the analytic spotlight on the formal organization. What are its properties? What are its basic "givens"? What probable impact will they have on the human personality? How will the human personality tend to react to this impact? What sorts of "chain reactions" are probable when these two basic components are brought together?

Formal Organizations Are Rational Organizations. Probably the most basic property of formal organization is its logical foundation or, as it has been called by students of administration, its essential rationality. It is the "mirror image" of the planners' conception of how the intended consequences of the organization may be best achieved. The underlying assumption made by the creators of formal organization is that man within respectable tolerances will behave rationally, i.e., as the formal plan requires him to behave. Organizations are formed with particular objectives in mind, and their structure mirrors these objectives. Although man may not follow the prescribed paths, and consequently the objectives might never be achieved, Simon (6) suggests that, by and large, man does follow these prescribed paths. He points out:

> Organizations are formed with the intention and design of accomplishing goals, and the people who work in organizations believe, at least part of the time, that they are striving toward these same goals. We must not lose sight of the fact that, however far organization may depart from the traditional description . . . nevertheless most behavior in organizations is intendedly rational behavior. By "intended rationality" I mean the kind of adjustment of behavior to goals of which humans are capable—a very incomplete and imperfect adjustment, to be sure, but one which nevertheless does accomplish purposes and does carry out programs.

Most of these experts emphasize that although no organizational structure will exemplify the maximum expression of the principles, a satisfactory aspiration is for optimum expression, which means modifying the ideal structure to take into account the individual (and any environmental) conditions. Moreover, they urge that the people must be loyal to the formal structure if it is to work effectively. Thus Taylor emphasizes that scientific management would never succeed without a "mental revolution." Fayol has the same problem in mind when he emphasizes the importance of esprit de corps.

However, it is also true that these experts have provided little insight into *why* they believe that people should undergo a "mental revolution," or why an esprit de corps is necessary if the principles are to succeed. The only hints usually found are that resistance to scientific management occurs because human beings "are what they are," or "because it's human nature." But, *why* does "human nature" resist formal organizational principles? Perhaps there is something inherent in the principles which causes human resistance. Unfortunately, there exists too little research that specifically assesses the impact of the formal organizational principles on human beings.

The formal organizational experts believe that logical, rational design, in the long run, is more human than creating an organization haphazardly. They argue that it is illogical, cruel, wasteful, and inefficient not to have a logical design. It is illogical because design must come first. It does not make sense to pay a large salary to an individual without clearly defining his position and its relationship to the whole. It is cruel because, eventually, the participants suffer when no clear organizational structure exists. It is wasteful because, unless jobs are clearly predefined, it is impossible to plan logical training, promotion, resignation and retirement policies. It is inefficient because the organization becomes dependent on personalities. The "personal touch" leads to "playing politics," which Mary Follett has described as a "deplorable form of coercion" (7).

Unfortunately, the validity of these arguments tends to be obscured in the eyes of the behavioral scientist because it implies that the only choice left, if the formal, rational, predesigned structure is not accepted, is to have no organizational structure at all, with the organizational structure left to the whims, pushes and pulls of human beings. Some human-relations researchers, on the other hand, have unfortunately given the impression that formal structures are "bad" and that the needs of the individual participants should be paramount in creating and administering an organization. However, a recent analysis of the existing research points up quite clearly that the importance of the organization as an organism worthy of self-actualization is now being recognized by those who, in the past, have focused largely on the individual (8).

In the past, and for the most part in the present, the traditional organizational experts based their "human architectural creation" on certain basic principles (more accurately, assumptions) about the nature of organization.

Although these principles have been attacked by behavioral scientists, the assumption is made in this paper that to date no one has defined a more useful set of formal organization principles. Therefore, the principles are accepted as "givens." This frees us to inquire about their probable impact on people, *if they are used as defined.*

In introducing these principles, it is important to note that, as Gillespie suggests, the roots of these principles may be traced back to certain "principles of industrial economics," the most important of which is the basic economic assumption held by builders of the industrial revolution that, "the concentration of effort on a limited field of endeavor increases quality and quantity of output" (9). It follows from the above that the necessity for specialization should increase as the quantity of similar things to be done increases.

Task (Work) Specialization. If concentrating effort on a limited field of endeavor increases the quality and quantity of output, it follows that organizational and administrative efficiency is increased by the specialization of tasks assigned to the participants in the organization (10). Inherent in this assumption are three others. *First,* that the human personality will behave more efficiently as the task becomes specialized. *Second,* that there can be found a one best way to define the job so that it is performed at greater speed (11). *Third,* that any individual differences in the human personality may be ignored by transferring more skill and thought to machines.

A number of difficulties arise with these assumptions when the properties of the human personality are recalled. *First,* the human personality, as we have seen, is always attempting to actualize its unique organization of parts resulting from a continuous, emotionally laden, ego-involving process of growth. It is difficult, if not impossible, to assume that this process can be choked off and the resultant unique differences of individuals ignored. This is tantamount to saying that self-actualization can be ignored. *Second,* task specialization requires the individual to use only a few of his abilities. Moreover, as specialization increases, it tends to require the use of the less complex doing or motor abilities which, research suggests, tend to be of lesser psychological importance to the individual. Thus the principle violates two basic "givens" of the healthy adult human personality. It inhibits self-actualization and provides expression for few, shallow, skin-surface abilities that do not provide the "endless challenge" desired by the healthy personality.

Chain of Command. The principle of task specialization creates an aggregate of parts, each performing a highly specialized task. However, an aggregate of parts busily performing their particular objective does not form an organization. A pattern of parts must be formed so that the interrelationships among the parts create the organization. Following the logic of specialization, the planners create a new function (leadership) whose primary responsibility is to control, direct and coordinate the interrelationships of the parts, and to make certain that each part performs its objective adequately. Thus the assumption is made that administrative and organizational efficiency is increased by arranging the parts in a determinate hierarchy of authority in which the part on top can direct and control the part on the bottom.

If the parts being considered are individuals, then they must be motivated to accept control, direction and coordination of their behavior. The leader, therefore, is assigned formal power to hire, discharge, reward and penalize the individuals in order that their behavior is molded toward the organization's objectives.

The impact of such a state of affairs is to make the individuals dependent on, passive and subordinate to the leader. As a result, the individuals have little control over their working environment. At the same time, their time perspective is shortened because they do not control the information necessary to predict their future. These requirements of formal organization act to inhibit four of the growth trends of personality because to be passive and subordinate and to have little control and short time perspective exemplify dimensions, in adults, of immaturity, not adulthood.

The planners of formal organization suggest three basic ways to minimize this admittedly difficult position. *First,* ample rewards should be given to those who perform well and who do not permit their dependence, subordination, passivity, etc., to influence them in a negative manner. The rewards should be material and psychological. Because of the specialized nature of the job, however, few psychological rewards are possible. It becomes important, therefore, that adequate material rewards are made available to the productive employee. This practice can lead to new difficulties, since the solution is, by its nature, not to do anything about the on-the-job situation (which is what is causing the difficulties) but to pay the individual for the dissatisfactions he experiences. The end result is that the employee is paid for his dissatisfaction while at work and his wages are given to him to gain satisfactions outside his immediate work environment.

Thus the management helps to create a psychological set which leads the employees to feel that basic causes of dissatisfaction are built into industrial life, that the rewards they receive are wages for dissatisfaction, and that if satisfaction is to be gained, the employee must seek it outside the organization.

To make matters more difficult, there are three assumptions inherent in the above solution that also violate the basic "givens" of human personality. *First,* the solution assumes that a whole human being can split his personality so that he will feel satisfied in knowing that the wages for his dissatisfaction will buy him satisfaction outside the plant. *Second,* it assumes that the employee is primarily interested in maximizing his economic gains. *Third,* it assumes that the employee is best rewarded as an individual producer. The work group in which he belongs is not viewed as a relevant factor. If he produces well, he should be rewarded. If he does not, he should be penalized even though he may be restricting production because of informal group sanctions.

The *second* solution suggested by the planners of formal organization is to have technically competent, objective, rational, loyal leaders. The assumption is made that if the leaders are technically competent, presumably they cannot have "the wool pulled over their eyes"; which should lead the employees to have a high respect for them. The leaders should be objective and rational and personify the rationality inherent in the formal structure. Being rational means that they must avoid becoming emotionally involved. As one executive states, "We must try to keep our personality out of the job." The leader must also be impartial. He does not permit his feelings to operate when he is evaluating others. Finally, the leader must be loyal to the organization so that he can inculcate the loyalty in the employees that Taylor, Fayol and others believe is so important.

Admirable as this solution may be, again it violates several of the basic properties of personality. If the employees are to respect an individual for what he does rather than for who he is, the sense of self-integrity, based on evaluation of the total self which is developed in people, is lost. Moreover, to ask the leader to keep his personality out of his job is to ask him to stop actualizing himself. This is not possible as long as he is alive. Of course, the executive may want to *feel* that he is not involved, but it is a basic "given" that the human personality is an organism always actualizing itself. The same problem arises with impartiality. No one can be completely impartial. As has been shown, the self concept always operates when we are making judgments. In fact, as May has pointed out, the best way to be impartial is to be as partial as one's needs predispose one to be but to be aware of this partiality in order to "correct" for it at the moment of decision (12). Finally, if a leader can be loyal to an organization under these conditions, there may be adequate grounds for questioning the health of his personality make-up.

The *third* solution suggested by many adherents to the formal organizational principles is to motivate the subordinates to have more initiative and to be more creative by placing them in competition with one another for the positions of power that lie above them in the organizational ladder. This solution is traditionally called "the rabble hypothesis." Acting under the assumption that employees will be motivated to advance upward, the formal organizational adherents add another assumption; that competition for the increasingly (as one goes up the ladder) scarcer positions will increase the effectiveness of the participants. Williams (13), conducting some controlled experiments, shows that the latter assumption is not necessarily valid for people placed in competitive situations. Deutsch (14), as a result of extensive controlled experimental research, supports Williams' results and goes much further to suggest that competitive situations tend to lead to an increase in tension and conflict and to a decrease in human effectiveness. Levy and Freedman confirm Deutsch's observations and go further to relate competition to psychoneurosis (15).

Unity of Direction. If the tasks of everyone in a unit are specialized, then it follows that the objective or purpose of the unit must be specialized. The principle of unity of direction states that administrative and organizational efficiency increases if each unit has a single (or homogeneous set of) activity (activities) that is planned and directed by the leader.[5]

This means that the work goal toward which the employees are working, the path toward the goal, and the strength of the barriers they must overcome to achieve the goal are defined and controlled by the leader. Assuming that the work goals do not ego-involve the employee (i.e., they are related to peripheral skin-surface needs), then ideal conditions for psychological failure have been created. The reader may recall that a basic "given" of a healthy personality is the aspiration for psychological success. Psychological success is achieved when each individual is able to define his own goals, in relation to his inner needs and the strength of the barriers to be overcome in order to reach these goals. Repetitive as it may sound, it is nevertheless true that the principle of unity of direction also violates a basic "given" of personality.

A BASIC INCONGRUENCY BETWEEN THE NEEDS OF A MATURE PERSONALITY AND THE REQUIREMENTS OF FORMAL ORGANIZATION

Bringing together the evidence regarding the impact of the formal organizational principles on the individual, it is concluded that there are some basic incongruencies between the growth trends of a healthy personality and the requirements of the formal organization. If the principles of formal organization are used as ideally defined, then the employees will tend to work in an environment where (1) they are provided control over their workaday world; (2) they are expected to be passive, dependent, subordinate; (3) they are expected to have a short-time perspective; (4) they are induced to perfect and value the frequent use of few skin-surface, shallow abilities; and (5) they are expected to produce under conditions leading to psychological failure.

All of these characteristics are incongruent to the ones healthy human beings

[5] The sacredness of these principles is questioned by a recent study. Herckscher concludes that the principles of unity of command and unity of direction are *formally* violated in Sweden. "A fundamental principle of public administration in Sweden is the duty of all public agencies to cooperate directly without necessarily passing through a common superior. This principle is even embodied in the constitution itself, and in actual fact it is being employed daily. It is traditionally one of the most important characteristics of Swedish administration that especially central agencies, but also central and local agencies of different levels, cooperate freely and that this is being regarded as a perfectly normal procedure."

are postulated to desire. They are much more congruent with the needs of infants in our culture. In effect, therefore, formal organizations are willing to pay high wages and provide adequate seniority if mature adults will for eight hours a day, behave in a less mature manner! *If the analysis is correct, this inevitable incongruency increases as (1) the employees are of increasing maturity; (2) as the formal structure, based on the above principles, is made more clear-cut and logically tight for maximum formal organizational effectiveness; (3) as one goes down the line of command; and (4) as jobs become more and more mechanized, i.e., take on assembly-line characteristics.*

The resultants of this lack of congruency are frustration, failure, short-time perspective and conflict. If the agents are predisposed to a healthy, more mature self-actualization:

(1). They will tend to experience frustration because their self-actualization will be blocked (16,17).

(2). They will tend to experience failure because they will not be permitted to define their own goals in relation to central needs, the paths of these goals, etc. (18,19).

(3). They will tend to experience short-time perspective because they have no control over the clarity and stability of their future (20).

(4). They will tend to experience conflict because, as healthy agents, they will dislike frustration, failure and short-time perspective which are characteristic of the present job. However, if they leave, they may not find a new job easily; and/or even if a new job is found, it may not be much different (21).

It can be shown that under conflict, frustration, failure and short-time perspective, the employees will tend to maintain self-integration by creating specific adaptive (informal) behavior such as:

1. Leaving the organization.
2. Climbing the organizational ladder.
3. Manifesting defense reactions such as daydreaming, aggression, ambivalence, regression, projection, etc.
4. Becoming apathetic and disinterested toward the organization, its make-up and goals. This leads to such phenomena as:
   a. Employees reduce the number and potency of the needs they expect to fulfill while at work.
   b. Employees "goldbrick," set rates, restrict quotas, make errors, cheat, slow down, etc.
5. Creating informal groups to sanction the defense reactions and apathy, distinterest and lack of self-involvement.
6. Formalizing the informal groups.
7. Evolving group norms that perpetuate the behavior outlined in items 3, 4, 5, and 6 above.
8. Evolving a psychological set that human or nonmaterial factors are becoming increasingly unimportant while material factors become increasingly important.
9. Acculturating the youth to accept the norms discussed in items 7 and 8.

The basic problem is to decrease the degree of dependency, subordination, submissiveness, etc. It can be shown that job enlargement, employee-centered (or democratic or participative) leadership are a few factors which, if used correctly, can go a long way toward ameliorating the situation. However, these are limited because their success depends on having employees who are ego-involved: highly interested in the organization. The adaptive behavior listed above predisposes the employee to disinterest, non-ego-involvement and apathy. The existence of such states of affairs, in turn, acts to require the more direct leadership pattern to "motivate" and control the disinterested employee. The directive leadership pattern, in turn, requires strong management controls if it is to succeed. But, as we have seen, directive leadership and management controls actually create the human problems that one is trying to solve.

This dilemma between the needs of the individuals and the demands of the organization is a basic, continual dilemma, posing an eternal challenge to the leader. How is it possible to create an organization in which it is possible for the individuals to obtain optimum expression and simultaneously, for the organization to obtain optimum satisfaction of its demands?

Although a few suggestions may be found in the literature, they are, by and large, untested and wanting in systematic rigor. Here lies a fertile field for future research in organizational behavior.

BIBLIOGRAPHY

1. White, R. W. *Lives in Progress,* p. 39 ff. New York, 1952.
2. White, R. W. *Op. cit.,* p. 347 ff.
3. Bakke, E. W. *Citizens Without Work.* New Haven, Conn.: Yale University Press, 1940.
4. Lewin, K. Times Perspective and Morale. In Lewin, G. W. (ed.): *Resolving Social Conflicts,* p. 105. New York, 1948.
5. Rogers, C. R. *Client-Centered Therapy.* New York, 1951.
6. Simon, H. A. *Research Frontiers in Politics and Government,* ch. 2, p. 30. Washington, D. C., 1955.
7. Bendix, R. *Work and Authority in Industry,* pp. 36-39.
8. Argyris, C. *The Present State of Research in Human Relations,* ch. 1. New Haven, Conn., 1954.
9. Gillespie, J. J. *Free Expression in Industry,* pp. 34-37. London, 1948.
10. Simon, H. A. *Administrative Behavior,* pp. 80-81. New York, 1947.
11. Friedman, G. *Industrial Society,* p. 54 ff. Glencoe, Ill., 1955.
12. May, R. *Historical and Philosophical Presuppositions for Understanding Therapy.* In Mowrer, O. H., *Psychotherapy Theory and Research,* pp. 38-39. New York, 1953.
13. Williams, L. C. S. Effects of Competition Between Groups in a Training Situation. *Occupational Psychology.* Vol. 30, no. 2 (April 1956): 85-93.
14. Deutsch, M. The Effects of Cooperation and Competition Upon Group Process. *Human Relations* 2 (1949): 129-52.
15. Levy, S., and Freedman, L. Psychoneurosis and Economic Life. *Social Problems* Vol. 4, no. 1 (July 1956): 55-67.
16. Barker, R. B., Dembo, T., and Lewin, K. *Frustration and Regression.* Iowa City, Iowa: University of Iowa, 1941.

17. Dollard, J., et. al. *Frustration and Agression.* New Haven, Conn., 1939.
18. Lewin, K., et al. Level of Aspiration. In Hunt, J. McV. (ed.): *Personality and the Behavior Disorders,* ch. 20, pp. 333-78.
19. Lippitt, R., and Bradford, L. Employee Success in Work Groups. *Personnel Administration,* Vol. 8 (Dec. 1945), ch. 4, pp. 6-10.
20. Lewin, K. Time Perspective and Morale. In Lewin, G. W. (ed.): *Resolving Social Conflicts,* pp. 103-24. New York, 1948.
21. Newcomb, T. M. *Social Psychology,* pp. 361-73. New York, 1950.

George Strauss

THE PERSONALITY–VERSUS–ORGANIZATION HYPOTHESIS

Over the years, out of the contributions of individuals such as Argyris (1957), Hertzberg (1960), Maier (1955), Maslow (1954), and McGregor (1960) has come a consistent view of human motivation in industry.[1] With due credit to Chris Argyris, I would like to call it the "personality-versus-organization" hypothesis. I will state this hypothesis briefly first and then criticize it.

(1). Human behavior in regard to work is motivated by a hierarchy of needs, in ascending order: physical, safety, social, egoistic, and self-actualization. By "hierarchy" is meant that a higher, less basic need does not provide motivation unless all lower, more basic needs are satisfied, and that, once a basic need is satisfied, it no longer motivates.

Physical needs are the most fundamental, but once a reasonable (satisficing, as Simon would put it) level of physical-need satisfaction is obtained (largely through pay), individuals become relatively more concerned with other needs. First they seek to satisfy their security needs (through seniority, fringe benefits, and so forth). When these, too, are reasonably satisfied, social needs (friendship, group support, and so forth) take first priority. And so forth. Thus, for example, hungry men have little interest in whether or not they belong to strong social groups; relatively well-off individuals are more anxious for good human relations.

[1] For an excellent summary of this hypothesis and its application, see Clark (1960-61). Somewhat the same position is taken by Merton (1957) and Selznick (1949); both suggest that organizational attempts to obtain conformity lead to unanticipated consequences, such as lack of innovation and even rebellion.

Only when most of the less pressing needs are satisfied will individuals turn to the ultimate form of satisfaction, self-actualization, which is described by Maslow (1943) as "the desire to become more and more what one is, to become everything that one is capable of becoming. . . . A musician must make music, an artist must paint, a poet must write, if he is to be ultimately happy. What a man *can* be, he *must* be." (p. 372)

(2). Healthy individuals desire to mature, to satisfy increasingly higher levels of needs. This, in practice, means that they want more and more opportunity to form strong social groups, to be independent, creative, to exercise autonomy and discretion, and to develop and express their unique personality with freedom.

(3). The organization, on the other hand, seeks to program individual behavior and reduce discretion. It demands conformity, obedience, dependence, and immature behavior. The assembly-line worker, the engineer, and the executive are all subject to strong pressures to behave in a programmed, conformist fashion.[2] As a consequence, many individuals feel alienated from their work.

(4). Subordinates react to these pressures in a number of ways, most of which are dysfunctional to the organization. Individuals may fight back through union activity, sabotage, output restriction, and other forms of rational or irrational (aggressive) behavior. Or they may withdraw and engage in regression, sublimation, childish behavior, or failure to contribute creative ideas or to produce more than a minimum amount of work. In any case, employees struggle not to conform (at least at first). To keep these employees in line, management must impose still more restrictions and force still more immature behavior. Thus, a vicious cycle begins.

(5). Management pressures often lead to excessive competition and splintering of work groups and the consequent loss of cooperation and social satisfaction. Or work groups may become even stronger, but their norms may now be antimanagement, those of protecting individuals against pressures from above.

(6). A subtle management, which provides high wages, liberal employee benefits, "hygienic," "decent" supervision, and not too much pressure to work, may well induce employees to *think* they are happy and not *dissatisfied.*[3] But they are not (or should not be) truly *satisfied;* they are apathetic and have settled for a low level of aspiration. They do as little work as they can get away with and still hold their job. This is an unhealthy situation which is wasteful both to the individual and to the organization.

(7). There seem to be some differences in emphasis among authorities as to whether the behavior of the typical subordinate under these circumstances will be rational (reality-oriented) or irrational (frustration-oriented). In any case,

[2] These three groups are discussed in Walker and Guest (1952); Shepard (1960); and Whyte (1956).

[3] Hertzberg, Mausner, and Snyderman (1960) distinguish between dissatisfiers (basically, the absence of "hygienic" factors such as good "supervision, interpersonal relations, physical working conditions, salary, company policies, and administrative practices, benefits and job security") (p. 113) and motivators (basically challenge, autonomy, and interesting work). Similar conclusions are reached by Guerin, Vernoff, and Feld (1960). The Hertzberg, Mausner, and Snyderman analysis is critized by Vroom and Maier (1960).

organizational pressures, particularly being subjected to programmed work, may lead to serious personality disturbances and mental illness.[4] Thus, traditional organizational techniques not only prevent the organization from operating at maximum efficiency, but, in terms of their impact on individual adjustment, they are also very expensive to society as a whole.

(8). The only healthy solution is for management to adopt policies which promote intrinsic job satisfaction, individual development, and creativity, according to which people will willingly and voluntarily work toward organizational objectives because they enjoy their work and feel that it is important to do a good job.[5] More specifically, management should promote job enlargement, general supervision, strong cohesive work groups, and decentralization. In a nutshell, management should adopt "power-equalization techniques."

CRITICISM

The above is, in a sense, a hypothesis as to human behavior in organizations. But it is more than a coldly objective hypothesis: it is a prescription for management behavior, and implicit in it are strong value judgments.[6] With its strong emphasis on individual dignity, creative freedom, and self-development, this hypothesis bears all the earmarks of its academic origin.

Professors place high value on autonomy, inner direction, and the quest for maximum self-development. As much as any other group in society, their existence is work-oriented; for them, creative achievement is an end in itself and requires no further justification. Most professors are strongly convinced of the righteousness of their Protestant ethic of hard work and see little incongruity in feeling that everyone should feel as they do.

And yet there are many individuals (perhaps the bulk of the population) who do not share the professor's values and would not be happy in the professor's job. Further, the technical requirements of many lines of work are very different from those of academia. Academic work is best accomplished by those with academic values, but it is questionable whether these values are equally functional in other lines of work—where creativity is not required to get the job done, but only the ability to follow orders.

[4] Recent evidence suggests that unskilled workers are significantly more likely to suffer from personality disturbances and psychosomatic illnesses than are skilled workers, and that these differences become manifest only after the individuals take up their work. (In other words, once individuals land in unskilled jobs, they tend to become more maladjusted.) (Kornhauser, 1962; French, Kahn, and Mann, 1962.)

[5] Perhaps the most general statement of this position is McGregor's Theory Y. See McGregor (1960).

[6] There seems to be a certain amount of confusion as to whether prescriptions for power-equalization are written from the point of view of organizational efficiency or that of mental health (and possibly the degree of confusion has increased since the primary source of research funds in this area has shifted from the military to the National Institute of Mental Health). There are those who claim that what is good for the individual will, in the long run, be good for the organization, and vice versa. Regardless, it is useful to keep one's criteria explicit.

In the pages which follow, I shall seek to revaluate the personality-versus-organization hypothesis. I shall suggest, first, that it contains many debatable value judgments, and, second, that it ignores what Harold Leavitt has called "organizational economics." I shall conclude that a broad range of people do not seek self-actualization on the job—and that this may be a fortunate thing because it might be prohibitively expensive to redesign some jobs to permit self-actualization.

VALUE JUDGMENTS

It seems to me that the hypothesis, as often stated, overemphasizes (1) the uniqueness of the personality-organization conflict to large-scale industry, (2) the universality of the desire to achieve self-actualization, and (3) the importance of the job (as opposed to the community or the home) as a source of need satisfaction. Thus, too little attention is given to economic motivation.[7]

The Uniqueness of the Problem

At least some authors seem to overdramatize the personality-organization conflict as something unique to large-scale organization (particularly to mass-production industry). But this conflict is merely one aspect of what has been variously characterized as the conflict between individual and society, individual and environment, desire and reality, id and superego. "Thus the formal organization . . . is not truly the real villain; rather any kind of organized activity, from the most democratic to the most authoritarian contains within itself the necessary conditions for conflict."[8]

Similarly, the impact of the industrial revolution on work satisfaction can be overemphasized. Much is made of "alienation" (dictionary meaning: turning away) from work. Comparisons are constantly made between the old-time craftsman who did the entire job and the mass-production worker of today. But I doubt whether the medieval serf or the Egyptian slave enjoyed much sense of autonomy or creativity (although one might perhaps argue that he had more of a sense of identification and less of a feeling of anomie than does his better-fed modern counterpart). Perhaps there is less job satisfaction today than there was 100 years ago. Obviously, there are no objective ways of measuring this, but my surmise is that the "turning away" has been less dramatic than some have suggested. There have been boring, programmed jobs throughout history.

Others are as skeptical as I am regarding the theory of increased alienation. In his conclusion to a survey of job-satisfaction studies, Robert Blauner (1960) questions "the prevailing thesis that most workers in modern society are alienated and estranged. There is a remarkable consistency in the findings that the vast majority of workers, in virtually all occupations and industries, are

[7] I must confess that many of these criticisms apply to my own writing. See Strauss and Sayles (1960), especially Chapters 4-8 and 12, chapters for which I was responsible. See the review by Brayfield (1962).

[8] Bennis (1959, p. 281). Ironically, some of those most concerned with the tyranny of the organization would substitute for it the tyranny of the participative group.

moderately or highly satisfied, rather than dissatisfied with their jobs . . . The real character of the [pre-mass production] craftsman's work has been romanticized by the prevalent tendency to idealize the past . . ." (pp. 352-53). And J. A. C. Brown (1954) asserts "that in modern society there is far greater scope of skill and craftsmanship than in any previous society, and that far more people are in a position to use such skills" (p. 207).

The Universality of the Desire for Self-Actualization

The basic hypothesis implies a strong moral judgment that people should want freedom and self-actualization,[9] that it is somehow morally wrong for people to be lazy, unproductive, and uncreative. It seems to me that the hypothesis overemphasizes their desire for security. It can even be argued that some of the personality-versus-organization writing has a fairly antisocial, even nihilistic flavor; it seems to emphasize individual freedom and self-development as the all-important values. Yet "mature" behavior does not mean freedom from all restrictions; it means successful adjustment to them.

As Eric Fromm has suggested, most people do not want complete freedom. They want to know the limits within which they can act (and this is true both on and off the job). To put it another way: most people are willing to tolerate and may even be anxious for a few areas of their life which are unpredictable and exciting, but they insist that, in a majority of areas, events occur as expected. The research scientist, for example, may relish the novelty and uncertainty of laboratory work, but he insists that his secretary be always on call, that his technician give predictable responses, and that his car start with complete regularity.

True, some people seek much broader limits than do others, and some are not too upset if the limits are fuzzy. However, there are many who feel most comfortable if they work in a highly defined situation. For them, freedom is a burden; they want firm, secure leadership. And there are many more who, if not fully happy with programmed work, find it rather easy to accomodate themselves to it.

Argyris, for example, might reply that such individuals are immature personalities who have adjusted to organizational restrictions by becoming apathetic and dependent. Were the organizational environment healthy, these individuals would react differently. But in many cases, the restrictions which made these people this way occurred in childhood or are present in the culture. Such individuals may be "too far gone" to react well to power equalization, and their attitude is not likely to be changed short of intensive psychotherapy. Indeed, many people may have internalized and made part of their self-concept a low level of aspiration regarding their on-the-job responsibilities and their ability to handle these. What psychologists call the *theory of dissonance* suggests that

[9] Though the concept of self-actualization is insightful, I tend to agree with Bennis (1959) that it "is, at best, an ill-defined concept . . . [and that] self-actualized man seems to be more myth than reality" (p. 279).

sudden attempts to increase their sense of autonomy and self-determination might be quite disturbing.

Impressive evidence of the need for self-actualization is provided by the preliminary results of the mental health studies, which suggest that poor mental health is correlated with holding low-skilled jobs. And yet the evidence is still not complete. Apparently, not everyone suffers equally from unskilled work, and some adjust more easily than others. (Perhaps these studies will help us to improve the prediction process, so that we can do a better job of selecting and even training people for this kind of work.)

Further, it is far from clear whether this lower mental health is caused primarily by the intrinsic nature of unskilled work or by the fact that such work pays poorly and has low status both off and on the job.[10] In so far as mental disturbances are caused by economic and social pressures at home, higher wages may be a better solution than improved human relations on the job or a rearrangement of work assignments.

A hasty glance at the research in this field, as summarized in two reviews (Kasl and French, 1962; Vroom and Maier, 1960; see also Guerin, et. al., 1960), makes it abundantly clear that unskilled workers are not the only ones to suffer from poor mental health. Depending on which study one looks at or what mental health index is used, one can conclude that executives, clerical personnel, salespeople, and lower-level supervisors *all* suffer from below-average mental health. The evidence makes one sympathize with the old Quaker, "All the world is queer save me and thee; and sometimes I think thee is a little queer."

The Job as the Primary Source of Satisfaction

There is an additonal value judgment in the basic hypothesis that the *job* should be a primary form of need satisfaction for everyone (as it is for professors). But the central focus of many peoples' lives is not the job (which is merely a "way of getting a living"), but the home or the community. Many people find a full measure of challenge, creativity, and autonomy in raising a family, pursuing a hobby, or taking part in community affairs. As Robert Dubin (1959) puts it:

> Work, for probably a majority of workers, and even extending into the ranks of management, may represent an institutional setting that is not the central life interest of the participants. The consequence of this is that while participating in work a general attitude of apathy and indifference prevails . . . Thus, the industrial worker does not feel imposed upon by the tyranny of Organizations, company, or union. (p. 161)[11]

[10] Both the Wayne State and the Michigan studies emphasize that no single factor explains the relationship. Kornhauser (1962) concludes: "Both on rational grounds and from empirical evidence, I see no reason to think that it is useful to single out one or a few of the job-related characteristics as distinctly important . . . If we are to understand why mental health is poorer in less-skilled, more routine factory jobs, we must look at the entire pattern of work and life conditions of people in these occupations–not just at single variables."

[11] Maslow (1954) himself suggests that self-actualization can be obtained off the job, as "an ideal mother[or] . . . athletically" (p. 373). Dubin's point may also be exaggerated. I

In my own interviewing experience in factories, I often ran across women who repeated variants of, "I like this job because it gets me away from all the kids and pressures at home." One girl even told me, "The job is good because it gives me a chance to think about God." Such individuals may feel little need for power equalization.

In any case, as Kerr, Dunlap, Harbison, and Myers (1960) predict, work, in the future, will doubtless be increasingly programmed and will provide fewer and fewer opportunities for creativity and discretion on the job. On the other hand, the hours will grow shorter and there will be a "new bohemianism" off the job. All this suggests the irreverent notion that *perhaps* the best use of our resources is to accelerate automation, shorten the work week just as fast as possible, forget about on-the-job satisfactions, and concentrate our energies on making leisure more meaningful.

Underemphasis on Economic Rewards

Since the hypothesis overemphasizes the job as a source of need satisfaction, it also underemphasizes the role of money as a means of motivation. The hypothesis says that, once employees obtain a satisficing level of economic reward, they go on to other needs and, presumably, are less concerned with money. However, the level of reward which is satisficing can rise rapidly over time. Further, money is a means of satisfying higher needs, too—ego, safety, and, for some, even self-actualization needs, for example, the individual who (perhaps misguidedly) seeks to live his life off the job engaging in "creative" consumption. True, employees expect much better physical, psychological, and social conditions on the job today than they did 50 years ago. But they also expect more money. There is little evidence that money has ceased to be a prime motivator.

"ORGANIZATIONAL ECONOMICS"

Perhaps the most fundamental criticisms of the personality-organization hypothesis is that it ignores (or at least misapplies) "organizational economics"; that is, it fails to balance carefully the costs and gains of power equalization. To be sure, most power-equalization advocates point out the hidden costs of autocracy: apathetic and resentful employees, turnover, absenteeism, sabotage, resistance to change, and all the rest. Traditional forms of supervision may be expensive in terms of the lost motivation and energy which might have been turned to organizational ends; they are even more expensive in terms of mental health. Yet some writers, in their moments of wilder enthusiasm, tend to overestimate the gain to be derived from eliminating autocracy and tend to underestimate the costs of power equalization.

---

would guess that for the most part those who participate actively (seek self-actualization) off the job also seek to participate actively on the job, as "an ideal mother [or] . . . athletically" (p. 373).

The Gains from Eliminating Autocracy

Carried to excess, anxiety and aggression are undoubtedly harmful to both the organization and the individual. But many psychological studies suggest that dissatisfaction and anxiety (and even aggression, depending on how it is defined) spur individuals to work harder—particularly in simple, highly programmed tasks. Autocratic, work-oriented bosses very often get out high production: on occasion, their subordinates even develop high morale and cohesive work groups.[12]

Still, beyond certain limits, dissatisfaction, anxiety, and aggression are not in the organization's interest. There is much more doubt about apathy and conformity. It is often argued that an apathetic worker who is subject to "hygienic" supervision will only work enough so as not to get fired, that he will never exercise creativity or imagination or put out an outstanding performance.

On many jobs, however, management has no use for outstanding performance. What is outstanding performance on the part of an assembly-line worker? That he works faster than the line? That he shows creativity and imagination on the job? Management wants none of these. *Adequate* performance is all that can be used on the assembly line and probably on a growing number (I know no figures) of other jobs in our society. Here the conformist, dependent worker may well be the best.[13] As Leavitt and Whisler (1958) put it, "The issue of morale versus productivity that now worries us may pale as programming moves in. The morale of programmed personnel may be of less central concern because less (or at least a different sort of) productivity will be demanded of them." (p. 46)

Even at the management level, there may be an increasing need for conforming, unimaginative types of "organization men" if Leavitt and Whisler's prediction comes true that "jobs at today's middle-management levels will become highly structured. Much more of the work will be programmed, i.e., covered by sets of operating rules governing the day-to-day decisions that are made." (p. 41) Despite the *organization man* it might be argued that nonconformity will be useful to the organization only in increasingly limited doses.

The Costs of Power-Equalization

On the other hand, power-equalization can be quite costly to the organization. To make general supervision or participative management work, many of the old-line autocratic supervisors must be retrained or replaced; this is an expensive process which may result in the demoralization or elimination of the organization's most technically competent individuals. Since it is extremely difficult to develop internalized motivation on many routine jobs, once the

[12] For a list of the conditions under which "authoritarian leadership might be as effective as its alternatives," see Wilensky (1957). Interestingly, the personality-organization hypothesis is strongly influenced by Freud. Yet Freud postulated that "productive work is partially a function of the expression of hostility to the leader" (Bennis, 1959, p. 292).

[13] For an outstanding example, see Goode and Fowler (1949).

traditional, external sanctions (monetary rewards, fear of discharge, and so forth) are removed, *net motivation* may fall on balance. And it is fairly meaningless to talk of permitting exercise of discretion to assembly-line workers or girls on a punch-card operation; the very nature of the technology requires that all essential decisions be centrally programmed.

"But if the nature of the job makes power-equalization techniques impractical," some may argue, "change the nature of the job." Rensis Likert (1961) puts this well:

> To be highly motivated, each member of the organization must feel that the organization's objectives are of significance and that his own particular task contributes in an indispensable manner to the organization's achievement of its objectives. He should see his role as difficult, important, and meaningful. This is necessary if the individual is to achieve and maintain a sense of personal worth and importance. When jobs do not meet this specification they should be reorganized so that they do. (p. 103)

True, there are many opportunities to redesign jobs and work flows[14] so as to increase various forms of job satisfaction such as autonomy and achievement. But whether such changes should be made is a matter for organizational economics.

In many instances these changes, when accompanied by appropriate forms of supervision and proper selection of personnel, may result in substantial increases of productivity. (Purely technological losses in efficiency may be more than offset by increased motivation, less work-flow friction, and so forth.) Obviously, in such instances organizational economics would dictate that the changes should be introduced.

But there are other areas where technological changes can be made only at a substantial cost in terms of productivity—and the impact of automation and information technology seems to be increasing the number of jobs where this may be true. Should we scrap the advances of technology in these areas in order to foster good human relations? Or should we say, "Thank God for the number of people who have made an apparent adjustment to routine jobs. Would that there were more." Perhaps—as has been suggested earlier—it would be best to devote our resources to ever-shortening the work week and helping people to enjoy their leisure more fully.

There seems to be considerable evidence (Argyris, 1960, Chap. 5) that a relatively stable situation can exist in which workers perform relatively routine, programmed jobs under hygienic supervision. Although these workers may not be satisfied (in the Hertzberg sense) and may be immature, apathetic and dependent (in the Argyris sense), they are not actively dissatisfied, they do not feel a need for additional responsibility, and they seek meaning in life from their home and community rather than from their jobs. To be sure, these individuals are maximizing neither their productive efforts nor their possible job

[14] See, for example, Davis and Werling (1960); Friedmann (1955); Chapple and Sayles (1961); Strauss and Sayles (1960), Chapters 2 and 16.

satisfaction. But both management and employees find the situation satisficing (in the Simon sense). Barring sudden change, it is stable. It may well be the best we are likely to get in many situations without costly changes in technology, child upbringing, and so forth.

THE PERSONALITY-ORGANIZATION HYPOTHESIS SUMMARIZED

My concern in this section has been with the personality-versus-organization hypothesis. I have tried to demonstrate:

1. Although many individuals find relatively little satisfaction in their work, this may not be as much of a deprivation as the hypothesis would suggest, since many of these same individuals center their lives off the job and find most of their satisfactions in the community and the home. With these individuals, power-equalization may not liberate much energy.
2. Individuals are not motivated solely to obtain autonomy, self-actualization, and so forth. With various degrees of emphasis, individuals also want security and to know what is expected of them. Power-equalization may certainly stir up a good deal of anxiety among those who are not prepared for it, and at least some individuals may be reluctant to assume the responsibility that it throws upon them.
3. Power-equalization techniques are not too meaningful when management needs no more than an "adequate" level of production, as is often the case when work is highly programmed. Under such circumstances, the costs entailed by modification in job design and supervisory techniques may be greater than the gains obtained from increased motivation to work.

All of the above does not mean either that the personality-organization hypothesis is meaningless or that power-equalization techniques are not useful. Quite the contrary. What it does mean is that many individuals can accommodate themselves to the demands of the organization without too much psychological loss, and for them the personality-organization conflict is not particularly frustrating. Similarly, in many circumstances the gains to the organization from power equalization may be moderate and more than offset by its costs.

For other individuals (for example, scientists working in large companies), the personality-organization conflict may be felt quite acutely. For the most part, these are the very individuals whose work cannot be programmed and from whom management wants more than merely "adequate" production.

All this reemphasizes the often-made point that no single style of leadership can be universally appropriate. The techniques which work on the assembly line will almost certainly fail with research scientists. Indeed, it is fair to predict that, over time, the differences among supervisory styles may increase. Perhaps, in the future, we shall have at one extreme research scientists and others doing creative work who will be putting in a 40-hour or longer work week under conditions of relative power-equalization. At the other extreme may be those who submit to close supervision on highly programmed jobs, but for only 20 hours or so. Shades of Brave New World: the alphas and the gammas!

* * *

BIBLIOGRAPHY

Argyris, Chris. *Personality and Organization.* New York: Harper & Row, Publishers, 1957.

———. *Understanding Organizational Behavior.* Homewood, Ill.: Irwin-Dorsey Press, 1960.

Bennis, Warren G. "Leadership Theory and Administrative Behavior," *Administrative Science Quarterly* 4 (December 1959).

Blauner, Robert. "Work Satisfaction and Industrial Trends in Modern Society." In Walter Galenson and Seymour Martin Lipset, *Labor and Trade Unionism,* New York: John Wiley & Sons, 1960.

Brayfield, Arthur H. "Treating Faint Workers," *Contemporary Psychology* 2 (March 1962): 92-93.

Brown, J. A. C. *The Social Psychology of Industry.* Baltimore: English Pelican edition, 1954.

Chapple, Elliot R., and Sayles, Leonard. *The Measure of Management.* New York: The Macmillan Company, 1961.

Clark, James V. "Motivation and Work Groups: A Tentative View," *Human Organization* 19 (Winter 1960-61): 199-208.

Davis, Louis E., and Werling, Richard. "Job Design Factors," *Occupational Psychology* 34 (April 1960): 109-132.

Dubin, Robert. "Industrial Research and the Discipline of Sociology." In *Proceedings of the 11th Annual Meeting,* Madison, Wisconsin: Industrial Relations Research Association, 1959.

French, John R. P., Jr.; Kahn, Robert L.; and Mann, Floyd C., eds. "Work Health and Satisfaction," *The Journal of Social Issues* 18 (July 1962).

Freidmann, George. *Industrial Society.* Glencoe, Ill.: The Free Press, 1955.

Goode, William J., and Fowler, Irving. "Incentive Factors in a Low-Morale Plant," *American Sociological Review* 14 (October 1949): 619-24.

Guerin, Gerald; Vernoff, Joseph; and Feld, Sheila. *Americans View Their Mental Health.* New York: Basic Books, Inc., 1960.

Hertzberg, Fredrick; Mausner; Bernard; and Snydermann, Barbara. *The Motivation to Work.* New York: John Wiley & Sons, 1960.

Kasl, Stanislov V., and French, John R. P., Jr. "The Effects of Occupational Status on Physical and Mental Health," *Journal of Social Issues* 18 (July 1962): 67-89.

Kerr, Clark; Dunlap, John T.; Harbison, Frederick H.; and Myers, Charles A. *Industrialism and Industrial Man: The Problems of Labor and Management.* Cambridge: Harvard University Press, 1960.

Kornhauser, Arthur. "Mental Health of Factory Workers: A Detroit Study," *Human Organization* 21 (Spring 1962): 43-6.

Leavitt, Harold J., and Whisler, Thomas, "Management in the 1980's," *Harvard Business Review* 36 (November 1958).

Likert, R. *New Patterns of Management.* New York: McGraw-Hill Book Co., Inc., 1961.

McGregor, Douglas. *The Human Side of Enterprise.* New York: McGraw-Hill Book Co., Inc., 1960.

Maier, Norman R. F. *Psychology in Industry,* 2nd ed. Boston: Houghton Mifflin Company, 1955.

Maslow, A. H. "A Theory of Human Motivation," *Psychological Review* 50 (July 1943): 372.

———. *Motivation and Personality.* New York: Harper & Row, Publishers, 1954.

Merton, Robert K. *Social Theory and Social Structure,* rev. enlarged ed. Glencoe: The Free Press, 1957.

Selznick, Philip. *TVA and the Grass Roots.* Berkeley: University of California Press, 1949.

Shepard, Herbert. "Nine Dilemmas in Industrial Research," *Administrative Science Quarterly* 1 (Fall 1960): 245-59.

Strauss, George, and Sayles, Leonard R. *Personnel: The Human Problems of Management.* Englewood Cliffs, N.J.: Prentice-Hall, Inc., 1960.

Vroom, Victor, and Maier, Norman R. F. "Industrial Social Psychology." *Annual Review of Psychology,* Paul Farnsworth, ed., Palo Alto: Annual Reviews, 1960, p. 12.

———. *Some Personality Determinants of the Effects of Participation.* Englewood Cliffs, N.J.: Prentice-Hall, Inc., 1960.

Walker, Charles R., and Guest, Robert H. *The Man on the Assembly Line.* Cambridge: Harvard University Press, 1952.

Whyte, William H., Jr. *The Organization Man.* New York: Simon and Schuster, Inc., 1956.

Wilensky, Harold W. "Human Relations in the Workplace." In *Research in Industrial Human Relations,* Arensberg and others, eds. New York: Harper and Row, Publishers, 1957, pp. 25-50.

Warren G. Bennis

THE COMING DEATH OF BUREAUCRACY

Not far from the new Government Center in downtown Boston, a foreign visitor walked up to a sailor and asked why American ships were built to last only a short time. According to the tourist, "The sailor answered without hesitation that the art of navigation is making such rapid progress that the finest ship would become obsolete if it lasted beyond a few years. In these words which fell accidentally from an uneducated man, I began to recognize the general and systematic idea upon which your great people direct all their concerns."

The foreign visitor was that shrewd observer of American morals and manners, Alexis de Tocqueville, and the year was 1835. He would not recognize Scollay Square today. But he had caught the central theme of our country: its preoccupation, its *obsession* with change. One thing is, however, new since de Tocqueville's time: the *acceleration* of newness, the changing scale and scope of change itself. As Dr. Robert Oppenheimer said, ". . . the world alters as we walk in it, so that the years of man's life measure not some small growth or rearrangement or moderation of what was learned in childhood, but a great upheaval."

How will these accelerating changes in our society influence human organizations?

A short while ago, I predicted that we would, in the next 25 to 50 years, participate in the end of bureaucracy as we know it and in the rise of new social systems better suited to the twentieth-century demands of industrialization. This forecast was based on the evolutionary principle that every age develops an organizational form appropriate to its genius, and that the prevailing form, known by sociologists as bureaucracy and by most businessmen as "damn bureaucracy," was out of joint with contemporary realities. I realize now that my distant prophecy is already a distinct reality so that prediction is already foreshadowed by practice.

I should like to make clear that by bureaucracy I mean a chain of command structured on the lines of a pyramid—the typical structure which coordinates the business of almost every human organization we know of: industrial, governmental, of universities and research and development laboratories,

From Warren G. Bennis, "The Coming Death of Bureaucracy," *Think*, (November-December, 1966), pp. 30-35.

military, religious, voluntary. I do not have in mind those fantasies so often dreamed up to describe complex organizations. These fantasies can be summarized in two grotesque stereotypes. The first I call "Organization as Inkblot"—an actor steals around an uncharted wasteland, growing more restive and paranoid by the hour, while he awaits orders that never come. The other specter is "Organization as Big Daddy"—the actors are square people plugged into square holes by some omniscient and omnipotent genius who can cradle in his arms the entire destiny of man by way of computer and TV. Whatever the first image owes to Kafka, the second owes to George Orwell's 1984.

Bureaucracy, as I refer to it here, is a useful social invention that was perfected during the industrial revolution to organize and direct the activities of a business firm. Most students of organizations would say that its anatomy consists of the following components:

1. A well-defined chain of command.
2. A system of procedures and rules for dealing with all contingencies relating to work activities.
3. A division of labor based on specialization.
4. Promotion and selection based on technical competence.
5. Impersonality in human relations.

It is the pyramid arrangement we see on most organizational charts.

The bureaucratic "machine model" was developed as a reaction against the personal subjugation, nepotism and cruelty, and the capricious and subjective judgements which passed for managerial practices during the early days of the industrial revolution. Bureaucracy emerged out of the organizations' need for order and precision and the workers' demands for impartial treatment. It was an organization ideally suited to the values and demands of the Victorian era. And just as bureaucracy emerged as a creative response to a radically new age, so today new organizational shapes are surfacing before our eyes.

First I shall try to show why the conditions of our modern industrialized world will bring about the death of bureaucracy. In the second part of this article I will suggest a rough model of the organization of the future.

FOUR THREATS

There are at least four relevant threats to bureaucracy:

1. Rapid and unexpected change.
2. Growth in size where the volume of an organization's traditional activities is not enough to sustain growth. (A number of factors are included here, among them: bureaucratic overhead; tighter controls and impersonality due to bureaucratic sprawls; outmoded rules and organizational structures.)
3. Complexity of modern technology where integration between activities and persons of very diverse, highly specialized competence is required.
4. A basically psychological threat springing from a change in managerial behavior.

It might be useful to examine the extent to which these conditions exist *right now:*

(1). Rapid and unexpected change. Bureaucracy's strength is its capacity to efficiently manage the routine and predictable in human affairs. It is almost enough to cite the knowledge and population explosion to raise doubts about its contemporary viability. More revealing, however, are the statistics which demonstrate these overworked phrases:

a. Our productivity output per man hour may now be doubling almost every 20 years rather than every 40 years, as it did before World War II.
b. The Federal Government alone spent $16 billion in research and development activities in 1965; it will spend $35 billion by 1980.
c. The time lag between a technical discovery and recognition of its commercial uses was: 30 years before World War 1, 16 years between the Wars, and only 9 years since World War II.
d. In 1946, only 42 cities in the world had populations of more than one million. Today there are 90. In 1930, there were 40 people for each square mile of the earth's land surface. Today there are 63. By 2000, it is expected, the figure will have soared to 142.

Bureaucracy, with its nicely defined chain of command, its rules and its rigidities, is ill-adapted to the rapid change the environment now demands.

(2). Growth in size. While, in theory, there may be no natural limit to the height of a bureaucratic pyramid, in practice the element of complexity is almost invariably introduced with great size. International operation, to cite one significant new element, is the rule rather than exception for most of our biggest corporations. Firms like Standard Oil Company (New Jersey) with over 100 foreign affiliates, Mobil Oil Corporation, The National Cash Register Company, Singer Company, Burroughs Corporation and Colgate-Palmolive Company derive more than half their income or earnings from foreign sales. Many others–such as Eastman Kodak Company, Chas. Pfizer & Company, Inc., Caterpillar Tractor Company, International Harvester Company, Corn Products Company and Minnesota Mining & Manufacturing Company–make from 30 to 50 percent of their sales abroad. General Motors Corporation sales are not only nine times those of Volkswagen, they are also bigger than the Gross National Product of the Netherlands and well over the GNP of a hundred other countries. If we have seen the sun set on the British Empire, we may never see it set on the empires of General Motors, ITT, Shell and Unilever.

LABOR BOOM

(3). Increasing diversity. *Today's activities require persons of very diverse, highly specialized competence.*

Numerous dramatic examples can be drawn from studies of labor markets and job mobility. At some point during the past decade, the U.S. became the first nation in the world ever to employ more people in service occupations than in the production of tangible goods. Examples of this trend:

a. In the field of education, the *increase* in employment between 1950 and 1960 was greater than the total number employed in the steel, copper and aluminum industries.

b. In the field of health, the *increase* in employment between 1950 and 1960 was greater than the total number employed in automobile manufacturing in either year.
c. In financial firms, the *increase* in employment between 1950 and 1960 was greater than total employment in mining in 1960.

These changes, plus many more that are harder to demonstrate statistically, break down the old, industrial trend toward more and more people doing either simple or undifferentiated chores.

Hurried growth, rapid change and increase in specialization—pit these three factors against the five components of the pyramid structure described on page 434, and we should expect the pyramid of bureaucracy to begin crumbling.

(4). Change in managerial behavior. There is, I believe, a subtle but perceptible change in the philosophy underlying management behavior. Its magnitude, nature and antecedents, however, are shadowy because of the difficulty of assigning numbers. (Whatever else statistics do for us, they most certainly provide a welcome illusion of certainty.) Nevertheless, real change seems underway because of:

a. A new concept of *man,* based on increased knowledge of his complex and shifting needs, which replaces an over simplified, innocent, push-button idea of man.
b. A new concept of *power,* based on collaboration and reason, which replaces a model of power based on coercion and threat.
c. A new concept of *organizational values,* based on humanistic-democratic ideals, which replaces the depersonalized mechanistic value system of bureaucracy.

The primary cause of this shift in management philosophy stems not from the bookshelf but from the manager himself. Many of the behavioral scientists, like Douglas McGregor or Rensis Likert, have clarified and articulated—even legitimized—what managers have only half registered to themselves. I am convinced, for example, that the popularity of McGregor's book, *The Human Side of Enterprise,* was based on his rare empathy for a vast audience of managers who are wistful for an alternative to the mechanistic concept of authority, i.e., that he outlined a vivid utopia of more authentic human relationships than most organizational practices today allow. Furthermore, I suspect that the desire for relationships in business has little to do with a profit motive per se, though it is often rationalized as doing so. The real push for these changes stems from the need, not only to humanize the organization, but to use it as a crucible of personal growth and the development of self-realization.[1]

[1] Let me propose an hypothesis to explain this tendency. It rests on the assumption that man has a basic need for transcendental experiences, somewhat like the psychological rewards which William James claimed religion provided—"an assurance of safety and a temper of peace, and, in relation to others, a preponderance of living affections." Can it be that as religion has become secularized, less transcendental, men search for substitutes such as close interpersonal relationships, psychoanalysis—even the release provided by drugs such as LSD?

The core problems confronting any organization fall, I believe, into five major categories. First, let us consider the problems, then let us see how our twentieth-century conditions of constant change have made the bureaucratic approach to these problems obsolete.

(1). Integration. The problem is how to integrate individual needs and management goals. In other words, it is the inescapable conflict between individual needs (like "spending time with the family") and organizational demands (like meeting deadlines).

Under twentieth-century conditions of constant change there has been an emergence of human sciences and a deeper understanding of man's complexity. Today, integration encompasses the entire range of issues concerned with incentives, rewards and motivations of the individual, and how the organization succeeds or fails in adjusting to these issues. In our society, where personal attachments play an important role, the individual is appreciated, and there is genuine concern for his well-being, not just in a veterinary-hygiene sense, but as a moral, integrated personality.

PARADOXICAL TWINS

The problem of integration, like most human problems, has a venerable past. The modern version goes back at least 160 years and was precipitated by an historical paradox: the twin births of modern individualism and modern industrialism. The former brought about a deep concern for and a passionate interest in the individual and his personal rights. The latter brought about increased mechanization of organized activity. Competition between the two has intensified as each decade promises more freedom and hope for man and more stunning achievements for technology. I believe that our society *has* opted for more humanistic and democratic values, however unfulfilled they may be in practice. It will "buy" these values even at loss in efficiency because it feels it can now afford the loss.

(2). Social influence. This problem is essentially one of power and how power is distributed. It is a complex issue and alive with controversy, partly because of an ethical component and partly because studies of leadership and power distribution can be interpreted in many ways, and almost always in ways which coincide with one's biases (including a cultural leaning toward democracy).

The problem of power has to be seriously reconsidered because of dramatic situational changes which make the possibility of one-man rule not necessarily "bad" but impractical. I refer to changes in top management's role.

Peter Drucker, over 12 years ago, listed 41 major responsibilities of the chief executive and declared that "90 percent of the trouble we are having with the chief executive's job is rooted in our superstition of the one-man chief." Many factors make one-man control obsolete, among them: the broadening product base of industry; impact of new technology; the scope of international operation; the separation of management from ownership; the rise of trade unions and general education. The real power of the "chief" has been eroding in most organizations even though both he and the organization cling to the older concept.

(3). Collaboration. This is the problem of managing and resolving conflicts. Bureaucratically, it grows out of the very same process of conflict and stereotyping that has divided nations and communities. As organizations become more complex, they fragment and divide, building tribal patterns and symbolic codes which often work to exclude others (secrets and jargon, for example) and on occasion to exploit differences for inward (and always fragile) harmony.

Recent research is shedding new light on the problem of conflict. Psychologist Robert R. Blake in his stunning experiments has shown how simple it is to induce conflict, how difficult to arrest it. Take two groups of people who have never before been together, and give them a task which will be judged by an impartial jury. In less than an hour, each group devolves into a tightly-knit band with all the symptoms of an "in group." They regard their product as a "master-work" and the other group's as "commonplace" at best. "Other" becomes "enemy." "We are good, they are bad; we are right, they are wrong."

RABBIE'S REDS AND GREENS

Jaap Rabbie, conducting experiments on intergroup conflict at the University of Utrecht, has been amazed by the ease with which conflict and stereotype develop. He brings into an experimental room two groups and distributes green name tags and pens to one group, red pens and tags to the other. The two groups do not compete; they do not even interact. They are only in sight of each other while they silently complete a questionnaire. Only ten minutes are needed to activate defensiveness and fear, reflected in the hostile and irrational perceptions of both "reds" and "greens."

(4). Adaptation. This problem is caused by our turbulent environment. The pyramid structure of bureaucracy, where power is concentrated at the top, seems the perfect way to "run a railroad." And for the routine tasks of the nineteenth and early twentieth centuries, bureaucracy was (in some respects it still is) a suitable social arrangement. However, rather than a placid and predictable environment, what predominates today is a dynamic and uncertain one where there is a deepening interdependence among economic, scientific, educational, social and political factors in the society.

(5). Revitalization. This is the problem of growth and decay. As Alfred North Whitehead has said: "The art of free society consists first in the maintenance of the symbolic code, and secondly, in the fearlessness of revision. . . Those societies which cannot combine reverence to their symbols with freedom of revision must ultimately decay. . . "

Growth and decay emerge as the penultimate conditions of contemporary society. Organizations, as well as societies, must be concerned with those social structures that engender buoyancy, resilience and a "fearlessness of revision."

I introduce the term "revitalization" to embrace all the social mechanisms that stagnate and regenerate, as well as the process of this cycle. The elements of revitalization are:

1. An ability to learn from experience and to codify, store and retrieve the relevant knowledge.
2. An ability to "learn how to learn," that is, to develop methods for improving the learning process.
3. An ability to acquire and use feed-back mechanisms on performance, in short, to be self-analytical.
4. An ability to direct one's own destiny.

These qualities have a good deal in common with what John Gardner calls "self-renewal." For the organization, it means conscious attention to its own evolution. Without a planned methodology and explicit direction, the enterprise will not realize its potential.

Integration, distribution of power, collaboration, adaptation and *revitalization*—these are the major human problems of the next 25 years. How organizations cope with and manage these tasks will undoubtedly determine the viability of the enterprise.

Against this background I should like to set forth some of the conditions that will dictate organization life in the next two or three decades.

(1). The environment. Rapid technological change and diversification will lead to more and more partnerships between government and business. It will be a truly mixed economy. Because of the immensity and expense of the projects, there will be fewer identical units competing in the same markets and organizations will become more interdependent.

The four main features of this environment are:

a. Interdependence rather than competition.
b. Turbulence and uncertainty rather than readiness and certainty.
c. Large-scale rather than small-scale enterprises.
d. Complex and multinational rather than simple national enterprises.

"NICE"—AND NECESSARY

(2). Population characteristics. The most distinctive characteristic of our society is education. It will become even more so. Within 15 years, two-thirds of our population living in metropolitan areas will have attended college. Adult education is growing even faster, probably because of the rate of professional obsolescence. The Killian report showed that the average engineer required further education only ten years after getting his degree. It will be almost routine for the experienced physician, engineer and executive to go back to school for advanced training every two or three years. All of this education is not just "nice." It is necessary.

One other characteristic of the population which will aid our understanding of organizations of the future is increasing job mobility. The ease of transportation, coupled with the needs of a dynamic environment, change drastically the idea of "owning" a job—or "having roots." Already 20 percent of our population change their mailing address at least once a year.

(3). Work values. The increased level of education and mobility will change the values we place on work. People will be more intellectually committed to their jobs and will probably require more involvement, participation and autonomy.

Also, people will be more "other-oriented," taking cues for their norms and values from their immediate environment rather than tradition.

(4). Tasks and goals. The tasks of the organization will be more technical, complicated and unprogrammed. They will rely on intellect instead of muscle. And they will be too complicated for one person to comprehend, to say nothing of control. Essentially, they will call for the collaboration of specialists in a project or a team-form of organization.

There will be a complication of goals. Business will increasingly concern itself with its adaptive or innovative-creative capacity. In addition, supragoals will have to be articulated, goals which shape and provide the foundation for the goal structure. For example, one might be a system for detecting new and changing goals; another could be a system for deciding priorities among goals.

Finally, there will be more conflict and contradiction among diverse standards for organizational effectiveness. This is because professionals tend to identify more with the goals of their profession than with those of their immediate employer. University professors can be used as a case in point. Their inside work may be a conflict between teaching and research, while more of their income is derived from outside sources, such as foundations and consultant work. They tend not to be good "company men" because they divide their loyalty between their professional values and organizational goals.

KEY WORD: "TEMPORARY"

(5). Organization. The social structure of organizations of the future will have some unique characteristics. The key word will be "temporary." There will be adaptive, rapidly changing *temporary* systems. These will be task forces organized around problems to be solved by groups of relative strangers with diverse professional skills. The groups will be arranged on an organic rather than mechanical model; they will evolve in response to a problem rather than to programmed role expectations. The executive thus becomes a coordinator or "linking pin" between various task forces. He must be a man who can speak the polyglot jargon of research, with skills to relay information and to mediate between groups. People will be evaluated not vertically according to rank and status, but flexibly and functionally according to skill and professional training. Organizational charts will consist of project groups rather than stratified functional groups. (This trend is already visible in the aerospace and construction industries, as well as many professional and consulting firms.)

Adaptive, problem-solving, temporary systems of diverse specialists, linked together by coordinating and task-evaluating executive specialists in an organic flux–this is the organization form that will gradually replace bureaucracy as we know it. As no catchy phrase comes to mind, I call this an organic-adaptive structure. Organizational arrangements of this sort may not only reduce the intergroup conflicts mentioned earlier; it may also induce honest-to-goodness creative collaboration.

(6). Motivation. The organic-adaptive structure should increase motivation and thereby effectiveness, because it enhances satisfactions intrinsic to the task. There is a harmony between the educated individual's need for tasks that are meaningful, satisfactory and creative and a flexible organizational structure.

There will also be, however, reduced commitment to work groups, for these groups will be, as I have already mentioned, transient structures. I would predict that in the organic-adaptive system, people will learn to develop quick and intense relationships on the job, and learn to bear the loss of more enduring work relationships. Because of the added ambiguity of roles, time will have to be spent on continual rediscovery of the appropriate organizational mix.

I think that the future I describe is not necessarily a "happy" one. Coping with rapid change, living in temporary work systems, developing meaningful relations and then breaking them–all augur social strains and psychological tensions. Teaching how to live with ambiguity, to indentify with the adaptive process, to make a virtue out of contingency, and to be self-directing–these will be the tasks of education, the goals of maturity, and the achievement of the successful individual.

NO DELIGHTFUL MARRIAGES

In these new organizations of the future, participants will be called upon to use their minds more than at any other time in history. Fantasy, imagination and creativity will be legitimate in ways that today seem strange. Social structures will no longer be instruments of psychic repression but will increasingly promote play and freedom on behalf of curiosity and thought.

One final word: While I forecast the structure and value coordinates for organizations of the future and contend that they are inevitable, this should not bar any of us from giving the inevitable a little push. The French moralist may be right in saying that there are no delightful marriages, just good ones. It is possible that if managers and scientists continue to get their heads together in organizational revitalization, they *might* develop delightful organizations–just possibly.

I started with a quote from de Tocqueville and I think it would be fitting to end with one: "I am tempted to believe that what we call necessary institutions are often no more than institutions to which we have grown accustomed. In matters of social constitution, the field of possibilities is much more extensive than men living in their various societies are ready to imagine."

part **3**

SOCIAL PSYCHOLOGY IN ORGANIZATIONAL BEHAVIOR

Parts 1 and 2 explored two complex sets of factors which are the basis for understanding the behavior of people in organizations. Part 1 treated individual behavior, and part 2 viewed the properties of organizations themselves. Part 3 centers on the relationships among people in the context of organizations. Emphasis is given to the manner in which the behavior of one person influences the behavior of others either intentionally or unintentionally. Social power, communication, attitudes, groups, and leadership are among the topics studied by social psychologists which have proved most valuable to practicing managers.

The concept of influence is helpful in integrating these overlapping topics. One of the central problems of organizations—in fact, the reason for their existence—is the coordination of individual effort to achieve certain specified goals. In many ways the problem of coordination is a problem of influence. Simply stated, influence occurs when changes in the behavior of one person are produced by the behavior of one or more other persons. Organizations are social devices for influencing behavior[1] toward the achievement of specific goals. In this section we are concerned with the sources and consequences of influence in organizations.

The selections view influence under the headings of power, communication, attitudes, group behavior, and leadership. The reader may find it helpful to consider how each of these topics relates to influence within organizations rather than to highlight the differences among the topics.

1. Here, behavioral changes are defined broadly to include both observable behavioral changes and internal changes, such as changes in perceptions, motives, attitudes, and expectations.

chapter **10**

Power and Influence

Almost everyone who has participated in a formal organization has experienced the consequences of power. Power is perhaps the key issue in most social units; its crucial role in human behavior has made it a focal point for theorists, researchers, and administrators. The disciplines of psychology, economics, political science, sociology, and anthropology have dealt extensively with the sources of power, but many students of organizational behavior have given little attention to the concept. Such important management theorists as Likert (1967) and Argyris (1964, 1970) have written books on organizations and organizational change without referring to power in their indexes;[1] other noted writers in the field have failed to give explicit attention to manifest and latent power in organizations. This lacuna is perhaps the fatal flaw in modern theories of organizational behavior.

It may be argued that, since terms such as "influence" have been substituted for "power," organizational behaviorsts have in fact dealt extensively with the phenomenon of power. This may be the case, but the preference of theorists to avoid using "power" explicitly may provide valuable insights for a student in the sociology of knowledge. Is the failure to use the word "power" indicative of value positions which introduce systematic biases and omissions in the work of theorists? For example, organizational behaviorists who most clearly espouse the "power-equalization" or participative management position seem to hold Theory Y assumptions; they also appear to neglect the functional outcomes of power in organizations as well as the broad development of stratification structures and dominance hierarchies among animals, including man. The widespread inattention to power may be symptomatic of a value position which has led to incomplete theory and inadequate suggestions for the practice of management.

1. These writers do, however, deal with the concept of power in their texts; in the above discussion it is the lack of specific attention to the concept that is being noted. For example, Argyris (1970) did view power explicitly in his treatment of entry points for intervention. While neither power nor influence was listed in the index, "openness," "trust" and "internal commitment" were cited no fewer than 53, 43, and 33 times, respectively! Control systems were given 10 index citations, but their dysfunctional consequences were the major focus of discussion.

Again, it could be argued that these writers have dealt with power by pointing to its dysfunctional consequences. At issue, however, is their insufficient consideration of the functional outcomes of power and reasons for pervasive and marked power differences among people. Many theorists have studied the undesired correlates of the use of power, but few currently fashionable models in organizational behavior incorporate the apparently successful use of power by such men as Vince Lombardi and by leaders in such organizations as the Marine Corps[2] and political "machines." How useful are Theory Y assumptions to a participant in the Democratic party in Chicago? The failure of leading thinkers in organizational behavior to deal with power has left a void between currently accepted theory and currently existing organizations.

Gouldner (1970) has argued that in a utilitarian culture social theory may function to reduce the tension which is created by the realization ". . . that things of power may lack morality and that things of value may lack power" (p. 85). Social theories that reduce the conflict between what is considered good (ideal) and what is (real) will be valued, especially by those with power. Theorists who appear to view power as "bad" have developed theories which deemphasize it and management strategies which advocate the reduction of power differentials. These systems (e.g., management by objectives, Theory Y, System 4, participative management) all seem to indicate that power and goodness need not be in conflict. These theories may be as widely accepted as they are because they resolve the tension hypothesized by Gouldner. Theories that focus on power may increase the tension and hence be less acceptable. While this position is highly speculative, it will perhaps stimulate discussion of some neglected issues.

THE READINGS

The first selection in this chapter is an overview of social power. In this paper Nord begins by summarizing some of the major ideas presented in the classic paper on social power by French and Raven (1959). He then reviews some of the research on power which has been reported since French and Raven first published their article. Nord points out that the concept of power is useful for understanding the behavior of entire organizations as well as individual and interpersonal behavior. He suggests that the magnitude of the power of the organization *vis-a-vis* its environment is both a cause and an effect of power relationships among the members of the organization.

In the last two papers Mulder and Krishnan examine the relationship between the distribution of social power and the practice of participative management. Both papers challenge the conventional wisdom in organizational behavior that

2. Recently an ex-major from the Marine Corps told me of how he successfully trained a group which had been torn by racial strife and value differences. His primary device was to exercise his power in a manner to induce the men to hate him more than they did each other. Similar strategies of training in the military are common, and many people will attest to the success of Marine Corps training in terms of such common criteria as morale and productivity. The point here is not to advocate such approaches as either good or generally applicable; it is rather to demonstrate how the values of behavioral scientists may have led them to omit important data from their thinking.

participative management can be implemented without substantial readjustments in the distribution of power. Mulder argues that participative management can often lead to greater disparities in the distribution of power. Krishnan reports on the attitudes of high-level executives toward the participation of lower-level participants in organizational decisions. He concludes that many executives attach far more importance to preserving traditional managerial prerogatives than to encouraging the participation of employees in organizational decisions.

REFERENCES

Argyris, C. *Integrating the Individual and the Organization.* New York: John Wiley & Sons, 1964.

Argyris, C. *Intervention Theory and Method: A Behavioral Science View.* Reading, Mass.: Addison-Wesley, 1970.

French, J. P. R., and Raven, B. "The Bases of Social Power." In D. Cartwright, *Studies in Social Power.* Ann Arbor, Mich.: University of Michigan Press, 1959, pp. 150-67.

Gouldner, A. W. *The Coming Crisis of Western Sociology.* New York: Basic Books, 1970.

Likert, R. *The Human Organization: Its Management and Value.* New York: McGraw-Hill Book Co., 1967.

Walter R. Nord

DEVELOPMENTS IN THE STUDY OF POWER

Bertrand Russell (1938) once commented, ". . . the fundamental concept in social science is Power, in the same sense in which Energy is the fundamental concept of Physics" (p. 12). Despite the importance of power in relationships among people, social scientists generally agree that we know relatively little about power. As Bennis (1974) wrote,

> If you think about the Victorian era . . . it was a period in which sex was a dominant issue expressed clearly either in its suppression or its celebration. By now it's easier for people to talk about sex on talk shows than to talk about finances. Finances are the next thing that will come into the open, as we become more of a public-sector society. Power is the last of the little dirty secrets. People who have it don't want to talk about it; people who don't have it don't want to talk about it. (p. 62)

There is much evidence to support Bennis's statement. However, although the topic of power has been neglected by social scientists, it has been the subject of more and more systematic studies during the last two decades. The purpose of this paper is to review the most important advances that have been made since publication of the influential work of French and Raven (1959).

In this selection, we will begin with a brief summary of French and Raven's paper. We will then examine some of the limitations of French and Raven's model as a guide for the study of power in organizations. Next, we will review some of the fundamental theoretical and empirical developments in the study of power that provide the basis for a clearer understanding of the power relationships that exist within organizations.

FRENCH AND RAVEN'S FIVE BASES OF POWER

In comparison with discussions of power by more macro-oriented theorists French and Raven's analysis of power was narrow in its scope. French and Raven were concerned primarily with understanding social influence in small groups. Moreover they were only concerned with one part of the influence process—the

Prepared especially for this volume.

psychological reasons why an individual is influenced by another person.

French and Raven distinguished five sets of reasons why one individual may be influenced by another. Each of these five sets corresponded to a particular type of power–reward power, coercive power, referent power, expert power and legitimate power. While these five types of power stem from different bases, they can, and often do, occur together.

Reward and coercive power are counterparts of each other. If an individual, who we will call Person, is influenced by some one else, who we will call Other, because Other has the ability to give Person rewards and/or remove aversive stimuli, then we say that Other has reward power over Person. Conversely if Person is influenced by Other because Other has the ability to remove positive and/or to administer negative stimuli, French and Raven suggest that Other has coercive power over Person.

In some ways the third type of power, referent power, can be viewed as an extension of reward power. If Other has referent power over Person, it is because Person identifies so closely with Other that Person comes to behave (and to even perceive and believe) in the same way that Other does. Thus Other is able to influence Person without monitoring Person's behavior and in fact may influence Person without even intending to.

The fourth type of power, expert power, arises from Person's perception that Other has valuable knowledge which will make it profitable for Person to follow Other's advice. Person is influenced by Other because Person respects Other's expertise.

The final type of power, legitimate power, stems from the internalized values of Person which lead him to believe that Other, by virtue of his position in the social structure, has the right to influence Person. For example, to the degree that a manager has legitimate power over his subordinates, his subordinates do what he asks them to do because they believe that he has the right to ask for and to receive such compliance. It is this type of power which is closest to what we normally mean when we talk about authority.

SOME LIMITATIONS OF FRENCH AND RAVEN'S MODEL FOR THE STUDY OF ORGANIZATIONS

French and Raven's work on power still serves as a useful introduction to the concept of social power, although it was published some time ago. However, since then there have been important new developments in our understanding of the role of power in human organization. While much of our knowledge is still derived from experiments conducted in psychological laboratories, there is a clear trend toward studies of the power process in ongoing organizations. In addition, as we have begun to study the interaction between organizations and their environments, we have become more aware that power relationships among people within an organization are influenced by the external power relationships of the organization.

French and Raven's model is of limited value in elucidating the complex power relationships within and among organizations. A major limitation of their model is that it describes only the behavior of individuals. As they wrote, "We . . . formulate our theory in terms of the life space of P, the person upon whom power is exerted." This formulation is too narrow in at least one important respect; it omits the power relationships that exist among other social units.

A second problem of their model stems from their definition of power, which equates power with influence and psychological change. In their words, ". . . we . . . define power in terms of influence, and influence in terms of psychological change." However, as Secord and Backman (1974) observed, it is useful to distinguish between power and influence, because ". . . a person might have considerable social power but rarely exercise it" (pp. 246-7). In other words, power may be latent; influence cannot. Since power in organizations is often latent, a more precise definition of power seems warranted. One such definition was provided by Olsen (1968). He defined social power as ". . . *the ability to affect social life (social actions, social order, or culture)* . . ." (p. 172). This definition, which includes latent power as well as influence under the heading of power, is more useful than French and Raven's for describing organizational processes.

Thirdly, French and Raven's model fails to deal with the psychological and behavioral consequences of the possession of power, the feeling of powerlessness, and the quest for power. Because of these shortcomings, the French and Raven model must be expanded if it is to be useful to our understanding of power in organizations.

POWER IN ORGANIZATIONS

Social power is pervasive; it has origins and effects at all levels of an organization. First, personalities of individuals are involved; different people appear to place different values on the gain and exercise of power. Second, in almost all organizations some people are more powerful than others. Disparities in power affect the behavior, feelings, and attitudes of both the powerful and the less powerful toward many aspects of their world, including themselves. Finally, the degree of power which the organization as a whole enjoys with respect to its environment, including its competitors and trading partners, influences the behavior of all members of the organization.

In reality the power of individuals, the distribution of power within the organization, and the power of the total system are interrelated. For example, differing needs for personal power affect the distribution of power within an organization; similarly, the internal distribution of power contributes to the effectiveness of an organization and consequently is a factor determining the power that the total system can exert within its environment. The direction of the relationships can also be reversed; the power of the whole organization influences the internal distribution of power and the degree to which individuals can satisfy their own needs for power. Even though the effects of these different aspects of power are closely interwoven, we will begin our analysis by treating the three topics separately.

Personality and the Need for Power

Individuals differ in the strength of their desire for power. Although discussions of these differences have taken place throughout history, recent investigations such as those of Winter (1973) and his colleagues have been particularly enlightening. Winter argued that an important determinant of the amount of power an individual exercises is the strength of his or her power motive, which Winter defined as a

> . . . disposition to strive for certain kinds of goals, or to be affected by certain kinds of incentives. People who have the power motive, or who strive for power, are trying to bring about a certain state of affairs—they want to feel "power" or "more powerful than. . . ." Power is their goal. (pp. 17-18)

After conducting a number of studies which demonstrated an association between the need for power and certain patterns of behavior, Winter concluded that the strength of a person's power motive can be used to predict such significant aspects of that individual's behavior as his

> . . . holding offices in organizations and having other positions of power, using interpersonal strategies that are likely to get power, controlling and even distorting information, and acquiring prestige. (p. 202)

Winter found that individuals with strong power needs tend to be attracted to occupations which afford them considerable scope in defining their roles, selecting their actions, advising and helping others, and controlling and evaluating the behavior of others. Consequently, people whose power motive is strong are drawn to such positions as business management, teaching, and psychology.

Several other writers have concluded that the need for power is related to success in modern business. Cummin (1967) administered measures of need for power to middle- and upper-level managers who worked in a number of business organizations. He classified the executives into high and low success groups on the basis of how their salaries compared to the salaries of other executives of comparable age. Cummin found that the most successful executives scored significantly higher in the need for power than did the less successful executives. He concluded that successful executives show a definite desire ". . . for increased responsibility and control under the organizational hierarchy" (p. 81). Similarly, Livingston (1971) suggested that the need for power is one of the most important factors determining an individual's advancement in modern corporations.[1]

In sum, individuals differ in their need for power. These differences, which influence how people behave, appear to be associated with differences in both success and the distribution of power in at least some modern organizations. However, the mere fact that people who currently hold positions of power have

[1] If upper-level managers have strong power needs, power equalization strategies advocated by some behavioral scientists will be unattractive to them. Evidence for this conclusion may be found in Krishnan's paper, reprinted in this chapter. Krishnan reported that the attitudes of corporate executives are quite incompatible with participative management.

strong needs for power does not prove that the need for power is the causal factor. It may be that the possession of power itself produces changes in an individual's personality, attitudes, and behavior toward others.

The Distribution of Power

Effects on the powerful. In organizations the various bases of power described by French and Raven tend to exist together; the individual who holds legitimate power is also apt to control sources of reward, coercive and information power and therefore is likely to be able to exercise a great deal of influence over others. Organizations are therefore a good setting for observations of the behavioral effects of unequal distribution of power.

There is considerable disagreement about how possession of power affects the powerful. As Kipnis (1972) has noted, a number of social scientists have reported that the possession of power may actually lead to compassionate behavior on the part of the power holder. By contrast, other social scientists believe ". . . that the very control of power induces individuals to act in an inequitable and exploitive manner towards the less powerful . . ." (p. 34). Kipnis and his colleagues have attempted to determine the validity of these two positions through a series of investigations of the behavior of individuals who hold power.

In one of these studies each subject was asked to supervise another person. Some of the supervisors were led to believe that they had a great deal of power over the workers; others were given less. Kipnis found that the amount of power given the supervisors affected their treatment of their workers. Subjects given a great amount of power attempted to influence the workers more frequently than did those with less power. Moreover, the longer the experiment continued, the greater became this difference in frequency. Kipnis also observed differences in the ways in which the supervisors attempted to influence the workers. Supervisors with less power used persuasion in only 16 percent of their attempts; for their other attempts they relied on the power that had been delegated to them, including promises of raises and threats of reductions in pay. Kipnis also observed that the supervisors who had been given power tended to devalue the work of their workers and to prefer to maintain psychological distance from them. In fact, when asked whether they would like to meet with the workers whom they had supervised in the experimental task, only 35 percent of the subjects with more power replied affirmatively; by contrast, 75 percent of the subjects with less power said they would like to meet their workers.

In comparison to the less powerful supervisors, the more powerful ones expressed more manipulative attitudes, showed less concern for the workers, and were less apt to believe that the workers wanted to do a good job. Kipnis concluded that

> . . . the control of power triggers a chain of events, which, in theory at least, goes like this: (a) with the control of power goes increased temptations [*sic*] to influence others' behavior. (b) As actual influence attempts increase, there arises the belief that behavior of others is not self-controlled, but is caused by the power holder, (c) hence, a devaluation of their performance. In addition, with increased influence attempts, forces are gen-

erated within the more powerful to (d) increase psychological distance from the less powerful and view them as objects of manipulation. (p. 40)

One of the most convincing demonstrations of the effects of power on the people who possess it was provided by the work of Zimbardo.[2] The men whom Zimbardo and his co-workers recruited for their experiment were, as far as could be determined, typical of many subjects used in psychological experiments; they were middle-class, Caucasian, college-age males. Half were randomly selected to serve as guards in a simulated prison, which had been constructed in the basement of the psychology building at Stanford University. The other subjects were assigned the role of prisoner.

A variety of techniques were used to recreate the actual psychological conditions of imprisonment. The prisoners were "deindividualized" and made powerless in relation to the guards. They were confined, dressed in prisoners' clothes, and made almost totally dependent on the guards.

The power gap produced startling results. Zimbardo observed that the guards quickly became highly aggressive and the prisoners very passive. As time went on, these qualities intensified. Among other things, the guards forced the prisoners to clean out the toilets with their bare hands.

> Typically the guards insulted the prisoners, threatened them, were physically aggressive, used instruments (night sticks, fire extinguishers, etc.) to keep the prisoners in line and referred to them in impersonal, anonymous, deprecating ways. . . . From the first to the last day there was significant increase in the guards' use of most of these domineering abusive tactics. (pp. 48-49)

In one of the more remarkable examples of the effect of power, by the fifth day guard A, who entered the experiment as a pacifist and a non-aggressive person, tried to force-feed a prisoner who would not eat. The aggression and sadism became so intense that the experimenters felt compelled to terminate the planned two-week experiment after six days.

While the data presented by Kipnis and Zimbardo were derived from psychological laboratories, similar effects are readily apparent in most organizations. The work of Rosenhan (see part 2) showed how the holders of power in mental institutions come to treat their patients as objects. However, one does not have to go to a prison or a mental hospital to see the effect of power on the behavior of the powerful. One need only visit a school or university to see a mild-mannered person turn into a tyrant when he teaches a class or questions a doctoral student during a dissertation "defense." One can enter almost any business organization and observe a variety of physical and social barriers separating the powerful from the rest. These range from such formal devices as executive lunchrooms and washrooms to social norms against the development of friendships between people at different levels of the organization.

Overall, it appears that the possession of power has important behavioral

[2] For a more complete description of this work, see "A Pirandellian Prison," in the *New York Times Magazine* for April 8, 1973, pp. 38-60.

effects. In McGregor's terms, there seems to be a tendency for powerful people to adopt Theory X assumptions about their subordinates. If power does act to induce Theory X assumptions, some fundamental beliefs of a number of organizational behaviorists must be reexamined. Theory Y assumptions may be incompatible with differentials in social power. The "authoritarian" behavior of a manager toward his subordinates may be a function not only of the manager's personality but of their social relationship, dictated by the formal structure itself.

Effects on the "powerless." Differences in social power also have important effects on the feelings of less powerful people. Lefcourt's paper (in part 1) described many of the consequences of the experience of powerlessness, and other writers have advanced similar ideas. Political scientists and philosophers have shown that most people view those who control economic and political power with a mixture of admiration and suspicion (Kipnis, 1972), fearing in particular that the powerful may become corrupt, mean, and self-serving.

One of the most dramatic statements of the effects of powerlessness is Michael Harrington's (1962) description of "the twisted spirit" of the American poor. He observed that the "culture of poverty" unleashes a vicious circle in which the poor are held back by the fatalism, pessimism, and feelings of alienation and powerlessness which are products of their total psychological experience. Their feelings of powerlessness act as self-fulfilling prophecies.

A parallel process seems to occur among the relatively powerless members of organizations. One set of consequences includes feelings of dependence and servility. As Gouldner (1970) noted, power

> . . . exists as a factor in the lives of subordinates shaping their behavior and beliefs, at every moment of their relations with those above them. Attitudes toward their superiors are continually influenced by the *awareness*—sometimes focal and sometimes only subsidiary—that superiors can give or withhold at will things that men greatly want, quite apart from their own agreement or consent, and that crucial gratifications depend upon allocations and decisions by their superiors. It is the sheer ability of the powerful to do this, quite apart from their *right* to do so, that is an independent, ever-present element in the servile attitudes that subordinates often develop toward their superiors. (p. 294)

In addition to producing feelings of dependence and servility, inequities in power also inhibit cooperative behavior (Nemeth, 1970).

The feelings associated with the experience of powerlessness are so common among members of modern organizations that most people can validate the observations of the social scientists through their own everyday experiences. Who has not experienced anger and frustration in response to an apparently arbitrary action of a boss or a seemingly worthless assignment made by a teacher? Anyone who has worked at a low level in an organization knows the tension and excitement that a casual visit from a member of the top brass can create.

Of course, the reactions that each of us has to the experience of powerlessness depend on our personality and on our perception of the situation. Some individuals typically comply happily with nearly all the demands or actions of an authority figure, perhaps rationalizing that what they are required to do will be for the best. Other individuals typically comply but experience hostility. They may express their anger directly and constructively to the power figure, lash out at the frustrating agent, or surpress their anger and appear to "keep their cool." Surpressed anger may be expressed indirectly to some third party when the power figure is not present or to the power figure but in disguised form at some later date. Still other individuals seem to resist authority figures at every turn. On different occasions all of us probably have experienced each of these reactions when we felt relatively powerless.

The power of lower-level participants. Underlying many discussions of power is the assumption that lower-level participants in organizations are, in reality, quite powerless. However, as Mechanic (1962) noted, these people often have a great deal of power and need only become aware of their resources. They may have access to certain people, information, and resources which would allow them to achieve their own goals or at least to thwart the efforts of higher-ranking individuals. Often, however, people continue to respond as if they were powerless. Why?

While there is no simple answer, Culbert (1974) provided some stimulating thoughts on the matter. Culbert coined the phrase "organization traps" to refer to shared assumptions in organizations which make people vulnerable ". . . to excessive influence by the system" (p. 20). When people accept these assumptions about themselves and their organizations, they tend to embrace the *status quo* rather than develop alternative ways of thinking and acting.

Culbert argued that to break out of these traps people must first become conscious of their assumptions and then develop new ideas that will allow them to act in new ways.

> Ultimately, we want organization members with various experiences to pool their perspectives and create a better, more complex picture of reality to guide the way the organization operates. (p. 151)

Culbert's ideas have several important implications for our discussion of powerlessness. First, an individual's perception of his organization may be a major cause of his feelings of powerlessness. Second, organizational power involves much more than just one person or a group of people exercising control over others. Rather, the system seems to take on power of its own. People are controlled by implicit assumptions that they share about the essential features of their organization. These assumptions comprise the culture of the organization and exert strong control over the behavior of the participants. Third, it is possible to conceive a deliberate strategy through which the "powerless" can exercise more influence within the system. Once the vicious cycle of powerlessness is broken and individuals begin to exert power, they will become psychologically more prepared to use power in the future. For example, as Raven and Kruglanski (1970) have noted, the exercise of power may boost an individual's self-esteem, free him from feelings of inferiority, despair and inaction, and cause him to be less fearful.

By way of summary, the distribution of power has important effects on the behavior of organizational participants. The possession of power may induce the powerful to neglect the interests of the powerless. Also, the absence of power is associated with feelings of inferiority, latent hostility, alienation, and fatalism. Furthermore, this process perpetuates itself. By contrast, as individuals begin to exercise power, they may become more confident and more able to exercise power.

Preservation of power. Employing various methods to maintain their position, the powerful usually resist anyone else's attempts to change the distribution of power within an organization. O'Day (1974) used the term "intimidation rituals" to refer to the devices that members of an organization's authority structure use to prevent change which they do not sanction.

O'Day suggested that there are two phases of intimidation, indirect and direct. The first step of indirect intimidation is called nullification and consists of the superior assuring the would-be reformer that his accusations or suggestions are merely the product of misunderstandings or misconceptions. If nullification fails to allay the reformer, management takes the second step–isolation. Now management separates the would-be reformer from other members of the organization in order to soften his impact and impede his efforts to mobilize support. Management isolates the individual or finds other ways to limit his communication links, restrict his freedom of movement, and reduce the resources available to him.

If indirect intimidation fails to curb the efforts of the reformer, the second phase–direct intimidation–becomes necessary. The first step of direct intimidation is defamation, whereby the authorities attempt to reduce the influence of the reformer over his potential followers by linking him publicly to questionable motives, gross incompetence, or even underlying psychopathology. If this step fails, the authorities resort to the final step–expulsion.

O'Day's analysis is a valuable complement to Culbert's; together these two treatments help us to understand some of the subtler attitudes and behaviors which affect the distribution and redistribution of power within organizations. Their analyses also clarify the forces for change latent in the existing distribution of power. Individuals and groups are continually gaining and losing power. As these changes occur, so do changes in the physical and psychological status of individuals who work in the organization and changes in the performance of the organization as a whole.

The distribution of power which exists at any one time influences important organizational decisions–what goals the organization will pursue and how organizational resources will be distributed among participants. These decisions play an important role in determining how effective the organization will be in its relationships with its environments and hence affect the power of the organization as a whole.

Organizational Power and the Environment

Organizations depend on their environments to survive; if they are unable to obtain resources from their environments, they cease to exist. They must be able to carry on profitable exchanges with various components of their environments, including suppliers, customers, and governmental bodies.

Organizations are more dependent on some elements of their environment than on others. As Thompson (1967) noted, the degree of dependence on any external element varies.

> . . . (1) in proportion to the organization's need for resources or performances which that element can provide and (2) in inverse proportion to the ability of other elements to provide the same resource or performance. (p. 30)

Dependence is the obverse of power; the more dependent an organization is on any particular element in its environment, the lower is the organization's power.

The nature of the relationship between an organization and its environment affects the amount of power available to various people within the organization in at least three ways. First, a number of forces in the environment act to constrain the ability of top management to exert influence over lower-level members of the organization. To the degree that the organization can affect these environmental constraints, high-level participants can exercise power over lower-level participants. Second, the more power the organization has *vis-a-vis* its environment, the greater will be the amount of power potentially available to all members of the organization. Third, the need for the organization to deal with various segments of its environment influences the status and power of the individuals who are responsible for dealing with those segments. For example, if a firm is very dependent on a particular element of its environment, the individuals who are charged with managing this relationship may be given a large share of the available resources. Let us look at these three types of effects in more detail.

Environmental constraints on treatment of lower-level participants. A major source of power for most work organizations is their ability to offer or deny membership. However, the amount of power an organization derives from this source depends on how highly members and potential members value membership. The value of membership is affected by such exogenous factors as the number and quality of alternative organizations in which the participant in question can conveniently work. Of course, not all individuals place the same value on membership. For example, some workers, usually the younger and more skilled ones, have more alternatives and are thus less dependent on the organization that employs them. In general, the degree of an organization's power is influenced by the demand for labor in the relevant labor market; when other jobs are plentiful and the cost of movement between jobs is small, the firm can exert less power over many of its members. However, when the demand for a particular set of job skills is weak and the cost of moving between jobs is high, the firm can exercise considerable power.

Laws and social norms, varying from state to state and nation to nation, also delimit the power of organizations by defining a number of responsibilities that employers have with respect to their employees. Formal regulations typically pertain to such things as working conditions, hours, and more recently the employment of women and minorities. The constraints imposed by social norms are more difficult to specify, but examples can be found in the discussions of cultural patterns elsewhere in this book. For instance, Japanese social norms relating to layoffs appear to constrain the typical employer there more than do such norms in the United States.

Other organizations in the environment, such as unions and similar professional organizations, also limit the power of the organization over its participants. For example, several decades ago, before unions became effective in instituting grievance procedures and other means for workers to protect and enhance their interests, the power of supervisors to take arbitrary action was far greater than it is today.

In brief, the greater the organization's power *vis-a-vis* certain elements of its environment, the more discretion it can exercise in its dealings with many of its participants. Moreover, in some ways the power of the organization in its environment can augment the power of all its members.

Net organizational power and the power of organizational members. Since every organization is related to a number of parts of its environment, the power of an organization is influenced by a complex set of relationships. As Thompson observed,

> . . . an organization may be relatively powerful in relation to those who supply its inputs and relatively powerless in relation to those who receive its outputs, or vice versa. (p. 31)

Thus, according to Thompson, we should not think of power as a generalized attribute of the organization. Rather, we can more usefully think of "net power" that results ". . . from a set of relationships between the organization and the several elements of its pluralistic task environment" (p. 31).

One of the major purposes for the existence of any organization is to increase the ability of its participants to accomplish ends that none of them could accomplish alone. In other words, organizations serve to increase the power that their members exercise in a certain domain. The degree to which an organization is successful in accomplishing its goals and in attracting and effectively utilizing resources from its environment is really a measure of the power of the whole organization. In this sense, a major objective of every organization is to increase its net power. Other things being equal, the greater the net power of the whole organization, the greater the power all individuals in the organization can exert. In order to see this point more clearly, consider the degree of power a firm has with respect to its customers.

If a firm is the only producer of a good that is vitally needed by a number of customers, the firm has considerable power over its customers. Consequently, the firm is often able to charge a high price for its output, and all members of the firm can benefit. Union members have a better chance of getting large wage increases than if the firm were operating on a narrower margin of profit. Managers are more apt to be granted budget increases.

Once we consider the fact that the power of the whole influences the power of the participants, we discover an important point–the total power of any member can be increased without that person gaining power in relation to other members; everybody can become more powerful, even though the internal distribution of power remains the same. In this respect power within the organization is similar to a non-zero-sum game–one person's gains are not necessarily another person's losses. However, many changes in an organization's net power are associated with changes in the power position of some of its members.

Environmental effects on the endogenous distribution of power. Actual and expected changes in the net power position of the organization can cause changes in the relative amount of power available to various participants. For example, large profits often enhance the status and prestige of "key" people; individuals who either have been or appear likely to be successful in dealing with elements of the environment on which the organization is most dependent are apt to be promoted or otherwise esteemed. Similarly, the relative power of whole groups of organizational participants may be altered as a result of exogenous threats to the organization.

The influence that any particular department can exert depends in part on the problems a firm faces in dealing with its environment. For example, during the oil embargo of 1973-1974, when the supply of raw materials necessary for production became tight, many purchasing departments gained significantly more influence on a number of decisions; at the same time such departments as sales found their power to have diminished considerably. The "strategic contingencies" theory of intraorganizational power developed by Hickson, Hinings, Lee, Schneck, and Pennings (1971) provides a comprehensive description of this process.

Hickson *et al.* began with the assumption that organizations can be conceived as open systems carrying on transactions with their environment. These systems are themselves made up of departments or subunits, each performing tasks that contribute to the ability of the organization to cope with its environment.

According to Hickson *et al.*, the distribution of power among departments is related to their interdependence. The more powerful departments are the less dependent ones, the ones on which other departments depend instead. Their power derives from their ability to control the "strategic contingencies" of other departments. Specifically, the power of a given department (let's call it Department A) is related to the degree to which information and/or resources needed by other departments for carrying out their tasks are (1) available from Department A, (2) unavailable from other sources, and (3) essential to the activities of the other departments. In the words of Hickson *et al.*, "The more contingencies are controlled by a subunit, the greater its power within the organization" (p. 222).[3]

[3] In a more recent paper Hinings, Hickson, Pennings, and Schneck (1974) presented

Clearly, the distribution of power will not be static, since the particular needs of the subunits will change, as will the abilities of the various departments to provide relevant information and resources. Many of these changes will, of course, be introduced exogenously as the organization's environment changes. As the challenges to the organization change, so does the nature and pattern of strategic contingencies among the departments. Although the internal distribution of power is subject to change with shifts in the organization's relationship with certain portions of its environment, redistribution of internal power is not automatic or immediate.

In fact, the rigidity of the power structure inhibits the organization's ability to deal with its environment. For example, consider a firm's decision to produce or not to produce a particular product. It is important that the individuals and departments with the most accurate information about such things as the quality of the product, consumer tastes, manufacturing costs, etc., should significantly influence the decision. However, often the existing distribution of power prevents them from doing so. In the extreme case, the decision may be based on a whim of the president rather than informed analysis. Generally, the more influential the people with the best, most relevant information are, the more successful the firm will be in dealing with its environment.

CONCLUSION

We have seen that power can act as both an independent and a dependent variable. The possession of power affects the behavior of the powerful and the less powerful. This behavior in turn influences the degree of power the different participants exercise.

We have also seen that power is a fundamental concept for the analysis of all organizations. It pertains to relationships among individuals, between individuals and organizations, and between organizations and their environments. Undoubtedly our ability to understand and manage organizations and other social systems awaits advances in our knowledge of social power.

REFERENCES

Bennis, W. G. "Conversation . . . with Warren Bennis." *Organizational Dynamics* 2 (1974): 51-66.

Culbert, S. A. *The Organization Trap.* New York: Basic Books, 1974.

Cummin, P. C. "TAT Correlates of Executive Performance." *Journal of Applied Psychology* 51 (1967): 78-81.

French, J. R. P., and Raven, B. "The Bases of Social Power." In *Studies in Social Power,* edited by D. Cartwright, pp. 150-167. Ann Arbor, Mich.: University of Michigan Press, 1959.

Gouldner, A. W. *The Coming Crisis of Western Sociology.* New York: Basic Books, 1970.

---

empirical support for their strategic contingencies theory. They studied a total of twenty-eight subunits from seven different organizations. They found that their theory predicted the power rankings of twenty-four of the twenty-eight subunits correctly.

Harrington, M. *The Other America.* Baltimore: Penguin Books, 1962.

Hickson, D. J.; Hinings, C. R.; Lee, C. A.; Schneck, R. E.; and Pennings, J. M. "A Strategic Contingencies' Theory of Intraorganizational Power." *Administrative Science Quarterly* 16 (1971): 216-229.

Hinings, C. R.; Hickson, D. J.; Pennings, J. M.; and Schneck, R. E. "Structural Conditions of Intraorganizational Power." *Administrative Science Quarterly* 19 (1974): 22-44.

Kipnis, D. "Does Power Corrupt?" *Journal of Personality and Social Psychology* 24 (1972): 33-41.

Livingston, J. S. "Myth of the Well-Educated Manager." *Harvard Business Review* 49 (1971): 79-89.

Mechanic, D. "Sources of Power of Lower Participants in Complex Organizations." *Administrative Science Quarterly* 7 (1962): 349-364.

Nemeth, C. "Bargaining and Reciprocity." *Psychological Bulletin* 74 (1970): 297-308.

O'Day, R. "Intimidation Rituals: Reactions to Reform." *Journal of Applied Behavioral Science* 10 (1974): 373-386.

Olsen, M. E. *The Process of Social Organization.* New York: Holt, Rinehart & Winston, 1968.

Raven, B. H., and Kruglanski, A. W. "Conflict and Power." In *The Structure of Conflict,* edited by P. Swingle, pp. 69-109. New York: Academic Press, 1970.

Russell, B. *Power.* New York: Norton & Co., 1938.

Secord, P. F., and Backman, C. W. *Social Psychology.* 2nd Ed. New York: McGraw-Hill, 1974.

Thompson, J. D. *Organizations in Action.* New York: McGraw-Hill, 1967.

Winter, D. G. *The Power Motive.* New York: Free Press, 1973.

Mauk Mulder

POWER EQUALIZATION THROUGH PARTICIPATION?

In recent years, participation has been widely used in social science literature to refer to practices intended to realize power equalization. It has been considered desirable to reduce differences in power between different levels in society, in organizations, and in groups; and participation in decision making by the less powerful members has been assumed to be one of the best means to this end.

The question is: What improvement can be expected from actual participation, and which effects of participation will persist in the future?

INTRODUCTION

Participation and Effectiveness

Participation is the most vital organizational problem of our time, and it is therefore astonishing that there have been so few investigations in this area, and that the theoretical basis for these studies has been so meager. Another organizational problem is how to make participation a reality. To elaborate this: participation in decision making by the less powerful will change the leadership functions of the more powerful; and new structures for leadership, decision making, and communication will develop. Connected with these structural variables is—as substantiated in much research—the effectiveness of an organization. For the individual members, feelings of well-being and their sense of self-realization are related to participation and its consequences.

In the development of new structures, however, participation is in danger of becoming a power struggle between those who stress the need for more participation by the lower levels of the organization and those who emphasize the necessity to preserve the capacity of the organization to function effectively and to survive. In the discussion and application of participation, little attempt has been made to formulate goals clearly, and to explore the functioning of participation procedures and the advantages of the different approaches. The result is

Mauk Mulder, "Power Equalization through Participation?" *Administrative Science Quarterly,* Vol. 16, No. 1, March 1971, pp. 31-37.

that those stressing participation and those stressing efficiency have often remained unreconciled, with the stronger party pressing for its objectives, while the other party complied as a result of weakness. Such a power struggle completely contradicts the concept of participation, which stresses that the use of power by the more powerful is rejectable and should be replaced by open communication on the basis of equality of all participants.

Need for Theoretical and Empirical Research

There is a great need for a theoretical framework for the problem of participation, and for gathering and analyzing empirical data. In Yugoslavia, Vidakovic (1965) stated that after more than a decade of self-government by the so-called work councils, the theory on self-government was inadequate, and reliable research data were lacking.

Empirical research, on an appropriate scale, has only very recently started in Dutch-speaking areas (Lammers (ed.), 1965; Coetsier, 1966; Drenth and Van der Pijl, 1966; Teulings, 1968; Van Zuthem and Wynia, 1967). In nearly all of these studies except Teulings's (1968), the survey method, using a verbal stimulus-verbal response mechanism, has been used for the attitude research. It is, of course, necessary to assess the expressed opinions of the involved classes of people, but it is far more important to find out what really happens. Van der Velden (1965, 1968) found clear evidence that the same respondents who had expressed quite a positive attitude about the functioning of their work council in their answers to survey questions were extremely negative about the council in their direct contacts with the participant observer. From this a conclusion is that research in this area should not be restricted to survey data. Thus, one means to an end for assessing the real ongoing processes is offered by systematic observation as it was applied, in addition to the survey technique, in the investigation by the Institute of Social Psychology at the State University at Utrecht (Van der Velden, 1965, 1968; Quint, 1967). An approach combining middle-range theorizing with strict testing of hypotheses in laboratory experiments is also more appropriate than relying only on large survey data.

Those who aim at power equalization see participation, or codetermination, as for example in the work councils, as the most appropriate way to achieve this goal. However, critical theorizing and research about the relation between participation as a means and reduction in inequality of power as a goal are needed.

It is necessary that participation be clearly defined; since it can vary from a process in which the less powerful—often on the initiative and with the consent of their superiors, although superiors make the final decisions—contribute their opinions, to a process in which group decisions come about. Strauss (1963: 43, 57, 60) stated that participation, however defined, is generally conceived of as a way of reducing power differences, and therefore equality is stressed. Communication among equals is usually explicitly mentioned in the application of participation procedures, as for example, in the pioneering Scanlon plan, in the appraisal interviewing procedures in management-development programs, and in the democratization programs in industrial organizations (Krulec, 1955; Lesieur,

1958; Unilever Group Management Personnel, 1967; Kolaja, 1965; Thorsrud and Emery, 1966). However, a formulation which proposes that participation is reduction of power inequality is too rough to be true, as may be made clear from the following: In the eyes of many European practitioners and scientists, work councils are a landmark of progressive thinking in industrial settings and could provide a model of participation, resulting in power equalization. However, members of work councils have very different functions in the organization. There is an obvious difference in formal power position between a manual laborer and a director. Also there are differences in the power of council members, based on expertness and access to relevant information (French and Raven, 1959). Managers and top specialists have more expertise and information about problems pertaining to their kind of organization than other organization members, simply because they spend more time on such problems. They know, for example, much more about financial resources, and about relationships between technology and production and between the organization and outside institutions. These are all of crucial significance for the survival of the system.

Managers and specialists also have more experience in communication and human relations. For example, in evaluation and promotion procedures, although the objective is a reciprocal discussion during the interview, it is doubtful that this is realized. The evaluators have many interviews with many, different evaluees. The evaluee, on the other hand, usually has only a few of these talks; therefore a wide difference between the relative expertness of evaluators and evaluees in such procedures is highly probable. Indeed, it is not by chance that in these evaluation programs, evaluators are often provided with special training, sometimes up to six months (Unilever Group Management Personnel, 1967; Morse and Reimer, 1956).

In addition, persons from the lower levels of the organization may not want to participate. Empirical investigations in Europe showed that members of organizations generally did not know very much about their work councils, although these were the most typical participation institutions. Thus, it is probable that the involvement and positive motivation for participation through delegates, as they function in work councils, are far less than suggested by the responses of members to the direct questions of surveys, which in themselves do not show a very positive picture of participation (Van de Vall, 1963).

Findings of Empirical Research

In research on the functioning of Dutch work councils, Van der Velden (1965, 1968) and Quint (1967) found that half the voluntary members of work councils were not strongly motivated to participate in decision making; the other half complained about having insufficient expertise, although these work councils had already been functioning for a fairly long period of time—some for more than eight years. This combination of low levels of motivation and expertness has appeared in all the investigations made in Dutch-speaking areas. Other researchers (Drenth and Van der Pijl, 1966; Van der Velden, 1965, 1968; Coetsier, 1966; Van Zuthem and Wynia, 1967) found that members of work councils were concerned with specific details in their personal interest areas, not with policy or organizational problems. They did not want participation when it involved codecision making. Expertise, including expertise in communication, is particularly lacking for problems of policy (Van de Vall, 1963; Van der Velden, 1965, 1968; Drenth and Van der Pijl, 1966; De Bruin, 1961; Ellemers, 1965; Philipsen, 1965).

Van der Velden (1965, 1968) reported from observational data that a few manager members of the work councils contributed 75 percent of the total communication in the work councils, and that two or three talkers from among the other members were responsible for two-thirds of the remaining 25 percent. In other European countries, similar data have been found (Coetsier, 1966; Thorsrud and Emery, 1966). Recently it has been suggested that successful participation is achieved by the Yugoslav work councils or workers' committees, where the laborers, having a large majority in this representative body, are assumed to function as the effective, collective leadership of the industrial enterprises. In research carried out on these Yugoslav councils, with observation methods as well as survey techniques, it was found that the managers and specialists were responsible for the greatest number of the proposals accepted by their councils (Kolaja, 1965), although they made up only a very small proportion of the total membership of the councils. The trade union and the Communist party consider that motivating the workers to participate in organizational affairs is their chief problem (Kolaja, 1965; Broekmeyer, 1968).

In his very extensive and intensive study of the entire Yugoslav development, Broekmeyer (1968) found:

1. Insufficient expertness among nonspecialist members of the Yugoslav work council; for example, 90 percent of the talkers in the council were specialists and had higher education (Broekmeyer, 1968: 269, see also 136). So the largest proportion of the members did not account for more than 10 percent of the communication.
2. Inadequate motivation of workers for general, important problem handling in the council; for example, when reactions were invited about proposals on very important questions, there was no response (Broekmeyer, 1968: 325).
3. Growth of a power elite, a small circle of the most competent and responsible people; for example, in one study, 703 of 738 activists fulfilled 6.4 functions per man (Broekmeyer, 1968: 123).

Broekmeyer (1968: 324, see also 267, 357) also reported that the leaders of the progressive movement of workers' self-government were not inclined to let others participate in their goal-directed efforts.

It is remarkable that Broekmeyer (1968: 191, 205, 367) stressed strong centralistic power as a prerequisite for the introduction and survival of the workers' self-government. These data are of some significance because they come from an ideological climate, Communist Yugoslavia, which could be assumed to be extremely favorable for the trend toward participation.

One can infer that participation does not automatically lead to reduction of power differences; in fact, very often the more powerful remain so in participation structures (Marrow *et al.*, 1968: 32, 52-53). Thus, the basic assumption of many of the theoretical and practical programs of participation, that participation leads to a decrease in power differences, is severely weakened. The following hypothesis can be formulated:

Hypothesis. When there are relatively large differences in the expert power of members of a system, an increase in participation will increase the power differences between members.

The greater expert power of managers and specialists mentioned earlier refers to potential power. Those with expertise must communicate with the less powerful to influence them effectively and to become powerful. Thus, when there are large differences in expert power, the introduction of greater participation provides the more powerful with an opportunity to exercise their influence over the less powerful, and thereby make their greater power a reality.

LABORATORY RESEARCH

Experiments designed by the present authors to test the above hypothesis were performed in 1967. Small groups were formed and two variables were experimentally manipulated: expert power and participation.

Expert power. All subjects had found individual solutions to a town-planning problem presented to them. Some members were provided with more relevant information than the others: one-half of these individuals who had more expertness had far more information than the other members; the other half of them had only a little more information than the other members.

In two experiments, the individual with the most expert power was also the formal boss, and thus also had position power or formal power. In a third experiment, no difference in formal power was introduced.

Participation. The time available for interpersonal discussion before the final decision was either very long, resulting in participation, or very restricted, resulting in little participation—see Golembiewski's (1965: 117) definition of participation.

In this way, four experimental treatments were created.

1. Small difference in expert power, little participation;
2. Small difference in expert power, great participation;
3. Large difference in expert power, little participation;
4. Large difference in expert power, great participation.

That the less powerful persons would have strong individual opinions about good solutions to the problem was experimentally manipulated before the participation phase started.

The most crucial data to be gathered from the experiments were to check whether the less powerful, as a consequence of the extent to which they communicated with the more powerful, demonstrated a factual shift from their original point of view and aligned themselves with the opposite point of view held by the more powerful. Subjects' perceptions that the more powerful had opposite opinions were experimentally manipulated.

In all three experiments, when the differences in expert power were small, differences in the amount of participation had no effect on changes in the viewpoints of the less powerful; that is, no difference appeared between treatments 1 and 2. When expert power differences were large however, the less powerful were strongly influenced under conditions of greater participation, as predicted. In a two-by-two table, 27.6 percent of the subjects in treatment 1 were influenced by the more powerful, 27.6 percent in treatment 2, 44.8 percent in treatment 3, and 86.3 percent in treatment 4. The trend in the data is significant at a level of $p < .05$. More participation enabled the more powerful to use their influence more effectively. A detailed discussion of the theoretical considerations, experimental design, and data are given in Mulder and Wilke (1970).

The general, unspecified assertion that participation of the less powerful in the preparation and execution of decision-making processes leads to a reduction of power differences is invalid. In the behavioral sciences, the only functional relationship which can be formulated in this regard is that: under certain conditions an increase of participation will lead to certain effects.

PARTICIPATION PREREQUISITES

One prerequisite for participation in the decision making of a group or organization is that members must be motivated to participate. Empirical data strongly suggest that such motivation is limited in work councils in the Netherlands, Yugoslavia, and a few other European countries. Participation is promoted primarily by members of the intellectual, often academic, levels of society. This is true for instance in Yugoslavia, for Sturanovic (Broekmeyer, 1968: 273) stated that Yugoslav laborers never asked for workers' self-government by work councils, but they received workers' self-government of the enterprises through work councils as a gift from the academicians. The intellectuals decide that more participation is needed, that certain structures such as work councils with certain rules of decision making are the most appropriate means, and that such participation is best. In other words, the intellectuals are making up the game, and the rules for the game. However, the game will not be played only by them, but also by others. The problem to be emphasized is whether, with regard to participation, the academicians are not acting and thinking too much on the basis of their own motives and abilities; perhaps these do not coincide with the motives and abilities of others. The preferences of nonintellectuals about participation have not been investigated. In the development of more participation by the have-nots in power, the concept of participation should be applied without restriction by those who advocate it with so much ardor. If the less powerful do not, to a greater degree, codetermine their own demands, society will be threatened by an enlightened despotism of the intellectuals.

Another, even more important prerequisite for participation, as indicated by the experimental findings of this study, is that differences in expertise should not be too great. In the present experiments it has been demonstrated that participation leads to the greater effective influence of the more powerful over the less powerful when the more powerful has considerably greater expert power. This is often the case for managers and top specialists, whose expert power is greater than that of other members of their organizations. Again, it appears from empirical data that in the Netherlands and Yugoslavia, for example, power differences between the director and the specialists on the one hand, and the workers on the other hand, are not at all decreased by participation procedures. Apparently, expertness and knowledge are required for good participation, but these are not at all equally divided among the members of the organization, or among the different levels of society. Possibilities for learning–through formal education, through opportunity for varied experience, and through means for self-actualization–have always been extremely unequal (see Inkeles, 1966: 273). People who come from groups underprivileged in this respect have to expend an extraordinary amount of energy when they want to contribute, by means of participation procedures, to the decision making which heretofore has been reserved for the top levels of their organizations.

On the basis of the foregoing, must we resign from the idea of participation? Certainly not. Research is needed to determine the prerequisites that will lead to the desired, effectual participation (see Dill, 1964; Lowin, 1968).

Some trends can already be identified from research data. First of all, it appears that motivation is learned; actual exertion of influence leads to a stronger motivation for further exertion of influence (Mulder, 1958). Also, the person's subjective experience of functioning on a high level of ability appears to be a determinant of his level of aspiration: volition is dependent upon ability. Motivation, then, is not a fixed given, and may increase to the necessary levels when promoting conditions can be created.

Since expertise is a strong prerequisite for participation, the most practical strategy for developing real participation would be to base it on sufficient expertness. There is an extensive area in which co-workers on lower organizational levels have great experience and expertness: the workers in a factory may not know too much, or virtually nothing, about problems of financing, macroeconomic factors influencing sales, or leadership training, but they do know about problems related to their own work. Thus, for all workers the preconditions of motivation and expertness necessary for real participation and decision-making problems–as, for example, structuring of the work process, design of new apparatus, structuring of adapted communication processes, and other matters important to workers and the organization–do exist, namely in the work site, where the work is actually carried out (see Marrow *et al.,* 1968: 26; Emery, 1966; Thorsrud and Emery, 1966; Van Beinum and De Bel, 1968). The approach of these investigators is in complete agreement with the theoretical emphasis on expert power suggested here, and it shows a way toward the realization of real, direct participation.

Without the necessary preconditions for participation, there exists the danger of false participation, which is to be avoided because the fact that people think they are participating is often sufficient to bring about feelings of satisfaction, involvement, productivity, and so forth (see Hoffman and Maier, 1965). Secondly, and worse, is that people may be engaged to participate in matters which are either completely unimportant or above their level of expertness. Such participation can be regarded as a learning process for which people are not rewarded: when they realize that they are not, in fact, contributing anything, they will have learned not to engage themselves in any other, possibly productive and useful, participation activities. It appeared from respondents to questionnaires in research in the Netherlands (Lammers (ed.), 1965; Lammers, 1967: 206), that bad participation was evaluated as worse than no participation at all, as has been demonstrated in earlier research.

Another danger which always exists in procedures involving participation through representatives, such as in the work councils, is that these representatives form an elite, and most members of the organization resign from actual participation, as substantiated by empirical data from European studies. When the whole system of participation through representatives boils down to the promotion of a small number of selected people from the lower levels to the higher levels of a small power elite, it is clear that this process is extraordinarily expensive in energy, loss of time, and so forth, and might be done in a better, more direct, and cheaper way.

No research data are known to us about an important aspect; that is, with regard to power a certain ambivalence manifests itself in social research and daily experience: although people may find it acceptable to be together with more powerful in certain conditions, a general trend is to prefer not to be dependent upon others. In this context, the participation idea is quite in line with such a preference. One disadvantage, however, presents itself in participation settings, that is, a possible loss of minimal psychological freedom. When someone's boss gives orders to him, he can resist. He can think, "what the boss doesn't see won't hurt him," or he can prevent the order from being carried out. He can also critically talk with others about it. But the mechanisms of resistance, obstruction, and catharsis are excluded from the participatory group after the decision has been made. The person is committed to the decision, and has to follow it without reserve. Some threat of tyranny by the participative group might realize itself (see Leavitt, 1965).

We are confronted with sociopsychological and economic costs attached to the different alternatives. Even in the case where participation through representation, as in work councils, could have observable, positive effects, this is not sufficient. A further step must always be to compare various participation procedures with each other; for example, on the one hand the costs which are connected with participation through work councils and the intended and realized outcomes, and on the other hand, the costs and benefits of alternative procedures such as direct participation in the work itself. On this basis, a choice must be made in each concrete situation.

If procedures do not allow equal influence and do not promote active participation, the outcomes or benefits in terms of individual self-realization and contribution to the effectiveness of an organization will be limited; and the costs, such as diminished and confused responsibility and division of roles, and endless discussions by everybody about anything, will be heavy. It is therefore important that more attention be directed toward research on participation.

REFERENCES

Broekmeyer, M. J.
1968 De Arbeidsraad in Zuidslavië. Meppel: Boom.

Coetsier, P.
1966 Organismen voor medezeggenschap in de onderneming–enn sociopsychologisch onderzoek. Antwerp: Standaard Wetenschappelijke Uitgeverij.

De Bruin, J. J.
1961 Een verslag van een onderzoek naar het oordeel van NVV–ondernemingsraadleden over het funktioneren van ondernemingsraden. Amsterdam: Arbeiderspers.

Dill, William R.
1964 "Desegregation or integration? Comments about contemporary research on organizations." In W. W. Cooper, H. J. Leavitt, and M. W. Shelly II (eds.), New Perspectives in Organizational Research: 39-52. New York: John Wiley.

Drenth, P. J. D., and J. C. Van der Pijl
1966 De ondernemingsraad in Nederland. The Hague: Commissie voor Opvoering van Productiviteit.

Ellemers, J. E.
1965 "De Israëlische kibboets ab systeem van medezeggenschap." Sociologische Gids, 5: 258-323.

Emery, F. E.
1966 The Democratization of the Work Place. London: Tavistock Institute of Human Relations.

French, John R. P., and Bertram Raven
1959 "The bases of social power." In Dorwin Cartwright (ed.), Studies in Social Power: 150-167. Ann Arbor: Institute for Social Research, University of Michigan.

Golembiewski, Robert T.
1965 "Small groups and large organizations." In James G. March (ed.), Handbook of Organizations: 87-141. Chicago: Rand McNally.

Hoffmann, L. R., and N. R. F. Maier
1965 "Quality and acceptance of problem solutions by members of homogeneous and heterogeneous groups." In I. D. Steiner and M. Fishbein (eds.), Current Studies in Social Psychology: 458-468. New York: Holt, Rinehart and Winston.

Inkeles, Alex
1966 "Social structure and the socialization of competence." Harvard Educational Review, 36: 265-283.

Kolaja, Jiri
1965 Workers' Councils: The Yugoslav Experience. London: Tavistock.

Krulec, G. K.
1955 "The Scanlon plan: cooperation through participation." Journal of Business, 2: 100-113.

Lammers, C. J.
1967 "Power and participation in decision-making in formal organizations." American Journal of Sociology, 73: 201-216.

Lammers, C. J. (ed.)
1965 Medezeggenschap en overleg in het bedrijf. Utrecht-Antwerp: Het Spectrum.

Leavitt, Harold J.
1965 "Applied organizational change in industry: structural, technological, and humanistic approaches." In James G. March (ed.), Handbook of Organizations: 1144-70. Chicago: Rand McNally.

Lesieur, Frederick G. (ed.)
1958 The Scanlon Plan. Cambridge: MIT Press.

Lowin, Aaron
1968 "Participative decision-making: a model, literature, critique and prescriptions for research." Organizational Behavior and Human Performance, 3: 68-106.

Marrow, A. J., D. G. Bowers, and S. E. Seashore
1968 Management by Participation. New York: Harper and Row.

Morse, N. C., and E. Reimer
1956 "The experimental change of a major organization variable." Journal of Abnormal and Social Psychology, 52: 120-129.

Mulder, Mauk
1958 Group Structure, Motivation and Group Performance. The Hague: Commissie voor Opvoering van Productiviteit and Moulton.

Mulder, Mauk, J. R. Ritsema van Eck, and R. D. de Jong
1970 "An organization in crisis and non-crisis situations." Human Relations, 23: in press.

Mulder, Mauk, and P. Veen, in collaboration with C. Roodenburg, J. Frenken, and H. Tielens
1970 Power Distance between Subject and More-powerful Other as a Determinant of Subject's Power Behavior on a Level of Reality. Working paper, Institute of Social Psychology, University at Utrecht.

Mulder, Mauk, and Henke Wilke
1970 "Participation and power equalization." Organizational Behavior and Human Performance, 5: 430-448.

Philipsen, H.
1965 "Medezeggenschap in de vorm van werkoverleg." In C. J. Lammers (ed.), Medezeggenschap en overleg in het bedrijf: 90-126. Utrecht-Antwerp: Het Spectrum.

Quint, J. G. H.
1967 De ondernemingsraad in een viertal bedrijven. Utrecht: Institute of Social Psychology, University at Utrecht.

Strauss, G.
1963 "Some notes on power-equalization." In Harold J. Leavitt (ed.), The Social Science of Organizations: 39-84. Englewood Cliffs: Prentice-Hall.

Teulings, A. W. M.
1968 "Belangenvertegenwoordiging en beraad in de ondermeningsraad." Mens en Onderneming, 22: 44-60.

Thorsrud, Einar, and F. E. Emery
1966 "Industrial conflict and industrial democracy." In J. R. Lawrence

(ed.), Operational Research and the Social Sciences: 439-447. London: Tavistock.

Unilever Group Management Personnel
1967 Manual on Evaluation of Managers, Specialists and Scientists in Unilever. Rotterdam: Unilever.

Van Beinum, H. J. J., and P. J. De Bel
1968 Improving Attitudes to Work Especially by Participation. Working paper, Netherlands School of Economics, Rotterdam.

Van de Vall, M.
1963 De vakbeweging in de welvaartstaat. Meppel: Boom.

Van der Velden, H. A.
1965 Feitelijk funktioneren van vier ondernemingsraden. Utrecht: Institute of Social Psychology, University at Utrecht.
1968 Medezeggenschap en overleg. Utrecht: Institute of Social Psychology, University at Utrecht.

Van Zuthem, J. J., and A. Wynia
1967 Medezeggenschap. Met 2 bijlagen. Een onderzoek naar de opvattingen over en wensen omtrent medezeggenschap in 42 industriele ondernemingen. The Hague: Stuwgroep Sociaal Wetenschappelijk Onderzoek.

Vidakovic, Z.
1965 "On the relationship between theory and empirical facts in the study of the workers' self-government." Sociologica, 2: 81-90.

Rama Krishnan

DEMOCRATIC PARTICIPATION IN DECISION MAKING BY EMPLOYEES IN AMERICAN CORPORATIONS

The purpose of economic activity in society is to enhance the need satisfactions of members along with the economic, social, and political security of the larger social unit. In authoritarian societies, the authority to make decisions concerning economic enterprises flows from top to bottom (central government authorities to the chief executive officer of the organization), and employees do not have any part either in determining the objectives and policies or the decision making processes used in implementing these objectives and policies.

Rama Krishnan, "Democratic Participation in Decision Making by Employees in American Corporations", *Academy of Management Journal,* 1974, Vol. 17, No. 2, pp. 339-347.

On the other hand, the basic structure of Western-free societies being much different, the method of operation of their business enterprises might be expected to be much different from that in the authoritarian systems. In the Western system the stockholders, through the board of directors, of which the chief executive officer is a highly influential member, determine the objectives and policies for the business enterprises. In implementing these objectives and policies, management personnel are assumed to have the right to manage their operations as they see fit. Neil Chamberlain, however, has pointed out:

> Except for authoritarian relations (for example in the military services at home, and in totalitarian societies generally abroad), people can be managed and directed only with their own consent. . . . The property rights of the stockholders, exercised for them by management, can be made meaningful only with the cooperation of all those who are actually needed to operate the business, including the workers (6, pp. 69-70).

Roethlisberger (13), Coch and French (7), Patchen (12), Beach (3), and others have concluded from their studies that participation by employees in decision making does positively contribute to improved effectiveness of the organization. On the other hand, Strauss (16) and Albrook (1) have raised questions as to the effectiveness of participatory management.

In recent times more attention has been given by American industries, especially the automobile industry, to the participative approach to decision making. In this context, *Life* magazine reported;

> . . . the long run answer to job boredom in the U.S. auto industry may nevertheless prove to be a mixture of shorter assembly lines, increased automation and *the kind of participatory industrial democracy that has been pioneered in some Norwegian and British businesses* (7, p. 38). [Emphasis added.]

The purpose of this study is to determine the viewpoints of executives in a large midwestern industrial area regarding the participatory industrial democracy which is becoming more common in Western European countries like Norway, Britain, Germany, and France.

METHOD

The questionnaire developed by the *Harvard Business Review (HBR)*[1] to ascertain the viewpoints of its subscribers on job security, participation, and/or philosophy was used in this study. The *HBR* study was considered to be limited by the nature of the population used in that survey (8, p. 16). To determine whether business executives in this country in general hold the same viewpoints as the *HBR* subscribers or if the findings are applicable only to an "elite" group of executives–better informed than the average businessman and intellectually more curious, as stated by the *HBR*–about 1,400 questionnaires were sent to all,

[1] My sincere appreciation to Professor David W. Ewing, Executive Editor, *Harvard Business Review,* for allowing use of the questionnaire.

90, manufacturing organizations in a large midwestern industrial area employing 100 or more people. The largest of these had more than 20,000 employees. A profile of the respondents is provided in a previous study (11, p. 661).

This report covers the aspect of employees' involvement, or participation, in decision making in business organizations. "Participation" as used in this paper means the mental and emotional involvement of an individual in group processes which encourages that person to contribute to group goals and share responsibility in them. The findings have been analyzed in terms of age, position held, size of organization, and job function, wherever applicable, and related to the *HBR* survey results.

RESULTS

The primary approach used in this study to determine the viewpoints of executives on participatory management practices was to provide certain incidents and situations in the questionnaire and ascertain the reactions of the respondents to them.

Employee Voting as a Method of Decision Making–One incident involved relocation of a plant for expansion purposes in which Richard Burdick, the president of Thermon Manufacturing Company of Houston, polled his employees to ascertain their wishes. Of the 80 employees polled, 70 percent voted to remove the plant to San Marcos, a small town in Texas, and the company decided to relocate as voted. The respondents were then asked to comment on certain aspects relating to this incident. The responses are indicated in Table 1. It can be seen from the answers that a clear majority (81 percent) do not favor voting by employees as a means of decision making on plant location. When the results are compared with the *HBR* study, the executives in this study area seem to be much more conservative, holding to their belief in the traditional managerial prerogatives. As against the 36.5 percent who supported such voting in the *HBR* study, only 19 percent of the respondents in this study support voting as a means of decision making (8). A recent report in *Business Week* pointed out that one of the main reasons for relocation of operations is the desire of the chief executive officer of the company to have the operations nearer to his family residence (18). From the data available, it appears that the executives in the businesses studied are more interested in upholding managerial prerogatives as they see them than in the operational efficiency of the organizations through retention of valuable employees.

TABLE 1. **Questions and Responses.**

	Question		*Present Study* %	*HBR Study* %
(1)	a) If your company were considering moving one of its offices or plants to another location, do you think the employees in the offices or plant should be asked to vote on the sites being considered by management?	Yes	19	36.5
		No	81	63.5
	b) If you answered "yes" to the preceding question, do	Yes	50	39

TABLE 1. **(continued)**

		Question		Present Study %	HBR Study %
		you think that management should feel obliged to make the location decision favored by employees if there is a strong preponderance of opinion one way or another?	No	50	61
(2)	a)	Plant location is not the only decision that has been referred on occasion to an employee vote. Suppose your company's policy toward hiring members of minority groups became controversial for some reason. Do you think employees should then be entitled to vote on the hiring policy or policies which they would most like to see followed?	Yes	9	15
			No	91	85
	b)	If you answered "yes" to the preceding question do you think management should feel obliged to take action favored by most employees, assuming there is a strong preference for one policy or another?	Yes	67	N.A.
			No	33	N.A.
(3)	i)	Whether all employees in the company should be subject to relocation by management as new plants and offices are opened, regardless of their desire to move.		20	29
	ii)	Whether retirement should be mandatory for all company employees at age 65 or some other age.		24	15
	iii)	Whether the company should continue working on certain controversial contracts for the Defense Department (e.g., chemical warfare, armaments for Latin American countries), or phase out of such work as soon as possible.		5	16
(4)	a)	He should let them argue their case before the directors if the petition is signed by 10% or more of company employees (assume roughly equal proportion of managers and nonmanagers).		–	7
	b)	He should let them argue their case before the directors if the petition is signed by 51% or more of company employees.		3	10
	c)	He should refuse them permission to talk at a board meeting and let the matter drop there.		10	6
	d)	He should inform the Board about the antiwar group's petition and go no farther unless the Board wishes to initiate action.		87	77
(5)	a)	If the dissidents don't like the way the company is run, they should get out.		12	8
	b)	The dissidents have a responsibility to society to press their case until they get a fair hearing from top management.		16	37
	c)	The dissidents should keep working at their cause but not push too hard because their primary responsibility is to follow orders.		22	16
	d)	The dissidents should state their views in a memo to the President, then shut up and go back to work.		45	29
	e)	Other.		5	10
(6)	a)	He should feel obliged to see them at his office.		19	23.5
	b)	He should feel obliged to promise to read a memorandum from them and then, if he likes, invite them to his office for a talk.		35	32.5

TABLE 1. (continued)

	Question	Present Study %	HBR Study %
	c) He should leave the whole thing in the hands of the manufacturing vice president.	6	2.3
	d) He has no obligation whatsoever to the managers and should have them fired if they bug him any longer.	–	0.1
	e) He should appoint an assistant to look into the matter but feel no obligation to do more.	6	3.2
	f) He should go to the offices of the young managers to discuss the problem with them.	28	29.2
	g) Other.	6	9.1
(7)	a) Since a board represents only the owners, it is under no obligation to learn the feelings of any employee group about a person who is being considered as the next chief executive.	33	17
	b) Directors should *never* select a new shief executive of a company without accurate knowledge first of his acceptability to key managerial or other employee groups.	10	12
	c) While the board should feel under no rigid obligation to consult any employees as described, such consultation may be so desirable that a board should normally be expected by stockholders to sound out key employee groups concerning their opinions about the new chief executive.	46	71 (c and d combined)
	d) In more and more cases, employee morale is such a crucial factor in management effectiveness that a board should be sure that the leading candidate actually meets with the approval of key employee groups before selecting him as chief executive.	11	

It was found that younger executives are more liberal; 36 percent of those below age 30 favor voting as a means of decision making, and all of these younger executives (100 percent) feel that once voting is allowed, the decision should be accepted by management. A surprising finding was that 27 percent of the top executives favor voting as opposed to 12 percent of second and 22 percent of lower level executives. This is contrary to the findings of the *HBR* study, where the responses were 33 percent, 37 percent, and 41 percent, respectively (8).

Another situation dealt with minority hiring. In this case, 91 percent of the respondents feel that minority hiring is not an issue on which voting should be used as a decision making tool, as compared to 85 percent in the *HBR* study (8). None of the respondents below 30 years of age favor voting by employees on this issue. The results of this study and that of *HBR* lead to the conclusion that hiring members of minority groups to any substantial extent can take place only through enlightened leadership on the part of the top managers of organizations.

The respondents were also asked questions on retirement age, relocation of employees, defense contracts, etc. It will be seen from the responses that even though employee preference is *not* binding on management, only a very small percentage (less than 25 percent) of executives felt that employees should be given the chance to express themselves on these issues affecting them and their organizations. However, since relocation and retirement age would affect jobs and family life personally, more of the study respondents (20 percent and 24 percent as compared to the 9 percent favorable on the issue of minority hiring) felt that employees should have a chance to vote on these two issues. The *HBR* study results were 29 percent and 15 percent respectively (8). However, if the situation is one in which values, social or moral, are involved, only a very small percentage of the respondents (5 percent as compared to 16 percent in the *HBR* study) felt that employees should be given a voice in the decision process.

To a question whether respondents' viewpoints would differ if the voting were limited to managerial employees (assuming a workable definition of managerial) as opposed to all employees, there was a substantial increase, to 43 percent, in favorable reactions to the voting procedure as a means of decision making. This supports the findings of the *HBR* study, wherein 41 percent responded favorable to the voting procedure when it is limited to managerial employees. This indicates that the respondents believe in the democratic procedure for select "elite" groups in business but not for all employees.

Employee Inputs and/or Consultation: Social and Ethical Responsibility— The preceding questions dealt with democratic participation by employees in decision making. The respondents were also asked their viewpoints on certain situations wherein employees merely wanted to present their case to their top management instead of taking direct part in decision making itself. In one case, a group of managers and engineers in a company, who believed in the views of the Business Executive Move for Vietnam Peace group, opposed the company's production of ammunition for wars unauthorized by Congress and making profits from defense production, and wanted the chief executive officer to argue their viewpoint before the Board of Directors at the next meeting. Towards this end, they started a petition among the employees. The chief executive officer felt that a public corporation should not take a position on a political issue. Of the respondents 97 percent do not think that employees should have the right to present their viewpoints directly to the top policy making body, as compared to 83 percent in the *HBR* study.

The respondents were also given two situations having social responsibility implications. One dealt with air and water pollution. A group of dissident middle management members having less than two years' service in the company felt that the company should do much more than just meet legal requirements in this area and cited as examples two other chemical companies which had gone beyond the legal requirements. The company president did not show any interest in their arguments. Only 16 percent of the respondents felt that employees should have a sense of social responsibility and try to influence the organizational decisions. The majority, 79 percent, felt that top management people know best and have the right to make organizational decisions as they see fit. In the *HBR* study, 37 percent of the executives chose this alternative indicating that the sense of social responsibility is much lower among the executives in the midwestern area studied. The younger executives below 34, however, show a higher degree of social responsibility. As against the 16 percent choice for all executives, 36 percent of this younger age group made this choice.

The second situation having social responsibility implications dealt with the concern of several young factory managers in a large multidivisional corporation on the issue of drugs being peddled inside the plant. Not having received any satisfaction from the manufacturing vice president, they personally wanted to present their case to the corporate president at headquarters instead of sending a memo, as suggested by the vice president. They sincerely felt that if the memo was sent it would not be read by the president. The respondents were asked to indicate the action the corporate president should take among the choices given in the questionnaire. Compared to the previous question, the responses indicate that the respondents seem more inclined to support the request of the young factory managers against the wishes of the manufacturing vice president. A total of 47 percent feel that the president should meet with the young managers. This need not mean that these executives support the rights of employees in presenting their viewpoints to top management. It is possible that this positive attitude towards the young managers' cause may stem from the fact that the drug problem is something which has affected their families, neighbors, and community, or they may feel that the request by the younger managers does not in any way question the authority of management. This inference can be drawn from the fact that an equal number (47 percent) indicated that the young managers should not have the right of direct access to the corporate president. An interesting finding is that more top level executives (38 percent) felt that the corporate president should go to the office of the younger managers and discuss the problem; this in contrast to the 21 percent of second and 29 percent of lower level executives. The *HBR* survey results in this area are similar in nature.

Employee Inputs and/or Consultation: **Chief Executive Selection**–Siegfried Fassbender has explained that in German industry, the executive committee, which has the operational responsibility for publicly held corporations, is nominated by the supervisory board, which in turn is elected by the stockholders and employees (9). Warren Bennis has predicted that industrial democracy in this country is inevitable in the future (4). In recent times, France has started to introduce such participative systems in French industrial plants. However, in the American system the directors are traditionally assumed to have the authority to select the chief executive officer of the corporation and the views of employees are not considered to be relevant. The respondents were asked to indicate their viewpoints in this area. It is very clear from the responses that the majority of executives surveyed (79 percent) do not believe in the concept of employee participation in the selection of the chief executive. This is contrary to the concept of authority set forth by Barnard, according to which authority is delegated upward and not downward as traditionally assumed. Barnard has explained:

> A person can and will accept a communication as authoritative only when four conditions simultaneously obtain: a) he can and does understand the communication; b) at the time of his decisions he believes that it is not inconsistent with the purposes of the organization; c) at the time of his

> decision he believes it to be compatible with his personal interest as a whole; and d) he is able mentally and physically to comply with it (2, p. 165).

Neil Chamberlain has expressed similar views (6). Only 11 percent of the respondents felt that prior approval by employees is necessary. The main variation from this general pattern occurs in the below 30 age group. Of this group, 27 percent felt that employee approval is necessary and another 36 percent indicated that acceptability or lack of acceptability should be ascertained before the chief executive is selected. When compared to the *HBR* study value of 17 percent, more executives (33 percent) in the midwestern industrial area believe that the board represents only the owners and need not concern itself with the feelings of employees in selecting the chief executive. The difference could be due to the fact that the *HBR* subscribers are better informed and intellectually more curious.

CONCLUSION

In 1971, the 500 largest industrial corporations, and 50 largest companies in banking, life insurance, diversified financial, retail, transportation and utilities fields combined owned $1.3 trillion in assets and employed 20.3 million persons (10). Compared to the $1.3 trillion assets of these business organizations, the GNP of the U.S. in 1971 was approximately $1.050 trillion (10). This provides some indication of the extent of the influence business institutions wield in this society. Paul Samuelson has pointed out that the executives and directors combined in a typical corporation own a very small fraction (3 percent) of the outstanding common stock, but still have the formal authority to control the business (14). Studies by Berle and Means, as early as 1932, indicate that the ownership and control of corporations are separate and that this has a negative effect on the efficiency of the free market mechanism in American industry (5). The business corporations, therefore, are controlled by executives, who manage the corporations, rather than by the legal owners of these corporations, the stockholders.

In discussing the influence of business in Europe, Jean-Jacques Servan-Schreiber, author of *The American Challenge,* stated: "The political people are figureheads most of the time. The real power is retained almost entirely by business executives." Servan-Schreiber in assessing the impact of such executive power has expressed the specific fear:

> This is not acceptable, and it will not be accepted. It will lead to revolt. And it will lead to revolt in America. It will not be a revolt against America, but against business (15, p. 66).

From the present study and the *HBR* one, it appears that the majority of business executives taking part in these studies do not take the view that employees should have the right to participate, through the democratic process, in making organizational decisions. They do not even favor allowing employees direct input to the decision making process through direct access to the top policy making body or presentation of their viewpoints to the chief executive, except when the nature of the problem is such that the traditional managerial prerogatives will in no way be affected. An absolute majority believe in the traditional managerial prerogatives. The executives do not think that direct involvement/participation by employees is desirable in business organizational decision making even though business as an institution has an overwhelming effect on the social system and the lives of the people in it.

REFERENCES

1. Albrook, Robert C. "Participative Management: Time for a Second Look," *Fortune,* Vol. 75, No. 5 (1967).
2. Barnard, Chester I. *The Functions of the Executive* (Cambridge, Mass.: Harvard University Press, 1938).
3. Beach, Dale S. *Personnel: The Management of People at Work* (New York: Macmillan, 1970).
4. Bennis, Warren G. *Changing Organizations* (New York: McGraw-Hill, 1966).
5. Berle, Adolf A., Jr., and Gardiner Means. *The Modern Corporation and Private Enterprise* (New York: Macmillan, 1932).
6. Chamberlain, Neil. "What is Management's Right to Manage," *Fortune* (July 1949).
7. Coch, L., and J. R. P. French, Jr. "Overcoming Resistance to Change," *Human Relations,* Vol. 1, No. 4 (1948).
8. Ewing David W. "Who Wants Corporate Democracy," *Harvard Business Review,* Vol. 49, No. 5 (1971), 12-28, 146-149.
9. Fassbender, Siegfried. "Management and Its Environment in Germany," in Joseph L. Massie and Jan Luytjes (Eds.), *Management in an International Context* (New York: Harper and Row, 1972).
10. *Fortune,* Vol. 85, No. 5 (May 1972).
11. Krishnan, Rama. "Business Philosophy and Executive Responsibility," *Academy of Management Journal,* Vol. 16 (1973), 658-669.
12. Patchen, Martin. "Labor-Management Consultation at TVA: It's Impact on Employees," *Administrative Science Quarterly,* Vol. 10, No. 2 (1965).
13. Roethlisberger, F. J. *Management and Morale* (Cambridge, Mass.: Harvard University Press, 1959).
14. Samuelson, Paul A. *Economics: An Introductory Analysis* (New York: McGraw-Hill, 1967).
15. "Servan-Schreiber Updates his 'Challenge,' " *Business Week,* October 14, 1972, pp. 63, 66 and 68.
16. Strauss, George. "Some Notes on Power Equalization," in Harold J. Leavitt (Ed.), *The Social Science of Organizations: Four Perspectives* (Englewood Cliffs, N.J.: Prentice-Hall, 1963).
17. "The Will to Work and Some Ways to Increase It," *Life,* September 1, 1972, p. 38.
18. "When Business Moves Where the Boss Lives," *Business Week,* September 30, 1972, p. 69.

chapter **11**

Communication

It is fashionable to diagnose organizational maladies as communications problems. While on a general level this conslusion may be valid, it does not lead directly to an appropriate therapy. Instead, attention is often diverted to the development of writing or speaking skills, to courses in persuasion, or to the sending of more, better, or streamlined memoranda. Frequently these remedies are attempted without consideration of the basic dynamics of communication. The extent to which a message accomplishes its goal may be determined more by the social context than by the "quality" of the message. More generally, the point which so many people miss is that the social context, in addition to the characteristics of the transmitter, determines what techniques of communication will be effective. Furthermore, even the best transmitters will fail if the intended recipients are unable and/or unwilling to receive and act on the messages.

HUMAN LIMITATIONS AND COMMUNICATION

Information theory is useful to an understanding of the technical process of communication. The engineers who originated this approach attempted to quantify information and deal with the flow of messages through channels from the transmitter to the receiver. Communication was seen as the degree of overlap between the message sent and the message received. Sources of discrepancy were treated as "noise." Efficiency of transmission was measured in terms of the energy input and the amount of information actually received.

Application of this model to human communication reveals a major problem: the human being is an inefficient processor of information. As Miller (1967) noted,

> . . . The most glaring result has been to highlight man's inadequacy as a communication channel. As the amount of input information is increased, for example, by increasing the size of the set of alternative stimuli, the amount of information that the man transmits increases at first but then runs into a ceiling, an upper limit that corresponds roughly to his channel capacity. This ceiling is always very low. Indeed, it is an act of charity to call man a channel at all. Compared to telephone or television channels, man is better characterized as a bottleneck. (p. 48)

Some communication errors are perceptual in origin, as noted in part 1. The well-known party game in which people transmit a message in sequence derives its amusement value from such errors; after passing through eight or ten people, the message usually bears little resemblance to its initial form. Other errors arise from more exclusively biological causes, such as the relatively limited human memory span. For example, most people can reliably repeat a string of only seven random digits. However, man's restricted channel capacity is only part of the story. Communication within organizations is complicated by social-psychological factors.

Organizations and Social-Psychological Distortions

Communication is crucial to organizations. Only through information transmission can the efforts of people be coordinated so that the organization can respond effectively to its environment. However, organizations themselves introduce "noise" into human communication.

Guetzkow (1965), for example, reported the case of a production manager who recorded the themes of his messages to his subordinates. Of 237 messages the manager saw 165 messages as containing instructions or decisions. However, his subordinates perceived only 84 messages in this way. The remainder of the messages they viewed as merely giving information or advice. Such differences cannot always be resolved by a better choice of words, since the discrepancy may result from different perceptions of the whole social context. The subordinates may have given less weight to the manager's position of authority than he himself did. Alternatively, the supervisor may have been seen as uninformed or incompetent. Also, any message with a high threat content for the receiver may have been distorted or ignored.

The hierarchical organizational structure can contribute directly to such distortions. While conducting a meeting of his subordinates, a vice president of one of our larger corporations made what he saw as a casual comment about a side issue which had arisen: "That's interesting; I'd like to hear more about that sometime." Much to his surprise, two weeks later one of his subordinates sent him a report on the topic which had obviously taken most of the subordinate's efforts since the meeting. This incident illustrates the extreme sensitivity of some people to cues from authority figures.[1] Downward information is often overweighted.

Another consequence of authority for intraorganizational communication is distortion of data sent upward. For example, it is very difficult for subordinates to convey unpleasant information to their superiors. When writing reports, which are condensations, the subordinates are more apt to omit undesirable elements than desirable ones. Carey (1951), after discussing his situation as a colonial administrator in Africa, concluded that his power created mistrust, which was manifested in the reluctance of his subordinates to give accurate information about unfavorable situations. Once he received several detailed reports

1. For example, students are very sensitive to cues from the professor about what information is "really important."

about damage to a bridge. In checking on the reports, he found that the bridge was not just badly damaged but had been completely washed away.[2]

The foregoing examples demonstrate some of the sociological and psychological blocks to successful communication. The model discussed by Marshall Rosenberg, in a selection that follows, suggests ways to remove the social-psychological barriers. He is concerned with the feelings communicated by the way a message is stated. If a method of communication can be devised that develops trust and communication of feelings, the blocks introduced by psychological threat can be reduced. Rosenberg stresses the importance of devoting attention both to sending and receiving. Rosenberg's technique can be extremely valuable for dealing with barriers to the flow of information within organizations.

COMMUNICATION IN ORGANIZATIONS

Gross's (1968) informative discussion classifies the sources of barriers to organizational communication into five groups. One type lies in certain motives of senders. Some senders are more interested in sounding good, influencing people, and building a record than in actually communicating. In fact, Gross suggests that many potential senders may not want to communicate, especially those who wish to avoid conflict.

A second group of barriers is in the messages themselves, which have a latent content of emotions, feelings, and attitudes more important than the overt message in influencing the response of the receiver.

Ambiguity—which frequently arises from the use of nonverbal or paralinguistic symbols which express the latent content—is the third source of error.[3] The nonverbal cues may be inconsistent with the verbal message. The responses to these inconsistencies often determine behavior, but the source of the behavior goes unrecognized by the participants. For example, an angry individual will often verbally deny his anger but communicate it in various nonverbal ways. The receiver often responds with some sort of anxiety, anger, or other emotion, even though he is not aware of the reason.

A fourth source of error, according to Gross, stems from certain characteristics of receivers, such as the psychological variables discussed earlier. Information is distorted by perceptual processes and perceptual sets of the receiver. People tend to see what they want or expect to see. Such behavior, while functional in some ways, has important dysfunctional consequences for communication.

A fifth set of barriers exists in the channels of communication themselves. For example, Gross cited evidence that the failure of the United States to be prepared for the Japanese attack on Pearl Harbor was the failure of communication channels. In this case, members of military intelligence failed to respond to

2. A student who wishes to learn for himself how these forces operate may compare his feelings about telling a fellow student the bad features of a professor's class and telling the professor himself. Also he may compare his feelings about confronting different professors. What characteristics of professors make it possible for them to get accurate feedback? What are the implications for managers?

3. The paper by Shulman in this section focuses on nonverbal communication.

a communication of the impending attack sent by lower-ranking officers in a unit which had low repute with the Intelligence Office. While the channels of communication existed in the formal sense, the value given to the information was affected by the channel through which it flowed. Messages must not only be sent and received; they must be sent through the appropriate channels.

CHANNELS OF COMMUNICATION IN ORGANIZATIONS

Classical theorists of management stressed lines of communication as a basic element in the design of the formal organization. For classical theorists, the lines on the organizational chart represented the communication channels. They advised that the channels of communication should be known, direct and short, and utilized consistently for all transmission of information. As noted above, however, communication which flows in the authority lines is often distorted by the responses of people to authority relationships. The influence of authority positions is not limited to subordinates; Gerard (1957) found the mere act of telling people that they are in a position of authority leads them to send more messages. Thus, the very structuring of hierarchical lines of communication introduces sources of "noise." Nevertheless, the authority channel is the most widely recognized line of communication in organizations.

Guetzkow pointed out another damaging effect of organizational hierarchy on communication by noting Read's (1962) finding that executives who aspired to higher positions were more inclined to withhold information that might be threatening to their status than were executives with lesser ambitions. Furthermore, this tendency was magnified by mistrust of superiors' motives and intentions concerning the executives' career and status.

Furthermore, the literature has shown that the structuring of communication channels affects the accomplishment of group tasks and feelings of satisfaction of group members. Some of the most frequently cited work in the field reports the effect of communication networks on people's behavior and feelings. For example, the circle pattern, pictured in Fig. 1(a), provides members of the group with more chance to participate and be responsible for decisions than does the wheel configuration in Fig. 1(b). Groups organized in circle patterns generally experience higher satisfaction for all participants and are more adaptable but tend to complete routine tasks somewhat more slowly than those organized according to the configuration in Fig. 1(b). In 1(b), where all lines of communication are between the central person and individual members, these peripheral members have no chance for intercommunication. Generally the central person is quite satisfied, but the rest of the group is less satisfied than members of a circle network. Groups like that in 1(b) have a great deal of difficulty adapting to newer tasks but are apt to carry out routine tasks faster.

Leavitt (1964), who did much of the early research on these networks, suggested that there is not one best network of communication. The suitability of a network depends instead on the type of task and the characteristics of the people involved (such variables as the need to get started rapidly, the size of the group,

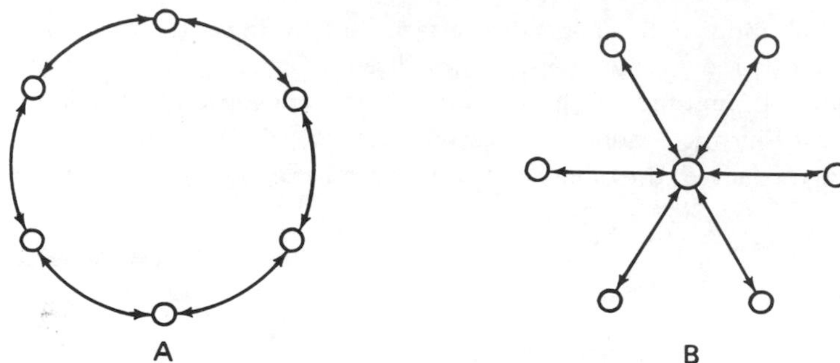

FIGURE 1. **Two types of communication network**

the security and self-esteem of the leader, and the confidence, values, and expectations of all group members). One-way communication can satisfy important needs. For example, Leavitt noted that one advantage of network (b) is that the leader can better hide his weaknesses from the group. Thus, while a great deal of the literature has argued for two-way open communication, the issue is not clear-cut. The "best" communication pattern is contingent on the situation, especially on the task. It should be noted, however, that the channels of communication are themselves independent variables with important consequences for organizational performance.

Although a great deal of attention has been given to formal channels, much communication does not follow the lines prescribed by organization charts. Guetzkow (1965) has classified other channels into four categories: information exchanges, task expertise, friendship, and status.

Guetzkow's information and task expertise channels are closely related. Information exchange channels carry messages which involve knowledge about both the internal and external operations of the organization. Often, this channel runs parallel to the authority channel, but information moves in the opposite or upward direction. In the expertise channel, information moves mainly laterally and diagonally in organizations from those who have competence to those who need it. Jasinski (1959) pointed out how crucial lateral and diagonal communication is for organizational effectiveness. Suppose that a factory does not provide formal channels between two foremen on the line or between the foremen of a line and the materials and maintenance departments. Because it is necessary to correct mistakes immediately to avoid costly delays, the foremen themselves may develop channels to allow successful internal coordination.

Another of Guetzkow's categories is the friendship channel that overlaps all the other channels. This channel, often called the grapevine, is apt to carry messages more relevant to individual needs than to organizational goals. Since individual needs and organizational goals are often incongruent, this channel can be one of the greatest sources of frustration to a manager. "Noise" in this channel is often of a personal nature. That is to say, issues of relatively minor importance to the sender may become central for the receiver, or vice versa, and unexpected reactions may result. While there is evidence that the grapevine can be extremely rapid and accurate, its distribution of information is uneven and does not encourage or permit a check on accuracy by either the receiver or the original source of the message. In addition, because this channel often carries emotionally potent and unwritten messages, there is a high probability of mouth-to-mouth distortion.

The friendship channel poses a further problem for organizations. Since information is a scarce and valued commodity, it is a source of power and status. Status incongruity and other violations of expected norms occur when a lower-level participant has more of this valued resource than someone at a higher level. Consider, for example, the case of an individual who receives important new information, of direct concern to his job performance, from his secretary. The incongruity can produce tension, hostility and resentment. Such feelings, coupled with probable distortion, make it difficult for the individual to accept related information when he receives it through more formal channels. The tension must be dealt with before effective communication can be reestablished.

Recovery from tensions generated by a communications leak can take years. For example, Nord (1968) reported on the consequences of such a leak for the merger of two furniture companies. The problems of the merger were compounded by lower-level participants having the information well ahead of plant managers. So much anxiety was created by the leaked information that substantial mistrust and hostility toward management developed.

Nord's study revealed another complication introduced by the friendship channel. Once the merger had taken place, people tended to exchange information with the same sources as before. In essence, it seems that the formal channels influence the development of the friendship channel. Once a friendship channel is developed, it may be resistant to organizational changes and create problems in the coordination of effort within a changed organization.

Finally, Guetzkow postulated the status channel, which transmits symbolic content. Although these cues are often fragmentary and ambiguous, they are important determinants of behavior in several ways. First, the transmission of nonsymbolic information is affected by and in turn affects status. As mentioned earlier, people who possess information are often esteemed by others. Symbolic information communicated through the status channel may also distort other information, as shown in the Pearl Harbor example. Information coming from low-status sources, even though accurate, often is not accepted or acted on in the organization.

Status symbols may have some other direct, dysfunctional consequences, often for the very goals organizations pursue. Universities, with their aim of educating students, offer a prime example. Students are frequently expected to address professors by a formal title and show "appropriate" respect. Does this practice reduce the open communication channels necessary for the free interchange of ideas? Clearly, the information carried in the status channel may inhibit the flow of information through other channels. Nevertheless, the information can also be useful by helping to define a stable social order.

Ethologists and other students of animal and human behavior have found that most social animals develop a status system, popularly known as a pecking order, which permits the dominant animals to assert their power symbolically, without physical conflict. Such status systems operate in human society. In small, face-to-face groups, one can observe a pecking order by noting who interrupts whom and who speaks to whom. In complex organizations the pecking order of the organizational hierarchy is supported by titles, size and location of office, dress, and a host of other status symbols. Patterns of expectation develop about how the people who possess these symbols should be treated. Adherence to these expectations can reduce anxiety, whereas violation of these expectations often produces tension. In many business organizations, the use of space and physical props operates to support the formal organizational hierarchy. In fact, a perceptive observer could walk into many organizations and accurately draw the organization chart just by observing the physical location and characteristics of the offices. Symbols thus communicate information which may help reduce tension by increasing each person's ability to predict what behavior will be shown toward him by others and what behavior of his own will be approved. Status symbols may have both functional and dysfunctional consequences.

People often appear to desire a high degree of predictability in their environment. Under conditions where intimate, face-to-face interaction is not possible, status symbols provide cues which help individuals to develop appropriate or at least tension-reducing expectations. Animals utilize similar cues. For example, bears are known to define their territory by scratching on trees, thus informing other bears that they can expect trouble if they violate the boundaries. Similarly, humans use "markers" to establish certain property rights. Engagement and wedding rings are common examples.

Goffman (1959) explored other functions of human symbols. People may employ props—such as a given model or brand of automobile—to convey a desired image to others. Thus, symbols may permit social definition of self in addition to tension reduction and social order.

The above discussion was written from a functional rather than from a moral perspective. Social critics who have pointed to the folly of status symbols have made important observations of the material waste and loss of human potential which the quest for status symbols often involves. Unfortunately, the social critics do not recognize the functional consequences of these symbols. More importantly, managers and others with power frequently are unaware of the dysfunctional consequences of these cues. Clearly, both functional and dysfunctional consequences arise from the large quantity of information which flows through the symbolic channel in organizations.

THE READINGS

The foregoing discussion has summarized many of the issues and problems of communication in organizations. Certainly, other readings in this book—especially those on perception, formal organization, power, and group behavior—are also relevant to communication. The piece by Townsend provides some clear, concise advice to the manager about the importance of open communication for dealing with conflict in organizations. In the second selection Gibb analyzes different types of interpersonal climates resulting from different types of messages that people send to each other. Rosenberg's paper presents a model for improving communication between people; his model describes a method for establishing the type of climate Gibb labeled "supportive." Shulman summarizes the growing body of work on nonverbal communication. Some estimates suggest that over 80 percent of face-to-face human communication is nonverbal. If, as many experts agree, interpersonal relationships are of growing importance in organizations, the work on nonverbal communication has great practical relevance.

REFERENCES

Cary, S. "Africa Yesterday: One Ruler's Burden." *The Reporter* 10 (May, 1951): 21-24.

Gerard, H. B. "Some Effects of Status, Role Clarity, and Group Goal Clarity upon the Individual's Relations to Group Process." *Journal of Personality* 25 (1957): 475-88.

Goffman, E. *The Presentation of Self in Everyday Life.* Garden City, N. Y.: Doubleday, 1959.

Gross, B. *Organizations and Their Managing.* New York: Free Press, 1968.

Guetzkow, H. "Communications in Organizations." In *Handbook of Organizations,* edited by J. G. March, pp. 534-73. New York: Rand-McNally, l965.

Jasinski, F. J. "Adapting Organization to New Technology." *Harvard Business Review* 37 (1959): 79-86.

Leavitt, H. J. *Managerial Psychology.* 2nd ed. Chicago: University of Chicago Press, 1964.

Miller, A. *The Psychology of Communication.* Baltimore: Penguin Books, 1967.

Nord, W. "Individual and Organizational Conflict in an Industrial Merger." In *Proceedings of the 11th Midwest Management Conference,* pp. 50-66. Madison, Wisc.: Academy of Management, 1968.

Read, W. H. "Upward Communication in Industrial Hierarchies." *Human Relations* 15 (1962): 3-16.

Robert Townsend

CONFLICT WITHIN THE ORGANIZATION

. . . a sign of a healthy organization—up to a point. A good manager doesn't try to eliminate conflict; he tries to keep it from wasting the energies of his people.

Conviction is a flame that must burn itself out—in trying an idea or fighting for a chance to try it. If bottled up inside, it will eat a man's heart away.

If you're the boss and your people fight you openly when they think you're wrong—that's healthy. If your men fight each other openly in your presence for what they believe in—that's healthy. But keep all the conflict eyeball to eyeball.

Jack R. Gibb

DEFENSIVE COMMUNICATION

One way to understand communication is to view it as a people process rather than as a language process. If one is to make fundamental improvement in communication, he must make changes in interpersonal relationships. One possible type of alteration—and the one with which this paper is concerned—is that of reducing the degree of defensiveness.

DEFINITION AND SIGNIFICANCE

Defensive behavior is defined as that behavior which occurs when an individual perceives threat or anticipates threat in the group. The person who behaves defensively, even though he also gives some attention to the common task, devotes an appreciable portion of his energy to defending himself. Besides talking about the topic, he thinks about how he appears to others, how he may be seen more favorably, how he may win, dominate, impress, or escape punishment, and/or how he may avoid or mitigate a perceived or an anticipated attack.

Such inner feelings and outward acts tend to create similarly defensive postures in others; and, if unchecked, the ensuing circular response becomes increasingly destructive. Defensive behavior, in short, engenders defensive listening, and this in turn produces postural, facial, and verbal cues which raise the defense level of the original communicator.

Defense arousal prevents the listener from concentrating upon the message. Not only do defensive communicators send off multiple value, motive, and affect cues, but also defensive recipients distort what they receive. As a person becomes more and more defensive, he becomes less and less able to perceive accurately the motives, the values, and the emotions of the sender. The writer's analyses of tape recorded discussions revealed that increases in defensive behavior were correlated positively with losses in efficiency in communication.[1] Specifically, distortions became greater when defensive states existed in the groups.

Jack Gibb, "Defensive Communication", *Journal of Communication,* No. 3, Sept. 1961, pp. 141-148.

[1] J. R. Gibb, "Defense Level and Influence Potential in Small Groups," in L. Petrullo and B. M. Bass (eds.), *Leadership and Interpersonal Behavior* (New York: Holt, Rinehart and Winston, Inc., 1961), pp. 66-81.

The converse, moreover, also is true. The more "supportive" or defense reductive the climate the less the receiver reads into the communication distorted loadings which arise from projections of his own anxieties, motives, and concerns. As defenses are reduced, the receivers become better able to concentrate upon the structure, the content, and the cognitive meanings of the message.

CATEGORIES OF DEFENSIVE AND SUPPORTIVE COMMUNICATION

In working over an eight-year period with recordings of discussions occurring in varied settings, the writer developed the six pairs of defensive and supportive categories presented in Table 1. Behavior which a listener perceives as possessing any of the characteristics listed in the left-hand column arouses defensiveness, whereas that which he interprets as having any of the qualities designated as supportive reduces defensive feelings. The degree to which these reactions occur depends upon the personal level of defensiveness and upon the general climate in the group at the time.[2]

TABLE I. **Categories of Behavior Characteristic of Supportive and Defensive Climates in Small Groups.**

Defensive Climates	*Supportive Climates*
1. Evaluation	1. Description
2. Control	2. Problem orientation
3. Strategy	3. Spontaneity
4. Neutrality	4. Empathy
5. Superiority	5. Equality
6. Certainty	6. Provisionalism

Evaluation and Description

Speech or other behavior which appears evaluative increases defensiveness. If by expression, manner of speech, tone of voice, or verbal content the sender seems to be evaluating or judging the listener, then the receiver goes on guard. Of course, other factors may inhibit the reaction. If the listener thought that the speaker regarded him as an equal and was being open and spontaneous, for example, the evaluativeness in a message would be neutralized and perhaps not even perceived. This same principle applies equally to the other five categories of potentially defense-producing climates. The six sets are interactive.

Because our attitudes toward other persons are frequently, and often necessarily, evaluative, expressions which the defensive person will regard as nonjudgmental are hard to frame. Even the simplest question usually conveys the answer that the sender wishes or implies the response that would fit into his value system. A mother, for example, immediately following an earth tremor that shook the house, sought for her small son with the question: "Bobby, where

[2] J. R. Gibb, "Sociopsychological Processes of Group Instruction," in N. B. Henry (ed.), *The Dynamics of Instructional Groups* (Fifty-ninth Yearbook of the National Society for the Study of Education, Part II, 1960), pp. 115-135.

are you?" The timid and plaintive "Mommy, I didn't do it" indicated how Bobby's chronic mild defensiveness predisposed him to react with a projection of his own guilt and in the context of his chronic assumption that questions are full of accusation.

Anyone who has attempted to train professionals to use information-seeking speech with neutral affect appreciates how difficult it is to teach a person to say even the simple "who did that?" without being seen as accusing. Speech is so frequently judgmental that there is a reality base for the defensive interpretations which are so common.

When insecure, group members are particularly likely to place blame, to see others as fitting into categories of good or bad, to make moral judgments of their colleagues, and to question the value, motive, and affect loadings of the speech which they hear. Since value loadings imply a judgment of others, a belief that the standards of the speaker differ from his own causes the listener to become defensive.

Descriptive speech, in contrast to that which is evaluative, tends to arouse a minimum of uneasiness. Speech acts which the listener perceives as genuine requests for information or as material with neutral loadings is descriptive. Specifically, presentations of feelings, events, perceptions, or processes which do not ask or imply that the receiver change behavior or attitude are minimally defense producing. The difficulty in avoiding overtone is illustrated by the problems of news reporters in writing stories about unions, communists, Negroes, and religious activities without tipping off the "party" line of the newspaper. One can often tell from the opening words in a news article which side the newspaper's editorial policy favors.

Control and Problem Orientation

Speech which is used to control the listener evokes resistance. In most of our social intercourse someone is trying to do something to someone else—to change an attitude, to influence behavior, or to restrict the field of activity. The degree to which attempts to control produce defensiveness depends upon the openness of the effort, for a suspicion that hidden motives exist heightens resistance. For this reason attempts of nondirective therapists and progressive educators to refrain from imposing a set of values, a point of view, or a problem solution upon the receivers meet with many barriers. Since the norm is control, noncontrollers must earn the perceptions that their efforts have no hidden motives. A bombardment of persuasive "messages" in the fields of politics, education, special causes, advertising, religion, medicine, industrial relations, and guidance has bred cynical and paranoidal responses in listeners.

Implicit in all attempts to alter another person is the assumption by the change agent that the person to be altered is inadequate. That the speaker secretly views the listener as ignorant, unable to make his own decisions, uninformed, immature, unwise, or possessed of wrong or inadequate attitudes is a subconscious perception which gives the latter a valid base for defensive reactions.

Methods of control are many and varied. Legalistic insistence on detail, restrictive regulations and policies, conformity norms, and all laws are among the methods. Gestures, facial expressions, other forms of nonverbal communication, and even such simple acts as holding a door open in a particular manner are means of imposing one's will upon another and hence are potential sources of resistance.

Problem orientation, on the other hand, is the antithesis of persuasion. When the sender communicates a desire to collaborate in defining a mutual problem and in seeking its solution, he tends to create the same problem orientation in the listener; and, of greater importance, he implies that he has no predetermined solution, attitude, or method to impose. Such behavior is permissive in that it allows the receiver to set his own goals, make his own decisions, and evaluate his own progress—or to share with the sender in doing so. The exact methods of attaining permissiveness are not known, but they must involve a constellation of cues and they certainly go beyond mere verbal assurances that the communicator has no hidden desires to exercise control.

Strategy and Spontaneity

When the sender is perceived as engaged in a stratagem involving ambiguous and multiple motivations, the receiver becomes defensive. No one wishes to be a guinea pig, a role player, or an impressed actor, and no one likes to be the victim of some hidden motivation. That which is concealed, also, may appear larger than it really is with the degree of defensiveness of the listener determining the perceived size of the suppressed element. The intense reaction of the reading audience to the material in the *Hidden Persuaders* indicates the prevalence of defensive reactions to multiple motivations behind strategy. Group members who are seen as "taking a role," as feigning emotion, as toying with their colleagues, as withholding information, or as having special sources of data are especially resented. One participant once complained that another was "using a listening technique" on him!

A large part of the adverse reaction to much of the so-called human relations training is a feeling against what are perceived as gimmicks and tricks to fool or to "involve" people, to make a person think he is making his own decision, or to make the listener feel that the sender is geniunely interested in him as a person. Particularly violent reactions occur when it appears that someone is trying to make a strategem appear spontaneous. One person has reported a boss who incurred resentment by habitually using the gimmick of "spontaneously" looking at his watch and saying, "My gosh, look at the time—I must run to an appointment." The belief was that the boss would create less irritation by honestly asking to be excused.

Similarly, the deliberate assumption of guilelessness and natural simplicity is especially resented. Monitoring the tapes of feedback and evaluation sessions in training groups indicates the surprising extent to which members perceive the strategies of their colleagues. This perceptual clarity may be quite shocking to the strategist, who usually feels that he has cleverly hidden the motivational aura around the "gimmick."

This aversion to deceit may account for one's resistance to politicians who are suspected of behind-the-scenes planning to get his vote, to psychologists whose listening apparently is motivated by more than the manifest or content-level interest in his behavior, or to the sophisticated, smooth, or clever person whose "oneupmanship" is marked with guile. In training groups the role-flexible person frequently is resented because his changes in behavior are perceived as strategic maneuvers.

In contrast, behavior which appears to be spontaneous and free of deception is defense reductive. If the communicator is seen as having a clean id, as having uncomplicated motivations, as being straightforward and honest, and as behaving spontaneously in response to the situation, he is likely to arouse minimal defense.

Neutrality and Empathy

When neutrality in speech appears to the listener to indicate a lack of concern for his welfare, he becomes defensive. Group members usually desire to be perceived as valued persons, as individuals of special worth, and as objects of concern and affection. The clinical, detached, person-is-an-object-of-study attitude on the part of many psychologist-trainers is resented by group members.

Speech with low affect that communicates little warmth or caring is in such contrast with the affect-laden speech in social situations that it sometimes communicates rejection.

Communication that conveys empathy for the feelings and respect for the worth of the listener, however, is particularly supportive and defense reductive. Reassurance results when a message indicates that the speaker identifies himself with the listener's problems, shares his feelings, and accepts his emotional reactions at face value. Abortive efforts to deny the legitimacy of the receiver's emotions by assuring the receiver that he need not feel bad, that he should not feel rejected, or that he is overly anxious, though often intended as support giving, may impress the listener as lack of acceptance. The combination of understanding and empathizing with the other person's emotions with no accompanying effort to change him apparently is supportive at a high level.

The importance of gestural behavioral cues in communicating empathy should be mentioned. Apparently spontaneous facial and bodily evidences of concern are often interpreted as espeically valid evidence of deep-level acceptance.

Superiority and Equality

When a person communicates to another that he feels superior in position, power, wealth, intellectual ability, physical characteristics, or other ways, he arouses defensiveness. Here, as with the other sources of disturbance, whatever arouses feelings of inadequacy causes the listener to center upon the affect loading of the statement rather than upon the cognitive elements. The receiver then reacts by not hearing the message, by forgetting it, by competing with the sender, or by becoming jealous of him.

The person who is perceived as feeling superior communicates that he is not willing to enter into a shared problem-solving relationship, that he probably does not desire feedback, that he does not require help, and/or that he will be likely to try to reduce the power, the status, or the worth of the receiver.

Many ways exist for creating the atmosphere that the sender feels himself equal to the listener. Defenses are reduced when one perceives the sender as being willing to enter into participative planning with mutual trust and respect. Differences in talent, ability, worth, appearance, status, and power often exist, but the low defense communicator seems to attach little importance to these distinctions.

Certainty and Provisionalism

The effects of dogmatism in producing defensiveness are well known. Those who seem to know the answers, to require no additional data, and to regard themselves as teachers rather than as co-workers tend to put others on guard. Moreover, in the writer's experiment, listeners often perceived manifest expressions of certainty as connoting inward feelings of inferiority. They saw the dogmatic individual as needing to be right, as wanting to win an argument rather than solve a problem, and as seeing his ideas as truths to be defended. This kind of behavior often was associated with acts which others regarded as attempts to exercise control. People who were right seemed to have low tolerance for members who were "wrong"–i.e., who did not agree with the sender.

One reduces the defensiveness of the listener when he communicates that he is willing to experiment with his own behavior, attitudes, and ideas. The person who appears to be taking provisional attitudes, to be investigating issues rather than taking sides on them, to be problem solving rather than debating, and to be willing to experiment and explore tends to communicate that the listener may have some control over the shared quest or the investigation of the ideas. If a person is genuinely searching for information and data, he does not resent help or company along the way.

CONCLUSION

The impliciations of the above material for the parent, the teacher, the manager, the administrator, or the therapist are farily obvious. Arousing defensiveness interferes with communication and thus makes it difficult–and sometimes impossible–for anyone to convey ideas clearly and to move effectively toward the solution of therapeutic, educational, or managerial problems.

Marshall B. Rosenberg

WORDS CAN BE WINDOWS OR WALLS

A friend of mine wrote a song entitled, "Words are Windows or They're Walls."[1] This phrase summarizes much that I have come to learn about the words people use in their relationships with one another. At times I see words serving as windows that allow me "to see into" the speaker's intentions and beliefs. At other times I see words serving as walls that obstruct the mutual understanding that will occur. In this article, I would like to outline a characteristic of language that serves to make words "walls," to describe how such language can interfere with working or living together, to outline characteristics that make words "windows" and to describe some of the procedures I use in helping people to learn to use words as windows rather than walls.

The main detriment to effective communication in working relationships involves the labeling of oneself or others. By labeling I refer to the use of words that describe static characteristics that exist "within" individuals. I would contrast words describing static characteristics that exist within persons with words describing processes or operations that go on between persons. For example, I would place the word "stupid" in the phrase, "John is stupid" in the category of words referring to static characteristics "within" John. In contrast, if I state "I am feeling frustrated because I do not know how to teach John," I am using words that describe processes or operations that exist in my *transactions* with John.

Associated with labels are expectations as to how a person should behave. For example, if I label John as stupid I might therefore expect that he would not be able to understand complicated messages. On the basis of this expectation I might then alter my behavior toward John by presenting information in a simplified way. My continuing to present information in this way could, of course, have consequences for John's behavior. His being exposed primarily to simplified information could prevent him from gaining experience in dealing with complicated messages. To the extent that intelligence is involved in learning

Prepared especially for this volume.

[1] Ruth Bebermeyer, *Words are Windows or They're Walls,* 1970.

to comprehend complicated messages, this sequence represents a self-fulfilling prophecy. I would like to diagram this process, since an understanding of it is crucial to an understanding of my concern about labels.

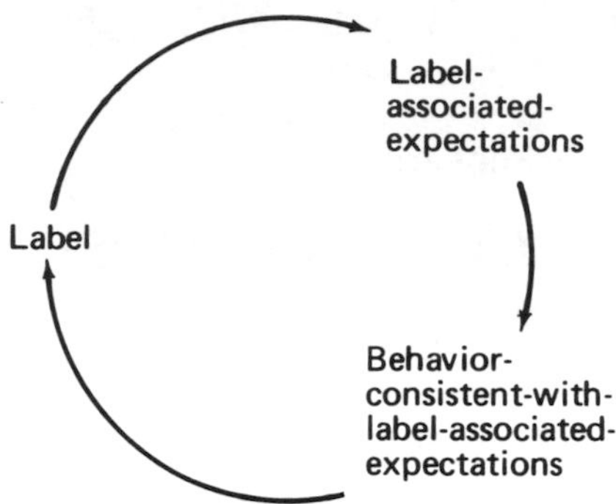

In the above example the label "stupid" led to label-associated expectations ("cannot comprehend complicated messages") which led to behavior consistent with label-associated expectations (presenting only simplified messages) which contributed to confirming the initial label ("stupid") by limiting the experience of the labeled person. The circle is complete and serves to perpetuate itself.

The nature of this "circular" process has a number of implications about interpersonal relations that are important to me. For example, when I see this self-fulfilling process, which can be associated with labeling, I can appreciate why John Paul Sartre states that it violates the integrity of persons to label them. In addition, I am led to recall that in the field of education the dangers of self-fulfilling prophecies associated with labeling have been documented by Rosenthal and Jacobson[2] in their study, *Pygmalion in the Classroom.* They discovered that teachers often initiate a "self-fulfilling" prophecy when they label students; that is, teachers' expectations of a student's performance associated with labels such as "high achiever," in effect, determine that performance.

In the area of working relationships, I find certain labels showing up with great regularity regardless of the nature of the working relationship. Perhaps the most common labels are conservative-liberal (or variations thereof). The "conservative" member of the pair engages in the process by labeling the other as a "liberal" (of course choice adjectives may precede the label). He then tends to "expect" certain things from him such as failing to respect standardized procedures. On the basis of such expectation, the "conservative" acts to impress the "liberal" with the importance of procedures (for example, lecturing him about the value of roles and procedures, reminding him repeatedly of the procedures, etc.). Such behavior on the part of the "conservative" is likely to be annoying to the "liberal" and increases his resistance to "adhering to

[2] R. Rosenthal and L. Jacobson, *Pygmalion in the Classroom: Teacher Expectation and Pupils' Intellectual Ability* (New York: Holt, Rinehart & Winston, 1968).

procedures." This of course confirms the prophecies of the "conservatives" about "liberals" not valuing procedures.

Or one can view this from the "liberal" point of view. Expecting that the "conservative" will resist innovation, the "liberal" does not openly communicate about the innovation, choosing to introduce it at the last moment, hopefully to minimize the opportunity for rebuttal. Such behavior on the part of the "liberal" is likely to provoke distrust on the part of the "conservative" and subsequent resistance to the innovation thereby confirming expectations of the "liberal" about "conservatives."

I would like to emphasize that labels can be equally self-defeating when applied to oneself as to others. Thus if an executive labels himself as an "organization man" he expects patterns of conformity from himself and rules out the possibility of his initiating or creating new patterns of behavior. The more he steeps himself in routine administrative activities, the more of an "organization man" he becomes.

I would also like to emphasize my belief that labels, whether "positive" or "negative," are limiting to one's development. Although labeling oneself as a "creative individual" in many organizations would be a "positive" label, I feel that it could be as limiting as labeling oneself as an "organization man." Labeling oneself as "creative" could lead one to ignore consideration and reverence of traditional procedures. Although this may perpetuate a person's labeling of himself in a positive way, I doubt that it would lead to his functioning either in an effective way regarding the organization or in a way that was fulfilling to himself.

In order to make words used to describe oneself and others windows rather than walls, I recommend learning to translate the labels one used into a language of feelings and objectives. More specifically, this requires skill in four areas: ability to note time and situational contexts in which behavior occurs; ability to make observations of behavior without interpreting the behavior; ability to report on one's affective state; and the ability to report on one's desires. I would now like to describe each of these skills in greater detail.

Ability to note time and situation contexts in which behavior occurs. In many instances of interpersonal communication, I find it particularly helpful to clearly denote the time and situational context in which I am embedding my message. For example: Person A has been late with three out of five reports in the last month. Person B, his supervisor, states, "I'm concerned because you don't get your reports in on time." I find myself easily falling into the habit of making such absolutistic statements when I am in Person B's position, perhaps because I believe it emphasizes my concern more sharply. Unfortunately, it also tends to get me into picayune hassles because it often motivates the other person to defend himself against the absolute nature of the statement. For example, I would not be surprised if Person A were to respond, "What do you mean? I was on time with my report last week!" I believe Person B would be further ahead were he to be more specific in his time and situational referents; perhaps stating, "Last Tuesday, and Wednesday, and Thursday, I was concerned because I did not get your reports by the time I expected to receive them."

I offer the following two statements to exemplify what I mean by clarifying the situational contexts of messages.

Statement 1. I do not like the familiarity which you *often show in our relationship.*

Statement 2. I do not like how I feel in relationship to you during business meetings.

By being specific about the situational context in which the behavior occurs in Statement 2, I believe the listener's ease of understanding is facilitated.

Ability to make observations of behavior without labeling or interpreting the behavior. This skill involves the ability of the speaker to differentiate between observable behavior and inferences. By observable behavior I refer to behavior that can be perceived in contrast to statements making inferences and interpretations of the observable behavior. Following are examples of observations of behavior that avoid labeling and a contrasting statement in which labels and observable behavior are not differentiated.

John did not submit his reports on schedule the last two weeks.	John is irresponsible in his report writing.
John's department met its quota the last six months.	John is an asset to the company.

Ability to report on one's affective state.[3] I find the reporting of one's affective state to have several advantages in interpersonal communication. To begin with, I find trust increases in proportion to the degree to which people are able to openly acknowledge their present feelings. Second, I find it aids in keeping the communication in the present thereby avoiding the boredom and vagueness that I see quickly settling into communications in which feelings are absent. Third, I find that people feel more alive the more they are in touch with their feelings.

I differentiate three stages in teaching people to report on their affective state. To begin with, I help people to become aware that they have feelings. As strange as it may seem, I find many people who have been oriented to the world in such a way that they seem totally unaware that they have feelings. To help them become aware of their feelings, I conduct various exercises in which the person is given the opportunity to focus on his feelings at the moment. After awareness, I help people to develop a differentiated vocabulary for describing their feelings. This is a particularly difficult problem using the English language as the English vocabulary for describing affective states is relatively sparse. For example, I am told the Japanese language has approximately 75 different words to describe differential feelings of love whereas I routinely hear only about four or five describing this emotion in English. After awareness of feelings and developing a differentiated vocabulary to describe them is left the step of verbally reporting them to others. For many people this is a terrifying step as the reporting of feelings often leaves individuals feeling painfully vulnerable.

[3] For those interested in a more thorough discussion of the advantages of reporting on one's affective state, I recommend John Powell, S.J., *Why Am I Afraid to Tell You Who I Am* (Chicago: Argus Communication, 1969).

Ability to report one's desires. The final skill I would like to describe is the ability to report on one's desires as explicitly as possible. This involves being able to state in measurable terms what would lead to satisfaction of your desires. For example, if someone says to me, "I would like you to be more considerate," I would have more difficulty fulfilling his desires than if he were to say, "I would like you to give me at least a week's notice before setting up a meeting."

In daily conversation, all four of the skills previously described could be contained in a single, short message. To exemplify:

> Yesterday, (specifying time context) during the business meeting (specifying situational context) when you brought up the matter of finances (observing behavior without labeling or interpreting) I was disappointed (reporting on one's affective state) because I wanted to finish the topic we started before going on to another (reporting on one's desires).

I frequently face the challenge of being asked to teach the communication skills described to teachers, parents, managers in industry and others as best I can in a relatively short time (usually two or three days). In learning these skills, the people I work with usually are changing from deeply ingrained habit patterns. I am far from solving the problems involved in making significant changes in longstanding communication patterns in a relatively short time,[4] but I would like to share some principles that have been helpful in bringing about the changes desired.

To begin with I try to be as explicit as possible about the objectives I have for the training sessions. I try to define in measurable terms what I would hope each participant would be able to accomplish by the end of the training program. The value of beginning an instructional program with measurable objectives has been described elsewhere and I won't go into it further at this point.[5] Second, I try to provide a learning environment that is as close to a real-life situation as possible. Thus through role playing and psychodrama I have people practice the communication skills in situations simulating real problems for them. Third, I try to maximize clear, concise feedback through the use of videotape and small group exercises. Fourth, I provide opportunity for as much actual practice of the new skills to be learned as possible. This practice involves immediately stopping a person if he departs from using the sought-for skills and enabling him to correct himself before going on. The concentration and attention that this requires usually leave participants exhausted physically and mentally.

At this point, I would like to mention two types of exercises that have not only been helpful in teaching the communication skills described, but which several participants also tell me have been very freeing to them psychologically.

The first type of exercise I call a *Label Detection Exercise.* I ask participants to detect and list the labels that they find themselves habitually applying to

[4] To complicate matters further, I often am asked to work with large numbers of people at a time.

[5] Robert F. Mager, *Preparing Instructional Objectives* (Palo Alto, Calif.: Fearon Publishers, Inc., 1962).

themselves and to others. Then I ask that the participant list the cost of this label; that is, I ask them to consider how labeling themselves as they do inhibits them from experiencing various possibilities in life, then I ask them to consider how labeling others as they do limits what they can experience with this other person. Thus one person labeled herself as "shy person" and she saw that by labeling herself as she did she expected "shy behavior" from herself and this kept her from approaching others at parties, limited the number of personal contacts she made in her work, and limited the initiative she exhibited even in intimate relationships. This same person frequently labeled others as "conceited." Labeling them in this way led her to expect that such persons would not be in need of any support or information from her. Thus, in these relationships she did not offer support or information even when she wanted to.

The other set of activities I call a *Label Transformation Exercise.* In this exercise I ask the participants to transform the labels in the Label Detection Exercise into the form of communication described in this paper; that is, I ask them to transform the label into a statement that (1) makes specific reference to time and situational contexts, (2) clearly differentiates between observations of behavior and labels, (3) reports on affective states, and (4) reports on desires.

Thus the label used by the person just referred to was transformed in the following way. The label of herself as "shy person" was transformed into the following statement, "Frequently when I am at parties (reference to time and situational context) I sit by myself and do not approach anyone (reference to observable behavior) and I'm afraid (reporting on affective state) because I want people to say that they like me and I don't want to chance this not happening" (report on desires). Once a label has been transformed in this way, I find people are freer to consider alternative possibilities of behavior than they were when labeling themselves.

The label this person used of others ("conceited") was transformed into the following statement, "Last week when we were working on the project (reference to time and situational context), Jack did not consult me (reference to observable behavior), and I was hurt (reporting on affective state) because I wanted to share what I had to offer in that project" (reporting on desires). Again I see this label transformation offering greater possibility of freedom of action than simply labeling the other person as "conceited."

In closing, when people read this article (reference to time and situation context) I'm afraid (reporting on affective state) that they might say "This is just a bunch of meaningless semantics" and not spend further time thinking about the article (reference to observable behavior) because I want them at least to spend time thinking to themselves, "I wonder how much of my life is being narrowed by how I label myself and others" (reporting on desires).

Arthur D. Shulman

A MULTICHANNEL TRANSACTIONAL MODEL OF SOCIAL INFLUENCE PROCESSES

For the most part, past research concerned with social influence has assumed unjustly that the major sources of influence affecting an individual are carried on spoken and written communication channels. This overemphasis is evidenced by the almost exclusive use of verbal channels within social influence research. As Ray Birdwhistell (1971) points out, the erroneous abstraction of verbal and written communication:

> . . . is justified on the premise that the *significant* aspect of communication is contained within this data . . . since these verbal or syntactic forms are carried along the audio-aural channel, that channel is examined as *the* communication channel, and the speech and the auditory apparatus, by logical extension, the organs of communications. Other sensorily based channels of interpersonal connection are either held constant as environmental variables of speech, . . . set aside as expressors of individual . . . states or dismissed as primitive contributors of interference . . . consistent with these premises and to this logic, communication is defended as a discontinuous single-channel process.

The purpose of this paper is to emphasize that nonverbal communications strongly influence and determine the course of social interaction. To facilitate this perspective a multichannel transactional model of social influence will be described. Though not independent, nor in any order of importance as will be stressed throughout this paper, the nonverbal channels of communication to be incorporated into a model of social influence processes are: the *proximic* mode concerned with spatial relations among interactants including eye contact and body orientation; *kinesic* modes or body motion; and *paralanguage* or the way in which things are vocalized, including pitch, range, intensity, hesitations, crying, etc. Other nonverbal modes as *dress, tactile, olfaction, temperature sensitivity,* and *extra sensory perception* which have not received as much attention as the above modes also will be considered potentially important nonverbal channels of social influence.

This article is an update of the article that appeared in the original edition of this volume.

These categories are by no means exhaustive, nor mutually exclusive. For instance, either body orientation or eye contact could be considered separate channels of communication or each could be grouped under kinesic or under proximic modes. However, for the sake of simplifying this presentation, they will be considered aspects of the proximic channel of communication. Furthermore, the current state of knowledge of nonverbal communication factors in social influence is at a descriptive stage. This stage is not only characterized by arbitrary assignment of behaviors to generic categories, and arbitrary separation of channels, but most important, the units and methods of analysis are still being defined.[1] Regardless of the methodological problems facing the social scientist, all of the nonverbal communications mentioned above are potential sources of influence and can best be put into perspective by briefly looking at the traditional ways social scientists have been formulating the social influence process.

In a recent social psychology text (1971), Edwin Hollander has elaborated on the idea that "all social influence appears to involve three essential elements which are not fixed but quite alterable in time." These elements are: (1) an influence source, (2) a communication or message, and (3) the recipient of the communication. These basic elements are evident in a two-step flow of communication concept formulated by Katz and Lazarsfeld (1955). They emphasized the social characteristics of the recipient's reference group affiliations which act as filters for the message. Bauer (1964) expanded the two-step flow by giving greater weight to the interaction of motives and social identities of both communicator and recipient. He specified that a message is interpreted by the recipient within the context of his own motives and group affiliations as well as his perception of those of the communicator. This viewpoint explicitly sees social influence as a two-way interaction, a transaction. Both parties adapt to and influence one another. Bauer's transactional model is presented graphically in Figure 1.

Implicit in Bauer's model is the idea that communication, whether written, verbal or nonverbal, is given on a specific channel at a specific point in time. Only one message, which is being interpreted by the recipient in terms of past messages, is transmitted and reacted to at a particular time. It is these assumptions that the multichannel transactional model challenges. The multichannel transactional model assumes that in any social interaction, many messages are transmitted to the recipient at the same time. Each of these messages is capable, separately and in combination, of influencing and directing social interaction. As Birdwhistell (1970) has pointed out, communication is a continuous process made up of overlapping discontinuous segments. In multisensory arrangements, these segments maintain or modify the interaction, influencing the behavior of both parties. That is, these arrangements affect and direct interactions in five ways by: (1) providing information not necessarily being sent by other audio-oral channels, (2) keeping the system of communication in operation, (3) regu-

[1] A more detailed discussion of the assignment of behaviors to generic categories and the problems of measurement can be found in Dittmann (1972), Lyons (1972) and vonCranach and Vine (1973).

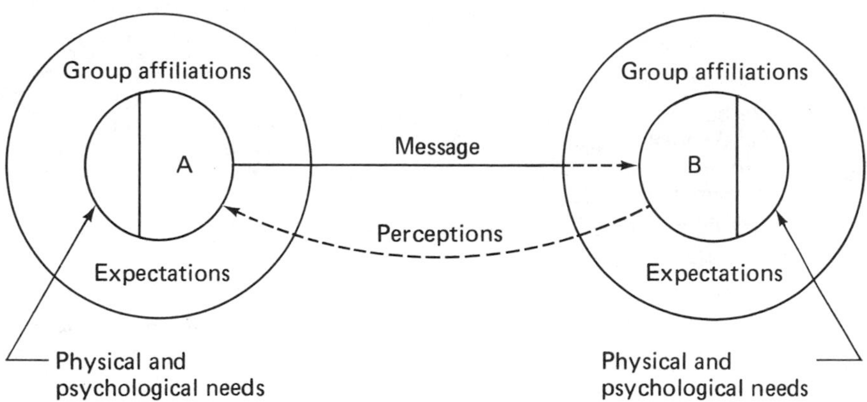

FIGURE 1. **Transactional model of social influence. The message is interpreted by B within the context of his own group affiliations and needs and his expectation mediated perception of those of A. The message being sent by A is in part, determined by his perception of B.**

lating the interaction process, (4) cross-referencing particular messages to comprehensibility in a particular context, and (5) relating the particular context to a larger context of which the interaction is but a special situation. A graphic description of this perspective is presented in Figure 2. As can be seen, the major extensions of Bauer's model have been the amplification of the communication unit and the emphasis on the continuous interplay of the behavior of the individuals involved.

The implications of this multichannel expansion may not be evident from inspection of Figure 2. The position can be taken that each channel can be analyzed separately in terms of Bauer's transactional model. In fact, most of the research on nonverbal social influence processes has done just that. This procedure has unfortunately resulted in the study of units out of context. The crucial point, however, is that each channel's message is *not* necessarily independent or the same. They are interdependent, modifying, negating, or reinforcing each other. Furthermore, the multichannel perspective brings to light the need to study the patterning of messages along the various channels, for depending upon the situation, each channel can appear as the major vehicle of social influence.[2] Before explicating these points further, attention will be drawn to how one situational factor–role expectations–fit into the multichannel transactional model.[3]

The nonverbal messages that are perceived and have meaning for the interactants are to a substantial degree dependent upon the expectations an individual

[2] That the situation can determine what channels carry what messages is readily seen in this writer's attempt to influence the reader within the confines of the written channel.

[3] Development of the multichannel model has been described elsewhere (Shulman and Stone, 1970) and will not be presented here. Such factors as the amount of information a given individual can physically take in as well as such factors as physical and psychological need states are also recognized as important determinants of social influence, but will not be considered within the context of this paper.

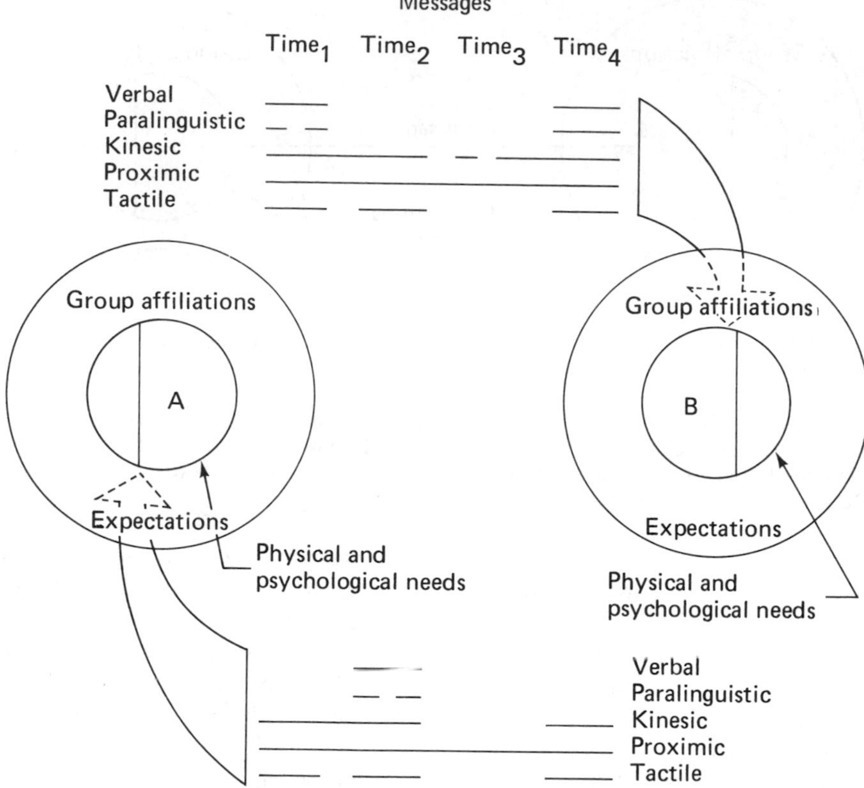

FIGURE 2. **Multichannel transactional model of social influence. In any given time period (seconds, minutes, hours), A is sending many messages simultaneously over the various channels. These messages are interpreted by B within the context of his group affiliations, needs and his expectation mediated perception of those of A. Concurrently, B is sending multimessages over the channels which in part, determine what A is sending.**

has for his behavior and for others' behavior. That is, within the multichannel transactional model, the expectations individuals have for their behavior within a given situation (their roles) provide a set of jointly agreed upon rules for conducting the interchange and, as such, act as information filters for each participant.[4] Furthermore, if we assume, as does Harry Stack Sullivan in his postulation of a need for consensual validation (1953) and Festinger (1950) in his presumption of a need for social reality, that expectation confirmation is a desired state, these expectations take on a motivational quality, one that not only affects what is perceived and decoded, but also how individuals will act

[4] A more detailed outline of the process of rule formulation and testing alluded to here can be found in Harre and Secord (1972).

within a given situation.[5] This fact is exemplified by the work of Goffman.

Goffman (1959, 1961) has suggested that not only does the situation demand certain behaviors, but that nonverbal behaviors in part provide feedback for the adequacy of one's role enactment in the eyes of the other. Furthermore, Goffman suggests that these nonverbal channels are used to indicate the aceptance of the image of self that one projects as affecting the particular role position occupied. Goffman has labeled this phenomenon role distance. Thus, the assembly-line worker appointed to an unwanted position of foreman may wear the required tie and jacket associated with his new position, but will wear the tie loosely, communicating his dissatisfaction with the new role assignment.[6]

Likewise, evidence that who the participants are, in terms of broad categories such as nationality, can determine how nonverbal behaviors are perceived and decoded is provided by the anthropologist, E. T. Hall.[7] Hall (1966) reports, for example, that Americans regard talking through a screen door while standing outside a house as not being inside the house or room in any sense of the word and act accordingly. On the other hand, Germans consider themselves as inside when talking through a screen door.[8] Similarly, within a culture, Jourard (1966) cites evidence for what each of us have experienced. The meaning of messages along the tactile channel is in part determined by the sex of interactants and whether the participants are marital partners. Additional examples for each of the nonverbal channels can be found in the excellent reviews of Argyle (1969), Duncan (1969), Mehrabian (1969), Hinde (1972), Harrison (1973), and von-Cranach and Vine (1973). These examples provide further insight into the current state of knowledge of nonverbal social influence channels. As previously indicated, the state is one characterized by descriptions with little theory. In reviewing these descriptive advances, Duncan (1969) suggests that the research can be divided into three interlocking phases: (a) differentiating and specifying the behaviors in question through a transcription or notation system; (b) discovering the extent and nature of internal structure exhibited by the behaviors; and (c) seeking relationships between the behaviors and external variables, such as personality characteristics and the situation. However, as previously noted, the investigators of nonverbal communicants have tended to look at each channel separately and only recently, as in the current work of Scheflin (1965)[9], Hall

[5] The motivational qualities of having one's expectations confirmed may not always be positive. Maddi (1968) and McClelland and Clark (1953) have evidence to suggest that only marked disconfirmation is viewed negatively with mild and moderate departure being viewed as positive.

[6] This example also demonstrates the need to include the nonverbal channel of dress within the multichannel transactional model. One of the few individuals who has started to explore this channel is Gregory Stone (1962).

[7] Hall is responsible for delineating the proximic channel and formulating a transcription system for these behaviors. Two other channels that have had much research also have their mentors, George Trager for paralanguage and Ray Birdwhistell for kinesics.

[8] Robert Sommer (1969) has experimentally verified Hall's observations of the potency of the proximic channel as a vehicle of social influence and has brought into focus the need for structural engineers and architects to take into consideration a behavioral basis for design.

[9] Scheflin, like other nonverbal communicator researchers, has concentrated on therapist-patient relationships. Within these relationships, Scheflin has found that nonverbal com-

(1966), Kendon (1973), Duncan (1974), Berman, Shulman, and Marwit (1975), and Shulman and Berman (1975), have investigators attempted to study the patterning of behavior via a multichannel perspective. The need for this perspective should be obvious to the reader who becomes conscious of the multimessages coming into him when interacting with another.

It is also becoming obvious to the social scientist who is finding that specific behaviors on each channel take on different connotations depending not only on the situation as previously mentioned, but also upon what else is being communicated. For instance, Mehrabian (1969) reports a number of instances where the external variables of attitude and status are curvilinearly related to proximic behaviors; his findings show the need to focus on the content, or patterning of behaviors across channels to understand the social influence process. For example, his summary of the research indicates that eye contact is slightly less than maximum for people who are either liked very much or slightly disliked. However, what attitude is being communicated can be described by looking at the distance between a communicator and his addressee. The more people like each other, the closer they will be.[10] These examples have been given to illustrate the level of sophistication of current description research. However, they give only minimal insight into the development of theory.

While there has been relatively little theory involved in research on separate nonverbal channels and much less from a multichannel transactional perspective, what little there is can be related to either (1) the information theory of Shannon and Weaver (1949) or (2) the writings of G. H. Mead (1924). Shannon and Weaver were most concerned with measuring information flow devoid of meaning and context.[11] Mead concentrated on the importance of gestures as taking on symbolic meaning. More recently, Abrahamson (1966), Rosenthal (1966), Argyle and Kendon (1967), and Argyle (1969) have implicitly called for a multichannel transactional perspective and have recently started to work with the channels as if they were not separate independent entities. Others as Hall,

---

munications play at least one unique function, that of regulation. According to Scheflin, nonverbal communication via proximic and kinesic channels may be employed to indicate that a new point is about to be made, that the communicator is taking an attitude relative to several points being made by himself or by his addressee, and he is temporarily removing himself from the communication situation. Further work on the regulatory implications of nonverbal behaviors can be found in a study by Condon and Ogston (1966).

[10] Mehrabian reports that the sex of the individual involved will also interact with these communication channels in encoding the message. For female communicators, body orientation toward the addressee, like their eye contact, is a parabolic function of attitude toward the addressee, such that the least direct orientation occurs for intensely disliked addressees, the highest degree occurs for addressees who are liked very much. For male communicators, the only significant difference occurs with intensely liked addressees, who receive a less direct body orientation. The slight decrease in the directness of orientation of males or females toward intensely liked addressees may be understood in terms of the tendency of communicators to assume a side-by-side and very close position when they communicate to such addressees (p. 370). Recently, Patterson (1973) has provided a summary of studies which suggests how attraction is related to the combined messages sent off by proximic cues, eye contact, and body orientation.

[11] See Dittmann (1972) for a readable account of the limitations of Shannon and Weaver's (1949) information theory.

Bateson and Goffman have proposed models which can be incorporated into the multichannel perspective. Hall's (1963, 1966) programs are extensive and will not be reviewed here. Bateson's and Goffman's models are not only multichannel in nature, but also are to a minimal degree transactional in nature. Their models, however, tend to classify the nonverbal behaviors in terms of an etiology of schizophrenia in Bateson's case, and in terms of impression formation and management in Goffman's case.

Bateson's model centers on the double-bind theory of schizophrenia. According to this theory, conflicting messages from a significant source may create a "double-bind" situation which can lead to schizophrenia. An example of such behavior would be a child sensing hostility from his mother's physical withdrawal via the proximic channel despite her concurrent, overlapping verbalization of love.

The use of nonverbal sources of influence by Goffman has already been mentioned above in terms of role distance. Focusing on nonverbal sources which give information about the communicator, Goffman (1959) separates the behaviors into two classes which differ in the perceived intent of the communicator. Some of these behaviors are perceived as under the control of the communicator, others are perceived as actions for which the communicator has no control and is unaware of. According to Goffman, these latter behaviors are used by the recipient as a test of the credibility of the controlled impressions given off by the communicator. Recently, Eckman and Freisen (1969, 1974) have reported experimental confirmation of Goffman's intentional-unintentional behavior classifications. They found that psychotic patients could manage their facial expressions and hide anxiety during psychiatric interviews, but that the person who they were interacting with perceived the person as anxious via uncontrolled leg movements. These movements were in fact kinesic communications that the patient was unaware of and unable to control. The fact that they were judged within the context of the occupational roles of the interactants and within the psychological interview setting is important. Calder (1974) has shown that how we perceive and presumably act is determined by the appropriateness of the exhibited behavior within a situational context (interview) and by the positions the individuals played within the situation.

CONCLUSION

The purpose of this article was to emphasize that nonverbal communications strongly influence and determine the course of social interaction. Specific meanings attributed to these communications and their functions are to a large degree dependent upon the context in which they occur. To facilitate this perspective, a multichannel transactional model of social influence was described. Within the 1972 edition of this book, this writer asked the question as to whether the model would be adopted or would social scientists continue to use the verbal, single-channel perspective. Since writing the 1972 version, enough evidence has become available to suggest that the perspective indeed has been adopted by social scientists. Part of this is due to the availability of video recording equipment and to computer technology for handling the multiple data points generated by such an approach. The practicing psychologist as well as the general public has also started to reject the single channel stimulus response approach and adopt a multichannel perspective. This evidence can be seen in the growth of sensitivity training laboratories and their attempt to have us become aware of the use of the many communication channels open to us and the use of transactional analysis which encourages us to examine the messages we send in terms of the multiple roles we play in a variety of situations. However, much work remains to be done both within the laboratory and within applied settings. Descriptions of the behavior patterns must be further refined. The existent knowledge base of how we communicate within the organizations we are in is for the most part lacking. Currently, within industry new communication systems, including video phone communication devices, audio conferencing devices, are being employed with the intent of cutting down the cost of travel. However, as each system is employed, other aspects of communication other than information exchange may no longer be feasible with the systematic restriction of behaviors usually found in face-to-face situations. As such, the interpersonal relationships that are maintained through the nonverbal behaviors may themselves change and break down.

REFERENCES

Abrahamson, M. *Interpersonal Accommodation.* Princeton: D. Van Nostrand, 1966.

Argyle, M. *Social Interaction.* New York: Atherton Press, 1969.

Argyle, M., and Kendon, A. "The Experimental Analysis of Social Performance." In *Advances in Experimental Social Psychology,* edited by L. Berkowitz. New York: Academic Press, 1967.

Bauer, R. A. "The Obstinate Audience: The Influence Process from the Point of View of Social Communication." *American Psychologist* 19 (1964): 319-328.

Berman, H. J.; Shulman, A. D.; and Marwit, S. "Comparison of Multidimensional Decoding of Affect from Audio, Video and Audiovideo Recordings." *Sociometry* (in press).

Birdwhistell, R. *Kinesics and Context.* Philadelphia: University of Pennsylvania Press, 1970.

Birdwhistell, R. "Communication: A Continuous Multichannel Process." In *Conceptual Bases and Applications of the Communicational Sciences.* New York: John Wiley & Sons, 1971.

Calder, B. J. "Informational Cues and Attributions Based on Role Behavior." *Journal of Experimental Social Psychology* 10 (1974): 121-125.

Condon, W. S., and Ogston, W. D. "Sound Film Analysis of Normal and Pathological Behavior Patterns." *Journal of Nervous and Mental Disease* 143 (1966): 338-347.

Dittmann, A. T. *Interpersonal Messages of Emotion.* New York: Springer Publishing Co., 1972.

Duncan, S. D., Jr. "Nonverbal Communication." *Psychological Bulletin* 72 (1969): 118-137.

Duncan, S. D., Jr. "On the Structure of Speaker-Auditor Interaction during Speaking Turns." *Language in Society* 2 (1974): 161-180.

Ekman, P., and Friesen, W. V. "Nonverbal Leakage and Clues to Deception." *Psychiatry* 32 (1969): 88-106.

Ekman, P., and Friesen, W. V. "Nonverbal Behavior and Psychopathology." In *The Psychology of Depression: Contemporary Theory and Research,* edited by R. J. Friedman and M. M. Katz. Washington, D.C.: Winston and Sons, 1974.

Festinger, L. "Informal Social Communication." *Psychological Review* 57 (1950): 271-282.

Goffman, E. *The Presentation of Self in Everyday Life.* Garden City, N.Y.: Doubleday Anchor, 1959.

Goffman, E. *Encounters.* Indianapolis: Bobbs-Merrill, 1961.

Hall, E. T. "A System for the Notation of Proximic Behavior." *American Anthropologist* 65 (1963): 1003-1026.

Hall, E. T. *The Hidden Dimensions.* New York: Doubleday, 1966.

Harre, R. and Secord, P. F. *The Explanation of Social Behavior.* Totowa, N.J.: Rowman and Littlefield, 1972.

Harrison, R. P. "Nonverbal Communication." In *Handbook of Communication,* edited by I. de Sola Pool, W. Schramm, N. Maccoby, F. Frey, and E. Parker. Chicago: Rand McNally, 1973.

Hinde, R. A., ed. *Nonverbal Communication.* Cambridge: Cambridge University Press, 1972.

Hollander, E. P. *Principles and Methods of Social Psychology.* New York: Oxford University Press, 1971.

Jourard, S. M. "An Exploratory Study of Body Accessibility." *British Journal of Social and Clinical Psychology* 5 (1966): 221-231.

Katz, E., and Lazarsfeld, P. F. *Personal Influence.* Glencoe, Ill.: Free Press, 1955.

Kendon, A. "The Role of Visible Behavior in the Organization of Social Interactions." In *Social Communication and Movement,* edited by M. von-Cranach and I. Vine. New York: Academic Press, 1973, 29-74.

Lyons, J. "Human Language." In *Nonverbal Communication,* edited by R. A. Hinde. Cambridge: Cambridge University Press, 1972, 49-85.

Maddi, S. R. "The Pursuit of Consistency and Variety." In *Theories of Cognitive Consistency,* edited by R. P. Abelson, E. Aronson, W. J. McGuire, T. M. Newcomb, M. J. Rosenberg, and P. H. Tannenbaum. Chicago: Rand McNally, 1968, 267-274.

McClelland, D., and Clark, R. A. "Antecedent Conditions for Affective Arousal." In *The Achievement Motive,* edited by D. McClelland, J. W. Atkinson, R. A. Clark, and E. L. Lowell. New York: Appleton-Century-Crofts, 1953, sections 2 and 10.

Mead, G. H. *Mind, Self, and Society.* Chicago: University of Chicago Press, 1924.

Mehrabian, A. "Significance of Posture and Position in the Communication of Attitude and Status Relationships." *Psychological Bulletin* 71 (1969): 359-372.

Patterson, M. "Compensation in Nonverbal Immediacy Behaviors: A Review." *Sociometry* 36 (1973): 237-252.

Rosenthal, R. *Experimenter Effects in Behavioral Research.* New York: Appleton-Century-Crofts, 1966.

Scheflin, A. E. *Stream and Structure of Communicational Behavior.* Philadelphia: Eastern Pennsylvania Psychiatric Institute, 1965.

Shannon, C. E., and Weaver, W. *The Mathematical Theory of Communication.* Urbana: University of Illinois Press, 1949.

Shulman, A. D., and Stone, M. "Expectation Confirmation-Disconfirmation as a Determinant of Interpersonal Behavior: A Study of Loudness of Voice." Paper presented at Southwestern Psychological Association Meetings, April 1970, St. Louis, Missouri.

Shulman, A. D., and Berman, H. J. "Role Expectations about Subjects and Experimenters in Psychological Research." *Journal of Personality and Social Psychology* 35, 2 (1975): 368-380.

Sommer, R. *Personal Space.* Englewood Cliffs, N.J.: Prentice-Hall, 1969.

Stone, G. P. "Appearance and the Self." In *Human Behavior and Social Processes,* edited by A. M. Rose. Boston: Houghton Mifflin, 1962, 128-147.

Sullivan, H. S. *The Interpersonal Theory of Psychiatry.* New York: Norton, 1953.

VonCranach, M., and Vine, I., eds. *Social Communication and Movement.* New York: Academic Press, 1973.

chapter **12**

Attitudes

An enormous amount of research on attitude development and change has been published. This book offers only a brief introduction to the concepts, theories, and implications for organizations. The major portion of our treatment of attitudes is a selection by Secord and Backman, who review some of the major approaches to attitude development and change.

Attitudes, like other concepts in the field of organizational behavior, may be defined in a variety of ways, depending on one's theoretical and/or practical orientation. Secord and Backman (1964) provided a widely used definition that alludes to the presence of affective, cognitive, and behavioral components in attitudes: ". . . certain regularities of an individual's feelings, thoughts and predispositions to act toward some aspect of his environment" (p. 97).[1]

It is generally believed that the outward effect of attitudes is to induce or inhibit behavior. It is difficult, however, to isolate this influence from the influence of other phenomena. Furthermore, a full understanding of attitudes requires measurement of the two internal components, feelings and thoughts, which may not be communicated accurately. The problem is compounded in many studies by attempts to compare and/or add together the attitudes of different people. Thus, our knowledge of attitudes and their consequences is limited by their nature and may be clouded by efforts to "average" them.

Attitude Research—A Moral Issue?

Incomplete though our knowledge of attitudes may be, there is much interest in manipulating them to achieve desired behavioral results.

The Skinner-Rogers controversy in part 1 focused on the ethical implications of attempts to control behavior. Skinner and his followers are never sure (and often give the impression that they do not care) what the mental processes of their subjects are. If attitudes do have important consequences for behavior, the potential ethical issues involved in attitude research are even greater than those

1. Recently, Zajonc (1969) emphasized that the cognitive organization of the component can have motivational properties as well.

involved in behavioral research. For example, when does attitude change become thought control? What constitutes legitimate influence of an individual's attitudes? What are possible ways to protect individuals from manipulation of attitudes? It is surprising that so many people, psychologists in particular, have reacted so vigorously on ethical grounds against the operant conditioners but have viewed the research on attitudes with such apparent ethical neutrality.[2] Perhaps it is because the effects of operant conditioning have been demonstrated to be so powerful, whereas knowledge about attitudes has not permitted such a high degree of control—*yet.* At any rate, it is important that we understand this research and explore its possible ethical implications. Secord and Backman's selection provides a useful beginning.

REFERENCES

Secord, P. F., and Backman, C. W. *Social Psychology.* New York: McGraw-Hill Book Co., 1964.

Zajonc, R. B. "Cognitive Theories in Social Psychology." In *The Handbook of Social Psychology.* 2nd ed., edited by G. Lindzey and E. Aronson, 1, pp. 320-411. Reading, Mass.: Addison-Wesley, 1969.

2. Only when attitude change is called brainwashing does it excite people very much. When it is called therapy, education, rehabilitation, management development, etc., it is generally applauded rather than feared by the masses, governmental leaders, and the social science "establishment." In many ways, these change processes can reasonably be described as types of brainwashing which are legitimated by the social system.

Paul F. Secord
Carl W. Backman

THEORIES OF ATTITUDE ORGANIZATION

In their enthusiasm for the new measurement techniques introduced by Thurstone in 1928 and Likert in 1932, investigators often studied attitudes almost apart from their relation to anything else. Today, psychologists and sociologists realize that the concept of attitude is most useful when studied in context: as a component of the personality of individuals, as serving functional or adjustive ends, or as a descriptive concept characterizing a prevailing mode of thought of the members of a category or subgroup. Context relating attitude to other variables is provided by theory. The years since World War II have seen the gradual development of theory appropriate to the study of attitude change. While none of the theories developed is as yet adequate, they nevertheless serve to integrate many investigations that formerly appeared to be unrelated. Moreover, much current research is generated by these theories.

Most of the theories are intrapersonal: they pertain to the relations of the three attitude components within an individual and specify various conditions that control these relations and produce changes in them. The remainder of this chapter will be devoted to a discussion of several representative theories in order to gain a perspective on the various empirical studies to be discussed in the chapters following.

CONSISTENCY AS AN ORGANIZING PRINCIPLE

One of the prevailing characteristics of human thought and behavior is its tendency to be consistent. If we like a person, we tend to attribute "good" traits to him, and we resist any suggestion that he might posess undesirable traits. We also have beliefs that are consistent with our behavior. Thus, after many news releases about the relation between lung cancer and smoking, a sample of respondents in Minneapolis were asked whether or not they believed the relation had been proved. Only 7 percent of the heavy smokers believed that it had, compared with 20 percent of the light smokers and 29 percent of the nonsmokers (Osgood, 1960). A good party Democrat is likely to give a friendly reception to speeches by any Democratic politician and unfriendly reception to speeches by any Republican politican.

* * *

In 1945 Lecky published a small book in which he attempted to explain much thought and behavior in terms of a single principle: the tendency of the individual to be self-consistent. He suggested that this single principle might substitute for the many principles of human behavior that had been developed for dealing with diverse areas of cognition and behavior. For example, he attempted to show how learning could be explained as well by a consistency principle as by conditioning. The process of forgetting was also explained by consistency: inconsistent elements drop out of memory. He even developed a theory of pleasure, based upon the idea that pleasure is experienced when the organism finds a way to make consistent some experience which is at first inconsistent.

Perhaps the father of modern consistency theory is Heider, who published an important paper on the topic in 1946 and in 1958 published a book-length monograph devoted to his "balance theory." In just the last decade, widespread interest in the principle of consistency has been evident. Many behavioral scientists are now assiduously devoting themselves to developing systematic theories based upon the principle, and many active research programs are in progress.

* * *

Only four of these theoretical approaches will be treated in any detail in this chapter: Rosenberg's theory of affective-cognitive consistency, Festinger's theory of cognitive dissonance, Katz and Stotland's motivational theory of attitude change, and Kelman's three-process theory of attitude change. Although Rosenberg's theory is not as broad as some . . . and has not produced as much extensive empirical study, it is chosen for discussion because it contributes to a better understanding of the nature of affective-cognitive components and the relation between them. Festinger's theory of cognitive dissonance has led to extensive research and has the special merit of demonstrating the relations between cognitive elements and behavior. The approaches of Katz and Stotland and of Kelman are discussed briefly in order to gain a broader perspective on approaches to attitude change other than consistency theory.

* * *

ROSENBERG'S THEORY OF AFFECTIVE-COGNITIVE CONSISTENCY

Rosenberg (1960*a*, 1960*b*) has concerned himself primarily with conceptualizing what happens *within the individual* when attitudes change. He is particularly interested in the relation between affective and cognitive components of an attitude. In general, past treatments have recognized both of these components, but have been unconcerned with specifying in any precise way how they are organized with respect to each other. Rosenberg attempts to remedy this deficiency. In addition, he extends the cognitive component of an attitude to include not only cognitions about the attitude object, but also *beliefs about* *the relations between that object and other important values of the person.* The affective component is defined in the usual manner as the positive or negative feeling that the individual has toward the attitude object. Thus, a person might have a negative feeling toward Republican congressmen. He also has certain beliefs about them that relate to other positively or negatively valued conditions. He might believe that Republican congressmen obstruct progress, that they hamper the economy, that they have outmoded views on taxation, and that their views on social welfare are inappropriate in a democratic nation.

Rosenberg's principal hypothesis is that the nature and strength of the feeling toward an attitude object are correlated with the cognitions associated with the attitude object. He makes the following statement:

> Strong and stable positive affect toward a given object should be associated with beliefs that it leads to the attainment of a number of important values, while strong negative affect should be associated with beliefs that the object tends to block the attainment of important values. Similarly, moderate positive or negative affects should be associated with beliefs that relate the attitude object either to less important values or, if to important values, then with less confidence about the relationships between these values and the attitude object. (1960*b*, p. 18)

Rosenberg (1953, 1956) has developed a procedure for determing the cognitive components of attitudes. He uses a set of 35 value statements, such as "all human beings having equal rights," "people being well-educated," "making one's own decisions," and "attaining economic security." The subject first categorizes each item in terms of its *value importance,* that is, how satisfying it is to him. To do this, he considers each value statement separately and rates its value importance by placing it in a category ranging from "gives me maximum satisfaction" (+10) through "gives me neither satisfaction nor dissatisfaction" (0) to "gives me maximum dissatisfaction" (-10). For example, if he values education highly, he might give a rating of +8 to "people being well-educated."

Second, the subject rates these value statements with respect to how well a particular attitude contributes to their realization. Suppose, for example, that the attitude concerns Federal aid to education. Taking the first value statement, "people being well-educated," he would rate Federal aid to education on a scale from +5 to -5, positive ratings implying that Federal aid interferes with its attainment. Ratings of the value of statements obtained in this fashion are termed the *perceived instrumentality* of the attitude object.

From ratings of value importance and perceived instrumentality, a *cognitive index* for the attitude object "Federal aid to education" may be obtained. This index represents the subject's pattern of beliefs about the extent to which Federal aid to education results in the attainment of or interference with the individual's values, weighted according to their importance. It is a quantitative measure of the extent to which a person's attitude is consistent with his values.

A principal finding by Rosenberg (1956) is that the index of cognitive structure is consistent with the affect of an attitude, as measured by an attitude scale. That is, if a subject has strong positive affect toward an attitude object, he is likely to have a high cognitive index for that attitude, believing it to be instrumental in attaining his positive values and in blocking negative values. The association between the affective component of an attitude and the cognitive index has been found to be greatest for the person's most salient values. A person's attitudes, then, are anchored in his important values in a highly consistent manner.

Of particular importance are the implications of Rosenberg's theory and methodology for understanding attitude change. . . . A basic proposition in his theory is as follows (Rosenberg, 1960*b*):

> When the affective and cognitive components of an attitude are mutually consistent the attitude is in a stable state; when the affective and cognitive components are mutually inconsistent (to a degree that exceeds the individual's present tolerance for such inconsistency) the attitude is in an unstable state and will undergo spontaneous reorganizing activity until such activity eventuates in either (1) the attainment of affective-cognitive consistency or (2) the placing of an "irreconcilable" inconsistency beyond the range of active awareness. (p. 22)

From this proposition it follows that if certain external forces bring about a change in either the affective or cognitive components of a previously stable attitude, pressures will arise to change the remaining component. Most studies previous to Rosenberg have emphasized change in cognitive components as a cause of change in affective components, stressing *rational* processes in attitude change. A good illustration is provided by certain attempts to change racial prejudice. Some attempts to change prejudice toward the Negro use communications designed to convince the individual of the unfavorable consequences of prejudice and of the lack of evidence concerning racial differences on important attributes. But if the person changes his beliefs in response to direct attempts of this kind, his new beliefs would be inconsistent with his negative affect, hence, according to this theory, he resists such approaches. To be successful, such pressures toward change would have to be strong and persistent, creating strong inconsistency between affect and cognition.

While most attitude studies have stressed change in cognitive components as a cause of shifts in affective components, Rosenberg has concentrated on demonstrating that a change in *affect* will produce cognitive changes (Rosenberg and Gardner, 1958; Rosenberg, 1960*c*). In one experiment, eight subjects who were in favor of the United States policy of giving economic aid to foreign nations were placed under deep hypnosis and their positive feeling reversed to a negative one. This was accomplished by giving each subject the following instructions while under deep hypnosis (Rosenberg, 1960*a*):

> After you awake, and continuing until our next meeting, you will feel very strongly opposed to the United States policy of giving economic aid to foreign nations. The mere idea of the United States giving economic aid to foreign nations will make you feel very displeased and disgusted. Until your next meeting with me you will continue to feel very strong and thorough opposition to the United States policy of economic aid to foreign nations. You will have no memory whatsoever of this suggestion's having been made . . . until the amnesia is removed by my giving you the signal at our next session. (p. 327)

Before and after hypnotic manipulation, subjects indicated the value importance and the perceived instrumentality on Rosenberg's 32 value statements with respect to their own attitude toward foreign aid and two other attitudes used as controls. As predicted, subjects made large-scale changes in both perceived instrumentality and value statements involving foreign aid. Since affect was not manipulated for the control attitudes, no appreciable changes occurred with respect to them. Typically, a subject changed from a position extremely supportive of foreign aid to one of extreme opposition. At the same time, many of his related beliefs changed. For example, if before the affect manipulation he believed that foreign aid would help to maintain such positive values as "the prevention of economic depression," he later believed that *abandonment* of foreign aid would prevent economic depression.

Sometimes, instead of changing the *instrumental* relation between attitude and value, a subject altered the strength or even the direction (positive or negative) of his values, to make them more consistent with the experimentally produced affect. For example, if a subject continued to believe that foreign aid would prevent economic depression, but shifted from extreme support of foreign aid to extreme opposition, he might change the value of economic depression from a negative one to a positive one, arguing that economic depression had certain beneficial effects upon the country. The effects observed in this experiment persisted in most instances for an entire week, at the end of which period the experimenter removed the affect change and explained the entire experiment to the subjects.

* * *

FESTINGER'S THEORY OF COGNITIVE DISSONANCE

The theory of cognitive dissonance, developed by Festinger (1957), has the great merit of linking attitude to overt behavior, a problem that has been troublesome throughout the history of attitude research. Critics often argued that the concept of attitude was useless, because no one could be sure that a person would behave in accordance with his verbally expressed attitudes. Dissonance theory recognizes this shortcoming and helps to remedy it by specifying the conditions under which attitudes and behavior do correspond.

Festinger introduces his theory by noting that the attitudes of an individual are normally consistent with each other, that he behaves in accordance with his attitudes, and that his various actions are consistent with each other. For example, if a person believes in democracy, he does not believe in fascism. If he believes a college education is a good thing, he tries to send his children to college. If he behaves conscientiously in doing his college assignments, he is likely to behave conscientiously on a job. Of particular interest is the question of what happens when inconsistencies occur.

By the term cognitive element is meant any knowledge, opinion, or belief about the environment, about oneself, or about one's behavior. The term *dissonance* is introduced to represent an inconsistency between two or more cognitive elements. Two cognitive elements are in a dissonant relation if, considering these two alone, *the obverse of one element would follow from the other.* For example, if a person knew that the most he could afford to pay for a new automobile was $2,500 and that he had just been persuaded to sign a contract to purchase one costing $3,000, there would be a dissonant relation between these two cognitive elements. On the other hand, two cognitive elements are consonant with one another if one follows from the other. Thus, the knowledge that you are getting wet is consonant with the knowledge that it is raining.

Relations between cognitive elements may be either relevant or irrelevant. Dissonance and consonance may only exist between relevant elements. Many cognitive elements have nothing to do with each other. A person may know that the cost of first-class mail is 5 cents an ounce and may also know that spark plugs ignite the gasoline in an engine. These elements are irrelevant to each other.

The magnitude of dissonance is a function of the proportion of all relevant cognitive elements that is dissonant. These elements are generally weighted according to their importance. Thus, the magnitude of dissonance may be expressed in terms of the following ratio:

$$\text{Dissonance} = \frac{\text{importance x no. of dissonant elements}}{\text{importance x no. of consonant elements}}$$

From this ratio,[1] it is clear that the more nearly equal the relative proportions of consonant and dissonant elements, the greater the dissonance is. If there are only a few dissonant elements and many consonant elements, dissonance is relatively low. The number of dissonant elements can never exceed the number of consonant elements, for this would lead to a change, removing the dissonance. Hence the maximum value that dissonance can reach is 1, which is approached when the proportions of dissonant and consonant elements are equal.

Actually, the magnitude of dissonance is represented in terms of a ratio in order to clarify the concept rather than to offer a measuring device. Dissonance cannot be directly measured, and in actual practice in experiments, conditions are compared only with respect to whether or not condition *A* represents a greater or a lesser amount of dissonance than condition *B*. At best, a series of conditions may be rank-ordered, but the exact quantities of dissonance present are not measured.

Reduction of Dissonance

Several propositions in dissonance theory have been stated as follows (Festinger, 1957):

[1] Strictly speaking, not even the ratio presented is correct. If there are relatively equal proportions of trivial dissonant and consonant elements, dissonance should be smaller than in the case of relatively equal proportions of highly important dissonant and consonant elements. But the formula shown would yield equal amounts of dissonance in these two special cases. Thus the ratio should be further weighted by the mean importance of all of the relevant elements. But this is mainly an academic point, since the ratio is not used to actually measure dissonance.

> The existence of dissonance, being psychologically uncomfortable, will motivate the person to try to reduce the dissonance and achieve consonance. (p. 30)
>
> When dissonance is present, in addition to trying to reduce it, the person will actively avoid situations and information which would likely increase the dissonance. (p. 3)
>
> The strength of the pressures to reduce the dissonance is a function of the magnitude of the dissonance. (p. 18)

Three ways of reducing dissonance are:

1. **Change of a behavioral cognitive element.** When knowledge of one's own behavior is dissonant with a belief, it is often simplest to change one's behavior. Thus if a person smokes but thinks it is bad for his health, he may stop smoking. Or if he realizes that "goofing off" instead of studying is inconsistent with knowledge that he intends to apply for medical school, he may stop goofing off.

2. **Change of an environmental cognitive element.** Sometimes the behavior of a person is dissonant with some environmental factor that can be changed. For example, he may reduce the dissonance between his knowledge that smoking causes cancer and his use of cigarettes by changing to a filter-tip brand. Perhaps the easiest aspect of the environment to change is the social or interpersonal environment. Thus a smoker bothered by dissonance may seek support from other persons who also smoke and who can present arguments and reassurance against the view that lung cancer is caused by smoking. He may, for example, point to the fact that many doctors smoke.

3. **Addition of new cognitive elements.** Sometimes it is difficult to change any of the cognitive elements that are involved in dissonance. Under these circumstances it is often possible to add new elements to outweigh the dissonant ones. A person who has purchased an automobile he cannot afford may convince himself that he is likely to get a substantial raise in pay, that he can readily borrow the additional money, or that he has probably overestimated his expenses and underestimated his income. The smoker worried about lung cancer may tell himself that smoking is relaxing and thus beneficial to his health.

IMPLICATIONS OF DISSONANCE THEORY

Many studies have explored various facets of dissonance theory, and more are in progress. One of these will be described to illustrate the usefulness of the theory in predicting attitude change. The experiment (Festinger and Carlsmith, 1959) chosen is of particular interest because it bears out predictions from dissonance theory opposite to those of common sense. From dissonance theory, the following hypothesis may be derived.

> 1. If a person is induced to say or do something opposite to his private attitude, he will tend to modify his attitude so as to make it consonant with the cognition of what he has said or done.

This is clear and obvious, but a second hypothesis is as follows:

2. The greater the pressure used to elicit the behavior contrary to one's private attitude (beyond the minimum needed to elicit it), the *less* his attitude will change.

To illustrate, if a person having a strong preference for Democratic candidates in an election were paid $5,000 to go out and persuade other persons to vote for Republican candidates, he would be less likely to switch his personal political preference than if he were to perform the same behavior for a fee of only $100. If $100 were just sufficient to elicit his acceptance of the task, this degree of reward would be more likely to result in a change in his own political preference than any other amount of reward. A greater amount of reward would appreciably strengthen the elements involved in working for a Republican victory and thereby would result in less dissonance and less pressure to change. It is at the point where the pressure to comply and one's political leanings are in approximately equal opposition that dissonance is at a maximum.

The following procedure was used to test the two hypotheses stated above. After completing a dull, boring "experimental" task, subjects were informed that a student helper usually brought in the next experimental subject and told him how enjoyable the experiment was. It was implied that this helper had failed to show up, and the student who had just completed the task was asked to serve in this capacity. Two magnitudes of reward for serving in this role were used for different groups of students: $1 and $20.

Here, then, is an experimental situation where the subject forms a strong private opinion that the task he has just engaged in is dull and boring, but where for a price (and presumably other considerations, such as his desire to cooperate with the experimenter), he agrees to tell a new subject that it is an enjoyable task. After they had served as helpers, subjects were interviewed and asked to rate their opinions concerning the experiment on an 11-point scale from maximum negative opinion to maximum positive opinion. As predicted, those who had received a reward of only $1 rated the experiment higher in terms of its enjoyability than those who had received $20.

In other words, if monetary reward is used as the pressure to win such compliance from a person, the prediction is that the more money he receives for complying, the less his attitude will change. The key to understanding the second hypothesis is the point that *dissonance is at its maximum* when the opposing cognitive elements are equal in strength and importance. Since the amount of attitude change is a function of the amount of dissonance, it is at the point where these opposing elements are equal that the greatest attitude change will occur. If opposing elements are made unequal by appreciably strengthening one set of elements but not the other, dissonance will be somewhat less, and attitude change will be smaller.

* * *

A FUNCTIONAL THEORY OF ATTITUDES

Katz (1960), and Katz and Stotland (1959) in a somewhat more formal presentation, have offered a functional approach to the study of attitudes. From their point of view, the motivational basis of an attitude is the key to understanding change and resistance to change. They note that situational factors and the communication directed toward attitude change will have different effects depending on the motivational basis of the attitude. The motivational basis is conceptualized in terms of the function which an attitude performs for the person. Katz has described four major functions of attitudes as follows:

1. The instrumental, adjustive, or utilitarian function. By this is meant that the individual strives to maximize the rewards and minimize the penalties which he experiences. Thus, he develops favorable attitudes toward those objects which result in reward and unfavorable attitudes toward those which lead to punishment.

2. The ego-defensive function. Attitudes may function to protect the person from acknowledgment of unpleasant truths about himself or of the harsh realities in his environment. For example, a person with considerable insecurity about his own worth may develop strong prejudice against minority groups so that he can regard himself as superior.

3. The value-expressive function. A person may derive satisfaction from expressing himself in terms of attitudes that are appropriate to his personal values and to his self concept. Thus, an individual with strong democratic-liberal values may receive much gratification by engaging in actions that foster such values.

4. The knowledge function. The individual is presumed to have a basic drive to understand, to make sense out of, to "structure" his experience. Elements of experience that are at first inconsistent with what a person knows are rearranged or changed so as to achieve consistency.

The value-expressive function and the knowledge function tie in closely with Festinger's theory of cognitive dissonance, as well as other consistency theories. The value-expressive function concerns consistency between values (a form of cognitive element) and cognitive elements representing behavior. The knowledge function resembles Festinger's proposition that a person is motivated to reduce dissonance and achieve consonance. Katz and Stotland apply the consistency principle primarily to single attitude objects: They suggest that affective, cognitive, and behavioral components involving a single attitude object move toward consistency. In their system, different attitudes often may be inconsistent with each other without creating strain.

The instrumental, adjustive, or utilitarian function and the ego-defensive function represent some elements of attitude theory not yet discussed, and they deserve further elaboration here. Katz (1960) notes that to change an attitude that serves an adjustive function, one of the following two conditions must prevail:

> (1) The attitude and the activities related to it no longer provide the satisfactions they once did, or (2) the individual's level of aspiration has been raised. The Chevrolet owner who had positive attitudes toward his old car may now want a more expensive car commensurate with his new status. (p. 177)

Shifts in the satisfactions obtained from various behaviors, then, result in associated changes in attitudes. When new behaviors which are somewhat inconsistent with current attitudes are rewarded, existing attitudes are modified. Similarly, experiences which are punishing lead to unfavorable attitudes toward the communicators or objects which incite the punishment. . . . Communications that arouse considerable anxiety or fear are likely to create unfavorable attitudes toward the communicator and his communication, a result consistent with theory.

Ego-defensive attitudes are readily aroused by any situation that threatens the individual. Prejudice toward minority groups is an example of an attitude that is sometimes ego-defensive. This attitude would be aroused by excessive competition, derogatory remarks by others, or any other threat to a person's status. Other factors arousing such attitudes include the direct encouragement of their expression by other persons, especially those who hold authoritative positions, and the building up of inhibited drives or impulses in the person such as sexual or aggressive feelings.

Most important is the point that persuasive communications that are effective with attitudes having other motivational bases are often ineffective with ego-defensive attitudes. Thus, communications that provide a great deal of information in support of changing an attitude may not work because such a change deprives the person of an attitude that serves to bolster his ego-defenses. To take one example, an individual whose prejudice toward the Negro is rooted in his own sense of inferiority and his hostile feelings resulting from emotional conflict will be highly resistant to information supporting the view that there is no innate difference between white and Negro. Similarly, promise of rewards for change or the threat of punishment are unlikely to have much effect, unless they are more powerful than the ego-defense motives. Threat of punishment in particular, because it increases defensiveness, may boomerang, that is, effect a change opposite to that intended by the communicator.

Not content with the conclusion that ego-defensive attitudes are more resistant to change than other kinds of attitudes, Katz identifies the conditions and types of persuasive communications which should be effective with ego-defensive attitudes. Two necessary conditions are the reduction of threat and the ventilation of feelings. The communication must come not from a threatening or anxiety-arousing person, but from one who creates a relaxed atmosphere. Opportunities to "blow off steam" reduce the strength of impulses that otherwise provide strong support for ego-defensive attitudes. Communications that help the person to acquire insight in a nonthreatening way into his own mechanisms of defense have the best possibility of changing ego-defensive attitudes.

* * *

KELMAN'S THREE-PROCESS THEORY OF ATTITUDE CHANGE

The last theory to be discussed is one proposed by Kelman (1961). His conception of the various means by which attitudes may be changed is particularly useful because the theory itself suggests the conditions under which attitude change will be manifested and those under which it will not, and because it also identifies the conditions leading to temporary change and those producing permanent change. His ideas have some resemblance to those of French and Raven (1959) on power. . . . Kelman (1961) suggests that there are three distinct processes of social influence: compliance, identification, and internalization.

(1) "*Compliance* can be said to occur when an individual accepts influence from another person or from a group because he hopes to achieve a favorable reaction from the other" (p. 62). Here the expression of opinion, even though the person privately disagrees with what he is expressing, is instrumental to gaining some reward or avoiding punishment. Thus an employee aware that his boss is proud of the jokes he tells may laugh heartily at them even though he does not think they are funny. In this way he avoids incurring his boss's displeasure. As might be expected, opinions of this sort are expressed only when they may be observed by the influencing agent.

(2) "*Identification* can be said to occur when an individual adopts behavior derived from another person or a group because this behavior is associated with a satisfying self-defining relationship to this person or group" (p. 63). This is a means of establishing or maintaining a desirable relation to the other person or group and of supporting the self-definition that is part of the relation. One form which identification takes is shown in attempts to be like the other person or to actually be the other person. This is commonly observed in children who copy the behavior and attitudes of their parents or other models. In another form of identification, the individual does not attempt to be like another person, but forms a relation to him that demands behavior quite different from his. The individual behaves in terms of the expectations that the other person has with respect to his behavior. For example, a patient behaves in accordance with the expectations of his doctor and adopts his advice and suggestions. A final form of identification maintains the individual's relation to a group in which his self-definition is anchored. Thus, a physician adopts the attitudes and behavior expected of him by his fellow physicians.

Identification, like compliance, does not occur because the behavior or attitude itself is intrinsically satisfying to the individual. It occurs because of the satisfying relation to another person or group, and it requires the activation of the relation in order for it to occur. Thus, in particular settings, an individual performs his role as a doctor, but there are some situations to which this role is not relevant, as for example situations relating to his wife or children. Unlike the compliance situation, however, the individual actually believes in the attitudes and actions that he adopts as a result of identification.

(3) "*Internalization* can be said to occur when an individual accepts influence because the induced behavior is congruent with his value system" (p. 65). Here the content of the induced attitude or behavior is intrinsically rewarding. The attitude or behavior helps to solve a problem or is demanded by the values of the individual. Thus a person with a liberal political attitude is likely to support a government program for medical care of the aged because one of the values to which he subscribes is that government should promote the public welfare.

Which of these various processes are likely to occur depends in part upon the *source of power of the influencing agent.* If he has strong control over rewards and punishment that the individual might receive, compliance is likely. For example, a child may often comply with the strictures of a stern parent even though his private feelings are in other directions. If on the other hand, the relation to the influence agent is a satisfying one, identification is likely to occur. Thus a daughter enjoying an affectionate relation to her mother may adopt many of her attitudes and behaviors. Finally, internalization occurs when the communicator is highly credible or believable. The recommendations of an expert are accepted if they appear to be congruent with one's values.

In a similar fashion, the conditions leading to the reaction of the individual vary for the different influence processes. When the influencing agent is in a position to closely observe an action or a statement of opinion, compliance is likely to occur. The child behaves well when the stern parent is watching him. Identification requires that the relation to the influence agent be a salient one: the situation must be dominated by the relation. The daughter adopts her mother's attitudes, for example, when playing the mother role toward her younger sister. Finally, attitudes or actions that have been internalized are likely to be expressed only when the values that were relevant to the initial acquisition are activated. The values with regard to honesty become particularly salient when the individual is taking an examination, for example.

These processes have somewhat different implications for permanence of the attitude change. An attitude adopted through compliance is likely to be abandoned if the agent exerting the initial influence loses control over the individual. Such attitudes are also likely to remain isolated from other attitudes and values. Behavior or attitudes initiated as a result of identification are maintained only so long as the relation to the influencing agent remains a satisfying one—and so long as the agent himself retains the attitude. Internalized attitudes are likely to persist as long as the values relevant to their adoption are maintained. A final point of importance is that particular situations are not necessarily pure examples of just one of these processes. Often two or more processes occur simultaneously, or all three may operate together. Thus, if an agent has powerful control over a person, but the relation is also a satisfying one, both compliance *and* identification are likely to occur. In addition, if the attitudes or actions required by this situation are also congruent with other attitudes held, internalization may take place.

* * *

SUMMARY AND CONCLUSIONS

Rosenberg's approach provides an explicit means of relating affective and cognitive components and demonstrates that attitude cognitions are instrumentally related to values. Unlike Festinger, however, he explicitly limits himself to "internal consistency," excluding from consideration behavioral elements as well as the various external conditions that might facilitate or block attitude change. The strength of Festinger's dissonance theory is the linkage it provides between behavior and attitude. This is especially evident in the forced-compliance situation, where behavior discrepant with existing attitudes is experimentally elicited.

Although Katz accepts consistency as the basis of the value function and knowledge function, he believes that consistency has certain limits. Along with his collaborator Stotland, he suggests that the principle is especially applicable to single attitude objects: the affective, cognitive, and behavior components toward a *single* object move toward consistency. Much inconsistency, however, may exist among different attitudes, according to Katz and Stotland. In a sense, dissonance theory provides for this by declaring that many cognitive elements are irrelevant to each other. But perhaps a theoretical system is needed that handles irrelevant as well as relevant elements. Katz stresses the importance of motivational factors conceived in terms long familiar to psychologists. In a wider sense, his adjustive and ego-defensive functions stress a broader consistency principle, embracing motivation and action.

Kelman, like Festinger, Rosenberg, and Katz, recognizes the role of internal consistency in attitude change. Like Katz, he suggests two other processes by which attitudes may be changed. He differs from all the other theorists in making a sharper distinction between overt and covert behavior—between public expression and private opinion. His three-process theory treats these two aspects of behavior as relatively independent of each other.

In contrast, Festinger is very explicit about the relation between these two facets of behavior. Speaking of compliance brought about by reward or threat of punishment, he states that if the compliant behavior is at variance with private attitudes, "dissonance inevitably follows from such a situation." It is likely, but not inevitable, that such dissonance will move the individual in the direction of private conformity in order to reduce the dissonance.

Kelman's approach attempts to specify conditions under which situations produce public conformity with little "dissonance" and others that produce more "dissonance" and probably lead to changes in private attitudes. His approach seems best suited to understanding long-term shifts in attitude occurring as a result of ongoing associations with other persons.

These four theories are only a sample chosen from a larger number of theories that have many points of similarity but some important differences. As a group, they make major contributions to the problems of attitude organization and change. Perhaps the most important general contribution of attitude theory is that it helps to solve the problem of *validity*. Throughout the history of attitude research, some psychologists and sociologists have been skeptical because, they asserted, the concept of attitudes was of doubtful validity. By this was meant that, unless it could be demonstrated that a person holding a particular position on an attitude continuum behaved in accordance with that position, the measurement of attitude was invalid. It was more or less assumed that there should be a direct correspondence between a person's overt behavior and his feelings and thoughts as indicated by his responses to an attitude test.

The relation between attitude and behavior is no longer conceptualized in such simple terms. Today we understand that it is necessary to have a theoretical structure that defines the conditions and the manner in which cognitive, affective, and behavioral elements do correspond to each other. The various theories permit us to devise experiments to study the manifold relations between cognitive, affective, and behavioral elements and the conditions that affect these relations. Thus, these theories enable us to make sense out of a great many otherwise unrelated phenomena. Present-day attitude theory, however, is by no means complete. The very existence of so many competing theories suggests that many problems remain to be solved. For example, a recent review of the early research on dissonance theory offers alternative interpretations of findings and points up many inadequacies in experimental design and analysis (Chapanis and Chapanis, 1964).

In the following three chapters,[2] the various research findings on attitude change will be described, and the theories already discussed will often be referred to in the attempt to explain the results of the various experiments. It will also become apparent that consistency theories are not entirely representative of attitude theory. Some investigators have attempted to apply learning theory to attitude research. Such theory assumes a greater diversity of motivation underlying attitude change than simply the need to restore consistency. The learning-theory approach also emphasizes attitude change as a process covering a broader span of time than is generally dealt with by consistency theories. To some extent, the theories of Katz and Stotland and of Kelman take learning theory into account, but further applications of learning theory to attitude change will be introduced from time to time in the chapters which follow.

BIBLIOGRAPHY

Chapanis, Natalia P., and Chapanis, A. Cognitive dissonance: Five years later. *Psychol. Bull.* 61 (1964): 1-22.

Festinger, L. *A theory of cognitive dissonance.* New York: Harper and Row, Publishers, Incorporated, 1957.

[2] [These three chapters refer to the Secord and Backman book] –Ed.

Festinger, L., and Carlsmith, J. M. Cognitive consequences of forced compliance. *J. abnorm. soc. Psychol.* 58 (1959): 203-10.

French, J. R. P., Jr., and Raven, B. H. The bases of social power. In D. Cartwright, ed. *Studies in social power.* Ann Arbor, Mich.: University of Michigan Press, 1959. p. 118-49.

Katz, D. The functional approach to the study of attitude change. *Publ. Opin. Quart.* 24 (1960): 163-204.

Katz, D., and Stotland, E. A preliminary statement to a theory of attitude structure and change. In S. Koch, ed., *Psychology: A study of a science.* Vol. 3. *Formulations of the person and the social context.* New York: McGraw-Hill Book Company, 1959. p. 423-75.

Kelman, H. C Processes of opinion change. *Publ. Opin. Quart.* 25 (1961): 57-78.

Rosenberg, M. J. The experimental investigation of a value theory of attitude structure. Unpublished doctoral dissertation, University of Michigan, 1953.

Rosenberg, M. J. Cognitive structure and attitudinal affect. *J. abnorm. soc. Psychol.* 53 (1956): 367-72.

Rosenberg, M. J. A structural theory of attitude dynamics. *Publ. Opin. Quart.* 24 (1960): 319-40. (a)

Rosenberg, M. J. An anlysis of affective-cognitive consistency. In C. I. Hovland and M. J. Rosenberg, eds., *Attitude organization and change.* New Haven, Conn.: Yale University Press, 1960. p. 15-64. (b)

Rosenberg, M. J. Cognitive reorganization in response to the hypnotic reversal of attitudinal affect. *J. Pers.* 28 (1960): 39-63. (c)

Rosenberg, M. J., and C. W. Gardner. Some dynamic aspects of post-hypnotic compliance. *J. abnorm. soc. Psychol.* 57 (1958): 351-66.

Walter R. Nord

ATTITUDES AND PERFORMANCE

Despite the abundance of studies on attitudes, the practical contributions of this research have been limited. This situation prompted Weick (1969) to remark that we have paid too much attention to such factors as cognitions, plans, and beliefs and too little to actions. He suggested that attitudes may be determined by behavior rather than vice versa. Attitudes may merely summarize behavior of the past. Weick's admonition to study behavior in organizations is well founded. At the same time, the work on attitudes and related concepts has contributed and will continue to contribute some interesting data about people in organizations.

Attitudes have received wide attention in the literature of organizational behavior and management. Such terms as "sentiments," "degree of job satisfaction," and "morale" have been employed to describe phenomena closely akin to what we have termed attitudes. While managers may be interested in the attitudes of people outside the organization for purposes of marketing and public relations, our concern here is primarily with the attitudes of organizational participants.

JOB SATISFACTION

The term "job satisfaction" seems to refer to a rather consistent set of feelings that people report about their work experiences. Ronan (1970) noted that the same seven basic dimensions of job satisfaction seem to be found by most researchers. These dimensions are

(a) The content of work, actual tasks performed, the control of work;
(b) supervision of the direct sort;
(c) the organization and its management;
(d) opportunities for advancement;
(e) pay and other financial benefits;
(f) co-workers; and
(g) working conditions. (pp. 2-3)

Apparently this list remains fairly consistent from job to job, although the importance of each item in determining job satisfaction varies.

Is satisfaction related to performance?[1] Most people assume that good feelings toward the organization will lead to effective performance. However, researchers have given up the hope of finding an invariant, positive relationship between measures of attitudes and organizational effectiveness or performance. Vroom (1964) reviewed 20 studies on the relationship of attitudes or job satisfaction to various criteria of effectiveness. He reported correlations ranging from +.86 to -.31, with a median of +.14. Clearly, such variation argues that there is unlikely to be any simple relationship between attitudes and performance. Rather, most research suggests a need to look at more narrowly defined criteria and attitudes toward particular aspects of the work environment.

Vroom (1969) concluded that the factors which make organizational membership seem attractive and satisfying are not the same as those which induce dependable and effective performance within the system. Vroom reached conclusions similar to those of Brayfield and Crockett (1955) in their comprehensive review; although job satisfaction seemed to be negatively related to voluntary turnover, absenteeism, and accident rates, the relationships that were found between job satisfaction and performance were inconsistent from study to study, some negative and some positive. A search for the conditions under which particular relationships exist is required. Research on job attitudes must take into account situational variables and the individuals' past experiences and present needs.

To date, no single theory has been able to account for all of these conflicting findings. Moreover, the various theorists make highly different assumptions and arrive at radically divergent conclusions. However, as Schwab and Cummings (1970) noted, most of the theoretical propositions about the relationship between performance and satisfaction can be classified into one of three categories.

One group of theorists suggests that satisfaction leads to performance. Schwab and Cummings assigned the label "human relations" to these theories. Herzberg's approach (see part 1) is a good example of this type of theory.

A second group of theorists maintains that satisfaction and performance are related under only some conditions. For example, Triandis (1959) suggested that strong pressure for production affects the relationship between these two variables. As pressures for production become stronger, job satisfaction is apt to decrease, but performance may either increase or decrease.

A number of other conditions may moderate the relationship between satisfaction and productivity. Herman (1973) hypothesized that satisfaction and productivity may be related to each other only when workers have a great deal of control over their own productivity.

Herman's research supported this expectation; when the work pace was not strictly determined by situational constraints, job attitudes were related to performance. However, a number of other conditions may influence the relationship between job satisfaction and performance. Quinn, Staines, and McCullough

[1] In this paper I will use the word performance synonomously with productivity. Moreover, I will use both "performance" and "productivity" broadly in that I will not distinguish among various types of performance. For example, I will not distinguish between quality and quantity of output as measures of performance.

(1974) suggested that other factors, such as skill levels and presence or absence of work-norms favorable to production, also moderate the relationship between satisfaction and productivity.

There is a growing amount of logical and empirical support for the proposition that the way organizational rewards are distributed moderates the satisfaction-performance relationship. Cherrington, Reitz, and Scott (1973) stated this point most clearly. They wrote,

> . . . there is no inherent relationship between satisfaction and performance, and . . . , as a matter of fact, one can produce just about any sort of a relationship between self-reports of satisfaction and performance that one wishes. (p. 153)
>
> We are led to postulate that there is no inherent relationship between satisfaction and performance, that variations in satisfaction and arousal are caused by the occurrence, non-occurrence, and other properties of reinforcing stimuli, and that one can produce varying degrees of covariation between satisfaction and performance by varying the contingencies between the performance and reinforcing events. (p. 154)

Cherrington *et al.* demonstrated the validity of their argument through a laboratory experiment. The participants began by scoring tests. After working for one hour, they received either $1 or $2 for their work so far. The experimenters told them that the better workers had received $2 and that the poorer workers had received only $1. Actually, the experimenters had distributed these rewards randomly, giving one-half of the workers $2 and the other half $1 without regard to performance. This procedure yielded four different groups of subjects. Workers in two of the groups had been appropriately rewarded, those who had not actually performed well and had received only $1 and those who had actually performed well and had received $2. The remaining subjects were inappropriately rewarded; some of these had actually not performed well but had received $2; other had actually performed well but had received only $1. After being informed about their rewards, the subjects were asked to rate their satisfaction with the task. They were then asked to score additional tests for another hour and afterwards were asked to report again their feelings of satisfaction.

The activity during the second hour of work was most interesting. The largest increases in productivity during this period were exhibited by the groups of appropriately reinforced participants. Moreover, while there was no general correlation between satisfaction and productivity for all subjects taken together, when the data collected from the appropriately and inappropriately rewarded subjects were analyzed separately, a consistent pattern emerged. During the second hour of performance, increases in productivity were positively correlated with the satisfaction that the subjects reported at the end of the second hour only for the workers who had earlier been appropriately rewarded. However, for the inappropriately reinforced subjects (even those who had performed poorly but had received $2) the correlations between performance and satisfaction were consistently negative.

This experiment demonstrates the importance of the nature of rewards as a factor moderating the relationship between satisfaction and performance. When rewards were contingent on performance, satisfaction and productivity went together. When rewards were not contingent on performance, satisfaction and productivity were negatively correlated.

More generally, the entire constellation of rewards given in an organization affects the relationship between performance and satisfaction with the organization. To the extent that the organization supports the satisfaction of needs by supporting productivity, a positive correlation between productivity and attitudes toward the organization might be expected. However, if the individual perceives the organization as reducing his need satisfaction by introducing barriers to his performance, he may be a high producer but have negative attitudes toward the organization.

Other sources of need satisfaction must also be considered. As we discussed earlier, an individual may experience need satisfaction from low productivity. When group norms restrict output, low productivity may well accompany a high degree of participation (i.e., long tenure, low absenteeism) in the organization and favorable attitudes toward the organization. The crucial factor seems to be the individual's perception of what behaviors lead to need satisfaction. Only when organization goals or requirements and individual needs are viewed as being satisfied by the same behavior can favorable attitudes toward the organization and performance be expected to be positively related. This relationship could be predicted from balance models discussed by Secord and Backman.

The balance models suggest that behavioral tendencies are associated with only a particular element of the environment. Behavioral predispositions to produce are apt to be much more closely associated and consistent with feelings and thoughts about the job itself than with feelings and thoughts about the supervisor, the organization, fringe benefits, and other features of the work environment not directly related to the job. There is no reason to expect attitudes toward a company in general to have any necessary relationship to behavioral tendencies to produce. Prediction of behavioral predispositions from affective expressions is likely to be successful only in cases in which both have to do with the same aspect of the environment.

The third group of theorists discussed by Schwab and Cummings conclude that performance causes satisfaction. Lawler's (1973) work (see Petrock and Gamboa's paper in part 1) is a major example of this type of theory. These theorists also stress the effect of the contingency of rewards in moderating the performance-satisfaction relationship. In fact, their theory applies only to situations in which an individual's rewards are a function of his or her performance. They argue that, if rewards are contingent on performance, things that lead to satisfaction (e.g., high pay) will follow from effective performance. Consequently, increments in performance are associated with increments in satisfaction. In other words, performance leads to satisfaction.

More recently, Quinn, Staines, and McCullough (1974) introduced some additional thoughts about the relationship between satisfaction and performance. First, they offered another possible explanation for the positive correlations sometimes observed between these two variables. They noted that both satisfaction and performance are produced by the same conditions, such as good supervision. Second, they observed that most attempts to explain this relationship have focused primarily on the satisfaction of individual workers and their own productivity. However, satisfaction may be related to the productivity of the community as a whole, because a company with satisfied workers will develop a community reputation as a "good place to work." Consequently, the company will have an opportunity to hire better workers, because individuals seeking employment will look into this company first.

Quinn *et al.* also noted that behavioral scientists and managers may have too readily accepted the assumption that increases in worker job satisfaction will yield higher profits because of an upward trend in output. Instead they suggested,

> *. . . the contribution of job satisfaction to productivity is probably less direct, and more likely to be reflected in reductions on the "cost" side of the ledger.* (p. 23)

In other words, many of the costs of job dissatisfaction are incurred when employees attempt to "escape" from work or even to "attack" the employer in direct and/or indirect ways.

Escape reactions. The two most prominent forms of escape behavior are turnover and absenteeism. A great deal of evidence suggests that job dissatisfaction is related to turnover. Quinn *et al.* wrote,

> A 1957 review of 24 previous studies reports that, in 21 of these research efforts, dissatisfied workers had a larger number of avoidable severances than did satisfied ones. Somewhat later (1964) a review of 7 studies bearing on the same question noted a significant association between job dissatisfaction and turnover in all of them. And a 1972 review of studies conducted since 1965 confirmed this conclusion. (p. 24)

Ronan (1970) came to a similar conclusion—people who are dissatisfied with their jobs are more likely to terminate their employment than people who are satisfied. However, Ronan stressed that their particular reasons for termination are quite specific to the particular organization involved.

Between absenteeism and job satisfaction, a negative correlation has been found in some studies but not in others. Apparently several variables moderate this relationship. For example, Quinn *et al.* noted that absenteeism may be less dependent on overall job satisfaction than on particular types of job satisfaction. For example, in one organization employees who worked in smaller plants were absent less than those who worked in larger plants, even though members of the two plants were equally satisfied with their work. However, employees from the smaller plants reported that they obtained greater satisfaction from the work itself and from their interpersonal relationships with their co-workers than did employees in the larger plants.

In addition to different types of job satisfaction, there are also different types of absenteeism, such as excused and unexcused. In one study Kerr, Kopelmeir, and Sullivan (1951) reported that high rates of unexcused absenteeism were associated with low job satisfaction but that the relationship did not hold for excused absenteeism.

Escape from work might take other forms, including accidents, drug use, and early retirement. However, as Quinn *et al.* concluded, there is little evidence giving clear support to relationships between any of these forms of escape and job dissatisfaction.

Attack reactions. Individuals may express their feelings of job dissatisfaction through grievance procedures, sabotage, theft, and other attacks against the organization. The evidence that worker dissatisfaction does result in such attacks is fragmentary.

Ronan noted that relatively little research had been done on the relationship between the rate of submission of grievances and job satisfaction. However, he did report that the use of grievance procedures may be positively related to absenteeism and negatively related to turnover. Moreover, he found some evidence that grievance rates are positively correlated with the number of work stoppages. Ronan suggested that grievances may be an important indicator of job dissatisfaction.

Quinn *et al.* discussed industrial sabotage and thefts as possible attack reactions. However, they reported only one relevant study, the 1972-73 Quality of Employment Survey. This survey provided only limited support for the expected positive correlation between dissatisfaction and attack reactions. In fact, such a relationship existed for only one stratum of workers; only for men who were thirty years of age or older was there a tendency for the more dissatisfied workers to engage in more forms of sabotage or theft. Clearly, more data must be collected before any definite statements about the relationship between dissatisfaction and attack behavior can be made.

Summary. The attitudes of individuals toward their jobs may have, at least under some conditions, important consequences for their employers. A full understanding of what particular conditions affect these relationships awaits further research. However, we have already noted several of these conditions. Most importantly, we have observed that performance will be less closely related to satisfaction in highly paced jobs and in jobs for which the rewards are not directly contingent on performance. Moreover, intra- and interorganizational differences interfere with our attempts at generalization from specific findings. Finally, as Schwab and Cummings (1970) observed, our efforts to develop theories about the relationship between satisfaction and performance have been premature. We do not have a good understanding of either satisfaction or performance taken alone. Perhaps in trying to study their interrelationship we have deceived ourselves into thinking that we know more about each than we really do.

ATTITUDES AND MANAGEMENT

Because there are so many possible sources of variance in attitudes, organization, and tasks, it is unlikely that anyone could devise a system of attitude development which would increase the effectiveness of members of all organizations. With this reservation in mind, managers can still derive useful insights from an understanding of management attitudes. Likert (1967) argued that work-related attitudes of organizational participants contribute directly, at least in the long run, to organization effectiveness. He maintained that a determination of the actual worth of an organization must include measures of the human assets as well as normal accounting data, and he proposed that much of this supplemental information should come from attitude surveys of organizational participants.

Likert advocated a particular style of management for developing favorable attitudes and hence increasing the value of the human assets. Field studies, conducted mainly by University of Michigan researchers, have shown that democratic or participatory management styles are associated with more positive attitudes toward the organization, more productive behavior on the part of organizational participants, and a greater realization of organizational goals. Likert suggested that System 4 (his term for participatory management) will enhance organizational performance. System 4, in Likert's view, changes the causal variable—managerial behavior toward people. These changes affect the intervening variables of attitudes and motivation and thereby lead to changes in organizational performance.

If reliable and valid measurement could be developed,[2] few behavioral scientists would be likely to disagree with Likert's argument for human-resource accounting. Organizational decisions often appear to overemphasize readily quantifiable variables and underestimate the effect of decisions on the human asset. Human-asset accounting could modify this dysfunctional imbalance.

Further investigation is required, however, before the influence of attitudes on organizational performance can be clearly understood. It would therefore be unwise to depend exclusively on anything as specific as System 4. A more fruitful approach would be some type of situational thinking (Pigors and Myers, 1965) or, better yet, a true systems view (Buckley, 1968; and Emery, 1969), which includes simultaneously the state of the individual's needs, his perceptions, the organizational structure and requirements, and many of the other variables treated in this book. All management systems influence the attitudes of participants. The type of attitudes each system fosters and the consequences of any particular set of attitudes depend on many factors.

Unresolved issues. While the concept of attitudes has important practical possibilities, their realization is apt to be hindered by several factors. First, our measures are less than satisfactory for many practical purposes. Second, there are substantial value questions involved in any attempt to measure and change attitudes. Third, there is the haunting suggesting of Weick (1969) that attitudes may develop after actions rather than before and thereby contribute relatively little to performance. Finally, there are intra- and interorganizational differences which make questionable the attempt to generalize from specific findings.

[2] Encouraging preliminary research in this direction was reported by Brummet, Flamholtz, and Pyle (1968).

REFERENCES

Brayfield, A. H., and Crockett, W. H. "Employee Attitudes and Employee Performance." *Psychological Bulletin* 52 (1955): 396-424.

Brummet, R. L.; Flamholtz, E. G.; and Pyle, W. C. "Human Resource Measurement—A Challenge for Accountants." *The Accounting Review* 43 (1968): 217-24.

Buckley, W., ed. *Modern Systems Research for the Behavioral Scientist.* Chicago: Aldine, 1968.

Cherrington, D. L.; Reitz, H. J.; and Scott, W. E. "Effects of Reward and Contingent Reinforcement on Satisfaction and Task Performance." In *Readings in Organizational Behavior and Human Performance,* edited by W. E. Scott and L. L. Cummings. Homewood, Ill.: Irwin, 1973.

Emery, F. E. *Systems Thinking.* Middlesex, Eng.: Penguin, 1969.

Herman, J. B. "Are Situational Contingencies Limiting Job Attitude-Job Performance Relationships?" *Organizational Behavior and Human Performance* 10 (1973): 208-224.

Kerr, W. A.; Kopelmeir, G.; and Sullivan, J. J. "Absenteeism, Turnover, and Morale in a Metals Fabrication Factory." *Occupational Psychology* 25 (1951): 50-55.

Lawler, E. E. *Motivation in Work Organizations.* Monterey, Calif.: Brooks/Cole, 1973.

Likert, R. *The Human Organization: Its Management and Value.* New York: McGraw-Hill Book Co., 1967.

Pigors, P., and Myers, C. A. *Personnel Administration: A Point of View and A Method.* 5th ed. New York: McGraw-Hill Book Co., 1965.

Quinn, R. P.; Staines, G. L.; and McCullough, M. R. *Job Satisfaction: Is There a Trend?* Manpower Research Monographs No. 30, U.S. Department of Labor, 1974.

Ronan, W. W. "Individual and Situational Variables Relating to Job Satisfaction." *Journal of Applied Psychology Monograph* 54, no. 1, part 2 (1970): 1-31.

Schwab, D. P., and Cummings, L. L. "Theories of Performance and Satisfaction: a Review." *Industrial Relations* 9 (1970): 409-430.

Triandis, H. C. "A Critique and Experimental Design for the Study of the Relationship between Productivity and Job Satisfaction." *Psychological Bulletin* 56 (1959): 309-312.

Vroom, V. H. "Industrial Social Psychology." In *The Handbook of Social Psychology,* 2nd ed. vol. 5, edited by G. Lindzey and E. Aronson, pp. 196-268. Reading, Mass.: Addison-Wesley, 1969.

Vroom, V. H. *Work and Motivation.* New York: John Wiley & Sons, 1964.

Weick, K. E. *The Social Psychology of Organizing.* Reading, Mass.: Addison-Wesley, 1969.

chapter **13**

Group Behavior and Organizations

Individualism is a central tenet of economic and social values in the United States. Many American politicians employ the rhetoric of personal initiative and freedom; few if any are elected on a platform advocating "from each according to his abilities, to each according to his needs." Our literature and history as taught in most public schools glorify rugged individualism. Politically and economically, individual dignity, freedom, power, and rewards are stressed in our explicit values.

In view of the widespread acceptance of these values and our success with an economic system based on individual initiative, it is no surprise that some people react strongly to any emphasis on groups rather than individuals. For instance, one recent presidential cabinet member did not differentiate between sociology and socialism; William H. Whyte, in his *Organization Man,* lamented the decreasing role of the individual in organizations; many managers do not have the understanding or the willingness to deal with the social side of man's behavior in organizations.

Despite such reactions, the increasing role of groups at all levels of modern organizations is becoming an accepted fact.[1] Bennis's paper in part 2 suggested that internal and external demands on modern organizations require much more interdependence and coordination of effort. Consider also Galbraith's (1967) description of the role of groups at middle and upper levels of management. He asserted that organizations are run by a technostructure, composed of everyone who participates in organizational decision making, and that the real accomplishments of large modern organizations depend on coordination of effort of many people rather than on genius. Further, ". . . the decision of modern

1. Groups themselves and awareness of groups are not new to organizations. As noted earlier, Frederick Taylor's "scientific management" was an outgrowth of his efforts to overcome "soldiering" (i.e., restrictive practices of informal groups). Mathewson (1931) described in great detail how groups influence individual behavior. Of course, the Hawthorne studies were most important in pointing to the influence of groups in organizations.

All of these efforts centered on blue-collar work groups. Although both Mathewson and the Hawthorne researchers reported that superiors as well as workers were involved in output restriction, generally output restriction has been considered a peer-group phenomenon.

business enterprises is the product not of individuals but of groups" (p. 65). According to Galbraith, such groups define the goals of the organization and ultimately determine the allocation of resources. The resulting allocation may be more in line with the goals of the technostructure than with the stated goals of the organization. Often even the president and other very high-level officers lack control or knowledge of what is happening in the organization. Certainly, the stockholders and the board of directors are apt to have relatively little influence. Galbraith's view leaves little place for individualism, even at the managerial level. Other modern critics have made similar assertions. For example, C. W. Mills argued in his *Power Elite* (1959) that group decision making and group processes are extremely important in the shaping of national policy.

Both friends and critics of modern society have pointed to the important role of groups in management, often drawing conclusions from personal observation or data of uncertain reliability. A survey of subscribers to the *Harvard Business Review* provides more firm evidence.

The survey, reported by Tillman (1960), explored the amount of time the respondents spent in groups and how they felt about it. The results revealed that an average executive spent 3½ hours per week in formal committee meetings and about one working day (9½ hours) per week in informal conferences and consultations with other executives. Interestingly, group work was more important at higher levels. Generally, upper-level executives served on more committees than did either lower- or middle-management people. Also, upper-level executives had more favorable feelings about committees than did lower-level executives. Overall, executives at all levels wholeheartedly agreed that committees are very useful for promoting coordination and sharing information. A variety of comments by the respondents reflected the theme that, in today's complex business world, committees are often the only way of coordinating the functions of the business and promoting communication among departments. In addition, committees were seen as means of inducing people to think about problems more clearly and deeply. Although there were many objections to committees—including feelings that they take too much time, prohibit the pinpointing of responsibility, and run the risk of undue compromises—the executives nevertheless perceived committees as contributing significantly to the realization of organizational goals. Tillman summarized their feelings by observing that

> The great majority of their suggestions led them to this conclusion: *the problem is not so much committees in management as it is the management of committees.* (p. 68)

Committees and task groups serve an important function in the operation of modern organizations. As the degree of specialization and the correlated requirements for coordination become greater, the role of groups will become even more important. Management's attitudes toward groups are changing. Much of the earlier literature of administration was devoted to how management can fight, or at least neutralize, work groups. It is increasingly evident that work groups are essential for the success of the organization.

GROUPS: FUNCTIONAL VIEW

Simply stated, the functional view of groups is that groups arise and endure to serve the needs of their members. An individual finds a group attractive because other members provide him with rewards which he cannot obtain as easily from any other source. When several people find each other to be sources of positive reinforcement, they are apt to form common patterns of exchange. Groups tend to dissolve or to be characterized by stress when the exchange of benefits is no longer favorable to all or some members.

The types of needs which are satisfied vary from one individual or situation to another because of variations in group tasks, organization structure surrounding the group, available technology, personalities of the group's members, cultural environment, and the degree of crisis. These and other factors influence the group process through their effect on individual needs.

Functions of Groups for Individuals

Groups help to satisfy a number of individual needs. Our knowledge about the functions of groups comes from research into both human and animal behavior. Some functions of groups are merely physiological, while others involve complex coordination of effort. One important function seems to be stress reduction.

The presence of other animals of the same species may be functional for individual survival. Etikin (1967) noted that, in water which has small quantities of harmful chemicals, goldfish survive better when in groups than when alone. Mice in cold environments tend to be able to survive better in groups, presumably because of heat and shelter provided by the animals' own bodies. Other research found that animals in a threatening situation experience less anxiety when another animal of the same species is present than when alone. Bovard (1959) provided additional evidence to support the stress-reducing properties of the mere presence of other animals.

Human groups have also been found to serve important functions. Schachter (1959) reported that the presence of others was valued by people under conditions of stress. Stotland (1959) found that peer groups provided support for members, allowing individuals to express more direct and overt hostility toward threatening power figures. Thus work groups may be a source of strength for subordinates.

Groups may also provide a means of self-definition—either through shared beliefs or values, as in religious and ethnic groups, or through interpersonal comparison (Festinger, 1954). A reward or personal ability, such as a particular grade in school, often has little meaning until one finds out how it compares with the attainment of other people.

Thus we see that the presence or absence of groups of different types has important functional and dysfunctional consequences for individuals and hence for organizations. The issue is not "are groups good or bad?" but "how can groups be best used to meet individual and organizational goals?" The functional view, focusing on individual needs, may give some insights into this question.

Groups in Organizations

Formal organizations affect the development of groups in a number of ways. First, most organizations require people to work physically close to each other on tasks that are interdependent. These conditions of proximity and common goals are, of course, two important elements from which groups develop. Moreover, a variety of events occur within an organization which affect the needs of individual participants. Often, these events (for example, the introduction of new policies and regulations) cause people to feel threatened by or hostile to certain elements of the organization. These feelings may induce some of an organization's participants to form groups for protection against certain features of the organization. In other words, the organization can stimulate needs within its members that they seek to satisfy by forming groups.

The nature of these groups varies widely. Some become very formal; others remain very informal. Some serve some very specific task need, whereas others satisfy individuals' needs for interaction. However, regardless of their original purpose, groups can come to serve other needs. For example, a group which has been formed for lunchtime card-playing can become a forum for a member who feels unjustly treated and wishes to mobilize support for his cause. More generally, once a group has formed, it becomes an on-going unit that can have a number of effects in the organization.

Tannenbaum (1966) summarized some of the important work on these effects. A central variable in this research is group cohesion—the degree of members' attraction to the group or the amount of "stick-togetherness" (Mikalachki, 1969) they exhibit. Considerable research has shown that membership in cohesive groups may serve to increase job satisfaction and to reduce absenteeism and turnover. Other studies have shown that groups whose members are strongly attracted to the group experience fewer work-related anxieties than do members of groups characterized by lower cohesiveness.

Mikalachki reviewed the literature on group cohesion and productivity and added some relevant data. He argued that cohesion may be either task-oriented or socially oriented. Only in the former case would we expect productivity to be enhanced by the cohesion.[2]

Attraction to a group is influenced by member qualities as well as organizational forces. For example, one is apt to be more attracted to people who share one's values than to others. Furthermore, personal relationships of individual members to the group affect its development. Aronson and Mills (1959) demon-

2. Mikalachki also suggested some important implications of group cohesion for administrators. He noted that supervision of noncohesive groups requires a great deal of time, because group members must be treated more individually than collectively. Furthermore, lack of cohesion may lead to the additional disadvantages of high turnover and tension and may require a supervisor to develop and monitor channels of communication. By contrast, highly cohesive task groups can be dealt with collectively and have less tension and turnover and a more integrated structure, which facilitates communication. Mikalachki suggests that administrators and industrial engineers may be well-advised to introduce conditions which are known to promote the development of highly cohesive task groups—". . . small groups whose members identify with [the groups'] formal goals, perform interdependent task roles, and show a high degree of concern for one another" (p. 79).

strated that a high "cost of entry" into a group may increase member commitment. In this sense, Marine training, fraternity hazing, and the rough treatment given to pro football rookies may be functional for the group. Group processes are also affected by the tendency of people to define themselves in terms of a group. (Often, especially in religious and ethnic groups, personal identity of individual members, as shown earlier, is dependent on the group.) An attack on groups central to one's identity arouses vigorous defenses and counterattacks. In this light the "irrational" behavior of unions, extremist political groups, and even management and other work groups becomes understandable.

THE READINGS

The following selections discuss the consequences of groups for individuals and highlight some issues of central importance to organizations. Cartwright and Lippitt attempt to tie together central findings on the social psychology of groups. Their focus on the relationship of individuals to groups is helpful for a consideration of ways to utilize groups effectively. The next article looks at the same issue from a different point of view. Schutz helps us understand how personal needs are related to group functioning and how interpersonal relationships within work groups can be improved. The paper by Zand discusses interpersonal trust both logically and empirically. He concludes that the degree of trust that exists among a group of people can be a significant determinant of their effectiveness in solving typical managerial problems. A final selection by the editor examines some additional ideas about groups in organization.

REFERENCES

Aronson, E., and Mills, J. "The Effects of Severity of Initiation on Liking for a Group." *Journal of Abnormal and Social Psychology* 59 (1959): 177-81.

Bovard, E. W. "The Effects of Social Stimuli on the Response to Stress." *Psychological Review* 66 (1959): 267-77.

Etikin, W. *Social Behavior from Fish to Man.* Chicago: University of Chicago Press, 1967.

Festinger, L. "A Theory of Social Comparison Processes." *Human Relations* 7 (1954): 117-40.

Galbraith, J. K. *The New Industrial State.* Boston: Houghton Mifflin, 1967.

Mathewson, S. B. *Restriction of Output among Unorganized Workers.* New York: Viking, 1931.

Mikalachki, A. *Group Cohesion Reconsidered.* London, Ont.: University of Western Ontario, 1969.

Mills, C. W. *The Power Elite.* New York: Oxford University Press, 1959.

Schachter, S. *The Psychology of Affiliation: Experimental Studies of the Sources of Gregariousness.* Stanford, Calif.: Stanford University, 1959.

Stotland, E. "Peer Groups and Reactions to Power Figures." In *Studies in Social Power,* edited by D. Cartwright, pp. 53-68. Ann Arbor, Mich.: University of Michigan, 1959.

Tannenbaum, A. S. *Social Psychology of the Work Organization.* Belmont, Calif.: Wadsworth Publishing Co., Inc., 1966.

Tillman, R. "Problems in Review: Committees on Trial." *Harvard Business Review* 38 (1960): 6-12, 162-73.

Dorwin Cartwright
Ronald Lippitt

GROUP DYNAMICS AND THE INDIVIDUAL

How should we think of the relation between individuals and groups? Few questions have stirred up so many issues of metaphysics, epistemology, and ethics. Do groups have the same reality as individuals? If so, what are the properties of groups? Can groups learn, have goals, be frustrated, develop, regress, begin and end? Or are these characteristics strictly attributable only to individuals? If groups exist, are they good or bad? How *should* an individual behave with respect to groups? How *should* groups treat their individual members? Such questions have puzzled man from the earliest days of recorded history.

In our present era of "behavioral science" we like to think that we can be "scientific" and proceed to study human behavior without having to take sides on these problems of speculative philosophy. Invariably, however, we are guided by certain assumptions, stated explicitly or not, about their observability, and about their good or bad value.

Usually these preconceptions are integral parts of one's personal and scientific philosophy, and it is often hard to tell how much they derive from emotionally toned personal experiences with other people and how much from coldly rational and "scientific" considerations. In view of the fervor with which they are usually defended, one might suspect that most have a small basis at least in personally significant experiences. These preconceptions, moreover, have a tendency to assume a homogeneous polarization—either positive or negative.

Consider first the completely negative view. It consists of two major assertions: first, groups don't really exist. They are a product of distorted thought processes (often called "abstractions"). In fact, social prejudice consists precisely in acting as if groups, rather than individuals, were real. Second, groups are bad. They demand blind loyalty, they make individuals regress, they reduce man to the lowest common denominator, and they produce what *Fortune* magazine has immortalized as "group-think."

In contrast to this completely negative conception of groups, there is the completely positive one. This syndrome, too, consists of two major assertions: first, groups really do exist. Their reality is demonstrated by the difference it

From Dorwin Cartwright and Ronald Lippitt, "Group Dynamics and the Individual," *International Journal of Group Psychotherapy* 7, (January, 1957): 86-102. Reprinted by permission of American Group Psychotherapy Association.

makes to an individual whether he is accepted or rejected by a group and whether he is part of a healthy or sick group. Second, groups are good. They satisfy deep-seated needs of individuals for affiliation, affection, recognition, and self-esteem; they stimulate individuals to moral heights of altruism, loyalty, and self-sacrifice; they provide a means, through cooperative interaction, by which man can accomplish things unattainable through individual enterprise.

This completely positive preconception is the one attributed most commonly, it seems, to the so-called "group dynamics movement." Group dynamicists, it is said, have not only *reified* the group but also *idealized* it. They believe that everything should be done by and in groups—individual responsibility is bad, man-to-man supervision is bad, individual problem-solving is bad, and even individual therapy is bad. The only good things are committee meetings, group decisions, group problem-solving, and group therapy. "If you don't hold the group in such high affection," we were once asked, "why do you call your research organization the Research Center FOR Group Dynamics? And, if you are for groups and group dynamics, mustn't you therefore be *against* individuality, individual responsibility, and self-determination?"

FIVE PROPOSITIONS ABOUT GROUPS

This assumption that individuals and groups must necessarily have incompatible interests is made so frequently in one guise or another that it requires closer examination. Toward this end we propose five related assertions about individuals, groups, and group dynamics, which are intended to challenge the belief that individuals and groups must necessarily have incompatible, or for that matter, compatible interests.

(1). Groups do exist; they must be dealt with by any man of practical affairs, or indeed by any child, and they must enter into any adequate account of human behavior. Most infants are born into a specific group. Little Johnny may be a welcome or unwelcome addition to the group. His presence may produce profound changes in the structure of the group and consequently in the feelings, attitudes, and behavior of various group members. He may create a triangle where none existed before or he may break up one which has existed. His development and adjustment for years to come may be deeply influenced by the nature of the group he enters and by his particular position in it—whether, for example, he is a first or second child (a personal property which has no meaning apart from its reference to a specific group).

There is a wealth of research whose findings can be satisfactorily interpreted only by assuming the reality of groups. Recall the experiment of Lewin, Lippitt, and White (15) in which the level of aggression of an individual was shown to depend upon the social atmosphere and structure of the group he is in and not merely upon such personal traits as aggressiveness. By now there can be little question about the kinds of results reported from the Western Electric study (18) which make it clear that groups develop norms for the behavior of their members with the result that "good" group members adopt these norms as their *personal* values. Nor can one ignore the dramatic evidence of Lewin, Bavelas, and others (14) which shows that group decisions may produce changes in individual behavior much larger than those customarily found to result from attempts to modify the behavior of individuals *as* isolated individuals.

(2). Groups are inevitable and ubiquitous. The biological nature of man, his capacity to use language, and the nature of his environment which has been built into its present form over thousands of years require that man exist in groups. This is not to say that groups must maintain the properties they now display, but we cannot conceive of a collection of human beings living in geographical proximity under conditions where it would be correct to assert that no groups exist and that there is no such thing as group membership.

(3). Groups mobilize powerful forces which produce effects of the utmost importance to individuals. Consider two examples from rather different research settings. Seashore (22) has recently published an analysis of data from 5,871 employees of a large manufacturing company. An index of group cohesiveness, developed for each 228 work groups, permitted a comparison of members working in high and in low cohesive groups. Here is one of his major findings: "Members of high cohesive groups exhibit less anxiety than members of low cohesive groups, using as measures of anxiety: (a) feeling 'jumpy' or 'nervous,' (b) feeling under pressure to achieve higher productivity (with actual productivity held constant), and (c) feeling a lack of support from the company" (p. 98). Seashore suggests two reasons for the relation between group cohesiveness and individual anxiety: "l) that the cohesive group provides effective support for the individual in his encounters with anxiety-provoking aspects of his environment, thus allaying anxiety, and 2) that group membership offers direct satisfaction, and this satisfaction in membership has a generalized effect of anxiety-reduction" (p. 13).

Perhaps a more dramatic account of the powerful forces generated in groups can be derived from the publication by Stanton and Schwartz (24) of their studies of a mental hospital. They report, for example, how a patient may be thrown into an extreme state of excitement by disagreements between two staff members over the patient's care. Thus, two doctors may disagree about whether a female patient should be moved to another ward. As the disagreement progresses, the doctors may stop communicating relevant information to one another and start lining up allies in the medical and nursing staff. The patient, meanwhile, becomes increasingly restless until, at the height of the doctors' disagreement, she is in an acute state of excitement and must be secluded, put under sedation, and given special supervision. Presumably, successful efforts to improve the interpersonal relations and communications among members of the staff would improve the mental condition of such a patient.

In general, it is clear that events occurring in a group may have repercussions on members who are not directly involved in these events. A person's position in a group, moreover, may affect the way others behave toward him and such personal qualities as his levels of aspiration and self-esteem. Group membership itself may be a prized possession or an oppressive burden; tragedies of major proportions have resulted from the exclusion of individuals from groups, and equally profound consequences have stemmed from enforced membership in groups.

(4). Groups may produce both good and bad consequences. The view that groups are completely good and the view that they are completely bad are both based on convincing evidence. *The only fault with either is its one-sidedness.* Research motivated by one or the other is likely to focus on different phenomena. As an antidote to such one-sidedness it is a good practice to ask research questions in pairs, one stressing positive aspects and one negative: What are the factors producing conformity? and what are the factors producing nonconformity? What brings about a breakdown in communication? and what stimulates or maintains effective communication? An exclusive focus on pathologies or upon positive criteria leads to a seriously incomplete picture.

(5). A correct understanding of group dynamics permits the possibility that desirable consequences from groups can be deliberately enhanced. Through a knowledge of group dynamics, groups can be made to serve better ends, for knowledge gives power to modify human beings and human behavior. At the same time, recognition of this fact produces some of the deepest conflicts within the behavioral scientist, for it raises the whole problem of social manipulation. Society must not close its eyes to Orwell's horrible picture of life in 1984, but it cannot accept the alternative that in ignorance there is safety.

To recapitulate our argument: groups exist; they are inevitable and ubiquitous; they mobilize powerful forces having profound effects upon individuals; these effects may be good or bad; and through a knowledge of group dynamics there lies the possibility of maximizing their good value.

A DILEMMA

Many thoughtful people today are alarmed over one feature of groups: the pressure toward conformity experienced by group members. Indeed, this single "bad" aspect is often taken as evidence that groups are bad in general. Let us examine the specific problem of conformity, then, in order to attain a better understanding of the general issue. Although contemporary concern is great, it is not new. More than 100 years ago Alexis de Tocqueville wrote: "I know of no country in which there is so little independence of mind and real freedom of discussion as in America. . . In America the majority raises formidable barriers around the liberty of opinion. . . The master (majority) no longer says: 'You shall think as I do or you shall die'; but he says: 'You are free to think differently from me and to retain your life, your property, and all that you possess, but they will be useless to you, for you will never be chosen by your fellow citizens if you solicit their votes; and they will affect to scorn you if you ask for their esteem. You will remain among men, but you will be deprived of the rights of mankind. Your fellow creatures will shun you like an impure being; and even those who believe in your innocence will abandon you, lest they should be shunned in their turn'" (25, pp. 273-75).

Before too readily accepting such a view of groups as the whole story, let us invoke our dictum that research questions should be asked in pairs. Nearly everyone is convinced that individuals should not be blind conformers to group norms, that each group member should not be a carbon copy of every other member, but what is the other side of the coin? In considering why members of groups conform, perhaps we should also think of the consequences of the removal of individuals from group membership or the plight of the person who really does not belong to any group with clear-cut norms and values. The state of anomie, described by Durkheim, is also common today. It seems as if people who have no effective participation in groups with clear and strong value systems either crack up (as in alcoholsim or suicide) or they seek out groups which will demand conformity. In discussing this process, Talcott Parsons writes: "In such a situation it is not surprising that large numbers of people should . . . be attracted to movements which can offer them membership in a group with a vigorous esprit de corps with submission to some strong authority and rigid system of belief, the individual thus finding a measure of escape from painful perplexities or from a situation of anomie" (17, pp. 128-29).

The British anthropologist, Adam Curle, has stressed the same problem when he suggested that in our society we need not four, but five freedoms, the fifth being freedom from that neurotic anxiety which springs from a man's isolation from his fellows, and which, in turn, isolates him still further from them.

We seem, then, to face a dilemma: the individual needs social support for his values and social beliefs; he needs to be accepted as a valued member of some group which *he* values; failure to maintain such group membership produces anxiety and personal disorganization. But, on the other hand, group membership and group participation tend to cost the individual his individuality. If he is to receive support from others and, in turn, give support to others, he and they must hold in common some values and beliefs. Deviation from these undermines any possibility of group support and acceptance.

Is there an avenue of escape from this dilemma? Certainly, the issue is not as simple as we have described it. The need for social support for some values does not require conformity with respect to all values, beliefs, and behavior. Any individual is a member of several groups, and he may be a successful deviate in one while conforming to another (think of the visitor in a foreign country or of the psychologist at a convention of psychiatrists). Nor should the time dimension be ignored; a person may sustain his deviancy through a conviction that his fate is only temporary. These refinements of the issue are important and should be examined in great detail, but before we turn our attention to them, we must assert that we do *not* believe that the basic dilemma can be escaped. To avoid complete personal disorganization man must conform to at least a minimal set of values required for participation in the groups to which he belongs.

PRESSURES TO UNIFORMITY

Some better light may be cast on this problem if we refer to the findings of research on conformity. What do we know about the way it operates?

Cognitive Processes. Modern psychological research on conformity reflects the many different currents of contemporary psychology, but the major direction has been largely determined by the classic experiment of Sherif (23) on the development of social norms in perceiving autokinetic movement and by the more recent study of Asch (1) of pressures to conformity in perceiving unambiguous visual stimuli.

What does this line of investigation tell us about conformity? What has it revealed, for instance, about the conditions that set up pressures to conformity? Answers to this question have taken several forms, but nearly all point out that social interaction would be impossible if some beliefs and perceptions were not commonly shared by the participants. Speaking of the origin of such cognitive pressures to uniformity among group members, Asch says: "The individual comes to experience a world that he shares with others. He perceives that the surroundings include him, as well as others, and that he is in the same relation to the surroundings as others. He notes that he, as well as others, is converging upon the same object and responding to its identical properties. Joint action and mutual understanding require this relation of intelligibility and structural simplicity. In these terms the 'pull' toward the group becomes understandable" (1, p. 484).

Consistent with this interpretation of the origin of pressures to uniformity in a perceptual or judgmental situation are the findings that the major variables influencing tendencies to uniformity are (a) the quality of the social evidence (particularly the degree of unanimity of announced perceptions and the subject's evaluation of the trustworthiness of the other's judgments), (b) the quality of the direct perceptual evidence (particularly the clarity or ambiguity of the stimuli), (c) the magnitude of the discrepancy between the social and the perceptual evidence, and (d) the individual's self-confidence in the situation (as indicated either by experimental manipulations designed to affect self-confidence or by personality measurements).

The research in this tradition has been productive, but it has emphasized the individual and his cognitive problems and has considered the individual apart from any concrete and meaningful group membership. Presumably any trustworthy people adequately equipped with eyes and ears could serve to generate pressures to conformity in the subject, regardless of his specific relations to them. The result of this emphasis has been to ignore certain essential aspects of the conformity problem. Let us document this assertion with two examples.

First, the origin of pressures to uniformity has been made to reside in the person whose conformity is being studied. Through eliminating experimentally any possibility that pressures might be exerted by others, it has been possible to study the conformity of people as if they existed in a world where they can see or hear others but not be reacted to by others. It is significant indeed, that conformity does arise in the absence of direct attempts to bring it about. But this approach does not raise certain questions about the conditions which lead to *social* pressures to conformity. What makes some people try to get others to conform? What conditions lead to what forms of pressure on others to get them to conform? The concentration of attention on the conformer has diverted attention away from the others in the situation who may insist on conformity and make vigorous efforts to bring it about or who may not exert any pressure at all on deviates.

A second consequence of this emphasis has been to ignore the broader social meaning of conformity. Is the individual's personal need for a social validation of his beliefs the only reason for conforming? What does deviation do to a person's acceptance by others? What does it do to his ability to influence others? Or, from the group's point of view, are there reasons to insist on certain common values, beliefs, and behavior? These questions are not asked nor asnwered by an approach which limits itself to the cognitive problems of the individual.

Group Processes. The group dynamics orientation toward conformity emphasizes a broader range of determinants. Not denying the importance of the cognitive situation, we want to look more closely at the nature of the individual's relation to particular groups with particular properties. In formulating hypotheses about the origin of pressures to uniformity, two basic sources have been stressed. These have been stated most clearly by Festinger and his co-workers (5), who propose that when differences of opinion arise within a group, pressures to uniformity will arise (a) if the validity or "reality" of the opinion depends upon agreement with the group (essentially the same point as Asch's), or (b) if locomotion toward a group goal will be facilitated by uniformity within the group.

This emphasis upon the group, rather than simply upon the individual, leads one to expect a broader set of consequences from pressures to uniformity. Pressures to uniformity are seen as establishing: (a) a tendency on the part of each group member to change his own opinion to conform to that of the other group members, (b) a tendency to try to change the opinions of others, and (c) a tendency to redefine the boundaries of the group so as to exclude those holding deviate opinions. The relative magnitudes of these tendencies will depend on other conditions which need to be specified.

This general conception of the nature of the processes that produce conformity emerged from two early field studies conducted at the Research Center for Group Dynamics. It was also influenced to a considerable extent by the previous work of Newcomb (16) in which he studied the formation and change of social attitudes in a college community. The first field study, reported by Festinger, Schachter, and Back (7), traced the formation of social groups in a new student housing project. As each group developed, it displayed its own standards for its members. The extent of conformity to the standards of a particular group was found to be related directly to the degree of cohesiveness of that group as measured by sociometric choices. Moreover, those individuals who deviated from their own group's norms received fewer sociometric choices than those who conformed. A process of rejection for nonconformity had apparently set in. The second field study, reported by Coch and French (3), observed similar processes. This study was conducted in a textile factory and was concerned with conformity to production standards set by groups of workers. Here an individual worker's reaction to new work methods was found to depend upon the standards of his group and, here too, rejection for deviation was observed.

The next phase of this research consisted of a series of experiments with groups created in the laboratory. It was hoped thereby to be able to disentangle the complexity of variables that might exist in any field setting in order to understand better the operation of each. These experiments have been reported in various publications by Festinger, Back, Gerard, Hymovitch, Kelley, Raven, Schachter, and Thibaut (2, 6, 8, 9, 11, 20). We shall not attempt to describe these studies in detail, but draw upon them and other research in an effort to summarize the major conclusions.

First, a great deal of evidence has been accumulated to support the hypothesis that pressures to uniformity will be greater the more members want to remain in the group. In more attractive or cohesive groups, members attempt more to influence others and are more willing to accept influence from others. Note that here pressures to conformity are high in the very conditions where satisfaction from group membership is also high.

Second, there is a close relation between attempts to change the deviate and tendencies to reject him. If persistent attempts to change the deviate fail to produce conformity, then communication appears to cease between the majority and the deviate, and rejection of the deviate sets in. These two processes, moreover, are more intense the more cohesive the group. One of the early studies which documented the process of rejection was conducted by Schachter (20) on college students. It has recently been replicated by Emerson (4) on high school students, who found essentially the same process at work, but he discovered that among his high school students efforts to influence others continued longer, there was a greater readiness on the part of the majority to change, and there was a lower level of rejection within a limited period of time. Yet another study, conducted in Holland, Sweden, France, Norway, Belgium, Germany, and England, found the same tendency to reject deviates in all of these countries. This study, reported by Schachter, et al. (21), is a landmark in cross-cultural research.

Third, there is the question of what determines whether or not pressures to uniformity will arise with respect to any particular opinion, attitude, and behavior. In most groups there are no pressures to uniformity concerning the color of necktie worn by the members. Differences of opinion about the age of the earth probably would not lead to rejection in a poker club, but they might do so in certain fundamentalist church groups. The concept of *relevance* seems to be required to account for such variations in pressures to uniformity. And, if we ask, "relevance for what?" we are forced again to look at the group and especially at the goals of the group.

Schachter (20) has demonstrated, for example, that deviation on a given issue will result much more readily in rejection when that issue is relevant to the group's goals than when it is irrelevant. And, the principle of relevance seems to be necessary to account for the findings of a field study reported by Ross (19). Here attitudes of fraternity men toward restrictive admission policies were studied. Despite the fact that there was a consistent policy of exclusion in these fraternities, there was, surprisingly, little evidence for the existence of pressures toward uniformity of attitudes. When, however, a field experiment was conducted in which the distribution of actual opinions for each fraternity house was reported to a meeting of house members together with a discussion of the relevance of these opinions for fraternity policy, attitudes then tended to change to conform to the particular modal position of each house. Presumably the experimental treatment made uniformity of attitude instrumental to group locomotion where it had not been so before.

SOURCES OF HETEROGENEITY

We have seen that pressures to uniformity are stronger the more cohesive the group. Shall we conclude from this that strong, need-satisfying, cohesive groups must always produce uniformity on matters that are important to the group? We believe not. We cannot, however, cite much convincing evidence since research has focused to date primarily upon the sources of pressures to uniformity and has ignored the conditions which produce heterogeneity. Without suggesting, then, that we can give final answers, let us indicate some of the possible sources of heterogeneity.

Group Standards about Uniformity. It is important, first, to make a distinction between conformity and uniformity. A group might have a value that everyone should be as different from everyone else as possible. Conformity to this value, then, would result not in uniformity of behavior but in nonuniformity. Such a situation often arises in therapy groups or training groups where it is possible to establish norms which place a high value upon "being different" and upon tolerating deviant behavior. Conformity to this value is presumably greater the more cohesive the group and the more it is seen as relevant to the group's objectives. Unfortunately, very little is known about the origin and operation of group standards about conformity itself. We doubt that the pressure to uniformity, which arises from the need for "social reality" and for group locomotion can simply be obliterated by invoking a group standard of tolerance, but a closer look at such processes as those of group decision making will be required before a deep understanding of this problem can be achieved.

Freedom to Deviate. A rather different source of heterogeneity has been suggested by Kelley and Shapiro (12). They reason that the more an individual feels accepted by the other members of the group, the more ready he should be to deviate from the beliefs of the majority under conditions where objectively correct deviation would be in the group's best interest. They designed an experiment to test this hypothesis. The results, while not entirely clear because acceptance led to greater cohesiveness, tend to support this line of reasoning.

It has been suggested by some that those in positions of leadership are freer to deviate from group standards than are those of lesser status. Just the opposite conclusion has been drawn by others. Clearly, further research into group properties which generate freedom to deviate from majority pressures is needed.

Subgroup Formation. Festinger and Thibaut (8) have shown that lower group-wide pressures to uniformity of opinion result when members of a group perceive that the group is composed of persons differing in interest and knowledge. Under these conditions subgroups may easily develop with a resulting heterogeneity within the group as a whole though with uniformity within each subgroup. This conclusion is consistent with Asch's (1) finding that the presence of a partner for a deviate greatly strengthens his tendency to be independent. One might suspect that such processes, though achieving temporarily a greater heterogeneity, would result in a schismatic subgroup conflict.

Positions and Roles. A more integrative achievement of heterogeneity seems to arise through the process of role differentiation. Established groups are usually differentiated according to "positions" with special functions attached to each. The occupant of the position has certain behaviors prescribed for him by the others in the group. These role prescriptions differ, moreover, from one position to another, with the result that conformity to them produces heterogeneity within the group. A group function, which might otherwise be suppressed by pressures to uniformity, may be preserved by the establishment of a position whose responsibility is to perform the function.

Hall (10) has recently shown that social roles can be profitably conceived in the context of conformity to group pressures. He reasoned that pressures to uniformity of prescriptions concerning the behavior of the occupant of a position and pressures on the occupant to conform to these prescriptions should be greater the more cohesive the group. A study of the role of aircraft commander in bomber crews lends strong support to this conception.

MORE THAN ONE GROUP

Thus far our analysis has proceeded as though the individual were a member of only one group. Actually we recognize that he is, and has been, a member of many groups. In one of our current research projects we are finding that older adolescents can name from 20 to 40 "important groups and persons that influence my opinions and behavior in decision situations." Indeed, some personality theorists hold that personality should be viewed as an "internal society" made up of representations of the diverse group relationships which the individual now has and has had. According to this view, each individual has a unique internal society and makes his own personal synthesis of the values and behavior preferences generated by these affiliations.

The various memberships of an individual may relate to one another in various ways and produce various consequences for the individual. A past group may exert internal pressures toward conformity which are in conflict with a present group. Two contemporaneous groups may have expectations for the person which are incompatible. Or an individual may hold a temporary membership (the situation of a foreign student, for example) and be faced with current conformity pressures which if accepted will make it difficult to readjust when returning to his more permanent memberships.

This constant source of influence from other memberships toward deviancy of every member of every group requires that each group take measures to preserve its integrity. It should be noted, however, that particular deviancy pressures associated with a given member may be creative or destructive when evaluated in terms of the integrity and productivity of the group, and conformity pressures from the group may be supportive or disruptive of the integrity of the individual.

Unfortunately there has been little systematic research on these aspects of multiple group membership. We can only indicate two sets of observations concerning (a) the intrapersonal processes resulting from multiple membership demands, and (b) the effects on group processes of the deviancy pressures which arise from the multiple membership status of individual members.

Marginal Membership. Lewin (13), in his discussion of adolescence and of minority group membership, has analyzed some of the psychological effects on the person of being "between two groups" without a firm anchorage in either one. He says: "The transition from childhood to adulthood may be a rather sudden shift (for instance, in some of the primitive societies), or it may occur gradually in a setting where children and adults are not sharply separated groups. In the case of the so-called 'adolescent difficulties,' however, a third state of affairs is often prevalent: children and adults constitute two clearly defined groups; the adolescent does not wish any longer to belong to the children's group and, at the same time, knows that he is not really accepted in the adult group. He has a position similar to what is called in sociology the 'marginal man' . . . a person who stands on the boundary between two groups. He does not belong to either of them, or at least he is not sure of his belongingness in either of them" (p. 143). Lewin goes on to point out that there are characteristic maladjustive behavior patterns resulting from this unstable membership situation: high tension, shifts between extremes of behavior, high sensitivity, and rejection of low status members of both groups. This situation, rather than fostering strong individuality, makes belonging to closely knit, loyalty-demanding groups very attractive. Dependency and acceptance are a welcome relief. Probably most therapy groups have a number of members who are seeking relief from marginality.

Overlapping Membership. There is quite a different type of situation where the person does have a firm anchorage in two or more groups but where the group standards are not fully compatible. Usually the actual conflict arises when the person is physically present in one group but realizes that he also belongs to other groups to which he will return in the near or distant future. In this sense, the child moves between his family group and his school group every day. The member of a therapy group has some sort of time perspective of "going back" to a variety of other groups between each meeting of the therapy group.

In their study of the adjustment of foreign students both in this country and after returning home, Watson and Lippitt (26) observed four different ways in which individuals cope with this problem of overlapping membership.

(1). Some students solved the problem by "living in the present" at all times. When they were in the American culture all of their energy and attention was directed to being an acceptable member of this group. They avoided conflict within themselves by minimizing thought about and contact with the other group "back home." When they returned to the other group they used the same type of solution, quickly shifting behavior and ideas to fit back into the new present group. Their behavior appeared quite inconsistent, but it was a consistent approach to solving their problem of multiple membership.

(2). Other individuals chose to keep their other membership the dominant one while in this country. They were defensive and rejective every time the present group seemed to promote values and to expect behavior which they felt might not be acceptable to the other group "back home." The strain of maintaining this orientation was relieved by turning every situation into a "black and white" comparison and adopting a consistently rejective posture toward the present, inferior group. This way of adjusting required a considerable amount of distorting of present and past realities, but the return to the other group was relatively easy.

(3). Others reacted in a sharply contrasting way by identifying wholeheartedly with the present group and by rejecting the standards of the other group as incorrect or inferior at the points of conflict. They were, of course, accepted by the present group, but when they returned home they met rejection or felt alienated from the standards of the group (even when they felt accepted).

(4). Some few individuals seemed to achieve a more difficult but also more creative solution. They attempted to regard membership in both groups as desirable. In order to succeed in this effort, they had to be more realistic about perceiving the inconsistencies between the group expectations and to struggle to make balanced judgments about the strong and weak points of each group. Besides taking this more objective approach to evaluation, these persons worked on problems of how the strengths of one group might be interpreted and utilized by the other group. They were taking roles of creative deviancy in both groups, but attempting to make their contributions in such a way as to be accepted as loyal and productive members. They found ways of using each group membership as a resource for contributing to the welfare of the other group. Some members of each group were of course threatened by this readiness and ability to question the present modal ways of doing things in the group.

Thus it seems that the existence of multiple group memberships creates difficult problems both for the person and for the group. But there are also potentialities and supports for the development of creative individuality in this situation, and there are potentialities for group growth and achievement in the fact that the members of any group are also members of other groups with different standards.

SOME CONCLUSIONS

Let us return now to the question raised at the beginning of this paper. How should we think of the relation between individuals and groups? If we accept the assumption that individuals and groups are both important social realities, we can then ask a pair of important questions. What kind of effects do groups have on the emotional security and creative productivity of the individual? What kinds of effects do individuals have on the morale and creative productivity of the group? In answering these questions it is important to be alerted to both good and bad effects. Although the systematic evidence from research does not begin to provide full answers to these questions, we have found evidence which tends to support the following general statements.

Strong groups do exert strong influences on members toward conformity. These conformity pressures, however, may be directed toward uniformity of thinking and behavior, or they may foster heterogeneity.

Acceptance of these conformity pressures, toward uniformity or heterogeneity, may satisfy the emotional needs of some members and frustrate others. Similarly, it may support the potential creativity of some members and inhibit that of others.

From their experiences of multiple membership and their personal synthesis of these experiences, individuals do have opportunities to achieve significant bases of individuality.

Because each group is made up of members who are loyal members of other groups and who have unique individual interests, each group must continuously cope with deviancy tendencies of the members. These tendencies may represent a source of creative improvement in the life of the group or a source of destructive disruption.

The resolution of these conflicting interests does not seem to be the strengthening of individuals and the weakening of groups, or the strengthening of groups and the weakening of individuals, but rather a strengthening of both by qualitative improvements in the nature of interdependence between integrated individuals and cohesive groups.

BIBLIOGRAPHY

1. Asch, S. E. *Social Psychology.* New York: Prentice Hall Inc., 1952.
2. Back, K. W. Influence Through Social Communication. *J. Abn. & Soc. Psychol.* 46: 1951, 9-23.
3. Coch, L., and French, J. R. P. Overcoming Resistance to Change. *Hum. Relat.* 1: 1948, 512-32.
4. Emerson, R. M. Deviation and Rejection: An Experimental Replication. *Am. Sociol. Rev.* 19: 1954, 688-93.
5. Festinger, L. Informal Social Communication. *Psychol. Rev.* 57: 1950, 271-92.

6. Festinger, L.; Gerard, H. B.; Hymovitch, B.; Kelley, H. H.; and Raven, B. The Influence Process in the Presence of Extreme Deviates. *Hum. Relat.* 5: 1952, 327-46.

7. Festinger, L.; Schachter, S.; and Back, K. *Social Pressures in Informal Groups.* New York: Harper & Row, Publishers, 1950.

8. Festinger, L., and Thibaut, J. Interpersonal Communication in Small Groups. *J. Abn. & Soc. Psychol.* 46: 1951, 92-99.

9. Gerard, H. B. The Effect of Different Dimensions of Disagreement on the Communication Process in Small Groups. *Hum. Relat.* 6: 1953, 249-71.

10. Hall, R. L. Social Influence on the Aircraft Commander's Role. *Am. Sociol. Rev.* 20: 1955, 292-99.

11. Kelley, H. H. Communication in Experimentally Created Hierarchies. *Hum. Relat.* 4: 1951, 39-56.

12. Kelley, H. H., and Shapiro, M. M. An Experiment on Conformity to Group Norms Where Conformity Is Detrimental to Group Achievement. *Am. Sociol. Rev.* 19: 1954, 667-77.

13. Lewin, K. *Field Theory in Social Science.* New York: Harper & Row, Publishers, 1951.

14. Lewin, K. Studies in Group Decision. In: *Group Dynamics: Research and Theory,* ed. D. Cartwright and A. Zander. Evanston: Row, Peterson, 1953.

15. Lewin, K.; Lippitt, R.; and White, R. Patterns of Aggressive Behavior in Experimentally Created "Social Climates." *J. Soc. Psychol.* 10: 1939, 271-99.

16. Newcomb, T. M. *Personality and Social Change.* New York: Dryden, 1943.

17. Parsons, T. *Essays in Sociological Theory.* rev. ed. Glencoe: Free Press, 1954.

18. Roethlisberger, F. J., and Dickson, W. J. *Management and the Worker.* Cambridge: Harvard University Press, 1939.

19. Ross, I. Group Standards Concerning the Admission of Jews. *Soc. Prob.* 2: 1955, 133-40.

20. Schachter, S. Deviation, Rejection, and Communication. *J. Abn. & Soc. Psychol.* 46: 1951, 190-207.

21. Schachter, S., et al. Cross-cultural Experiments on Threat and Rejection. *Hum. Relat.* 7: 1954, 403-39.

22. Seashore, S. E. *Group Cohesiveness in the Industrial Group.* Ann Arbor: Institute for Social Research, 1954.

23. Sherif, M. *The Psychology of Social Norms.* New York: Harper & Row, Publishers, 1936.

24. Stanton, A. H., and Schwartz, M. S.: *The Mental Hospital.* New York: Basic Books, 1954.

25. Tocqueville, A. *Democracy in America,* Vol. 1. New York: Alfred A. Knopf, 1945 (original publication, 1835).

26. Watson, J., and Lippitt, R. *Learning Across Cultures.* Ann Arbor: Institute for Social Research, 1955.

William C. Schutz

INTERPERSONAL UNDERWORLD

Although the businessman must spend a major part of his time dealing with other people, he has in the past had little help in overcoming the difficulties that inevitably arise when people get together. The terms which have been used to describe these problems—terms like "disciplinary problems," "human relations troubles," or the currently popular "communications difficulties"—have served only to hide the real difficulties, for they are descriptions of symptoms. The real causes must be sought at a deeper level; they lie in interpersonal relations.

In every meeting of two or more people two levels of interaction occur. One is the overt—the play that is apparently being played. The other is the covert—like a ballet going on in back of the performance on the interpersonal stage—a subtle struggle for attention and status, for control and influence, and for liking and warmth. This ballet influences the performance by pushing the overt players into unusual postures and making them say and do unusual things. Thus, the objective, hardheaded executive is overtly very resistant to a splendid idea suggested by the brash young fellow who may someday replace him. But this example is much too obvious. The ballet's effect on the actors is usually more subtle.

The importance of these covert factors can hardly be overestimated. The productivity of any particular group is profoundly influenced by them. One of the main functions of this article is to attempt to dispel the idea that strong interpersonal differences existing within a group setting can be effectively handled by ignoring them—as if by the magic of closing your eyes you could make problems go away. Rather, interpersonal problems must be understood and dealt with. If ignored, they are usually transformed so that they are not expressed directly as open hostility but find their expression through the task behavior of the group. Failure to allow these group processes to work in a direct fashion will decrease the group's productivity.

The types of behavior that result from interpersonal difficulties are various. In many cases it is difficult to recognize their connection with interpersonal relations in the work situation. To illustrate some of these more subtle

Abridged from William C. Schutz, "Interpersonal Underworld," *Harvard Business Review,* 36 (July-August, 1958): 123-35.

connections, I shall describe several behaviors resulting from, or symptomatic of, interpersonal difficulties, and then present a sampling of situations giving rise to these behaviors.

BEHAVIORAL SYMPTOMS

Generally, interpersonal problems lead individuals to resist each other and each other's influence in various overt, but more often covert, ways. Each individual may oppose, delay, fail to support, or sabotage another. The mechanisms to be discussed here are largely covert, or unconscious; the individual does these things without being aware of his intention to resist or obstruct.

Communications Problems

These days "communications problems" are greatly emphasized as a source of industrial difficulty. This emphasis, however, seems misplaced. For one thing, problems which are caused by communications are due not to *inadequate* communication but to *too adequate* communication, since what is transmitted most accurately between people is how they feel rather than what they say. Thus, if the boss really feels his research scientist is not very important, that feeling will be communicated to the scientist much more readily than any words that pass between them. For another thing, communications difficulties are primarily the *result* of interpersonal difficulties; they arc seldom themselves a primary *cause* of problems. Resisting another person is often accomplished through the medium of communication. Thus:

> A person may find it difficult to understand what is being said, or, sometimes, actually not hear what is said. Often a person feels confused; he just cannot follow all the things that are going on. Another sign of resistance is incoherent speech, mumbling, not bothering to make a point clear, or not making sure that the listener has heard. All of these occurrences impede the process of verbal communication.
>
> Resistance may also take the form of forgetting to pick up a message that was to have been left on one's desk. Or one may forget to mail a memo or leave a message of importance to someone else; or the message may be garbled, ambiguous, or actually contain a factual error. Similarly, misreading and misinterpretation increase greatly in situations of interpersonal strife.

Individually, these behaviors all appear to be simple human failings and, indeed, in many cases may be only that. However, it is always a good bet, especially when the incidents recur, that they are unconsciously motivated by interpersonal differences. In short, interpersonal problems frequently find expression through the obstruction of valid communication. Excessive communications problems can usually be interpreted as a symptom of interpersonal trouble.

Loss of Motivation

Another expression of interpersonal problems is the loss of motivation to work on a task. In innumerable ways the individual's work becomes ineffective because he lacks the desire to produce. The accumulation of many minor inefficiencies amounts to the equivalent of losing the services of a group member or a part of one or more members' resources and abilities. For example:

> If a group member is supposed to look up some information which is needed for other members of the group to complete their work, he may just miss getting to the company library before Friday night closing time. Therefore he will have to wait over the weekend and, in the meantime, hold up two other people who are waiting for his report. Or perhaps some morning he will oversleep when he should be at the committee meeting.
>
> Another individual does only what is required of him and nothing extra. If he works from nine to five, he will leave promptly at five, for he considers his work a chore, a task to be accomplished and nothing more. If something goes wrong because of someone else's error, he will make no effort to compensate for it. If he is not very busy and someone else needs a hand, he will not lend it. All in all, he will do only the very minimum required to retain his job.
>
> Another manifestation of a man's loss of motivation is a sudden realization that his outside interests and commitments are much stronger than he had thought when the group began. He finds that he has conflicting meetings and other things to do which force him to leave meetings early, to arrive late, or perhaps even to miss one. Or he may have reports to write that prevent him from coming or working for this committee.
>
> Chronic absenteeism or lateness is still another manifestation of an interpersonal difficulty. Perhaps a group member has an actual illness or some commitment at home that prevents his coming; there may be any one of a large number of reasons for his absence or lateness, many of which are rational. But these situations may happen too often to make the whole pattern a rational one. If a man has a meeting and the snow is heavy, it may be that he cannot make the meeting because of the traffic situation; but if it were a meeting which he really wanted to attend, the snow would not be a great enough obstacle to prevent him from going.
>
> Also, a loss of motivation very frequently expresses itself in an actual feeling of physical tiredness. Handling emotional and interpersonal difficulties is hard work, especially if it involves holding back certain strong feelings. This work actually makes the individual so tired that he has great difficulty in bringing himself to work and to persevere on a job once it is begun. It often happens that an individual who feels completely exhausted in one part of his work situation miraculously perks up when a new task comes along or when he goes home to a more enjoyable activity. Again, this is not a case of deliberate malingering. The person actually feels tired. When the conflict-inducing situation is removed, the tiredness lifts.

In general, what is happening is that a person suddenly finds that other groups in which his interpersonal relations are happier are more important than the present group, and hence his motivation to work in the situation is reduced.

A man will seek a situation in which he is happiest and will attempt to avoid unpleasant situations as far as possible. In other words, he escapes the situation by withdrawing his involvement.

Indiscriminate Opposition

Another category of responses to interpersonal difficulties involves direct blockage of action. This mechanism is often quite overt and conscious, but it likewise has many covert and unconscious forms.

A symptom of a bad relationship is resistance to suggestions. It may happen that an individual in the group makes suggestions which are opposed by another member regardless of their merit. As soon as the first member begins to talk, the second man—because he feels hostile to the first—feels a surge of resistance or reluctance to accept anything he is going to hear. This is, of course, not beneficial from the standpoint of the group, because a very good suggestion may be rejected for irrelevant personal reasons.

The manner in which such opposition is manifested is often very subtle. If an antagonist makes a suggestion, rather than use direct attack an individual may say smilingly, "That sounds interesting, but perhaps if we tried this other method it would be even more effective." Another technique is to postpone a decision on an opponent's suggestion. The parliamentary procedure of "tabling" is one formal method, as are setting up investigating committees, considering other matters first, offering amendments, or being unavailable for a meeting to decide on the suggestion. Undoubtedly the experienced businessman can extend this list indefinitely. Again, it is important to note that, although the techniques are often deliberately used, they are perhaps used even more often without the user's awareness of his motivation.

Operational Problems

There are several ailments of total group functioning that are symptomatic of interpersonal difficulties. In most cases, difficulty in reaching decisions is a sure indication of interpersonal strife. This usually implies that the group is unable to tell anybody *no,* since to make such a decision involves saying *yes* to the proponents of another view. Compromises are then put through that satisfy neither side and that certainly do not accomplish the task as effectively as the group could under optimal conditions. The compromise is really one between the individuals who are in conflict, and not a compromise, essentially, of the issues of the case.

Another symptom of interpersonal problems in a group is inefficient division of labor. If the relationships among the men are poor, difficulties arise as soon as it comes time to assign different roles and divide the labor so that the group can operate more effectively. Strongly held interpersonal feelings prevent the group from saying *no* to somebody who wants to be in a particular position in the group but whom the other members consider unsuited to that position. This person may, therefore, be put into the role anyway, to the detriment of the functioning of the group. For example:

> In one group of marketing personnel there was a man of clearly outstanding abilities regarding ideas for the solution of the group's problem. Because of his strength and dominance in the group he was accepted as the leader. One result of this was that he was not in a very good position to express his ideas, since as the leader he had to assume a conciliator role; thus, his virtue as a member who could contribute to the substance of the group's task was diminished.
>
> A second result was that he could not act as a good administrator, that is, could not effectively coordinate the efforts of the other group members. So, by not being able to say *no* to this person, or by not being able to discuss more openly the best use to be made of his abilities, the group lost in two very important ways.

Another frequent instance of this difficulty is putting a man who is extremely capable in a subordinate role, with the result that his abilities cannot be utilized by the group. Thus:

> In a different group the phenomenon opposite to the previous example occurred, resulting in equal injury to the group's performance. Because of personal hostility from several other members the most competent man was relegated to the role of secretary. There his time was consumed taking minutes, and his stellar abilities were wasted.

In general, then, ability to place men properly within a group is one indication of good basic interpersonal relations, while inability is a sign that there must be something wrong among the people that prevents them from using their resources optimally.

Task Distortions

Interpersonal difficulties are almost invariably reflected in a group's performance on its task, although at times these effects are more obvious than at others. Here are three examples of interpersonal problems being expressed directly in work behavior, taken from groups of eight graduate students working on actual industrial problems at the Harvard Business School:

> One of these groups was working on the problem of bringing out a new product for a major manufacturer. The members developed a marketing strategy for this product in which the big stress was on the image that the product would present to consumers. In fact, they put so much stress on the image that they neglected certain other factors.
>
> My observations of this group in operation indicated the reason for the inefficient emphasis. From the beginning certain men were assigned by the group, not to the actual task, but to the presentation to be made to the company at the completion of the work. Some of them became very concerned with the impression *they* would make–in fact more concerned with this than with the impression the product would make. Therefore, they unconsciously sought the aspect of their assigned task which would allow them to work on their interpersonal problem and anxiety and concentrated on it to the consequent neglect of other factors which were also important.

> Another group evolved a marketing strategy for bringing out a family of products. On examination, it appeared that this product family was not particularly well integrated. In addition, there was reason to believe that a single product would be more effective.
>
> From interviews with the individual members and from observations of their working as a group, it became clear that the family of products was a compromise solution. Certain members of the group had wanted one product; others had wanted a different one. Instead of trying to work out these differences of opinion in terms of marketing considerations, the group decided implicitly to bring out the whole family as a solution to their interpersonal problem.
>
> Still another group devised a marketing solution with a heavy emphasis on a decentralized distribution system. But the company representatives immediately wondered about the wisdom of using such autonomous distributors, since company-hired distributors should lead to more profits. The group was at a loss to justify its own suggestion.
>
> Again, observations of the group throughout the term indicated a possible reason. The group had had a serious interpersonal blowup at one point, and the members had decided to go their separate ways. The result of this decision was autonomous operation by the individual members of the group. Apparently the group members were unconsciously influenced by the fact that their group could operate more effectively as autonomous individuals.

Interpersonal problems are often worked out on some aspect of the task that closely approximates the relationship which is of concern to the group (company to dealer, company to consumer, and so forth). In this way the tensions generated by the interpersonal problems can be relieved by symbolically displacing them into the work situation. The drawback of this phenomenon is that, although it appears that the group is very task-oriented, its work may in fact be quite inappropriate and inefficient at many points.

COMMON ISSUES

We have looked at some of the behaviors which may be considered symptomatic of inadequate interpersonal relations. Certain problem situations that occur in group and interpersonal dealings with great frequency generate these symptoms. As an illustration of the nature of the problems and some of their vicissitudes, I shall now discuss three of them.

Consensus for Decision

In every group, sooner or later, a decision-making apparatus must be agreed on. Whether it be consensus, majority rule, unanimity, or any other method, there must be some *modus operandi* for the group to make decisions. By consensus I mean, here, that everyone in the group is agreed that a certain course of action is best for the group, regardless of whether or not he individually agrees with it. Ordinarily, if the group does not have consensus and a decision goes through, the group pays. For instance:

> Let us suppose that a group, perhaps a committee, has gotten together with the task of deciding a particular issue. The issue has come to a vote, and the vote is fairly decisive, say six to two. The two people in the minority, however, do not really feel that they have had an opportunity to express their feelings about the issue. Although they are committed to go along with the decision, they have an inner reluctance to do so. This covert reluctance may manifest itself in any of the symptoms already mentioned. Perhaps the most common symptom is a loss of interest, although this situation could be expected to give rise to any of them.

The question of consensus is central in decision making. In a deeper sense, consensus means that everyone in a group feels that the group understands his position and his feelings about it; and he feels, then, that the group should take a particular course of action even though he does not personally agree. If the individual is not allowed to voice his own feelings and reasons for voting against the particular issue, he will, at least unconsciously, resist the efficient functioning of the group from that point on. If consensus is not required, decisions can often be made more quickly (for example, by majority rule or by fiat), but delay will probably result, due to the unacknowledged members having various ways of resisting once the decision has been made and the action is undertaken.

The ability to detect a lack of consensus is, of course, a very important attribute for a group leader. A few rules of thumb might be of help here. The clue is that it is very difficult to find out whether there is a consensus unless each person is allowed to speak; for lack of disagreement does not necessarily indicate that the group has consensus. Frequently people simply are reluctant to raise their objections. However, if each member is asked separately whether or not he assents to the issue, the group leader can usually pick up objections:

> He may be able to spot disagreement by noticing such things as changes in tone of voice. In one group the leader asked if everyone agreed on a suggested course of action. As he went around the room he got the following responses: *yes, yes, yes, yes, yes, okay.* This leader, being fairly astute, immediately began to question the man who had said *okay,* because this man apparently could not quite bring himself to be like the other members of the group with regard to this decision. This inability is usually a good indication of an objection. The individual is reluctant to object directly because of the weight of all the other members disagreeing with him.
>
> After this man had been quizzed for a while, it became clear that he did have a strong objection. Once he was allowed to talk it out, he went along with the group and was quite willing to say *yes* and, in fact, to pitch in and work with the decision that was finally made.
>
> Another good indicator of lack of consensus is any attempt by a member to postpone a decision by further discussion or by further action of some kind. Comments like, "What is it we are voting on?" or "Weren't we supposed to discuss something else first?" or "I have no objection to that, but . . . " all indicate that the individual is not yet ready to cast a positive vote for a given decision. He probably has an objection that ought to be brought out into the open and discussed.

Allowing the objector to raise his point for discussion is not just a hollow gesture. The objector will be more likely to go along with the final decision–or he may eventually carry the day because he reflects some objections that other people had but were not aware of. Whether the group actually changes its vote or not, it will be more likely to reach a correct decision. This opportunity for the group to discuss a previously covert factor is very important for its effectiveness.

Authority Problem

Another group phenomenon that leads to reduced effectiveness concerns the relationship of the group members to the leader of the group. (The term *leader* will be used loosely to mean the person who is, in the eyes of the group members, supposed to head the group–usually a formal leader, a designated person who has a higher title.) It is the nature of such relationships that members of the group have ambivalent feelings toward the authority figure–both positive and negative feelings. The negative feelings can be particularly disturbing since it usually is hard for people to express such feelings directly, because their jobs may be in jeopardy or because they feel that they should not attack an authority figure.

Since the hostility must be expressed, however, they often transfer it to another member of the group. Some other member, usually one with characteristics similar to those disliked in the leader, will be attacked more than he realistically should be for his behavior in the group. He will be attacked not only for what he does, but also because the attack that the group would like to level toward the leader is displaced onto him. The term *scapegoat* is often used for this person. For example, if the group members are dissatisfied because the leader is not giving sufficient direction to the group, the dissatisfaction may be vented toward a silent or nonparticipating member, the member in the group who comes closest to having the characteristic of the leader which the group members do not like. For example:

> In one marketing group the leader offered the group very little direction, far less than most members would have liked. Subsequently, everyone began to get very angry with one group member who did not say much and who occasionally missed meetings because of his other commitments. The group attacked him for his lack of interest and unwillingness to contribute to the group.
>
> A key to what was really happening is found in the fact that he was actually quite interested and was contributing a great deal, thus making the attack somewhat undeserved; but significantly, the characteristics which angered the group members were precisely those that covertly irritated them about the leader. Apparently they displaced their aggression from the leader, whom they felt they could not attack directly, onto a group member who had similar attributes.

This same mechanism operates when the boss is too *authoritarian.* Somebody in the group who has similar tendencies will be severely attacked, again as a displacement of the attack they would like to level at the boss.

With regard to dealing with this phenomenon, perhaps the most useful thing to be said is that there are times when a leader, in order to allow a group to operate more effectively, must himself become the scapegoat. If he can absorb some of the hostility that is really meant for him or perhaps in some cases even absorb some of the hostility meant for other group members, he can be most useful in helping a group to function more effectively. Of course, in order to do this the leader must be aware that the hostility is not necessarily directed at him personally; it is just an inevitable consequence of group activity that hostility does arise. If he can absorb the hostility directly, it does not have to be deflected into the group where it is most destructive to the group and to the group's ability to fulfill its purposes. An important part of a leader's role is to be a scapegoat occasionally in order that the group may proceed and operate more effectively. This situation brings to mind an old saying, "A good king is one whose subjects prosper."

The Problem Member

Another frequently occurring group difficulty is the presence of a problem member, one of the most difficult of all interpersonal problems for a group to deal with. Problem members are of two main types—the overactive member and the underactive member. Either can disrupt group functioning, and both are usually difficult to handle.

The overactive problem member dominates the group's attention far more than his abilities warrant. The difficulties arise partly because the apparent intensity of his feelings leads to a general reluctance of the group to hurt the individual while at the same time they cannot curtail his destructive activities. To illustrate what can happen in such a situation:

> In one five-man group of military personnel working on a series of tactical problems, Mac immediately took over control of the group. Because he was reasonably competent and highly forceful, he went unchallenged for several meetings. The other group members were not very compatible, so they had a difficult time handling Mac. Gradually some members began losing interest in the group until one discussion of a very trivial topic, the postal rates from Washington to Chicago, came up in one of their rest periods. The exchange that followed was amazing in that Mac was attacked severely and at length by the other group members for his dogmatically stated opinion about postal rates. The group used this topic to vent their stored-up feelings toward Mac. By this time, however, the group had no resources to cope with these strong feelings, and it quickly disintegrated after the conflict.

The optimal solution to the problem represented by this member is to handle him in such a way that he can be retained in the group and his resources made use of and still not be allowed to obstruct the group's functioning:

> Another group had this problem with Bob. But this group quickly deposed Bob and set up a leader of considerably less intellect but with superior coordinating abilities. For a short time after they had deposed Bob the group made sure he realized he was not going to run the group; then they gradually allowed him back into the group by paying more attention to his

ideas. Finally, after about ten meetings, his ideas were highly influential and sought by the group, although he was not allowed to dominate. In this way the group took care of the problem presented by an overactive member and was still able to utilize his abilities. This is an ideal solution and the sign of a strong, compatible group.

Someone who will not become integrated into the group also poses a problem for the group. The lack of commitment of this member, perhaps even a lack of willingness to work, constitutes a serious group problem. One solution is to eject the member from the group. This is a solution only insofar as it removes the source of a difficulty; it does not allow the group to utilize the man's abilities. The problem member often serves a useful function by enabling other members to direct their hostility toward him, so that they do not have to deal with the real differences among themselves. Thus, it is not unusual that if a chronically negative member is absent, the group finds that it still has disagreements.

FRAMEWORK FOR BEHAVIOR

Now that I have described examples of several interpersonal problem situations and various reactions to them, I shall present a brief outline of a theory of interpersonal behavior. In order to deal with interpersonal behavior it is necessary to have an understanding of the *general* principles of this behavior, since formulas for handling *specific* situations are of limited value at best. The following theory is by no means the only one extant in psychological literature, but it is offered as a possible framework for understanding phenomena of the type under discussion here.

Interpersonal Needs

The basis for evolving this theory of interpersonal behavior is the individual's *fundamental interpersonal relations orientation* or, to abbreviate, FIRO. The basic assumption of this approach is that people need people. Every human being, because he lives in a society, must establish an equilibrium between himself and his human environment – just as he must establish an equilibrium between himself and the physical world. This social nature of man gives rise to certain interpersonal needs, which he must satisfy to some degree while avoiding threat to himself. Although each individual has different intensities of need and different mechanisms for handling them, people have three basic interpersonal needs in common:

The Need for Inclusion. This is the need to maintain a satisfactory relation between the self and other people with respect to interaction or belongingness. Some people like to be with other people all the time; they want to belong to organizations, to interact, to mingle. Other people seek much less contact; they prefer to be alone, to interact minimally, to stay out of groups, to maintain privacy.

If a continuum were to be drawn between these two extremes, every person could be placed at a point (or region) at which he feels most comfortable. Thus, to a certain degree each individual is trying to belong to a group, but he is also trying to maintain a certain amount of privacy. From the other point of view he wishes to some degree to have people initiate interaction toward him through invitations and the like, and also wishes to some degree that people would leave him alone. For each dimension these two aspects may be distinguished: (1) the behavior he initiates toward others, his expressed behavior; and (2) the behavior he prefers others to express toward him, his wanted behavior. This distinction will prove valuable in the discussion of compatibility.

The Need for Control. This is the need to maintain a satisfactory relation between oneself and other people with regard to power and influence. In other words, every individual has a need to control his situation to some degree, so that his environment can be predictable for him. Ordinarily this amounts to controlling other people, because other people are the main agents which threaten him and create an unpredictable and uncontrollable situation. This need for control varies from those who want to control their entire environment, including all the people around them, to those who want to control no one in any situation, no matter how appropriate controlling them would be.

Here, again, everyone varies as to the degree to which he wants to control others. In addition, everyone varies with respect to the degree to which he wants to be controlled by other people, from those who want to be completely controlled and are dependent on others for making decisions for them to those who want to be controlled under no conditions.

The Need for Affection. This is the need to maintain a satisfactory relation between the self and other people with regard to love and affection. In the business setting this need is seldom made overt. It takes the form of friendship. In essence, affection is a relationship between two people only, a dyadic relationship. At one extreme individuals like very close, personal relationships with each individual they meet. At the other extreme are those who like their personal relationships to be quite impersonal and distant, perhaps friendly but not close and intimate.

Again between these two extremes everyone has a level of intimacy which is most comfortable for him. From the other side, each individual prefers that others make overtures to him in a way that indicates a certain degree of closeness.

To clarify the various orientations in these three areas, Exhibit 1 presents the extreme positions taken on each of the dimensions. Everyone fits somewhere between these two extremes, most of them in the middle.

EXHIBIT 1. **Extreme types on the three interpersonal dimensions**

Expressed Behavior		*Dimension*	*Wanted Behavior*	
Extreme High	Extreme Low	Inclusion	Extreme High	Extreme Low
Oversocial	Undersocial		Social-Compliant	Countersocial
Autocrat	Abdicrat	Control	Submissive	Rebellious
Overpersonal	Underpersonal	Affection	Personal-Compliant	Counterpersonal

GROUP COMPATIBILITY

This theory of interpersonal relations can be very useful to businessmen in determining the compatibility of the members of a group. If at the outset we can choose a group of people who can work together harmoniously, we shall go far toward avoiding situations where a group's efforts are wasted in interpersonal conflicts.

Our theoretical framework is designed to handle this problem. Suppose we consider in more detail the two aspects for each one of the three interpersonal dimensions. One aspect is what we *do* with relation to other people; let us call this "e" for *expressed* behavior. The second is what we *want* from other people, how we want them to act toward us; let us call this "w" for *wanted* behavior. Then we can use "e" and "w" to try to find out how people will relate to each other in the *inclusion* dimension ("I"), the *control* dimension ("C") and the *affection* dimension ("A"), as shown schematically in Exhibit 2.

EXHIBIT 2. **Schema of interpersonal behaviors**

Expressed Behavior	*Dimension*	*Wanted Behavior*
I initiate interaction with people	Inclusion	I want to be included
I control people	Control	I want people to control me
I act close and personal toward people	Affection	I want people to get close and personal to me

If we make a ten-point scale, from zero to nine, and say that in each of the two aspects of the three dimensions everyone has some propensity, some preferred behavior, we can characterize each person by six scores: e^I, w^I, e^C, w^C, e^A, w^A.

In the course of my research I have developed a questionnaire, called FIRO-B (the "B" refers to *behavior),* comprising a check list of 54 statements designed to measure an individual's propensities in each of these six categories. . . The resulting scores for each need area can be plotted on a diagram, as in Exhibit 3.

Two Kinds

Note that in Exhibit 3 there are two diagonals, which may be used to explain two different kinds of compatibility—"originator compatibility" (oK) and "interchange compatibility" (xK). Individuals can be located on these diagonals from their scores on FIRO-B.

In popular literature there are at least two well-known and apparently contradictory maxims relating to the bases of compatibility: "Opposites attract," and "Birds of a feather flock together." Considering the diagonals on Exhibit 3 might aid us in coming to a sensible resolution of these maxims, since there seems to be some truth in each of them:

Originator Diagonal. Let us take an example in the control dimension and consider the lower right to upper left line. The people who fall in the lower right quadrant are the ones who want to control others and do not want to be controlled themselves. These people can be called autocrat-rebels; they want to be the bosses and do not want anyone else to tell them what to do. In the upper left quadrant we have just the opposite. These are abdicrat-submissives; they want to be told what to do, and they do not want to control anyone else.

For smooth functioning it would appear that if we had one autocrat-rebel, we would not want another one, since they would both want to give orders and neither would want to take them. This is called *competitive* incompatibility. Also, if we had two abdicrat-submissives, a situation would be created wherein both people want someone to tell them what to do and neither wants to do the telling. This is called *apathetic* incompatibility. However, if we have one autocrat-rebel and one abdicrat-submissive, the relationship will probably be harmonious, since one person wants to give orders and the other wants to take them.

Interchange Diagonal. Now, consider the other diagonal on the diagram. Let us take affection for an example this time. In the upper right quadrant are the people who express a lot of close personal behavior, and want the same expressed to them. These are the people of "high interchange," and they can be called overpersonal-personal-compliants. They like an atmosphere in which there is a lot of affection; so, for instance, they would like a party better than a board of directors meeting. In the lower left quadrant are people of "low interchange," who like neither to give nor to receive affection. They can be called underpersonal-counterpersonals. They do not want anyone to get very close to them, nor do they want to get very close to anyone. They like their relations rather reserved, cool, and distant.

EXHIBIT 3. **Graphic representation of interpersonal dimensions**

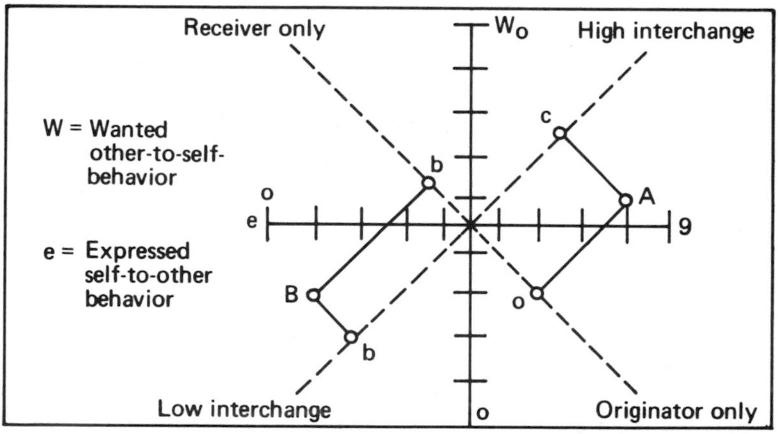

Here the complementary idea of the originator diagonal—that opposites attract—does not apply; for, if one person likes to be very close and personal and the other person does not, they are going to threaten each other. One who likes to keep his relations reserved is not going to like it when the other makes overtures; and, in the reverse direction, the one who wants very close relations is not going to be very happy if the other does not. So it seems reasonable that the situation would lead to harmony more readily if the people involved were close on this diagonal, unlike the situation on the originator diagonal.

In the inclusion dimension, again, it would be better if both interacting persons were very close to being either very high or very low on this diagonal so that one would not always want to be with people while the other wanted to stay home and read a book. Hence, on the interchange diagonal the "birds of a feather" maxim seems most appropirate; people should be similar in their values along this diagonal.

Predictable Relations

To exemplify the working of the technique let us consider Exhibit 3 for the control area.

From FIRO-B, we learn that A has a score of 8 on e^c, and 5 on w^c, while B has a score of 1 on e^c and 1 on w^c. These points are plotted on the diagram. Each score, for illustrative purposes, may be divided into two components, one on each diagonal. These components are represented by a_x and a^o and b_x and b^o on the diagram.

The measure of interchange compatibility (xK) of A and B is proportional to the distance between a_x and b_x. A smaller distance means a more similar orientation toward the amount of interchange of control that should exist in a relation. In the example, A believes that relations should involve a great deal of influence and control, while B's preference is for less structured, more laissez-faire relations. Their compatibility in this regard is reflected in he relatively large distance between a_x and b_x.

Originator compatibility (oK) is proportional to the sum of a^o and b^o. Optimal originator compatibility occurs when one score is to the left of the midpoint of the diagonal and the other score is exactly the same distance to the right of the midpoint. In our example this is almost exactly true; thus A and B have high originator compatibility. A wishes to control others but not to be controlled, while B wishes to be controlled but not to control or influence others very much. Hence they complement each other.

Our conclusion then about this pair is the following: they disagree as to the atmosphere they desire regarding mutual influence and control. A likes structured hierarchies while B prefers more permissive relations. However, when there is a situation of a certain structure, they are compatible with regard to the roles they will take in relation to each other. A will take the influential, responsible position, and B will take the subordinate role.

These psychological considerations can very easily be converted into formulas, and in research work and practical applications this is done. There have been several experiments performed which indicate the usefulness of this approach. These experiments demonstrate that groups of from two to eight can be composed—based on FIRO-B scores—in such a way that their productivity, and to some extent their interaction, is predictable. Much research is still to be done to improve the accuracy of these predictions, but the results are highly encouraging.[1]

[1] See William C. Schutz, op. cit. [FIRO, New York, 1958]

GROUP DEVELOPMENT

Another major point in the theory is that every group, no matter what its function or composition, given enough time, goes through the three interpersonal phases of inclusion, control, and affection in the same sequence. To illustrate:

> Recently I was interviewing a member of a group, which had just completed 30 meetings, to get an idea of her feeling about the experience. In response to the question, "How would you describe what happened in this group?" she replied, "Well, first you're concerned about the problem of where you fit in the group; then you're wondering about what you'll accomplish. Finally, after a while, you learn that people mean something. Your primary concern becomes how people feel about you and about each other."

In or Out

First, *the inclusion phase centers around the question of "in or out."* It begins with the formation of the group. When people are confronted with each other, they must first find the place where they fit in. This involves being in or out of the group, establishing oneself as a specific individual, and seeing if one is going to be paid attention to and not be left behind or ignored. This anxiety area gives rise to individual-centered behavior such as overtalking, extreme withdrawal, exhibitionism, recitation of biographies and other previous experience.

At the same time the basic problem of commitment to the group is present. Each member is implicitly deciding to what degree he will become a member of the group, how much investment he will withdraw from his other commitments and invest in this new relationship. He is asking, "How much of myself will I devote to this group? How important will I be in this setting? Will they know who I am and what I can do, or will I be indistinguishable from many others?" This is, in short, the problem of identity. He is, in effect, deciding primarily on his preferred amount of inclusion initiation with the other members—just how much actual contact, interaction, and communication he wishes to have.

Hence, the main concerns of the formative process are "boundary problems," problems that have to do with entering into the boundaries of a group and belonging to that group. These are problems of inclusion.

Characteristic of groups in this phase is the occurrence of what have been called "goblet issues." The term is taken from an analogy to a cocktail party where people sometimes pick up their cocktail glass, or goblet, and figuratively peer through it to size up the other people at the party. Hence, they are issues that in themselves are of minor importance to the group members but serve as vehicles for getting to know people, especially in relation to oneself.

Often a goblet issue is made of the first decision confronting a group. In some groups discussions leading to a decision about such an issue continue for an unbelievably long time and then never reach a conclusion. But there has been a great deal of learning in that the members have gained a fairly clear picture of each other. Each member knows who responds favorably to him, who sees the things the way he does, how much he knows as compared to the others, how the leader responds to him, and what type of role he can expect to play in the group. Acquiring this knowledge is the unconscious purpose of the goblet issue.

The frustrating experience of having groups endlessly discuss topics of little real interest to anyone is very common. Every group finds its own goblet issues within the framework of its aim. "The weather" is fairly universal; "rules of procedure" is common in formal groups; "Do you know so-and-so?" often characterizes new acquaintances from the same location; relating incidents or telling stories has a goblet element for business gatherings; and "Where are you from?" often serves for military settings. Mark Twain apparently overlooked the fact that nobody really *wants* to "do anything about the weather"—they just want to use it as a topic for sizing up people. These discussions are inevitable, and, contrary to all outward appearances, they do serve an important function. Groups which are not permitted this type of testing out will search for some other method of obtaining the same personal information, perhaps using as a vehicle a decision of more importance to the work of the group.

Top or Bottom

After the problems of inclusion have been sufficiently resolved, control problems become prominent. *This phase centers around the problems of "top or bottom."* Once members are fairly well established as being together in a group, the issue of decision-making procedures arises. This involves problems of sharing responsibility and its necessary concomitant, distribution of power and control. Characteristic behavior at this stage includes leadership struggles; competition; and discussion of orientation to the task, structuring, rules of procedure, methods of decision making, and sharing the responsibility for the group's work. The primary anxieties at this phase revolve around having too much or too little influence. Each member is trying to establish himself in the group so that he has the most comfortable amount of interchange and the most comfortable degree of initiation with the other members with regard to control, influence, and responsibility.

Near or Far

Finally, following a satisfactory resolution of these phases, problems of affection become focal. *This phase centers on the issue of "near or far."* The individuals have come together to form a group; they have differentiated themselves with respect to responsibility and power. Now they must become emotionally integrated. At this stage it is characteristic to see such behavior expressed through positive feelings, direct personal hostility, jealousies, pairing behavior, and, in general, heightened emotional feeling between pairs of people.

The primary anxieties at this stage have to do with not being liked or close enough to people or with being too intimate. Each member is striving to obtain his most favorable amount of affectional interchange and most comfortable position regarding initiating and receiving affection–deciding, like Schopenhauer's porcupines, how to get close enough to receive warmth, yet avoid the pain of sharp quills.

Tightening the Bolts

These are not distinct phases. The group development postulate asserts that these problem areas are *emphasized* at certain points in a group's growth, but all three problem areas are always present. Similarly, some people do not always go along with the central issue for the group. For certain individuals a particular problem area will be so personally potent that it will transcend the current group issue. The area of concern for any individual will result from his own problem areas and those of the group's current phase. Perhaps a close approximation to the developmental phenomena is given by the tire-changing model:

> When a person changes a tire and replaces the wheel, he first sets the wheel in place and secures it by tightening the bolts one after another just enough so the wheel is in place and the next step can be taken. Then the bolts are tightened further, usually in the same sequence, until the wheel is firmly in place. Finally each bolt is gone over separately to secure it.

In a similar way, the need areas are worked on until they are handled satisfactorily enough to continue with the work at hand. Later on they are returned to and worked over to a more satisfactory degree. If one need area has not been worked out well on the first sequence, it must receive more attention on the next cycle.

APPLICATIONS OF THEORY

The next question is: What can we do about these problems so as to utilize this information practically? This is more difficult. The above analysis is derived largely from experience with experimental research on small groups selected for this purpose. Solutions for the problems observed are largely, though not entirely, speculative and can only be offered as suggestions which should be explored carefully in each individual case before being adopted.

More specifically, the interpretations presented here can be looked upon as suggestions for *diagnosis.* The more men in business can become aware of the basic factors underlying their interpersonal difficulties, the better they will be able to meet these difficulties. As in the practice of medicine, if the disease is properly diagnosed, the doctor has a better chance of curing it than if it is improperly or superficially diagnosed, even though a correct diagnosis by no means guarantees a cure.

Clearing the Air

Serious interpersonal difficulties that are left covert only smolder and erupt at the expense of efficiency and productivity. The most effective way covert difficulties can be dealt with is by first making them overt. For example:

> In one marketing group, the leader finally told one member that he did not like the way he was acting in the group and that he felt he should contribute more. After a brief but difficult and bitter exchange the two began to tell each other their feelings about the situation. They managed to clear the air, and the situation improved markedly.

When successful, overt discussion is like a cold shower: it is approached with apprehension, the initial impact is very uncomfortable, but the final result justifies the tribulations.

To summarize, "interpersonal problems" include difficulties such as members who are withdrawn from a group; personal hostilities between members; problem members who are either inactive and unintegrated or overactive and destructive; power struggles between group members; members battling for attention; dissatisfaction with the leadership in the group; dissatisfaction with the amount of acknowledgment that an individual's contributions are getting, or dissatisfaction with the amount of affection and warmth exhibited in the group.

If it becomes quite clear to the group members that their difficulties are so severe that their activity is being impaired, then bringing the issues out in the open and talking about them will help. It is somewhat difficult, however, to tell exactly when a problem is so severe that it is holding the group up. Perhaps some of the earlier discussion of symptoms will be useful for assessing the effect of interpersonal factors on the group.

It might be helpful to view groups (including anywhere from two to twenty people) on a continuum–from those that are completely compatible, that is, able to work well together, to those that are completely incompatible, that is, incapable of working together. Any particular group can be placed somewhere along this continuum. To illustrate:

> The members of the group at the extreme compatible end of the continuum are able to work well together within a relatively short time with a minimum of difficulty and can operate effectively over a period of time on a wide variety of problems. They need no training or new awareness.
>
> The group at the incompatible end, however, cannot work effectively. The interpersonal problems that cause the task difficulties are so deepseated in the personalities of the individual members that no amount of outside assistance will be worthwhile. It would take so long before this group could operate effectively that, from a practical standpoint, any kind of training of the group members or any awareness of their problems would be unfruitful.
>
> Between these two extreme types are groups that profit more or less by the kind of awareness which has been discussed. If a group is relatively near the compatible end, with a minimum of awareness and a minimum of discussion of its difficult problems, it will become a smoothly functioning group. If interpersonal problems in a group are very minor, they can usually be ignored without impairing the group seriously; or, if the

problems exist between two members, they can often work out their difficulties by themselves outside the group.

With groups near the incompatible end much more intensive work has to be done to get through their problems so that they can function effectively. Such work should probably be guided by someone who is experienced with group process and can help group members to work out their difficulties.

Another advantage of this approach operates more through the individuals than the group. If the individual members can gain the kind of awareness of their own needs in situations as discussed in this article, then this in itself will help them to understand their reactions to other people and, perhaps, to operate more effectively. In addition, it is often helpful to point out to group members that other people have the same basic needs; for, if they understand what other people are trying to do, they may be more tolerant of other people's behavior. Since everyone has these needs, everyone tries to get the same thing from other people, even though each may use different adaptive patterns for achieving his ends. To illustrate such a mechanism:

> It generally is felt that if an individual has an excessively strong negative reaction to another individual in the setting of a work group, the individual who is irritated fears deep down within himself that he is like the one who annoys him, that he himself has the trait that is so annoying. It is threatening for him to see it in some other individual, and he must immediately deny it and attack it, almost as if he were trying to deny to himself that he is like this.

Awareness of mechanisms of this type may help in understanding what is happening in the group and one's own reaction in the situation.

CONCLUSION

The time seems to have come for the businessman to make use of some of the social scientists' more recent findings on the unconscious, or covert, factors in human interaction. Since the businessman does deal so heavily in interpersonal relations, his skill and success are dependent on his ability to understand interpersonal relations and to deal effectively with them. Thus, it becomes important for him to gain a more basic understanding instead of simply trying out panaceas that aim only at the symptoms of the problems and not at the basic problems themselves. He must understand the vast interpersonal underworld that operates beneath the overt, observable behavior.

As I have already pointed out, current interest in what are called "communications problems" provides an example of the symptomatic approach, for these problems are symptoms of poor interpersonal relations rather than primary causes of operational difficulties. It is an error, therefore, to try to attack the problems of communication by building more effective physical lines of communication, when the trouble really lies in the relation between individuals. The way to attack the basic problem would seem to be to investigate what is going on among the individuals themselves and try to improve those relations.

If it is true that the unconscious factors are so all-important to understanding groups, then we ought to find out exactly how these factors do affect what the businessman is usually primarily interested in—namely, effective operation. In this article I have tried to illustrate the inadequacy of attempting to operate by ignoring interpersonal difficulties and attending to the task only, since in reality the interpersonal factors somehow find their way into the task and directly affect the productivity of the group. No matter how much people try to keep interpersonal problems out by ignoring them, they will turn up in subtle forms such as loss of motivation, tiredness, or the group member's preoccupation with outside tasks; or they may get entangled directly with the solution of the task and have to be worked out in the body of the problem.

I have offered a theoretical framework which may be of some help in understanding the structure of these interpersonal problems in an attempt to aid in the diagnosis of interpersonal behavior. Such a diagnosis may then leave the businessman in a better position to deal with what actually occurs. I have tried to suggest possible lines of solution, but these attempts are offered in a much more speculative manner. Although they are based on rather extensive experience with psychological phenomena, they are only suggestions that the individual businessman must try out and adapt to his own needs.

Dale E. Zand

TRUST AND MANAGERIAL PROBLEM SOLVING

There is increasing research evidence that trust is a salient factor in determining the effectiveness of many relationships, such as those between parent and child (Baldwin *et al.,* 1945), psychotherapist and client (Fiedler, 1953; Seeman, 1954), and members of problem-solving groups (Parloff and Handlon, 1966). Trust facilitates interpersonal acceptance and openness of expression, whereas mistrust evokes interpersonal rejection and arouses defensive behavior (Gibb, 1961).

During the past fifteen years many managers have been introduced to programs, variously called sensitivity training (Bradford *et al.,* 1964), grid laboratories (Blake and Mouton, 1964), or group workshops (Schein and Bennis, 1965), to improve their skills in developing trust and thus, presumably, their managerial effectiveness. It has been difficult, however, to show a direct correlation between trust and managerial effectiveness in a working organization (Dunnette and Campbell, 1968; House, 1967), so that there is a need to clarify the theoretical basis for assertions about trust and managerial effectiveness and to devise experiments to test them.

INTRODUCTION

Rogers (1961) found that in an effective helping relationship, one participant (counselor, therapist, helper) behaved in ways that developed trust and the other experienced an increase in trust, and concluded that the development of trust is a crucial initial factor and a necessary continuing element in such a relationship. He summarized extensive research in which an increase in trust appeared to be causally related to more rapid intellectual development, increased originality, increased emotional stability, increased self-control and decreased physiological arousal to defend against threat.

The level of trust in a relationship affects the degree of defensiveness. Gibb (1961) found that members of small groups that developed a "defensive climate," had difficulty concentrating on messages, perceived the motives, values, and

Dale E. Zand, "Trust & Managerial Problem Solving," *Administrative Science Quarterly,* Vol. 17, No. 2, June 1972, pp. 229-238.

emotions of others less accurately, and increased the distortion of messages. Other studies suggest that some interpersonal trust is required for effective problem solving in a group. Parloff and Handlon (1966) found that intensive, persistent criticism increased defensiveness and mistrust among members of a group and decreased their ability to recognize and accept good ideas. Meadow *et al.* (1959) reported that defensiveness induced a lasting decrease in problem-solving effectiveness. They found that groups penalized for poor ideas and admonished to produce only good ideas while working on early problems produced poorer solutions to later problems when these restrictions were removed than groups that were not penalized and admonished during their early problem assignments.

This paper: (1) analyzes the concept of trust, (2) presents a model of the interaction of trust and problem-solving behavior, and (3) reports the results of an experiment that attempted to test several hypotheses derived from the model.

ANALYSIS OF CONCEPT

Trusting behavior, following Deutsch (1962), is defined here as consisting of actions that (a) increase one's vulnerability, (b) to another whose behavior is not under one's control, (c) in a situation in which the penalty (disutility) one suffers if the other abuses that vulnerability is greater than the benefit (utility) one gains if the other does not abuse that vulnerability. For example, a parent is exhibiting trusting behavior in hiring a baby sitter so he can see a movie. The action significantly increases his vulnerability, since he cannot control the baby sitter's behavior after leaving the house. If the baby sitter abuses that vulnerability, the penalty may be a tragedy that may adversely affect the rest of his life; if the baby sitter does not abuse that vulnerability, the benefit will be the pleasure of seeing a movie. Thus trust, as the term will be used in this paper, is not a global feeling of warmth or affection, but the conscious regulation of one's dependence on another that will vary with the task, the situation, and the other person.

MODEL

The following model, based on Gibb (1964), conceptualizes the transforming of one's inner state of trust (or mistrust) into behavior that is trusting (or mistrusting) through (1) information, (2) influence, and (3) control.

One who does not trust others will conceal or distort relevant information, and avoid stating or will disguise facts, ideas, conclusions and feelings that he believes will increase his exposure to others, so that the information he provides will be low in accuracy, comprehensiveness, and timeliness; and therefore have low congruence with reality. He will also resist or deflect the attempts of others to exert influence. He will be suspicious of their views, and not receptive to their proposals of goals, their suggestions for reaching goals, and their definition of criteria and methods for evaluating progress. Although he rejects the influence of others, he will expect them to accept his views. Finally, one who does not trust will try to minimize his dependence on others. He will feel he cannot rely on them to abide by agreements and will try to impose controls on their behavior when coordination is necessary to attain common goals, but will resist and be alarmed at their attempts to control his behavior.

When others encounter low-trust behavior, initially they will hesitate to reveal information, reject influence, and evade control. This short cycle feedback will reinforce the originator's low trust, and unless there are changes in behavior, the relationship will stabilize at a low level of trust.

All of this behavior, following from a lack of trust, will be deleterious to information exchange, to reciprocity of influence, and to the exercise of self-control, and will diminish the effectiveness of joint problem-solving efforts.

To the objective uncertainty inherent in a problem, for example, unavailable facts and unknown causal relationships between actions and results, low trust will add social uncertainty; that is, uncertainty introduced by individuals withholding or distorting relevant information and concepts.

Persons lacking trust attempting to solve a problem jointly will attempt to minimize their vulnerability. There will be an increase in the likelihood of misunderstanding or misinterpretation. The social uncertainty induced by their low trust will increase the probability that underlying problems may go undetected or be avoided, and that inappropriate solutions may be more difficult to identify. If the group is incapable of breaking out of this ineffective pattern of problem solving, it may seize an expedient solution as a device to end its work and dissolve itself.

Persons who trust one another will provide relevant, comprehensive, accurate, and timely information, and thereby contribute realistic data for problem-solving efforts. They will have less fear that their exposure will be abused, and will therefore be receptive to influence from others. They will also accept interdependence because of confidence that others will control their behavior in accordance with agreements, and therefore will have less need to impose controls on others, (see Figure 1). Consequently they will contribute to a decrease in social uncertainty, and be less likely to misinterpret the intentions and the behavior of others. As a result, underlying problems are more likely to be identified and examined, and solutions more likely to be appropriate, creative, and long-range.

Hypotheses

It is not assumed here that trust alone will solve a technical problem; it is assumed that group members collectively have adequate knowledge, experience, and creativity to define and solve a complex problem. It is also assumed that it is possible to increase or decrease trust in members of a problem-solving group.

On the basis of the model described, the following differences can be predicted in the problem-solving behavior of groups with high and low trust.

An increase in trust will increase the exchange of accurate, comprehensive, and timely information. Problem-solving groups with high trust will:

Hypothesis 1. Exchange relevant ideas and feelings more openly,
Hypothesis 2. Develop greater clarification of goals and problems.

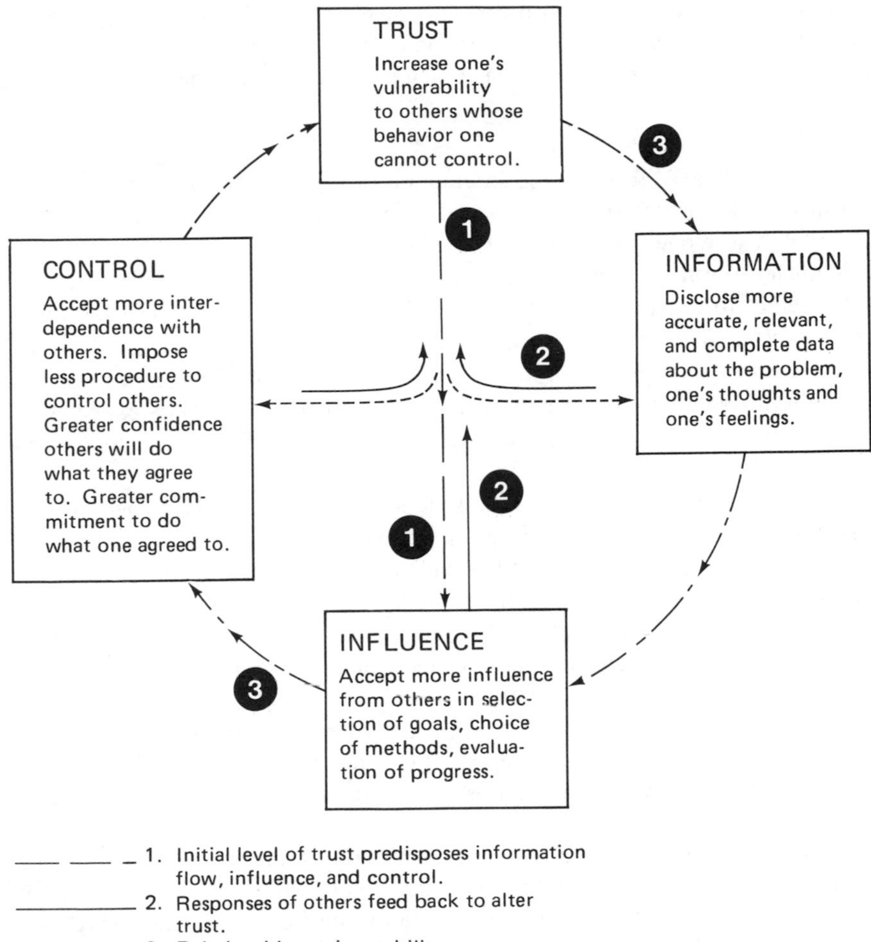

FIGURE 1. **A model of the relationship of trust to information, influence, and control**

An increase in trust will increase the willingness to influence others and the receptivity to the influence of others. Hence, problem-solving groups with high trust will:

Hypothesis 3. Search more extensively for alternative courses of action,
Hypothesis 4. Have greater influence on solutions.

Finally, an increase in trust will increase willingness to control one's own behavior, will increase confidence in the reliability of others, and will decrease efforts to control the behavior of others, all of which will contribute to increased satisfaction and motivation. Hence, problem-solving groups with high trust will:

Hypothesis 5. Be more satisfied with their problem-solving efforts,

Hypothesis 6. Have greater motivation to implement conclusions,
Hypothesis 7. See themselves as closer and more of a team,
Hypothesis 8. Have less desire to leave their group to join another.

Dynamics of Trust

Trust takes form in the interaction of two (or more) people, and the dynamics of this interaction is illustrated in Figure 2.

Let P denote one person and O the other. If (1) P lacks trust, (2) he will disclose little relevant or accurate information, be unwilling to share influence, and will attempt to control O. (3) Assume O also lacks trust, (4) perceives P's initial behavior as actually untrusting, and (5) concludes he was right to expect P to be untrustworthy; then (6) he will feel justified in his mistrust of P. Since (7) P sees O's behavior as untrusting, he (8) will be confirmed in his initial expectation that O would not be trustworthy and (2) P will behave with less trust than when he entered.

The interaction will continue around the loop inducing O and P to behave with less and less trust until they arrive at an equilibrium level of low trust, each attempting to minimize his vulnerability and to maximize his control of the other. In the process the effectiveness of problem solving will decrease. After interaction has continued, each will tend to hold more firmly to his entering beliefs. They will not have a reliable basis for accepting or sharing influence, and the mutual resistance to influence will arouse feelings of frustration in both. If they have a deadline, each will attempt to impose controls on the other. If P is O's organizational superior, he may command O's compliance, which will reinforce O's mistrust. Usually, by the middle of the meeting the level of trust will be lower than the initial level.

Gibb (1964) offers support for the dynamics of this interaction. In observing small group behavior he noted that the defensive behavior of a listener generated cues which subsequently increased the defensiveness of the communicator, resulting, if unchecked, in a circular pattern of escalating defensiveness.

The pattern of spiral reinforcement illustrated in Figure 2 would operate constructively if it is assumed that both P and O entered the relationship with trust in the other. Gibb (1964) observed that when defensiveness was reduced, members were better able to concentrate on the content and meaning of a message, became more problem oriented, and were less concerned about imposing controls on each other's behavior.

METHOD

The spiral reinforcement model of the dynamics of trust (Figure 2) has been presented to establish a theoretical rationale for the methods used to induce different levels of trust, but this study did not focus on a test of the spiral reinforcement model. The aim of this study was to examine the relation between trust and problem-solving effectiveness as formulated in the eight hypotheses.

To test the hypotheses derived from the model, the research was designed so that half of the experimental groups started work on a business-management

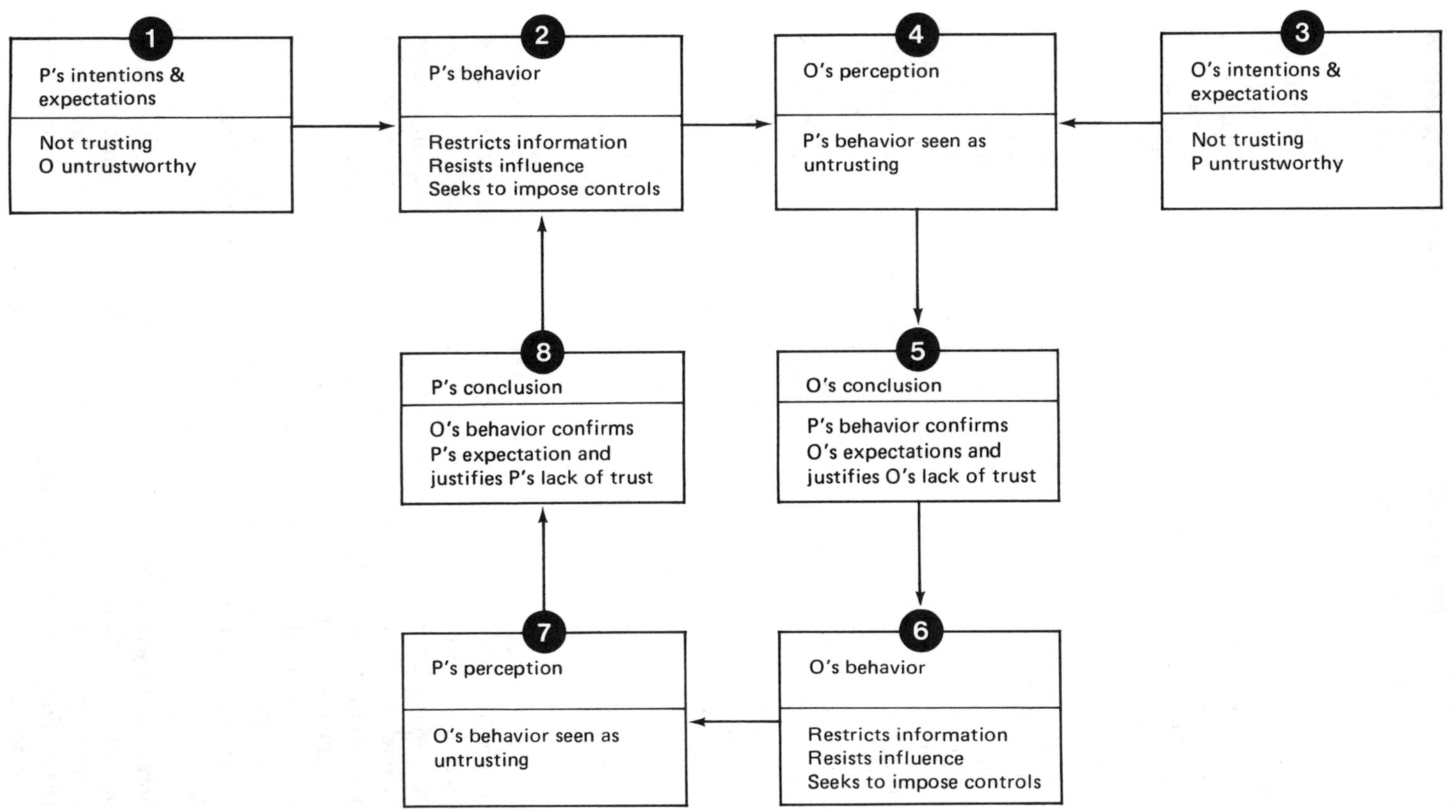

FIGURE 2. **A model of the interaction of two persons with similar intentions and expectations regarding trust**

problem with a mental set toward low trust and half with a mental set toward high trust. Mental set, as used here, includes intentions as to one's behavior, expectations as to the behavior of others, feelings such as anxiety or discomfort, and cognitive frame used to interpret events and form perceptions. In this research trust was not examined as a personality variable; that is, an element of individual character, but as an induced attitude, one that the individual could alter in a situation in which he was led to intend and to expect trust (or mistrust) from others as he attempted to solve a problem. Because trust as a personality trait was not relevant, and to avoid alerting the subjects to the issue of trust, no prior measures were taken of the subjects' attitude toward trust.

Subjects. Because of their high potential for top management, upper-middle managers from all functions and product divisions of a large, international electronics company were periodically selected by their superiors, after discussion with the corporate personnel staff, to attend an off-site, four week, in-residence program in management development given several times a year that accepted sixteen managers at a time. Eight managers in each program, were randomly chosen to be subjects and distributed into two problem-solving groups, each with four members. The remaining eight managers were observers; each was randomly assigned to a group with four members and each group observed one problem-solving group. Data were gathered in eight programs providing a total of sixty-four subjects in sixteen problem-solving groups and fifty-nine observers (five programs were short one manager) in sixteen observing groups. There were no subordinates, superiors, or peers from the same department or division in any program. Interviews confirmed that the subjects and the observers did not know about the experiment, which was designed as a learning event embedded in the program.

Problem. The central problems involved (1) developing a strategy to increase short-term profits without undermining long-term growth of a medium-sized electronics company with very low return on investment, outdated manufacturing facilities, whose labor force had been cut 25 percent and whose top management personnel had been changed and reorganized two years before, and (2) obtaining commitment to implement such a program despite strong managerial disappointment because expectations of immediate investment for expansion and modernization would not be met. The situation, a variation of one described by Maier *et al.* (1959), involved four executive roles: president and vice presidents for marketing, manufacturing, and personnel. Subjects were randomly assigned to the roles.

Procedure. All subjects and observers were given a written description of the production, marketing, financial, and personnel difficulties of the company.

In the presence of the observers, subjects were told they were to conduct a meeting lasting thirty minutes in the president's office to make appropriate management decisions. Ostensibly, they were to demonstrate their decision-making competence to their fellow managers, the observers.

Each subject was then given an additional written statement with factual and attitudinal information relevant to his function. He had no knowledge of the role information given to other subjects. The subjects privately read and absorbed this problem information for twenty-five minutes so there would be minimal need to refer to it during the meeting.

Treatments. Subjects were randomly assigned to one of two group conditions: an entering mental set toward high or low trust.

The factual data about production, marketing, finance, and so on was identical in both conditions, and all vice presidents were led to expect that the president would announce approval of a long-studied plant expansion.

In both conditions the president's statement told him that on the preceding day, he had received an ultimatum from the board of directors demanding an increase in profits within one year or else he would be forced to resign. Furthermore, he was told that expansion was not feasible because it would reduce short-term profits, take more than a year to build and start up a new plant, and the board was not likely to approve the financing, so as a first step toward increasing profits, he would have to announce his decision against expansion. The vice presidents had no knowledge of the president's dilemma when they started their thirty-minute problem-solving meeting.

Induction of Conditions of Trust. The induction of the two levels of trust was accomplished by operating on the following entering beliefs of subjects: (1) the task competence of others, (2) norms on introducing information and new ideas, (3) norms on attempts to influence managers outside of one's primary responsibility, (4) likelihood that others would abuse trusting behavior, and (5) competitiveness or collaborativeness for rewards.

In a high-trust group, a manager's entering mental set toward trust was shaped by the following paragraph, which followed the factual information in the role statement:

> You have learned from your experiences during the past two years that you can trust the other members of top management. You and the other top managers openly express your differences and your feelings of encouragement or of disappointment. You and the others share all relevant information and freely explore ideas and feelings that may be in or out of your defined responsibility. The result has been a high level of give and take and mutual confidence in each other's support and ability.

Subjects in low-trust groups had a similar paragraph in their role information, but worded to induce a decrease in trust.

The reward system was operated on by information placed only in the president's statement. In the high-trust condition, the president was led to see his relation to his vice presidents as collaborative. His role statement said that "although the Board's decision considered you specifically, since you appointed the current top management team it is likely that the Board will go outside for a successor and possibly other vice presidents."

In the low-trust condition the president was led to see his relation to his vice presidents as potentially competitive. His role statement said that since the board's ultimatum pertained to him, it was possible that they might appoint one of the vice presidents as his successor. The vice presidents in both conditions were given no information about whether their relation to the president was potentially competitive or collaborative.

All subjects were told that "whenever information is incomplete, introduce whatever facts and experiences seem reasonable under the circumstances."

Observers. In addition to reading the written general description of the company's problems, before observing the problem-solving meeting, the observers were told of the vice presidents' factual basis for seeking and expecting to get final approval for plant expansion and that the president had received a one-year ultimatum from the board the preceding day, but they were given no information about the attitudinal parts of the statements.

Measures. After thirty minutes, group discussion was stopped and each subject and observer completed a questionnaire with eight or nine items. The respondent was to indicate whether in his group, or the group he observed, there was "much" or "little" of the property described in each item.

The items were: (1) trust, (2) openness about feelings, (3) clarification of the group's basic problems and goals, (4) search for alternative courses of action, (5) mutual influence on outcomes, (6) satisfaction with the meeting, (7) motivation to implement decisions, (8) closeness as a management team as a result of the meeting. The subjects' questionnaire had a ninth item: "As a result of this meeting would you give little or much serious consideration to a position with another company?" The written statement could only suggest to each subject an entering mental set toward high or low trust. By the end of the meeting each subject's level of trust would depend on the extent to which his entering beliefs were confirmed by the behavior of the other managers.

RESULTS

Measures of Trust. The responses of subjects and of observers are reported separately in Table 1, with the chi-square value for each item.

The subjects' rating of level of trust confirms that the induction of high and low trust was successful ($p < .001$) after one-half hour of problem discussion. This result, although not a direct test of the spiral reinforcement model, does offer support for it.

Since the observers used only their personal standards for their ratings, it is noteworthy that they had little difficulty recognizing the behavior indicative of low or high trust ($p < .001$).

The hypotheses about differences between groups with high or low trust were confirmed by the responses of the subjects (items 2-9, $p < .001$) and observers (items 3-9, $p < .001$; item 2, $p < .05$).

Qualitative Differences. There were also observable qualitative differences in the comprehensiveness and creativity of the problem solving of the two groups.

High-Trust Groups. In the high-trust groups the president consistently disclosed voluntarily the board's demand for better short-term performance. These

TABLE 1. **Frequency of Response to Each Item by Subjects and Observers Under High Trust and Low Trust with Chi-Square Values for Differences.**

		Subjects			*Observers*		
		Condition			*Condition*		
Item	*Response*	*High trust*	*Low trust*	x^2*	*High trust*	*Low trust*	x^2**
1. Trust	Much	30	9	28.1	19	7	16.7
	Little	2	23		6	26	
2. Openness about feelings	Much	31	15	26.4	15	12	4.2
	Little	1	17		7	21	
3. Clarification of problems and goals	Much	24	10	10.8	18	7	12.9
	Little	8	22		8	26	
4. Search	Much	21	6	13.8	11	5	14.7
	Little	11	26		11	28	
5. Influence	Much	29	6	30.8	19	2	32.0
	Little	3	26		6	31	
6. Satisfaction	Much	28	7	25.6	20	2	32.7
	Little	4	25		6	31	
7. Motivation to implement conclusions	Much	30	10	26.6	19	4	22.2
	Little	2	22		7	29	
8. Closeness as a team	Much	27	9	19.1	17	5	16.6
	Little	5	23		9	28	
9. Desire to take a job in another company	Much	8	22	10.8			
	Little	24	10				

*$p < .001$ for all x^2 values in this column.
**$p < .001$ for all x^2 values in this column except item 2 for which $p < .05$.

teams, after initial frustration with the disapproval of immediate expansion, dealt with the short-range plans to increase profitability and then began to design long-range plans for modernization and expansion that they would present to the board.

Short-range plans emerging from the discussion among the vice presidents included straightforward proposals to review the product line, to identify and promote sales of high-profit items, and to cut back output of low-profit items. Their more creative proposals, flowing from substantial changes in their perceptions, included, for example, leasing space in a nearby vacant plant, rearranging work flow, selectively modernizing equipment that would provide greatest cost benefits and require minimal capital, subcontracting standard components, and rapidly converting two new products from research to production. In one group the managers agreed to invest their personal savings to help finance modernization, to show the board their strong commitment to the company's future.

Low-Trust Groups. In low-trust groups, the vice presidents had difficulty understanding the basis for the president's decision against expansion and his desire for short-range profits. In several groups they asked him if there were reasons behind his decision other than those he had disclosed, but he steadfastly refused to reveal information about the board's demands. As a result the vice presidents in low-trust groups could not sense how close the company might be to reorganization and possibly dissolution. They spent most of the meeting disagreeing with the president by repeating their basic arguments for immediate expansion. Finally, after prolonged frustration, the president would impose directives on the group. Usually he would demand review of the product line to eliminate low-profit items. If there was any creativity it came from the president, who was desperately seeking a solution in spite of the resistance of his vice presidents. Occasionally, the president would propose that it might be possible to lease space in a nearby vacant plant, but his idea would be discarded as unworkable by the belligerent vice presidents. In several groups the president threatened to dismiss a vice president.

Conversation among subjects of the low-trust groups after they had answered the questionnaire, showed the high defensiveness and antagonism they had induced in each other. For example, half the vice presidents said that they were so discouraged they had started to think of looking for another job in the middle of the meeting, and several said they hoped the president's plane would be hijacked or crash. The president usually retorted that he had decided to dismiss them before the next meeting.

Discussion. One might contend that the managers were attempting to follow rigidly the attitude toward trust suggested in their briefing, but in the debriefing interviews, the managers said that after their meeting had started, their level of trust varied in response to the behavior of the other managers. In low-trust groups, for example, about half of the vice presidents said that by the end of the meeting they found themselves trusting one or another vice president more than they expected to and trusting the president much less than when they had started.

That the pattern of spiral reinforcement requires all members of a group to hold similar intentions to trust (or not trust) may be too stringent a condition. The following anecdotal evidence suggests that several members with similar intentions may be sufficient. An unanticipated incident illustrates how difficult it may be for one person acting alone to break the reinforcement pattern even though he has formal power. In one low-trust group, in an effort to behave with trust toward his vice presidents, the president early in the meeting disclosed that the board wanted better profit performance in one year or else might ask for his resignation, but this attempt to show trust did not alter the emergence of low-trust behavior among the vice presidents. Indeed, in interviews after the meeting, the vice presidents said they interpreted the president's statement as a means of shifting blame to the board for his decision not to approve expansion, so that instead of increasing their trust, his behavior confirmed their mistrust. Also, they interpreted the president's comment that he might be forced to resign as evidence that the board did not trust him, so they should not either. Two vice presidents in this group said that by the middle of the meeting they were thinking about how they might hasten the president's resignation. It seems that behaving with high trust towards others who are not trusting will not necessarily induce trust, and if one does so it is wise to limit one's increase in vulnerability.

Another illustration of the difficulty of interrupting the spiral reinforcement pattern occurred in a high-trust group, in which the president did not reveal the board's demand for short-term profits. The vice presidents said that the president seemed troubled, and asked him if he was explaining all the reasons behind his decision not to expand. In the debriefing interviews, after they learned about the president's predicament, one vice president turned to the president and said "Why didn't you tell us? We could have done so much more to help you and ourselves." The group's level of trust had remained high, but the creativity and comprehensiveness of its solutions had suffered in comparison with other high trust groups.

Because of the many limitations of the experiment—that is, the small number of subjects, data gathered over several years, the study conducted within the context of a management development program—the study was restricted to conditions in which all managers in a group had the same initial level of trust. The condition of mixed trust, in which some members would tend to trust and others would tend to mistrust, was not included; but one could predict that the effects on creativity and comprehensiveness of solutions, and on motivations to implement solutions might be intermediate between those of the high-trust and low-trust groups. The two incidents described above are consistent with such a prediction.

Furthermore the problem used in this study was quite complex, required that the participants generate the alternatives, and had no unique, optimal solution. There might be less of a difference in the output of high-trust and low-trust groups working on highly structured problems; that is, problems with clear, tangible goals, with well-defined information, with alternatives provided, and with a unique solution. Theoretically, the structure inherent in the problem might reduce a group's susceptibility to the social uncertainty generated by low-trust behavior. On the basis of the data in Table 1, however, it would seem that, given similar member competence, groups that develop high trust would solve problems more effectively than low-trust groups, that is, they would do better in locating relevant information, in using their members' skills to generate alternatives, and in eliciting commitment.

The data also indicate that patterns of low-trust and high-trust group behavior are recognizable by untrained observers. Possibly the consistency between the responses of subjects and observers was increased by the fact that they were all managers in one company, presumably exposed to a common organizational culture, but any such effect was probably offset by the fact that they came from widely separated divisions, and some were foreign nationals who had worked in overseas subsidiaries.

Finally, this study revealed that theory and research on group forces have had only a minor impact on the thinking of managers. The managers in this study were among the best educated and the most sophisticated to be found in corporate organizations. After completing the questionnaires, but without any information about the trust model, they were brought together and asked for their explanation of what had happened in the two groups. They consistently responded that the outcomes were the result of the personalities of the men (who had been randomly assigned to the different roles) or the president's style (which they interpreted as autocratic or democratic) or the time he stated his decision not to expand (early or late in the meeting). The possibility that a shared level of trust, that is, a group force or a belief held by several or all members of a group, could constitute a social reality which could significantly affect problem-solving effectiveness was not mentioned.

CONCLUSIONS

The findings of this study confirm the hypotheses derived from the model. The results indicate that it is useful to conceptualize trust as behavior that conveys appropriate information, permits mutuality of influence, encourages self-control, and avoids abuse of the vulnerability of others.

It appears that when a group works on a problem, there are two concerns: one is the problem itself, the second is how the members relate to each other to work on the problem. Apparently in low-trust groups, interpersonal relationships interfere with and distort perceptions of the problem. Energy and creativity are diverted from finding comprehensive, realistic solutions, and members use the problem as an instrument to minimize their vulnerability. In contrast, in high-trust groups there is less socially generated uncertainty and problems are solved more effectively.

This study also offers qualitative support for the spiral-reinforcement model. It suggests that mutual trust or mistrust, among members of a group, are likely to be reinforced, unless there is marked or prolonged disconfirming behavior. Exactly what disconfirmation is needed and how much requires further investigation.

Finally, this research offers evidence that a social phenomenon, trust, can significantly alter managerial problem-solving effectiveness.

Dale E. Zand is a professor of management in the Graduate School of Business Administration at New York University.

REFERENCES

Baldwin, Alfred L., Joan Kalhorn, and Fay Hoffman Breese
1945 "Patterns of parent behavior." Psychological Monograph, 58, 268, pp. 1-75.

Blake, Robert R., and Jane S. Mouton
1964 The Managerial Grid. Houston: Gulf Publishing.

Bradford, Leland P., Jack R. Gibb, and Kenneth D. Benne
1964 T-Group Theory and Laboratory Method. New York: John Wiley.

Deutsch, Morton
1962 "Cooperation and trust: some theoretical notes." In Marshall R. Jones (ed.), Nebraska Symposium on Motivation. Lincoln, Nebraska: University of Nebraska Press, pp. 275-319.

Dunnette, Marvin D., and John P. Campbell
1968 "Laboratory education: impact on people and organizations." Industrial Relations, 8, 1, pp. 1-27.

Fiedler, Fred E.
1953 "Quantitative studies on the role of therapists' feelings toward

their patients." In Orval H. Mawrer (ed.), Psychotherapy: Theory and Research. New York: Ronald Press, Ch. 12.

Gibb, Jack R.
1961 "Defense level and influence potential in small groups." In Luigi Petrillo and Bernard M. Bass (eds.), Leadership and Interpersonal Behavior. New York: Holt, Rinehart Winston, pp. 66-81.
1964 "Climate for trust formation." In Leland P. Bradford, Jack R. Gibb and Kenneth D. Benne (eds.), T-Group Theory and Laboratory Method. New York: John Wiley, pp. 179-301.

House, R. J.
1967 "T-group education and leadership effectiveness: a review of the empiric literature and a critical evaluation." Personnel Psychology, 20, 1, pp. 1-32.

Maier, Norman R. F., Allen R. Solem, and Ayesha A. Maier
1959 Supervisory and Executive Development. New York: John Wiley, pp. 308-315.

Meadow, Arnold S., Sidney J. Parnes, and Hayne Reese
1959 "Influence of brainstorming instructions and problem sequence on creative problem-solving tests." Journal of Applied Psychology, 43, pp. 413-416.

Parloff, Morris B., and Joseph H. Handlon
1966 "The influence of criticalness on creative problem solving dyads." Psychiatry, 29, pp. 17-27.

Rogers, Carl R.
1961 On Becoming A Person. Boston: Houghton Mifflin, pp. 39-58.

Seeman, Julius
1954 "Counselor judgments of therapeutic process and outcome." In Carl R. Rogers and Rosalind F. Dymond (eds.), Psychotherapy and Personality Change. Chicago: University of Chicago Press, Ch. 7.

Schein, Edgar H., and Warren G. Bennis
1965 Personal and Organizational Change Through Group Methods. New York: John Wiley.

Walter R. Nord

GROUPS AND ORGANIZATIONS: SOME CONCLUDING THOUGHTS

The preceding selections demonstrate that groups have powerful effects on individuals and hence on organizations. Groups have become an increasingly important vehicle of management. Rather than seeking to resist groups, as previous theorists did, current management scholars stress the utilization of groups. In fact, Likert (1967) has viewed management as a highly group-oriented process. He has argued that groups of people are required for the performance of many tasks and that these task groups, superimposed on organizational charts, should be the vehicles for coordination and decision making. Likert and many other behavioral scientists see the effective utilization of groups as a necessary condition for organizational success.

The group-centered view of management runs counter to cultural bias in favor of the individual. Furthermore, the lack of group leadership and problem-solving skills in our society has generated negative attitudes toward groups as decision-making instruments. Fortunately, knowledge about the nature of group decisions, the behavior of groups, and strategies for the effective use of groups has been expanded by recent research.

THE QUALITY OF GROUP DECISIONS

The issue of group vs. individual decisions is very complex, and the evidence is mixed. Kelley and Thibaut (1969) reviewed the literature in depth and formulated several hypotheses. They stressed that their conclusions should not be viewed as established facts, since often the amount of supporting evidence was small and outweighed conflicting data by only a small margin.

First, Kelley and Thibaut suggested that success in problem-solving by groups depends on the characteristics of the problem undertaken. In general, both very difficult and very easy problems are better handled by individuals, but problems of moderate difficulty are more effectively solved by groups.

Second, Kelley and Thibaut noted that group discussions usually generate pressures toward uniformity. Numerous studies have shown that individuals can

This article is an update of the article that appeared in the original edition of this volume.

be influenced by group pressure to make inaccurate judgments. However, whether pressures towards conformity in a decision-making group are, on balance, dysfunctional cannot be discerned from those results. Successful pressures for uniformity may be useful if they are exerted by the most competent group members on each decision. Thus, while individual opinions contributing to a group decision tend to be more uniform than those leading to aggregated individual decisions, the consequences in terms of effectiveness will vary from group to group and from decision to decision.

Third, groups tend to act more slowly than individuals. Kelley and Thibaut observed that most often groups require more time to solve a problem than individuals. However, even when groups act faster, the total output/man-hour is apt to be considerably less for groups than for individuals.

Fourth, groups suffer from the fact that *inter*personal coordination tends to be more difficult to accomplish than is *intra*personal coordination. While this statement is clearly true for physical or motor tasks, Kelley and Thibaut noted that it is also true for such complex mental tasks as designing crossword puzzles.

Fifth, groups need to develop organization, and this takes time. In other words, over a period of time groups tend to become relatively more effective.

Sixth, a number of studies have confirmed the finding that groups tend to make decisions involving more risk than do individuals. This finding has interesting implications for organizations. Kelley and Thibaut suggested that the dynamics of this shift toward more risk taking may be the result of a diffusion of responsibility and a "rhetorical advantage" inherent in the English language, favoring those who advocate the more risky position.[1]

Finally, there is the question of how individual member motivation is influenced by group conditions. Much evidence indicates that under a wide variety of conditions participation in decision making increases a member's understanding of the decision and commitment to it. The group decision may then be more likely to result in appropriate action than the decision made by experts[2] not personally responsible for implementation.

Like so many issues in organizational behavior, the relevant question is not an "either-or" one; rather the issue is better seen as: Which method of decision making is more useful for particular purposes under a certain set of circumstances? A variety of factors which influence the effectiveness of group decision making, including the environment, the nature of the task, the people, and the organization, have been investigated. From the organization's viewpoint, the question can be treated only in systems terms, not in absolute terms. Attempts at group decision making may be ineffective for a variety of reasons. In some cases group decision efforts may fail because the formal leader is not able or willing to accept

[1] The "risky-shift" phenomenon is coming under attack. For example, Belovicz and Finch (1971) suggest that the shift may be an artifact of one particular type of measuring instrument.

[2] Certainly the degree of expertise is a limiting condition. A minimum level of competence is required on the part of at least some of the group members if the group is to make effective decisions.

group decisions for psychological reasons. Both task and social-emotional factors play central roles in effective organizational decisions.

GROUP DYNAMICS AND SUCCESS

Effective management of modern organizations demands attention to both task and emotional needs. Certainly, the growing use of T-groups, teambuilding, and related training experiences is oriented in this direction. Such special training can enhance both the objective quality of decisions and the psychological involvement of group members in the decision, the organization, and the group itself. Effective groups are apt to be those whose members are able to recognize and control the social forces which affect its dynamics, so that these forces work to increase rather than inhibit task performance. In other words, effective groups require both leaders and members who are aware of the psychological processes in a group and who are able to deal with them to satisfy both emotional and task needs.

Usually groups devote most of their conscious effort toward the accomplishment of their tasks. They concentrate on the development of goals, action plans, procedures for making decisions, the assignment of specific tasks to individuals, and the evaluation of performance. Considerably less attention is given to the socio-emotional or maintenance issues, which according to Bennis, Berlew, Schein, and Steele (1973) are concerned with the relationship itself. They wrote,

> . . . these issues most often have to do with tensions that result from either just being together or from trying to do a task. They can be characterized by such questions as: How close or distant, are the partners with each other, and how do they want to be? How do the members *feel* about each other? How shall hostility and other *disruptive feelings* be handled in the relationship? . . . How will *evaluations* of one another be handled? (p. 380)

Often the maintenance issues determine whether a group will be successful or not. Group members who mistrust each other, who feel treated unfairly, or who are uncomfortable with how their efforts are being evaluated or how decisions are being arrived at will not be motivated to help the group achieve its objectives. They will be unlikely to contribute fully to the group's decision-making process and cannot be counted on to do their best to implement any decision that has been made. Argyris (1964) provided a case in point. He noted,

> For example, in some situations . . . mathematicians and engineers dealing with highly technical issues developed strong emotional attachments to these issues. During discussions held to resolve technical, rational issues, the emotional involvements tended to block understanding. Since the men did not tend to deal with emotions their inhibiting effects were never explored. On the contrary, they were covered up by the use of technical, rational arguments. Since these arguments were attempts by people to defend themselves or attack others, there was a tendency for the rationality of the arguments to be weak. This, in turn, troubled the receiver of the argument, who tended to attack obvious rational flaws immediately. The attack tended to increase the degree of threat experienced by the first person and he became even more defensive . . . . (pp. 106-7)

Improved capabilities to manage the social-psychological processes of groups are needed. The Rosenberg model presented earlier and Schein's (1969) and Walton's (1969) informative books are helpful for the development of these skills.

Instrumental relationships. The groups of most interest to organizational behaviorists and managers are instrumental groups, those whose ultimate function is the performance of a task. Some instrumental groups are more effective than others. Often, differences in effectiveness are due to factors other than intergroup differences in the competence of group members. In particular, the social-emotional climate of a group (Schutz's "interpersonal underworld") is known to have an important effect on the group's ability to accomplish its tasks.

Bennis, Berlew, Schein, and Steele (1973) developed a scheme that can help the manager to understand and improve the climate of an instrumental group. They began with the assumption that the personal orientation of the members toward each other and the attitude of the members toward attainment of the group's goal affect the climate of any group. The personal orientation of the parties toward each other may vary from friendly to antagonistic. The orientation of the participants with respect to goal-attainment may be either cooperative or competitive. The orientation is cooperative when ". . . the effort of each member is seen as collaborative and useful to the other . . ." (p. 376). The orientation is competitive when ". . . the attainment of goals by one member is seen as a threat to the goal attainment of the other" (p. 376). Combinations of these two sets of feelings yield four possible group climates:

1. friendly cooperation
2. antagonistic competition
3. friendly competition
4. antagonistic cooperation

The results of these four climates are quite different. In friendly cooperation the individuals generally have positive feelings toward each other and view their interaction as necessary for achieving a common goal. Such a climate is conducive to effective performance. Not only do the individuals share a strong commitment to achievement of the task, but their friendly orientation reflects liking, respect, and trust of each other. These feelings help the participants to deal with the interpersonal conflicts that often arise when highly motivated people are working together.

In contrast, the psychological condition of antagonistic competition is conducive to failure. Each person feels that he is in a win-lose situation; if his goals are to be accomplished, the goals of the other person cannot be. Moreover, the individuals involved are apt to mistrust and not care for each other. Such feelings make it difficult for the individuals to deal with the interpersonal tensions that inevitably arise as people work together. Moreover, the individuals are not motivated to help each other, since helping the other person can be damaging to oneself. In short, participants do not communicate well about either the task or the social-emotional aspects of the group's process.

In the two climates discussed so far, the personal orientation of the parties toward each other and their attitudes toward the goals are mutually consistent. The motivation to cooperate is consistent with feelings of friendliness; similarly, competitive orientation is consistent with an antagonistic orientation toward competitors. By contrast, the two other climates involve mixed or inconsistent feelings.

In friendly competition the individuals have a positive orientation toward each other but are often competing with each other. Bennis *et al.* used the example of two Nobel laureate physicists, Lee and Yang, to illustrate this point. Each of these scientists sustained interest in his work by racing with the other to arrive at his own solutions.[3]

The fourth type of instrumental relationship, antagonistic cooperation, is often found in organizations. Frequently people who have negative personal orientations toward one another are forced to share their resources to achieve a common goal. This climate is conducive to strong feelings of frustration. Individual participants are highly committed to achieving the same goal and perceive themselves as needing the resources of the other individuals involved. However, the low degree of trust and the strong negative feelings of the parties toward each other make it difficult for them to work together. The group's ability to accomplish the task is subverted by the fact that its members are unable to deal with and to resolve conflicts that all groups experience in working on a task. Underlying their interaction are many "sensitive issues" relative to interpersonal relationships within the group that the members avoid discussing for fear that such intense conflict would result that the group could not function at all.

Bennis *et al.* summarized the practical implication of the different types of instrumental relationships well. They wrote,

> There is a clear trend toward "the rich get richer and the poor get poorer." In Friendly Cooperation where tensions and difficulties tend to be lower than [in] the other three, the tendencies are toward freer discussion of both task and maintenance. Conversely in Antagonistic Cooperation, for instance, a good deal of tension is generated by the process of working together, and the situation is loaded against dealing with it, thus allowing the problems to build, making it still more difficult to share information and so on. (p. 383)

This quotation illustrates the need for managers to understand the processes we have discussed so far in this chapter. Each individual brings his or her own perceptions, motivations, personalities, and interpersonal styles into the organization. As these individuals work together on different tasks, the interaction of the various aspects of their personalities creates climates and "interpersonal underworlds" that often determine the ability of each group to accomplish its tasks. Successful leaders are able to manage this interpersonal underworld so that it facilitates rather than inhibits group performance. The papers in this sec-

[3] Of course, in many ways the Bennis *et al.* model is an oversimplification. Often individuals who are cooperating on some things are competing on others. For example, consider two managers working on a project under one supervisor. They are cooperating to get the job done but also competing for approval and positive evaluations from the boss.

tion on group dynamics, interpersonal behavior, and interpersonal trust revealed some of the determinants of the structure of this interpersonal underworld. The earlier section on communication and the section on leadership that follows provide suggestions for management of the interpersonal underworld in such a way that both the rich and the poor get richer.

Groups which support individuality. Much modern writing on groups has seen them as functional, necessary, inevitable, but costly to individual growth. While it is recognized that social approval and peer relations are important for the stability and identity of individuals, both advocates and critics of groups emphasize that to attain the approval of one's peers one must often sacrifice the expression of individuality and conform to group norms. Benne (1961), however, explored the possibility that groups could be developed to reward nonconformity and innovation.

He argued that the pressures for conformity need not suppress individuality. Citing his own experiences in sensitivity-training groups, he proposed that under some circumstances interpersonal relationships enhance individuality and freedom. For example, an environment can be created that will help members move beyond the traditional mode of stereotyping each other. In this climate people can explore and examine the social and psychological forces which often seem so powerful that they control our behavior. Benne leaves us with the provocative challenge to provide ways of using authority and peer-group relations to promote individual freedom and growth as well as group and organizational goals. The establishment of groups and organizations which support individual growth requires an understanding of group processes. Additional insights can be acquired through an exploration of the topic of leadership, to which we now turn.

REFERENCES

Argyris, C. *Integrating the Individual and the Organization.* New York: John Wiley & Sons, 1964.

Belovicz, M., and Finch, F. "A Critical Analysis for the 'Risky Shift' Phenomenon." *Organizational Behavior and Human Performance* 6 (1971): 150-68.

Benne, K. D. "The Use of Fraternity." *Daedalus: Journal of the American Academy of Arts and Sciences* (1961): 233-46.

Bennis, W. G.; Berlew, D. E.; Schein, E. H.; and Steele, F. I., eds. *Interpersonal Dynamics,* 3rd ed. Homewood, Ill.: Dorsey, 1973.

Kelley, H. H., and Thibaut, J. W. "Group Problem Solving." In *The Handbook of Social Psychology,* edited by G. Lindzey and E. Aronson. 2nd ed. vol. 4. Reading, Mass.: Addison-Wesley, 1969. pp. 1-101.

Likert, R. *The Human Organization: Its Management and Value.* New York: McGraw-Hill Book Co., 1967.

Schein, E. H. *Process Consultation: Its Role in Organizational Development.* Reading, Mass.: Addison-Wesley, 1969.

Walton, R. E. *Interpersonal Peacemaking: Confrontations and Third-Party Consultation.* Reading, Mass.: Addison-Wesley, 1969.

chapter **14**

Leadership

Although systematic investigations of leadership are relatively new, Gross (1964) pointed out that since ancient times writers of all persuasions have sought to advise leaders of better methods to conduct affairs. Particularly influential in the past were such writers as Confucius, Plato, Aristotle, contributors to the Bible, and Machiavelli, who collectively admonished leaders to be wise, bold, good, willing to compromise, unscrupulous and well-advised. More recently, advice has been contributed by representatives of various schools of thought about formal organizations—the "scientific management," classical, and human-relations schools. Currently psychologists, sociologists, political scientists, and business academicians and practitioners all contribute theories, principles, and even "how-to" books for leadership.

Their advice has found an eager audience. As we mentioned earlier, many practicing managers expect communication and motivation to resolve organizational problems. Perhaps an equally large number expect to find the panacea in leadership. This state of buyer readiness and the willingness of writers to supply ready answers have combined to generate a number of fads in management. Strategies which succeeded under one set of circumstances have been applied uncritically to other situations for which they were not as well suited. Costly failures have resulted. Recently, substantial controversy and more critical thinking have developed about both the role of leadership and the desired type of leadership for organizations.

F. W. Taylor and the classical theorists provide a convenient starting point for the study of leadership in modern organizations. We have already mentioned that these writers tended to focus advice on the design of tasks and the structuring of organizations, assuming relatively passive responses by lower-level participants.[1] After publication of the Hawthorne studies, lower-level people could no longer be viewed as passive, but attention was still given to leadership. Since then, managers have been increasingly encouraged to consider the effect of leadership strategies on the organization as a social-psychological system.

1. In the classical literature the writing of Mary Parker Follett was a major exception to this view.

SOME LEADERSHIP ISSUES

What Is Leadership?

Although there is no general agreement on the precise meaning of the term, Gibb (1969a) offered a definition which encompasses many of the ideas put forth by others. He refers to leadership as the influence of one person on another. Since this influence is often felt by several people, we could say that leaders are those members of a group who most significantly influence the group. If influence is the mark of a leader, then formal authority over a group is neither necessary nor sufficient for leadership. The formal head of a group is not a leader if he does not significantly influence the other members, and the actual leader need not occupy a position of formal authority.[2] Also, it is clear that leadership is not just a social position or a set of personality traits; it is a form of social interaction.

Leadership Style

How should a leader behave? This frequently asked question has received a variety of answers, generally falling into two categories and suggesting a false dichotomy; a manager should be concerned either with structure or with human relations. For many practitioners and consultants the search for the "one best way" of leadership continues; leader behavior is seen as either good or bad in relation to some particular set of assumptions or theories, the validity of which is often questionable.

A leadership study conducted in the late 1930s by Lewin and his colleagues and reported by Lippitt and White (1958) served to direct attention to "democratic" leadership as a viable management strategy. This experiment investigated the effects of authoritarian, democratic, and laissez-faire leadership on the functioning of children's groups. The most important findings were those concerning differences between the authoritarian and democratic groups. In comparison with democratic leadership, authoritarian leadership produced groups which tended to be more submissive and dependent on the leader, to be characterized by more aggressive and domineering relationships among the group members, to have less group unity, to engage in less work-minded conversation, to be less constructive in work activity in the absence of the leader, and to become more disrupted by frustrating situations. This study, generally taken to show the superiority of democratic leadership over authoritarian leadership, has stimulated much research and is important in the history of the controversy highlighted by the selection by Dubin in this section. Much of this controversy concerns the design and interpretation of research, but hidden in the debates are important value issues as well.

Americans often perceive dictatorial or authoritarian political systems as a threat to their values and way of life. Some respond to this threat by seeing

2. As French and Raven noted (1959), there are at least five bases of power, of which formal or legitimate authority is only one.

democratic leadership as good and authoritarian leadership as bad, without recognizing that authoritarian leadership within an organization may be quite unrelated to authoritarian political systems. The issue is also influenced by questions of strength and rights. Often a democratic leader may be labeled weak or a move toward more participation by lower-level participants may be seen as a challenge to the legitimate rights of managers.

The issue of authoritarian vs. democratic leadership is beginning to fade, and an awareness is growing that leadership is a relative phenomenon. Many variables interact to influence what will be a successful leadership pattern in any particular situation. In fact, in many cases different styles of leadership may be unrelated to differences in performance.

The Contribution of Leadership to Performance

No one has precisely measured how important leadership is for the accomplishment of group and organizational goals. While much conflict in the published literature exists over leadership styles, considerably less can be found over the more basic issue—whether differences in leadership style are very important. To some degree this controversy is implicit in differences in what theorists take as problematic in their work. For example, Katz and Kahn (1966) pointed out that some people, such as McGregor and Likert, view leadership as the primary determinant of organizational performance. On the other hand, March and Simon's (1958) highly regarded book on organizations contains no mention of leadership in either the table of contents or the index.

Two authors have treated the issue of the importance of leadership style directly. Homans (1965) argued that behavior of the first-line supervisor may have relatively little effect on the productivity of the work group; he noted that technology and work methods are far more important factors. Nevertheless, the behavior of top management may be of great importance. Thus, the magnitude of the effect of leadership styles varies throughout the organizational hierarchy. Perrow (1970) labeled the idea that leadership is the answer to organizational problems an "important prejudice." He argued that, while leadership may be an influential variable, it is certainly not the most significant and in fact may be viewed as a dependent rather than an independent variable. Dubin, in the selection which follows, maintains that the magnitude of the effects of different leadership styles is a function of the type of technology.

Personality vs. Situational Factors

In spite of a great deal of research, few if any personality traits have been shown to be consistently related to leadership. Gibb (1969b) made several important observations about the role of personality traits in leadership. First, some traits have been found more consistently among leaders than among nonleaders. However, these traits are neither necessary nor sufficient conditions for leadership; rather their contribution to leadership is influenced by how well they meet the needs of the group in a particular situation. To quote Gibb,

> The traits of leadership are any or all of these personality traits which, in *any particular situation,* enable an individual to (1) contribute significantly to group locomotion in the direction of a recognized goal and (2) be perceived as doing so by fellow group members. Second, there is abundant evidence that member personalities do make a difference to group performance, and there is every reason to believe that they do affect that aspect of the group's behavior to which the leadership concept applies. (p. 227)

While no traits can be viewed as universal determinants of leadership, many studies have shown that such characteristics as dominance, intelligence, self-confidence, and empathy or interpersonal sensitivity often contribute to leadership.

Gibb (1969b) noted four possible explanations for the relatively limited relationship that has been found between personality and leadership. First, the existing devices for personality measurements are inadequate. Second, since leadership itself is a complex pattern of roles, characterized by much inconsistency, no specific traits are universally required. Third, since the groups whose leadership has been studied have differed widely from each other, some of the effects of personality which may occur in more similar groups may have been concealed. Finally, situational factors may be so powerful as to override personality variables. These last two explanations suggest that leadership must be viewed in the context of a particular group of people at a particular time. The needs of group members are central in the determination of what type of individual behavior will influence the group.

Leaders—People Who Meet Group Needs

In sharp contrast to the view that leaders are people who control the group is the position that leaders are people who function to serve the needs of the group for his or her influence. Only if the members perceive that their needs will be met if they follow a particular person will that person be influential. This be met if they follow a particular person will that person be influential. This idea is often called the functional view of leadership.

The functional approach supports the notion that groups exist to meet the needs of their members. Leaders are just group members who are especially helpful in meeting certain needs important to the group. Considerable research is consistent with this view.

One early study, by Merei (1949), demonstrated that groups can limit the power of "leaders" who do not meet the needs and expectations of members. For this research children who were rated by teachers as being leaders were separated from the rest of their peers. The remaining children were divided into groups and allowed to play together for several periods. Then one leader was introduced into each of these groups, and the leader's influence on the group was observed. The results showed that a group which had a tradition of playing together was stronger than the leader. Leaders from the normal situation generally were not able to influence the new groups unless they took into account the group norms and practices which had developed. This study is important because it showed that leadership is influenced by group norms and group values. Again, leadership is not a set of traits but is an interaction of people under certain conditions. Previous group history is one relevant condition.

Other support for the functional view of leadership comes from Hamblin's (1958) study on the effect of a crisis upon leadership. Hamblin observed groups engaged in a complex task. After having learned the rules, some of the groups were exposed to a crisis situation; the rules under which the task could be performed were radically changed. During the crisis leadership in the group was affected in two ways. The group members were far more willing to follow a strong leader, and leaders who did not respond rapidly and decisively to the crisis were rejected and replaced by others.

Perhaps the clearest demonstration of the functional nature of leadership has come from Bales (1958), who specified classes of behavior which appeared to be necessary for satisfactory group performance. Members who provided this behavior to the group tended to be influential. In observing discussion groups, which had no formal leader, Bales discovered that he could classify the behavior of influential group members into 12 categories, which could then be grouped into three characteristics: "activity," "task ability," and "likeability." Different leaders exhibited contrasting combinations of the categories. In Bales's view an individual whose behavior strongly shows all three characteristics corresponds to the traditional leader, the "great man." An individual who demonstrates a great deal of activity and task ability may be termed a task specialist. An individual who is active but is most concerned with social-emotional matters is generally ranked high on likeability and is called a social specialist. The task and social specialists each seem to display behaviors which satisfy a set of needs felt by group members—desires to get the job accomplished and to manage social tensions and feelings. The "great man," of course, is able to meet both sets of needs. Since the "great man" is relatively rare, there are often two or more leaders in a group.

The functional nature of the leadership role is demonstrated by changes in the group's preference for various types of leadership behavior. For example, early in the history of a task group, members tend to be interested in getting on with the job; accordingly, they support and approve the behavior of the task specialist. Later, however, interpersonal tensions often appear, and the behavior of the social specialist becomes more desired and approved. In general, groups appear to have two sets of needs, and individuals whose behavior functions to satisfy them tend to become leaders.

Considerable research supports this two-factor view. For example, the work of Fleishman, which is treated in detail by Dubin, distinguished between "initiation of structure" (task orientation) and "consideration" (social-emotional orientation). Similarly, *The Managerial Grid* developed by Blake and Mouton (1964) was composed of the dimensions of "concern for production" and "concern for people." A great deal of current management training and thinking rests on an assumption of the dual nature of group needs and hence leadership.

A corollary of this two-factor view of leadership and groups is the idea that, if groups do have these two sets of needs. then successful groups are apt to be those which satisfy both sets. Tensions arising from any unresolved needs are apt to interfere with the group's progress toward satisfaction of its other needs. For example, unresolved hostility in a group can prevent rational discussions of tasks.

A NEW ROLE FOR LEADERS IN ORGANIZATIONS

Increasingly, many leaders appear to be required to stimulate, facilitate, and utilize group resources rather than to plan, direct, and control. The resources of group members are more relevant for a problem than those of the formal leader. The advice of the classical theorists, so widely accepted in our society, provides inadequate guidelines for meeting these new demands.

A major problem for leadership in the future may well be a conflict between the cultural definition of a leader and the actual requirements of many leadership roles. For example, leaders are commonly thought to be the most competent, the strongest, the most aggressive, and the most intelligent people in a group. As tasks of managers increasingly require the coordination of the efforts of experts, a person with the foregoing characteristics is apt to be less successful than in the past. In many cases, the leader may best act as a facilitator of intragroup communication and an agent who helps the group use its own resources. Directing and controlling produce dependence on the director and inhibit the communication needed for the group to best use its own resources. The work of Maier (1967) has made these general points well.

Maier argued that in many situations the leader contributes most to a group task not by presenting ideas but by enhancing the group's ability to generate its own ideas. In this case the leadership function is one of clarifying, supporting novel ideas which might otherwise be rejected prematurely, reflecting, and helping to integrate. Such a leader must be aware of group dynamics and skillful in helping the group to move in constructive directions. In many ways, leadership behavior of management and professional groups should resemble the behavior of a facilitator more than that of a director.

In general, different organizational situations require different leadership behavior. A successful leader is aware of the wide spectrum of relevant variables and is able to help the group to achieve organizational goals. Organizational leadership is as complex as organizations themselves.

TOWARD A RESOLUTION OF THE ISSUES

In general, much of the literature documents the trend toward seeing leadership as closely related to group behavior and individual needs. The dominant view of leadership in organizational behavior appears to emphasize social and psychological factors far more than structural and task factors. This trend contrasts sharply with the "scientific" and classical management positions. The emphasis given to a concern for people in the writings of Likert and McGregor is now widely shared in the thoughts of both students and practitioners of management. McMurry (1958) and others, however, have argued that this concern for people has been oversold in the quest for more "democratic" leadership.

The selections which follow center on the effects on performance of different styles of leadership. The first selection, by Dubin, reviews and evaluates the literature on democratic or group-centered leadership. He presents the major findings of important research but challenges their relevance for many supervisory jobs. In many cases variability in output is almost exclusively a function of technological factors rather than of human motivation. Dubin's article is followed by a selection prepared by the editor which reconsiders the issues raised by Dubin and others and provides a bridge to the other papers in this chapter.

REFERENCES

Bales, R. F. "Task Roles and Social Roles in Problem-Solving Groups." In *Readings in Social Psychology.* 3rd ed., edited by E. E. Maccoby, T. M. Newcomb, and E. L. Hartley. New York: Holt, Rinehart & Winston, 1958. pp. 437-47.

Blake, R. R., and Mouton, J. S. *The Managerial Grid.* Houston: Gulf Publishing Co., 1964.

French, J. R., and Raven, B. H. "The Bases of Social Power." In *Studies in Social Power,* edited by D. Cartright. Ann Arbor, Mich.: Institute for Social Research, 1959. Pp. 150-67.

Gibb, C. A. *Leadership.* Baltimore: Penguin Books, Inc., 1969a.

_____ "Leadership." In *The Handbook of Social Psychology.* 2nd ed., vol. 4, edited by G. Lindzey and E. Aronson. Reading, Mass.: Addison-Wesley, 1969b. pp. 205-82.

Gross, B. *The Managing of Organizations.* vol. 1. New York: The Free Press, 1964.

Hamblin, R. L. "Leadership and Crisis." *Sociometry* 21 (1958): 322-35.

Homans, G. C. "Effort, Supervision, and Productivity." In *Leadership and Productivity,* edited by R. Dubin, G. C. Homans, F. C. Mann, and D. C. Miller. San Francisco: Chandler Publishing Co., 1965. pp. 51-67.

Katz, D., and Kahn, R. L. *The Social Psychology of Organizations.* New York: John Wiley & Sons, 1966.

Likert, R. *The Human Organization: Its Management and Value.* New York: McGraw-Hill Book Co., 1967.

Lippitt, R., and White, R. K. "An Experimental Study of Leadership and Group Life." In *Readings in Social Psychology.* 3rd ed., edited by E. E. Maccoby, T. M. Newcomb, and E. L. Hartley. New York: Holt, Rinehart & Winston, 1958. pp. 496-511.

Maier, N. R. F. "Assets and Liabilities in Group Problem Solving: The Need for an Integrative Function." *Psychological Review* 74 (1967): 239-49.

March, J. G., and Simon, H. A. *Organizations.* New York: John Wiley & Sons, 1958.

McMurry, R. N. "The Case for Benevolent Autocracy." *Harvard Business Review* 36 (1958): 82-90.

Merei, F. "Group Leadership and Institutionalization." *Human Relations* 2 (1949): 23-39.

Perrow, C. *Organizational Analysis: A Sociological View.* Belmont, Calif.: Wadsworth Publishing Co., Inc., 1970.

Robert Dubin

SUPERVISION AND PRODUCTIVITY: EMPIRICAL FINDINGS AND THEORETICAL CONSIDERATIONS

TECHNOLOGY, SUPERVISION AND PRODUCTIVITY

The most notable consequence of advances in technology . . . is the man-hour productivity increases with transfer of labor operations from men to machines. In the United States, for example, over-all man-hour productivity has risen about three percent per year, at least since World War I, and probably had increased at an even higher annual rate from the turn of the century until then. Increases in man-hour productivity have been largely the consequence of the efficiency built into machines, a major fact to keep in mind when considering productivity and the influences that bear upon it.

Technology and Management Structure

Only recently has there been reborn an interest in the core feature of the modern industrial world—the technologies upon which it is grounded. Social scientists and management theorists have been preoccupied for several decades with "human problems" and human relations in work organizations. A recent analysis could discover fewer than three dozen research studies in the American, British, French, and German literature empirically dealing with social aspects of the man-machine relationship.[1] This paucity is a harsh commentary on the neglect of technology during the current preoccupation with the psyche of man in industry.

The idea that special technologies have associated with them variations in the structure and function of management is a recent notion that has challenged traditional managerial thinking. Research by Joan Woodward[2] on British

From Robert Dubin "Supervision and Productivity: Empirical Findings and Theoretical Considerations". In Robert Dubin, George Homans, Floyd C. Mann, Robert Miller, *Leadership in Productivity: Some Facts of Industrial Life* pp. 10-50. Reprinted by permission of Chandler Publishing Company,©1965.

[1] See the study by Martin Meissner, "Behavioral Adaptations to Industrial Technology" (unpublished Ph.D. dissertation, Dept. of Sociology, University of Oregon, 1963).

[2] Joan Woodward, *Management and Technology* (London: Her Majesty's Stationery Office, 1958).

industry has emphasized the importance of technology in structuring management. Woodward's small monograph, *Management and Technology,* has precipitated lively controversy since its publication in 1958.

Woodward classified approximately 100 English firms according to a simple feature of the technology characterizing their production. She distinguished (1) those firms that produced goods in small batches or in units, from (2) the large-batch and mass-production firms and both of these from (3) companies employing continuous-process production. Among the 24 small-batch and unit-production firms, she found that the median number of levels of management authority was only 3, with a range from 2 to 4. . . Among the 31 mass-production firms, the median number of levels of management authority was 4; the range was from 3 to 8 or more, with 13 of the 31 firms having 5 or more levels of authority as contrasted with none among the unit-production firms. In the 25 companies employing continuous-process technologies, the median number of levels of management was 6, with but 2 firms having only 4 levels of authority; the rest had 5 or more, and 10 had 7 or more.

Thus, on the simple feature of levels of authority in the firm, it became clear that the production technology was a determinant of managerial structure. Technology made a difference in the structure of management in spite of a high level of communication between and among the managerial groups in Great Britain, and certainly in the South East Essex area where the study was made. Furthermore, British management practice has been strongly influenced by British management theorists, particularly Lyndall Urwick, which could result in great similarities in the structure of management in spite of technological differences among the companies. The fact that there is such marked technological impact on the structure of management leads one to believe that the technology of an industry is an essential influence structuring management and also, at least by inference, the functions and character of supervision.

A closer look at the system of supervision in terms of span of control and ratio of managers and supervisors to workers likewise reveals the technological factor dominant. Woodward found that for the unit-production companies, the median span of control (number of persons controlled) by first-line supervision was between 21 and 30. The median span rose to between 41 and 50 in mass-production industries. In process-production companies, however, the median span of control of first-line supervisors was lowest, between 11 and 20 workers. Furthermore, the distribution of companies according to their span of control, for each type of technology, was characteristically different. . .

Turning to the ratio of managers and supervisors to other personnel, the impact of technology is also significant. . . The ratio of managers and supervisory staff to other personnel is lowest in unit-production and highest in continuous-process industries, with mass-production industries falling in between. The differences are very sharp. In continuous-process production the ratio of managers and supervisors to other personnel is between 1 to 7 and 1 to 8, whereas in unit production the ratio ranges from 1 to 24 to as low as 1 to 49. In mass production, the ratio ranges from 1 to 14 through 1 to 18. It should be noted that the ratio of management personnel to workers is little affected by size of firm for mass-production and continuous-process technologies. With a unit-production technology there are more workers per supervisor for firms with about 1000 employees than for either smaller or larger firms, but regardless of company size, fewer managers and supervisors are required for unit-production technologies than for mass-production or continuous-process technologies. The simple measure of the ratio of managers and supervisors to other personnel is clearly related to the technology employed in the industry and is relatively little influenced by the size of the firm.

Technology and Responsibility

Some implications of the impact of technology on the location of responsibility for production are interesting to examine. In continuous-process industries like oil and gas manufacture, the high ratio of managers and supervisors to other personnel is probably a consequence of: (1) the potentiality of an error causing substantial loss in the process should it go on unattended and unnoticed, and (2) the resultant concentration in the ranks of managers and supervisors of inspection and control functions with respect to the technological process. Thus, with high-speed and continuous-process technologies the direct control of technology itself is transferred from operatives to management. (A similar transfer is characteristic of data-processing operations, where control of machines becomes critical, especially in programming the machines, and many of the control and surveillance functions in monitoring quality and quantity of output are transferred from worker level to management.)

As technology in the future tends toward continuous-process manufacture, there will be a shift of control of product quality and quantity from workers to supervisory and managerial personnel. The supervisor will become more immediately involved in the control of output than he is at present. The manager of the machine in continuous-process technologies is no longer primarily the supervisor of people but rather the supervisor of the technology.

On the other hand, in unit production where the time dimension for the production of the unit of output is relatively long, and where the individual is likely to be involved in the production of substantial subassemblies or of the entire product, the control of actual output and quality can be maintained at the worker-operator level. Relatively high levels of skills may be required at the worker level; skills including not only the technical performance of work operations, but also some knowledge about correction of operating errors, inspection, and control. Where the control functions reside in the hands of the worker, the need for supervision is reduced. Woodward's study confirms the consequence, which is a low ratio of managers and supervisors to workers.

The analog to worker-centered responsibility is to be found in the industrial research laboratory, where typically there is unit production (the individual research project), and where there is "colleague authority" in Marcson's sense.[3] Colleague authority means reference to peers rather than to research managers of problems requiring decision. Much is made in the supervision of research

[3] Simon Marcson, op. cit. [*The Scientist in American Industry* (Princeton: Industrial Relations Section, Princeton University, 1958]

activities of the need for maximizing colleague authority and the individual scientist's control of quantity and quality of production. The fact is, however, as Woodward's data show, that the opportunity for fixing production responsibility at the worker level exists alike in manual operations and in scientific and intellectual operations, providing the manual operations involve *unit-production technologies.*[4] The supervisory problems of maintaining quantity and quality of output are the same for highly technical people in research and development activities and for workers in unit-production industrial operations.

Technology and Managerial Costs

There are several secondary productivity consequences of variations in supervisory staffing in relation to technology. The simple per worker costs of supervision are considerably less in unit production than in continuous-process production, with mass production midway position between these two. Insofar as management is counted as an indirect cost of production, unit-production systems save money, all other things being equal.

Commitment to the organization on the part of workers and the skill necessary to make the commitment effective in high-quality work vary with the nature of technology. In continuous-process production, commitment may be minimal since supervisors and managers assume the burden of being sure the technological processes are performed adequately. Commitment must presumably be much higher in unit production, since those same responsibilities devolve directly on the worker.

Considerable "cost" may be impressed into the production process if inappropriate supervisory styles are applied under given technological conditions. If close supervision is used in unit production, it may fail or be inefficient. "Democratic" supervision in continuous-process production may prove extremely costly where errors are made in the process operations.

Another way of looking at one of the consequences of the impact of technology on supervision is to note that unit-production technologies have the most "flat" managerial structure and also the fewest managers and supervisors in relation to other personnel. Thus, the total number of managers and the complexity of the managerial structure are both minimal in unit production. On the other extreme, in process production, the number of authority levels in management is highest and the ratio of managers and supervisors to other personnel is also highest. In going from unit production to continuous-process production (mass production lying between unit and continuous production) there is a shift toward the total management component in staffing the enterprise, with more levels of managers and more managers per worker. Management of managers and supervisors, as distinct from management of workers, becomes a critical problem in continuous-process industries. In the area

[4] A recent popular article by Vance Packard described two instances where worker-centered responsibility was effective, and in both cases a unit-production technology was employed. See "A Chance for Everyone to Grow," *Reader's Digest* 83 (November 1963): 114-18.

of managing managers we have minimal knowledge and a great deal of speculation.[5]

There is a high probability that it will become increasingly difficult to view the costs of management as "overhead" or "indirect" in continuous-process technologies because so much of the total manpower investment will be in the managerial component. Managers carry relatively high unit prices. The sheer size of the managerial payroll will surely have an impact on production-cost analyses and may bring the development of new ideas regarding the costliness of managers in production.

In passing, mention may be made of other organizational variables that affect complexity of managerial structure. Organizational centralization and decentralization and the structures that flow from them also produce variations in supervisory practices. The technological variable is not the only one that affects managerial practices, and, either directly or indirectly, the productivity of workers.

SUPERVISORS AND GROUP ATMOSPHERES

The question put at the beginning of this chapter implies: What atmospheres created by supervisors affect productivity of their subordinates?

This problem has been approached polemically and with relatively inadequate research. It is useful to begin with a statement of one view of the supervisor's role in creating a working-group atmosphere.

Maier[6] observed: "We are entering a period in work relations where mental cruelty is becoming an appropriate charge in a grievance committee meeting as it is in the divorce court."[7] Specifically, self-determination of behavior is more acceptable than determination by others: "It is apparent that a person accepts his own decisions more often than he does another's. Group decisions are more readily accepted, but may sacrifice quality."[8] Nevertheless: "When production is a matter of coordination of group activity, it can be increased by stimulating the group to decide on a goal. In such cases the goal set should be unanimously approved. . . Group decision thus becomes an extremely important factor in determining the performance of a team of workers."[9]

Maier's thinking starts with the mental well-being or psychic comfort of the worker and concludes that somehow or other this is positively related to production. The argument is a very tenuous one and it may be accurate. However, the evidence is meager and when marshaled gives weak support to the conclusion. Participation in decisions about own behavior does not necessarily lead to maximizing own behavior to achieve organizational objectives, with a payoff in mental comfort. Even the evidence of the quality of group decisions

[5] One of the early students of this problem was Melville Dalton. See his "Managing the Managers," *Human Organization* 14 (1955) 4-10.

[6] Norman R. F. Maier, *Psychology in Industry* 2nd ed. (Boston: Houghton Mifflin Company, 1955).

[7] Ibid., p. 137.

[8] Ibid., p. 141.

[9] Ibid., pp. 151-52.

calls into serious doubt the effectiveness of groups in making production decisions. For example, the original work by Taylor[10] made clear that even in the number of ideas produced in group discourse while "brainstorming" the group output was measurably less than individual output under similar circumstances.

Drucker[11] has pointed out that the trend in modern industrial work emphasizes individual jobs as well as group or team jobs. He noted that many maintenance jobs are individual jobs and that these will increase in number with increasing automation of industry. Furthermore, many sales jobs are individual jobs, and these will also increase in number as secondary economic activity provides an increasing proportion of employment opportunities. An important corrective to current emphasis on the "groupness" of industrial work is to realize that there are now and will probably be an increasing proportion of all jobs which will *not* be performed in groups but will be performed individually and outside of group contexts. For individual jobs, the group theory of motivation simply will not apply and new studies will be necessary to find out how the lone worker can be moved to a high level of productivity and sustained there as a member of a modern work organization. This area is one of present ignorance among industrial psychologists and sociologists as well as among management practitioners.

Superior-Subordinate Interaction

A more analytical reading of the group-dynamics literature was presented by Arensberg and Tootel, who drew the following conclusions:

> But the Mayoites seem to have misread their own data. Reanalysis shows that their "teamwork" and "informal organization" are less multifactorial results, or even steady states, than emergent results of prior and continuous managerial and flow-of-work changes. The process took the form of this definite order of development: (1) an increase of managerial initiative, (2) followed by an increase of inter-worker communication, (3) followed by an increase of redressive up-the-line action of the worker upon foreman or spokesman, (4) which resulted in further changes of rewarding sorts in managerial actions, (5) changing individual attitudes, (6) reaching expression as group attitudes or morale (the "norms" of Homans), (7) which won informal sanction by the workers on one another, (8) and stimulated further releases of individual output and productivity.[12]

Arensberg and Tootel go on to state: "It is worthwhile reiterating the discovery of the 'interactionists' that this process, and the gain in productivity it brings about, seems to have *very delicate and narrow limits.*[13] Their summary is worthy of note:

[10] D. W. Taylor, P. C. Berry, and C. H. Block, "Does Group Participation When Using Brainstorming Facilitate or Inhibit Creative Thinking," *Administrative Science Quarterly* 3 (1958): 23-47.

[11] Peter Drucker, *The Practice of Management* (New York: Harper and Bros., 1951).

[12] Conrad M. Arensberg and Geoffrey Tootel, "Plant Sociology: Real Discoveries and New Problems," in Mirra Komarovsky (ed.), *Common Frontiers in the Social Sciences* (Glencoe: Free Press, 1957), p. 316.

[13] Ibid.

Indeed, present evidence suggests that the release of productivity is not so much limited by human capacity or by "diminishing returns" of maximization, as older efficiency doctrines have it, as it is dependent upon some "feedback" between worker initiative and managerial facilitation. The next advance in our understanding will come when we work out the empirical characteristics of this process.[14]

At a later point in their paper, Arensberg and Tootel conclude with:

. . . the finding that the process of the social release of productivity, in the empirical studies so far made, is not a matter of offering rewards alone . . . We must remember that a plant is not only a place of performance tests and output scores. It is a power situation where a lesser-powered group is performing a test imposed and surveyed by a higher. Even if the management with consummate skill were to use all the goals of its employees there is both theoretical and empirical reason to doubt that the human "contented cows" stay contented under continuous driving. A "strain" is likely to develop.

. . . If, however, for any reason the cumulative process of change . . . which we are discussing, gets under way, a different outcome may ensue. In that case, such a process might move the relevant social system comprising the two groups *toward* some "fusion" so that a common system of shared values might develop about the performance in question.[15]

The statement starts with "the release of productivity" and ends with a "common system of shared values." These are two different things. It still remains to be proved that the shared values are always or ever goals apropos of productivity. This distinction has been recognized by Bakke in his discussion of the "fusion process."[16]

Shared Goals

Perhaps the best single piece of empirical evidence bearing on the issue of a shared goal as the stimulus to high-level group effort is found in the celebrated "Robbers Cave Experiment."[17] Two groups of boys in a boy's camp achieved fusion in the solution of a common problem, after they had been deliberately placed in antagonism to each other, only when they realized that the continuous flow of behavior in each group depended on overcoming this mutual problem. The groups were driven into each other's arms and into cooperation by the need jointly to solve a problem bigger than each could handle separately. Thus, fusion was achieved between two antagonistic groups in overcoming a common obstacle.

It is worth emphasizing that there is a difference between (1) maintaining steady states in a social system and (2) the reaction of the social system to

[14] Ibid., p. 317.

[15] Ibid., p. 332.

[16] E. Wight Bakke, *The Fusion Process* (New Haven: Yale Labor and Management Center, 1953).

[17] Muzafer Sherif, *Intergroup Conflict and Cooperation: The Robbers Cave Experiment* (Norman, Okla.: University Book Exchange, 1961).

blockages or obstacles against the normal flow of activities. Empirical evidence does indicate that "fusion" can develop among diverse groups in overcoming obstacles that they face in common. Such evidence appears in Sherif's studies and in the earlier studies of Kurt Lewin, who examined the problems of group decision to achieve eating-habit changes under wartime shortages of food.[18] Sociologists have long called attention to the fact that national unity and social cohesion are usually the products either of acute crises in the social system or of attack from outside. In wars and other major social crises, many intrasocietal differences are set aside in favor of overcoming the obstacles confronting the society as a whole. Fires, floods, and other disasters in industrial establishments automatically override differences between union and management as they work together to overcome the obstacle and restore the plant to productive effectiveness. In a mine disaster, a union and its members, normally struggling against management, may temporarily set aside antagonisms in the common concern to save the men trapped underground. All these instances bear on the fact that "fusion" of groups with different goals can be achieved when they are simultaneously confronted with a common obstacle that halts the normal flow of behavior in the groups.

The maintenance of a steady state like high productivity, and the accompanying values necessary to sustain it, has not been shown to be the product of the "fusion" of diverse goals and values of the groups involved. Even the neglected and important research of Blake and Mouton[19] has dealt only with problem solving but not with steady-state maintenance.

It is not the purpose here to assert that maintenance of a steady state of high output is impossible, or that it may not be the product of a "fusion" of diverse group values. There is, however, no present empirical evidence to show that the fusion of group values is what sustains steady states in social systems. It is time to devote attention to actual measurement and analysis of this connection.

Supervisor as Environment for Workers

One of the direct consequences of Woodward's work was a study by Thurley and Hamblin[20] of five English firms. The purpose of the study was to focus attention on supervisory behaviors that could be directly associated with technological feature of the work. A number of the findings are highly significant for understanding the functions of direct supervision but are beyond the subject matter of this chapter. One technical factor affecting what the supervisor does on his job was the variability of the operations supervised. Supervisors devoted much attention to meeting schedules and to planning

[18] Kurt Lewin, *Field Theory in Social Science* (Dorwin Cartwright, ed.) (New York: Harper and Bros., 1951).

[19] Some of which is summarized in Robert R. Blake and Jane S. Mouton, "Competition, Communication, and Conformity," and "Conformity, Resistance and Conversion," both in I. A. Berg and B. M. Bass (eds.), *Conformity and Deviation* (New York: Harper & Row, Publishers 1961).

[20] K. E. Thurley and A. C. Hamblin, *The Supervisor and His Job* (London: Her Majesty's Stationery Office, 1963). Comments are based on a prepublication copy of this study.

sequences of operations as well as to overcoming blockages against continuity of product rather than producers. The supervisors also spent significant amounts of time checking machinery—in one department of an electronics company this activity reached 16 percent of the supervisors' total working time. Dealing with contingencies was another major consumer of supervisors' attention and time.

What is important here is to note that the supervisor is constantly caught up with duties focusing on plans, schedules, machines, and overcoming contingencies that interfere with meeting output expectations. In short, supervisors are supervising technical processes and machines, meeting output standards, and maintaining quality controls. People are relatively incidental and instrumental to these preoccupations, the more so as the technology approaches continuous-flow operations.

Workers, too, perceive this operating system and probably in terms not unlike those of the supervisor. Worker expectations of supervisors are molded just as much as are the behaviors of supervisors by the technical and organizational environment.

Structuring of the supervisor's work responds to technical and organizational imperatives, as will appear in the studies of Fleishman, and consideration for the worker as individual decreases as the technology becomes more complicated and the production schedule demands higher rates of continuous output.

MULTIPLE GOALS OF SUPERVISION

Supervisors are not solely oriented toward building and maintaining the productive level of those supervised. Indeed, as theorists like Maier have indicated, the mental health or psychic well-being of workers may be a coördinate goal of the efforts of supervision, along with productivity. Beside the notion of psychic well-being can be set those of morale, of loyalty, of commitment to organization, as other goals toward which supervisory practices may be directed. These all relate to the connection between employee and organization. In addition, there is an extremely large body of studies and theory dealing with such goals of supervision as maintenance of safety, reduction of employee turnover, minimization of employee grievances, reduction of scrap and other losses, quality control, and plant and equipment maintenance.

It is notable that in pursuit of this incomplete list of goals toward which supervisory behaviors are directed a vast range of activities is to be found, many of which are independent of each other. The supervisor's jobs are many and varied, and it should not be at all surprising to find numerous empirical situations in which the supervisor is little, if at all, concerned with people or with productivity. Certainly, under circumstances of complete machine pacing, for example, the variability in productivity that can be attributed to supervisory practices is probably extremely small.

Morale, feelings of well-being, attitudes toward the company, acceptance or nonacceptance of supervisors, cohesiveness of the work group, employee turnover, or grievance incidence rates are in and of themselves important subjects for study and analysis. Because, however, the major test applied by operating management to any innovations in supervisory practices is the influence these may have on productivity, the authors of studies relating supervisory practices to other outcomes often gratuitously conclude that their results support the belief that productivity will also be positively affected. It is important to keep in mind that the various goals toward which supervisory practices are directed are not necessarily interrelated.

Worker Morale as a Goal

A number of studies of supervisory behavior concern its influence on morale of workers. Almost invariably the author will conclude that if the supervisor's behavior can raise morale, then there are probably associated increases in productivity. The study may clearly demonstrate that morale does vary according to the behaviors of supervisors, but the conclusion that morale change in turn influences productivity remains unsupported. Indeed, Dubin[21] has pointed out that high morale in a work group may be the basis for successful sabotage of management's productivity goals, and Seashore[22] has shown that high-cohesion work groups may deviate from production norms on *both* the high and the low sides. Since Seashore's data also show that high-cohesion work groups tend to be high-morale groups, his findings support Dubin's conclusion.

As part of the Yale study of automobile assembly-line workers, Turner[23] showed that the attitudes of workers toward the job itself and toward their own foremen were independent. In particular, Turner found that if the job was of primary importance to the workers, then the foreman and his behaviors made relatively little difference in their orientation toward the organization. "It was as if the nature of the job and the nature of supervision, as perceived by workers, were almost separate influences on workers' over-all attitudes."[24]

Kahn, one of the principal investigators in the Michigan researches, concluded the survey of the Michigan studies of supervisors and workers as follows: "None of the major indices of satisfaction (job, supervision, company, etc.) proved either to relate to productivity or to mediate significantly between productivity and such independent variables as role differentiation, delegation, or employee orientation."[25]

Turning directly to evidence on morale, Kahn stated the following:

> This research, . . . did not provide positive evidence on the matter of morale in relation to productivity. . . . Indices of worker satisfaction were developed by means of factor analysis, which showed four well-defined dimensions of satisfaction: satisfaction with supervision, with the job itself, with the company as a whole, and with the extrinsic rewards of money, mobility, etc. None of these indices was significantly related to productivity.

[21] Robert Dubin, *The World of Work* (Englewood Cliffs, N. J.: Prentice-Hall Inc., 1958), especially Chapter 12.

[22] Stanley E. Seashore, *Group Cohesiveness in the Industrial Work Group* (Ann Arbor: Institute for Social Research, University of Michigan, 1954).

[23] Arthur N. Turner, "Foreman, Job, and Company," *Human Relations* 10 (1957): 99-112.

[24] Ibid., p. 111

[25] Robert L. Kahn, "The Prediction of Productivity," *Journal of Social Issues* 12 (1956): 41-49, 44.

In line with a statement already made in this chapter, Kahn stated: "The notion that supervision (among other things) determines satisfaction, which in turn determines productivity, has been considerably discredited in our eyes.[26]

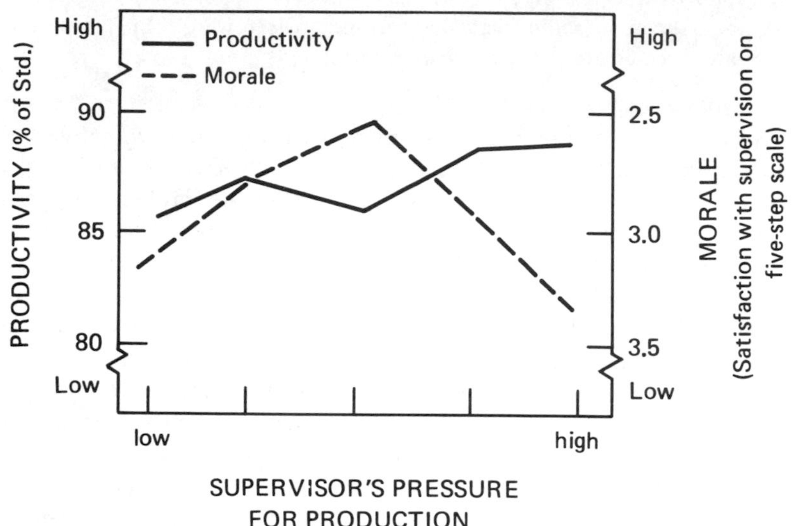

FIGURE 1. **The Relation of Productivity and Morale to Supervisor's Pressure for Production (Redrawn from Rensis Likert, "Developing Patterns in Management," cited in footnote 27.)**

Likert[27] has presented some other Michigan data which show that productivity increases with supervisor's pressure for more output (Figure 1). Morale also increases up to about the mid range of supervisory pressure for output, after which it declines, just as sharply as it increased. Thus, even the data used by one of the strongest exponents of worker autonomy shows that pressure *does* produce more productivity and even increases morale through a portion of the range of increasing supervisory pressure. This observation suggests that social systems respond to leadership pressures in "putting the heat on" and holding subordinates to high expectations. In an organized production situation, workers expect to be asked to produce and be held to reasonable levels of output. Furthermore, if the supervisory pressure is not excessive workers' morale goes up with increasing pressure!

Worker Autonomy as a Goal

Management literature is replete with a theme that worker autonomy is a viable goal for supervisory practices. Generally the worker autonomy sought is one best described as the condition wherein workers require little supervision. Sometimes autonomy is specified as the condition requiring minimum "close

[26] Ibid., from pp. 46 and 47.

[27] Rensis Likert, "Developing Patterns in Management," in American Management Association, *Strengthening Management for the New Technology* (New York: The Association, 1955).

supervision." The definition of autonomy is almost always in the supervisor-worker context. On its face, worker autonomy should be an acceptable condition for many workers, and it is obviously an aid to supervisors since it reduces their burden.

Kahn,[28] in summarizing the human-relations research program at the University of Michigan, showed that in the studies of clerical and railroad workers the high-productivity groups were supervised in a general fashion rather than in a close or detailed one. This demonstration was the beginning of the repeated emphasis in the Michigan studies, castigating close and detailed supervision and pleading for worker autonomy as one of the important requisites for high output. The idea has persisted to the present and is given renewed emphasis by Likert.[29] But the study of British industry by Argyle, Gardner, and Ciofi[30] did not demonstrate autonomy as a central variable in productivity. These data have never been incorporated into the thinking of the Michigan group.

Perhaps these disparate findings can be reconciled by noting that both railroad and clerical workers, the samples from which the Michigan group drew its conclusions, are involved in unit- or batch-production systems. Woodward's studies of technology and management show that the ratio of supervisors to workers is very low in such systems. A correlate of this low ratio, one noted earlier, is that the responsibility of individual workers may be maximal in such systems. A further correlate is that workers in unit-production technologies will produce most when given only general supervision. This relation is to be attributed to the technology rather than to a general principle that all work situations demand maximum autonomy for workers.

The study by Argyle, Gardner, and Ciofi was based on 90 foremen in eight British factories manufacturing electric motors and switchgear. These factories would all probably be classified as employing large-batch or quasi-mass production, with basic technological features different from those in the routine clerical work in a large insurance company and in the railroad gangs studied by the Michigan group. The British study revealed that the only dimension of supervisory behavior which bore a significant relationship to measured output of the departments supervised was punitive or nonpunitive correction by the foreman of worker mistakes and errors. When general supervision was combined with nonpunitive behavior and democractic relations with employees, these three dimensions of supervisor behavior were positively and significantly correlated with output, but together they accounted only for 18 percent of the variance in output.

Likert reproduced the results of one of his earliest studies in *New Patterns of*

[28] Robert L. Kahn, op. cit. in note 25.

[29] In his widely acclaimed book, *New Patterns of Management* (New York: McGraw-Hill Book Company, 1961).

[30] Michael Argyle, Godfrey Gardner, and Frank Ciofi, "The Measurement of Supervisory Methods," *Human Relations* 10 (1957):295-313, and by the same authors, "Supervisory Methods Related to Productivity, Absenteeism, and Labour Turnover," *Human Relations* 11 (1958):23-40.

Management[31] in which he compared the difference between superior and mediocre life-insurance agencies. The data show that an attitude of cooperation with his sales agents by the agency manager was found more often among managers of agencies judged superior in performance. The descriptions of the managers were based on agents' evaluations. Furthermore, these same successful managers gave considerably more autonomy to their agents than the less successful managers.

It is not surprising, in view of these results secured when he made one of his first studies of managerial behavior, that Likert would conclude that considerate, nondirective leadership characteristics symbolize modern industrial statesmanship. However, it is obvious that selling life insurance is a classical unit-production process, a one-customer-one-sale situation. Each sale is a unit by itself, typically taking place away from the office and therefore removed from the point of supervision. It would seem evident that the technology associated with selling life insurance would make autonomy of sales agents an important condition of success.

Evidence is by no means conclusive in support of the contention that worker autonomy is essential for high individual productivity. Indeed, when worker autonomy (of which general supervision instead of close supervision is the foreman facet) is combined with two other dimensions of supervisory behavior found significant in combination in the English factories, the combination still accounts for less than one-fifth of the variance in productivity. Further, there is reason to believe that worker autonomy may be relevant to batch- or unit-production technologies, but probably not to mass-production technologies and almost certainly not to continuous-process technologies.

Consideration for Workers as a Goal

Another popular goal of supervision is to develop considerate treatment of subordinates. This supervisory stance may be characterized as being employee-centered. The presumption underlying a belief in employee-centered supervision is that considerate treatment will be repaid by devoted effort and possibly higher output.

Kahn reviewed the study of two groups of employees in a large business office, the Prudential study.[32] One group was given employee-centered supervision and the other was given just the opposite. Both groups showed a significant increase in productivity. The employee-centered supervision produced an increase in favorable employee attitudes toward supervisors and the company, while the authoritarian-led group showed a marked decrease in employee satisfaction. This classic study, often cited in support of the employee-centered supervision ethic, provides data to show that employee-centeredness is *not* the critical factor that determines individual productivity. If anything, the most direct conclusion from this study is that productivity can either be forced or be encouraged with about the same outcomes with respect to output. Obviously, it is other outcomes that distinguish the two methods of supervision.

[31] Rensis Likert, op. cit. in note 27.
[32] Robert L. Kahn, op. cit. in note 25.

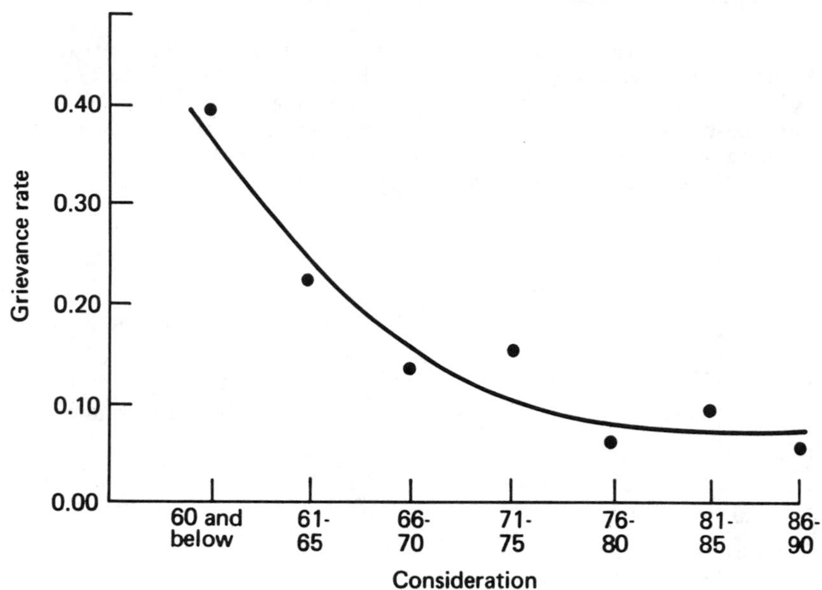

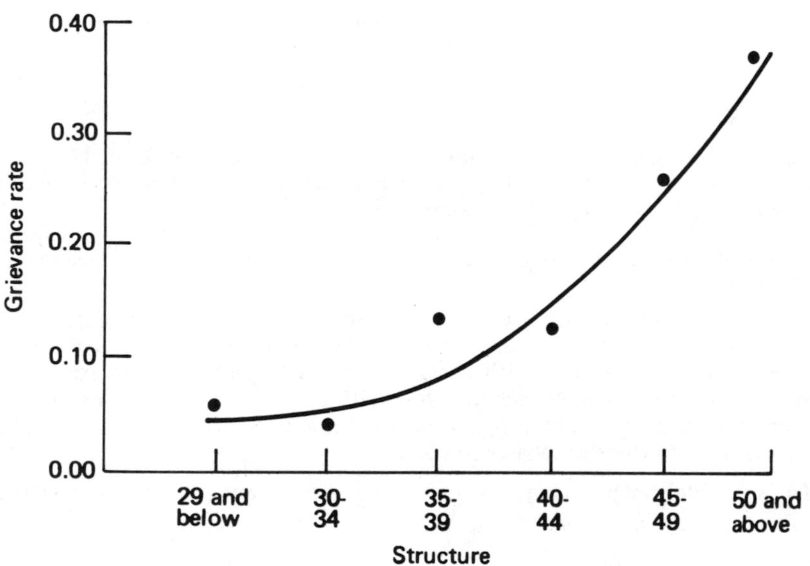

FIGURE 2 (portion). See legend on page 608.

Kahn further reported on the heavy-industry study among 20,000 workers engaged in the manufacture of tractors and earthmoving equipment:

> Like the earlier studies, the research in the tractor factory showed that the foremen with the best production records were the ones who were most skilled at and most concerned with meeting employee needs for information, support, assistance, but they were no less concerned with production . . . The foremen with the best production records, in short, were both production-centered and employee-centered.

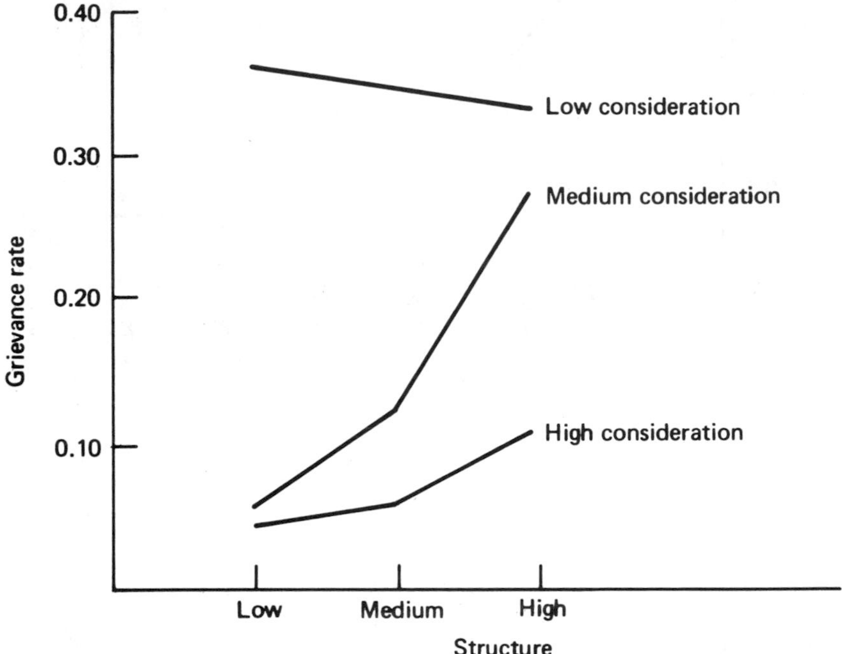

FIGURE 2. **Leadership Behavior and Grievances (Redrawn from E. A. Fleishman and E. F. Harris, "Patterns of Leadership Behavior Related to Employee Grievances and Turnover," cited in footnote 34.)**

It is especially desirable to pay attention to one of Kahn's major conclusions:

> It thus appeared that the continuum of supervisory behavior which placed employee-centeredness at one end and production-centeredness at the other was less in accord with the facts than a four-fold classification of supervisors which would include two additional types—the supervisor who combined employee and production orientation and the supervisor who gave neither of these emphases to his role.[33]

In the Fleishman, Harris study[34] of 57 foremen in a motortruck manufacturing plant, it was found that as the degree of consideration shown

[33] Ibid., pp. 44 and 45.

[34] E. A. Fleishman and E. F. Harris, "Patterns of Leadership Behavior Related to Employee Grievances and Turnover," *Personnel Psychology* 15 (1962):45-53.

toward subordinates increased the grievance rate decreased (Fig. 2). This decrease is not a straight-line relationship but is a curvilinear one. The greatest amount of decrease in the grievance rate comes as consideration increases from the lowest levels to near the mid point of consideration.

The structuring of the work relationship as measured on a scale of structuring behaviors by the foremen shows a curve in the opposite direction. The more structure imposed upon work by the supervisor the higher the grievance rate. The most marked increase in the grievance rate occurs only after the mid point in the structuring behavior of the foreman is reached.

However, when the two factors of consideration and structure are combined and related to the grievance rate, a very interesting fact emerges. When low consideration for employees is consistent, then the more structuring the behavior of the foreman the *lower* is the grievance rate. On the other hand, when high consideration for employees is shown consistently by the foreman, then the more the structuring the higher is the grievance rate. The grievance rate goes up most markedly if medium consideration is shown toward employees and structuring goes from low to high.

Employee-turnover rates have a pattern almost exactly like those of grievances when related to foreman consideration and structuring of the work situation. It is again notable that the curvilinear relationships show that the major rate of change in employee turnover occurs at the low end of the consideration scale, with a moderate degree of consideration materially reducing the turnover rate, and with further increase in consideration having no further influence in reducing turnover. Similarly, an increase in structure up to about the mid point produces no increase in turnover, but beyond the mid point it makes for a marked increase in turnover.

This study provides good evidence of the consequences of supervisory behavior for turnover and grievances; but again, it should be emphasized, neither of these have been demonstrated to be directly related to productivity. Multiple goals of supervision are illustrated here and it is demonstrated quite adequately that differences in supervisory practices will produce measurable differences in turnover and grievance behaviors of employees.

Attention is especially directed to the curvilinear relationships. To know that some structuring of work for subordinates does not induce high grievance rates among them and that they begin to grieve in material amounts only when supervisory structuring of work behavior becomes marked is quite different from thinking that the more structuring the more grievances, or the less structuring of work the fewer grievances. Yet, most of the precepts of management and supervision are couched in linear terms.

The related study by Fleishman, Harris, and Burtt[35] revealed that "... there was a clear-cut tendency for the divisions that were under the pressure of time to have foremen who were most inclined toward initiating structure and vice versa. There was also a very marked tendency for the foremen in the most demanding

[35] E. A. Fleishman, E. F. Harris and R. D. Burtt, *Leadership and Supervision in Industry* (Columbus: Ohio State University Press, 1955).

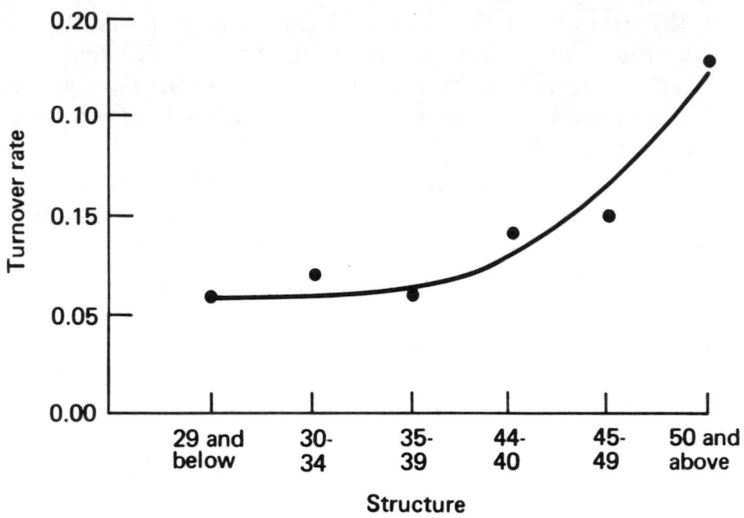

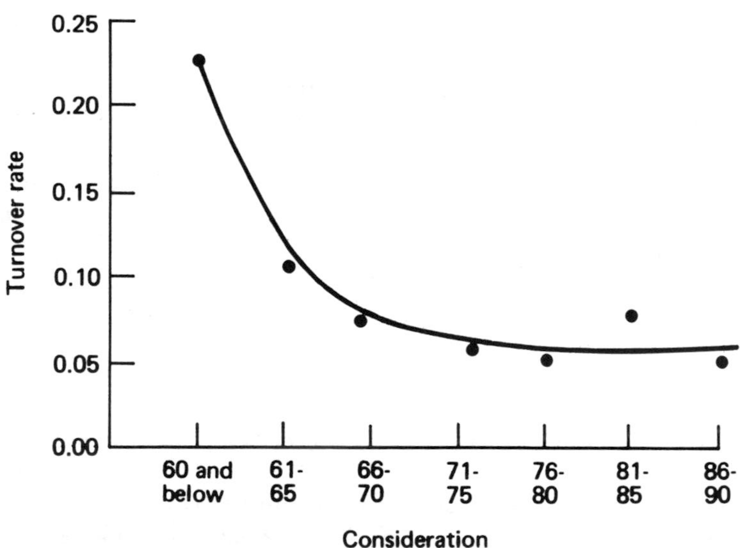

FIGURE 3. Leadership Behavior and Turnover Rates (Redrawn from E. A. Fleishman and E. F. Harris, "Patterns of Leadership Behavior Related to Employee Grievances and Turnover," cited in footnote 34.)

divisions to operate with the least consideration."[36] This is a study of the motor truck manufacturing plant of International Harvester Company, a unit-production technology in the final assembly line but one accompanied by mass-production technologies in the parts departments and in some subassembly departments. Thus, the authors' emphasis on time pressures leading to more structuring and less consideration might well give way to emphasis on the character of the technology in which little worker autonomy is needed to get the work out, hence the prevalence of supervisory structuring of work for subordinates.

The authors add: "The results go on to show that the more efficient foremen, as rated by the boss, are inclined to show more initiation Structure and less Consideration. This appears to be a function of the demandingness of the time schedule."[37]

The theme that technology affects supervisory behaviors appeared in this early study by Fleishman, Harris, and Burtt. However, neither they nor subsequent analysts recognized what Woodward later discovered. The following quotation explains:

> Results indicate that there appears to be a difference between production and nonproduction departments in the requisite kinds of leadership. [This is one way of stating the difference in this sample between mass-production and unit- or batch-production technologies in Woodward's terms.] In the nonproduction departments, the foremen who are rated most proficient by their own supervisors apparently motivate their work groups to get the job done by creating a friendly atmosphere and by considerate behavior with a minimum of emphasis on work methods, standards, and structuring of activities. [In production departments foremen play a difficult role. Their] considerate behavior is very good from the morale standpoint, but not so good for proficiency as judged by the foreman's own boss.[38]

In the Fleishman and Peters study[39] of the effectiveness of middle managers in a continuous-production operation, soap and detergent manufacture, 39 managers in the ranks between line foremen and plant managers were studied. The major conclusions are: (1) "there is an absence of relationship between leadership attitudes and rated effectiveness," and (2) "no particular combination of Structure and Consideration attitudes was predictive of effectiveness ratings."[40] Here the managers' efficiency was rated by their own superiors.

Thus, for production workers in unit and small-batch technologies, the factors of high consideration and low structure do have a bearing on rated departmental efficiency and foreman proficiency, if not on output. In mass production, efficiency and effectiveness are positively related to low consideration by the foreman and much structuring of the work situation by

[36] Ibid., p. 99.
[37] Ibid., p. 99.
[38] Ibid., p. 103-4.
[39] E. A. Fleishman and D. R. Peters, "Interpersonal Values, Leadership Attitudes and Managerial 'Success'," *Personnel Psychology* 15 (1962):127-43.
[40] Ibid., p. 136.

him. In managing middle managers, neither consideration nor structuring relates to rated efficiency of performance.

Sensitivity to Workers as a Goal

A firmly established notion stemming from the group dynamics tradition has been that supervisors who are sensitive to the needs of their subordinates have an important requisite for being effective leaders. The insensitive supervisor is presumably an ineffective leader. The idea that "sensitivity" is an essential ingredient of supervisory practice has even been incorporated into a formal training program called "sensitivity training."[41]

In a study by Nagle[42] a questionnaire was administered to supervisors to measure their sensitivity, and six plant executives rated departments as to their productivity. Then these data on 14 departments composed of office workers in a large industrial organization were correlated. It was found that there was a correlation of .82 between supervisor sensitivity and rated productivity of the department.

The meaning of "sensitivity" is variously interpreted. According to Fiedler,[43] sensitivity means the ability to discriminate clearly among subordinates on the basis of their characteristics. Thus Cleven and Fiedler,[44] in their study of steel-mill open-hearth supervisors, took note of discrimination as exercised by pit foremen and melters, the supervisors most directly involved in open-hearth operations. They found that those whose crews had good production records discriminated more sharply between the most- and the least-liked coworkers; those whose crew production records were below average discriminated less sharply.

This meaning of sensitivity, sensitivity to the differences among subordinates and the ability to use this information effectively to supervise them, may be the factor which accounts for the high correlation that Nagle found between supervisor's sensitivity and the attributed productivity of his group. The Cleven and Fiedler results were obtained in a batch-production situation and the Nagle results in a unit-production technology (office work). These are similar technologies and demand high worker autonomy. The results of the two studies may legitimately be put together to support the opinion that in such a technology sensitivity to the individual characteristics of the worker is one of the supervisor traits which is successful in getting a high level of productivity from workers. That is, the supervisor may well give different kinds of autonomy to individual workers in accord with their special personalities and other characteristics. The more successful supervisor may be the one best able to

[41] See the description of "sensitivity training" in Robert Tannenbaum, Fred Massarik, and Irving Weschler, *Leadership and Organization* (New York: McGraw-Hill Book Company 1961).

[42] B. F. Nagle, "Productivity, Employee Attitude, and Supervisor Sensitivity," *Personnel Psychology* 7 (1954):219-33.

[43] Fred E. Fiedler, *Leadership Attitudes and Group Effectiveness* (Urbana: University of Illinois Press, 1958) summarizes the several studies made by Fiedler in this area.

[44] W. A. Cleven and Fred E. Fiedler, "Interpersonal Perceptions of Open Hearth Foremen and Steel Production," *Journal of Applied Psychology* 40 (1956):312-14.

perceive these individual characteristics (discriminate them, in Fiedler's terms) in order to tailor his own actions to the individual's unique qualities.

Worker Participation as a Goal

A particularly important study in the analysis of supervisory practices was that by French and Coch,[45] in which the effects of employee participation in a decision affecting them were measured. It was concluded that those who participated in decisions regarding work changes ultimately reached somewhat higher levels of output than a comparable group of workers who were told to change their methods of work. This study has been the cornerstone of theory concluding that worker participation is desirable for efficiency reasons and improvement of output levels.

Wickert[46] studied employee turnover and feelings of ego involvement in the day-to-day operations of telephone operators and female service representatives in the Michigan Bell Telephone Company. About 700 women were studied. The principal finding was that those who stayed with the company had a greater feeling of involvement in the day-to-day operations of the company than those who left. Specifically, those who stayed tended to say (1) they had a chance to make decisions on the job, and (2) they felt they were making an important individual contribution to the success of the company. It will be noted that telephone operators and service representatives are all involved in unit production, since they each have to depend upon someone initiating a call or a service request before they go into action. Under these circumstances of technology a material degree of autonomy is probably essential in maintaining levels of output. A chance to make decisions on the job and contribute to company success are measures of participation. It might be concluded, however, that these aspects of participation in work are mediated by the need for autonomy that comes from the technology employed.

In Rice's study of the Indian weaving shed,[47] a comparison was made of production before and after a change in the organization of the work. The individual workers in the experimental weaving groups revised the production process from what had previously been a confused and relatively unstructured one. The data demonstrate that the subsequent steady state of output was markedly and significantly higher after the workers reorganized the work themselves. Furthermore, the rate of cloth damage in the weaving mill was lower than before reorganization of production.

Several comments need to be made about this study. The self-organizing productive groups increased their efficiency by about 18 percent if we take the before-reorganization figures as the base. This improvement tends to give the impression, as Rice suggests, that the self-organization of work is one means for

[45] Lester Coch and John R. P. French, Jr., "Overcoming Resistance to Change," *Human Relations* 1 (1948):512-32.

[46] F. R. Wickert, "Turnover and Employee's Feelings of Ego-Involvement," *Personnel Psychology* 4 (1951):185-97.

[47] A. K. Rice, "Productivity and Social Organization in an Indian Weaving Shed," *Human Relations* 6 (1953):297-329.

increasing efficiency considerably. But a disturbing feature of this situation also must be taken into account. The original structuring of the work situation, which continued to obtain in the nonexperimental groups in the same company, was one in which there were confused task and worker relationships, and no perceptible internal work-group structure. Thus the base from which change was measured in this study may be an instance of industrial "anarchy," or near anarchy, in which the designs of the production processes themselves were scarcely adequate.

Under these circumstances, any attention to the *organization* of work, whether management-initiated or worker-initiated, undoubtedly would have produced significant increases in productivity. Weaving, being a continuous-process production technology over short time spans, would require high structure for adequate performance. In the light of Fleishman's results it seems probable that structuring itself is what may have improved productivity in the Indian weaving shed, not worker participation. It may not, therefore, be desirable or warranted to draw the conclusion that high autonomy and participation in decisions by the Indian weavers are what really produced higher output.

Likert, in an early paper,[48] made the point that

> Available research findings indicate, therefore, that when . . . the amount of participation used is less than or very much greater than expected, an unfavorable reaction is likely to be evoked. Substantially greater amounts of participation than expected appear to exceed the skill of the subordinate to cope with it and produce a negative reaction because of the threatening nature of the situation to the subordinate. The available theory and research findings suggest that the best results obtain when the amount of participation used is somewhat greater than expected by the subordinate, but still within their capacity to respond to it effectively.

Likert had made this point as early as 1952, but it is a point that is rarely given attention by those who urge participative management as the be-all and end-all of supervisory practice.

Likert clearly argued for an optimal rather than a maximal level of participation of subordinates in decision making relative to their own destinies. That is, there is a curvilinear relation between worker participation and such consequences as output. This relation recalls Fleishman's studies of initiating structure and consideration which relate in a curvilinear fashion to turnover and absenteeism. That is to say, over part of the range of consideration and initiating structure for subordinates there is no material change in their reactions, but beyond a critical point their reactions become prompt and decisive.

The general conclusion that emerges is that employee participation is probably not linearly related but rather curvilinearly related to aspects of working behavior. Likert has pointed out that his own researches have indicated that supervisory behavior in excess of normal expectations will not be favorably accepted by subordinates. This disfavor may be particularly likely if the

[48] Rensis Likert, "Effective Supervision: An Adaptive and Relative Process," op. cit., p. 329.

supervisor invites participation beyond the subordinate's normal level of acceptance. This conclusion recalls Barnard's "zone of indifference," in which reactions of the subordinate become significant only if the supervisor exceeds the tolerance limits customarily adopted by the subordinate.[49]

Rewarding Workers as a Goal

One of the important functions of supervisors is that of rewarding subordinates. In modern industrial firms the immediate supervisor has relatively little connection with monetary rewards, except perhaps to recommend promotions and pay increases. There remains, however, a range of nonfinancial rewards that each supervisor can monitor in influencing his subordinates. Surprisingly little research has been directed at finding out what effects such rewards have.

In the interesting study by Zaleznik, Christensen, and Roethlisberger,[50] 50 industrial workers were analyzed to determine the influences of social factors on productivity. Among the major findings was the fact that individuals with high status and high status congruence (agreement between self-conception and other's perception that they are properly placed in a social system) tended to produce at the normal or expected levels of output more than they tended to deviate from "on-line" output. On the other hand, of individuals with low status and low status congruence twice as many were deviant in output as were "on-line."

In analyzing status by itself it was found that the high-status people were average in productivity and "on-line" more than they deviated, while the low-status people deviated more than they were "on-line" in output. However, when status congruence was examined by itself the relationship turned out to be nonsignificant between that and level of productivity.

The study showed that when both management and the peer group rewarded the workers, more of them produced "on-line" than were deviant by a ratio of eight to three. Similarly when management did not reward the worker but the group did, more produced "on-line" by the ratio of six to three. However, when management rewarded the individual and the group did not, or when neither rewarded, then the preponderance was deviancy by the individual from the "on-line" expectations of output. When management alone rewarded the worker, he tended to produce below norm. When neither rewarded the worker, however, he tended to produce above average.

Another way of examining the influences of the social factors on productivity is to look at the character of group membership and its impact on productivity. Those who were regular members of a group tended to produce in the ratio of 14 at the expected average to six "off-line." Those who were perceived by the group as being deviant individuals were predominantly "off-line" in output in the ratio of ten to three who were "on-line," while isolates from the group

[49] Chester I. Barnard, *The Functions of the Executive* (Cambridge, Mass.: Harvard University Press, 1938).

[50] Abe Zaleznik, Charles R. Christensen, and Fritz J. Roethlisberger, *The Motivation, Productivity, and Satisfaction of Workers* (Cambridge, Mass.: Harvard University Press, 1958).

tended to produce "off-line" in the ratio of nine to three who were "on-line." Thus, being a deviant or isolate from the work group meant that the individual would not produce at the expected norm of output. It is interesting to note that those who were deviants from the work group tended to produce higher than the norm, while those who were isolates from the work group tended to produce below standard.

These results, suggestive as they are, must be approached cautiously since the numbers on which they are based are small, there being only 45 workers in the total sample for whom full data were available. The conclusions can be treated as suggesting the following speculations.

It seems that individual productivity is influenced by (1) the location of an individual in a social group, (2) the status accorded to him by those in his social environment, and (3) the sources of social rewards coming to him. The smallness of the sample precludes any cross tabulations to isolate the impact of rewards vs. social position when these are considered simultaneously.

What seems especially notable is that individual productivity varies with social factors in the work situation that may not be within the influence range of the supervisor. Indeed, strange as it may seem, insofar as supervisors manipulate nonfinancial rewards without parallel rewards coming from the peer work group, the worker response may be output lower than the norm! This finding is significant for reinforcement theorists in the realm of industrial incentives. Complicating the reinforcement theorist's problem even further is the finding that nonreward produces output higher than normal! Maybe if we really want high productivity, the social payoffs with which we reward industrial workers should be withheld!

The study just analyzed calls attention to the importance of the working peer group as a source of reward and reinforcement of individual behavior. This importance turns attention to the characteristics of peer groups. Among those features studied that bear on productivity is peer-group cohesivesness.

Seashore's study[51] of group cohesiveness in the industrial work group showed (Fig. 4) that among low-productivity groups, worker-perceived pressure for productivity decreased as the group cohesiveness increased. When the condition of maximum group cohesiveness was approached the perceived degree of pressure for productivity went up markedly. This tendency contrasted with that in groups of high productivity, which perceived a declining degree of pressure for productivity as group cohesiveness increased.

For the low-productivity group, management pressure for productivity was perceived only if the group was highly cohesive. Thus, one of the consequences of cohesiveness in low-productivity groups is to provide the opportunity for supportive rebellion against management. This conclusion is further supported by the general summing up by Seashore: "High cohesive groups differ more frequently and in greater amount than low cohesive groups from the plant norms of productivity. These deviations are toward both high and lower productivity."[52]

[51] Stanley E. Seashore, op. cit.
[52] Ibid., p. 98.

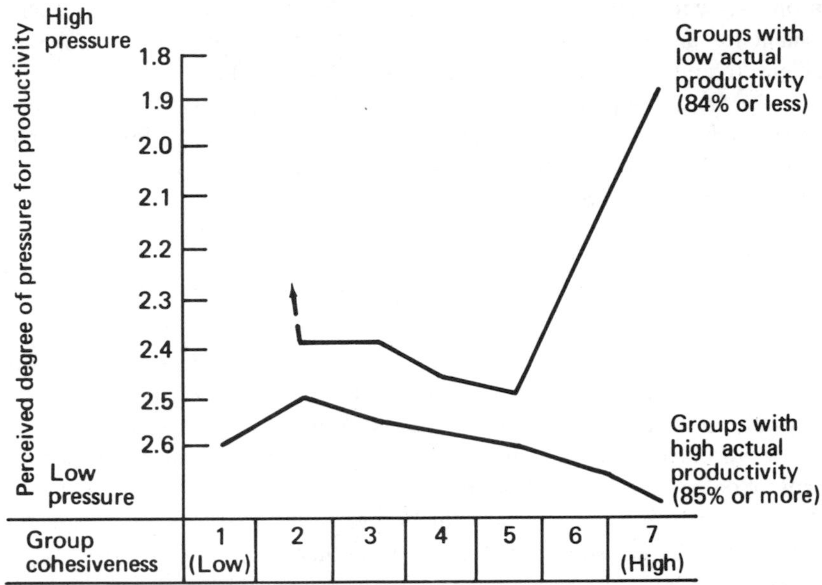

FIGURE 4. **Relationship between Group Cohesiveness and Perceived Degree of Pressure for Productivity. The measure of perceived degree of pressure for productivity is based on response to the question, "How hard do you usually have to work in order to get your work done?" A high numerical score represents relatively low pressure. (Redrawn from Stanley Seashore,** *Group Cohesiveness in the Industrial Work Group,* **cited in footnote 22.)**

CONCLUSION

Supervision does make some difference in productivity. Supervisory practices also affect other aspects of work. The details of these conclusions depart significantly from current views, and are both unique and surprising.

(1). Supervisory behavior affects the productivity of individuals by being appropriate to the work setting. One key to describing the characteristics of work settings is to know the nature of the technologies employed. The descriptive task has just begun but the results are promising. By drawing simple distinctions between unit- and mass-production technologies, and viewing continuous production as another type of technology, supervisory styles are found appropriate to each technological type. The more a production process resembles a unit or batch technology, the greater is the probability that worker autonomy and its supervisory counterpart–general rather than close supervision–will be appropriate. The more a technology resembles a continuous-production system the more appropriate will close supervision be.

(2). This first proposition leads directly to the second. There is no "one best" method of supervision. As in all human systems, there is variability in the systems of supervision of industrial and commercial work. Several styles of supervision are effective, but they are individually successful only in relation to appropriate work settings. Variety in supervisory behaviors may no longer be considered a challenge to choose the "one best" for all settings, but rather as a challenge to understand where each does or does not work.

(3). As far as empirical data take us, it seems clear that the influence of supervisory behaviors on productivity is small. The studies are few in number, however, and not adquately designed to measure magnitude of influence of supervision on productivity.

(4). Supervision of industrial and commercial work has many functions. The variety of areas in which supervisors act is the consequence of their having numerous functional contributions to make. For a given situation supervision may have relatively little to do with individual productivity, and yet supervisors, because they perform many other functions, may retain importance in work organizations. Executives must therefore constantly face the difficult problem of organizational design and the choice of operating goals for supervisors. If, for example, top management wants workers to be happy this goal may be attained by appropriate supervisory behaviors.

(5). The goals of supervision and the behaviors of supervisors are independent of each other in one sense and linked in another. A variety of goals may be assigned to supervisors, and those selected do not appear to be limited or determined by any features of organizational structure or process. Thus, consideration of workers may be emphasized in unit production, in mass production, or in process production if top management chooses consideration as a goal. Supervisory practices in each technological system will be different although directed toward the same goal. It is in this sense that the goals of supervision and the behaviors of supervisors are independent of each other.

On the other hand, goals and behaviors are linked through technology since behaviors necessary to achieve a particular goal must be appropriate to the operating situation. For example, consideration of workers in unit-production technologies may exhibit itself by providing workers with maximum opportunities to pace their own work, while in continuous-production technologies the same consideration may be most appropriately expressed as detailed concern with safety or physical comfort of the worker.

(6). It is now possible to take a sophisticated view of the impact of supervision on working behaviors. Most analysts up to this time have assumed that whatever the linkage, it tended to be a linear one. That is, a unit change in a particular supervisory behavior was assumed to produce a corresponding change in worker response throughout the range of supervisory action. This view is simply false. Many behaviors have thresholds above which the behavior is responded to by others, but below which the behaviors produce little or no effect. Thresholds were revealed, for example, in the relationship between supervisory consideration and worker responses in terms of grievances and absenteeism. This phenomenon was also discovered in the relation between opportunity to participate in decisions and worker responses to the opportunity.

(7). A supervisory practice in the low range may have one effect on worker response, but in the high range may produce exactly the opposite effect. This disparity was exhibited in the consequence of supervisory pressure for worker morale. At least in some demonstrable instances the relationship between supervisory behavior and worker response is nonlinear and may even be parabolic. Evidence supports the contention that if a little bit of a supervisory behavior may be good, a lot may be very bad indeed. This optimization notion is sometimes overlooked in the theory and practice of personnel administration.

(8). An important technological trend is making for a fundamental shift in industry from the management of people to the management of things. The detailed study of continuous-process manufacture showed the highest ratio of managers to other workers for any type of technology. It has been inferred that this high ratio reflects the need for supervisor surveillance of high-speed production processes to insure that product runs are error-free, since large numbers of defects can be produced by the time the process is halted to correct an error. As supervisors supervise machines more and people less, they will become increasingly responsible for production. Supervisory controls will not be controls on speed of output, since output will be machine or process-paced. The supervisors will be largely concerned with controlling quality, and the operating contingencies that influence the go-no-go performance of the production process.

(9). Knowledge of leadership and supervision as they affect working behavior is almost exclusively the result of studying American industrial practices. A few important English studies have been cited here, and additional studies dealing with other national economics are scattered through the literature.[53] Culture does make a difference in supervisory practices. It follows, then, that caution is necessary in applying present knowledge to cultural settings different from those in which the knowledge was gained. Generalizations may work universally, but then again they may not. We have no *a priori* reason for guessing which of these two outcomes will obtain.

(10). All the studies of human relations and supervision tell little about how much productivity is affected by individual supervisory practices. Only one study attempted to tease out the answer to this question and it suggested that not more than one-fifth of the variance in productivity can be accounted for by a combination of three supervisory practices. The Western Electric and other researches showed that fellow workers influence the individual's output. Advances in technology produce steady increases in man-hour productivity. There has never been a proper analysis of variance to assay that relative importance of simultaneous factors affecting individual output. It is certainly time to turn empirical attention to just this kind of problem.

[53] I cite just two studies conducted in Scandinavian countries which have been scarcely noticed by American scholars although both are significant contributions. K. Raino, *Leadership Qualities: A Theoretical Inquiry and an Experimental Study of Foremen* (Helsinki: Annales Academiae Scientiarum Fennicae, Series B, vol. 95.1, 1955); Uno Remitz, *Professional Satisfaction among Swedish Bank Employees* (Copenhagen: Munksgaard, 1960).

Walter R. Nord

LEADERSHIP: SOME IMPORTANT DEVELOPMENTS

Current models of leadership contrast sharply with those of the classical management era, which were drawn from the administrative structures of the Roman Catholic Church and military organizations. The classical models stressed authority, discipline, and control and looked on leadership as determined by organizational position, which one attained through ability. Most modern theorists, on the other hand, hold a subordinate-centered view, stressing the interdependence of leader and group and defining leadership as a form of interaction between the two. Considerable evidence has been accumulated that, in most organizations, attention of a group leader or head to social-emotional needs often pays dividends in organizational effectiveness. It has recently been suggested that the advocates of a subordinate-centered approach have overstated their case. A new synthesis now seems to be developing.

Interactionist View of Leadership

We have seen throughout this book that most organizational phenomena are the product of multiple, interacting forces. Perhaps no topic reflects this multivariate perspective more plainly than that of leadership. Gibb (1969) has provided a clear statement of the interactionist view of leadership. He stressed that groups are vehicles for satisfying the needs of individuals. As group members interact, a structure emerges from individuals' expectations about the behavior of others. While all groups develop some type of role differentiation, particular roles develop as a product of the needs experienced in the group. The needs are influenced by the task, the size of the group, and a host of other variables. Personality traits, abilities, and skills of members influence how each will be perceived by other members and thus play a part in the development and performance of roles within the group. Leadership, then, is one aspect of the more general process of role differentiation; like any other type of role differentiation, leadership is a function of the dynamic interaction of personal attributes and variables in the social system. As Gibb says,

This article was prepared especially for this volume.

> Both leadership structure and individual leader behavior are determined in large part by the nature of the organization in which they occur. Leadership structure is relative, also, to the population characteristics of the group, or, in other words, to the attitudes and needs of the followers. Leadership inevitably embodies many of the qualities of the followers, and the relation between the two may often be so close that it is difficult to determine who influences whom and to what extent. For this reason, it is possible for leadership to be nominal only. (p. 271)

With this interactionist view in mind, one can more easily understand both the advocates and the critics of democratic-participative leadership.

DEMOCRATIC LEADERSHIP RECONSIDERED

Currently an important group of organizational behaviorists relies heavily on the idea of involving organizational participants in the decision-making process in order to win their commitment to organizational goals. A great deal of research has supported the view that the democratic approach to leadership can produce positive changes in organizational performance. However, Dubin and others have suggested that this research has been too narrowly conceived.

In the preceding selection Dubin noted that the research which has found participative leadership to be far superior has been confined to studies of batch-type operations. Democratic management may be most valuable for the unprogrammed tasks characteristic of many managerial, research, and craft jobs. A logical implication is that democratic leadership may have fewer benefits in divisions, departments, organizational levels, or organizations in which the operations are less variable.

Mann (1965) showed that organizational level is an important determinant of the demands placed on a supervisor. The mix of supervisory skills required at lower levels is likely to be weighted in favor of technical rather than administrative competence; at intermediate levels the technical skills are less necessary and the administrative more so. Top management positions require even more administrative ability but relatively little technical proficiency. Competence in a third area, human relations, is important throughout the organization but probably more essential at lower levels, where motivation is likely to be a greater problem.

Additional support for Mann's ideas has come from Nealey and Fiedler (1968), who concluded that the skills required of second-level managers are often quite different from those needed at the first level. They reviewed research which used as indices of a supervisor's effectiveness the satisfaction of his subordinates and the rating of his performance by his superior. At the first or lowest level of supervision, most successful supervisors scored high on both consideration and initiation of structure. Successful second-level supervisors, on the other hand, scored high on consideration but low on initiation of structure. Successful first-level supervisors tended to have low Least Preferred Co-worker (LPC)[1] scores,

[1] The LPC scale is a device developed by Fiedler to measure the degree to which a person describes his least-preferred co-worker in positive terms. A high LPC score indicates an un-

whereas successful second-level supervisors tended to have high ones. These differences may be, at least in part, a reflection of the different needs and characteristics of the people reporting directly to first- and second-level supervisors.

Mann (1965) suggested that different stages of organizational growth also affect the type of leadership required. Lippitt and Schmidt (1967) further explored of this idea. They viewed the development of organizations as progressing through the stages of birth, youth, and maturity. At each stage an organization faces different critical concerns and key issues. At birth, organizations are concerned with creating and surviving and must decide what to risk and what to sacrifice. During youth—when organizations are concerned with gaining stability, reputation, and pride—the critical activities are organizing, reviewing, and evaluating. At maturity, organizations are concerned with achieving uniqueness and adaptability and contributing to society, so they must decide whether and how to change and share. The central concerns at each stage require different skills and temperaments. The human-relations skills appear to assume their greatest importance in the mature phase, since many people may feel threatened by change. In contrast, technical and administrative skills are more important at the earlier stages than later.

Leadership and Organizational Climate

We have suggested that a variety of organizational factors dictate which leadership style will be most appropriate. However, the actual behavior of a leader will also be influenced by the manner in which he himself is supervised.

Correlation between the behavior of a supervisor and that exhibited by his boss was reported by Fleishman (1953). Men who worked for considerate bosses were reported to be more considerate toward their subordinates than were men working under less considerate bosses. A similar chain of effect was shown for initiation of structure. Furthermore, the success of supervisory training programs was also influenced. Foremen who had taken part in human-relations training programs tended to continue practicing what they had learned only if their supervisors maintained a supportive climate. Foremen whose supervisors scored low in consideration tended to revert to former patterns of behavior. Clearly, supervision and supervisory training cannot be divorced from the organizational system in which the participants function.

Similarly, Sykes (1962) reported that supervisors who had been trained in a program emphasizing human relations and group participation became very frustrated when their organization refused to adapt to their new, human-relations view. The top executives seemed unwilling to practice themselves what they had encouraged their subordinates to learn. As a result, a group that had been highly successful from the organization's point of view before training became highly dissatisfied, and a large percentage of these men left the organization. Prior to the training program there had been almost no turnover within this group.

Nealey and Fiedler (1968) suggested that second-level leadership in an organi-

---

derlying motive to obtain good relations with others in the group, and a low LPC score indicates a leader who stresses task accomplishment.

zation can have an even more important effect on the productivity of the group than first-level leadership. They summarized several studies which supported this idea and noted that the second-level superior can make his influence felt through direct contacts with the group and through various administrative programs.

Additional evidence suggests that the degree of influence which subordinates perceive their supervisor to have with his superiors may be a determinant of the effectiveness of a given leadership style. For example, Pelz (1952) found that when subordinates perceived their supervisor as powerful in the organizational hierarchy, his "going to bat" for them and siding with them in disputes with management tended to be associated with supervisory effectiveness. On the other hand, supervisors who followed these same practices but were not perceived as having power in the hierarchy received negative reactions from their subordinates. Pelz concluded that "social closeness" and "siding with" employees only raise employee satisfaction if the supervisor has enough influence to produce actual benefits for this group.

A similar argument about the consequences of an individual's power position for leadership was made by Fiedler (1965), who proposed that the state of leader-member relations, the type of group tasks, and the power position of the leader all interact to determine which of two leadership styles will have a higher probability of success. He characterized one style as controlling, structuring, or active and the second as permissive, passive and considerate. In Table 1, cells marked CAS indicate those conditions under which controlling, active, structuring leadership is most apt to be effective, and those marked PPC indicate those conditions which favor a permissive, passive, considerate style.

TABLE 1. **Summary of Fiedler's Work on the Relationship Between Effective Leadership Style and Situational Factors.**

	Leader-Member Relations			
	Good		*Poor*	
Leader Power Position	*Task Structured*	*Task Unstructured*	*Task Structured*	*Task Unstructured*
Strong	CAS	CAS	PPC	PPC
Weak	CAS	PPC	PPC	CAS

Although Fiedler's data are more suggestive than conclusive, he provides a useful model for relating effective leadership styles to organizational conditions.

In summary, the importance of organizational climate for leadership has been amply demonstrated. In addition, most of the recent writers pay particular attention to the role of task and organizational structure. Since Dubin has so comprehensively shown the role of technology in organizational leadership, little more need be added here. What remains is to spell out for management the implications of our knowledge of leadership. For this purpose, an extremely perceptive paper by Tannenbaum and Schmidt (1958) is very helpful.

An Integrative View of Leadership Behavior: Tannenbaum and Schmidt's View

Tannenbaum and Schmidt assumed that boss-centered leadership and subordinate-centered leadership are merely opposite ends of a continuum. Leadership is not simply Theory X or Theory Y but rather may be exercised in a variety of ways ranging between two extremes. The alternatives open to a manager include making a decision and announcing it, selling his decision, presenting his ideas and inviting questions, presenting a tentative decision subject to change, presenting the problem, getting suggestions and then making his own decision, and requesting the group to make a decision within prescribed limits. A further possibility, not mentioned by Tannenbaum and Schmidt, is that of asking the group to make a decision and define its own limits. Of course, a manager varies his behavior along this continuum from one situation to another. Tannenbaum and Schmidt examined some of the factors that determine which alternative will seem to be most appropriate. One group of factors relates to the manager himself, another to the other members of the group, and a third to the situation at hand. The manager chooses not just any leadership style but one consistent with his own personality—his values, his confidence in his subordinates, his leadership inclinations, and his feelings of security in the situation. The wise leader also bases his choice on his subordinates' individual needs for independence, their tolerance for ambiguity, their willingness to accept responsibility, their interest and expertise in the problem, their understanding of organizational goals, and their experience in decision making. Among the situational factors to be considered, Tannenbaum and Schmidt included the degree of time pressure, the type of problem, the ability of the group to work together, and the type of organization.

A successful manager, then, is one who is aware of the situation, the people he is dealing with, himself, and the dynamic interaction of these factors. An understanding of these relationships is important, but it is useful only to the degree that it influences behavior. This point is best summarized by Tannenbaum and Schmidt themselves:

> Thus, the successful manager of men can be primarily characterized neither as a strong leader nor as a permissive one. Rather, he is one who maintains a high batting average in accurately assessing the forces that determine what his most appropriate behavior at any given time should be and in actually being able to behave accordingly. Being both insightful and flexible, he is less likely to see the problems of leadership as a dilemma. (p. 101)

THE READINGS

The last two selections treat some recent developments in our knowledge about leadership. In the first paper Vroom and Yetton discuss how the manager must employ different leadership styles in order to cope effectively with different types of problems. Although Vroom and Yetton's model is conceptually similar to Tannenbaum and Schmidt's perspective, their work may prove to be one of the most important recent developments in organizational behavior. They have done more than just demonstrate that different leadership styles are appropriate for different types of problems. By specifying a number of dimensions that can be used to distinguish different types of problems and linking these different sets of problems to rather specific actions, they have provided a means for translating theory into action. Moreover, they have developed a set of instruments that can be used for both training managers and conducting research on leadership style.

The second selection is from the concluding chapter of Mintzberg's excellent book, in which he tried to answer the question "What do managers do?" On the basis of his observations of managers at work and his knowledge of previous research on leadership, Mintzberg classified the demands on managers into a series of roles that occupants of managerial positions must play. The portion of Mintzberg's chapter reprinted here summarizes some of his most important ideas on the nature of managerial work.

REFERENCES

Fielder, F. E. "Engineer the Job to Fit the Manager." *Harvard Business Review* 43 (1965): 115-22.

Fleishman, E. A. "Leadership Climate, Human Relations Training, and Supervisory Behavior." *Personnel Psychology* 6 (1953): 205-22.

Gibb, C. A. "Leadership." In *The Handbook of Social Psychology*. 2nd ed. vol. 4, edited by G. Lindzey and E. Aronson. Reading, Mass.: Addison-Wesley, 1969. pp. 205-82.

Lippitt, G. L., and Schmidt, W. H. "Crises in a Developing Organization." *Harvard Business Review* 45 (1967): 102-12.

Mann, F. C. "Toward an Understanding of the Leadership Role in Formal Organization." In *Leadership and Productivity,* edited by R. Dubin, G. C. Homans, F. C. Mann, and D. C. Miller. San Francisco: Chandler Publishing Co., 1965. pp. 68-103.

Nealey, S. M., and Fiedler, F. E. "Leadership Functions of Middle Managers." *Psychological Bulletin* 70 (1968): 313-29.

Pelz, D. C. "Influence: A Key to Effective Leadership in the First-Line Supervisor." *Personnel* 29 (1952): 209-17.

Sykes, A. J. M. "The Effect of a Supervisory Training Course in Changing Supervisors' Perceptions and Expectations of the Role of Management." *Human Relations* 15 (1962): 227-43.

Tannenbaum, R., and Schmidt, W. H. "How to Choose a Leadership Pattern." *Harvard Business Review* 36 (1958): 95-101.

Victor H. Vroom
Philip W. Yetton

LEADERSHIP AND DECISION-MAKING: BASIC CONSIDERATIONS UNDERLYING THE NORMATIVE MODEL

One of the most persistent and controversial issues in the study of management is that of participation in decision-making by subordinates. Traditional models of the managerial process have been autocratic in nature. The manager makes decisions on matters within his area of freedom, issues orders or directives to his subordinates, and monitors their performance to ensure conformity with these directives. Scientific management, from its early developments in time and motion study to its contemporary manifestations in mathematical programming, has contributed to this centralization of decision-making in organizations by focusing on the development of methods by which managers can make more rational decisions, substituting objective measurements and empirically validated methods for casual judgments.

In contrast, social psychologists and other behavioral scientists who have turned their attention toward the implications of psychological and social processes for the practice of management have called for greater participation by subordinates in the problem-solving and decision-making processes. The empirical evidence provides some, but not overwhelming, support for beliefs in the efficacy of participative management. Field experiments on rank-and-file workers by Coch and French (1948), Bavelas (reported in French 1950), and Strauss (reported in Whyte 1955) indicate that impressive increases in productivity can be brought about by giving workers an opportunity to participate in decision-making and goal-setting. In addition, several correlational field studies (Katz, Maccoby, and Morse 1950; Vroom 1960) indicate positive relationships between the amount of influence supervisors afford their subordinates in decisions that affect them and individual or group performance.

On the other hand, in an experiment conducted in a Norwegian factory,

French, Israel, and Ås (1960) found no significant differences in production between workers who did and those who did not participate in decisions regarding the introduction of changes in work methods. To complicate the picture further, Morse and Reimer (1956) compared the effects of two programs of change, each of which was introduced in two divisions of the clerical operations of a large insurance company. One of the programs involved increased participation in decision-making by rank-and-file workers, while the other involved increased hierarchical control. The results show a significant increase in productivity under both programs, with the hierarchically controlled program producing the greater increase.

The investigations cited constitute only a small portion of those which are relevant to the effects of participation. The reader interested in a more comprehensive review of that evidence should consult Lowin (1968), Vroom (1970), and Wood (1974). We conclude, as have other scholars who have examined the evidence, that participation in decision-making has consequences that vary from one situation to another. Given the potential importance of this conclusion for the study of leadership and its significance to the process of management, social scientists should begin to develop some definitions of the circumstances under which participation in decision-making may contribute to or hinder organizational effectiveness. These could then be translated into guidelines to help leaders choose leadership styles to fit the demands of the situations they encounter.

In this and the following chapter, one approach to dealing with this important problem will be described. A normative model is developed which is consistent with existing empirical evidence concerning the consequences of participation and which purports to specify a set of rules that *should* be used in determining the form and amount of participation in decision-making by subordinates in different classes of situations. This chapter presents the basic assumptions that have guided the development of the normative model and the situational attributes that are contained within it.

BASIC ASSUMPTIONS

1. The normative model should be constructed in such a way as to be of potential value to managers or leaders in determining which leadership methods they should use in each of the various situations that they encounter in carrying out their formal leadership roles. Consequently, it should be operational in that the behaviors required of the leader should be specified unambiguously.

To be operational, a prescriptive statement must permit the person to determine whether or not he is acting in accordance with the statement. The statement "in case of headache, take one aspirin tablet at intervals of four hours" is quite operational in this sense. It specifies the activities to be performed and the conditions under which they are to be performed. On the other hand, the statement "to maintain one's health, one should lead a clean life" is not operational. The activities subsumed by "leading a clean life" are subject to many differences in interpretation, and there is no clear indication in the statement of the conditions under which the activities are to be carried out.

Many of the prescriptions of behavioral scientists are far closer in operationality to the second statement than to the first. Leaders are told to exhibit maximum concern for people and for production or to develop relationships with subordinates that are supportive. Such prescriptions have some informational value but fall short of the degree of operationality that we believe could be achieved.

2. There are a number of discrete social processes by which organizational problems can be translated into solutions, and these processes vary in terms of the potential amount of participation by subordinates in the problem-solving process.

The term participation has been used in a number of different ways. Perhaps the most influential definitions have been those of French, Israel, and Ås (1960) and Vroom (1960), who define participation as a process of joint decision-making by two or more parties. The amount of participation of any individual is the amount of influence he has on the decisions and plans agreed upon. Given the existence of a property such as participation that varies from high to low, it should be possible to define leader behaviors representing clear alternative processes for making decisions that can be related to the amount of participation each process affords the managers' subordinates.

A taxonomy of decision processes created for normative purposes should distinguish among methods that are likely to have different outcomes but should not be so elaborate that leaders are unable to determine which method they are employing in any given instance. The taxonomy to be used in the normative model is shown in table 2.1.

The table contains a detailed specification of several alternative processes by which problems can be solved or decisions made. Each process is represented by a symbol (AI, CI, GII, DI) which will be used throughout this book as a convenient method of referring to each process. The letters in this code signify the basic properties of the process (A stands for autocratic; C, for consultative; G, for group; and D, for delegated). The roman numerals that follow the letters constitute variants on that process. Thus AI represents the first variant on an autocratic process; AII, the second variant; and so on.

It should be noted that the methods are arranged in two columns corresponding to their applicability to problems which involve the entire group or some subset of it (hereafter called group problems) or a single subordinate (hereafter called individual problems). If a problem or decision clearly affects only one subordinate, the leader would choose among the methods shown in the right-hand column; if it had potential effects on the entire group (or subset of it) he would choose among the methods shown in the left-hand column. Those in both columns are arranged from top to bottom in terms of the opportunity for subordinates to influence the solution to the problem. The distinction between group and individual problems can be illustrated with the following examples.

GROUP PROBLEMS

A. Sharply decreasing profits for the firm has resulted in a directive from top management that makes it impossible to take on any new personnel even to re-

TABLE 2.1. **Decision Methods for Group and Individual Problems.**

Group Problems		*Individual Problems*	
AI.	You solve the problem or make the decision yourself, using information available to you at the time.	AI.	You solve the problem or make the decision by yourself, using information available to you at the time.
AII.	You obtain the necessary information from your subordinates, then decide the solution to the problem yourself. You may or may not tell your subordinates what the problem is in getting the information from them. The role played by your subordinates in making the decision is clearly one of providing the necessary information to you, rather than generating or evaluating alternative solutions.	AII.	You obtain the necessary information from your subordinate, then decide on the solution to the problem yourself. You may or may not tell the subordinate what the problem is in getting the information from him. His role in making the decision is clearly one of providing the necessary information to you, rather than generating or evaluating alternative solutions.
CI.	You share the problem with the relevant subordinates individually, getting their ideas and suggestions without bringing them together as a group. Then *you* make the decision, which may or may not reflect your subordinates' influence.	CI.	You share the problem with your subordinate, getting his ideas and suggestions. Then you make a decision, which may or may not reflect his influence.
CII.	You share the problem with your subordinates as a group, obtaining their collective ideas and suggestions. Then you make the decision, which may or may not reflect your subordinates' influence.	GI.	You share the problem with your subordinate, and together you analyze the problem and arrive at a mutually agreeable solution.
GII.	You share the problem with your subordinates as a group. Together you generate and evaluate alternatives and attempt to reach agreement (consensus) on a solution. Your role is much like that of chairman. You do not try to influence the group to adopt "your" solution, and you are willing to accept and implement any solution which has the support of the entire group.	DI.	You delegate the problem to your subordinate, providing him with any relevant information that you possess, but giving him responsibility for solving the problem by himself. You may or may not request him to tell you what solution he has reached.

place those who leave. Shortly after this directive is issued, one of your five subordinates resigns to take a job with another firm. Your problem is how to rearrange the work assignments among the remaining four subordinates without reducing the total productivity of the group.

B. You have been chosen by your firm to attend a nine-week senior executive program at a famous university. Your problem is to choose one of your subordinates to take your place during your absence.

C. You have two main projects under your direction with three subordinates assigned to each. One of these projects is three months behind schedule with only six months remaining before the work *must* be completed. Your problem is to get the project back on schedule to meet the completion date.

INDIVIDUAL PROBLEMS

D. As principal of an elementary school, you often handle disciplinary cases. Over the last six months, one of your fifteen teachers has referred an inordinately large number of cases to your attention. This fact, combined with other information you have received, leads you to believe that there is a serious breakdown of discipline within that teacher's classroom.

E. The cost figures for section *B* have risen faster than those of the other three similar sections under your direction. The manager of section *B* is your immediate subordinate.

F. You have the opportunity to bid on a multi-million-dollar government contract. While the decision will be made by top management, you have to formulate a recommendation that has a high probability of being accepted. You have only one subordinate who is a specialist in the area in which the contract is to be granted, and you will have to rely heavily on him to present and defend the recommendation to top management. As you see it, there are at least three options: to bid as prime contractor; to bid as subcontractor for another firm planning to bid as prime contractor; or to do nothing.

The person in the leadership position could presumably employ any one of the alternatives on the left-hand side of table 2.1 (AI, AII, CI, CII, GII) for problems *A, B,* and *C* and could employ any one of the alternatives on the right-hand side of table 2.1 (AI, AII, CI, GI, DI) for problems *D, E,* and *F.* Since the two sets of alternatives have three common decision processes (AI, AII, CI), this categorization effectively eliminates from consideration *GI* and *DI* as relevant decision processes for group problems (like *A, B,* and *C*) and eliminates CII and GII for individual problems (like *D, E,* and *F*). The reader can verify for himself the appropriateness of these exclusions.

Table 2.2 shows the relationship between the methods shown in table 2.1 and those described in prior taxonomies. Our methods appear as row headings, and the names of other authors or researchers appear as column headings. If there seems to be correspondence between the definition of one of our methods and that used by a given author, his term appears in the intersection of row and column. A vacant cell, defined by the intersection of a column and row, indicates that the investigator whose name heads the column does not recognize any style corresponding to that in the row heading. If a column is partitioned within a row, it means that the investigator uses a finer breakdown than that employed in the model. Similarly, if a column entry cuts across two or more rows, it indicates that the model employs a finer breakdown than that made by the investigator. The relationships presented in table 2.2 are matters of judgment and are merely intended to suggest the correspondence or lack of correspondence existing between the taxonomy that is used here and those which were previously employed.

3. No one leadership method is applicable to all situations; the function of a normative model should be to provide a framework for the analysis of situational requirements that can be translated into prescriptions of leadership styles.

The fact that the most effective leadership method or style is dependent on the situation is becoming widely recognized by behavioral scientists interested in problems of leadership and administration. A decision-making process that is optimal for a quarterback on a football team making decisions under severe time constraints is likely to be far from optimal when used by a dean introducing a new curriculum to be implemented by his faculty. Even the advocates of participative management have noted this "situational relativity" of leadership styles. Thus, Argyris (1962) writes:

> No one leadership style is the most effective. Each is probably effective under a given set of conditions. Consequently, I suggest that effective leaders are those who are capable of behaving in many different leadership styles, depending on the requirements of reality as they and others perceive it. I call this "reality-centered" leadership. (1962, p. 81)

We must go beyond noting the importance of situational factors and begin to move toward a road map or normative models that attempt to prescribe the most appropriate leadership style for different kinds of situations. The most comprehensive treatment of situational factors as determinants of the effectiveness and efficiency of participation in decision-making is found in the work of Tannenbaum and Schmidt (1958). They discuss a large number of variables, including attributes of the manager, his subordinates, and the situation, which ought to enter into the manager's decision about the degree to which he should share his power with his subordinates. But they stop at this inventory of variables, and do not show how these might be combined and translated into different forms of action.

4. The most appropriate unit for the analysis of the situation is the particular problem to be solved and the context in which the problem occurs.

While it is becoming widely recognized that different situations require different leadership methods, there is less agreement concerning the appropriate units for the analysis of the situation. One approach is to assume that the situations that determine the effectiveness of different leadership styles correspond to the environment of the system. Thus, Bennis (1966) argues that egalitarian leadership styles work better when the environment of the organization is rapidly changing and the problems with which it has to deal are continually being altered. If this position were extended to provide the basis for a comprehensive normative model, one would prescribe different leadership styles for different systems but make identical prescriptions for all leadership roles within a system.

Alternatively, one might assume that the critical features of the situation concern the role of the leader, including his relations with his subordinates. Examples would include Fiedler's (1967) three dimensions of task structure, leadership position power, and leader-member relations. Implicit is the assumption that all problems or decisions made within a single role require a similar leadership style. Normatively, one might prescribe different amounts or forms of participation for two different leaders but prescribe identical amounts or forms of participation for all problems or decisions made by a single leader within a single role.

TABLE 2.2. **Correspondence Between Decision Processes Employed in the Model and Those of Previous Investigators.**

<table>
<tr><th></th><th>Lewin, Lippitt, and White (1939)</th><th>Maier (1955)</th><th colspan="3">Tannenbaum and Schmidt (1958)</th><th colspan="2">Heller (1971)</th><th colspan="2">Likert (1967)</th></tr>
<tr><td>AI
AII</td><td>Autocratic leadership</td><td>Autocratic management</td><td>Manager makes decision and announces it</td><td>Manager sells decision</td><td>Manager presents ideas and invites questions</td><td>Own decision with detailed explanation</td><td>Own decision without detailed explanation</td><td>Exploitive authoritative (system 1)</td><td>Benevolent authoritative (system 2)</td></tr>
<tr><td>CI
CII</td><td rowspan="2"></td><td>Consultative management</td><td>Manager presents tentative decision, subject to change</td><td colspan="2">Manager presents problem, gets suggestions, makes decision</td><td colspan="2">Prior consultation with subordinate(s)</td><td colspan="2">Consultative (system 3)</td></tr>
<tr><td>GI</td><td></td><td colspan="3"></td><td colspan="2" rowspan="2">Joint decision-making with subordinate(s)</td><td colspan="2"></td></tr>
<tr><td>GII</td><td>Democratic leadership</td><td>Group decision</td><td>Manager defines limits, asks group to make decision</td><td colspan="2">Manager permits group to make decisions within prescribed limits</td><td colspan="2">Participative group (system 4)</td></tr>
<tr><td>DI</td><td>Laissez-faire leadership</td><td></td><td colspan="3"></td><td colspan="2">Delegation of decision to subordinate(s)</td><td colspan="2"></td></tr>
</table>

The approach taken here is to select the properties of the problem to be solved as the critical situational dimensions for determining the appropriate form or amount of participation. Different prescriptions would be made for a given leader for different problems within a given role. It should be noted that constructing a normative model with the problem rather than the role or any organizational differences as the unit of analysis does not rule out the possibility that different roles and organizations may involve different distributions of problem types that, in aggregate, may require different modal styles or levels of participation.

5. The leadership method used in response to one situation should not constrain the method or style used in other situations.

Implicit in the use of the attributes of the particular problem to be solved or decision to be made as the unit of analysis is the assumption that problems can be classified such that the relative usefulness of each alternative decision process is identical for all problems in a particular classification. A corollary to this assumption is that the process or method used on problems of one type does not constrain that used on problems of a different type. It is only in this way that prescriptions could be made for a given problem without knowing the other problems encountered by a leader or his methods for dealing with them.

This assumption is necessary to the consttuction of a normative model founded on problem differences. It may seem inconsistent with the view, first proposed by McGregor (1944), that consistency in leadership style is desirable because it enables subordinates to predict their superiors' behavior and to adapt to it. However, predictability does not preclude variability. There are many variable phenomena which can be predicted quite well because the rules or processes that govern them are understood. The antithesis of predictability is randomness, and, if McGregor is correct, a normative model to regulate choices among alternative leadership styles should be deterministic rather than stochastic. The model to be developed here is deterministic; the normatively prescribed method for a given problem type is a constant.

CONCEPTUAL AND EMPIRICAL BASIS OF THE MODEL

A model designed to regulate, in some rational way, choices among the decision methods shown in table 2.1 should be based on sound empirical evidence concerning their likely consequences. The more complete the empirical base of knowledge, the greater the certainty with which one can develop the model and the greater will be its usefulness. In this section we will restrict ourselves to the development of a model concerned only with group problems and, hence, will use only the methods shown in the left-hand column of table 2.1. A comparable model for individual problems will be discussed in chapter 9.

We will now consider the empirical evidence that can at present be brought to bear on such a normative model. You will note that much of the evidence is incomplete, and future research should prove helpful in providing a firmer foundation for a model. In this analysis it is important to distinguish three classes of outcomes that influence the ultimate effectiveness of decisions. These are: (1)

the quality or rationality of the decision, (2) the acceptance of the decision by subordinates and their commitment to execute it effectively, and (3) the amount of time required to make the decision.

The evidence regarding the effects of participation on each of these outcomes or consequences has been reviewed elsewhere (Vroom 1970). He concluded that

> the results suggest that allocating problem solving and decision-making tasks to entire groups as compared with the leader or manager in charge of the groups, requires a greater investment of man hours but produces higher acceptance of decisions and a higher probability that the decisions will be executed efficiently. Differences between these two methods in quality of decisions and in elapsed time are inconclusive and probably highly variable. . . . It would be naive to think that group decision-making is always more "effective" than autocratic decision-making, or vice versa; the relative effectiveness of these two extreme methods depends both on the weights attached to quality, acceptance and time variables and on differences in amounts of these outcomes resulting from these methods, neither of which is invariant from one situation to another. The critics and proponents of participative management would do well to direct their efforts toward identifying the properties of situations in which different decision-making approaches are effective rather than wholesale condemnation or deification of one approach. (Vroom 1970, pp. 239-40)

Stemming from this review, an attempt has been made to identify these properties of the situation, which will be the basic elements in the model. These problem attributes are of two types: (1) those which specify the importance for a particular problem of quality and acceptance (see *A* and *E* below), and (2) those which, on the basis of available evidence, have a high probability of moderating the effects of participation on each of these outcomes (see *B, C, D, G,* and *H* below). The following are the problem attributes used in the present form of the model.

A. The importance of the quality of the decision

According to Maier (1955, 1963), decision quality refers to the "objective or impersonal" aspects of the decision. For groups embedded within formal organizations with specifiable goals, the relative quality of a set of alternative decisions can be expressed in terms of their effects, if implemented with equal expenditure of energy, on the attainment of those goals.

The first attribute refers to what Maier (1963) has termed the quality requirement for the decision. There are some problems for which the nature of the solution reached within identifiable constraints is not at all critical. The leader is (or should be) indifferent among the possible solutions since their expected value is equal, provided that those who have to carry them out are committed to them. Typically, the number of solutions that meet the constraints is finite, and the alternatives are obvious or do not require substantial search. In such instances, there is no technical, rational, or analytic method of choosing among the alternatives.

In Maier's new-truck problem (Maier 1955), the issue of which of the five truck drivers should get the new truck has no quality requirement. The foreman is (or should be) indifferent among the various possible alternatives provided they are accepted by the men. On the other hand, the problem of which truck should be discarded to make way for the new one does have a quality requirement. The five present trucks vary in age and condition, and a decision to discard other than the poorest truck in the set would be irrational.

While on a consulting assignment, the senior author encountered another problem which may help to illustrate the meaning of the term "quality requirement." A plant manager and his staff were about to move into a new plant. On inspecting the plans, he discovered that there were insufficient reserved parking places (directly in front of the building) to accommodate all six of his department heads. The design of the building permitted only four such parking places with all other cars having to park across the street in a large parking lot. There was no possible way to increase the number of parking spaces without modifying the design of the structure, and the costs would be prohibitive. Any solution to the parking-space allocation problem would have satisfied the plant manager provided it had the support of his department heads, each of whom, incidentally, expected to receive a reserved parking place. The problem had no quality requirement since he was indifferent among all possible solutions which met the constraints.

In both of the examples given, the constraints were imposed on the leader by forces outside him. The foreman had only one new truck to allocate among his drivers, and the plant manager could do nothing to increase the size of the reserved parking lot. In other instances, the quality requirement can be eliminated from the problem if the leader *imposes* constraints on the possible solutions. By attaching suitable constraints, quality requirements can be eliminated from such problems as the choice of personnel to be assigned to work on each shift, the design of a vacation schedule showing when each person should take his vacation, and the selection of a time at which to hold a meeting.

At the other end of the dimension specified by this attribute are so-called strategic decisions (Ansoff 1965), which involve the allocation of scarce resources and are not easily reversible. At what level should we price out products? What new businesses should we acquire? Where should we locate our plants? What is the most effective advertising policy? These are just a few of the problems and decisions which have marked consequences for the effectiveness of the organization. No leader should be indifferent among possible alternative courses of action. Even though the relative consequences of the alternatives may not be known at any given point in time, the specific course chosen is going to make a difference in the degree to which the system attains its goals. In such instances, the variance in contribution to organizational objectives of alternative courses of action is large, and the rational quality of the decision is of central importance.

The function of this attribute in the model is to determine the relevance to the choice of decision process of such considerations as the nature and location of information or expertise necessary to generate and evaluate alternatives. If the quality of the decision is unimportant, then attributes *B, C, D,* and *G* below can be shown to be irrelevant to the prescription of that process.

B. The extent to which the leader possesses sufficient information/ expertise to make a high quality decision by himself

The quality of the decisions reached by any decision-making process is dependent on the resources the leader is able to utilize. One of the most critical of these resources is information. If a rational solution to the problem is to be obtained, alternatives must be generated and evaluated in terms of their organizational consequences. Any such activities require the use of the relevant information and expertise by participants in the decision process.

It is possible to distinguish two different kinds of information that are potentially relevant to problem-solving in an organizational setting. One is information necessary to the task of evaluating the relative quality or rationality of different alternatives. The other is information concerning the preferences of subordinates and their feelings about the alternatives.

These two kinds of information and associated expertise need not be correlated. One leader may be extremely knowledgeable about the terrain to be traversed and its possible pitfalls, and he may have worked out an elegant means of attaining the external objective. However, he may be completely unaware of the preferences of his men. Another may be uninformed about the external environment but highly sensitive to the attitudes and feelings of his subordinates. A low correlation between these two components of information is suggested by research on role differentiation in problem-solving groups. Task facilitative leadership tends to be carried out by different persons than socio-emotional leadership (Bales and Slater 1955).

The information referred to in attribute *B* deals with the external goals and the consequences of actions on the part of the system for their attainment. In other words, we are interested only in the degree to which the leader possesses facts and skills relevant to the quality of the decision. Thus, in evaluating the level of this attribute in the case of a head dietician in a hospital faced with the task of preparing the week's menus, one would be concerned with such things as her knowledge of the components of a balanced diet, the availability and cost of different food products, and the existence of special dietary requirements among the patient load. One would not be concerned with the kinds of foods that her staff liked to consume, prepare, or deliver. Similarly, in evaluating the information possessed by a university department chairman faced with the problem of selecting a text to be used by members of his department in teaching the introductory course, the relevant questions would concern his knowledge of the alternatives as they relate to the goal of education and not his information regarding the preferences of those assigned to teach the course.

In defining this attribute solely in terms of information or expertise in matters relating to the quality of the decision, we intend not to render unimportant the task of having decisions accepted by subordinates, but rather to recognize the conceptual and empirical independence of the two kinds of information. As will be seen later in the description of other problem attributes, acceptance requirements are an integral part of the framework being developed.

The decision-making processes shown in table 2.1 differ in terms of the amount of information and expertise that can be brought to bear on the problem. For example, in AI, only information available to the leader may be utilized in problem-solving, whereas in GII the information base extends to all group members including the leader.

There has been little research on the determinants of whether the leader's information is adequate to deal with the problems he encounters. Since he has been selected by somewhat different criteria, may have received special training, and has access to different information, there is strong *a priori* reason to believe that his information base will be different from (and in most cases superior to) that of the average group member. However, its absolute level must be assumed to be variable with the nature of the problem. There are undoubtedly some situations in which the leader possesses all of the necessary information and others for which his information is critically deficient. In the model, this attribute determines the importance of choosing a decision-making process that augments the information base of the decision.

Kelley and Thibaut (1969) have reviewed the literature on group and individual problem-solving and have advanced a set of hypotheses concerning the conditions in which a group solution is likely to be higher than, equal to, or lower in quality than that of the best member of the group. The studies were conducted principally on ad hoc leaderless groups in laboratory settings, so it is not clear that the best member would always have been a formal leader. However, their hypotheses may ultimately prove fruitful in relating variation on the attribute defined above to problem differences.

Kelley and Thibaut (1969) suggest that: (1) group decisions are likely to be above the level of the most proficient member when the problem has multiple parts and when group members have uncorrelated (complementary) deficiencies and talents; (2) groups are likely to perform at the level of the most proficient member when the problem is simple (very few steps are required for its solution) and the solution is highly verifiable by all persons in possession of the original facts; and (3) groups are likely to do less well than the best member when the solution requires thinking through a series of interrelated steps or stages, applying a number of rules at each point, and always keeping in mind conclusions reached at earlier points.

C. The extent to which subordinates, taken collectively, have the necessary information to generate a high quality decision

This attribute is similar to *B* above except that it deals with the resources of subordinates rather than the leader. There are some situations in which these resources may in fact be very small. For example, the problem may be a highly technical one, and the subordinates may lack any of the knowledge needed to deal with it. On the other hand, in problems with multiple parts and where the level of information needed to deal with these parts is uncorrelated, the potential contribution of subordinates may be very high. This attribute is relevant to the choice of a decision process only when the information available to the leader is deficient. It determines whether the information search activities can be conducted within the group as part of the decision-making activity or whether, in order to obtain a high quality decision, it will be necessary to go outside the group for the necessary information.

D. The extent to which the problem is structured

A distinction is frequently made between problems or decisions that are structured or programmed and those which are unstructured or nonprogrammed (Simon 1960). Structured problems are those for which the alternative solutions or methods for generating them and the parameters for their evaluation are known. There are typically specific procedures within the organization for handling them. Under these circumstances, the decision is made once all the necessary information has reached a central source, in this case the leader. The process is essentially that of the "wheel" in communication net experiments, which has been found to be more efficient for the solution of simple problems that less centralized networks (Shaw 1964).

However, if the problem is unstructured and the relevant information widely dispersed among persons, the organizational task is somewhat different. Under these circumstances it is less clear what information is relevant, and empirical evidence appears to favor a less centralized network which permits those with potentially relevant information to interact with one another in the course of solving the problem. This process is more akin to that in the circle networks, which have been found to be more effective in solving complex problems (Shaw 1964). Within the model, this attribute bears on the relative efficiency of information collection activities that involve interaction among subordinates (that is, CII and GII) and those which do not involve such interaction (AII and CI).

E. The extent to which acceptance or commitment on the part of subordinates is critical to the effective implementation of the decision

In most situations, the effectiveness of an organizational decision is influenced both by its quality or rationality and by the extent to which it is accepted by subordinates. A decision can be ineffective because it did not utilize all of the available information concerning the external environment or because it was resisted and opposed by those who had to implement it.

The distinction between quality and acceptance is reminiscent of Bales's (1949) distinction between problems of the group involving goal achievement and adaptation to external demands and problems involving internal integration and expression of emotional tensions. Bales divides problems into two groups, adaptive-instrumental problems and integrative-expressive problems. In the framework being developed, quality and acceptance requirements are seen not as discrete types or even as opposite ends of a single continuum but rather as two separable dimensions. Just as the quality of the decision varies in importance from one problem to another, so also does the acceptance of the decision by subordinates, and there is no necessary correlation between these two dimensions.

There are two classes of situations in which acceptance of the decision by subordinates may be regarded as irrelevant to its effective implementation. One of these is what Maier (1970) has termed "outsider problems." In an "outsider problem," the subordinates are not involved in the execution of the decision. One may still desire their participation in order to enhance the quality of the solution, but the decision will be implemented by the leader or some other group. Acceptance by this particular set of persons is not critical to the ultimate success or failure of the decision.

The second type of situation in which acceptance or commitment to the decision by subordinates is not critical is that in which subordinates will be required to execute the decision but its nature is such that compliance on their part, rather than acceptance or commitment, is sufficient. Typically in such situations, subordinates' actions necessary for implementation of the decision are specific; the leader is able to monitor or observe these actions, and he controls rewards and punishments, which he is able to mete out accordingly. Both in the larger society and in organizations, people carry out directives to which they feel no personal commitment and, in fact, may be strongly opposed. The forces operating on them are "induced" forces rather than "own" forces (Lewin 1935), and the conditions necessary for the successful induction of a force must be present. The actions must be observable by others who wish to see the directive carried out, and these others must control rewards and/or penalties, which are meted out in accordance with the degree of compliance observed.

Acceptance becomes more critical as the effective execution of the decision requires initiative, judgment, or creativity on the part of subordinates or when one or more of the conditions necessary for obtaining compliance breaks down; for example, the leader is unable to monitor subordinates' behavior and reward or punish deviations. Within the model, the interaction of this attribute with the following one determines the importance of attempting to develop subordinates' commitment to the final solution by employing a participative decision-making process.

F. The prior probability that the leader's autocratic decision will receive acceptance by subordinates

The relationship between participation in decision-making and the acceptance of decisions by subordinates is marked but probably not invariant with the nature of the problem and the context within which it occurs. Thus, Vroom (1960) found that the effects of participation varied with the subordinate's need for independence and authoritarianism. Similarly, in a field experiment in a Norwegian factory, French, Israel, and Ås (1960) discovered that the effects varied with subordinates' perceptions of the legitimacy of their participation, and Marrow (1964) has provided a brief account of some of the problems that occurred when the Harwood Manufacturing Company attempted to increase participation in decision-making, which had proved highly successful in their plants in the United States, in their newly acquired subsidiary in Puerto Rico.

It appears that participation is not a necessary condition for the acceptance of decisions. There are some circumstances in which the leader's decision has high prior probability of being accepted by subordinates. These circumstances are predictable from a knowledge of the relationship between the leader and his subordinates. French and Raven (1959) distinguish among five bases of power all of which are defined in terms of the relationship between the source and object of influence. Three of these bases (legitimate power, expert power, and referent power) are hypothesized to produce "own" forces on the object of influence to engage in the indicated action, thereby conforming to our definition of acceptance. Thus, the subordinates may accept the leader's decision because they believe that it is his legitimate right to make that decision by virtue of the position he occupies (legitimate power), because he is the acknowledged expert and the only one capable of taking all the necessary factors into consideration (expert power), or because he is strongly admired by them (referent power). In such situations, it is not at all difficult for the leader to "sell" his decision to his subordinates, thereby gaining the necessary acceptance.

There are many situations in which the prior probability of acceptance of a decision by subordinates will vary with the nature of the solution adopted. Some alternatives may be acceptable to subordinates and some may not. In effect, the prior probability of acceptance becomes a property of a solution rather than a property of the problem. To deal with the potential complexities introduced by this state of affairs, the following guidelines are suggested. For problems with a quality requirement (attribute *A*), the relevant prior probability of acceptance is that of the highest quality alternative known to the leader. Thus, if the leader had worked out a solution to a complex production scheduling problem using critical path analysis and were convinced that it would work and would be superior to the present method and other alternatives known to him, one would be interested in the prior probability that this new method would be accepted by his subordinates.

For problems without a quality requirement, the relevant prior probability of acceptance is the highest value for any of the solutions meeting the constraints specified. In a case described earlier in this chapter—that of the plant manager assigning four reserved parking places among his six department heads—the level specified for prior probability would be that of the most palatable alternative to his subordinates.

This attribute is relevant to the choice of method only where acceptance is required in order for the decision to be effectively implemented (attribute *E*). It, in turn, determines whether participation in decision-making is necessary in order to attain that acceptance.

G. The extent to which subordinates are motivated to attain the organizational goals as represented in the objectives explicit in the statement of the problem

In all problems, there are one or more goals to be achieved. Ultimately, it is the attainment of those goals that determines whether the problem is actually solved. In effect, the general goal of organizational effectiveness is replaced by surrogate and more operational goals such as improving the safety record, reducing costs by 30 percent, or reorganizing to adapt to a cut in manpower while maintaining volume.

It is assumed that the quality of the decision reached is dependent not only on the information or expertise of those participating in it, but also on their disposition to use their information in the service of the goals stated in the problem. This phenomenon has seldom been examined in laboratory experiments on group problem-solving, where participants are motivated to solve the problem as accurately and as quickly as possible. But in formal organizations, there are many situations in which the goals of the group members may be in conflict with those stated in the problem. For example, decisions concerning the wage levels or the work loads of the participants may be among those which personal rather than organizational goals might dominate the search for and evaluation of alternatives.

This problem attribute is similar to what Maier (1963) terms "mutual interest," and to the potential amount of trust that the leader can place in his subordinates to solve the problem in the best interest of the organization. It determines the potential risk to the quality of the decision of methods like GII in which the leader relinquishes his final control over the decision.

H. The extent to which subordinates are likely to be in disagreement over preferred solutions

Conflicts or disagreements among group members over the appropriate solution are quite common features of decision-making in organizations. It is possible for group members to agree on a common goal but disagree over the best means of attaining it. Such disagreements can result from access to different information or from the fact that personal gains or losses from different solutions are negatively correlated.

There is substantial evidence from the literature in social psychology (see Brown 1965) to indicate that interaction among people tends to increase their similarity in attitudes and opinions. Members of a group with initially wide variance in individual judgments will tend to converge on a common position. This process seems to be enhanced when the issue is relevant to their interaction and when the problem is of mutual interest. Thus, Kelley and Thibaut (1969) note in their review of the literature on group problem-solving that "group problem discussion generates pressures toward uniformity" (p. 71). This attribute determines the importance of choosing a decision-making process (CII and GII) in which subordinates interact in the process of solving the problem, as opposed to those (AII and CI) in which no such interaction takes place.

Table 2.3 shows the same eight problem attributes expressed in the form of questions which might be used by a leader in diagnosing a particular problem before choosing his leadership method. In phrasing the questions, technical language has been held to a minimum. Furthermore, the questions have been phrased in yes-no form, translating the continuous variables defined above into dichotomous variables. For example, instead of attempting to determine how important the decision quality is to the effectiveness of the decision (attribute *A*), the leader is asked in the first question to judge whether there is any quality component to the problem. Similarly, the difficult task of specifying exactly how much information the leader possesses that is relevant to the decision (attribute *B*) is reduced to a simple judgment by the leader concerning whether he has sufficient information to make a high quality decision.

TABLE 2.3. **Problem Attributes.**

A. If decision were accepted, would it make a difference which course of action were adopted?
B. Do I have sufficient information to make a high quality decision?
C. Do subordinates have sufficient additional information to result in a high quality decision?
D. Do I know exactly what information is needed, who possesses it, and how to collect it?
E. Is acceptance of decision by subordinates critical to effective implementation?
F. If I were to make the decision by myself, is it certain that it would be accepted by my subordinates?
G. Can subordinates be trusted to base solutions on organizational considerations?
H. Is conflict among subordinates likely in preferred solutions?

Expressing what are obviously continuous variables in dichotomous form greatly simplifies the problem of incorporating these attributes into a model that can be used by leaders. It sidesteps the problem of scaling each problem attribute and reduces the complexity of the judgments required of leaders.

It has been found that managers can diagnose a situation quickly and accurately by answering this set of eight questions.

REFERENCES

Ansoff, H. I. 1965. *Corporate strategy.* New York: McGraw-Hill.

Argyris, C. 1962. *Interpersonal competence and organizational effectiveness.* Homewood, Illinois: Irwin.

Bales, R. F. 1949. *Interaction process analysis: a method for the study of small groups.* Cambridge, Mass.: Addison-Wesley.

Bales, R. F., and Slater, P. E. 1955. Role differentiation in small groups. In *Family, socialization and interaction process,* by T. Parsons, R. F. Bales et al. Glencoe, Ill.: Free Press.

Bennis, W. G. 1966. *Changing organizations.* New York: McGraw-Hill.

Brown, R. 1965. *Social psychology.* New York: Free Press.

Coch, L., and French, J. R. P., Jr. 1948. Overcoming resistance to change. *Human Relations* 1: 512-32.

French, J. R. P., Jr. 1950. Field experiments: changing group productivity. In *Experiments in social process: a symposium on social psychology,* edited by J. G. Miller. New York: McGraw-Hill.

French, J. R. P., Jr.; Israel, J.; and Ås, D. 1960. An experiment on participation in a Norwegian factory. *Human Relations* 13: 3-19.

French, J. R. P., Jr., and Raven, B. 1959. The bases of social power. In *Studies in social power,* edited by D. Cartwright. Ann Arbor, Mich.: Institute for Social Research.

Heller, F. A. 1971. *Managerial decision making.* London: Tavistock.

Katz, D.; Maccoby, N.; and Morse, N. C. 1950. *Productivity, supervision, and morale in an office situation.* Ann Arbor: University of Michigan, Institute for Social Research.

Kelley, H., and Thibaut, J. 1969. Group problem solving. In *Handbook of social psychology,* edited by G. Lindzey and E. Aronson, vol. 4, pp. 1-101. Reading, Mass.: Addison-Wesley.

Korman, A. K. 1966. "Consideration," "initiating structure," and organizational criteria—a review. *Personnel Psychology* 19: 349-61.

Lewin, K. 1935. *A dynamic theory of personality.* New York: McGraw-Hill.

_____. 1951. *Field theory in social science,* edited by D. Cartwright. New York: Harper.

Lewin, K.; Lippitt, R.; and White, R. K. 1939. Patterns of aggressive behavior in experimentally created social climates. *Journal of Social Psychology* 10: 271-99.

Likert, R. 1967. *The human organization.* New York: McGraw-Hill.

Lowin, A. 1968. Participative decision making: a model, literature critique, and prescriptions for research. *Organizational Behavior and Human Performance* 3: 68-106.

McGregor, D. 1944. Getting effective leadership in the industrial organization. *Advanced Management* 9: 148-53.

Maier, N. R. F. 1955. *Psychology in industry.* 2nd ed. Boston: Houghton-Mifflin.

_____. 1963. *Problem-solving discussions and conferences: leadership methods and skills.* New York: McGraw-Hill.

_____. 1970. *Problem solving and creativity in individuals and groups.* Belmont, Calif.: Brooks-Cole.

Marrow, A. J. 1964. Risk and uncertainties in action research. *Journal of Social Issues* 20: 5-20.

Morse, Nancy C., and Reimer, E. 1956. The experimental change of a major organizational variable. *Journal of Abnormal and Social Psychology* 52: 120-29.

Shaw, M. E. 1964. Communication networks. In *Advances in experimental psychology,* edited by L. Berkowitz, vol. 1, pp. 111-47. New York: Academic Press.

Simon, H. A. 1960. *The new science of management decision.* New York: Harper.

Tannenbaum, R., and Schmidt, W. 1958. How to choose a leadership pattern. *Harvard Business Review* 36: 95-101.

Vroom, V. H. 1960. *Some personality determinants of the effects of participation.* Englewood Cliffs, N.J.: Prentice-Hall.

_____. 1970. Industrial social psychology. In *Handbook of social psychology,* edited by G. Lindzey and E. Aronson, vol. 5, pp. 196-268. Reading, Mass.: Addison-Wesley.

Whyte, W. F. 1955. *Money and motivation: an analysis of incentives in industry.* New York: Harper.

Wood, M. J. 1974 (in press). Power relationships and group decision making in organizations. *Psychological Bulletin.*

Henry Mintzberg

A COMPREHENSIVE DESCRIPTION OF MANAGERIAL WORK

DEFINITION AND BASIC PURPOSES

The manager is that person in charge of a formal organization or one of its subunits. He is vested with formal authority over his organizational unit, and this leads to his two basic purposes. First, the manager must ensure that his organization produces its specific goods or services efficiently. He must design, and maintain the stability of, its basic operations, and he must adapt it in a controlled way to its changing environment. Second, the manager must ensure that his organization serves the ends of those persons who control it (the "influencers"). He must interpret their particular preferences and combine these to produce statements of organizational preference that can guide its decision-making. Because of his formal authority the manager must serve two other basic purposes as well. He must act as the key communication link between his organization and its environment, and he must assume responsibility for the operation of his organization's status system.

TEN WORKING ROLES

These basic purposes are operationalized through ten interrelated roles, performed by all managers. The roles fall into three groupings–three *interpersonal* roles, which derive from the manager's authority and status, three *informational* roles, which derive from the interpersonal roles and the access they provide to information, and four *decisional* roles, which derive from the manager's authority and information.

As *figurehead,* the simplest of managerial roles, the manager is a symbol, required because of his status to carry out a number of social, inspirational, legal, and ceremonial duties. In addition, the manager must be available to certain parties who demand to deal with him because of his status and authority. The *figurehead* role is most significant at the highest levels of the organizational hierarchy.

From pp. 166-173, *The Nature of Managerial Work* by Henry Mintzberg.

The *leader* role defines the manager's interpersonal relationships with his subordinates. He must bring together their needs and those of the organization to create a milieu in which they will work effectively. The manager motivates his subordinates, probes into their activities to keep them alert, and takes responsibility for the hiring, training, and promoting of those closest to him. The societal shift toward greater organizational democracy will cause managers to spend more time in the *leader* role.

The *liaison* role focuses on the manager's dealings with people outside his own organizational unit. He develops a network of contacts in which information and favors are traded for mutual benefit. The manager spends a considerable amount of time performing this role, first by making a series of commitments to establish these contacts, and then by engaging in various activities to maintain them. For some managers this role is paramount. In the managerial diad, for example, the chief executive generally focuses on outside work and the second in command concentrates on internal operations (notably the *leader* and the decisional roles). Line sales managers, because their orientation is external and interpersonal, give special attention to this role, and to the other two interpersonal roles as well.

Through the *leader* and *liaison* roles, the manager gains access to privileged information and he emerges as the "nerve center" of his organization. He alone has formal access to every subordinate in his own organization, and he has unique access to a variety of outsiders, many of whom are nerve centers of their own organizations. Thus the manager is his organization's information generalist, that person best informed about its operations and environment.

As *monitor* the manager continually seeks and receives internal and external information from a variety of sources to develop a thorough knowledge of his milieu. Because a good part of this information is current and nondocumented, the manager must take prime responsibility for the design of his own information system, which is necessarily informal. Managers in new jobs, particularly, spend considerable time on the *monitor* and *liaison* roles in order to build up their information systems and bring themselves up to the level of knowledge needed for effective strategy-making.

As *disseminator* the manager transmits some of his internal and external information to subordinates. In this way, he maintains their only access to certain privileged information. Some of this information is of a factual nature; some relates to the values of the organization's influencers.

As *spokesman* the manager transmits information to individuals outside his organizational unit. He acts in a public relations capacity, lobbies for his organization, informs key influencers, tells the public about the organization's performance, and sends useful information to his liaison contacts. Furthermore, the manager must serve outsiders as an expert in the industry or function in which his organization operates. Managers of staff groups, because their subunits are highly specialized and oriented to analysis, spend considerable time in this expert capacity as well as giving relatively more attention to the other informational roles.

Because of his formal authority and special information, the manager must take responsibility for his organization's strategy-making system—the means by which decisions important to his organizational unit are made and interrelated. Strategy is made through four decisional roles.

As *entrepreneur* the manager is responsible for the initiation and design of much of the controlled change in his organization. He continually searches for new opportunities and problems and he initiates improvement projects to deal with these. Once started, an improvement project may involve the manager in one of three ways. He may delegate all responsibility to a subordinate, implicitly retaining the right to replace him; he may delegate responsibility for the design work but retain responsibility for authorizing the project before implementation; or he may supervise the design work himself. Senior managers appear to maintain supervision at any one time over a large inventory of these projects. Each is worked on periodically, with each step followed by a period of delay during which the senior manager waits for the feedback of information or the occurrence of an event.

As *disturbance handler* the manager is required to take charge when his organization faces a major disturbance. Since each subordinate is charged with a specialized function, only the manager is able to intervene when the organization faces a novel stimulus that is unrelated to any particular function and for which it has no programmed response. In effect, the manager again acts as his organization's generalist—the problem-solver who can deal with any kind of stimulus. Disturbances may reflect an insensitivity to problems, but they may also result from the unanticipated consequences of bold innovation. Hence we may expect to find many disturbances in the work of managers of both innovative and insensitive organizations. One can also expect to find the *disturbance handler* role emphasized following a period of intense innovation; a period of major change must be followed by a period in which the change is consolidated. Furthermore, managers of small companies and those in line production jobs, especially at lower levels in the hierarchy are likely to give the greatest attention to the *disturbance handler* role (and to the other decisional roles) because they tend to be most involved with the day-to-day maintenance of the workflow.

As *resource allocator* the manager oversees the allocation of all his organization's resources and thereby maintains control of its strategy-making process. He does this in three ways. First, by scheduling his own time the manager implicitly sets organizational priorities. Issues that fail to reach him fail to get support. Second, the manager designs the basic work system of his organization and programs the work of subordinates. He decides what will be done, who will do it, and what structure will be used. Third, the manager maintains ultimate control by authorizing, before implementation, all major decisions made by his organization. The authorization decisions are difficult ones to make; the issues are complex, but the time that can be devoted to them is short. The manager can ease the difficulty by choosing the person rather than the proposal. But when he must decide on the proposal, the manager makes use of loose models and plans that he develops implicitly from his nerve-center information. The models describe in a conceptual way a great variety of the internal and external situations that the manager faces. The plans—in the form of anticipated improvement projects–exist as his flexible vision of where the organization might go. Such plans serve as the common frame of reference against which he can evaluate, and hence interrelate, all proposals.

Finally, as *negotiator* the manager takes charge when his organization must have important negotiations with another organization. As *figurehead* he represents his organization, as *spokesman* he speaks for it, and as *resource allocator* he trades resources in real-time with the opposite party.

To summarize, the manager must design the work of his organization, monitor its internal and external environment, initiate change when desirable, and renew stability when faced with a disturbance. The manager must lead his subordinates to work effectively for the organization, and he must provide them with special information, some of which he gains through the network of contacts that he develops. In addition, the manager must perform a number of "housekeeping" duties, including informing outsiders, serving as *figurehead,* and leading major negotiations.

Thus, the popular view of the manager as the one who must take the broad view, do the unprogrammed work, and buttress the system where it is imperfect is only partly correct. Managers must also do their share of regular work and must involve themselves in certain ongoing organizational activities.

BASIC JOB CHARACTERISTICS

It has been noted that the manager must take responsibility for the operation of his organization's strategy-making system, that he alone must find and process a significant amount of its important information, and that he must also perform a number of "housekeeping" duties. Added to all this is the open-ended nature of his job. There are no clear mileposts in the job of managing, never an indication that nothing more need be done for the moment, always the nagging thought that something could be improved if only the time could be found. Hence the manager's burden of responsibility is inherently great.

His problem is further compounded. The current and speculative nature of so much of the manager's information means that it is verbal. But the dissemination of verbal information is time-consuming. Hence the manager faces a "dilemma of delegation." He has unique access to much important information, but he lacks a formal and efficient means of disseminating it. The result is that the manager finds it difficult to delegate certain tasks with confidence, since he has neither the time nor the means to send along all the necessary information.

The net effect of all this is that the manager's time assumes a great opportunity cost. He carries this great burden of responsibility, yet he cannot easily delegate his tasks. As organizations become increasingly large and complex, this burden increases, particularly for senior managers. Unfortunately, these men cannot significantly increase their available time or significantly improve their abilities to manage. Hence the leaders of large complex bureaucracies face the real danger of becoming major obstructions in the flow of decisions and information.

These points explain a number of distinctive characteristics that can be observed in managerial work. The manager feels compelled to perform a great quantity of work and the pace he assumes is unrelenting. The manager seems to have little free time during the workday and he takes few breaks. Senior managers appear unable to escape from their work after hours because of what they take home and because their minds are constantly turned to their jobs.

The manager's activities are characterized by brevity, variety, and fragmentation. The vast majority are of brief duration, on the order of seconds for foremen and minutes for chief executives. A great variety of activities are performed, but with no obvious patterns. The trivial are interspersed with the consequential so that the manager must shift moods quickly and frequently. There is great fragmentation of work, and interruptions are commonplace. The characteristics of brevity and fragmentation, apparently present in virtually all managers' jobs, are most pronounced for those who are closest to the "action"—top managers of small organizations, managers at lower levels in the hierarchy, particularly in production jobs, and managers working in the most dynamic environments.

Interestingly, the manager shows signs of preference for brevity and interruption in his work. No doubt, he becomes conditioned by his workload. He develops an appreciation for the opportunity costs of his own time and he lives with the awareness that, no matter what he is doing, there are other, perhaps more important, things that he might do and that he must do. A tendency toward superficiality becomes the prime occupational hazard of the manager.

In choosing activities the manager gravitates where possible to the more active elements in his work—the current, the well-defined, the nonroutine. Very current information—gossip, hearsay, speculation—is favored; routine reports are not. Time scheduling reflects a focus on the definite and the concrete, and activities tend to deal with specific rather than general issues. These characteristics are clearly found in the activities of chief executives and most become even more pronounced at lower levels of the hierarchy. The manager's job is not one that breeds reflective planners; rather, it produces adaptive information manipulators who favor a stimulus-response milieu.

The manager's work is essentially that of communication and his tools are the five basic media—mail, telephone, unscheduled meetings, scheduled meetings, and tours. Managers clearly favor the three verbal media, many spending on the order of 80 percent of their time in verbal contact. Some managers, such as those of staff groups, spend relatively more time alone. But the greatest share of the time of almost all managers is spent in verbal communication. The verbal media are favored because they are the action media, providing current information and rapid feedback. The mail, which moves slowly and contains little "live action" material, receives cursory treatment. Mail processing tends to be treated as a burden.

The informal media—the telephone and the unscheduled meeting—are generally used for brief contacts when the parties are well known to each other and when information or requests must be transmitted quickly. In contrast, scheduled meetings allow for more formal contacts, of longer duration, with large groups of people, and away from the organization. Of special interest is the flow of incidental, but often important, information at the beginning and end of scheduled meetings. Scheduled meetings are used for the special purposes of ceremony, strategy-making, and negotiation. Managers in large organizations and top managers of public organizations spend more time in scheduled meetings and other formal activities, while the work of lower-level managers and managers in dynamic environments tends to exhibit less formality.

Tours provide the manager with the opportunity to observe activity informally. Yet, managers apparently spend little time in this medium, perhaps because it involves nonspecific activity that is nonaction oreinted.

An analysis of the characteristics of the manager's interactions with other people shows that he stands between his own organizational unit and an extensive network of contacts. These can include his unit's clients, suppliers, and associates, his peers and colleagues, and their superiors and subordinates. Nonline relationships are a significant component of every manager's job, generally consuming one-third to one-half of his contact time. Managers in large organizations appear to have greater ranges of these contacts and better communication patterns. Much of their horizontal communication, however, appears to be with small cliques of colleagues that serve as centers for specialized information. Subordinates consume about one-third to one-half of the manager's time. He interacts with a wide variety of subordinates, freely bypassing formal channels of authority to get the information he desires. Finally, the evidence suggests that managers spend relatively little time with their superiors, only about one-tenth of their contact hours.

It has been implied in a number of the above conclusions that the burden of his work results in the manager's being carried along by his job to a large extent. The evidence concerning who initiates the manager's contacts and what types of contacts he engages in would appear to bear this out. Nevertheless, the strong incumbent (in any but the most highly structured jobs) can control his own work in subtle ways. In the first place, he is responsible for many of his initial commitments which later lock him into a set of ongoing activities. In the second place, the strong manager can turn to his own advantage those activities in which he must engage; he can extract information, lobby for his causes, or implement changes.

An analysis of the roles further suggests a blend of duties and rights. The duties come with the roles of *figurehead, spokesman, disturbance handler,* and *negotiator.* But in the roles of *leader, entrepreneur,* and *resource allocator,* the manager has the opportunity to put his stamp on his organizational unit and set its course.

SCIENCE IN THE JOB

The evidence suggests that there is no science in managerial work. That is to say, managers do not work according to procedures that have been prescribed by scientific analysis. Indeed, the modern manager appears to be basically indistinguishable from his historical counterparts. He may seek different information, but he gets most of it in the same old way, by word of mouth. He may make decisions dealing with modern technology, but he uses the same intuitive (that is, nonexplicit) procedures or "programs" in making them.

Managers use a whole repertoire of general-purpose programs in their work. Faced with a particular task, the manager chooses, combines, and sequences a set of programs to deal with it. We can identify a number of general-purpose programs—such as information dissemination, alternative selection, and negotiation. There are other general-purpose programs that are more difficult to isolate, such as those associated with the *leader* role. In addition, the manager has some special purpose programs. He uses one—the scheduling program—to control his activities and determine the sequence of tasks to be executed.

The current reality is that all these programs are locked in the manager's brain, not yet described by the management researcher. There can be no science of managing until these programs are demarcated, their contents specified, the set of them linked into a simulation of managerial work, and particular ones subjected to systematic analysis and improvement.

part **4**

TOWARD SOME ANSWERS?

The first three sections of this book explore some of the controversies in the basic foundation areas of psychology, sociology, and social psychology. In general, the controversy seems to grow when the knowledge is applied to organizations. Despite conflict, the existing concepts have been shown to have practical relevance now and great potential for the future. That this potential has gone unrealized may be the result of a futile hope for across-the-board answers to management problems, a hope that has eclipsed the more realistic idea of situational relativity in the minds of many people. In this final section, our theme of concepts and controversy is applied to some of the more popular strategies for contemporary management: participative management, management by objectives, organizational development, Theory Y, and the systems approach. The theoretical merits of these and other, closely related approaches have already been debated; our emphasis at this point is on the practice of these strategies. Given the controversy in the foundation areas, we can expect less than perfect agreement on strategies.

PARTICIPATIVE MANAGEMENT

As noted earlier, effective leadership styles depend on many variables, including the work group, supervisor personality, the organization, and the nature of the task. However, as the paper by Krishnan in part 3 suggested, leadership style is also influenced by some general value judgments. The roles that these value judgments can play are well documented in the heated controversies which have taken place about participative management.

Perhaps the best known of these "debates" was the series of exchanges between Gomberg and Bennis (1966) and Gomberg and Marrow (1966). The Gomberg-Bennis Marrow controversy centered around the famous Harwood experiments conducted by Coch and French (1948), a cornerstone study of the introduction of change through participative techniques. Gomberg was involved with the Harwood Corporation on the union side. He argued that what the researchers termed "worker participation" was perceived by the group of workers as insidious control. More generally, while Gomberg acknowledged the merits of the Lewinian value structure, he argued that its proponents (Bennis and others) failed to provide a strategy for implementation which would enable the manager to fulfill his primary objective of getting the job done profitably. To do so, he must make decisions and exercise power in ways which will be pleasing to some people and frustrating to others. Gomberg questioned whether participative methods would permit the necessary decisions to be made and carried out.

Gomberg was unhappy with the democratic approach for other reasons, too. He questioned the morality of attempts to use quasi-psychotherapeutic techniques for industrial purposes. He also charged that the human-relations approach had confused democracy with decentralization. For Gomberg, decentralization was not a technique of democracy but a means of maintaining central control while allowing relatively unimportant decisions to be handled on the periphery. In addition, Gomberg suggested that so-called democratic management may be just an attempt to break up groups of workers. Finally, Gomberg speculated that the successes of participative management might have been based on fear, on the part of relatively powerless workers, about the consequences of failure to go along with the new techniques.

The advocates of democratic management, of course, take serious issue with Gomberg. Bennis, in his reply, noted that he favored democracy mainly because he felt it to be efficient under many conditions. In addition, he questioned Gomberg's understanding of the Harwood experiments. In a later exchange (Gomberg and Marrow, 1966), Marrow, president of the Harwood Company and an important social scientist, joined the debate. Marrow took issue with Gomberg's charge that participative management was not apt to be consistent with organizational needs by pointing to Harwood's strong competitive position. He also countered Gomberg's argument that participative management produced worker hostility toward management by pointing to Harwood's good relationships with employees. In his final reply Gomberg (1966) questioned whether Harwood's management was in fact democratic. He cited a statement by French, one of the original Harwood researchers, to the effect that management at Harwood laid out and followed a policy of fairness and openness. This approach, according to Gomberg, differed little from General Electric's policy of Boulwarism, in which management offered what it believed would be a fair settlement for a union contract and stuck with it. The one difference between the two, according to Gomberg, was that Boulware did not call his approach democratic or participative management. Gomberg suggests that behavioral scientists and "industrial democrats" have failed to distinguish between a benevolent paternal style of autocracy and democracy. He concluded that benevolent autocracy does not satisfy some important needs of individual workers.

In contrast to Gomberg, there are a number of people who believe that benevolent autocracy may be a very desirable form of corporate governance. McMurry (1958) has provided a most articulate statement of this view. McMurry argued that the characteristics of subordinates and leaders in organizations, as well as the characteristics of organizations themselves, are much more consistent with some type of autocracy.

In order to help people know where they stand and what is expected of them and to focus on goals for individual performance and growth, McMurry would institute conferences to review employee performance. Such conferences, in McMurry's view, are to be instructive, not critical or admonitory. Also, McMurry would introduce surveys of employees' opinions on a regular basis to find out where problems exist and how to deal with them. This is a technique of Likert (1967) himself. In a sense, McMurry has taken an in-between view, recognizing the important role of power and the effect power has on people in the organizations and, at the same time, the desirability and practicality of at least some elements of the democratic or participative approach to management.

McMurry maintained that people want and require considerable direction from above in modern organizations. If this is true, his choice of autocracy over democracy would seem appropriate. However, it may be that autocratic practices in the past have brought about the conditions which McMurry sees as necessitating autocratic practices in the present. The democratic theorists would argue that this cycle may be broken by management styles which encourage more participation by all organizational members in decisions which affect their work.

In this respect their ideas appear to represent an advance beyond those of McMurry and Gomberg; at the same time, however, the democratic theorists may be faulted for having given inadequate attention to power as a variable, despite its importance in organizations. They seem to have been more concerned with power equalization than with the study of power itself. It is certainly laudable to note that power has dysfunctional consequences and to strive to eliminate them, but it is not possible to do so by neglecting the subject of power in both research and therapies. While the views of Gomberg, McMurry, and others are highly debatable, they are nevertheless notable for their attention to an important organizational variable sidestepped in the writings of many current organizational behaviorists.

More recently Gomberg (1973) has updated his attack on applied behavioral scientists. In his paper "Job Satisfaction: Sorting Out the Nonsense," he evaluated a number of instances of the introduction of participative management and job enrichment. He charged that behavioral scientists have overlooked the contributions that trade unionism can make to participative management. He suggested that the behavioral scientists are basically indifferent to the goal of managerial democracy and/or are ignorant of what changes are required for it to exist.

In sum Gomberg continues to argue strongly against one of the basic themes of the human relations approach. The schemes devised by human relationists for increasing the participation of lower-level members in organizational decisions are limited in scope. For the most part these strategies do not transfer real power, but only allow lower-level members to participate in ways carefully circumscribed by upper-level managers.

Although Gomberg's attacks on the participative aspects of human relations are among the most hard hitting, other writers seem to share some of his basic observations. One of the most insightful analyses of why managers often may not encourage and achieve real participation from their subordinates can be found in an excellent book by Miles (1975).

Based on some of his earlier research Miles suggested that there are three alternative theories or models which managers have about the management of people. One model, the traditional view, resembles McGregor's Theory X in that the manager assumes his or her subordinates find work distasteful and cannot be counted on to control or direct their own work behavior. Miles second model, the human relations model, is similar to the traditional view, but adds recognition of human social needs and the desires of people to be treated with dignity. This approach encourages managers to treat their subordinates with consideration. However, Miles pointed out that the purpose of these efforts is to more or less lubricate the machinery of the traditional organizational structure by improving morale and overcoming resistance to authority. As Miles noted, the participative mechanisms which emerge from the human relations approach

> are aimed at preventing and/or resolving conflict within the structure rather than at utilizing the full range of capabilities of members, inefficiency will exist to the degree that these capabilities are under-valued by management's assumptions. Moreover, if the participative devices divert work-relevant energy and capability rather than use them, a double cost is incurred. (p. 84)

Miles' third model, the human resources approach, stems from a very different set of assumptions and implies the need for a redesign of work and of organizational structures to encourage the full participation of people at all levels in the organization. It is based on assumptions which hold that people want to contribute to meaningful goals and can exercise far more responsible and creative role-direction than they are normally required to do in most work organizations. According to Miles, a manager who is guided by the human resources model values the participation of individuals because the decisions and outcomes which result are superior to what would occur without their inputs.

Which of the three models describes the perspective of the typical manager? Miles reports that the attitudes of most American managers are closely aligned with the human relations perspective. He writes

> . . . most sociotechnical systems operate with traditional structures, policies, and practices, laid over with a thin veneer of human relations modifications. (p. 233)

Thus Miles' observations parallel Gomberg's. While managers frequently talk about the merits of participation, they often are advocating only a limited form of participation—a form which does not conflict to any great extent with the existing hierarchical distribution of power.

Why should these attitudes be so widely shared? Miles provided some thoughtful answers. Among other things he suggested that the human relations model is a ". . . comforting collection of concepts and prescriptions. . ." which promises ". . . to allow the manager to retain his role as controller of the system while minimizing conflict and gaining the compliance of . . . subordinates" (pp. 233-34). Managers are motivated to achieve accountability from their subordinates and are acutely aware that they themselves are accountable to their superiors. Consequently they may prefer to achieve predictable behavior through a human relations approach than to tolerate the ambiguity they perceive inherent in the human resources view" (pp. 233-34). Moreover, Miles observed that the human relations viewpoint has been widely disseminated and is well developed compared to the human resources perspective. By contrast, the human resources model is new, not fully developed, and often misunderstood. Finally, Miles suggested that managers may not perceive their subordinates as really having important inputs to make.

Miles' discussion provides us with some insights as to why managers advocate participative management but often do not practice it. Moreover, these insights give us some clues as to why certain "participative" strategies such as management by objectives and organizational development may often fail to achieve the outcomes which, based on what appears to be a sound body of evidence and theory, we expect them to produce.

MANAGEMENT BY OBJECTIVES (MBO)

A second modern strategy for applying the findings of behavioral science is management by objectives. The popularity of this approach can be partially explained by its demonstrated success. However, its positive reception may be due to its consistency with both a hierarchical view of organizations and with entrepreneurial values demanding that individuals be given autonomy to work and rewards commensurate with their achievements. Drucker (1954) is generally credited with coining the phrase "management by objectives." McGregor (1960) drew on Drucker to develop a means of implementing his Theory Y approach. More recently, Odiorne (1965) dealt at length with the implementation of MBO in systems terms.

Hunt (1972) observed that MBO is the most important structural change in the management of organizations in the last twenty years. He wrote,

> We believe it will replace the traditional authority structure by placing control in the lap of each and every member. This will make it possible to eliminate many of the petty and irritating structural controls which are forced on members because they *have to be made to perform* a job. . . . (p. 353)

Hunt is suggesting that what is innovative about MBO is not the idea of using objectives in management—objectives have been used for a long time—but that it involves individuals at all levels of the organization in the process of establishing the goals.

Those who manage by objectives work jointly with their subordinates to identify organizational and individual goals, to define responsibility for each manager by specifying expected results, to measure actual results, and to utilize them as a means of assessing and improving individual performance. Recently, a research report by the National Industrial Conference Board (1968) suggested that management by objectives should be considered as management with objectives, because MBO is only one of many strategies that can be followed simultaneously. It is not a total system of management. Rather, it is a technique to supplement others. Further, the NICB report noted that management by objectives is not a standardized technique. Instead, the introduction, evolution, and form of the objectives programs vary among companies.

The strategy also has had mixed results. Most companies which have adopted it have reported both benefits and problems, the benefits generally outweighing the problems. Common benefits included better management performance, more complete planning, better control (since the objectives and plans themselves are the major tools of control), improved subordinate-superior relationships, and better development of managerial abilities. Common problems included the relatively long time period required for supervisors to learn to manage by objectives, an overemphasis on the objectives alone (which means a failure to tend to other important problems), confusion and difficulty resulting from attempts to use MBO as a tool for appraisal, and problems in changing administrative procedures to support rather than conflict with the objectives program.

Generally, MBO has been well received by both theorists and practicing managers. In many ways its acceptance is due to its success as well as its consistency with the prevailing assumptions and values of the culture in which it evolved. The procedure is oriented toward reward for results, toward individual freedom and variation, toward measurement, and toward reevaluation and readjustment.

However, Levinson (1970) has attacked the approach as being much more consistent with hierarchy than with effective management of people. While not rejecting MBO as a technique, Levinson argued that its current implementation is more consistent with the methods of Frederick Taylor and industrial engineering than with the true integration of individual and organizational purposes. According to Levinson, characteristically top management sets the corporate goals, and the individual manager is limited to choosing which of those goals to pursue and helping to select the statistics which his superiors will use to evaluate his work. In essence then, MBO is ". . . based on a short-term, egocentrically oriented perspective and an underlying reward-punishment psychology" (p. 128). It treats a person differently from a rat in a maze only in allowing him to select ". . . his own bait from a limited range of choices" (p. 128). A subordinate's personal objectives are seldom taken into account, since top-level executives assume that they alone have the prerogative to determine objectives, provide rewards and targets, and drive people who work for the organization. Under such conditions individual managers come to view appraisal as a hostile, destructive act and find it difficult to give constructive criticism. Levinson concluded that executives can improve MBO by exploring its underlying psychological assumptions, by utilizing group appraisal, and by considering the personal goals of the individual ahead of organizational goals. Unless these changes are made, Levinson considers the technique, as currently practiced, to be self-defeating in the long run.

While Hunt (1972) believed that MBO represents a most important structural change, he noted some of the same problems that Levinson did:

> . . . unless MBO is seen as only *one* ingredient of a change of the whole system, then it remains yet another single variable solution and will have limited success. It must be combined with concurrent changes in other variables, especially attempts to satisfy individual needs. (p. 353)

In other words, the introduction of MBO represents only one change in a complex social system. This change, by itself, is insufficient to bring about the humanistic outcomes that the proponents of MBO believe it will produce.

The reading by Tosi and Carroll presents evidence related to Levinson's and Hunt's arguments. They, too, indicated the need for more research on the implementation and consequences of management by objectives.

ORGANIZATIONAL DEVELOPMENT

Although "organizational development" (OD) is a relatively new term, many of the concepts and techniques it includes have been discussed and used for some time. Because of its diverse lineage OD is an ambiguous concept. As Kahn (1974) observed, OD ". . . is a new label for a conglomerate of things. . . . What that label refers to depends to a considerable extent upon the doer or writer" (pp. 485-86). OD is a convenient label rather than a precise concept, but it refers to a somewhat homogeneous constellation of ideas and strategies.

Friedlander and Brown (1974) observed that OD is emerging as both a recognized profession and a field of academic study. There are a number of academic courses and even degree programs preparing students for OD work. Moreover, there are several professional organizations and even one accrediting agency for OD practitioners.

More importantly, Friedlander and Brown were able to develop a simple, albeit general, overview that describes most of the essential features of OD. They wrote,

> The framework we shall use in reviewing OD views organizations as composed of people with different sets of values, styles, and skills; technologies with different characteristics; and processes and structures which reflect different kinds of relationships between people or between people and their work. . . . OD is a method for facilitating change and development in people (e.g., styles, values, skills), in technology (e.g., greater simplicity, complexity), and in organizational processes and structures (e.g., relationships, roles). The objectives of OD can generally be classified as those optimizing human and social improvement or as those optimizing task accomplishment or more likely as some (often confused) blend of the two. (p. 314)

Thus, OD treats many of the problems we have dealt with throughout this book. It recognizes that organizations are complex human and technical systems that are constantly restructuring themselves in order to achieve those outcomes that permit them to survive in their environments.

From what we have said, it may appear that OD is the ultimate form of application of the concepts that have been advanced by applied behavioral scientists. OD seems to be individually as well as systems-oriented, and directed toward the achievement of organizational goals. Certainly OD includes a number of the concepts that we have discussed as needed for the improvement of organizations. However, its promise has yet to be fulfilled; in fact, the efficacy of OD has been questioned by a number of behavioral scientists, including Warren Bennis, who had been one of the early OD enthusiasts.

During the 1960s Bennis was one of the leaders in predicting the death of bureaucracy (see his paper in part 2 of this book). He stressed the need for participative management and the importance of honest, open communication among individuals within organizations. However, in the late 1960s Bennis left his professional role and became an administrator at the University of Buffalo and later president of the University of Cincinnati.

Since his transition from theorist to practitioner Bennis's ideas about OD have undergone important changes. Bennis (1974) has come to believe that bureaucracy is the inevitable form of organization in large-scale enterprises. He has rejected the notion that achievement of consensus through trust, openness, confrontation, and feedback can be a viable process for making decisions in large, complex organizations. Bennis (1973) noted,

> . . . the problem in our institutions today are basically size and scale, an incessant, turbulent and imposing environment (like federal and state government), diverse and basically conflicting constituencies, politics, economics, and technology—and their phenomenal rate of change. Consensus is chimerical under these conditions, a "good old days" myth, perpetuated by OD practitioners and as appropriate to today's organizations as buggy whips are to GM. (p. 391)

Bennis noted that OD theorists have overlooked several other things. First, they have given inadequate attention to the pressures that time creates for administrators. Bennis (1973) observed, "There is the reality of the time in which people have to work, and we have to negotiate a trade-off between trust, group development, and achievement of tasks" (p. 394). Moreover, he observed that to date most OD approaches have not conceptualized power adequately and have failed to deal with the pressures exerted by interest groups both inside and outside organizations. As president of the University of Cincinnati, Bennis has become very aware of the constraints that the environment imposes on administrators. Various constituencies outside the university claim 80% of this time, leaving him little to devote to the development of relationships with his own staff.

While his thoughts have changed, Bennis has not fully rejected OD. He tries to adhere to the values he advanced in his earlier writings, as evidenced by his desire to serve as a "role model" of these attributes. Moreover, he has asked a leading OD practitioner to work with him and his staff at the University of Cincinnati.

While Bennis's experiences are not necessarily representative of those that individuals would encounter elsewhere, they do reveal some of the difficulties of introducing OD even where top management is highly knowledgeable about and committed to the process. Just as MBO constitutes only one set of changes in a complex organization, so does OD. Unless other changes are made concurrently, OD as currently conceived may be very difficult to implement.

Organizational development poses other problems for both researchers and managers. First, Kahn (1974) has pointed to the absence of data about the efficacy of OD as well as the conceptual and methodological difficulties likely to be encountered by researchers who attempt to collect such information. Second, Friedlander and Brown (1974) noted that OD has been developed and attempted within a very narrow range of organizations—primarily business and industrial firms. Its applicability to other types of organizations is largely unknown. Finally, Friedlander and Brown noted that OD practitioners and researchers often may emphasize the goal of task accomplishment and other interests of management more than they stress other ends, such as human fulfillment. Consequently, in the words of Friedlander and Brown, "OD as a field runs the risk of encouraging and implementing subtle but persuasive forms of exploitation, curtailment of freedom, control of personality, violation of dignity, intrusion of privacy—all in the name of science and of economic and technological efficiency" (p. 335).

Our discussion of OD has pointed to some of its assets and liabilities. The paper by French, which appears later in this part, examines a number of the assumptions and approaches embodied in organizational development.

TOWARD SOME RESOLUTION

The article by Morse and Lorsch in many ways summarizes the major points developed in this book. Theory Y often provides a useful orientation for management toward human behavior, but it is more sound in some situations than others. The same is true of Theory X or perhaps any general orientation. What matters most is that one's management orientation, whatever its nature, should be chosen deliberately, not assumed a priori.

The final article in this section is the editor's assessment of the state of knowledge of organizational behavior and implications for the development of managers. The article is designed to help integrate the material and to suggest some of the paths that students of organizational behavior may find rewarding. Every section of this book stresses the effect of the interaction of multiple variables on the behavior or organizational participants. Organizational behavior must be both multi- and interdisciplinary. This last selection suggests that people must be prepared to seek answers and to deal realistically with highly complex human situations. Thus, rather than supplying the answers, this paper offers a strategy for obtaining them.

REFERENCES

Bennis, W. G. "An O.D. Expert in the Cat Bird's Seat." *Journal of Higher Education* 44 (1973): 389-98.

Bennis, W. G. "Conversation . . . with Warren Bennis." *Organizational Dynamics* 2 (1974): 51-66.

Coch, L., and French, J. R. P. "Overcoming Resistance to Change." *Human Relations* 1 (1948): 512-32.

Drucker, P. *The Practice of Management.* New York: Harper & Row, Publishers, 1954.

Friedlander, F., and Brown, L. D. *Organization Development.* In Rosenzweig, M. R., and Porter, L. W. (Eds.) *Annual Review of Psychology* 25 (1974): 313-41.

Gomberg, W. "Democratic Management—Gomberg Replies." *Trans-action* 3 (1966): 48.

Gomberg, W. Job Satisfaction: Sorting Out the Nonsense. *AFL-CIO American Federationist,* June, 1973.

Gomberg, W., and Bennis, W. G. "The Trouble with Democratic Management, and a Reply: When Democracy Works." *Trans-action* 3 (1966): 30-36.

Gomberg, W., and Marrow, A. "Democratic Management—The Debate Continues." *Trans-action* 3 (1966): 35-37, 56.

Hunt, J. W. *The Restless Organization.* New York: John Wiley, 1972.

Kahn, R. L. "Organizational Development: Some Problems and Proposals." *Journal of Applied Behavioral Science* 10 (1974): 485-502.

Levinson, H. "Management by Whose Objectives?" *Harvard Business Review* 48 (1970): 125-34.

Likert, R. *The Human Organization.* New York: McGraw-Hill Book Co., 1967.

McGregor, D. *The Human Side of Enterprise.* New York: McGraw-Hill Book Co., 1960.

McMurry, R. N. "The Case for Benevolent Autocracy." *Harvard Business Review* 36 (1958): 82-90.

Maier, N. R. F. "Assets and Liabilities in Group Problem Solving: The Need for an Integrative Function." *Psychological Review* 74 (1967): 239-49.

Managing by—and with—Objectives. Personnel Policy Study No. 212. New York: National Industrial Conference Board, Inc., 1968.

Miles, R. E. *Theories of Management: Implications for Organizational Behavior and Development.* New York: McGraw-Hill Book Co., 1975.

Odiorne, G. S. *Management by Objectives.* New York: Pitman Publishing Corp., 1965.

Tannenbaum, R., and Schmidt, W. H. "How to Choose a Leadership Pattern." *Harvard Business Review* 36 (1958): 95-101.

Henry L. Tosi
Stephen J. Carroll

MANAGERIAL REACTION TO MANAGEMENT BY OBJECTIVES

Interest in the "management by objectives" approach has been growing steadily since it was popularized in the fifties by Drucker and McGregor.[1] Odiorne describes the process as one in which

> . . . the superior and the subordinate managers of an organization jointly define its common goals, define each individual's major areas of responsibility in terms of the results expected of him and use these measures as guides for operating the unit and assessing the contribution of each of its members.[2]

While the major discussion of benefits of this approach tends to center around the possibility of more objective performance evaluation, other values may accrue. If goals are set and understood by the subordinate, frustration and anxiety resulting from ambiguity surrounding job expectations may be reduced. Higher levels of performance may be achieved. If the goals are progressively more difficult from period to period, and the participation of the subordinate leads to increased levels of ego-involvement in their attainment, higher levels of motivation may obtain.

For the most part, "management by objectives" has been implemented on the

From Henry L. Tosi and Stephen J. Carroll "Managerial Reaction to Management by Objectives," *Academy of Management Journal* 11, (December, 1968): 415-26. Reprinted by permission.

[1] Peter Drucker, *The Practice of Management* (New York: Harper and Row, Publishers, 1954) and Douglas McGregor, "An Uneasy Look at Performance Appraisal," *Harvard Business Review* (May-June, 1957). As an indication of the growing interest, see for example Charles L. Hughes, *Goal Setting* (New York: AMA, 1966); Raymond F. Valentine, *Performance Objectives for Managers* (New York: AMA, 1966); J. D. Batten, *Beyond Management by Objectives* (New York: AMA, 1966); Earnest C. Miller, *Objectives and Standards of Performance in Financial Management* (New York: AMA, 1968); Nathaniel Stewart, *Strategies of Managing for Results* (Englewood Cliffs, N.J.: Prentice-Hall, Inc., 1966); George Odiorne, *Management by Objectives* (New York: Pitman, 1965). Textbooks include George Strauss and Leonard R. Sayles, *Personnel* (Englewood Cliffs, N.J.: Prentice-Hall, Inc., 1967); Wendell French, *The Personnel Management Process* (Boston: Houghton Mifflin Company); Paul Pigors and Charles A. Myers, *Personnel Administration* (New York: McGraw-Hill Book Company. 1965).

[2] Odiorne.

basis of its apparent theoretical practicability and advantages. There has been only limited research examining its effects. One set of studies was conducted by Raia.[3] A large firm implemented "Goal Setting and Self Control," a variant of management by objectives. By the end of the first program year productivity had increased, managers were more aware of the firm's goals, and specific goals had been set in more areas than had been the previous experience. Prior to the program, productivity was decreasing at the rate of 4 percent per month. After the program was instituted, the trend reversed and was increasing at 3 percent per month. Raia concluded that:

> A contribution of the program in the area of performance appraisal has been quite significant. There was unanimous agreement among the line managers in the department, particularly plant managers, the Goals and Controls had simplified the evaluation of the individual's performance. The statement by the manager who, while being interviewed, remarked that he was now judged by his job performance and not "by the way I comb my hair," is quite meaningful.

Among the other advantages cited were better planning of resource utilization, pinpointing of problem areas, and improved communications and mutual understanding.

A follow-up study of the same program sheds additional light on the Goal Setting Program.[4] This study generally supports the findings of the first. The level of goal attainment increased, there were continuing increases in productivity and improved managerial planning and control. Some managers, however, felt the program was "easy to beat." There seemed to be an overemphasis on production or measureable goals. Some of the participants reevaluated their initial feeling about appraisal and felt that the program did not provide adequate incentives to improve performance. The managers asked, "What does it mean to the individual when he fails to meet certain goals?" They were not able to link the goal setting program to the organization's reward system.

The study by Meyer, Kay, and French examined the effect of a Work Planning and Review Program.[5] The basic features of this program are very similar to management by objectives.

> In WPR discussion, the managerial subordinates do not deal in generalities. They consider specific objectively defined work goals and establish the yardstick for measuring performance. These goals stem, of course, from broader departmental objectives and are defined in relation to the individual's position in the departments.

Managers using this system were compared to those operating under the traditional performance appraisal method used in the company studied. Those

[3] Anthony P. Raia, "Goal Setting and Self Control," *Journal of Management Studies II,* 1 (Feb., 1965): 34-53 and "A Second Look at Goals and Controls," *California Management Review* (Summer, 1966), pp. 49-58.

[4] Raia, "A Second Look . . . ."

[5] Herbert H. Meyer, Emanuel Kay, and John R. P. French, Jr., "Split Roles in Performance Appraisal," *Harvard Business Review* 43 (Jan.-Feb., 1965): 123-29.

managers operating under the old appraisal method did not change in the areas measured.

> The WPR group, by contrast, expressed significantly more favorable attitudes on almost all questionnaire items. Specifically, their attitudes changed in a favorable direction over the year that they participated in the new WPR program with regard to:
> 1. Amount of help the manager was giving them in improving performance on the job and the degree to which the manager was receptive to new ideas;
> 2. The ability of the manager to plan;
> 3. The extent to which the managers made use of their abilities and experience;
> 4. The degree to which they felt the goals they were shooting for were what they *should be;*
> 5. The extent to which they received help from the manager in planning for future job opportunities;
> 6. The value of the performance discussions they had with their managers.

In addition to changes in attitudes, the authors concluded that the members of the WPR group were much more likely to have taken specific actions to improve performance than those who were continuing to operate within a traditional performance appraisal approach.

Mendleson found that while there was no significant relationship between the *extent* of goal setting within a superior-subordinate pair of managers and the superior's *ratings of his subordinate's present performance,* there was, on the other hand, a positive relationship between *goal setting and the superior's rating of his subordinate's promotability.*[6]

The research evidence points to three general conclusions. First, changes in performance and attitude, which seem positive and desirable, appear to be associated with management by objectives. Secondly, some signals of caution must be noted. Last, the number of researches in this topic is limited.

THE CURRENT STUDY

The management by objectives program studied here was implemented in a large manufacturing firm. The company produces both industrial and consumer products. It is a large national concern with sales, manufacturing, and distribution locations dispersed throughout the United States.

The *work planning and review* program (WPR is the program designation by the company) was instituted at the initiative and the authority of a new vice president of personnel. He found, on joining the company, that the appraisal system was essentially based on "personality traits and characteristics." The Personnel Department began developing manuals and procedures necessary for the change to an objectives-oriented appraisal system. These were prepared and

[6] Jack L. Mendleson, "Managerial Goal Setting: An Exploration Into Meaning and Measurement" (unpublished dissertation, Michigan State University, 1967).

distributed. Meetings were held with the top management group in the company to discuss the use and rationale underlying the objectives approach. They were instructed to implement it in their own units. Needless to say, the degree of implementation and management support varied within different departments.

Essentially, the purposes of the program are to motivate managers and improve individual job performance. Goals were to be set in two areas, performance and self-improvement. The performance goals were described in the instruction manual as those

> things to be accomplished, changes to be made, and standards of performance to be met. This is a plan of action for the year. *Be Specific.* Indicate how each item is to be accomplished. Show priorities, when each item is to begin and when it is to be completed. Indicate specific amounts, dates or quality. Don't try to include everything; just the important things.

A self-improvement plan was also to be devised. Managers were instructed to

> select a few, preferably not more than three or four, items for personal improvement–ways to expand your knowledge or improve your effectiveness. *Be Specific.*

This study basically reports the results of in-depth interview with 48 managers at all levels ranging from vice president to foremen. Some additional data, in the form of supporting correlation coefficients, have been included from the more extensive questionnaire survey of managers in the company. Table 1 shows the distribution of managers at various organizational levels who participated in the interview phase of the study.

TABLE 1.

Vice President	6
Director	12
Middle Management	20
Lower Management	10
Total	48

The mail questionnaire was distributed to 150 managers in the company. Of the 120 responses, there were at least 98, and in some cases slightly more, usable replies for calculating the correlation coefficient.

FINDINGS

The study is one phase of a more complete examination of the program. This phase deals with four general areas. First we were concerned with the manager's perceptions of the underlying rationale, problems, and advantages associated with an objectives approach. From this naturally follows a set of suggested changes to improve the approach.

Philosophy, Rationale, and Purpose of the Program

During the interview, each manager was asked the following question: "What are the purposes of the program as you see them? What is the rationale for this approach? Table 2 below presents a summary of the responses.

TABLE 2. **Philosophy and Rationale of the Objectives Approach.**

RATIONALE	*n**	%
1. To Link Evaluation to Performance	17	35.4
2. Aid Manager in Planning	12	25.0
3. Motivate Managers	11	22.9
4. To Increase Boss/Subordinate Interaction & Feedback	11	22.9
5. Development of Management Potential	8	16.6
6. Link Company Objectives to Department Objectives	8	16.6
7. Managers Know What Their Job Is	6	12.5
8. Give Management Information About What's Going On at Lower Levels	4	8.3
9. Management Club to Pressure Performance	3	6.25
10. No Mention	7	14.5

n=48 Managers

*The totals are more than 48 since a respondent may have cited more than one advantage.

Those purposes cited most frequently tend to parallel those stated in the company manuals. The largest percentage (35 percent) felt that an objectives program was intended to link the evaluation of an individual to his actual performance rather than to personality or to other personal characteristics. About 25 percent considered the approach as useful as a planning aid. Increased feedback and the positive motivational effect of the objectives approach were mentioned by 22 percent of the respondents.

The magnitude, or rather lack of it, of the percentages suggests little general agreement among managers about the underlying philosophy and rationale of the program. Only one item, "the attempt to relate evaluation to performance," was noted by more than 30 percent of the respondents. It could be that those items which were cited most frequently, i.e., evaluation, feedback, planning, and motivation, may well be the respondents' verbalization of the content of the organization policy. There seemed to be no central item or set of items around which the responses clustered. Perhaps the attempts to introduce and initiate the program did not substantially affect the attitudes and knowledge of the managers about the program.

Advantages

The managers interviewed were asked the advantages of the objectives program. They reported advantages as indicated below in Table 3. By far the major advantage was that one was more likely to "know what is expected of him by his boss." Over 58 percent of the managers noted this advantage. One marketing executive said:

Now we can focus our evaluation on what people do, rather than what they are. This is the best thing we have for evaluating the performance of our men. And it has a substantial motivational effect. These goals set up a challenge for them. I have seen changes in men's work habits after I began to use this approach. I have been able to watch improvements occur in some of my men.

TABLE 3. **Advantages of Management by Objectives.**

ADVANTAGE	*n**	*%*
1. I Know What is Expected of Me	28	58.6
2. It Forces Planning and Setting Target Dates	20	41.6
3. It Forces Boss/Subordinate Feedback & Communication	15	31.2
4. Increases Awareness of Company Goals	9	18.7
5. Documented Goals Relating Evaluation to Performance	8	16.6
6. Focus on Self-Improvement	7	14.5
7. I Know Where I Stand	6	12.5
8. Coordinates Activity toward Company Objectives	6	12.5
9. Subtle Pressure and Motivation to Perform Better	5	10.4
10. Improves Performance if Used	4	8.3
11. Only a General Help	3	6.2
12. No Advantages Mentioned	5	10.4
n=48		

*The total responses are more than 48 since a manager may have noted more than one advantage.

An engineer felt that

> . . . while I did not have much to say in what the final determination of my goals were, at least I knew what my boss wanted and I knew what to do. I think this motivated me to work harder, or at least to work on those things that I knew were important to him. I also knew whether or not I achieved targets set for me.

The next item cited most frequently (41 percent) was that the program forced more planning, specification of projects, and setting target dates. As one of the managers indicated:

> There is a kind of discipline involved in this program. I had to sit down and think about what I am going to be doing next year. I need to spell out what kind of resources are required and when I expect a particular project to be accomplished. This is a great help to me in determining what priorities should exist. Of course, it is an advantage to have these priorities verified by your boss.

Several managers (31.2 percent) felt that it forced bosses to interact with their subordinates, providing more communication and feedback. One of the respondents, who had recently joined the firm, thought it to be

> . . . a fantastic idea to have a voice along with your boss in setting individual goals. Not only do you get a chance to put your two cents worth in but it gives your boss the benefit of the individual's thinking. I

> thought it was a psychological lift. I like the fact that they ask me what I thought my goal levels should be. I think the chance to sit down with your boss is important.

Another manager said:

> I like the fact that I sit down with my boss to set these objectives. Every time I sit down and talk with him, I can't help but learn more about what he expects of me. Anything that does that is a help.

The advantages cited are fairly consistent with those one would have expected and those found earlier by Raia.[7] The most frequently cited advantages he noted were (1) planning, (2) pinpointing problem areas, (3) objective performance measures, and (4) improved communications. Meyer, Kay, and French similarly found better planning, improved appraisal, and a greater acceptance of the goals set as some of the positive effects. It seems reasonable to conclude that objectives oriented programs increase certainty about job requirements, result in a more comfortable feeling about the kind of criteria used in evaluation, and create a situation which ostensibly forces superiors to communicate with subordinates.

Problems Encountered

A number of managers (37.5 percent) indicated no problems with the objectives approach. The major problem, cited by 43 percent of the managers, was compliance with the formal procedural requirements, the process of completing forms, updating changes, and providing other information to the personnel unit. Raia also found this a major irritant and dubbed it the "paperwork problem."[8]

Some (20.8 percent) felt that the objectives approach was not used to its full potential in the organization. One of the respondents said:

> I am not sure that many managers know how to use and develop objectives and goals. Everyone seems to think in terms of "target dates." Some jobs just don't lend themselves to that kind of goal. We need to recognize that different kinds of goals and objectives might be required for different functions, different jobs, and maybe even different managerial levels. Yet if you look at these review sheets all the goals look the same–a project designation and a target date. And besides, the self-improvement goals really seem to just be an appendage and not an integral part of the process.

In general, with the exception of the problems cited above, the problems and disadvantages cited tend to be fairly well distributed across the range of items listed in Table 4.

[7] Raia, "Goal Setting . . . ."
[8] Raia, "Goal Setting . . . ."

TABLE 4. **Problems and Disadvantages Associated with Management and Objectives.**

PROBLEM	*n**	*%*
Excessive Formal Requirements	21	43.7
Not Used to Full Potential	10	20.8
Need to Consider Different Goals for Different Jobs and Levels	7	14.5
Never Get Good Feedback	7	14.5
I Was Never Really Involved in the Program	7	14.5
It is Undesirable to Commit Oneself to Goals Formally	5	10.5
Lack of Information About Personal Characteristics	2	4.2
No Real Problems	18	37.5

n=48

*More than one response from each subject was possible.

Additional insight into the problem areas was obtained by asking the subjects "How would you improve the program?" Table 5 lists the suggestions and the percentage of executives reporting them.

TABLE 5. **Suggestions for Improving the Objectives Program.**

SUGGESTIONS	*n**	*%*
1. Insure Review and Feedback	24	50.0
2. Develop a Way to Update Goals so that Changes Can be Noted	20	41.6
3. Use by Top Management so that *Their* Goals are Known at Lower Levels	19	39.5
4. Include "Personal" Evaluations in Addition to Goals	16	33.3
5. Top Management Support for the Program	15	31.2
6. Increase the Understanding of the Program and How to Set Goals	12	24.9
7. Include "Normal Job Requirements"	10	20.8
8. Due Dates of Program are Incompatible with Unit Planning and Control Cycles	7	14.5
9. Insure "Real" Participation and Involvement in Goal Setting	5	10.4
10. Others	11	22.9

n=48

*More than one response from each manager was possible.

The major responses to this question point to a lack of top management support, use, and reinforcement. This is, of course, a reiteration of item 2 in Table 4 above—the program was "not used to full potential." Note that in Table 5, with the exception of item 2, the major suggestions focus on the manner in which the program is implemented by superiors. Obviously, the respondent's perception of how his boss uses the MBO process has an impact on the manner in which the subordinate uses and reacts to it.

If we turn to the mail questionnaire, we begin to get some additional light shed upon specific managerial behavior associated with the subordinates' satisfaction with the objectives process. The responses to items on the mail questionnaire indicate that the individual's satisfaction with the WPR program is highly correlated with items describing conditions dealing with goal clarity, feedback, and management support for the program. The frequency of feedback is importantly related to satisfaction with Work Planning and Review. The items below are those which were significantly correlated with *Satisfaction with Work Planning and Review.*[9]

FREQUENCY OF FEEDBACK

How often were you given feedback on progress toward performance goals?	.42
How often were you given feedback on progress toward self-improvement?	.29
The kind of feedback you get from your boss about performance.	-.22

The questionnaire responses also illustrate the importance of specific *managerial support* for WPR. The items below describe supervisory behavior directed toward the program.

SUPPORT FOR THE PROGRAM

How much interest do you think the company has in the program?	.34
How much interest do you think your boss has in the program?	.46
How much time does your boss devote to WPR?	.44
How concerned do you feel your boss would be if you failed to achieve the goals established for your job to a significant degree?	-.29

Although other factors, such as the type of job and level of management, may affect the precision with which targets and goals may be described, the perceptions of managers about how clearly goals have been spelled out and can be measured may also be a function of the manner in which the boss uses the program. The following items show the relationship between *satisfaction with WPR* and items describing *goal characteristics.*

GOAL CLARITY AND IMPORTANCE

What was the level of difficulty of your self-improvement goals?	.29	
The extent to which performance goals met the most pressing needs of the department and the company.	.21	(xx)
How clearly were performance goals stated with respect to expected results?	.44	
The extent to which the relative importance of performance goals was pointed out to you.	.33	
The difficulty the boss has in measuring your performance.	-.26	

There is an important point (Table 5, Item 2) which should not be overlooked. Over 40 percent of the managers indicated that after their goals had been set, their time had been preempted by higher levels of management and they were placed to work on another project. In most cases, this change was not noted formally on the Review Forms. While most agreed that their immediate superior took this into consideration in evaluation, some expressed concern that if their boss left and a new man came in, "he would find that I did not achieve

[9] The correlation coefficients reported were calculated from an n of at least 98 and all are significant at the .01 level except the one marked (xx) which is at the .05 level. Negative correlations should be reversed in sign. They appear because responses were reversed in the questionnaire.

any of the objectives on the form, and consequently, my performance might be evaluated lower than it is." Several expressed a degree of anxiety and threat because they had to commit themselves to goals on paper which may well change due to demands upon them over which they have little control.

CONCLUSIONS

Perhaps the most notable limitation in the management-by-objectives literature has been a consistent avoidance of a discussion of its problems. Its proponents have been essentially positive, stressing the advantages as an appraisal technique and a motivational tool. Goal-oriented systems do not eliminate all the problems that might have been attributable to "trait oriented" appraisal systems. Our findings, especially the negative implications, are similar to those found elsewhere.[10] Problems of appraisal and motivation do not fade into the sunset when this method is used. If anything, the demands are more rigorous and problems probably magnified when members' expectations about feedback and appraisal are raised and not met. It seems to us that the apologists for these methods have long avoided subjecting them to the same scrutiny applied to the "old" techniques. Yet the unanticipated consequences seem to be of sufficient magnitude that they must be taken into account. Management by objectives is not the sovereign remedy that some seem to suggest. The implications of its use, especially the problems of implementation, need to be evaluated more completely. These have been discussed elsewhere.[11] To move toward an objectives-oriented system probably constitutes a fundamental change in the managerial orientation and style which may well require an alteration of the general organization climate. We believe the data from this study point to some major areas which require attention.

Use by Managers

Satisfaction with WPR is positively related to subordinate's perceptions of boss (r=.46) and company (r=.34) interest in the program and how much time the boss spends on it (r=.44). This, we believe is strong evidence of the link between managerial support and the degree to which the program is accepted by an individual. It is only when all levels of management reinforce the use of the program by subordinates by *using the system themselves* that benefits can obtain. One manager said, "I have never been asked by my boss whether or not I used the system. I don't know whether he really cares about it." Obviously the fundamental requirement of executive support *and use* is critical before any substantial benefits can occur. One manager said:

> We ought to go at this full blast or not at all. I haven't had to answer to my boss to the fact that I haven't set objectives yet this year. We need

[10] Raia, "Goal Setting . . . ."
[11] Henry L. Tosi, "Management Development and Management by Objectives: An Interrelationship," *Management of Personnel Quarterly* 4 no. 2 (Summer, 1965).

> some indication that management is really behind us. I can't really be sure. I think the program is beneficial.

The Formulation of Goals

Greater attention must be given to introducing not only the philosophy, but the mechanics of goal setting. The importance of the goal itself is significant. From the questionnaire, it was found that managers who were satisfied with WPR felt that the goals represented the unit's most pressing needs (r=.21), that the importance of the goals was made clear to him (r=.33), that the goals were clearly stated (r=.44), and the boss had less difficulty in measuring his performance with some objective criteria (r=.26). Managers must either intuitively be able to set goals or learn how to set them properly to get the full benefits of the objectives approach.

Provide Feedback

Now more than ever, the managers want feedback. They seem to recognize the attempt to link performance with evaluation (see Table 2, #1), and believe it to be of benefit to "know what is expected" (Table 3, #1), yet only a few mention feedback as an advantage. Just 12 percent felt that they "knew where they stood" (see Table 3, #7), and the major suggestion for improvement, noted by the majority, was to "insure feedback" (Table 5, #1). This is also reflected by the comment that the "program was not used to its full potential" (Table 4, #2). This was also reflected in the responses to the mail questionnaire. Those who were more satisfied with WPR also reported relatively frequent feedback about progress toward performance goals (r=.42) and self-improvement goals (r=.29) and the objectivity of the feedback (r=.22). This suggests a failure to effectively use the whole program cycle. There was apparently some "work planning" and it seems that it was positively valued by the respondents. Yet this developed expectancies for performance "review," which apparently did not occur to their satisfaction. Benefits did not accrue, which might have, had the planning and review cycle been completed.

Program Maintenance over Time

There may be a tendency for these objective-oriented systems to have only a short-range impact. The enthusiasm in the early stages seems to fade into disenchantment in later periods. For instance, Raia detected the beginnings of managerial dissatisfaction in his follow-up study. He noted a tendency to revert to production goals, more easily measured. Questions were raised of the value and meaning of the Goals and Controls Program. Some managers sensed a lack of top management support, lack of incentive, and a tendency to play "the reporting game."

Similar indications were found in this study. One manager maintained that:

> . . . everyone was interested in this a year ago. This year, it just fell between the chairs. No one picked it up, except personnel. My boss never asked me about it, I haven't set my objectives yet.

Another suggested that he could

> . . . not guess what would happen if goals were missed. I don't know anyone who has ever gotten any "negative" feedback. I don't believe everyone in the company met all their goals. What good is it if we don't know how well we did?

Enthusiasm and support wane. The novelty wears thin and the need to cope with the difficulties of an objectives approach may force managers toward the path of least resistance, compliance with the minimum formal requirements, use of unimaginative goals, and only surface support. The program must be kept viable and relevant. This is supported by the respondents to the mail survey. Those satisfied with the program were those, who for one reason or the other, found that WPR was applicable to their job (r=.66) and was helpful to them in the performance of their duties (r=.52).

Recognize the Constraints of Participation

Relevance may be increased by participation. If so, then managers must be cognizant that "mutual goal setting" may require a reallocation of influence in setting goals. The subordinate has to be given the opportunity to participate. The superior must be willing to relinquish some influence. If this redistribution does not occur, participation will not work. *Participation is power redistribution,* and power means some control over the work environment. For instance, those managers in the questionnaire study who were satisfied with WPR also felt they had control over the means to achieving their performance goals (r=.36).

SUMMARY

These problems cited above tend to be the practical limitations of the objectives approach. To obtain benefits, the necessary condition is to use it. Constant review is needed to insure that the program fills a legitimate need in the organization, a need which operating managers sense exists. There is a kind of motion and effort economy that tends to drive unimportant, unnecessary, and most importantly, unrequired activities from a manager's list of priorities. The objectives approach cannot be sold in books, meetings, or theory. It can only be sold in practice.

Wendell French

ORGANIZATION DEVELOPMENT–OBJECTIVES, ASSUMPTIONS AND STRATEGIES

Organization Development refers to a long-range effort to improve an organization's problem solving capabilities and its ability to cope with changes in its external environment with the help of external or internal behavioral-scientist consultants, or change agents, as they are sometimes called. Such efforts are relatively new but are becoming increasingly visible within the United States, England, Japan, Holland, Norway, Sweden, and perhaps in other countries. A few of the growing number of organizations which have embarked on organization development (OD) efforts to some degree are Union Carbide, Esso, TRW Systems, Humble Oil, Weyerhaeuser, and Imperial Chemical Industries Limited. Other kinds of institutions, including public school systems, churches, and hospitals, have also become involved.

Organization development activities appear to have originated about 1957 as an attempt to apply some of the values and insights of laboratory training to total organizations. The late Douglas McGregor, working with Union Carbide, is considered to have been one of the first behavioral scientists to talk systematically about and to implement an organization development program.[1] Other names associated with such early efforts are Herbert Shepard and Robert Blake who, in collaboration with the Employee Relations Department of the Esso Company, launched a program of laboratory training (sensitivity training) in the company's various refineries. This program emerged in 1957 after a headquarters human

[1] Richard Beckhard, W. Warner Burke, and Fred I. Steele, "the Program for Specialists in Organization Training and Development," mimeographed, NTL Institute for Applied Behavioral Science, Dec. 1967, p. ii; and John Paul Jones, "What's Wrong With Work?" in *What's Wrong With Work?* (New York: National Association of Manufacturers, 1967), p. 8, For a history of NTL Institute for Applied Behavioral Science, with which Douglas McGregor was long associated in addition to his professorial appointment at M.I.T. and which has been a major factor in the history of organization development, see Leland P. Bradford, "Biography of an Institution," *Journal of Applied Behavioral Science,* III:2 (1967), 127-143. While we will use the word "program" from time to time, ideally organization development is a "process," not just another new program of temporary quality.

relations research division began to view itself as an internal consulting group offering services to field managers rather than as a research group developing reports for top management.[2]

Objectives of Typical OD Programs

Although the specific interpersonal and task objectives of organization development programs will vary according to each diagnosis of organizational problems, a number of objectives typically emerge. These objectives reflect problems which are very common in organizations:

1. To increase the level of trust and support among organizational members.
2. To increase the incidence of confrontation of organizational problems, both within groups and among groups, in contrast to "sweeping problems under the rug."
3. To create an environment in which authority of assigned role is augmented by authority based on knowledge and skill.
4. To increase the openness of communications laterally, vertically, and diagonally.
5. To increase the level of personal enthusiasm and satisfaction in the organization.
6. To find synergistic solutions[3] to problems with greater frequency. (Synergistic solutions are creative solutions in which 2 + 2 equals more than 4, and through which all parties gain more through cooperation than through conflict.)
7. To increase the level of self and group responsibility in planning and implementation.[4]

Difficulties in Categorizing

Before describing some of the basic assumptions and strategies of organization development, it would be well to point out that one of the difficulties in writing about such a "movement" is that a wide variety of activities can be and are subsumed under this label. These activities have varied all the way from inappropriate application of some "canned" management development program to highly responsive and skillful joint efforts between behavioral scientists and client systems.

Thus, while labels are useful, they may gloss over a wide range of phenomena. The "human relations movement," for example, has been widely written about as though it were all bad or all good. To illustrate, some of the critics of the movement have accused it of being "soft" and a "hand-maiden of the Establish-

[2] Harry D. Kolb, Introduction to *An Action Research Program for Organization Improvement* (Ann Arbor: Foundation for Research in Human Behavior, 1960), p. i.

[3] Cattell defines synergy as "the sum total of the energy which a group can command." Daniel Katz and Robert L. Kahn, *The Social Psychology of Organizations* (New York: John Wiley and Sons, 1966), p. 33.

[4] For a similar statement of objectives, see "What is OD?" *NTL Institute: News and Reports from NTL Institute for Applied Behavioral Science,* II (June 1968), 1-2. Whether OD programs increase the overall level of authority in contrast to redistributing authority is a debatable point. My hypothesis is that both a redistribution and an overall increase occur.

ment," of ignoring the technical and power systems of organizations, and of being too naively participative. Such criticisms were no doubt warranted in some circumstances, but in other situations may not have been at all appropriate. Paradoxically, some of the major insights of the human relations movement, e.g., that the organization can be viewed as a social system and that subordinates have substantial control over productivity have been assimilated by its critics.

In short, the problem is to distinguish between appropriate and inappropriate programs, between effectiveness and ineffectiveness, and between relevancy and irrelevancy. The discussion which follows will attempt to describe the "ideal" circumstances for organization development programs, as well as to point out some pitfalls and common mistakes in organization change efforts.

Relevancy to Different Technologies and Organization Subunits

Research by Joan Woodward[5] suggests that organization development efforts **might be more relevant to certain kinds of technologies and organizational levels, and perhaps to certain workforce characteristics, than to others.** For example, OD efforts may be more appropriate for an organization devoted to prototype manufacturing than for an automobile assembly plant. However, experiments in an organization like Texas Instruments suggest that some manufacturing efforts which appear to be inherently mechanistic may lend themselves to a more participative, open management style than is often assumed possible.[6]

However, assuming the constraints of a fairly narrow job structure at the rank-and-file level, organization development efforts may inherently be more productive and relevant at the managerial levels of the organization. Certainly OD efforts are most effective when they start at the top. Research and development units—particularly those involving a high degree of interdependency and joint creativity among group members—also appear to be appropriate for organization development activities, if group members are currently experiencing problems in communicating or interpersonal relationships.

Basic Assumptions

Some of the basic assumptions about people which underlie organization development programs are similar to "Theory Y" assumptions[7] and will be repeated only briefly here. However, some of the assumptions about groups and total systems will be treated more extensively. The following assumptions appear to underlie organization development efforts.[8]

[5] Joan Woodward, *Industrial Organization: Theory and Practice* (London: Oxford University Press, 1965).

[6] See M. Scott Myers, "Every Employee a Manager," *California Management Review,* X (Spring 1968), 9-20.

[7] See Douglas McGregor, *The Human Side of Enterprise* (New York: McGraw-Hill Book Company, 1960), pp. 47-48.

[8] In addition to influence from the writings of McGregor, Likert, Argyris, and others, this discussion has been influenced by "Some Assumptions About Change in Organizations," in notebook "Program for Specialists in Organization Training and Development," NTL Institute for Applied Behavioral Science, 1967; and by staff members who participated in that program.

ABOUT PEOPLE

- Most individuals have drives toward personal growth and development, and these are most likely to be actualized in an environment which is both supportive and challenging.
- Most people desire to make, and are capable of making, a much higher level of contribution to the attainment of organization goals than most organizational environments will permit.

ABOUT PEOPLE IN GROUPS

- Most people wish to be accepted and to interact cooperatively with at least one small reference group, and usually with more than one group, e.g., the work group, the family group.
- One of the most psychologically relevant reference groups for most people is the work group, including peers and the superior.
- Most people are capable of greatly increasing their effectiveness in helping their reference groups solve problems and in working effectively together.
- For a group to optimize its effectiveness, the formal leader cannot perform all of the leadership functions in all circumstances at all times, and all group members must assist each other with effective leadership and member behavior.

ABOUT PEOPLE IN ORGANIZATIONAL SYSTEMS

- Organizations tend to be characterized by overlapping, interdependent work groups, and the "linking pin" function of supervisors and others needs to be understood and facilitated.[9]
- What happens in the broader organization affects the small work group and vice versa.
- What happens to one subsystem (social, technological, or administrative) will affect and be influenced by other parts of the system.
- The culture in most organizations tends to suppress the expression of feelings which people have about each other and about where they and their organizations are heading.
- Suppressed feelings adversely affect problem solving, personal growth, and job satisfaction.
- The level of interpersonal trust, support, and cooperation is much lower in most organizations than is either necessary or desirable.
- "Win-lose" strategies between people and groups, while realistic and appropriate in some situations, are not optimal in the long run to the solution of most organizational problems.
- Synergistic solutions can be achieved with a much higher frequency than is actually the case in most organizations.
- Viewing feelings as data important to the organization tends to open up many avenues for improved goal setting, leadership, communications, problem solving, intergroup collaboration, and morale.
- Improved performance stemming from organization development efforts needs to be sustained by appropriate changes in the appraisal, compensa-

[9] For a discussion of the "linking pin" concept, see Rensis Likert, *New Patterns of Management* (New York: McGraw-Hill Book Company, 1961).

tion, training, staffing, and task-specialization subsystem—in short, in the total personnel system.

Value and Belief System of Behavioral Scientist-Change Agents

While scientific inquiry, ideally, is value-free, the applications of science are not value-free. Applied behavioral scientist-organization development consultants tend to subscribe to a comparable set of values, although we should avoid the trap of assuming that they constitute a completely homogenous group. They do not.

One value, to which many behavioral scientist-change agents tend to give high priority, is that the needs and aspirations of human beings are the reasons for organized effort in society. They tend, therefore, to be developmental in their outlook and concerned with the long-range opportunities for the personal growth of people in organizations.

A second value is that work and life can become richer and more meaningful, and organized effort more effective and enjoyable, if feelings and sentiments are permitted to be a more legitimate part of the culture. A third value is a commitment to an action role, along with a commitment to research, in an effort to improve the effectiveness of organizations.[10] A fourth value—or perhaps a belief—is that improved competency in interpersonal and intergroup relationship will result in more effective organization.[11] A fifth value is that behavioral science research and an examination of behavioral science assumptions and values are relevant and important in considering organizational effectiveness. While many change agents are perhaps overly action-oriented in terms of the utilization of their time, nevertheless, as a group they are paying more and more attention to research and to the examination of ideas.[12]

The value placed on research and inquiry raises the question as to whether the assumptions stated earlier are values, theory, or "facts." In my judgment, a substantial body of knowledge, including research on leadership, suggests that there is considerable evidence for these assumptions. However, to conclude that these assumptions are facts, laws, or principles would be to contradict the value placed by behavioral scientists on continuous research and inquiry. Thus, I feel that they should be considered theoretical statements which are based on provisional data.

[10] Warren G. Bennis sees three major approaches to planned organizational change, with the behavioral scientists associated with each all having "a deep concern with applying social science knowledge to create more viable social systems; a commitment to action, as well as to research . . . and a belief that improved interpersonal and group relationships will ultimately lead to better organizational performance." Bennis, "A New Role for the Behavioral Sciences: Effecting Organizational Change," *Administrative Science Quarterly,* VIII (Sept. 1963), 157-158; and Herbert A. Shepard, "An Action Research Model," in *An Action Research Program for Organization Improvement,* pp. 31-35.

[11] Bennis, "A New Role for the Behavioral Sciences," 158.

[12] For a discussion of some of the problems and dilemmas in behavioral science research, see Chris Argyris, "Creating Effective Relationships in Organizations," in Richard N. Adams and Jack J. Preiss, eds., *Human Organization Research* (Homewood, Ill.: The Dorsey Press, 1960), pp. 109-123; and Barbara A. Benedict, *et al.,* "The Clinical Experimental Approach to Assessing Organizational Change Efforts," *Journal of Applied Behavioral Science,* (Nov. 1967), 347-380.

This also raises the paradox that the belief that people are important tends to result in their being important. The belief that people can grow and develop in terms of personal and organizational competency tends to produce this result. Thus, values and beliefs tend to be self-fulfilling, and the question becomes "What do you choose to want to believe?" While this position can become Pollyannaish in the sense of not seeing the real world, nevertheless, behavioral scientist-change agents, at least this one, tend to place a value on optimism. It is a kind of optimism that says people can do a better job of goal setting and facing up to and solving problems, not an optimism that says the number of problems is diminishing.

It should be added that it is important that the values and beliefs of each behavioral science-change agent be made visible both to himself and to the client. In the first place, neither can learn to adequately trust the other without such exposure—a hidden agenda handicaps both trust building and mutual learning. Second, and perhaps more pragmatically, organizational change efforts tend to fail if a prescription is applied unilaterally and without proper diagnosis.

Strategy in Organization Development: An Action Research Model

A frequent strategy in organization development programs is based on what behavioral scientists refer to as an "action research model." This model involves extensive collaboration between the consultant (whether an external or an internal change agent) and the client group, data gathering, data discussion, and planning. While descriptions of this model vary in detail and terminology from author to author, the dynamics are essentially the same.[13]

Figure 1 summarizes some of the essential phases of the action research model, using an emerging organization development program as an example. The key aspects of the model are **diagnosis, data gathering, feedback to the client group, data discussion and work by the client group, action planning, and action.** The sequence tends to be cyclical with the focus on new or advanced problems as the client group learns to work more effectively together. Action research should also be considered a process, since, as William Foote Whyte says, it involves ". . . a continuous gathering and analysis of human relations research data and the feeding of the findings into the organization in such a manner as to change behavior."[14] (Feedback we will define as nonjudgmental observations of behavior.)

Ideally, initial objectives and strategies of organization development efforts stem from a careful **diagnosis** of such matters as interpersonal and intergroup problems, decision-making processes, and communication flow which are currently being experienced by the client organization. As a preliminary step, the behavioral scientist and the key client (the president of a company, the vice president in charge of a division, the works manager or superintendent of a plant,

[13] For further discussion of action research, see Edgar H. Schein and Warren G. Bennis, *Personal and Organizational Change Through Group Methods* (New York: John Wiley and Sons, 1966), pp. 272-274.

[14] William Foote Whyte and Edith Lentz Hamilton, *Action Research for Management* (Homewood, Ill.: Richard D. Irwin, 1964), p. 2.

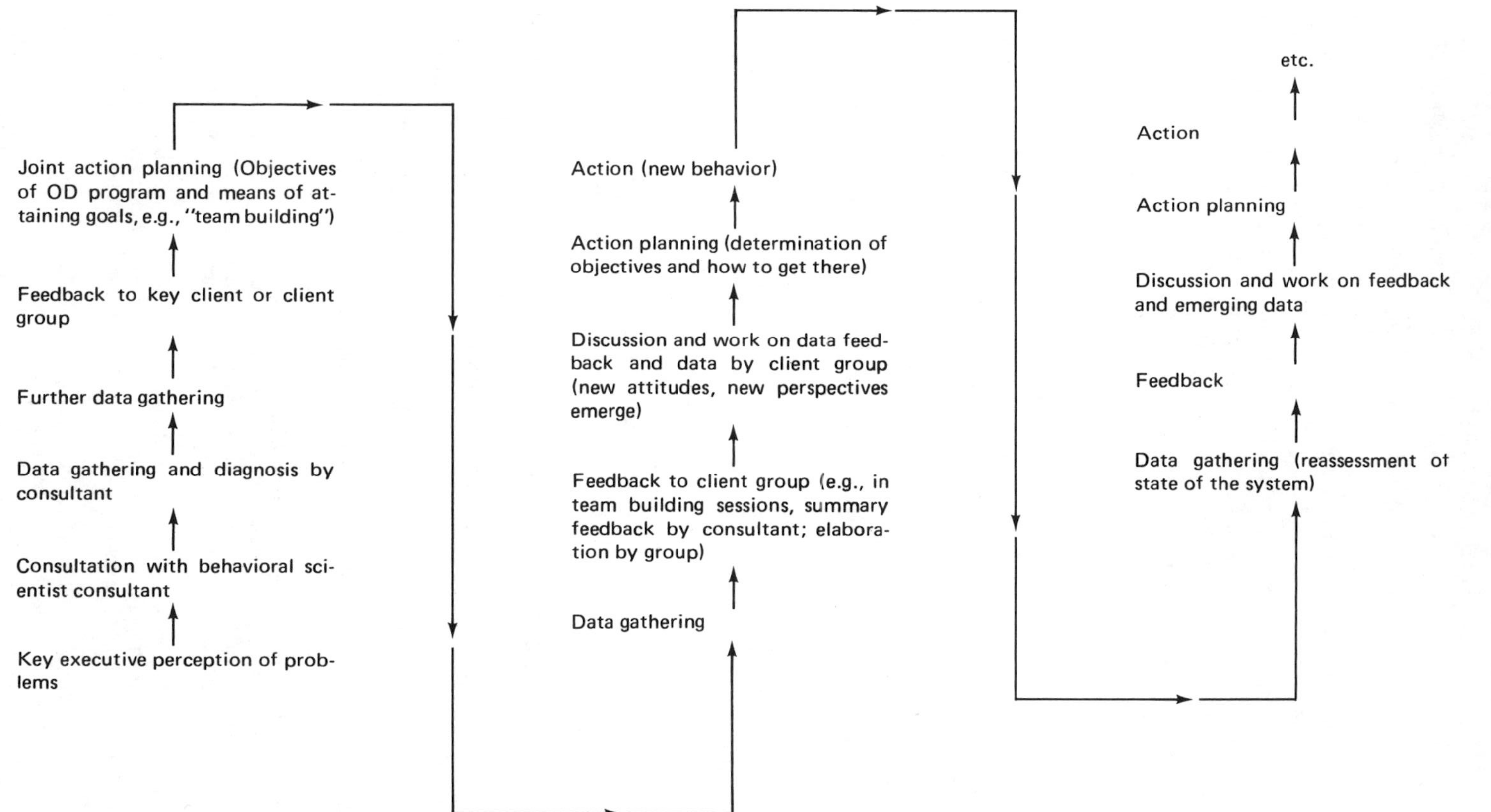

FIGURE 1. **An action research model for organization development**

a superintendent of schools, etc.), will make a joint initial assessment of the critical problems which need working on. Subordinates may also be interviewed in order to provide supplemental data. The diagnosis may very well indicate that the central problem is technological or that the key client is not at all willing or ready to examine the organization's problem-solving ability or his own managerial behavior.[15] Either could be a reason for postponing or moving slowly in the direction of organization development activities, although the technological problem may easily be related to deficiencies in interpersonal relationships or decision making. The diagnosis might also indicate the desirability of one or more additional specialists (in engineering, finance, or electronic data processing, for example) to simultaneously work with the organization.

This initial diagnosis, which focuses on the expressed needs of the client, is extremely critical. As discussed earlier, in the absence of a skilled diagnosis, the behavioral scientist-change agent would be imposing a set of assumptions and a set of objectives which may be hopelessly out of joint with either the current problems of the people in the organization or their willingness to learn new modes of behavior. In this regard, it is extremely important that the consultant **hear and understand** what the client is trying to tell him. This requires a high order of skill.[16]

Interviews are frequently used for **data gathering** in OD work for both initial diagnosis and subsequent planning sessions, since personal contact is important for building a cooperative relationship between the consultant and the client group. The interview is also important since the behavioral scientist-consultant is interested in spontaneity and in feelings that are expressed as well as cognitive matters. However, questionnaires are sometimes successfully used in the context of what is sometimes referred to as survey feedback, to supplement interview data.[17]

Data gathering typically goes through several phases. The first phase is related to diagnosing the state of the system and to making plans for organizational change. This phase may utilize a series of interviews between the consultant and the key client, or between a few key executives and the consultant. Subsequent phases focus on problems specific to the top executive team and to subordinate teams. (See Fig. 2.)

Typical questions in data gathering or "problem sensing" would include:

[15] Jeremiah J. O'Connell appropriately challenges the notion that there is "one best way" of organizational change and stresses that the consultant should choose his role and intervention strategies on the basis of "the conditions existing when he enters the client system" (*Managing Organizational Innovation* [Homewood, Ill.: Richard D. Irwin, 1968], pp. 10-11).

[16] For further discussion of organization diagnosis, see Richard Beckhard, "An Organization Improvement Program in a Decentralized Organization," *Journal of Applied Behavioral Science*, II (Jan-March 1966), 3-4, "OD as a Process," in *What's Wrong with Work?*, pp. 12-13.

[17] For example, see Floyd C. Mann, "Studying and Creating Change," in Timothy W. Costello and Sheldon S. Zalkind, eds., *Psychology in Administration–A Research Orientation* (Englewood Cliffs: Prentice-Hall, 1963), pp. 321-324. See also Delbert C. Miller, "Using Behavioral Science to Solve Organization Problems," *Personnel Administration*, XXXI (Jan.-Feb. 1968), 21-29.

What problems do you see in your group, including problems between people, that are interfering with getting the job done the way you would like to see it done?; and what problems do you see in the broader organization? Such open-ended questions provide wide latitude on the part of the respondents and encourage a reporting of problems as the individual sees them. Such interviewing is usually conducted privately, with a commitment on the part of the consultant that the information will be used in such a way as to avoid unduly embarrassing anyone. The intent is to find out what common problems or themes emerge, with the data to be used constructively for both diagnostic and feedback purposes.

Two- or three-day offsite **team-building or group problem-solving sessions** typically become a major focal point in organization development programs. During these meetings the behavioral scientist frequently provides **feedback** to the group in terms of the themes which emerged in the problem-sensing interviews.[18] He may also encourage the group to determine which items or themes should have priority in terms of maximum utilization of time. These themes usually provide substantial and meaningful data for the group to begin work on. One-to-one interpersonal matters, both positive and negative, tend to emerge spontaneously as the participants gain confidence from the level of support sensed in the group.

Different consultants will vary in their mode of behavior in such sessions, but will typically serve as **"process" observers and as interpreters of the dynamics of the group interaction** to the degree that the group expresses a readiness for such intervention. They also typically encourage people to take risks, a step at a time, and to experiment with new behavior in the context of the level of support in the group. Thus, the trainer-consultant(s) serves as a stimulant to new behavior but also as a protector. The climate which I try to build, for example, is: "Let's not tear down any more than we can build back together."[19] Further, the trainer-consultant typically works with the group to assist team members in improving their skills in diagnosing and facilitating group progress.[20]

It should be noted, however, that different groups will have different needs along a task-process continuum. For example, some groups have a need for intensive work on clarifying objectives; others may have the greatest need in the area of personal relationships. Further, the consultant or the chief consultant in a team of consultants involved in an organization development program will play a much broader role than serving as a T-group or team-building trainer. He will

[18] For a description of feedback procedures used by the Survey Research Center, Univ. of Michigan, see Mann and Likert, "The Need for Research on the Communication of Research Results," in *Human Organization Research,* pp. 57-66.

[19] This phrase probably came from a management workshop sponsored by NTL Institute for Applied Behavioral Science.

[20] For a description of what goes on in team-building sessions, see Beckhard, "An Organizational Improvement Program," 9-13; and Newton Margulies and Anthony P. Raia, "People in Organizations–A Case for Team Training," *Training and Development Journal,* XXII (August 1968), 2-11. For a description of problem-solving sessions involving the total management group (about 70) of a company, see Beckhard, "The Confrontation Meeting," *Harvard Business Review,* XLV (March-April 1967), 149-155.

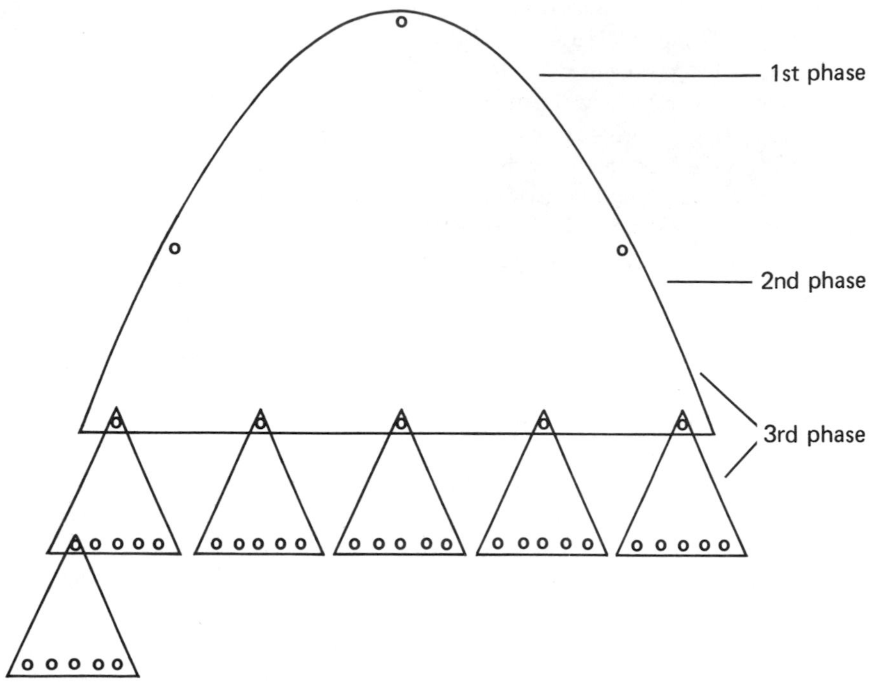

1st phase. Data gathering, feedback and diagnosis—consultant and top executive only.

2nd phase. Data gathering, feedback, and revised diagnosis—consultant and two or more key staff or line people.

3rd phase. Data gathering and feedback to total top executive team in "team-building" laboratory, with or without key subordinates from level below.

4th and additional phases. Data gathering and team-building sessions with 2nd or 3rd level teams.

Subsequent phases. Data gathering, feedback, and interface problem-solving sessions across groups.

Simultaneous phases. Several managers may attend "stranger" T-Groups; courses in the management development program may supplement this learning.

FIGURE 2. **Organization development phases in a hypothetical organization**

also play an important role in periodic data gathering and diagnosis and in joint long-range planning of the change efforts.[21]

[21] For a description of actual organization development programs, see Paul C. Buchanan, "Innovative Organizations–A Study in Organization Development," in *Applying Behavioral Science Research in Industry* (New York: Industrial Relations Counselors, 1964), pp. 87-107; Sheldon A. Davis, "An Organic Problem-Solving Method of Organizational Change," *Journal of Applied Behavioral Science,* III:1 (1967), 3-21; Cyril Sofer, *The Organization from Within* (Chicago: Quadrangle Books, 1961); Alfred J. Marrow, David G. Bowers, and

Laboratory Training and Organization Development

Since organization development programs have largely emerged from T-group experience, theory, and research, and since laboratory training in one form or another tends to be an integral part of most such programs, it is important to focus on laboratory training per se. As stated earlier, OD programs grew out of a perceived need to relate laboratory training to the problems of ongoing organizations and a recognition that optimum results could only occur if major parts of the total social system of an organization were involved.

Laboratory training essentially emerged around 1946, largely through a growing recognition by Leland Bradford, Ronald Lippitt, Kenneth Benne, and others, that human relations training which focused on the feelings and concerns of the participants was frequently a much more powerful and viable form of education than the lecture method. Some of the theoretical constructs and insights from which these laboratory training pioneers drew stemmed from earlier research by Lippitt, Kurt Lewin, and Ralph White. The term "T-Group" emerged by 1949 as a shortened label for "Basic Skill Training Group"; these terms were used to identify the programs which began to emerge in the newly formed National Training Laboratory in Group Development (new NTL Institute for Applied Behavioral Science).[22] "Sensitivity Training" is also a term frequently applied to such training.

Ordinarily, laboratory training sessions have certain objectives in common. The following list, by two internationally known behavioral scientists,[23] is probably highly consistent with the objectives of most programs:

SELF OBJECTIVES

- Increased **awareness** of own feelings and reactions, and own impact on others.
- Increased **awareness** of feelings and reactions of others, and their impact on self.
- Increased **awareness** of dynamics of group action.
- **Changed attitudes** toward self, others, and groups, i.e., more respect for, tolerance for, and faith in self, others, and groups.
- Increased **interpersonal competence**, i.e., skill in handling interpersonal and group relationships toward more productive and satisfying relationships.

Stanley E. Seashore, *Management by Participation* (New York: Harper and Row, 1967); Robert R. Blake, Jane S. Mouton, Louis B. Barnes, and Larry E. Greiner, "Breakthrough in Organization Development," *Harvard Business Review,* XLII (Nov.-Dec. 1964), 133-155; Alton C. Bartlett, "Changing Behavior as a Means to Increased Efficiency," *Journal of Applied Behavioral Science,* III:3 (1967), 381-403; Larry E. Greiner, "Antecedents of Planned Organization Change," *ibid.,* III:1 (1967), 51-85; and Robert R. Blake and Jane Mouton, *Corporate Excellence Through Grid Organization Development* (Houston, Texas: Gulf Publishing Company, 1968).

[22] From Bradford, "Biography of an Institution." See also Kenneth D. Benne, "History of the T Group in the Laboratory Setting," in Bradford, Jack R. Gibb, and Benne, eds., *T/Group Theory and Laboratory Method* (New York: John Wiley and Sons, 1964), pp. 80-135.

[23] Schein and Bennis, p. 37.

ROLE OBJECTIVES

- Increased **awareness** of own organizational role, organizational dynamics, dynamics of larger social systems, and dynamics of the change process in self, small groups, and organizations.
- **Changed attitudes** toward own role, role of others, and organizational relationships, i.e., more respect for and willingness to deal with others with whom one is interdependent, greater willingness to achieve collaborative relationships with others based on mutual trust.
- Increased **interpersonal competence** in handling organizational role relationships with superiors, peers, and subordinates.

ORGANIZATIONAL OBJECTIVES

- Increased **awareness** of, **changed attitudes** toward, and increased **interpersonal competence** about specific organizational problems existing in groups or units which are interdependent.
- **Organizational improvement** through the training of relationships or groups rather than isolated individuals.

Over the years, experimentation with different laboratory designs has led to diverse criteria for the selection of laboratory participants. Probably a majority of NTL-IABS human relations laboratories are "stranger groups," i.e., involving participants who come from different organizations and who are not likely to have met earlier. However, as indicated by the organizational objectives above, the incidence of special labs designed to increase the effectiveness of persons already working together appears to be growing. Thus terms like "cousin labs," i.e., labs involving people from the same organization but not the same subunit, and "family labs" or "team-building" sessions, i.e., involving a manager and all of his subordinates, are becoming familiar. Participants in labs designed for organizational members not of the same unit may be selected from the same rank level ("horizontal slice") or selected so as to constitute a heterogeneous grouping by rank ("diagonal slice"). Further, NTL-IABS is now encouraging at least two members from the same organization to attend NTL Management Work Conferences and Key Executive Conferences in order to maximize the impact of the learning in the back-home situation.[24]

In general, experienced trainers recommend that persons with severe emotional illness should not participate in laboratory training, with the exception of programs designed specifically for group therapy. Designers of programs make the assumptions, as Argyris states them,[25] that T-Group participants should have:

1. A relatively strong ego that is not overwhelmed by internal conflicts.

[24] For further discussion of group composition in laboratory training, see Schein and Bennis, pp. 63-69. NTL-IABS now include the Center for Organization Studies, the Center for the Development of Educational Leadership, the Center for Community Affairs, and the Center for International Training to serve a wide range of client populations and groups.

[25] Chris Argyris, "T-Groups for Organizational Effectiveness," *Harvard Business Review,* XLII (March-April 1964), 60-74.

2. Defenses which are sufficiently low to allow the individual to hear what others say to him.
3. The ability to communicate thought and feelings with minimal distortion.

As a result of such screening, the incidence of breakdown during laboratory training is substantially less than that reported for organizations in general.[26] However, since the borderline between "normalcy" and illness is very indistinct, most professionally trained staff members are equipped to diagnose severe problems and to make referrals to psychiatrists and clinical psychologists when appropriate. Further, most are equipped to give adequate support and protection to participants whose ability to assimilate and learn from feedback is low. In addition, group members in T-Group situations tend to be sensitive to the emotional needs of the members and to be supportive when they sense a person experiencing pain. Such support is explicitly fostered in laboratory training.

The duration of laboratory training programs varies widely. "Micro-Labs," designed to give people a brief experience with sensitivity training, may last only one hour. Some labs are designed for a long weekend. Typically, however, basic human relations labs are of two weeks duration, with participants expected to meet mornings, afternoons, and evenings, with some time off for recreation. While NTL Management Work Conferences for middle managers and Key Executive Conferences run for one week, team-building labs, from my experience, typically are about three days in length. However, the latter are usually only a part of a broader organization development program involving problem sensing and diagnosis, and the planning of action steps and subsequent sessions. In addition, attendance at stranger labs for key managers is frequently a part of the total organization development effort.

Sensitivity training sessions typically start with the trainer making a few comments about his role—that he is there to be of help, that the group will have control of the agenda, that he will deliberately avoid a leadership role, but that he might become involved as both a leader and a member from time to time, etc. The following is an example of what the trainer might say:

> This group will meet for many hours and will serve as a kind of laboratory where each individual can increase his understanding of the forces which influence individual behavior and the performance of groups and organizations. The data for learning will be our own behavior, feelings, and reactions. We begin with no definite structure or organization, no agreed-upon procedures, and no specific agenda. It will be up to us to fill the vacuum created by the lack of these familiar elements and to study our group as we evolve. My role will be to help the group to learn from its own experience, but not to act as a traditional chairman nor to suggest how we should organize, what our procedure should be, or exactly what our agenda will

[26] Based on discussions with NTL staff members. One estimate is that the incidence of "serious stress and mental disturbance" during laboratory training is less than one percent of participants and in almost all cases occurs in persons with a history of prior disturbance (Charles Seashore, "What is Sensitivity Training," *NTL Institute News and Reports,* II [April 1968], 2).

include. With these few comments, I think we are ready to begin in whatever way you feel will be most helpful.[27]

The trainer then lapses into silence. Group discomfort then precipitates a dialogue which, with skilled trainer assistance, is typically an intense but generally highly rewarding experience for group members. What goes on in the group becomes the data for the learning experience.

Interventions by the trainer will vary greatly depending upon the purpose of the lab and the state of learning on the part of the participants. A common intervention, however, is to encourage people to focus on and own up to their own feelings about what is going on in the group, rather than to make judgments about others. In this way, the participants begin to have more insight into their own feelings and to understand how their behavior affects the feelings of others.

While T-Group work tends to be the focal point in human relations laboratories, laboratory training typically includes theory sessions and frequently includes exercises such as role playing or management games.[28] Further, family labs of subunits of organizations will ordinarily devote more time to planning action steps for back on the job than will stranger labs.

Robert J. House has carefully reviewed the research literature on the impact of T-Group training and has concluded that the research shows mixed results. In particular, research on changes as reflected in personality inventories is seen as inconclusive. However, studies which examine the behavior of participants upon returning to the job are generally more positive.[29] House cites six studies, all of which utilized control groups, and concludes:

> All six studies revealed what appear to be important positive effects of T-Group training. Two of the studies report negative effects as well . . . all of the evidence is based on observations of the behavior of the participants in the actual job situations. No reliance is placed on participant response; rather, evidence is collected from those having frequent contact with the participant in his normal work activities.[30]

[27] *Ibid.*, 1.

[28] For a description of what goes on in T-groups, see Schein and Bennis, pp. 10-27; Bradford, Gibb, and Benne, pp. 55-67; Dorothy S. Whitaker, "A Case Study of a T-Group," in Galvin Whitaker, ed., *T-Group Training: Group Dynamics in Management Education,* A.T.M. Occasional Papers, (Oxford: Basil Blackwell, 1965), pp. 14-22; Irving R. Weschler and Jerome Reisel, *Inside a Sensitivity Training Group* (Berkeley: University of California, Institute of Industrial Relations, 1959); and William F. Glueck, "Reflections on a T-Group Experience," *Personnel Journal,* XLVII (July 1968), 501-504. For use of cases or exercises based on research results ("instrumented training") see Robert R. Blake and Jane S. Mouton, "The Instrumented Training Laboratory," in Irving R. Weschler and Edgar H. Schein, eds., *Five Issues in Training* (Washington: National Training Laboratories, 1962), pp. 61-76; and W. Warner Burke and Harvey A. Hornstein, "Conceptual vs. Experimental Management Training," *Training and Development Journal,* XXI (Dec. 1967), 12-17.

[29] Robert J. House, "T-Group Education and Leadership Effectiveness: A Review of the Empiric Literature and a Critical Evaluation," *Personnel Psychology,* XX (Spring 1967), 1-32. See also Dorothy Stock, "A Survey of Research on T-Groups," in Bradford, Gibb, and Benne, pp. 395-441.

[30] House, *ibid.*, pp. 18-19.

John P. Campbell and Marvin D. Dunnette,[31] on the other hand, while conceding that the research shows that T-Group training produces **changes in behavior**, point out that the usefulness of such training in terms of **job performance** has yet to be demonstrated. They urge research toward "forging the link between training-induced behavior changes and changes in job-performance effectiveness."[32] As a summary comment, they state:

> . . . the assumption that T-Group training has positive utility for organizations must necessarily rest on shaky ground. It has been neither confirmed nor disconfirmed. The authors wish to emphasize . . . that utility for the organization is not necessarily the same as utility for the individual.[33]

At least two major reasons may account for the inconclusiveness of research on the impact of T-Group training on job performance. One reason is simply that little research has been done. The other reason may center around a factor of cultural isolation. To oversimplify, a major part of what one learns in laboratory training, in my opinion, is how to work more effectively with others in group situations, **particularly with others who have developed comparable skills.** Unfortunately, most participants return from T-Group experiences to environments including colleagues and superiors who have not had the same affective (emotional, feeling) experiences, who are not familiar with the terminology and underlying theory, and who may have anxieties (usually unwarranted) about what might happen to them in a T-Group situation.

This cultural distance which laboratory training can produce is one of the reasons why many behavioral scientists are currently encouraging more than one person from the same organization to undergo T-Group training and, ideally, **all** of the members of a team and their superior to participate in some kind of laboratory training together. The latter assumes that a diagnosis of the organization indicates that the group is ready for such training and assumes such training is reasonably compatible with the broader culture of the total system.

Conditions and Techniques for Successful Organization Development Programs

Theory, research, and experience to date suggest to me that **successful** OD programs tend to evolve in the following way and that they have some of these characteristics (these statements should be considered highly tentative, however):

- There is strong pressure for improvement from both outside the organization and from within.[34]

[31] John P. Campbell and Marvin D. Dunnette, "Effectiveness of T-Group Experiences in Managerial Training and development," *Psychological Bulletin,* LXX (August 1968), 73-104.

[32] *Ibid.,* 100.

[33] *Ibid.,* 101. See also the essays by Dunnette and Campbell and Chris Argyris in *Industrial Relations,* VIII (Oct. 1968), 1-45.

[34] On this point, see Larry E. Greiner, "Patterns of Organization Change," *Harvard Business Review,* XLV (May-June 1967), 119-130.

- An outside behavioral scientist-consultant is brought in for consultation with the top executives and to diagnose organizational problems.
- A preliminary diagnosis suggests that organization development efforts, designed in response to the expressed needs of the key executives, are warranted.
- A collaborative decision is made between the key client group and the consultant to try to change the culture of the organization, at least at the top initially. The specific goals may be to improve communications, to secure more effective participation from subordinates in problem solving, and to move in the direction of more openness, more feedback, and more support. In short, a decision is made to change the culture to help the company meet its organizational goals and to provide better avenues for initiative, creativity, and self-actualization on the part of organization members.
- Two or more top executives, including the chief executive, go to laboratory training sessions. (Frequently, attendance at labs is one of the facts which precipitates interest in bringing in the outside consultant.)
- Attendance in T-Group program is voluntary. While it is difficult to draw a line between persuasion and coercion, OD consultants and top management should be aware of the dysfunctional consequences of coercion (see the comments on authentic behavior below). While a major emphasis is on team-building laboratories, stranger labs are utilized both to supplement the training going on in the organization and to train managers new to the organization or those who are newly promoted.
- Team-building sessions are held with the top executive group (or at the highest point where the program is started). Ideally, the program is started at the top of the organization, but it can start at levels below the president as long as there is significant support from the chief executive, and preferably from other members of the top power structure as well.
- In a firm large enough to have a personnel executive, the personnel-industrial relations vice president becomes heavily involved at the outset.
- One of two organizational forms emerges to coordinate organization development efforts, either (a) a coordinator reporting to the personnel executive (the personnel executive himself may fill this role), or (b) a coordinator reporting to the chief executive. The management development director is frequently in an ideal position to coordinate OD activities with other management development activities.
- Ultimately, it is essential that the personnel-industrial relations group, including people in salary administration, be an integral part of the organization development program. Since OD groups have such potential for acting as catalysts in rapid organizational change, the temptation is great to see themselves as "good guys" and the other personnel people as "bad guys" or simply ineffective. Any conflicts between a separate organization development group and the personnel and industrial relations groups should be faced and resolved. Such tensions can be the "Achilles heel" for either program. In particular, however, the change agents in the organization development program need the support of the other people who are heavily involved in human resources administration and vice versa; what is done in the OD program needs to be compatible with what is done in selection, promotion, salary administration, appraisal, and vice versa. In terms of systems theory, it would seem imperative that one aspect of the human resources function such as any organization development program must be highly interdependent with the other human resources activities including

selection, salary administration, etc. (TRW Systems is an example of an organization which involves top executives plus making the total personnel and industrial relations group an integral part of the OD program.[35])

- Team-building labs, at the request of the various respective executives, with laboratory designs based on careful data gathering and problem diagnosis, are conducted at successively lower levels of the organization with the help of outside consultants, plus the help of internal consultants whose expertise is gradually developed.
- Ideally, as the program matures, both members of the personnel staff and a few line executives are trained to do some organization development work in conjunction with the external and internal professionally trained behavioral scientists. In a sense, then, the external change agent tries to work himself out of a job by developing internal resources.
- The outside consultant(s) and the internal coordinator work very carefully together and periodically check on fears, threats, and anxieties which may be developing as the effort progresses. Issues need to be confronted as they emerge. Not only is the outside change agent needed for his skills, but the organization will need someone to act as a "governor"—to keep the program focused on real problems and to urge authenticity in contrast to gamesmanship. The danger always exists that the organization will begin to punish or reward involvement in T-Group kinds of activities per se, rather than focus on performance.
- The OD consultants constantly work on their own effectiveness in interpersonal relationships and their diagnostic skills so they are not in a position of "do as I say, but not as I do." Further, both consultant and client work together to optimize the consultant's knowledge of the organization's unique and evolving culture structure, and web of interpersonal relationships.
- There needs to be continuous audit of the results, both in terms of checking on the evolution of attitudes about what is going on and in terms of the extent to which problems which were identified at the outset by the key clients are being solved through the program.
- As implied above, the reward system and other personnel systems need to be readjusted to accommodate emerging changes in performance in the organization. Substantially improved performance on the part of individuals and groups is not likely to be sustained if financial and promotional rewards are not forthcoming. In short, management needs to have a "systems" point of view and to think through the interrelationships of the OD effort with the reward and staffing systems and the other aspects of the total human resources subsystem.

In the last analysis, the president and the "line" executives of the organization will evaluate the success of the OD effort in terms of the extent to which it assists the organization in meeting its human and economic objectives. For example, marked improvements on various indices from one plant, one division, one department, etc., will be important indicators of program success. While human resources administration indices are not yet perfected, some of the measuring devices being developed by Likert, Mann, and other show some promise.[36]

[35] See Sheldon A. Davis, "An Organic Problem-Solving Method."

[36] See Rensis Likert, *The Human Organization: Its Management and Value* (New York: McGraw-Hill Book Company, 1967).

Summary Comments

Organization development efforts have emerged through attempts to apply laboratory training values and assumptions to total systems. Such efforts are organic in the sense that they emerge from and are guided by the problems being experienced by the people in the organization. The key to their viability (in contrast to becoming a passing fad) lies in an authentic focus on problems and concerns of the members of the organization and in their confrontation of issues and problems.

Organization development is based on assumptions and values similar to "Theory Y" assumptions and values but includes additional assumptions about total systems and the nature of the client-consultant relationship. Intervention strategies of the behavioral scientist-change agent tend to be based on an action-research model and tend to be focused more on helping the people in an organization learn to solve problems rather than on prescriptions of how things should be done differently.

Laboratory training (or "sensitivity training") or modifications of T-group seminars typically are a part of the organizational change efforts, but the extent and format of such training will depend upon the evolving needs of the organization. Team-building seminars involving a superior and subordinates are being utilized more and more as a way of changing social systems rapidly and avoiding the cultural-distance problems which frequently emerge when individuals return from stranger labs. However, stranger labs can play a key role in change efforts when they are used as part of a broader organization development effort.

Research has indicated that sensitivity training generally produces positive results in terms of changed behavior on the job, but has not demonstrated the link between behavior changes and improved performance. Maximum benefits are probably derived from laboratory training when the organizational culture supports and reinforces the use of new skills in ongoing team situations.

Successful organization development efforts require skillful behavioral scientist interventions, a systems view, and top management support and involvement. In addition, changes stemming from organization development must be linked to changes in the total personnel subsystem. The viability of organization development efforts lies in the degree to which they accurately reflect the aspirations and concerns of the participating members.

In conclusion, **successful organization development tends to be a total system effort; a process of planned change—not a program with a temporary quality; and aimed at developing the organization's internal resources for effective change in the future.**

This article is largely based on the forthcoming second edition of my *The Personnel Management Process: Human Resources Administration* (Boston: Houghton Mifflin Company, 1970), chap. 28.

John J. Morse
Jay W. Lorsch

BEYOND THEORY Y

During the past 30 years, managers have been bombarded with two competing approaches to the problems of human administration and organization. The first, usually called the classical school of organization, emphasizes the need for well-established lines of authority, clearly defined jobs, and authority equal to responsibility. The second, often called the participative approach, focuses on the desirability of involving organization members in decision making so that they will be more highly motivated.

Douglas McGregor, through his well-known "Theory X and Theory Y," drew a distinction between the assumptions about human motivation which underlie these two approaches, to this effect:

Theory X assumes that people dislike work and must be coerced, controlled, and directed toward organizational goals. Furthermore, most people prefer to be treated this way, so they can avoid responsibility.

Theory Y—the integration of goals—emphasizes the average person's intrinsic interest in his work, his desire to be self-directing and to seek responsibility, and his capacity to be creative in solving business problems.

It is McGregor's conclusion, of course, that the latter approach to organization is the more desirable one for managers to follow.[1]

McGregor's position causes confusion for the managers who try to choose between these two conflicting approaches. The classical organizational approach that McGregor associated with Theory X does work well in some situations, although, as McGregor himself pointed out, there are also some situations where it does not work effectively. At the same time, the approach based on Theory Y, while it has produced good results in some situations, does not always do so. That is, each approach is effective in some cases but not in others. Why is this? How can managers resolve the confusion?

A NEW APPROACH

Recent work by a number of students of management and organization may help to answer such questions.[2] These studies indicate that there is not one best

John J. Morse and Jay W. Lorsch, "Beyond Theory Y," *Harvard Business Review* 48 (May-June, 1970): 61-68.

[1] Douglas McGregor, *The Human Side of Enterprise* (New York; McGraw-Hill Book Company, Inc., 1960), pp. 34-35 and pp. 47-48.

[2] See for example Paul R. Lawrence and Jay W. Lorsch, *Organization and Environment*

organizational approach; rather, the best approach depends on the nature of the work to be done. Enterprises with highly predictable tasks perform better with organizations characterized by the highly formalized procedures and management hierarchies of the classical approach. With highly uncertain tasks that require more extensive problem solving, on the other hand, organizations that are less formalized and emphasize self-control and member participation in decision making are more effective. In essence, according to these newer studies, managers must design and develop organizations so that the organizational characteristics *fit* the nature of the task to be done.

While the conclusions of this newer approach will make sense to most experienced managers and can alleviate much of the confusion about which approach to choose, there are still two important questions unanswered:

1. How does the more formalized and controlling organization affect the motivation of organization members? (McGregor's most telling criticism of the classical approach was that it did not unleash the potential in an enterprise's human resources.)
2. Equally important, does a less formalized organization always provide a high level of motivation for its members? (This is the implication many managers have drawn from McGregor's work.)

We have recently been involved in a study that provides surprising answers to these questions and, when taken together with other recent work, suggests a new set of basic assumptions which move beyond Theory Y into what we call "Contingency Theory: the fit between task, organization, and people." These theoretical assumptions emphasize that the appropriate pattern of organization is *contingent* on the nature of the work to be done and on the particular needs of the people involved. We should emphasize that we have labeled these assumptions as a step beyond Theory Y because of McGregor's own recognition that the Theory Y assumptions would probably be supplanted by new knowledge within a short time.[3]

THE STUDY DESIGN

Our study was conducted in four organizational units. Two of these performed the relatively certain task of manufacturing standardized containers on high-speed, automated production lines. The other two performed the relatively uncertain work of research and development in communications technology. Each pair of units performing the same kind of task were in the same large company, and each pair had previously been evaluated by that company's management as containing one highly effective unit and a less effective one. The study design is summarized in Exhibit 1.

(Boston: Harvard Business School, Division of Research, 1967); Joan Woodward, *Industrial Organization: Theory & Practice* (New York: Oxford University Press, Inc., 1965); Tom Burns and G.M. Stalker, *The Management of Innovation* (London: Tavistock Publications, 1961); Harold J. Leavitt, "Unhuman Organizations," HBR July-August 1962, p. 90.

[3] McGregor, op. cit., p. 245.

Characteristics	*Company I (predictable manufacturing task)*	*Company II (unpredictable R&D task)*
Effective performer	Akron containers plant	Stockton research lab
Less effective performer	Hartford containers plant	Carmel research lab

EXHIBIT 1. **Study design in "fit" of organizational characteristics**

The objective was to explore more fully how the fit between organization and task was related to successful performance. That is, does a good fit between organizational characteristics and task requirements increase the motivation of individuals and hence produce more effective individual and organizational performance?

An especially useful approach to answering this question is to recognize that an individual has a strong need to master the world around him, including the task that he faces as a member of a work organization.[4] The accumulated feelings of satisfaction that come from successfully mastering one's environment can be called a "sense of competence." We saw this sense of competence in performing a particular task as helpful in understanding how a fit between task and organizational characteristics could motivate people toward successful performance.

Organizational Dimensions

Because the four study sites had already been evaluated by the respective corporate managers as high and low performers of tasks, we expected that such differences in performance would be a preliminary clue to differences in the "fit" of the organizational characteristics to the job to be done. But, first, we had to define what kinds of organizational characteristics would determine how appropriate the organization was to the particular task.

We grouped these organizational characteristics into two sets of factors:

1. Formal characteristics, which could be used to judge the fit between the kind of task being worked on and the formal practices of the organization.
2. Climate characteristics, or the subjective perceptions and orientations that had developed among the individuals about their organizational setting. (These too must fit the task to be performed if the organization is to be effective.)

We measured these attributes through questionnaires and interviews with about 40 managers in each unit to determine the appropriateness of the organization to the kind of task being performed. We also measured the feelings of competence of the people in the organizations so that we could link the appropriateness of the organizational attributes with a sense of competence.

MAJOR FINDINGS

The principal findings of the survey are best highlighted by contrasting the highly successful Akron plant and the high-performing Stockton laboratory.

[4] See Robert W. White, "Ego and Reality in Psychoanalytic Theory," *Psychological Issues* 3, No. 3 (New York: International Universities Press, 1963).

Because each performed very different tasks (the former a relatively certain manufacturing task and the latter a relatively uncertain research task), we expected, as brought out earlier, that there would have to be major differences between them in organizational characteristics if they were to perform effectively. And this is what we did find. But we also found that each of these effective units had a better fit with its particular task than did its less effective counterpart.

While our major purpose in this article is to explore how the fit between task and organizational characteristics is related to motivation, we first want to explore more fully the organizational characteristics of these units, so the reader will better understand what we mean by a fit between task and organization and how it can lead to more effective behavior. To do this, we shall place the major emphasis on the contrast between the high-performing units (the Akron plant and Stockton laboratory), but we shall also compare each of these with its less effective mate (the Hartford plant and Carmel laboratory respectively).

Formal Characteristics

Beginning with differences in formal characteristics, we found that both the Akron and Stockton organizations fit their respective tasks much better than did their less successful counterparts. In the predictable manufacturing task environment, Akron had a pattern of formal relationships and duties that was highly structured and precisely defined. Stockton, with its unpredictable research task, had a low degree of structure and much less precision of definition (see Exhibit 2).

Characteristics	*Akron*	*Stockton*
1. Pattern of formal relationships and duties as signified by organization charts and job manuals	Highly structured, precisely defined	Low degree of structure, less well defined
2. Pattern of formal rules, procedures, control, and measurement systems	Pervasive, specific, uniform, comprehensive	Minimal, loose, flexible
3. Time dimensions incorporated in formal practices	Short-term	Long-term
4. Goal dimensions incorporated in formal practices	Manufacturing	Scientific

EXHIBIT 2. **Differences in formal characteristics in high-performing organizations**

Akron's pattern of formal rules, procedures, and control systems was so specific and comprehensive that it prompted one manager to remark:

"We've got rules here for everything from how much powder to use in cleaning the toilet bowls to how to cart a dead body out of the plant."

In contrast, Stockton's formal rules were so minimal, loose, and flexible that one scientist, when asked whether he felt the rules ought to be tightened, said:

"If a man puts a nut on a screw all day long, you may need more rules and a job definition for him. But we're not novices here. We're professionals and not the kind who need close supervision. People around here *do* produce, and produce under relaxed conditions. Why tamper with success?"

These differences in formal organizational characteristics were well suited to the differences in tasks of the two organizations. Thus:

Akron's highly structured formal practices fit its predictable task because behavior had to be rigidly defined and controlled around the automated, high-speed production line. There was really only one way to accomplish the plant's very routine and programmable job; managers defined it precisely and insisted (through the plant's formal practices) that each man do what was expected of him.

On the other hand, Stockton's highly unstructured formal practices made just as much sense because the required activities in the laboratory simply could not be rigidly defined in advance. With such an unpredictable, fast-changing task as communications technology research, there were numerous approaches to getting the job done well. As a consequence, Stockton managers used a less structured pattern of formal practices that left the scientists in the lab free to respond to the changing task situation.

Akron's formal practices were very much geared to *short-term* and *manufacturing* concerns as its task demanded. For example, formal production reports and operating review sessions were daily occurrences, consistent with the fact that the through-put time for their products was typically only a few hours.

By contrast, Stockton's formal practices were geared to *long-term* and *scientific* concerns, as its task demanded. Formal reports and reviews were made only quarterly, reflecting the fact that research often does not come to fruition for three to five years.

At the two less effective sites (i.e., the Hartford plant and the Carmel laboratory), the formal organizational characteristics did not fit their respective tasks nearly as well. For example, Hartford's formal practices were much less structured and controlling than were Akron's, while Carmel's were more restraining and restricting than were Stockton's. A scientist in Carmel commented:

"There's something here that keeps you from being scientific. It's hard to put your finger on, but I guess I'd call it 'Mickey Mouse.' There are rules and things here that get in your way regarding doing your job as a researcher."

Climate Characteristics

As with formal practices, the climate in both high-performing Akron and Stockton suited the respective tasks much better than did the climates at the less successful Hartford and Carmel sites.

Perception of structure: The people in the Akron plant perceived a great deal of structure, with their behavior tightly controlled and defined. One manager in the plant said:

"We can't let the lines run unattended. We lose money whenever they do. So we make sure each man knows his job, knows when he can take a break, knows how to handle a change in shifts, etc. It's all spelled out clearly for him the day he comes to work here."

In contrast, the scientists in the Stockton laboratory perceived very little structure, with their behavior only minimally controlled. Such perceptions encouraged the individualistic and creative behavior that the uncertain, rapidly changing research task needed. Scientists in the less successful Carmel laboratory perceived much more structure in their organization and voiced the feeling that this was "getting in their way" and making it difficult to do effective research.

Distribution of influence: The Akron plant and the Stockton laboratory also differed substantially in how influence was distributed and on the character of superior-subordinate and colleague relations. Akron personnel felt that they had much less influence over decisions in their plant than Stockton's scientists did in their laboratory. The task at Akron had already been clearly defined and that definition had, in a sense, been incorporated into the automated production flow itself. Therefore, there was less need for individuals to have a say in decisions concerning the work process.

Moreover, in Akron, influence was perceived to be concentrated in the upper levels of the formal structure (a hierarchical or "top-heavy" distribution), while in Stockton influence was perceived to be more evenly spread out among more levels of the formal structure (an egalitarian distribution).

Akron's members perceived themselves to have a low degree of freedom vis-à-vis superiors both in choosing the jobs they work on and in handling these jobs on their own. They also described the type of supervision in the plant as being relatively directive. Stockton's scientists, on the other hand, felt that they had a great deal of freedom vis-à-vis their superiors both in choosing the tasks and projects, and in handling them in the way that they wanted to. They described supervision in the laboratory as being very participatory.

It is interesting to note that the less successful Carmel laboratory had more of its decisions made at the top. Because of this, there was a definite feeling by the scientists that their particular expertise was not being effectively used in choosing projects.

Relations with others: The people at Akron perceived a great deal of similarity among themselves in background, prior work experiences, and approaches for tackling job-related problems. They also perceived the degree of coordination of effort among colleagues to be very high. Because Akron's task was so precisely defined and the behavior of its members so rigidly controlled around the automated lines, it is easy to see that this pattern also made sense.

By contrast, Stockton's scientists perceived not only a great many differences among themselves, especially in education and background, but also that the coordination of effort among colleagues was relatively low. This was appropriate for a laboratory in which a great variety of disciplines and skills were present and individual projects were important to solve technological problems.

Time orientation: As we would expect, Akron's individuals were highly oriented toward a relatively short time span and manufacturing goals. They responded to quick feedback concerning the quality and service that the plant was providing. This was essential, given the nature of their task.

Stockton's researchers were highly oriented toward a longer time span and scientific goals. These orientations meant that they were willing to wait for long-term feedback from a research project that might take years to complete. A scientist in Stockton said:

> "We're not the kind of people here who need a pat on the back every day. We can wait for months if necessary before we get feedback from colleagues and the profession. I've been working on one project now for three months and I'm still not sure where it's going to take me. I can live with that, though."

This is precisely the kind of behavior and attitude that spells success on this kind of task.

Managerial style: Finally, the individuals in both Akron and Stockton perceived their chief executive to have a "managerial style" that expressed more of a concern for the task than for people or relationships, but this seemed to fit both tasks.

In Akron, the technology of the task was so dominant that top managerial behavior which was not focused primarily on the task might have reduced the effectiveness of performance. On the other hand, although Stockton's research task called for more individualistic problem-solving behavior, that sort of behavior could have become segmented and uncoordinated, unless the top executive in the lab focused the group's attention on the overall research task. Given the individualistic bent of the scientists, this was an important force in achieving unity of effort.

All these differences in climate characteristics in the two high performers are summarized in Exhibit 3.

As with formal attributes, the less effective Hartford and Carmel sites had organization climates that showed a perceptibly lower degree of fit with their respective tasks. For example, the Hartford plant had an egalitarian distribution of influence, perceptions of a low degree of structure, and a more participatory type of supervision. The Carmel laboratory had a somewhat top-heavy distribution of influence, perceptions of high structure, and a more directive type of supervision.

COMPETENCE MOTIVATION

Because of the difference in organizational characteristics at Akron and Stockton, the two sites were strikingly different places in which to work. But these organizations had two very important things in common. First, each organization fit very well the requirements of its task. Second, although the

Characteristics	*Akron*	*Stockton*
1. Structural orientation	*Perceptions of tightly controlled behavior and a high degree of structure*	*Perceptions of a low degree of structure*
2. Distribution of influence	*Perceptions of low total influence, concentrated at upper levels in the organization*	*Perceptions of high total influence, more evenly spread out among all levels*
3. Character of superior-subordinate relations	*Low freedom vis-à-vis superiors to choose and handle jobs, directive type of supervision*	*High freedom vis-à-vis superiors to choose and handle projects, participatory type of supervision*
4. Character of colleague relations	*Perceptions of many similarities among colleagues, high degree of coordination of colleague effort*	*Perceptions of many differences among colleagues, relatively low degree of coordination of colleague effort*
5. Time orientation	*Short-term*	*Long-term*
6. Goal orientation	*Manufacturing*	*Scientific*
7. Top executive's "managerial style"	*More concerned with task than people*	*More concerned with task than people*

EXHIBIT 3. **Differences in "climate" characteristics in high-performing organizations**

behavior in the two organizations was different, the result in both cases was effective task performance.

Since, as we indicated earlier, our primary concern in this study was to link the fit between organization and task with individual motivation to perform effectively, we devised a two-part test to measure the sense of competence motivation of the individuals at both sites. Thus:

The *first* part asked a participant to write creative and imaginative stories in response to six ambiguous pictures.

The *second* asked him to write a creative and imaginative story about what he would be doing, thinking, and feeling "tomorrow" on his job. This is called a "projective" test because it is assumed that the respondent projects into his stories his own attitudes, thoughts, feelings, needs, and wants, all of which can be measured from the stories.[5]

The results indicated that the individuals in Akron and Stockton showed significantly more feelings of competence than did their counterparts in the lower-fit Hartford and Carmel organizations.[6] We found that the organization-task fit is simultaneously linked to and interdependent with both individual motivation and effective unit performance. (This interdependency is illustrated in Exhibit 4.)

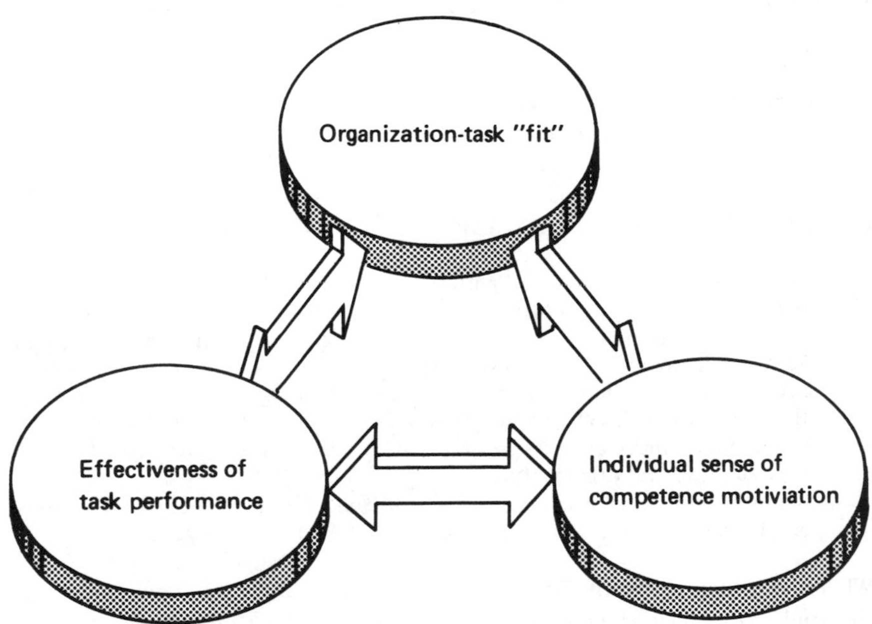

EXHIBIT 4. **Basic contingent relationships**

[5] For a more detailed description of this survey, see John J. Morse, *Internal Organizational Patterning and Sense of Competence Motivation* (Boston: Harvard Business School, unpublished doctoral dissertation, 1969).

[6] Differences between the two container plants are significant at .001 and between the research laboratories at .01 (one-tailed probability).

Putting the conclusions in this form raises the question of cause and effect. Does effective unit performance result from the task-organization fit or from higher motivation, or perhaps from both? Does higher sense of competence motivation result from effective unit performance or from fit?

Our answer to these questions is that we do not think there are any single cause-and-effect relationships, but that these factors are mutually interrelated. This has important implications for management theory and practice.

CONTINGENCY THEORY

Returning to McGregor's Theory X and Theory Y assumptions, we can now question the validity of some of his conclusions. While Theory Y might help to explain the findings in the two laboratories, we clearly need something other than Theory X or Y assumptions to explain the findings in the plants.

For example, the managers at Akron worked in a formalized organization setting with relatively little participation in decision making, and yet they were highly motivated. According to Theory X, people would work hard in such a setting only because they were coerced to do so. According to Theory Y, they should have been involved in decision making and been self-directed to feel so motivated. Nothing in our data indicates that either set of assumptions was valid at Akron.

Conversely, the managers at Hartford, the low-performing plant, were in a less formalized organization with more participation in decision making, and yet they were not as highly motivated like the Akron managers. The Theory Y assumptions would suggest that they should have been more motivated.

A way out of such paradoxes is to state a new set of assumptions, the Contingency Theory, that seems to explain the findings at all four sites:

1. Human beings bring varying patterns of needs and motives into the work organization, but one central need is to achieve a sense of competence.
2. The sense of competence motive, while it exists in all human beings, may be fulfilled in different ways by different people depending on how this need interacts with the strengths of the individuals' other needs—such as those for power, independence, structure, achievement, and affiliation.
3. Competence motivation is most likely to be fulfilled when there is a fit between task and organization.
4. Sense of competence continues to motivate even when a competence goal is achieved; once one goal is reached, a new, higher one is set.

While the central thrust of these points is clear from the preceding discussion of the study, some elaboration can be made. First, the idea that different people have different needs is well understood by psychologists. However, all too often, managers assume that all people have similar needs. Lest we be accused of the same error, we are saying only that all people have a need to feel competent; in this *one* way they are similar. But in many other dimensions of personality, individuals differ, and these differences will determine how a particular person achieves a sense of competence.

Thus, for example, the people in the Akron plant seemed to be very different from those in the Stockton laboratory in their underlying attitudes toward uncertainty, authority, and relationships with their peers. And because they had different need patterns along these dimensions, both groups were highly motivated by achieving competence from quite different activities and settings.

While there is a need to further investigate how people who work in different settings differ in their psychological makeup, one important implication of the Contingency Theory is that we must not only seek a fit between organization and task, but also between task and people and between people and organization.

A further point which requires elaboration is that one's sense of competence never really comes to rest. Rather, the real satisfaction of this need is in the successful performance itself, with no diminishing of the motivation as one goal is reached. Since feelings of competence are thus reinforced by successful performance, they can be a more consistent and reliable motivator than salary and benefits.

Implications for Managers

The major managerial implication of the Contingency Theory seems to rest in the task-organization-people fit. Although this interrelationship is complex, the best possibility for managerial action probably is in tailoring the organization to fit the task and the people. If such a fit is achieved, both effective unit performance and a higher sense of competence motivation seem to result.

Managers can start this process by considering how certain the task is, how frequently feedback about task performance is available, and what goals are implicit in the task. The answers to these questions will guide their decisions about the design of the management hierarchy, the specificity of job assignments, and the utilization of rewards and control procedures. Selective use of training programs and a general emphasis on appropriate management styles will move them toward a task-organization fit.

The problem of achieving a fit among task, organization, and people is something we know less about. As we have already suggested, we need further investigation of what personality characteristics fit various tasks and organizations. Even with our limited knowledge, however, there are indications that people will gradually gravitate into organizations that fit their particular personalities. Managers can help this process by becoming more aware of what psychological needs seem to best fit the tasks available and the organizational setting, and by trying to shape personnel selection criteria to take account of these needs.

In arguing for an approach which emphasizes the fit among task, organization, and people, we are putting to rest the question of which organizational approach—the classical or the participative—is best. In its place we are raising a new question: What organizational approach is most appropriate given the task and the people involved?

For many enterprises, given the new needs of younger employees for more autonomy, and the rapid rates of social and technological change, it may well be that the more participative approach is the most appropriate. But there will still be many situations in which the more controlled and formalized organization is desirable. Such an organization need not be coercive or punitive. If it makes sense to the individuals involved, given their needs and their jobs, they will find it rewarding and motivating.

CONCLUDING NOTE

The reader will recognize that the complexity we have described is not of our own making. The basic deficiency with earlier approaches is that they did not recognize the variability in tasks and people which produces this complexity. The strength of the contingency approach we have outlined is that it begins to provide a way of thinking about this complexity, rather than ignoring it. While our knowledge in this area is still growing, we are certain that any adequate theory of motivation and organization will have to take account of the contingent relationship between task, organization, and people.

Walter R. Nord

SOME PARTING THOUGHTS

The preceding paper by Morse and Lorsch indicated the direction that organizational behavior is now taking. As the controversy in this book has demonstrated, effective management of human resources requires a systems approach, a consideration of individual elements and their relationships and interdependencies. In this concluding note, several possible steps for the development of such an approach will be considered.

The traditional approach of students of management has been to focus on one set of variables–be it technology, structure, individual behavior, group behavior, or even organizational environment–and to attempt to hold constant all other variables. Such an approach will continue to have only limited success, because it disregards the true dynamics of organizations. Advocates of multidimensional approaches or systems views have often made an equally serious error by proposing that, since everything in the system is interrelated, everything must be dealt with at once. Meaningful research and guidelines for action then become impossible to develop, since so many variables are involved.

The approach suggested here assumes that the systems people are correct in saying that everything is interrelated. At the same time, it contends that some things are more interdependent than others and that some things have more powerful effects than others. This view demands a search not for variables which have merely statistically significant effects but for those which have the most powerful effects. Such a guideline permits the development of a body of knowledge based on scientifically rigorous research, conducted within a holistic framework and centered on variables which have important practical effects. It is through the use of this systems perspective that applied behavioral scientists will make their greatest contributions.[1]

The application of systems thinking to organizations is not new. Some early sociologists such as Saint Simon, Comte, and Durkheim were systems-oriented. In the area of organizational theory, Mary Parket Follett in 1933 (1949) noted,

> You will understand that I am simplifying when I speak of A, B, C and D adjusting themselves to one another. They are, of course, at the same time

[1] Books edited by Buckley (1969) and Emery (1969) are excellent sources for the student of organizational behavior who wishes to develop further a systems perspective.

> adjusting themselves to every other factor in the situation. Or it would be more accurate to say that all the factors in the situation are going through this process of reciprocal relating. . . . I am trying to express a total which shall include all the actors in a situation not as an additional total but as a relational total—a total where each part has been permeated by every other part. (p. 79)

Although organizations have long been seen as complex systems, this awareness has not found its way into management action. Even the most systems-oriented people, when confronted by a problem, tend to engage in limited search behavior, to make present decisions similar to past decisions, and to focus on a relatively limited set of variables. Furthermore, people find it difficult to act in accordance with systems considerations. More than an increased cognitive appreciation of systems is needed. Successful management requires affective and behavioral changes as well; specific possible changes are discussed in the remainder of this concluding note.

NEEDED COGNITIVE CHANGES

The cognitive needs may be viewed in three parts. First, the student of management must acquire an awareness and understanding of the individual concepts or elements themselves. It is on this level that the individual readings in this book may be most useful. While topics have been separated for analytical purposes, they are actually overlapping and interwoven. Each provides a way of thinking about some elements of the system. However, as the relatedness of these separate topics reveals, an understanding of the individual elements is not adequate. It is at this point in our reasoning that the structure of this book becomes important. Many conflicting findings are due to effects of variables other than the ones taken as problematic. Therefore, the second cognitive need is that people be trained to think in terms of interrelationships rather than mere cause and effect. In many ways our language, logic, and organization of knowledge by discipline rather than by problem predispose modes of thought that are not readily adapted to the idea of interrelatedness. Such books as those mentioned in footnote 1 by Emery and Buckley may be very helpful in suggesting new ways of thinking for the behavioral scientist.

A major advantage of the systemic perspective is the emphasis it forces us to give to the influence of the environment on an organization. Until recently the analysis of many organizational behaviorists ignored or understated the role that the firm's environment plays. Consequently, we are prone to assume that our ideas are universally applicable when they are not. Even now, many of the most popular approaches in organizational behavior have a strong, implicit flavor of being the "one best way." For the most part we seem to have become more sophisticated and recognized that what is the best approach for a particular situation depends on a number of elements in the environment. However, we have yet to develop a good way of conceptualizing the environment so that we can be confident about what will work in any given case.

The third set of cognitive needs involves research methods. Gradually, rigorous research on complex systems is becoming more feasible. The current approaches and issues involved in organizational research were well summarized in March's (1965) *Handbook of Organizations.* The three chapters by Scott, Weick, and Cohen and Cyert all dealt with approaches to the study of organizational systems. Most researchers who have sought to study organizations as systems have done some type of field study, and the field methods discussed by Scott were generally systems-oriented. However, the other two chapters presented additional ways of conducting research in systems terms. Weick suggested that laboratory experimentation could incorporate many of the appropriate properties of organizational systems. He argued convincingly that, for a wide variety of problems, the control permitted by laboratory methods could be exercised without a sacrifice of the data's relevance to natural organizations. He contented that an important correspondence between laboratory situations and actual organizations can often be maintained, because organizational problems have many extraneous and superfluous details. Weick seems to have been suggesting that organizations are indeed systems but that, since some things are not highly interrelated with others, many elements can be studied without consideration of the states of the other variables. Obviously, some elements can be studied in the laboratory more realistically than others. Finally, the chapter by Cohen and Cyert suggested organizational simulation as a research approach to organizational systems. In many ways computer simulation may provide a valuable tool by which students of management may analyze the micro-components of organizations to obtain implications for the dynamics of the system as a whole.

The work of Campbell and Stanley (1963) and of Webb, Campbell, Schwartz, and Sechrest (1966) has provided two additional ways of thinking about systems research. Campbell and Stanley outlined various designs for carrying out research in naturalistic settings with some of the rigor of the experimental method. These designs, ranging from weaker, quasi-experimental to very well controlled, point to the possibility of highly controlled research on systems. A fine example of the potential of such thinking was provided by Rosen's (1969) study of leadership. Rosen collected premeasures on a variety of dimensions of supervision and of group preferences and performance. He then experimentally studied the relationship between different leadership styles and group composition by reassigning the supervisors. Rosen's work demonstrated that such research is possible, though costly in terms of time and effort. He also found that the process by which the particular experimental changes were introduced had important effects. He concluded from the results of such an experiment within an on-going social system that the search for causal relationships among organizational variables may not be very promising. Rather, some type of systems equilibrium model, which searches for both equilibrium-disturbing and equilibrium-restoring variables, might be more fruitful. Nevertheless, his work and that of Campbell and Stanley demonstrate the possibilities of precise research in on-going systems.

The work of Webb *et al.* presented some creative ways for obtaining data in on-going social situations. Data collected from archives, erosion and accretion methods, and simple observations all seem to have substantial potential for organizational research.[2] Since organizations are relatively permanent social systems and keep a substantial body of records quite amenable to research, the analyst will find many sources of data already developed and waiting to be discovered; he may need to generate few himself.

It can be seen from the foregoing that cognitive tools for systems thinking are being developed. There is a growing body of concepts and ideas about the separate aspects of organizational behavior. Furthermore, greater attention is being devoted to the development of systems perspectives. Finally, research methods exist which permit attention to complex relationships without the sacrifice of too much control. Thus, on the cognitive level, the field of organizational behavior is becoming better equipped to deal with organizations as systems. How can individual managers translate their new awareness into action?

FEELING AND RESPONDING IN SYSTEMS TERMS

Lawrence and Lorsch (1969) argued that man is limited, in his rational capacities, to attending to about seven variables at a time. They promoted the concept of "bounded rationality" to warn the reader that they were unable to treat all the interdependencies of organizational systems at one time. They seemed to be taking a reasonable approach for exploration and perhaps even consultation. Complex organizations may require managers to act on the basis of more than the seven variables they can process cognitively. Fortunately, man has an affective side, which processes additional information rapidly and usefully.

One of the purposes of this book has been to create affective as well as cognitive change. New feelings about organizations and human behavior are needed if an ability to operate in systems terms is to be taught. Until recently, education in organizational behavior and other subjects has tended to be almost exclusively cognitive. In addition, education is often oriented toward providing answers to problems defined on only one or a very few dimensions. Hopefully, the reader now will be uncomfortable when he or she hears of a simple theoretical model that purports to solve organizational problems.

Another purpose of this book is to develop the reader's intuitive feeling about systems. There are two major reasons why I have stressed this goal. First, integration of knowledge from the various disciplines on which organizational behavior has been built is accomplished better through a systemic perspective than any other viewpoint I know of. Second, the systemic approach is a useful one for managers who are attempting to anticipate and solve organizational problems. Real problems are inevitably open-ended; to cope with such problems a manager must have a framework that enables him or her to deal simultaneously with a number of diverse elements. Moreover, the multivariate nature of organizational processes means that rarely can any two problems be treated in exactly the same way. A systemic perspective, with its emphasis on the complex interaction of elements, encourages managers to attend to differences among problems rather than foster a search for generalized solutions.

[2] The suggestion of Webb *et al.* of employing hidden recording devices is also a possibility, although it introduces certain ethical, legal, and practical problems.

In many applied areas the case method has served this purpose. However, the viewpoints of case writer and reader are likely to intrude, limiting the variables to be included in the writeup and those to be stressed in the analysis. The student is not required to search actively for data in a complex world and may not even have to impose his own structure on the data he uses. Especially in the behavioral area, cases and experiences in which the student is an active participant may provide the best vehicle for teaching organizational behavior. Written cases cannot induce the feelings of an on-going situation nearly as adequately as more direct experiences. The use of internship programs, where actual experience and academic training are combined, may prove to be most beneficial.[3] More easily developed methods may include the use of classrooms and schools themselves as actual cases in organizational dynamics. More traditional role-playing, T groups, and newer types of simulations may be useful. All types of experiences in other subject areas can facilitate the learning of organizational behavior if time and encouragement are provided for consideration of issues of possible relevance.

In addition, Vaill (1969) has outlined a valuable supplement to the case method. He developed a data bank containing information required for analysis of a case. The data were not structured in the normal manner of a case but rather were stored in a computer. Each piece of information could be purchased at a price calculated to represent its cost of collection. The students could buy information up to the limits of a budget, which was not large enough to permit purchase of all the data. Vaill noted that this approach made students more aware of the utility of planning, of theories or models as guides, of the need to determine the relevance of data, and of the variety of ways to diagnose a social system.

A systems view may require a reconsideration of the process by which people are taught to think. Management of organizations in the future will require an ability to deal with the many variables which comprise the organizational climate. Litwin and Stringer (1968) suggested some teaching techniques to help students to acquire this ability. Since organizational climates are composed of many stimuli operating simultaneously, Litwin and Stringer proposed the use of technology which simulates these climatic conditions. They argued that, since lectures, discussions, and film tend to create or present only discrete or sequential stimuli, they are consistent with outdated views of environments which emphasize specific or discrete qualities of stimuli. These older technologies are not adequate for teaching responses to situations in which the total configuration of the environment is central. New technologies that communicate along many channels at the same time may produce an emotional involvement and a realistic simulation of environments that other teaching methods cannot.

In addition to new technologies, it would seem that other educational changes

[3] An article by Livingston (1971), "Myth of the Well-Educated Manager" questions whether important managerial skills can be acquired in the normal classroom. How much experience in organizations and the management of people must management training include in order to be maximally beneficial?

are necessary. In fact, the whole process of education, especially in applied areas, may need to be reexamined. Educational systems have been highly concerned with content while neglecting process. Postman and Weingartner's (1969) application of McLuhan's idea merits repeating: it is the process of education, rather than the content, which produces the most learning. While the emphasis on process often is taken to mean the exclusion of content, the choice is not really "either - or." Rather, the question is one of developing a process which supports the desired learning outcomes. If modern organizations are going to demand that people have an awareness and feel for systems, clearly the process by which people are taught must parallel these needs. Particularly in the field of organizational behavior, the process of teaching must be consistent with the view of the world and the responses that are the ends of the teaching.

CONCLUSION

Since intellectual and affective changes are interdependent, any science has an important affective component. Butterfield (1957), one of the leading scholars of the history of science, has noted that the great discoveries in science have been related to changes in the feelings of people. Writing about the development of science between 1300 and 1800, Butterfield commented,

> It would appear that the most fundamental changes in outlook, the most remarkable turns in the current intellectual fashion may be referable in the last resort to an alteration of men's feelings for things, an alteration at once so subtle and so generally pervasive that it cannot be attributed to any particular writers or any influence of academic thought as such. . . . Subtle changes like this—the result not of any book but of the new texture of experience in a new age—are apparent behind the story of the scientific revolution, a revolution which some have tried to explain by a change in man's feelings for matter itself. (p. 130)

Perhaps the great discoveries in organizational behavior await similar changes in men's feelings about organizations.

Once we are fully aware of the systemic nature of organizations, we can see that changes in the environments in which organizations function will lead to changes within organizations. Since so few predictions of even the near future seem to be accurate, I will refrain from such speculation. However, I will make one observation in the hope of stimulating the student to continue to update his knowledge in this field. There is a strong probability that social and economic conditions will be so different in a few years that currently accepted practice in organizational behavior will look foolish.

Webb (1975) noted that much of the knowledge that comprises the substance of organizational behavior in the 1970s was developed while many nations of the world were experiencing unprecedented levels of economic growth and psychological comfort. However, Webb suggested (as did Scott in part 2 of this book) that the conditions that permitted rapid growth in the recent past no longer exist. Today, a major challenge to many American organizations is not growth but minimization of decay.

If the constraints on economic growth are becoming increasingly stringent, as many futurists predict, then the climate in which people work may be very different from what it has been in the recent past. Consequently, the ideas discussed throughout this book must be subjected to continuous scrutiny. As Webb (1975) wrote,

> How robust will the humanistic values inherent in participative management be when organizations struggle for their very survival? Can we preserve openness and concern for others when people are fighting to maintain their private empires, departments or even their jobs?
>
> . . . As the organizational growth curve flattens or declines, we should expect an increase in compliance through fear, an upsurge in inter-departmental rivalries for scarce resources and a reduction in willingness to share information and feelings. (p. 5)

Webb noted that the subject matter and pedogogical techniques needed to prepare managers for these conditions may be very different from those in vogue today. For example, organizational behaviorists may need to teach "power juggling and conscious manipulative tactics" (p. 6).

Again, my point is not that Webb's predictions are necessarily correct. What I wish to leave the reader with is a strong appreciation for contingency and systemic approaches discussed in this book for the management of people. No point of view presented in this volume is necessarily right or wrong. Each may well lead to effective management under some conditions but to ineffective management under others. Thus, the controversies that dominate the study of organizational behavior are capable of at least partial resolution at both theoretical and applied levels. I believe that such resolution for both theorists and managers is facilitated when the various points of view are thoroughly understood and related, both cognitively and affectively, to organizations as complex social systems.

REFERENCES

Bennis, W. G. *Organizational Development: Its Nature, Origins, and Prospects.* Reading, Mass.: Addison-Wesley, 1969.

Buckley, W., ed., *Modern Systems Research for the Behavioral Scientist.* Chicago: Aldine Publishing Company, 1969.

Butterfield, H. *The Origins of Modern Science 1300-1800.* rev. ed. New York: The Free Press, 1957.

Campbell, D. T., and Stanley, J. C. "Experimental and Quasi-Experimental Designs for Research." In *Handbook of Research on Teaching,* edited by N. L. Gage, pp. 171-246. Chicago: Rand McNally & Co., 1963.

Emery, F. E. *Systems Thinking.* Middlesex, England: Penguin, 1969.

Follett, M. P. *Freedom and Co-ordination.* L. Urwick, ed. London: Management Publications Trust, 1949.

Lawrence, P., and Lorsch, J. *Developing Organizations: Diagnosis and Action.* Reading, Mass.: Addison-Wesley, 1969.

Litwin, G. H., and Stringer, R. A. *Motivation and Organizational Climate.* Boston: Harvard University Graduate School of Business, 1968.

Livingston, J. S. "Myth of the Well-Educated Manager." *Harvard Business Review* 49 (Jan.-Feb., 1971): 79-89.

March, J. G., ed., *Handbook of Organizations.* Chicago: Rand McNally & Co., 1965.

Postman, N., and Weingartner, C. *Teaching as a Subversive Activity.* New York: The Delacorte Press, 1969.

Rosen, N. A. *Leadership Change and Work-Group Dynamics: An Experiment.* Ithaca, N.Y.: Cornell University Press, 1969.

Vaill, P. B. "An Approach to Social Systems Diagnosis: The Data Bank." Paper presented at the meeting of the American Psychological Association, Sept., 1969.

Webb, E. J. "The Fate of Romeo in the World of Cassius." *The Teaching of Organization Behavior* 1 (1975): 5-6.

Webb, E. J.; Campbell, D. T.; Schwartz, R. D.; and Sechrest, L. *Unobtrusive Measures: Nonreactive Research in the Social Sciences.* Chicago: Rand McNally & Co., 1966.

Index

AUTHOR

SUBJECT